T0201281

Security in Fixed and Wireless Networks
(2nd Edition)

Security in Fixed and Wireless Networks
(2nd Edition)

Guenter Schaefer and Michael Rossberg

Technische Universitaet Ilmenau, Germany

Library of Congress Cataloging-in-Publication Data

Schaefer, Guenter (Telecommunications engineer), author.
  [Netzsicherheit, Algorithmische Grundlagen und Protokolle. English]
  Security in fixed and wireless networks / Dr Guenter Schaefer, Technische Universitaet
Ilmenau, Michael Rossberg, Technische Universitaet Ilmenau.
      pages   cm
  Includes bibliographical references and index.
  ISBN 978-1-119-04074-3 (cloth : alk. paper) 1. Computer networks–Security measures.
2. Wireless communication systems–Security measures. 3. Computer security. I. Rossberg,
Michael, author. II. Title.
  TK5105.59.S3313   2003
  005.8—dc23

                              2015034626

A catalogue record for this book is available from the British Library.

Set in 10/13pt, NewCenturySchlbkLTStd by SPi Global, Chennai, India.
Printed and bound in Singapore by Markono Print Media Pte Ltd

1 2016

Contents

About the authors

Guenter Schaefer studied computer science at Universitaet Karlsruhe, Germany, from 1989 to 1994. Between 1994 and 1999 he was a researcher at the Institute of Telematics, Universitaet Karlsruhe. After obtaining his PhD degree (1998) he worked at Ecole Nationale Supérieure des Télécommunications, Paris, France (1999–2000). Between 2000 and 2005 he was a researcher at Technische Universitaet Berlin in the Telecommunication Networks Group. Since 2005 he has been full professor of computer science at the Technische Universität Ilmenau, leading the Telematics/Computer Networks research group. His research interests lie in the areas of network security, networking protocols, mobile communications and innovative communication services/architectures, and he regularly gives courses on network security, networking subjects and the basics of computer science (programming, algorithms etc.).

Michael Rossberg studied computer science at Technische Universitaet Ilmenau, Germany, from 2002 to 2007. Since 2007 he has been a researcher at the Telematics/Computer Networks research group. In 2011 he obtained his PhD in computer science with a thesis on peer-to-peer-based autoconfiguration of large-scale IPsec VPNs. His research interests lie in network security, resilience against denial-of-service attacks and performance evaluation/optimisation. Since December 2013 he has served as a lecturer in the Telematics and Computer Networks research group.

Preface to the second edition

Since the publication of the first edition of this book, 12 years ago, many developments have taken place in the field of network security. Indeed, the innovations are so numerous that we decided to develop this second edition of the book in a team, therefore Michael Rossberg and myself now jointly maintain the book.

The evolution of the topic required not only a rigorous revision of the existing chapters, but also the addition of new material in order to take new developments into account. For example, quite a number of new cryptographic algorithms are discussed in the new edition, including new attacks and security insights on former ones. Nevertheless, we decided to keep the discussion of some historic approaches, like DES and MD5, as they serve as a foundation of the newer developments and are well suited to explain important concepts. We extended the chapter on asymmetric cryptography with an introduction to cryptography based on elliptic curves, as this approach plays a more and more important practical role due to the improvements in calculating discrete logarithms. The chapter on mobile Internet communication and Mobile IP has been dropped from the second edition because Mobile IP has not been widely adopted in the open Internet, only in very controlled environments.

Furthermore, the book has been extended by the addition of a completely new part, which covers the protection of whole communications infrastructures against targeted attacks on integrity and availability. The chapter on Internet firewalls from the first edition has been integrated into this part of the book, for obvious reasons.

In its resulting structure this second edition serves well as a foundation for two or three consecutive college-level courses, but it is also possible to teach some aspects independently. For example, a three-step approach could cover IT security foundations (Part I) in a first course, their application to networks (Parts II and III) in a second course and the protection of communications infrastructures in a final third course, and it may be possible to attend the last course without the first and second ones. In this latter case, only some central ideas from the first part of the book need to be studied first. A division into two lectures would cover essential parts of the first part of the book and discuss their application to networks. To cover all topics in the first three parts, one must plan for at least 4 hours of lectures per week. The protection of communications infrastructures would be the second independently held lecture in this case. We have had good experience with the two-step approach, which we have used for teaching at TU Ilmenau in recent years.

Please note that all chapters and sections in this book that are marked by an asterisk may safely be skipped during reading and teaching without impairing the understanding of subsequent material.

At this point we want to thank our students and the many other people who have helped us with their numerous questions and suggestions to present the teaching material in its current form. We would also like to thank two members of our research group who contributed slides to the lectures, which also served as a first foundation for the second edition of the book, Prof. Dr.-Ing. Thorsten Strufe and Dr.-Ing. Mathias Fischer. Prof. Dr. Martin Dietzfelbinger from the Complexity Theory and Efficient Algorithms research group provided us with valuable comments on our chapter on asymmetric cryptography, which we were largely able to integrate into this second edition. The responsibility for any errors that still might appear in the book despite all the help that was available, of course, lies with us. We will, therefore, continue to appreciate any comments or suggestions regarding the content of this book.

Ilmenau, July 2015
Guenter Schaefer and Michael Rossberg

Preface to the first edition

This book has evolved during my time as a technical assistant in the department of telecommunications networks at the Technical University of Berlin. It is based on my lecture Network Security that I have been presenting at the university since the winter semester of 2000/2001.

I therefore particularly want to express my warm gratitude to the head of this department, Professor Adam Wolisz, for the wonderful opportunities he has given me for my work. He has supported my plans to write a textbook on network security from the very beginning.

Dipl.-Ing. Mr. Andreas Hess offered to read and edit the entire first draft of my text. I am sincerely grateful to him for his fast turnaround times and numerous helpful suggestions for changes and improvements.

Mrs. Hedwig Jourdan von Schmüger translated the German version of the book into English. She not only had a good grasp of the technical content but also had a knack for dealing with my often rather long German sentences. I want to thank her for the very good working relationship we had.

This gratitude also extends to the editorial staffs of dpunkt.verlag and John Wiley & Sons, who were so helpful with both the German and English versions of the book. Their constant support and guidance made my task much easier. I also appreciate the helpful input from the various reviewers who provided useful and constructive comments.

Lastly, I want to thank the students who attended my lectures for their numerous questions and suggestions that gave me many ideas for how to structure this book.

The responsibility for any errors that still might appear in this book despite all the help that was available, of course, lies with me. I will, therefore, continue to appreciate any comments or suggestions regarding the content of this book.

Berlin, December 2003
Guenter Schaefer

Part I

Foundations of Data Security Technology

Part I

Foundations of Data Security Technology

1   Introduction

It is now a well-known fact that, despite all the benefits, the digital revolution with its omnipresent networking of information systems also involves some risks. This book looks at a specific category of risks, the category of risks that evolve as a result of eavesdropping and the manipulation of data transmitted in communication networks and the vulnerability of the communication infrastructure itself. In particular, measures are discussed that can be taken to minimise them.

Protecting transmitted data

Mankind very early on recognised the need to protect information that was being transferred or stored, and so the desire to protect information from unauthorised access is probably as old as writing itself. For example, reliable early records on protective measures describe a technique used by the Spartans around 400 BC. The technique entailed writing messages on a leather strip that was wrapped around a stick of a specific diameter. Before the message was delivered, the leather strip was removed from the stick, and a potential attacker who did not have a stick with the same diameter, because he did not know the diameter or anything about the technique, could not read the message. In a sense this was an implementation of the first 'analogue' encryption.

First substitution ciphers

In the fourth century BC, the Greek Polybius developed a table of bilateral substitution that defined how to encode characters into pairs of symbols and their corresponding reinstatement, thereby specifying the first 'digital' encryption method. Of the Romans we know that they often protected their tactical communication by using simple monoalphabetic substitution methods. The most widely known one was probably the 'Caesar cipher', named after its creator Julius Caesar, in which each character of the alphabet is shifted upwards by three characters. Thus, 'A' becomes 'D', 'B' becomes 'E', etc.

Origins of
cryptanalysis

The Arabs were the first people to develop a basic understanding of the two fundamental principles of *substitution*, that is, pure character replacement, and *transposition*, that is, changing the sequence of the characters of a text. When they evaluated a method they also considered how a potential attacker might analyse it. They were therefore aware of the significance of relative letter frequency in a language for the analysis of substitution ciphers because it gave some insight into substitution rules. By the beginning of the fifteenth century, the Arabic encyclopaedia 'Subh al-a'sha' already contained an impressive treatment and analysis of cryptographic methods.

In Europe, cryptology originated during the Middle Ages in the papal and Italian city-states. The first encryption algorithms merely involved vowel substitution, and therefore offered at least some rudimentary protection from ignorant attackers who may not have come up with the idea of trying out all the different possible vowel substitutions.

Protection of
infrastructure

Not wanting to turn the entire development of cryptology into a scientific discipline at this juncture, we can deduce from the developments mentioned that special importance has always been given to protecting information. However, a second category of risks is increasingly becoming a major priority in the age of omnipresent communication networks. These risks actually affect communication infrastructures rather than the data being transmitted. With the development and expansion of increasingly complex networks, and the growing importance of these networks not only to the economic but also to the social development of the modern information society, there is also a greater demand for ways to secure communication infrastructures from deliberate manipulation. For economic operation it is important to ensure that the services provided by communication networks are available and functioning properly as well as that the use of these services can be billed correctly and in a way that everyone can understand.

1.1   Content and Structure of this Book

In this book equal treatment is given to the two task areas in network security mentioned: *security of transmitted data* and *security of the communication infrastructure*. We start by introducing central terms and concepts and providing an overview of the measures available for information security.

Building on this introductory information, the rest of the chapters in Part 1 deal with the *fundamental principles of data security technology*. Chapter 2 uses basic concepts to introduce cryptology. Chapter 3 covers the use and functioning of *symmetric ciphering schemes*, whereas Chapter 4 is devoted to *asymmetric cryptographic algorithms*. Chapter 5 introduces *cryptographic check values* for the detection of message manipulation. Generating secure, non-predictable random numbers is the subject of Chapter 6. In a sense, the algorithms in these four chapters constitute the *basic primitives* of data security technology upon which the cryptographic protection mechanisms of network security are based. Chapter 7 discusses *cryptographic protocols* and introduces the authentication and key exchange protocols that are central to network security. Chapter 8 enlarges the topic in the context of scenarios with *group communication*. This deeper discussion may be skipped in an introductory course without impairing the understanding of further book chapters. Part 1 concludes with Chapter 9, which provides an introduction to the principles of access control.

Part 1 of the book deals with fundamental principles

Part 2 of this book focuses on the architectures and protocols of *network security*. It starts with Chapter 10, which examines general issues relating to the integration of security services in communication architectures. Chapter 11 discusses security protocols of the data link layer, Chapter 12 examines the security architecture for the Internet protocol *IPsec* and Chapter 13 closes Part 2 by describing security protocols for the transport layer.

Part 2 introduces architectures and protocols for network security

Part 3 of the book presents the field of *secure wireless and mobile communication*. Chapter 14 differentiates the additional security aspects that arise in mobile communications compared with conventional fixed networks, and presents approaches of a more conceptual nature for maintaining the confidentiality of the current location area of mobile devices. The other chapters in this part examine concrete examples of systems. Chapter 15 deals with the security functions of the IEEE 802.11 standard for wireless local networks and includes an in-depth discussion of the weaknesses of former versions of the standard. Chapter 16 introduces the security functions for the current standards for mobile wide-area networks, that is, *GSM*, *UMTS* and *LTE*.

Part 3 is devoted to wireless and mobile communication

While Parts 1 to 3 of the book mainly concentrate on the security of communication processes between end systems, the fourth and last part of the book deals with *protection of large networks and the communication infrastructure*. Chapter 17 first describes the basic problem of protecting systems in open networks and provides a short overview of systematic threat analysis. It also discusses

Part 4 deals with protection of communication infrastructures.

the problem of protecting end systems as a requirement for secure network operation. Chapter 18 deals with *denial-of-service attacks*, which affect end systems as well as the communication infrastructure. Chapters 19 and 20 cover the security of fundamental communication infrastructure services: *routing* and *name resolution*. *Internet firewalls* as the main means for realising subnet-related access control are introduced in Chapter 21. Since attacks cannot always be prevented through the proactive security measures described in these chapters, it often makes sense to introduce additional control through *intrusion detection systems* and/or *intrusion prevention systems*. The principles of such systems and existing techniques are introduced in Chapter 22. Finally, Chapter 23 deals with difficulties in the management of large security infrastructures.

The field of network *security is currently* *marked by a* *major dynamic*   Before our attentive and inquisitive readers get too involved in the further content of this book, they should be made aware that the field of network security has developed into a very active field during the last few years. Consequently, extensive improvements are constantly being made to existing security protocols and new protocols are being developed and introduced. Doing justice to the speed of this development in a textbook thus becomes a very difficult if not impossible undertaking. We therefore ask for the reader's understanding if a detail or two has already been resolved in a way that deviates from our interpretation in a particular chapter or totally new protocols have established themselves in the meantime and are not dealt with in this book. It is precisely because of the rapid developments in this field that the priority of this book is to provide the reader with a fundamental understanding of the central principles presented and to describe them on the basis of concrete and relevant sample protocols.

1.2   Threats and Security Goals

The terms *threat* and *security goal* play an important role in assessing the risks in communication networks, therefore they will first be defined in general terms.

Definition 1.1 *A* **threat** *in a communication network is a potential event or series of events that could result in the violation of one or more security goals. The actual implementation of a threat is called an* **attack***.*

Definition 1.1 is kept quite abstract and refers to the term *security goal* defined below. The following examples clarify the types of threats that exist:

Examples of concrete threats

- a hacker intruding into the computer of a company;
- someone reading someone else's transmitted e-mails;
- a person altering sensitive data in a financial accounting system;
- a hacker temporarily shutting down a web site;
- somebody using or ordering services and goods in someone else's name.

The term *security goal* is another concept that is easier to explain with examples because at first glance security goals can vary considerably depending on the respective application scenario:

Examples of security goals

- Banks:
  - protection from deliberate or unintentional modification of transactions;
  - reliable and non-manipulable identification of customers;
  - protection of personal identification numbers from disclosure;
  - protection of personal customer information.
- Administration:
  - protection from disclosure of sensitive information;
  - use of electronic signatures for administrative documents.
- Public network operators:
  - restriction of access to network management functions to authorised personnel only;
  - protection of the availability of the services offered;
  - guarantee of accurate and manipulation-safe billing of use of services;
  - protection of personal customer data.
- Corporate and private networks:
  - protection of the confidentiality of exchanged data;
  - assurance of the authenticity of messages (details follow).
- All networks: Protection from intrusion from outside.

Some of the security goals listed above are of course relevant to several different application scenarios — even if they are not

General definition of security goals

repeated in the categories above. However, security goals can also be defined from a purely technical standpoint without being based on a concrete application scenario.

Definition 1.2 *In the field of network security, a distinction can be made between the following* **technical security goals***:*

- **Confidentiality:** *Transmitted or stored data and/or details about the communication itself, e.g. the identity of sender or receiver, should only be disclosed to authorised entities.*
- **Data integrity:** *It should be possible to detect unintentional or deliberate changes to data. This requires that the identification of the originator of the data is unique and cannot be manipulated.*
- **Accountability:** *It must be possible to identify the entity responsible for a particular event, e.g. use of a service.*
- **Availability:** *The services implemented in a system should be available and function properly.*
- **Controlled access:** *Only authorised entities should be able to access certain services and data.*

Not all security experts and standards see the last goal to be full-fledged, but rather already covered by the first two goals. However, for communication networks it is often reasonable to restrict access to the network, even though there is no direct threat by any unauthorised access for that network itself.

General technical threats   Like security goals, threats can be viewed from a primarily technical standpoint and therefore *technical threats* are distinguished as follows:

- *Masquerade:* An entity pretends to have the identity of another entity.
- *Eavesdropping:* An entity reads information that is meant for someone else.
- *Authorisation violation:* An entity uses services or resources although it does not have appropriate permission.
- *Loss or modification of information:* Certain information is destroyed or changed.
- *Forgery:* An entity creates new information using the identity of another entity.
- *Repudiation:* An entity falsely denies having participated in a particular action.
- *Sabotage:* Any action that is aimed at reducing the availability or correct functioning of services or systems. In the context of computer networks these attacks are usually referred to by the term *denial-of-service (DoS)*.

Technical security goals	Technical threats						
	Masque-rade	Eaves-dropping	Authori-sation violation	Loss or modification of information	Forgery of information	Repudiation of events	Sabotage (e.g. by overload)
Confidentiality	x	x	x				
Data integrity	x		x	x	x		
Accountability	x		x	x		x	
Availability	x		x	x			x
Controlled access	x		x		x		

These terms can be used as the basis for creating a general classification that clarifies which security goals are in danger of being exposed to which threats. Table 1.1 provides an overview of this classification. The table can be read in two different ways. On one hand, it shows that information confidentiality is threatened by the technical threats of masquerade, eavesdropping and authorisation violation; on the other hand, it can also be directly inferred from the table that forgery primarily threatens the security goals of data integrity, accountability and controlled access.

Table 1.1
Technical security goals and threats

In reality, a concrete attack often involves a combination of the threats mentioned above. An intrusion into a system often involves sniffing the access identification and related passwords. The identity of the sniffed identification is then provided for the access check with the latter representing a masquerade. Thus, Table 1.1 serves more the purpose of illustration than a definition of the abilities or possibilities of the different attacker types.

Real attacks often combine several threats

1.3 Network Security Analysis

When appropriate action is taken to counteract the above-mentioned threats to an actual application scenario, the counter-measures being considered first have to be evaluated carefully for the given network configuration. This requires a detailed *security analysis* of the network technology with an assessment of the risk potential of technical threats to the entities communicating in the network, along with an evaluation of the cost in terms of resources and time, that is, computing capacity, storage, message transfer, of executing known attack techniques.

Note: Unknown attack techniques are generally not possible to evaluate!

Sometimes the detailed security analysis of a given network configuration or a specific protocol architecture will be needed to convince an organisation's financial controlling of the need for further security measures. Additionally, since the attack techniques as well as the network configuration are normally subjects of constant change, a security analysis and the respective derivation of risks needs to be constantly re-evaluated. In larger organisations it is advantageous to install a security management according to ISO 27001 [ISO13]. This includes, for example, the introduction of dedicated staff for IT security.

In any case, a key issue for security analyses is the question: 'How can the complexity of the overall system be effectively reduced?' Some fundamental techniques will be covered in Chapter 17 in more depth, but as a rule a detailed security analysis of a specific protocol architecture may be structured according to the following finely granulated *attacks at the message level*:

- Passive attacks: Eavesdropping on protocol data units (PDUs);
- Active attacks: Delay, replay, deletion and insertion of PDUs.

Combination   For any security analysis, one basic assumption needs to be that
of attacks   an actual hacker would have to be able to combine the attacks listed above in order to use them to construct more complex attacks from these basic building blocks interpreted as attack primitives. A 'successful attack' at the message level therefore requires that:

- the attack produces no directly detectable side effects for other communication processes, e.g. for other connections or connectionless data transmission;
- the attack produces few side effects for other PDUs in the same connection or in connectionless data transmission between the entities participating in the communication.

Otherwise, there is the inherent risk of attack detection and therefore the attacker may not be able to combine the building blocks to a more complex attack.

When a security analysis is produced for protocol architectures, each individual layer in the architecture should be checked for the attacks mentioned above.

Figure 1.1 shows the layered architecture typically used in communication systems today. In this architecture the end systems communicate with one another over a network of intermediate systems. The protocol functions are organised into five layers:

- The lowest layer is the *physical layer*, which is responsible for transmitting bit streams over a physical medium, e.g. line or radio transmission link.

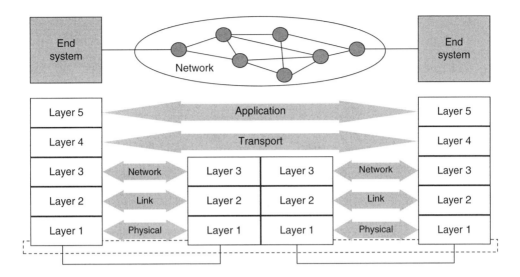

The *data link layer* above it combines multiple bits from the transmitted bit stream into transmission frames and carries out transmission that is protected against errors between two systems connected over a physical medium. It performs two basic tasks. When a shared medium is available to several systems, it coordinates access to the shared medium *(medium access control, MAC)*. It also takes appropriate measures to detect transmission errors so that defective frames received at the receiver are detected and can be discarded.

Figure 1.1
Architecture of layered communication systems

- The *network layer* is responsible for the communication between end systems that are normally linked to one another over several intermediate systems. The main task of this layer therefore is routing and forwarding through the transmission network between the two end systems.
- The *transport layer* enables an exchange of data between the processes of the end systems. The key tasks of this layer are addressing applications processes, detecting errors at the end-to-end level and, with a reliable service, implementing measures for error recovery, e.g. through retransmission.
- Above the transport layer the *application layer* – as its name suggests – implements applications-specific protocols that are as diverse as the applications run in the end systems.

Only the three lower layers up to the network layer are normally implemented in the (intermediate) systems of the transmission network.

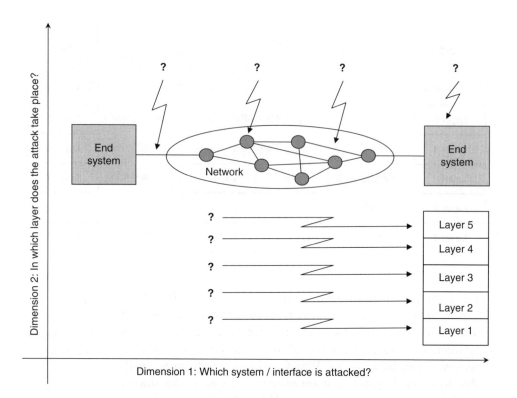

Figure 1.2
Dimensions of the security analysis of layered protocol architectures

According to the description given above, a security analysis of layered protocol architectures can be structured along two dimensions (also compare Figure 1.2):

- First the *systems and interfaces at risk* in the network configuration being analysed must be identified. For example, publicly accessible end systems, gateways to public networks as well as non-secure transmission routes (particularly in the case of wireless transmission) pose special security risks.
- The security analysis is also structured according to the *layer* in which an attack can take place. Attacks do not necessarily have to occur in the application layer. On the contrary, depending on the intentions of the hacker, the main attack point can be the layers below the transport layer.

A detailed security analysis is very useful for identifying the security risks that dominate in a particular network configuration. It can be used as the basis for selecting appropriate security measures to reduce these risks. The following section provides a general overview on this subject.

1.4 Information Security Measures

Many different security measures are available, each dealing with specific aspects of an information processing system and its embedding into the work processes supported by the system:

- *Physical security measures* include lock systems and physical access controls, tamper proofing of security-sensitive equipment and environmental controls such as motion detectors, etc.
- *Personnel security measures* begin with a classification of the security-specific sensitivity of a position and also include procedures for employee screening and security training and awareness.
- *Administrative security measures* include procedures for the controlled import of new software and hardware, detection of security-relevant occurrences through maintenance and regular checks of event logs as well as an analysis of known security breaches and incidents.
- *Media security measures* are aimed at safeguarding the storage of information. Procedures and control mechanisms are implemented to identify, reproduce or destroy sensitive information and data carriers.
- *Radiation security measures* are designed to prevent or limit electromagnetic emission from computer systems and peripheral devices (especially monitors) that a hacker could note and use to eavesdrop on information.
- *Life-cycle controls* monitor the design, implementation and introduction of information processing systems. The specification and control of standards to be upheld for programming and documentation are geared towards achieving a 'reliable' development process.
- *System security measures* for computers, operating systems and the applications run on computers are designed to secure information that is stored and processed in computing systems.
- Expanding on the latter category, *communication security measures* are designed to protect information while it is being transmitted in a communication network. In conjunction with the measures that protect the network infrastructure itself, they form the category of *network security measures*.

*A secure inform-
ation processing
process requires
a comprehensive
catalogue of measures*

The last category mentioned, network security, is the main subject of this book. However, it should be emphasised that a careful application of the entire catalogue of measures listed above is necessary to guarantee the security of information processing processes. This is due to the fact that a security system is only as secure as its weakest component. For example, a sophisticated password system that prevents the use of easily guessed passwords is minimally effective if users write their passwords on media that are not adequately protected or if a hacker can use a telephone call to induce someone to divulge a password ('social engineering').

1.5   Important Terms Relating to Communication Security

This section introduces the terms *security service, cryptographic algorithm* and *cryptographic protocol*, which are central to network security, and explains their relationship to one another.

Definition 1.3 *A* **security service** *is an abstract service that seeks to achieve a specific security objective.*

*Implementation of
security services*

A security service can be implemented through either cryptographic or conventional means. For example, one way to prevent a file stored on a USB stick from being read by an unauthorised entity is to ensure that the file is encrypted before it is stored. On the other hand, the same goal can be achieved if the stick is locked up in a secure safe. Normally, the most effective approach is a combination of cryptographic and conventional methods.

*Fundamental
security services*

In its generalisation, Definition 1.3 gives the impression that a multitude of different security services exist. Actually the number is surprisingly small; precisely five fundamental security services are distinguished:

- As subsequent discussions in this book will show, *authentication* is the most important of all security services because it allows manipulation-safe identification of entities.
- To a certain extent the security service *data integrity*, which ensures that data generated by a specific entity cannot undetectably be modified, is the 'little brother' of the authentication service.
- *Confidentiality*, which is aimed at preventing information from being made known to unauthorised entities, is probably the most widely known security service.

- The security service *access control* checks that only entities that have proper authorisation can access certain information and services in a specified way.
- The aim of the *non-repudiation* service is to enable the unique identification of the initiators of certain actions, such as the sending of a message, so that these completed actions cannot be disputed after the fact. In contrast to the authentication service this evidence can be provided to third parties.

Definition 1.4 *A* **cryptographic algorithm** *is a mathematical transformation of input data (e.g. data, keys) to output data.*

Cryptographic algorithms play an important role in the realisation of security services. However, a cryptographic algorithm used on its own is not sufficient because it also has to be embedded in a semantic context. This usually occurs as part of the definition of a *cryptographic protocol*.

Definition 1.5 *A* **cryptographic protocol** *is a procedural instruction for a series of processing steps and message exchanges between multiple entities. The aim is to achieve a specific security objective.*

The last two terms defined for cryptographic algorithms and protocols are of such fundamental significance for network security that they are dealt with in several chapters. However, the next chapter will first introduce the general basics of cryptology.

2 Fundamentals of Cryptology

This chapter introduces the basic concepts of cryptology [Sim94a, Riv90]. The first section starts with a definition of the general terms cryptology, cryptography and cryptanalysis. Section 2.2 follows with a basic classification of the cryptographic algorithms that occur within the area of network security. Section 2.3 introduces basic issues relating to cryptanalysis. Subsequently, Section 2.4 introduces comparative numbers to assess the possibilities of successful attacks based on the estimated computing and memory efforts. Section 2.5 examines the properties of encryption schemes important to communication and presents a breakdown of the different schemes. Lastly, Section 2.6 looks at the main tasks involved in the management of cryptographic keys, which is of central importance in the use of cryptographic methods.

2.1 Cryptology, Cryptography and Cryptanalysis

The term *cryptology* refers to the science of secure and, as a rule, confidential communication. The word itself derives from the two Greek words *kryptós* (hidden) and *lógos* (word). Cryptology comprises two main areas:

■ *Cryptography* analyses and develops methods for transforming unsecured *plaintext* into *ciphertext* that cannot be read by unauthorised entities. The term is made up from the two words *kryptós* and *gráphein* (writing). As the field has developed over the last 40 or so years, additional categories of algorithms have been added to the main subject of pure encryption schemes. These algorithms are generally also considered cryptographic algorithms although they do not realise encryption in a true sense.

Cryptanalysis is a complementary discipline to cryptography

■ In some respects, *cryptanalysis*, sometimes also called *cryptological analysis*, represents the antagonist of cryptography because it is the science and partly also the art of recovering plaintext from ciphertext without initial knowledge of the key that was used. The term comes from the two Greek words *kryptós* and *analýein* (loosening, untying). Cryptanalysis is an essential extension of cryptography, which means that a cryptographer has always also to be a cryptanalyst so that the methods he or she develops can actually accomplish what is expected of them.

2.2 Classification of Cryptographic Algorithms

Main applications of cryptography

There are two main applications of cryptography that are important in connection with network security:

■ Data *encryption*, which is a transformation of plaintext into ciphertext, as well as the inverse operation *decryption*, sometimes also referred to as *ciphering* and *deciphering*, respectively.

■ Data *signing*, which is a manipulation-evident calculation of the checksum. On the basis of a *signature check*, the checksum makes it possible to determine whether data was modified, due to either errors or deliberate manipulation, after it was created and signed. It is important to make a distinction between *signing* as it is defined here and the generating of a *digital signature*. The latter additionally allows attesting the authenticity of data to third parties.

Some cryptographic algorithms can be used for both applications, whereas others are secure and/or can be efficiently used for only one of the applications.

Classification according to number of keys

At a general level, cryptographic algorithms can be classified according to how many different keys they use:

■ *Symmetric cryptographic algorithms* use *one* key, which means that a message is decrypted with the same key that was used to encrypt it or a signature is checked with the same key that created it.

■ *Asymmetric cryptographic algorithms* use *two* different keys for encryption and decryption or signing and signature check.

The two keys cannot be selected independently of the other and instead must be constructed as a pair specifically in accordance with the cryptographic algorithm.

■ *Cryptographic hash functions* use *no* key. This means that they implement a transformation from input data that is defined only by the specific algorithm but not through an additional key. This category of algorithms is mainly used to create cryptographic check values (see Chapter 5) and to generate pseudo-random numbers (see Chapter 6).

A separate chapter is devoted to each of these categories. However, we will first present some general observations on cryptanalysis and on the characteristics and classification of encryption algorithms.

2.3 Cryptanalysis

Cryptanalysis is essentially the process used to obtain the corresponding plaintext or even the appropriate key from ciphertext. Depending on the cryptanalyst's requirements, a distinction is made between the following classic types of cryptanalysis:

■ *Exhaustive search of key space*: Also called *brute-force attack*,   *Brute-force attack*
this is basically the simplest but usually also the most time-consuming form of attack. First it makes an assumption about the algorithm used to encrypt a plaintext and then it successively tries out all possible keys to decrypt an intercepted ciphertext. If the ciphertext can be represented in 'intelligible' plaintext with one of the keys, it is then assumed that the key being sought has been discovered. Statistically this involves searching through half the key space. Because this form of attack can basically be used against every cryptographic scheme, it imposes an upper limit for the effort required to break arbitrary cryptographic schemes. The effort required increases exponentially with the length of the key.

■ *Analysis based only on known-ciphertext*: This form of crypt-   *Known-ciphertext*
analysis is based on the assumption that certain properties of a plaintext will be retained even with encryption. For example, simple ciphers retain the relative frequency of individual letters or combinations of letters. With this attack form, different ciphertexts $C_1, C_2, \ldots$, all created with the same key K, are available to the cryptanalyst. This means

that plaintexts $P_1, P_2, \ldots$ exist so it holds that $C_1 = E(K, P_1)$, $C_2 = E(K, P_2), \ldots$ with $E(K, P)$ representing the encryption of plaintext P with key K. Thus the objective of the cryptanalyst is to determine either as many plaintexts $P_1, P_2, \ldots$ as possible or even the key K.

Known-plaintext
- ■ *Analysis based on known-plaintext pairs*: With this form of analysis the cryptanalyst has access to a set of known-plaintext pairs $(P_1, C_1), \ldots, (P_i, C_i)$, all of which have been generated with the same key K. The objective is to discover key K or at least an algorithm that can be used to obtain the plaintexts of other ciphertexts $C_{i+1}, \ldots$.

Chosen plaintext
- ■ *Analysis based on chosen plaintext*: In this case, the cryptanalyst not only has access to pairs of plaintexts and ciphertexts generated with the same key, but can also choose plaintexts $P_1, P_2, \ldots P_i$ him- or herself and gain knowledge about the corresponding ciphertexts $C_1, C_2, \ldots, C_i$ that were encrypted with the same key K. The objective of this analysis is to determine the unknown key K or at least an algorithm for decrypting other ciphertexts from pairs $(P_{i+j}, C_{i+j}), j > 1$.

Chosen ciphertext
- ■ *Analysis based on chosen ciphertext*: This attack form is very similar to the previous one. The only difference is that the cryptanalyst specifies ciphertexts $C_1, C_2, \ldots C_i$ and gains knowledge about the corresponding plaintexts $P_1, P_2, \ldots P_i$ that are all decrypted with the same key K. Here again the objective of the analysis is to determine the unknown key K or at least an algorithm for decrypting other ciphertexts from pairs $(P_{i+j}, C_{i+j}), j > 1$.

Related key attacks
- ■ *Analysis based on relations between keys*: Cryptanalysts may exploit the fact that some systems use different keys over time, when these keys have some kind of algebraic relation to each other. This relatively new method to break cryptographic algorithm became well known for its effectiveness to break into wireless LANs.

Unpublished cryptographic methods usually do not offer sufficient security
An important assumption with all the forms of analysis listed is that the cryptanalyst knows how the cryptographic algorithm functions. This assumption, which is now generally accepted as being a prudent one, relates to the principle named after the Flemish cryptographer August Kerckhoff. It states that the strength of a cryptographic method must be based completely on the secrecy of the key and not the secrecy of the algorithm [Ker83]. This principle is supported by the fact that extensive cryptanalytic studies by a large number of experienced cryptanalysts provide a statement about the

security of a cryptographic algorithm. A popular aphorism among cryptographers states that 'anyone can design a cryptographic algorithm that he cannot break himself.'

Besides generic forms of cryptanalysis, more specialised techniques like *differential cryptanalysis* [BS90, BS93] and *linear cryptanalysis* [Mat94] have become established over the last two decades. Both techniques are specialisations of the basic forms discussed above: differential cryptanalysis implements a special form of chosen plaintext analysis and linear cryptanalysis is a special form of known-plaintext analysis.

The cryptanalysis of asymmetric cryptographic methods can usually not be organised into the classification just described because it starts at a special place: the construction of matching key pairs. As the section on asymmetric cryptography explains in detail, these key pairs are constructed using mathematical attributes specified by the concrete cryptographic algorithm. The cryptanalyst tries to exploit these attributes by computing the appropriate private key from the public key of the two keys. Cryptanalysis of asymmetric methods therefore actually represents a separate discipline of mathematical research – more accurately, a subfield of number theory – and works with means different from those in the classic cryptanalysis of symmetric methods. Overall it is directed more towards completely breaking cryptographic algorithms than only calculating some plaintexts or keys from actual ciphertexts.

Cryptanalysis of asymmetric methods

Asymmetric cryptanalysis is aimed at completely breaking algorithms

2.4 Estimating the Effort Needed for Cryptographic Analysis

As mentioned above, the easiest way to attack any cryptographic algorithm is by systematically trying out all potential keys. For example, all possible keys are iterated and used to decrypt a ciphertext until an 'intelligible' plaintext is found. The probability is relatively high that the key discovered this way is the right key, and the cryptanalyst will be fairly certain of having found the right key by the time a second ciphertext is encrypted into intelligible plaintext with the same key. Since the number of possible keys with all the methods being used today is finite, this approach will inevitably be successful *sometime*. This section will look into the question of 'when' this sometime will be and related issues.

Which circumstances and which means are needed to carry out a specific cryptanalysis?

An estimation of the effort required for an attack on a cryptographic method usually includes the following:

- An estimate of the average number of steps needed, with one step possibly consisting of a sequence of complex calculations.
- An assumption of the number of steps that can be executed in one time unit. This is usually also based on a technical assumption, e.g. an upper bound for the increase of the achievable computation power like the generally recognised Moore's Law, which basically estimates that the achievable processing speed doubles every 18 months.
- An estimate of the memory needed for an analysis.

Goal is an estimate of the magnitude of the effort

The estimates needed are not an exact calculation of the actual effort. What is of interest instead is an assessment of the magnitude involved. Additive and multiplicative constants are therefore not important. What is important is only the term that calculates the magnitude, and with algorithms for cryptographic attacks it should be exponentially in the length of the key used.

For example, for the brute-force attack described earlier, one work step involves identifying the key being checked in this step, decrypting the recorded ciphertext and checking whether the plaintext recovered from it is intelligible. To simplify matters more, it is usually assumed that only the decryption is the dominant value.

Table 2.1

Average times needed for an exhaustive search for a key

Key length (bit)	Number of keys	Time req. with 1 encryption per μs	Time req. with 10^6 encryptions per μs
32	4.3×10^9	35.8 min	2.15 ms
56	7.2×10^{16}	1142 years	10.01 years
128	3.4×10^{38}	5.4×10^{24} years	5.4×10^{18} years
256	1.2×10^{77}	3.7×10^{63} years	3.7×10^{57} years

Estimating the development of processing times using Moore's Law

Table 2.1 lists the resulting times of a brute-force attack for different key lengths and different decryption speeds. Note that the value of 10^6 decryptions per microsecond (μs) was realistic for the DES algorithm and the technology available in the mid-1990s. Over the last few decades Moore's Law has been a relatively reliable estimate of the development of these processing times because the hardware logic required for an attack did not change. What should be exempted explicitly from such estimates are principal scientific developments in respect to the underlying computation model. A principal example is the methods of *quantum informatics* that are not yet ready for practical implementation but are theoretically designed [CU98].

Reference	Magnitude
Seconds in a year	3×10^7
Seconds since creation of solar system	2×10^{17}
Clock cycles per year at 50 MHz	1.6×10^{15}
Binary numbers of length 64	1.8×10^{19}
Binary numbers of length 128	3.4×10^{38}
Binary numbers of length 256	1.2×10^{77}
Number of 75-digit prime numbers	5.2×10^{72}
Number of electrons in the universe	8.4×10^{77}

Table 2.2
Reference values for estimating the computational effort of cryptanalytic methods

When such results are evaluated, it is useful to know some of the comparison values that relate the computed value to the magnitudes of the world around us. Table 2.2 lists some of these values.

What the two tables show is that the time needed for a brute-force calculation of a 128-bit long key exceeds the age of our solar system. The assumption that such an attack is not practical is therefore justified.

The estimated number of electrons that exist in our universe is another useful comparison value because it represents – even if the number is on the high side – an upper limit for the maximum memory space available to an attacker. This is of course based on a technological assumption that at least one electron is needed to store an information unit.

The table contains one last important value, the magnitude of the number of 75-digit prime numbers. The significance of prime numbers to asymmetric cryptography is clarified in Chapter 4. The only important point to mention here is that prime numbers exist in sufficient number for the probability that the same prime number will be selected twice during a random selection of large prime numbers to be minimal.

The practicality of cryptanalytic schemes can be evaluated based on a comparison of time and material requirements against reference values of the world around us

2.5   Characteristics and Classification of Encryption Algorithms

This section introduces two characteristics of encryption algorithms that are important for message transfer, and presents an initial categorisation of these schemes.

Assume that a sender wants to send a series of plaintexts $P_1, P_2, \ldots$ to a receiver. Because the messages are confidential, the sender first encrypts them into ciphertexts $C_1, C_2, \ldots$ and then transmits these to the receiver. There are two characteristics of the encryption method that are important:

Error propagation

- *Error propagation* in an encryption scheme characterises the effect of bit errors during the transmission of ciphertext on plaintexts $P_1', P_2', \ldots$ reconstructed after decryption. Depending on the cryptographic method used, a bit error in the ciphertext can result in a single bit error or a larger number of defective bits in the plaintext.

  The error propagation of a cryptographic method should be considered particularly in connection with *error-correcting codes*. By transmitting redundant information such codes enable certain errors, e.g. single-bit errors or even bursty errors up to a certain length, to be corrected automatically at the receiver. When they are used simultaneously with an encryption method that propagates transmission errors, it is important that encryption takes place first before the redundant information of the error-correcting code is computed. This ensures the error-correcting properties of the code, thereby also reducing the probability of errors in defective recovered plaintexts.

Synchronisation feature

- In contrast, the *synchronisation feature* of an encryption scheme describes the effect of a lost ciphertext C_i on plaintexts $P_{i+1}, P_{i+2}, \ldots$ reconstructed from subsequent correctly transmitted ciphertexts $C_{i+1}, C_{i+2}, \ldots$. Depending on the method used, it can turn out that such a loss has no effect on following plaintexts, that some subsequent plaintexts are falsified or even that all the following ciphertexts are incorrectly deciphered, and therefore explicit synchronisation is required between sender and receiver.

At the topmost level, encryption schemes can be categorised according to the following dimensions:

Type of operations

- According to the type of operations used for mapping plaintext to ciphertext:

  - *Substitution* maps elements of the plaintext, e.g. bits, letters or groups of bits or characters, to other elements.
  - *Transposition* rearranges the sequence of the elements of a plaintext.

Most encryption methods today combine both basic techniques because pure substitution or transposition ciphers do not offer adequate security.

- According to the number of keys used:

  - *Symmetric encryption methods* use the same key for decryption as for encryption.
  - *Asymmetric encryption methods* use two different but matching keys for the two complementary operations.

- According to the way in which the plaintext is processed:

  - *Stream ciphers* work on bit streams, which means that they encrypt plaintext one bit after another. Many stream ciphers are based on the idea of linear feedback shift registers that realise very efficient encryption. However, a multitude of cryptographic weaknesses has already been discovered in this method because of the sophisticated mathematical theory that exists for this field. The use of stream ciphers based on feedback shift registers is therefore often discouraged [Sch96, Chapters 16 and 17]. Most stream ciphers do not incorporate error propagation but instead react with great sensitivity to any loss of synchronisation and in such cases require explicit resynchronisation.
  - *Block ciphers* transform blocks of length b bits with the parameter b always dependent on the actual algorithm used.

2.6 Key Management

If cryptographic measures are used to protect data in a system, the management of the keys required for this purpose becomes a critical task. This is because data loses its cryptographic protection if the keys used to encrypt it are known. The tasks involved in key management are discussed in detail below:

- *Key generation* is the creation of the keys that are used. This process must be executed in a *random* or at least *pseudo-random-controlled* way because hackers will otherwise be able to execute the process themselves and in a relatively short time will discover the key that was used for security. Pseudo-random-controlled key generation means that keys are created according to a deterministic approach but each possible key has the same probability of being created from the method. Pseudo-random generators must be initialised with a real random value so that they do not always produce the same keys. If the process of key generation is not reproducible, it is referred to as 'truly random' key generation. The generation of random numbers is dealt with at length in Chapter 6.

If keys are needed for a symmetric cryptographic method, the output of a random or pseudo-random generator can be deployed as a key. On the other hand, key pairs produced for asymmetric cryptographic algorithms based on mathematical problems of factorisation or discrete logarithms require the generation of random and large prime numbers [Bre89].

Key distribution ■ The task of *key distribution* consists of deploying generated keys in the place in a system where they are needed. In simple scenarios the keys can be distributed through direct (e.g. personal) contact.

If larger distances are involved and symmetric encryption algorithms are used, the communication channel again has to be protected through encryption, therefore a key is needed for distributing keys. This necessity supports the introduction of what is called *key hierarchies*. The three-tier hierarchy of the IBM key management scheme [DP89, pages 143 ff.] is an early example. The scheme distinguishes between two *master keys* at the top level, a number of *terminal keys* at the next level and, lastly, *session keys* at the third level. Public keys of asymmetric cryptographic schemes (compare Chapter 4) generally can be made known. They only require that authenticity is guaranteed but not confidentiality.

Key storage ■ When *keys are stored*, measures are needed to make sure that they cannot be read by unauthorised users. One way to address this requirement is to ensure that the key is regenerated from an easy to remember but sufficiently long password (usually an entire sentence) before each use, and therefore is only stored in the memory of the respective user. Another possibility for storage is manipulation-safe crypto-modules, which are available on the market in the form of processor chip cards at a reasonable price [RE08, VV96].

Key recovery ■ *Key recovery* is the reconstruction of keys that have been lost. The simplest approach is to keep a copy of all keys in a secure place. However, this creates a possible security problem because an absolute guarantee is needed that the copies of the keys will not be tampered with [Sch96, pages 181 f.]. The alternative is to distribute the storage of the key fragments to different locations, which minimises the risk of fraudulent use so long as there is an assurance that all or a least a certain number of fragments are required to reconstruct the keys.

■ *Key invalidation* is an important task of key management, particularly with asymmetric cryptographic methods. If a private key is known, then the corresponding public key needs to be marked as invalid. This task is complicated by the fact that public keys are possibly stored in public directories worldwide and numerous but non-accessible copies of these keys may exist.   *Key invalidation*

■ The *destruction of no longer required keys* is aimed at ensuring that messages ciphered with them also cannot be decrypted by unauthorised persons in the future. It is important to make sure that all copies of the keys have really been destroyed. In modern operating systems this is not a trivial task since storage content is regularly transferred to hard disk through automatic storage management and the deletion in memory gives no assurance that copies of the keys no longer exist. In the case of magnetic disks, so-called EEPROMs (electrically erasable programmable read-only memory) and flash-based storage devices, these have to be overwritten or destroyed more than once to guarantee that the keys stored on them can no longer be read, even with sophisticated technical schemes.   *Destruction of no longer required keys*

2.7 Summary

Cryptology is the science of secure communication based on an algorithmic transformation of communicated data. It consists of the two fields of *cryptography* and *cryptanalysis*. Two main applications are of special interest in the context of network security: data *encryption* to hide its meaning and data *signing*, which is the generation of cryptographically secure check values to verify the authenticity of a message.   *Main cryptography applications for network security are encryption and signing*

A number of different cryptanalysis methods exist and they are usually categorised according to which information is available to cryptanalysts for an attack. The simplest form of attack consists of trying out all possible keys. Since the effort required for this form of attack grows exponentially according to key length, an attacker will reach the physical limits of our universe if the keys are long enough.

This book presents
an essential selection
of algorithms

The following chapters examine a range of cryptographic algorithms that are of central importance to network security. We have purposely limited the selection because it is not the goal of this book to present a comprehensive introduction to the field of cryptology. Our aim instead is to provide a fundamental understanding of how cryptographic methods work as the basis for explaining their use in the protocols and architectures of network security.

Figure 2.1
Overview of
cryptographic
algorithms presented
in this book

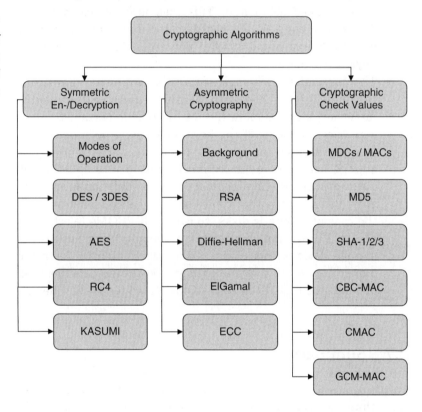

Content of the
chapters on crypto-
graphic algorithms

Figure 2.1 presents an overview of the algorithms discussed in this book. The following chapter deals with symmetric encryption methods and Chapter 4 is devoted to asymmetric cryptographic algorithms. Chapter 5 provides an introduction to the field of cryptographic checksums.

2.8   Supplemental Reading

[Ker83]   KERCKHOFF, A.: La Cryptographie Militaire. In:
          Journal des Sciences Militaires (1883), January 1883.
          The important principle stating that a cryptographic

algorithm has to provide security even if its functioning has been made known to a possible adversary was first formulated in this historically interesting article on the state of technology in the field of encryption in the late 19th century.

[Riv90]   RIVEST, R.: Cryptography. In: VAN LEEUWEN, J. (Ed.): Handbook of Theoretical Computer Science Vol. 1, Elsevier, 1990, pp. 717–755.

[Sim94a]   SIMMONS, G. J.: Cryptology. In: *Encyclopaedia Britannica*, Britannica, 1994.

2.9   Questions

1.   How much computation is required for a brute-force attack on a ciphertext in an optimal case, in an average case and in the worst case?

2.   Can it make sense for error-correcting coding to be provided in layer $n + 1$ of a protocol stack and encryption in layer n? If yes, which requirements have to be met?

3.   The *Caesar-cipher*, named after Julius Caesar, shifts every letter in the alphabet upward by three positions (thus 'A' becomes 'D,' 'B' becomes 'E', etc.). How many possible keys can be used? How many keys are theoretically possible with this scheme?

4.   Can there be any benefit to a cryptographic algorithm that is designed with a finite length key but is based on a theoretically undecidable problem of computer science?

3 Symmetric Cryptography

Symmetric encryption schemes use the same key for enciphering and deciphering. This key must be kept secret and should only be known to entities that need the key to read encoded ciphertexts. This chapter explains the basic encryption modes of symmetric encryption algorithms and describes DES, AES, RC4 and KASUMI, which are some of the most widely used algorithms.

3.1 Encryption Modes of Block Ciphers

In Section 2.5 we established that block ciphers do not encrypt or decrypt a bit stream bit by bit but instead in blocks, with the block length b specified by the encryption algorithm. This leads us to the question of how messages with a length different than b can be encrypted. To keep the discussion simple, we will assume below that the length of the message is a multiple of the block length b. This assumption can be applied to any messages that use known data processing methods, for example adding a '1' bit and a variable number of '0' bits until reaching the next multiple of b.

How can messages with a different length than the block size of the cipher be encrypted?

At this point one could come to the conclusion that message *padding* would completely solve the problem of the encryption of different length messages: all that is still needed is that each block of the length b has to be encrypted individually. Actually this describes one possible procedure. However, as shown in the following, the approach has a serious cryptographic drawback. As a result, alternative procedures were developed. These procedures are generally referred to as *encryption modes* and are explained below, but before giving more details a formal notation is introduced, which is also valid in the following chapters.

Using padding alone to fill blocks and block-wise message processing is not enough

Security in Fixed and Wireless Networks, Second Edition.
Guenter Schaefer and Michael Rossberg.
Copyright © 2014 by dpunkt.verlag GmbH, Heidelberg, Germany.
Title of the German original: Netzsicherheit   ISBN 978-3-86490-115-7
Translation Copyright © 2016 by John Wiley & Sons, Ltd., All rights reserved

Notation   Because keys for symmetric schemes have to be kept secret, they are normally always agreed between two entities A and B. When more than one key is involved, it is useful if the two entities are noted as the index of the key so that a key between A and B can be identified as $K_{A,B}$, for example. However, this indexing is often dispensed with when it is implicitly clear or immaterial which entities have agreed key K. The encryption of a plaintext P into a ciphertext C is often noted as $C = E(K_{A,B}, P)$ through the function E for encrypt. Its complementary operation is expressed by the function D for decrypt and it holds that $D(K_{A,B}, E(K_{A,B}, P)) = P$. For space reasons the notations $E_{K_{A,B}}(P)$ or, even shorter, $\{P\}_{K_{A,B}}$ are sometimes used to denote encryption of a message.

A plaintext message P is segmented into blocks $P_1, P_2, \ldots$ of the same length j, with $j \leq b$ and j normally a factor of b. The corresponding ciphertext blocks are of the same length and are noted with $C_1, C_2, \ldots$.

Electronic Code   The procedure described above in which a message P is en-
Book Mode   crypted through a separate enciphering of the individual message blocks P_i is called *Electronic Code Book Mode (ECB)* and is illustrated in Figure 3.1.

Figure 3.1
Electronic Code
Book Mode

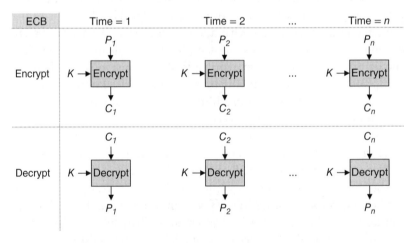

If an error occurs during the transmission of a ciphertext block C_i, the entire decrypted plaintext block P_i' is always falsified. However, the blocks that follow are correctly decrypted again and no subsequent errors occur even if one or more ciphertext blocks are lost. On the other hand, if the number of 'lost' bits has a value other than the block size b of the encryption procedure, then explicit resynchronisation is required between sender and receiver. The main disadvantage of this scheme is that identical plaintext blocks are mapped to identical ciphertext blocks. This characteristic makes the procedure vulnerable to a number of cryptographic analysis schemes, for example it is simple to detect when a message is sent twice, and it therefore should not be used in general.

Mapping the same plaintext blocks to identical ciphertexts should be avoided, therefore with *Cipher Block Chaining Mode (CBC)* plaintext blocks P_i are XORed to previous ciphertext block C_{i-1} before encryption. Consequently, when the blocks are decrypted, the value obtained after decryption of received ciphertext C_i still has to be XORed with the previous ciphertext C_{i-1} to recover the correct plaintext P_i. An *initialisation vector (IV)* is agreed as value C_0 between sender and receiver for the encryption and decryption of the first message block. This value does not have to be hidden from attackers and can be transmitted in plaintext before the actual message is sent. An overview of this mode is shown in Figure 3.2 and the following equations give additional clarification of the relationships described:

Cipher Block Chaining Mode

$$C_i = E_K(C_{i-1} \oplus P_i)$$
$$D_K(C_i) = D_K(E_K(C_{i-1} \oplus P_i))$$
$$D_K(C_i) = C_{i-1} \oplus P_i$$
$$C_{i-1} \oplus D_K(C_i) = C_{i-1} \oplus C_{i-1} \oplus P_i$$
$$C_{i-1} \oplus D_K(C_i) = P_i$$

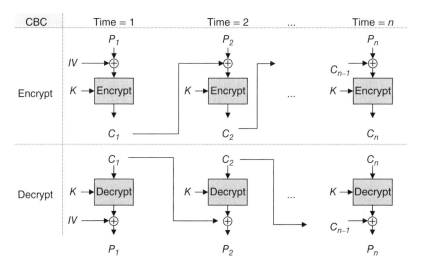

Figure 3.2
Cipher Block Chaining Mode

If one or more bit errors occur in ciphertext block C_i, the entire deciphered plaintext block P_i' is falsified, as are the corresponding bits in following block P_{i+1}'. The loss of ciphertext block C_i also results in a falsification of the following block P_{i+1}'. However, the scheme resynchronises itself automatically after one block has been incorrectly deciphered as long as complete blocks are lost.

Processing shorter message blocks

In some instances message blocks even shorter than those with a b bit length require encryption. An example is confidential interactive terminal communication, where individual characters should ideally be encrypted and then transmitted immediately after being typed in by the user.

Using padding alone to achieve block size wastes bandwidth and leads to cryptographic weaknesses

A naïve approach in this case would be to 'pad' each message block of length j up to length b and then to encrypt and transmit it. A downside of this approach would be an undesirable increase in the data being transmitted because a b length block would have to be transmitted for each j length block, for example one character. With character-orientated applications and a cipher with a 128-bit block length, this would amount to a sixteenfold increase in the transmission bandwidth required.

Such an approach may also lead to cryptographic weaknesses, for example when incomplete plaintext blocks are filled with predetermined bit patterns. In this case the encryption of a single byte will result in only 256 different ciphertexts and might allow the attacker to build a dictionary that maps ciphertexts to plaintexts.

Ciphertext Feedback Mode

The increase in required transmission bandwidth can be avoided using a more suitable mode. The *Ciphertext Feedback Mode (CFB)* encrypts message blocks of length j bits using a block cipher with a block size of b bits. All message blocks P_i in the following discussion have a length of j bits.

The scheme works with a register. An initialisation vector is written into the register before the first message block is processed. The key is used to encipher the register content before the encryption of each message block. From the value obtained the j higher-valued bits are XORed with the plaintext that is being encrypted. The resulting ciphertext is then written in the j lower-valued bits of the register, which previously was left-shifted by j bits. This feedback of the ciphertext also explains how the name of the scheme originated. Messages are decrypted with the same procedure. The decryption function of the encryption procedure is not required, as shown by the following equations in which $S(j, X)$ denotes the higher-valued j bits of X and R_i denotes the content of register R in the encryption or decryption of plaintext block P_i:

$$R_1 = IV$$
$$R_i = (R_{i-1} \times 2^j \mod 2^b) + C_{i-1}$$
$$C_i = S(j, E_K(R_i)) \oplus P_i$$

$$S(j, E_K(R_i)) \oplus C_i = S(j, E_K(R_i)) \oplus S(j, E_K(R_i)) \oplus P_i$$
$$S(j, E_K(R_i)) \oplus C_i = P_i$$

Figure 3.3 presents an overview of this encryption mode with a second register showing the selection of j higher-valued bits after encryption of the register content. Unlike the one discussed above, this register does not store the status of the procedure and in an actual implementation can just as easily be omitted.

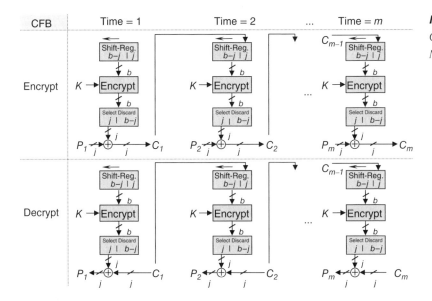

Figure 3.3
Ciphertext Feedback Mode

If a bit error occurs during the transmission of a ciphertext block C_i, a bit error then appears in the same place of corresponding plaintext block P_i'. Furthermore, the error also occurs in the register and produces completely distorted plaintext blocks until it is completely shifted out of the register by subsequent ciphertext blocks. Likewise, if a ciphertext block is lost, the following blocks will be decrypted incorrectly until subsequent ciphertext blocks lead to a resynchronisation of the register content between sender and receiver.

The concept of encryption using an XOR-operation with a pseudo-random sequence is also realised through the *Output Feedback Mode (OFB)*. In contrast to CFM, it is not the recovered ciphertext C_i that is fed back into the register but the j higher-valued bits of the enciphered register content. The block cipher in this mode therefore generates a pseudo-random bit sequence, which is completely independent of the plaintext being encrypted.

Output Feedback Mode

Figure 3.4

Output Feed-
back Mode

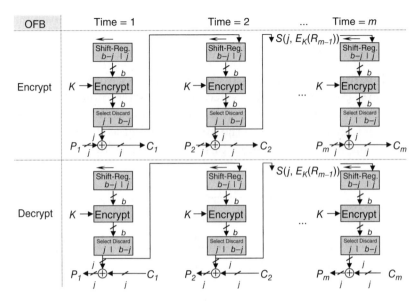

This results in the following relationships (also see Figure 3.4):

$$R_1 = IV$$
$$R_i = (R_{i-1} \times 2^j \bmod 2^b) + S(j, E_K(R_{i-1}))$$
$$C_i = S(j, E_K(R_i)) \oplus P_i$$
$$S(j, E_K(R_i)) \oplus C_i = S(j, E_K(R_i)) \oplus S(j, E_K(R_i)) \oplus P_i$$
$$S(j, E_K(R_i)) \oplus C_i = P_i$$

If a bit error occurs between the encryption and decryption of a ciphertext block, then a bit error will also appear in the corresponding place in the plaintext block. Output Feedback Mode, therefore, does not lead to error propagation. However, the loss of one or more message blocks has a disruptive effect on all subsequent blocks and an explicit resynchronisation of the procedure is required.

Cryptographically,
error propaga-
tion is desirable

The characteristic of OFB that it does not propagate errors may be considered an advantage from a data processing view but from a cryptographic standpoint it is usually considered a disadvantage because it means that attackers can make controllable alterations to texts protected by encryption. This is based on the fact that each modified bit in a ciphertext results in exactly one modified bit in the plaintext after decryption. Even if an attacker cannot know which value the corresponding bit will hold after decryption, he or she can deliberately inverse it. The fact that such an attack can be useful will also be shown in the discussion on the use of security protocols to protect communication in wireless local area networks in Chapter 15.

Another important point to remember with encryption in OFB mode is that the scheme will be completely insecure if the same pseudo-random sequence is used to encrypt two different messages. In a case like this, the XOR-operation of the two ciphertexts produces the XOR-operation of the two corresponding plaintexts, which means that an attacker who knows one of the two plaintexts merely has to compute the pseudo-random sequence and the other plaintext using a simple XOR-operation.

Multiple use of the same pseudo-random sequence with OFB is not secure!

Apart from the presented modes, which only encrypt data, more sophisticated ones exist that not only encrypt, but also authenticate data in the same step. However, details will not be given before Section 5.5 as they require the introduction of further cryptographic primitives.

3.2 Data Encryption Standard

The *Data Encryption Standard (DES)* was introduced in the mid-1970s. In 1973 the American National Bureau of Standards, today called the *National Institute of Standards and Technology (NIST)*, had invited proposals for a national encryption standard that would meet the following requirements:

- provide a high level of security;
- be completely specified and easy to understand;
- provide security only on the basis of the secrecy of its keys and not on the basis of the secrecy of the algorithm itself;
- potentially be available to all possible users;
- be adaptable for use in diverse applications;
- be implementable in electronic devices;
- be efficient to use;
- be capable of being validated;
- be exportable.

Requirements of the algorithm

None of the submissions in response to the first call met these requirements, and it was not until the second call that IBM submitted the algorithm Lucifer, which turned out to be an encouraging candidate. Lucifer was a symmetric block cipher that worked on 128-bit length blocks and used 128-bit long keys.

IBM's algorithm Lucifer was the only promising submission for the second call

The National Bureau of Standards requested help from the *National Security Agency (NSA)* in assessing the security of the algorithm. The NSA, the largest foreign secret service in the USA, is widely recognised as it has a staff of highly competent crypto-graphers and mathematicians. The results of the NSA are usually confidential and therefore not intended to become public know-ledge. This makes it difficult to make an exact assessment of the 'cryptographic lead' the NSA enjoys ahead of other cryptographers in the world. That it has had the lead for a long time has been historically proven and the development history of DES also sup-ports this.

Modifications to the algorithm by the NSA

The NSA reduced the block size of the algorithm to 64 bits and its key length to 56 bits. It also made modifications to the internal structure of the substitution tables. These changes were the cause of extensive discussions among cryptographers and it was not until the 1990s that some of these changes could be understood.

Despite all the criticism it attracted, the algorithm was standardised in 1977 [NIS77, NIS88] and released for securing 'non-confidential' government data. Since the algorithm was freely available in the USA, it was also used by private-sector companies and quickly developed into the standard algorithm for encryption. Until the mid-1990s, permission to export DES products from the USA was subject to stringent conditions due to the terms of the US Weapons Act.

***Figure 3.5**
Overview of the
DES algorithm*

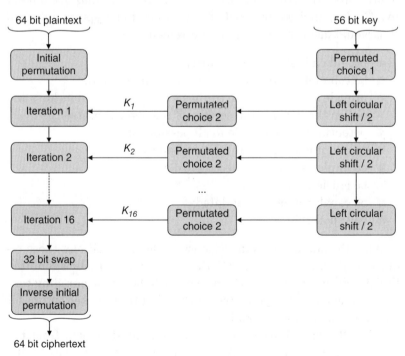

Figure 3.5 shows how the DES algorithm is structured. A 64-bit long data block first undergoes an *initial permutation* and is then processed in 16 *iterations*, also called *rounds*. A different *round key* is computed in each round and linked to the data block. After the last iteration, the two 32-bit long halves of the data block are interchanged and the resulting block undergoes a new permutation, which is an inverse operation to the initial permutation. In the illustration, the data block is being worked on in the left half and the key in the right half.

Functioning of DES

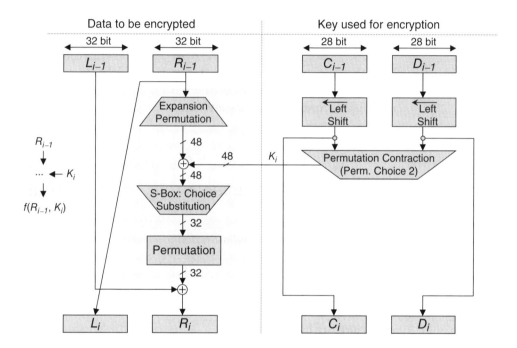

The internal structure of an iteration step is shown in Figure 3.6, where again one half shows a data block being processed and the other half shows the key. The data block is worked on in two halves with the result of the ith iteration step denoted in the following as L_i and R_i. The left half L_i simply receives the content of the right half R_{i-1} from the previous step. For computing the right half, function $f(R_{i-1}, K_i)$ from the previous step R_{i-1} and the round key K_i are applied to the content of the right half and the resulting value XORed to the content of the left half L_{i-1} of the previous step. The function f first expands and permutes the content of R_{i-1} with the duplication of 16 of the 32 bits, thereby creating a value of the length of 48 bits. This is XORed with the 48-bit long round key and

Figure 3.6
One round in the DES algorithm

the result of this operation in turn is mapped to a 32-bit long value through eight *substitution boxes (S-boxes)*. During the mapping with the substitution boxes, a 6-bit long value is mapped to a 4-bit long value in each box according to a rule that has been specified for each box. The value obtained according to the substitution boxes is then permuted to obtain the result of function f.

Computation of round key   For the computation of round key K_i the round key is also divided into two halves. In each iteration, both halves are shifted circularly to the left by 1 or 2 bits. The round determines whether the half is shifted one or two positions. After this operation, the 56 bits of the key are mapped to 48 bits to obtain round key K_i.

DES decryption   Decryption with DES uses the same procedure except that the round keys are applied in the reverse. The following computations help to show how the encryption function of DES is reversed. In each step i the two halves of the data block being processed are modified according to the equations:

$$L_i = R_{i-1}$$
$$R_i = L_{i-1} \oplus f(R_{i-1}, K_i)$$

Register content before the first step   For decryption the initial data block $L_0'||R_0'$ before the first iteration step is:

$$L_0' \ || \ R_0' = InitialPermutation(ciphertext)$$

Also:

$$ciphertext = InitialPermutation^{-1}(R_{16} \ || \ L_{16})$$

and therefore overall:

$$L_0' \ || \ R_0' = R_{16} \ || \ L_{16}$$

After one step   After the first iteration step:

$$L_1' = R_0' = L_{16} = R_{15}$$
$$R_1' = L_0' \oplus f(R_0', K_{16}) = R_{16} \oplus f(R_{15}, K_{16})$$
$$= [L_{15} \oplus f(R_{15}, K_{16})] \oplus f(R_{15}, K_{16}) = L_{15}$$

This relationship continues in all rounds of the decryption because it holds that:

$$R_{i-1} = L_i$$
$$L_{i-1} = R_i \oplus f(R_{i-1}, K_i) = R_i \oplus f(L_i, K_i)$$

Therefore after the 16th round it holds that: *After 16 steps*

$$L'_{16} \| R'_{16} = R_0 \| L_0$$

At the end the two 32-bit long halves of the data block are reversed and the resulting block undergoes inverse initial permutation so that the results of the decryption are:

$InitialPermutation^{-1}(L_0 \| R_0) =$

$InitialPermutation^{-1}(InitialPermutation(plaintext)) = plaintext$

In the underlying construction scheme of the DES algorithm, the   *Feistel network*
data block being encrypted is divided into two halves and encrypted in several iterations with alternating round keys according to the equations above. This scheme is also called a *Feistel network* after its creator Horst Feistel. Because of its relatively well-researched cryptographic attributes, which have not shown any inherent weaknesses, this structure has been used as the underlying basis for numerous other modern block ciphers in addition to DES. One of these is the *KASUMI* cipher, which will be discussed later in this chapter.

Independent cryptographers criticised the NSA because it   *Security of DES*
weakened the algorithm by reducing the block size to 64 bits and the key length to 56 bits. They claimed that the reductions made the algorithm vulnerable to brute-force attacks, even if at the time these would have had to be extremely powerful attackers, such as the secret service of a government. In addition, the NSA modified the structure of the internal substitution boxes of the algorithm. Because independent cryptographers did not have the opportunity to evaluate the latter modifications, it was long suspected that these changes had weakened the algorithm, too. This meant that the NSA could have been deciphering messages without ever being in possession of the key.

This suspicion has not ever been confirmed. On the contrary, it   *Resistance against*
became obvious in the early 1990s that DES could not be broken   *differential*
by the attack technique of differential cryptanalysis [BS90, BS93]   *cryptanalysis*
published in 1990 and the reason was precisely because of the structure of the substitution boxes and the number of iterations carried out in the algorithm. Sources at the NSA subsequently disclosed that it had already known about this attack technique in the 1970s and strengthened DES accordingly.

It is the short key length of DES that has continued to be   *Key length is main*
its main weakness. Even 'average' attackers have been able to   *weakness*
carry out brute-force searches through entire key spaces since the mid-1990s, and this now makes DES an insecure option.

Multiple encryption
Because it was already possible to predict this potential inadequacy of DES in the 1970s through an estimation of technological development in terms of computing speed, consideration could be given early enough to the use of multiple encryption with different keys in order to increase the overall security attainable with the DES algorithm.

Certain algebraic properties can make multiple encryption ineffective
What has to be taken into account, however, is that multiple encryption only results in a longer effective key length if the encryption algorithm does not show certain algebraic properties. If, for example, DES were *closed*, that is, a third key K_3 exists for all keys K_1, K_2 so that $E(K_2, E(K_1, M)) = E(K_3, M)$ for all messages M, then double encryption using different keys K_1, K_2 would not increase the effective key length. By a complete search of the key space, an attacker in this case would always find a key K_3 that correctly deciphers all messages doubly encrypted with K_1 and K_2.

A similar inadequacy would occur with triple encryption if DES were *pure*, that is, if a K_4 were to exist for all K_1, K_2, K_3 so that $E(K_3, E(K_2, E(K_1, M))) = E(K_4, M)$ for all messages M. Because DES is neither closed nor pure, multiple encryption for the purpose of extending the effective key length is possible in principle.

Meet-in-the-middle attack with double encryption
Double encryption with two different keys is still insecure because it can be broken with a *meet-in-the-middle* attack. Although the key length with DES in this case is 112 bits, *double DES* can be broken with an effort of 2^{56}. All an attacker needs are a few plaintext-ciphertext pairs $C = E(K_2, E(K_1, P))$ that were encrypted with the same key $K = K_1 || K_2$. What the attacker is 'interested' in is the value X, which is always 'in the middle' between the two encryption steps, so that:

$$X = E(K_1, P) = D(K_2, C)$$

An attacker will take advantage of this fact to construct all possible combinations of type $K_1 || K_2$ keys, with K_1 and K_2 initially un-

Construction of two tables
known. First, two tables $T_1[0, 2^{56}]$ and $T_2[0, 2^{56}]$ are set up, with the first one containing the values of $X = E(K_1, P)$ for all possible values of K_1 and the second one containing the values of $X = D(K_2, C)$ for all possible values of K_2. Then both tables are sorted according to the values of X and compared against each other value by value. A possible candidate for the tuple (K_1, K_2) is found for all matching values of X.

A DES plaintext is always mapped to one of 2^{64} possible ciphertexts due to its block size of 64 bits, therefore with 2^{112} possible values for (K_1, K_2), on average $2^{112}/2^{64} = 2^{48}$ 'false alarms' will occur after the first plaintext-ciphertext pair. With each further pair for which both tables have been constructed the probability of such a falsely assumed key value reduces by a factor of 2^{64}. As a result, the probability of a false key after the second pair reduces to 2^{-16}.

Overall this means that the average effort required for the cryptanalysis of a double DES is of the magnitude of 2^{56}, which only represents a minimal increase in security compared to a simple DES, the compromising of which requires an average effort of 2^{55}. This improvement is, therefore, well below the anticipated increase of the average effort to 2^{111} that one would expect of a cryptographic scheme with a key length of 112.

The attack method described can be dealt with through the following triple encryption scheme, which was proposed by W. Tuchman in 1979:

Triple DES (3DES)

$$C = E(K_3, D(K_2, E(K_1, P)))$$

The use of the decryption function D in the middle of the scheme enables devices that implement triple encryption to be used together with devices that only carry out simple encryption. In this case, the three keys are set to the same value, with the resulting security again only being the same as that of simple encryption.

Triple encryption can be used with either two ($K_1 = K_3$) or three different keys, in which case three different keys are often given explicit preference. While meet-in-the-middle attacks are theoretically also possible with triple encryption, one of the two calculated tables would require 2^{112} entries. However, according to the considerations in Section 2.4 this is impractical. Until now there has been no publicity about viable attacks on this scheme and so it is considered secure. However, the drawback of multiple encryption compared with simple encryption is that performance is reduced by a third. Consequently, it is more beneficial to use an encryption algorithm that already offers a longer key length for simple encryption to start with. The following section describes the efforts that have gone into standardising such a scheme.

3DES is considered rather secure

Main drawback of multiple encryptions is reduced performance

3.3 Advanced Encryption Standard

In January 1997 the NIST made an official announcement of its plans to develop an *Advanced Encryption Standard (AES)*. As with DES earlier, its principle objective was to develop an encryption standard that could be used to protect sensitive government data.

Again, as with DES, it was assumed that as a standard AES would also find wide acceptance in the private sector.

Worldwide call for submission of algorithms

In September 1997 a formal request was published inviting cryptographers from all over the world to submit algorithms for the AES proposal. The conditions stipulated that the algorithms submitted had to be unclassified, published and available without licensing fees worldwide. The algorithms were also required to use a symmetric block cipher and support a minimum block size of 128 bits as well as key lengths of 128, 192 and 256 bits.

In August 1998 the first AES conference set up to identify possible candidates was held. NIST subsequently nominated a selection of 15 algorithms as candidates and requested comments on them.

Five candidates selected after the second AES conference

A second AES conference took place in March 1999, and the results of various analytic studies carried out by the professional world of cryptography since the first conference were discussed. After this conference, NIST announced in April 1999 that it had narrowed its selection and that five algorithms were now candidates for the final choice of the AES standard. These were the *MARS, RC6, Rijndael, Serpent* and *Twofish* algorithms. Another request was made for an intensive analysis of the five algorithms with attention given not only to purely cryptographic aspects but also to implementation considerations, issues relating to possible patent rights in respect to intellectual property and other overall recommendations.

Selection of Rijndael algorithm as future AES

The third and last AES conference was held in May 2000. After an intensive evaluation of its findings, NIST published the Rijndael algorithm as the official proposal for AES in October 2000.

The main justification for selecting the Rijndael algorithm was that it effectively met the central requirements for a secure, efficient, easy-to-use and flexible algorithm. Even though all five candidates still under consideration during the last round were about evenly matched regarding meeting security requirements on the basis of the known level of technology, Rijndael was particularly impressive because of some of its other attributes. It shows good performance in hardware and software implementations, requires minimal effort in key preparation (thus supporting fast key change), needs minimal memory and uses operations that

Security against timing and power analyses

are relatively simple to protect from timing and power analyses. With *timing analyses* an attacker uses the timely behaviour of a cryptographic algorithm to obtain feedback on the current key being used, whereas with *power analyses* similar conclusions are reached on the basis of power demand.

A first version of the standard was published in February 2001 and allowed a three-month comment period. After a further revision, AES was officially adopted as a standard on 26 November 2001 [NIS01] and came into effect on 26 May 2002.

Publication of AES standard

```
// Algorithm: Rijndael_Encrypt
// Input:     in  = 16 octets of plaintext (Nb = 4)
//                w  = the key prepared for
//                      No. + 1 rounds
// Output:     out = 16 octets of ciphertext

void Rijndael_Encrypt(byte in[4*Nb], byte out[4*Nb],
                      word w[Nb*(Nr+1)]) {
  byte state[4,Nb];

  state = in; // Copying of plaintext
              // to state matrix

  AddRoundKey(state, w[0, Nb-1]);

  for (round = 1;  round <= Nr - 1; round++) {
    SubBytes(state);
    ShiftRows(state);
    MixColumns(state);
    AddRoundKey(state, w[round*Nb, (round+1)*Nb-1]);
  }

  SubBytes(state);
  ShiftRows(state);
  AddRoundKey(state, w[Nr*Nb, (Nr+1)*Nb-1]);

  out = state; // Copying of state matrix
               // to output
}
```

Figure 3.7
Overview of Rijndael encryption

The Rijndael algorithm can be used with different block sizes and key lengths. As part of the AES standardisation the block size was specified as 128 bits even though the algorithm description in [NIS01] still reflects the flexibility of the algorithm (compare Figure 3.7), giving the block size as parameter Nb in 32-bit words ($Nb = 4$). The values 128, 192 and 256 bits are specified for the key length. Depending on the key length, the algorithm iterates internally in 10, 12 or 14 rounds (parameter Nr), with a negligible difference between the last round and the other rounds.

Parameterisation of Rijndael

The encryption function of Rijndael operates on a state matrix of four-times four octets into which the plaintext being encrypted

Functioning of Rijndael

is initially written and is based on four different operations. In each round, an octet substitution is first carried out on the basis of an S-box *(SubBytes)* and then the columns of the state matrix are interchanged according to line-specific rules *(ShiftRow)*. The subsequent *MixColumns operation* executes a matrix multiplication using a specifically defined matrix with the octets interpreted as elements of the field $GF(2^8)$ and not as numbers. Mathematically, this results in a polynominal multiplication carried out modulo $x^4 + 1$ with the fixed matrix

$$\begin{pmatrix} 02 & 03 & 01 & 01 \\ 01 & 02 & 03 & 01 \\ 01 & 01 & 02 & 03 \\ 03 & 01 & 01 & 02 \end{pmatrix}$$

Each number in the matrix actually represents the coefficients of a term, for example 03 is $x + 1$. Details for calculating with this so-called Galois field will be given in Section 4.8.3, as more algebraic background knowledge needs to be introduced first. The inverse matrix over $GF(2^8)$ (modulo $x^4 + 1$) required for the decryption function is:

$$\begin{pmatrix} 0e & 0b & 0d & 09 \\ 09 & 0e & 0b & 0d \\ 0d & 09 & 0e & 0b \\ 0b & 0d & 09 & 0e \end{pmatrix}$$

The product of the matrices in $GF(2^8)$ is the identity matrix. The MixColumn operation is not carried out in the last round, which only executes three operations.

The last operation in each round is an XOR-operation with a round-specific key *(AddRoundKey)*. The round key is computed beforehand in an initialising operation before actual encryption, which is not explained further here.

Decryption func-tion of Rijndael   The decryption function of Rijndael can be realised in two different ways. The variant shown in Figure 3.8 uses the same key schedule for the round key as encryption does but computes the inverse functions for the operations described above in a different sequence.

Proof that the encryption and decryption functions of Rijndael are complementary to one another is not as readily evident as with the DES algorithm. Rijndael clearly uses more complex operations

```
// Algorithm: Rijndael_Decrypt
// Input:     in  = 16 octets ciphertext
//            w   = the key prepared for
//                  No. + 1 rounds
// Output:    out = 16 octets plaintext

void Rijndael_Decrypt(byte in[4*Nb], byte out[4*Nb],
                      word w[Nb*(No.+1)]) {
  byte state[4,Nb];

  state = in; // Copying of ciphertext
              // to state matrix

  AddRoundKey(state, w[Nr*Nb, (Nr+1)*Nb-1]);

  for (round = Nr - 1;  round >= 1; round--) {
    InvShiftRows(state);
    InvSubBytes(state);
    AddRoundKey(state, w[round*Nb, (round+1)*Nb-1]);
    InvMixColumns(state);
  }

  InvShiftRows(state);
  InvSubBytes(state);
  AddRoundKey(state, w[0, Nb-1]);

  out = state; // Copy state matrix
               // to the output
}
```

Figure 3.8
Overview of Rijndael decryption

and does not follow a Feistel structure. This book therefore will not discuss this standard further and interested readers are referred to the AES Standard [NIS01] or a textbook with a focus on cryptography like [PPP09].

After more than a decade since the standardisation of AES there are still no notable weaknesses known. Nevertheless, there have been some critical statements by cryptanlysts: the *SubBytes* function is the only non-linear function of AES. Because of the simple structure it possible to express the whole AES algorithm by large matrix operations, which has, however, not led to any attacks, yet. The first attack on AES with a full number of rounds was not published until 2011 [BKR11]. Nevertheless, with an effort of $2^{126.1}$ operations for AES with a 128-bit key length, $2^{189.7}$ operations of the 192-bit version and $2^{254.4}$ operations for AES with a full key length of 256 bits, this is attack is still far from being practical. Still this has been the first really noteworthy advance in the analysis of AES in more than a decade.

Security of AES today

3.4   RC4 Algorithm

The RC4 algorithm realises a still widely used stream cipher and was created by Ron Rivest in 1987. The operations of the algorithm were not published until 1994, when an anonymous announcement appeared on a mailing list.

Encryption in   RC4 operates in OFB, that is, a pseudo-random bit sequence
OFB mode $RC4(IV, K)$, which is dependent only on the key K being used and an initialisation vector IV, is generated through the algorithm and XORed to the plaintext P being encrypted. Decryption is then realised through an XOR-operation of the ciphertext with the same pseudo-random bit sequence:

$$C = P \oplus RC4(IV, K)$$
$$P = C \oplus RC4(IV, K)$$

The pseudo-random bit sequence is often also referred to as a *keystream*.

Initialisation vectors   For the security of the algorithm it is essential that a keystream
must never be reused!   used to encrypt a plaintext P_1 is never used to encrypt another plaintext $P_2 \neq P_1$. An initialisation vector IV must therefore be combined with a static key K, thus ensuring that two different plaintexts are never encrypted with the same initialisation vector $IV_1 = IV_2$. If this condition is violated, an XOR-operation of the two ciphertexts C_1 and C_2 can compute the XOR-operation of the two plaintexts P_1 and P_2. If $IV_1 = IV_2$, then:

$$C_1 \oplus C_2 = P_1 \oplus RC4(IV_1, K) \oplus P_2 \oplus RC4(IV_2, K)$$
$$= P_1 \oplus RC4(IV_1, K) \oplus RC4(IV_1, K) \oplus P_2$$
$$= P_1 \oplus P_2$$

Known-   If the attacker in this case knows one of the two plaintexts, for ex-
plaintext attack   ample P_1, then he or she can use it to compute the other plaintext (known-plaintext attack). This possibility was not taken into account in the standardisation of wireless local networks in the IEEE 802.11 standard therefore the security protocol defined in the standard has serious shortcomings (compare Chapter 15).

The RC4 algorithm can be operated with different length keys and initialisation vectors, with the maximum overall length being

```
// Algorithm: RC4_Init
// Input:     key = the key of the length
//                  KeyAndIvLen already linked to an
//                  initialisation vector that can
//                  only be used once
//
// Ouput:     i, n = 2 state indices modulo 256
//                  s = state field with 256 entries

void RC4_Init(byte* key; int& i, n; byte s[256]) {
  unsigned int keyIndex, stateIndex;
  byte a;

  // Padding s[] with 0 up to 255
  for (i = 0; i < 256; i++) S[i] = i;

  // Compute initial state field s
  keyIndex = 0; stateIndex = 0;
  for (i=0; i < 256; i++) {
    stateIndex = stateIndex + key[keyIndex] + a;
    stateIndex = stateIndex & 0xff; // modulo 256
    a = s[i];
    s[i] = s[stateIndex];
    s[stateIndex] = a;
    if (++keyIndex >= KeyAndIvLen) keyIndex = 0;
  }
  i = 0; n = 0; // Initialise state indices
}
```

Figure 3.9
*Initialisation of RC4
algorithm*

2048 bits. The algorithm operates on a state field $s[\,]$ with 256 entries and two indices i and n for this field. These variables are initialised in a preliminary step using the initialisation vector and the key (compare Figure 3.9).

Figure 3.10 illustrates how RC4 computes a pseudo-random bit sequence and is used in encryption and decryption.

In terms of the security of RC4, it should be noted that the *Security of RC4* variable key length of up to 2048 bits means that the algorithm can be operated so that it is secure from brute-force attacks that use resources available in our universe and are based on known technologies — possible future technologies such as quantum informatics explicitly excluded. However, a significant reduction in key length, for example to 40 bits, can make operation of the algorithm insecure. For example, the standard specification for keys in the SSL protocol is 40 bits, which *de facto* provides no security (see also Chapter 11). For a long time RC4 with 40-bit

Figure 3.10

*Encryption or
decryption with
the RC4 algorithm*

```
// Algorithm:   RC4_Process
// Input:         in = the plaintext or ciphertext
//                       being processed
//                   len = length of inut
// In/output: i, n = 2 state indices modulo 256
//                     s = state field with 256
//                            entries
// Output:        out = the resulting ciphertext
//                         or plaintext

void RC4_Process(byte* in, int len; int& i, n;
                    byte s[256], byte* out) {
    int  j;
    byte a, b;

    for(j = 0; j < len; j++) {
      i = (i+1) & 0xff; // Addition modulo 256
      a = s[i];
      n = (n+a) & 0xff; // Addition modulo 256
      b = s[n];
      s[i] = b;
      s[n] = a;
      out[j] = in[j] xor s[((a+b) & 0xff)];
    }
}
```

*Encryption with
40-bit long keys
offers no security!*

*Improper key
scheduling
affects security*

*Potential counter-
measures*

long keys had special export status, which is evident by its former wide use in diverse software products, in particular web browsers. As mentioned earlier, this does not provide any considerable level of security. The situation has changed as a result of a relaxing of export rules in the USA and products that use RC4 with 128-bit long keys may now be sold in most countries.

Attacks on RC4 mainly concentrate on weaknesses regarding the derivation of the initial state from the key material. For example, depending on the method used to combine the key and the initialisation vector, the key can be discovered using known plaintext-ciphertext pairs by a related key attack. It is sufficient for the attacker to know the first octet of the encrypted plaintexts. Depending on the method used to generate the initialisation vectors, the attacker needs around a quarter of a million to two million such pairs (P_i, C_i), encrypted with the same key K and different initialisation vectors IV_i. The fundamental attack technique was presented at a conference in August 2001 [FMS01]. Subsequently, this method has been heavily refined.

A commentary by Ron Rivest describes how to counter this shortcoming through careful preparation of the key with the initialisation vector [Riv01], that is, by using the output of a cryptographic hash function or by rejecting the first 256 bytes of the RC4 output. The authors of different related key attacks [Mir02, Kle08] recommend rejecting even more bytes of the initial key stream. Currently these are at least the first 3072 bytes. Chapter 15 will show that this shortcoming is not just of theoretical interest. For the recent advances in the cryptanalysis of RC4, it seems reasonable that RC4 contains even more weaknesses, therefore a usage of the cipher should be avoided if possible.

3.5   The KASUMI algorithm

In addition to the algorithms already presented, a number of other encryption and authentication techniques are used in mobile communication applications. This is due to the low energy and power resources of the terminal devices and the space limitations on the smart cards used. In the past this has led to the development of specially adapted ciphers, often with borderline security. The A5/1 and A5/2 algorithms, for example, which were used in GSM and early versions of UMTS, can now be broken in real-time [BBK08].

Ciphers for mobile networks

In mobile networks the main algorithm that is currently used is KASUMI [ETS12a]. Depending on the standard it is also referred to as A5/3 for 64-bit key length and A5/4 or UEA1 for 128-bit key length. It is a block cipher that is designed for high speeds in hardware and can be realised with fewer than 10,000 gates per chip. Like RC4 and DES, KASUMI goes back to a company development. It is a modified version of Mitsubishi Electric's MISTY1 algorithm.

KASUMI uses a key that is 128 bits long and operates with a block size of 64 bits. To realise the encryption the algorithm cycles through eight rounds of a Feistel network. In the rounds the data is split into two blocks. The left block is modified by means of two non-linear functions FL and FO, as shown in Figure 3.11. The sequence in which FL and FO are applied changes in each round. As in DES, the modified data is linked with the unchanged subblock via an XOR operation, and the sequence of the subblocks is changed. For decryption these steps simply have to be processed in reverse order.

The KASUMI procedure

In view of the small number of rounds, the security of KASUMI essentially depends on how successful the functions FL and FO are at quickly combining the input and the key. The function FL only plays a limited role. It divides the input value into two 16-bit values, which are then modified by means of two simple logic operations.

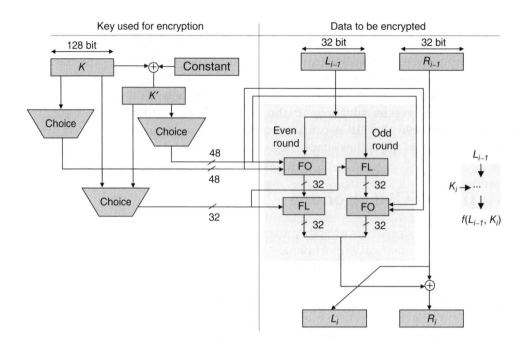

Figure 3.11

One round of the KASUMI algorithm

FO is much more complex: it is itself a small Feistel network, which in each of three rounds changes a 16-bit data block. The function that modifies the data within FO is referred to in the standard as FI. It too is a Feistel network, consisting of four rounds. Since the 16-bit input data is split into 7- and 9-bit wide parts, it is also referred to as a *irregular Feistel network*.

Security of KASUMI

    The multiple, recursive use of a Feistel structure is intended to ensure the security properties of KASUMI, despite the comparatively small number of rounds. However, because of the short block length there is nevertheless a risk that, for example, dictionaries might be created in the not too distant future. In addition, a number of cryptographic attacks have occurred in recent years. As early as 2001, for instance, a so-called *impossible differential attack* on a KASUMI that was reduced to six rounds was published [Küh01]. In this case, certain internal states of the algorithm can be ruled out and the complexity of an attack is reduced to $\mathcal{O}(2^{100})$. Other attacks on KASUMI have come to light in which the attacker can presumably infer relations between keys. Such related keys may exist in situations where a key is slightly modified for each packet by including the initialisation vector in the block cipher. In this case the time complexity is reduced to values between $\mathcal{O}(2^{76.1})$ [BDK05] and $\mathcal{O}(2^{32})$ [DKS10]. At any rate, in mobile networks such attacks should not occur, since, for instance, no initialisation vectors are incorporated in key material.

Nevertheless, the standardisation committees are aware of the risk that KASUMI may be significantly weakened in the near future. For this eventuality they have specified another encryption algorithm referred to as SNOW 3G (or UEA2 and UIA2) [ETS12b]. SNOW 3G is a stream cipher that is based on a linear-feedback shift register and can be implemented in fewer than 7500 gates. However, initial attacks against SNOW 3G have come to light, which are also based on related keys [KY11]. For LTE networks AES has therefore been specified as standard, in addition to SNOW.

Alternative algorithm SNOW 3G

3.6 Summary

At an initial level, symmetric encryption methods can be divided into *block ciphers*, which operate on blocks of a fixed length, and into *stream ciphers*, which in principle encrypt each bit individually.

A range of different encryption modes exists for block ciphers, with the main objective being to ensure that identical plaintext blocks are not mapped continuously to identical ciphertext blocks. *CBC* and *OFB* are the two most frequently used modes.

Encryption modes

The DES algorithm that was standardised in the 1970s realises a symmetric block cipher with a block length of 64 bits and a key length of 56 bits. Even though no attack method much more effective than brute-force has been discovered in the more than 35 years since it was introduced, since the mid-1990s the algorithm has been considered insecure due to its short key length. The now frequently used variant of *triple-DES (3DES)* encryption with a selectable 112 or 168 bit key length displays relatively poor performance behaviour due to the required computation of three iterations with 16 rounds each.

DES

In the mid-1990s development therefore began on a successor to the standard, the *AES*. Numerous submissions were made from around the world, and after an international public review process the *Rijndael* algorithm was selected. The new AES algorithm implements a symmetric block cipher with a block length of 128 bits and a variable key length of 128, 192 or 256 bits.

AES

The symmetric stream cipher *RC4* is implemented through a pseudo-random bit generator, the output of which is XORed (OFB mode) to the plaintext or ciphertext being worked on. RC4 can operate with variable key lengths of up to 2048 bits. It should be noted, however, that before each plaintext is encrypted the key first has to be linked to an initialisation vector in order to ensure that two different plaintexts are not encrypted with the same output stream.

RC4

Depending on how this key is prepared, the scheme can be insecure. If the key is prepared 'carelessly', it can be computed from around one quarter of a million plaintext-ciphertext pairs. Because of the recent advances in breaking RC4, it should not be used any more.

KASUMI   Mobile networks are usually secured by specially designed cryptographic algorithms. The standardisation committees try to balance the achieved efficiency and security properties as much as possible. Current networks often use the KASUMI block cipher, which makes use of a recursive Feistel structure to secure data and takes only an extreme low number of gates in hardware. Because of security reservations and the increased hardware performance, LTE standardises the use of AES also for mobile networks.

3.7   Supplemental Reading

[ETS12a]   ETSI/SAGE: *Specification of the 3GPP confidentiality and integrity algorithms; Document 2: Kasumi specification.* 3GPP Release 11., 2012

[FMS01]   FLUHRER, S.; MANTIN, I.; SHAMIR, A.: Weaknesses in the Key Scheduling Algorithm of RC4. In: *Selected Areas in Cryptography, Lecture Notes in Computer Science* Vol. 2259, Springer, 2001, pp. 1–24

[Mil03]   MILLER, M.: *Symmetrische Verschlüsselungsverfahren: Design, Entwicklung und Kryptoanalyse klassischer und moderner Chiffren (German).* Teubner, 2003

[NIS77]   NIST (NATIONAL INSTITUTE OF STANDARDS AND TECHNOLOGY). *FIPS (Federal Information Processing Standard) Publication 46: Data Encryption Standard.* 1977

[NIS01]   NIST (NATIONAL INSTITUTE OF STANDARDS AND TECHNOLOGY). *FIPS (Federal Information Processing Standard) Publication 197: Specification for the Advanced Encryption Standard (AES).* 2001

[Riv01]   RIVEST, R.: *RSA Security Response to Weaknesses in Key Scheduling Algorithm of RC4.* 2001. – http://www.rsa.com/rsalabs/node.asp?id=2009

3.8 Questions

1. Is it possible to produce a code dictionary with an encryption algorithm that is operated in ECB mode and has a block length of 128 bits?

2. Is there a significant cryptographic advantage to keeping an initialisation vector (if it is used) secret?

3. What is the difference between Ciphertext Feedback Mode and Output Feedback Mode? How does this affect the characteristics of error propagation and synchronisation?

4. Assume that a block cipher has a 56-bit key length and a 128-bit block length. Can a 'lengthening' of the effective key length using double encryption also be broken in this case through a meet-in-the-middle attack with a still 'justifiable' use of resources? What is the probability in this case of a tuple (K_1, K_2) falsely being assumed to be a key after the nth plaintext-ciphertext pair?

5. What is the main drawback of the DES algorithm?

6. Why does double encryption with two different keys not produce an exponential increase of the search space in the cryptanalysis?

7. How can the block length of DES be securely increased with the help of a Feistel structure?

8. Why is the AES algorithm faster than 3DES?

9. Why can the effective key length with RC4 simply be adjusted?

10. How can reuse of keystream occur when deploying RC4?

4   Asymmetric Cryptography

This chapter introduces the fundamentals of asymmetric cryptography. It starts with a brief explanation of the basic concept and two main applications of the scheme followed by some preliminary mathematical background needed to understand the algorithms. The chapter continues with an explanation of the three central algorithms by Rivest, Shamir and Adleman (RSA), Diffie and Hellman, and ElGamal. The concluding section gives a short overview on the use of this class of algorithms with specific mathematical fields, so-called elliptic curves, which offer more efficient computation based on shorter keys while maintaining a comparable degree of security.

4.1   Basic Idea of Asymmetric Cryptography

The central idea behind asymmetric cryptography is the use of a different key for decryption from the one used for encryption, or the use of a different key to check a signature than the one used to create this signature. It should also be possible for one of these two keys, indicated as $+K$ below, to be made public without the possibility of it being used to calculate the appropriate private key $-K$ or to decrypt a message encrypted with key $+K$. Expressed in more formal terms, it should not be computationally feasible to use random ciphertext $c = E(+K, m)$ and key $+K$ to compute a plaintext message $m = D(-K, c) = D(-K, E(+K, m))$. In particular, this implies that it should not be feasible to compute key $-K$ from key $+K$.

One of the two keys of a pair can be made public

Key $-K$ is normally referred to as a *private key* and $+K$ as a *public key*. In contrast to symmetric cryptography where keys are basically agreed between two (or more) entities A and B and

Basic notation

Security in Fixed and Wireless Networks, Second Edition.
Guenter Schaefer and Michael Rossberg.
Copyright © 2014 by dpunkt.verlag GmbH, Heidelberg, Germany.
Title of the German original: Netzsicherheit   ISBN 978-3-86490-115-7
Translation Copyright © 2016 by John Wiley & Sons, Ltd., All rights reserved

consequently referred to as $K_{A,B}$, asymmetric cryptography allows the allocation of exactly one key pair $(-K_A, +K_A)$ to each entity A. This results in important advantages for key management because

Asymmetric cryptography is advantageous for key management

now only n key pairs instead of $n \times (n-1)/2$ are needed for secure pairwise communication between the entities from a group of n entities. Furthermore, these keys no longer have to be distributed over confidential channels and instead the keys $+K_x$ of arbitrary instance x can be made public.

The two main applications of asymmetric cryptography are:

- *Encryption:* When an entity B enciphers a message with public key $+K_A$, it can be assured that only A will be able to decrypt it with its private key $-K_A$.
- *Signing:* When an entity A encrypts a message with its private key $-K_A$, then all entities using key $+K_A$ can decipher it. However, as only A is in possession of private key $-K_A$, it is the only entity that can encrypt the message. The ciphertext acts *de facto* as a *signature* of the message.

Authenticity of public keys is essential

It is essential that all entities have the assurance that they really know the correct public key of $+K_A$, that is, the public keys must be authentic. Compared with symmetric cryptography, where keys $K_{A,B}$ must be authentic and distributed over a confidential channel, with asymmetric cryptography the property of authenticity suffices.

Asymmetric methods enable electronic signatures

Another important difference compared with symmetric cryptography is that signatures created using asymmetric methods can also be checked by independent third parties. When signatures are created with a symmetric key $K_{A,B}$, an independent third party is, in principle, not able to distinguish which of the two entities A or B created the signature since both entities know key $K_{A,B}$. In contrast, asymmetric schemes permit the unique allocation of a signature to owner A of key $-K_A$ that was used to produce the signature. Electronic signatures can be realised on this basis.

First publication on asymmetric cryptography

The basic concept of asymmetric schemes described so far along with their possible applications was first published in 1976 by Diffie and Hellman in the article 'New Directions in Cryptography', which was considered a scientific milestone at the time [DH76]. In addition to describing the fundamental idea behind cryptography, this article defined a mathematical algorithm that could be used by two entities to negotiate a shared secret over a public channel. The algorithm was named the *Diffie–Hellman key exchange* after its creators. However, this algorithm only implements key exchange and is not an asymmetric cryptographic scheme with any of the attributes listed earlier or deployable for encryption and decryption or signing and signature checking. So although the article made an announcement about asymmetric cryptography and described its properties, it was not able to provide a concrete algorithm to meet its requirements.

The difficulty in developing such a scheme lies in finding an algorithm for encryption and decryption as well as a procedure for the construction of matching key pairs $(+K, -K)$. The scheme needs to ensure that it is impossible to decrypt an encrypted message $E(+K, m)$ if $+K$ is known. The scheme should also meet a number of relevant practical requirements:

Requirements of asymmetric cryptography

- the key length should be manageable;
- encrypted messages should not be arbitrarily longer than non-encrypted ones, even if a small constant factor is acceptable;
- encryption and decryption should not consume too many resources (time, memory).

After the article [DH76] was published, a number of scientists worked on constructing a practical algorithm that would meet the requirements described above. The basic idea was to use a problem familiar from the fields of computer science or mathematics that would be 'difficult' — in the best case only with an exponential effort — to solve if only $+K$ were known and 'simple' to solve (with a polynomial effort) if $-K$ were known. The following three problems particularly came to mind:

Construction of concrete algorithms

- The *knapsack problem*, familiar from computer science, consists of ideally packing a knapsack of a specific capacity, i.e. filling it with objects of maximum total value without exceeding a certain total weight. Merkle, in particular, researched asymmetric schemes based on this problem, but all of them proved to be insecure and could, therefore, not be considered viable from a practical standpoint.

Knapsack problem

- The *integer-factorisation* problem, which consists of factorising a integer number into its prime factors. This problem forms the basis of the *RSA algorithm*, named after its creators Rivest, Shamir and Adleman. This was the first secure asymmetric algorithm invented and it still represents one of the most important asymmetric algorithms as it is in wide practical use.

Factorisation problem

- The *problem of the discrete logarithm*, which involves finding the logarithm of a number for a given base in finite fields, is the cornerstone of the key exchange algorithm by Diffie–Hellman as well as for the asymmetric cryptographic

Problem of the discrete logarithm

scheme according to ElGamal, both of which have great practical significance today.

Lattice-based cryptography

■ More current research focuses on the construction of asymmetric ciphers with the help of lattices. Lattices are sets of points or vectors in $\mathbb{R}^n$ that are spanned by a common basis. The problem for an attacker lies in the difficulty of solving mathematical problems in the lattice without the knowledge of such a basis. Lattice-based approaches are currently of no practical meaning. Nevertheless, as they are immune to attacks by quantum computers, they may gain more importance in future. A major drawback of these algorithms is that ciphertexts are significantly longer than plaintexts.

How schemes of practical importance function will be explained in the following sections. First, an understanding of some mathematical principles is required.

4.2   Mathematical Principles

This section introduces the mathematical principles of asymmetric cryptography. Most of the relationships presented build on one other so that no previous mathematical knowledge is required other than what is normally taught in school. Readers who have a sound mathematical background may find the explanations somewhat detailed and are requested to have some patience.

Divisibility

In the following, let $\mathbb{N}$ denote all positive integers and $a, b, k, n \in \mathbb{N}$. We say a divides b (Notation: '$a|b$') when an integer $k \in \mathbb{N}$ exists so that $a \times k = b$. A positive integer $a \geq 2$ is called *prime* when its only divisors are 1 and a.

Remainder with division

Moreover, r is the remainder of a divided by n when $r = a - \lfloor a/n \rfloor \times n$, with $\lfloor x \rfloor$ being the positive integer that is smaller than or equal to x. For this and all following definitions we assume n to be a natural number truly greater than zero. For example, 4 is the remainder of 11 divided by 7, since $4 = 11 - \lfloor 11/7 \rfloor \times 7$. For the remainder r of the division of a by n we also write $a \bmod n$. Generally a may also be an element of all integer numbers $\mathbb{Z}$, that is, it may be negative. However, negative numbers will have only a minor part in the following, and the only consequence is that definitions are done over $\mathbb{Z}$. Thus, they include all integers.

Congruence modulo of a number

We say b is *congruent* a *modulo* n when b has the same remainder as a when divided by n. n therefore divides the difference $(a - b)$ and we write $b \equiv a \pmod{n}$. Particular attention should be paid here to the different way in which $x \bmod y$ and $x \pmod y$ are written. Whereas $x \bmod y$ denotes a concrete number, namely the remainder that results when x is divided by y, the style $x \,(\bmod\, y)$ is a more detailed specification of a congruence and to an extent represents a rounding off of character $\equiv$. Without this detail there would be no clear reference to the number to which the two other numbers are actually congruent.

Examples:

$$4 \equiv 11 \quad (\bmod\ 7), \qquad 25 \equiv 11 \quad (\bmod\ 7), \qquad 11 \equiv 25 \quad (\bmod\ 7),$$

$$11 \equiv 4 \quad (\bmod\ 7), \qquad -10 \equiv 4 \quad (\bmod\ 7)$$

Because the remainder r of division by n is always smaller than n, *Residue class* we often represent the set $\{x \bmod n \mid x \in \mathbb{Z}\}$ through its elements $\{0, 1, \ldots, n-1\}$. Each element a of this set always stands for an entire set of numbers that all produce the same remainder a when divided by n. These sets are also called *residue classes*. Normally they are noted as $[a]_n := \{x \mid x \in \mathbb{Z} : x \equiv a \,(\bmod\, n)\}$ and their combined set as $\mathbb{Z}_n := \{[a]_n \mid a \in \mathbb{Z}\}$.

The study of remainders with division by a number leads to *modular arithmetic*; some of its properties and computing rules are summarised in Table 4.1.

Characteristic	Expression
Commutative laws	$(a + b) \bmod n = (b + a) \bmod n$
	$(a \times b) \bmod n = (b \times a) \bmod n$
Associative laws	$[(a + b) + c] \bmod n = [a + (b + c)] \bmod n$
	$[(a \times b) \times c] \bmod n = [a \times (b \times c)] \bmod n$
Distributive law	$[a \times (b + c)] \bmod n = [(a \times b) + (a \times c)] \bmod n$
Identities	$(0 + a) \bmod n = a \bmod n$
	$(1 \times a) \bmod n = a \bmod n$
Inverses	$\forall\, a \in \mathbb{Z}_n : \exists (-a) \in \mathbb{Z}_n : a + (-a) \equiv 0 \ (\bmod\ n)$
	$p \text{ is prime} \Rightarrow \forall\, a \in \mathbb{Z}_p : \exists (a^{-1}) \in \mathbb{Z}_p : a \times (a^{-1}) \equiv 1 \ (\bmod\ p)$

Definition 4.1 *A natural number c is called the* **greatest common divisor (GCD)** *of two natural numbers a and b when c divides both numbers a and b and c also is the greatest number with this property. Therefore, each other common divisor d of a and b is also a divisor of c. Formally:*

Table 4.1
Properties of modular arithmetic

$$c = gcd(a, b) :\Leftrightarrow (c \mid a) \wedge (c \mid b) \wedge [\forall\, d : (d \mid a) \wedge (d \mid b) \ \Rightarrow \ d \le c]$$

The greatest common divisor of two numbers a and b will usually be referred to by $\gcd(a, b)$. The following theorem can be used as the basis for efficiently computing the greatest common divisor of two numbers:

Theorem 4.1 *For all positive integer numbers a and b the greatest common divisor of a and b is equal to the greatest common divisor of b and $a \bmod b$:*

$$\forall a, b \in \mathbb{Z}^+ : \gcd(a, b) = \gcd(b, a \bmod b)$$

Proof of this theorem is presented in two arguments:

- As the GCD of a and b divides a as well as b, it also divides each linear combination of them, in particular the linear combination $(a - \lfloor a/b \rfloor \times b) = a \bmod b$. Therefore $\gcd(a, b) \mid \gcd(b, a \bmod b)$.
- As the GCD of b and $a \bmod b$ divides b as well as $a \bmod b$, it also divides each linear combination of them, in particular also the linear combination $\lfloor a/b \rfloor \times b + (a \bmod b) = a$. Therefore $\gcd(b, a \bmod b) \mid \gcd(a, b)$. □

Recursive compu- Theorem 4.1 directly leads to the correctness of using the *Euclidean* *tation of GCD* *algorithm* to compute the GCD of two numbers, formulated in a notation based on programming language C in Figure 4.1.

Figure 4.1
Euclidean algorithm

```
// Algorithm: Euclidean
// Input:     two natural numbers a, b
// Ouput:     the greatest common divisor of a, b

uint Euclid(uint a, b) {
    if (b == 0) return a;
    else            return Euclid(b, a mod b);
}
```

It is often helpful to use an extended form of the Euclidean algorithm along with the greatest common divisor c to compute another two coefficients m and n with c representing the linear combination of a and b so that $c = \gcd(a, b) = m \times a + n \times b$. This algorithm is shown in Figure 4.2.

Proof by full induction   The correctness proof for the extended Euclidean algorithm is carried out by full induction:

- Base case $(a, 0)$: $\gcd(a, 0) = a = 1 \times a + 0 \times 0$;
- Induction hypothesis: the extended Euclidean algorithm computes c', m', n' correctly.

■ Induction of $(b, a \bmod b)$ to (a, b):

$$c = c' = m' \times b + n' \times (a \bmod b)$$

$$= m' \times b + n' \times (a - \lfloor a/b \rfloor \times b)$$

$$= n' \times a + (m' - \lfloor a/b \rfloor \times n') \times b \quad \square$$

```
// Algorithm: Extended Euclidean
// Input:     two natural numbers a, b
// Output     numbers c, m, n, so that:
//                c = gcd(a, b) = m * a + n * b
// Note:      Floor(x) computes the greatest
//                integer number <= x

struct{uint c, m, n}  ExtendedEuclidean(uint a, b) {
  uint c', m', n';

  if(b == 0)
    return {a, 1, 0};

  (c', m', n') = ExtendedEuclidean(b, a mod b);
  (c, m, n)    = (c', n', m' - Floor(a / b) * n');
  return {c, m, n};
}
```

Figure 4.2
Extended Euclidean algorithm

It can also be shown that the runtime of both Euclidean algorithms is of the magnitude of $O(\log b)$, if elementary operations are assumed to take place in constant time. The proof of this assessment will not be dealt with here and the reader is referred to [CLR01, Section 33.2] for additional information. If the required effort of single operations grows with the bit length of the numbers, a complexity of $O(\log^2 b)$ arises, whereas b is assumed to be the larger one of the two numbers. The discussion of the two Euclidean algorithms can be summarised with the following lemma:

Runtime of Euclidean algorithms

Lemma 4.1 *Let* $a, b \in \mathbb{Z}$ *and* $c = \gcd(a, b)$. *We then have numbers* $m, n \in \mathbb{Z}$ *so that* $c = m \times a + n \times b$.

We can use this lemma to prove the following theorem:

Theorem 4.2 *(Euclid) When a prime number* p *divides the product of two integers* a *and* b, *then it is dividing at least one of the two numbers:*

$$p \mid (a \times b) \Rightarrow (p \mid a) \vee (p \mid b)$$

Proof of this theorem is provided by two arguments:

- If $p \mid a$, then proof would exist.
- If not, then $\gcd(p, a) = 1$ holds.

$$\Rightarrow \exists\, m, n \in \mathbb{Z} : 1 = m \times p + n \times a$$

$$\Leftrightarrow b = m \times p \times b + n \times a \times b$$

However, as p divides the product $(a \times b)$, then p divides both summands of the equation and therefore also divides the sum, which is b. $\square$

Theorem 4.2, proven above, is useful in turn for proof of the *fundamental theorem of arithmetic*:

Fundamental theorem of arithmetic   **Theorem 4.3**   *The factorisation of a natural number is unique up to the sequence of its prime factors.*

For proof of this theorem we will show that each integer with non-unique factorisation has a real divisor with non-unique factorisation. A contradiction occurs if the number is reduced to a prime number due to a repeated application of this argument. As the correct inference is that a false statement cannot be derived from a true assumption, the assumption therefore must be wrong (basic principle of proof through contradiction). Let us assume therefore that n is a number with non-unique factorisation, that is:

Proof through contradiction

$$n = p_1 \times p_2 \times \ldots \times p_r$$

$$= q_1 \times q_2 \times \ldots \times q_s$$

The prime factors are not necessarily all different but the second factorisation is not merely a reordering of the first.

Because p_1 divides the number n, it also divides the product $q_1 \times q_2 \times \ldots \times q_s$. A repeated application of Theorem 4.2 results in at least one q_i that is divisible by p_1. However, as q_i is a prime number, p_1 and q_i have to be equal so that we can divide by p_1 and thus arrive at n/p_1, which must be a number with non-unique factorisation. $\square$

Division by factors with congruencies   We can use Theorem 4.3 to prove the following corollary that gives the conditions for dividing a factor on both sides of a congruence:

Corollary 4.1   *Let $a, b, c, m \in \mathbb{Z} \backslash \{0\}$, $\gcd(c, m) = 1$ and furthermore $(a \times c) \equiv (b \times c)\,(\mathrm{mod}\ m)$. This implies that $a \equiv b\,(\mathrm{mod}\ m)$.*

For proof: As $(a \times c) \equiv (b \times c) \pmod{m}$, it follows that the difference between $(a \times c)$ and $(b \times c)$ has to be divisible by m without remainder, that is, $\exists n \in \mathbb{Z} : (a \times c) - (b \times c) = n \times m$

$$\Leftrightarrow \quad (a - b) \quad \times \quad c \quad = \quad n \quad \times \quad m$$

$$\Leftrightarrow \overbrace{p_1 \times \ldots \times p_i} \times \overbrace{q_1 \times \ldots \times q_j} = \overbrace{r_1 \times \ldots \times r_k} \times \overbrace{s_1 \times \ldots \times s_l}$$

The second line of this equivalence shows the separate components of the line above factorised into their unique prime factors according to Theorem 4.3. However, the same prime factors have to appear on both sides of the equation (again because of Theorem 4.3). Furthermore, the prime factors of c all differ from the prime factors of m since c and m are assumed to be relatively prime ($gcd(c, m) = 1$). Consequently, $q_1, \ldots, q_j$ can be successively divided by all of them without one of the prime factors $s_1, \ldots, s_l$ being eliminated. An equation of the form $a - b = n' \times m$ is all that still remains. This in turn means that $(a - b)$ can be divided by m without remainder, which is equivalent to $a \equiv b \pmod{m}$. $\square$

Definition 4.2 *(Euler's Φ function) Let $\Phi(n)$ denote the number of positive integers $a_1, \ldots, a_t$ that are smaller than n and relatively prime to n, i.e. $\forall\, i \in \{1, \ldots, t\} : (a_i < n) \wedge \gcd(a_i, n) = 1$.* *Euler's Φ function*

The best way to understand this function is to look at a few examples: $\Phi(4) = 2$ (as $\{1, 3\}$ are relatively prime to 4), $\Phi(6) = 2$ (as $\{1, 5\}$ are relatively prime to 6), $\Phi(7) = 6$ (as $\{1, 2, 3, 4, 5, 6\}$ are relatively prime to 7), $\Phi(15) = 8$ (as $\{1, 2, 4, 7, 8, 11, 13, 14\}$ are relatively prime to 15). Basically it holds for all prime numbers p that $\Phi(p) = p - 1$ since prime numbers are only divisible by 1 and themselves.

Even though the review of a set of numbers that are smaller than a number and are relatively prime to this number would not initially appear to be particularly beneficial, it does provide 'raw material' for one of the most important asymmetrical cryptographic schemes, the RSA algorithm. The following central theorem serves as its foundation: *Mathematical principle of RSA algorithm*

Theorem 4.4 *(Euler) Let n and b be natural numbers ≥ 1 and relatively prime to one another, i.e. $\gcd(b, n) = 1$. Then it holds that $b^{\Phi(n)} \equiv 1 \pmod{n}$.* *Euler's theorem*

To prove this theorem, we consider $t = \Phi(n)$ and $\{a_1, \ldots, a_t\}$, the set of numbers that are prime to n. We also define the set $\{r_1, \ldots, r_t\}$ as the remainders $b \times a_i \bmod n$ so that it always holds that $b \times a_i \equiv r_i \pmod{n}$:

- Note that $i \neq j \Rightarrow r_i \neq r_j$. The reason is that a pair (i, j) of indexes could otherwise be found so that $b \times a_i \equiv b \times a_j \pmod{n}$. However, as $\gcd(n, b) = 1$, with Corollary 4.1 this would imply that $a_i \equiv a_j \pmod{n}$, which is not possible because all a_i are per definition different natural numbers between 0 and n.

- We could also deduce that all r_i are relatively prime to n since each common divisor k of r_i and n, i.e. with $n = k \times m$ and $r_i = p_i \times k$ for suitable m and p_i, would also be a divisor of a_i:

$$b \times a_i \equiv (p_i \times k) \pmod{k \times m}$$

$$\Rightarrow \exists s \in \mathbb{Z} : (b \times a_i) - (p_i \times k) = s \times k \times m$$

$$\Leftrightarrow (b \times a_i) = s \times k \times m + (p_i \times k)$$

Since k divides each of the two summands on the right side, it also has to divide the left side. As b is assumed to be relatively prime to n, it would consequently have to divide a_i, which would, however, be a contradiction to the definition of a_i, since a_i per definition is relatively prime to n.

- $\{r_1, \ldots, r_t\}$ is consequently a set of $\Phi(n)$ different integers that are all relatively prime to n. This means that the numbers are exactly the same as those in set $\{a_1, \ldots, a_t\}$, but normally in a different sequence. This therefore brings us to the conclusion that $r_1 \times \ldots \times r_t = a_1 \times \ldots \times a_t$.

- Let us now study the congruence:

$$
\begin{aligned}
r_1 \times \ldots \times r_t &\equiv b \times a_1 \times \ldots \times b \times a_t &&\pmod{n} \\
\Leftrightarrow r_1 \times \ldots \times r_t &\equiv b^t \times a_1 \times \ldots \times a_t &&\pmod{n} \\
\Leftrightarrow r_1 \times \ldots \times r_t &\equiv b^t \times r_1 \times \ldots \times r_t &&\pmod{n}
\end{aligned}
$$

Since all r_i are relatively prime to n, we can apply Corollary 4.1 and divide by the product $r_1 \times \ldots \times r_t$ to arrive at $1 \equiv b^t \pmod{n} \Leftrightarrow 1 \equiv b^{\Phi(n)} \pmod{n}$. $\square$

Even though we will use Theorem 4.4 to prove the basis of the RSA algorithm, we still need an additional result that can help us to compute the Euler's Φ function for the product of two numbers. To provide proof, we first derive a much more powerful result, the *Chinese remainder theorem*:

Chinese remainder theorem

Theorem 4.5 *(Chinese remainder theorem) Let $m_1, \ldots, m_r$ be positive integers that pair-wise are relatively prime to one another, i.e. $\forall i \neq j : \gcd(m_i, m_j) = 1$. Let furthermore $a_1, \ldots, a_r$ be arbitrary integers. Then there exists an integer a so that a fulfils all the* *following congruencies:*

$$a \equiv a_1 \pmod{m_1}$$

$$a \equiv a_2 \pmod{m_2}$$

$$\ldots$$

$$a \equiv a_r \pmod{m_r}$$

Furthermore, a is unique modulo $M := m_1 \times \ldots \times m_r$.

To prove this theorem, we first define the number $M_i := (M/m_i)^{\Phi(m_i)}$ for all $i \in \{1, \ldots, r\}$.

- As M_i is by definition relatively prime to m_i, we can apply Theorem 4.4 and know that $M_i \equiv 1 \pmod{m_i}$.
- As M_i is divisible by m_j for all $j \neq i$, we also know that $\forall\, j \neq i : M_i \equiv 0 \pmod{m_j}$.
- We can therefore define the solution of simultaneous congruencies as:

  Constructing the solution of simultaneous congruencies

  $$a := a_1 \times M_1 + a_2 \times M_2 + \ldots + a_r \times M_r$$

  Based on the two arguments on congruencies satisfied by M_i given above, it holds that a actually meets all required congruencies of the form $a \equiv a_i \pmod{m_i}$.
- To show the uniqueness of this solution modulo M, we will look at an arbitrarily different integer b, which fulfils the r required congruencies. As $a \equiv c \pmod{n}$ and $b \equiv c \pmod{n}$ imply that also $a \equiv b \pmod{n}$, it holds that:

  Uniqueness of the solution modulo M

  $$\forall\, i \in \{1, \ldots, r\} : a \equiv b \pmod{m_i}$$

  $$\Rightarrow \forall\, i \in \{1, \ldots, r\} : m_i \mid (a - b)$$

  $$\Rightarrow M \mid (a - b) \text{ since all } m_i \text{ pair-wise are relatively prime}$$

  $$\Leftrightarrow a \equiv b \pmod{M} \quad \square$$

We will now use Theorem 4.5 to prove the following lemma that helps us to compute Euler's Φ function for the product of two relatively prime numbers:

Computation of Φ function for the product of relatively prime numbers

Lemma 4.2 *Let $m, n \in \mathbb{Z}^+$ and $\gcd(m, n) = 1$. It then holds that:*

$$\Phi(m \times n) = \Phi(m) \times \Phi(n)$$

For the proof of the lemma let us consider an arbitrary positive integer a, which is smaller than $(m \times n)$ and relatively prime to $(m \times n)$. In other words, a is one of the numbers that is counted by $\Phi(m \times n)$:

■ Let us consider the tuple $a \rightarrow (a \bmod m, a \bmod n)$. The number a is relatively prime to m and also to n as it would otherwise divide the product $(m \times n)$.

This makes $(a \bmod m)$ relatively prime to m and $(a \bmod n)$ relatively prime to n, as $a = \lfloor a/m \rfloor \times m + (a \bmod m)$, which means that if a common divisor of m and $(a \bmod m)$ exists, it too would have to divide a.

A tuple $(a \bmod m, a \bmod n)$ therefore corresponds to each number a that is counted by $\Phi(m \times n)$, with $(a \bmod m)$ counted by $\Phi(m)$ and $(a \bmod n)$ counted by $\Phi(n)$.

■ On the basis of the second result of Theorem 4.5, the uniqueness of a solution a modulo $(m \times n)$ for the simultaneous congruencies, i.e.:

$$a \equiv a \bmod m \quad (\bmod\ m)$$

$$a \equiv a \bmod n \quad (\bmod\ n)$$

we can deduce that distinct integers counted by $\Phi(m \times n)$ correspond to different tuples $(a \bmod m, a \bmod n)$.

Another way to understand this is through the assumption that two numbers $a \neq b$ counted by $\Phi(m \times n)$ correspond to the same pair $(a \bmod m, a \bmod n)$. However, this assumption creates a contradiction since b would also have to fulfil the two congruencies:

$$b \equiv a \bmod m \quad (\bmod\ m)$$

$$b \equiv a \bmod n \quad (\bmod\ n)$$

$\Phi(m \times n)$
counts at most
$\Phi(m) \times \Phi(n)$ numbers

According to the second part of Theorem 4.5, the solution of these congruencies is uniquely modulo $(m \times n)$. Consequently, all corresponding pairs must be different. The number of integers that can be counted by $\Phi(m \times n)$ is therefore limited by the number of distinct pairs of numbers that can be counted by $\Phi(m)$ and $\Phi(n)$.

$$\Phi(m \times n) \leq \Phi(m) \times \Phi(n)$$

■ Let us now consider a number pair (b, c) in which b is counted by $\Phi(m)$ and c by $\Phi(n)$. Using the first part of Theorem 4.5, we can construct a unique positive integer that is smaller than and relatively prime to $(m \times n)$ and fulfils the two following congruencies:

$$a \equiv b \quad (\bmod\ m)$$

$$a \equiv c \quad (\bmod\ n)$$

However, as per definition of Euler's Φ function, a maximum of $\Phi(m \times n)$ different numbers can exist that are smaller than and relatively prime to $(m \times n)$, the number of pairs of the type $(a \bmod m, a \bmod n)$ can at most amount to $\Phi(m \times n)$:

At most $\Phi(m) \times \Phi(n)$ can be $\Phi(m \times n)$

$$\Phi(m \times n) \geq \Phi(m) \times \Phi(n) \quad \square$$

We have used Lemma 4.2 to prove all mathematical principles needed to understand how the RSA algorithm functions. The following section uses this basis to provide a clear overview of the actual algorithm.

4.3 The RSA Algorithm

The RSA algorithm was invented in 1977 by Rivest, Shamir and Adleman and is based on Theorem 4.4. The way it functions is relatively easy to explain.

Let p and q be large prime numbers that are distinct from one another and $n = p \times q$. We also assume to know two natural numbers $e, d \in \mathbb{N}$ so that $d \times e \equiv 1 \pmod{\Phi(n)}$. How such numbers are calculated will be explained later.

Prerequisites of RSA algorithm

Let M be a natural number that represents an encrypted message and is smaller than and relatively prime to n. If, for example, M should encode a text message, one can specify that letters {A, B, ..., Z} are encoded by numbers $\{10, 11, \ldots, 35\}$ and the blank by the number 99. The character string 'HELLO' would then be represented by the number 1714212124. If necessary, the number can also be broken up into blocks of smaller numbers: 17142 12124.

Encoding messages as numbers

To encrypt M, one computes:

Encryption

$$E = M^e \bmod n$$

This computation can be executed efficiently using the *Square and Multiply algorithm*, sometimes also called the *Repeated Squaring algorithm* [CLR01, Section 33.6].

To decrypt encrypted message E again, one computes:

Decryption

$$M' = E^d \bmod n$$

The correctness of the RSA algorithm can be explained on the basis of the following two observations:

Correctness

- As $d \times e \equiv 1 \pmod{\Phi(n)} \Rightarrow$

$$\exists k \in \mathbb{N} : (d \times e) - 1 = k \times \Phi(n)$$
$$\Leftrightarrow (d \times e) = k \times \Phi(n) + 1$$

- Therefore, it holds that:

$$M' \equiv E^d \equiv M^{(e \times d)} \equiv M^{(k \times \Phi(n)+1)} \equiv 1^k \times M \equiv M \pmod{n} \quad \square$$

With RSA keys can be used in both directions As $(d \times e) = (e \times d)$, this operation also works in the opposite direction, that is, the number d can be used for encryption and the associated e for decryption. This characteristic of the RSA algorithm enables the same key pair to be used for the two following operations:

- receiving messages that have been encrypted with one's own public key;
- sending messages that through encryption were signed with one's own private key.

Creating RSA keys The following steps are required to create a key pair that can be used with RSA:

1. Randomly choose two large prime numbers p and q (each with about 200 to 300 decimal points).
2. Compute $n = p \times q$ and $\Phi(n) = (p-1) \times (q-1)$ (Lemma 4.2).
3. Choose an e and compute using the extended Euclidean algorithm c, d as well as $\gcd(e, \Phi(n))$ so that $e \times d + \Phi(n) \times c = \gcd(e, \Phi(n))$.

   The value e may be chosen randomly. However, many implementations use $e = 65537$, and as this number is large enough to cause distortion it contains only 2 bits that are set. Thus, the Square and Multiply algorithm runs rather quickly. If $\gcd(e, \Phi(n)) \neq 1$, then continue to choose a new e, p or q values, until you find an e that is relatively prime to $\Phi(n)$. Note that this construction ensures that $e \times d \equiv 1 \pmod{\Phi(n)}$.
4. The public key is the pair (e, n).
5. The private key is the pair (d, n).

Security of RSA The security of this scheme is based on the difficulty of factorising the large natural number n into its prime factors $p \times q$, since it is simple to compute $\Phi(n)$ and thus d if p and q are known.

We will not delve into why it is 'difficult,' i.e. computationally too intensive, to factorise large integers using schemes already known to us because this would require an extensive discussion on the mathematical relationships relevant in this context. At this juncture we will content ourselves with the somewhat vague statement that when p and q fulfil certain properties the runtime of the best-known algorithms is superpolynomial in the number of digits of n.

However, we should briefly point out some pitfalls in conjunction with the implementation of RSA so the reader has a certain basic awareness of the dangers that exist for those who are inexperienced at working with the relevant mathematical relationships:

Potential pitfalls when implementing RSA

■ For example, if p and q are chosen in an 'unfortunate' way, algorithms may exist that can factorise n efficiently. RSA encryption that uses keys constructed this way will therefore not be secure.

■ Therefore, p and q should be about the same bit length and be sufficiently large. Likewise, the difference $(p - q)$ should not be too small.

■ Should a small encryption exponent be selected for the public key, which enables operations with a public key to be executed noticeably more quickly, then there are other constraints to be considered, e.g.:

$$\gcd(p - 1, 3) = 1 \text{ and } \gcd(q - 1, 3) = 1$$

■ The security of RSA strongly depends on whether the prime numbers p and q are truly random because otherwise it is easy for attackers to imitate this process and guess the factorisation of n relatively quickly. It goes without saying that all cryptographic schemes should have a 'sufficiently random' key creation process.

We have one concluding comment to make in regard to the security of RSA implementations. It is our recommendation that users either work with an existing and widely used implementation or, if it is their own implementation, make sure to have it checked by an appropriately experienced mathematician or, better yet, a cryptographer.

RSA implementations should be checked by cryptographers

4.4 The Problem of the Discrete Logarithm

Section 4.1 mentioned that asymmetric cryptography can be implemented on the basis of the factorisation of large natural numbers as well as the *problem of the discrete logarithm*. This section deals with the mathematical principles relevant to the problem of the discrete logarithm.

Definition 4.3 *(Finite group) A* **group** *$(S, \oplus)$ is a set S together with a binary operation $\oplus$ for which the following properties hold:*

Finite group

- **Closure:** $\forall\, a, b \in S : a \oplus b \in S$
- **Identity:** $\exists\, e \in S : \forall\, a \in S : e \oplus a = a \oplus e = a$
- **Associativity:** $\forall\, a, b, c, \in S : (a \oplus b) \oplus c = a \oplus (b \oplus c)$
- **Inverse element:** $\forall\, a \in S : \exists\, b \in S : a \oplus b = b \oplus a = e$

*If a group $(S, \oplus)$ also satisfies the commutative law $\forall a, b \in S : a \oplus b = b \oplus a$, then it is called an **Abelian group**. If a group $(S, \oplus)$ only has a finite set of elements, i.e. $|S| < \infty$, then it is called a **finite group**.*

Examples   The following examples clarify this further:

$(\mathbb{Z}_n, +_n)$
- Group $(\mathbb{Z}_n, +_n)$ of the residue classes modulo n with the operation Addition modulo n, which is defined as follows:
  - $\mathbb{Z}_n := \{[0]_n, [1]_n, \ldots, [n-1]_n\}$
  - $[a]_n := \{b \in \mathbb{Z} \mid b \equiv a \,(\mathrm{mod}\ n)\}$
  - $+_n$ is defined so that $[a]_n +_n [b]_n = [a+b]_n$

  is a finite Abelian group. Direct proof can be calculated using the computing rules of modular arithmetic (also see Table 4.1).

$(\mathbb{Z}_n^*, \times_n)$
- Group $(\mathbb{Z}_n^*, \times_n)$ of the residue classes modulo n with the operation Multiplication modulo n, which is defined as follows:
  - $\mathbb{Z}_n^* := \{[a]_n \in \mathbb{Z}_n \mid \gcd(a, n) = 1\}$
  - $\times_n$ is defined so that $[a]_n \times_n [b]_n = [a \times b]_n$

  is a finite Abelian group. Direct proof can be calculated here too using the computing rules of modular arithmetic.

  Note that $\mathbb{Z}_n^*$ only contains those elements from $\mathbb{Z}_n$ for which inverse elements modulo n exist. Z_{15}^* is presented here explicitly as an example:

$$\mathbb{Z}_{15}^* = \{[1]_{15}, [2]_{15}, [4]_{15}, [7]_{15}, [8]_{15}, [11]_{15}, [13]_{15}, [14]_{15}\}, \text{ as}$$

$$1 \times 1 \equiv 1 \quad (\mathrm{mod}\ 15), \qquad 2 \times 8 \equiv 1 \quad (\mathrm{mod}\ 15),$$

$$4 \times 4 \equiv 1 \quad (\mathrm{mod}\ 15), \qquad 7 \times 13 \equiv 1 \quad (\mathrm{mod}\ 15),$$

$$11 \times 11 \equiv 1 \quad (\mathrm{mod}\ 15), \qquad 14 \times 14 \equiv 1 \quad (\mathrm{mod}\ 15)$$

Equivalence classes represented by elements   When it is clear from the context that group $(\mathbb{Z}_n, +_n)$ or $(\mathbb{Z}_n^*, \times_n)$ is meant, then the equivalence classes $[a]_n$ are often represented by their elements a and the operations '$+_n$' and '$\times_n$' are noted with '$+$' or '$\times$'.

Finite fields   **Definition 4.4** *(Finite fields) A **field** $(S, \oplus, \odot)$ is a set S together with two binary operations $\oplus$ and $\odot$ so that the following holds:*

- *$(S, \oplus)$ and $(S \backslash \{e_\oplus\}, \odot)$ are Abelian groups, i.e. in regard to the addition it is only the neutral element that does not need to have an inverse element in regard to $\odot$ in S, and*

- $\forall\, a, b, c \in S : a \odot (b \oplus c) = (a \odot b) \oplus (a \odot c)$, *i.e. both operations must satisfy the* **distributive law**.

If a field $(S, \oplus, \odot)$ *only has a finite set of elements, i.e.* $|S| < \infty$, *it is called a* **finite field**.

Thus $(\mathbb{Z}_p, +_p, \times_p)$ is a finite field for all prime numbers p, which can be proven by the computing rules of modular arithmetic (see Table 4.1).

Definition 4.5 *(Primitive root, generator) Let* $(S, \circ)$ *be a group*   *Primitive root* $g \in S$ *and* $g^a := g \circ g \circ \ldots \circ g$, *i.e.* g *is linked* a *times with itself,* $a \in \mathbb{Z}^+$. *Then* g *is called a* **primitive root** *or a* **generator** *of* $(S, \circ)$ *precisely when:*

$$\{ g^a \mid 1 \leq a \leq |S| \} = S$$

1 is therefore a primitive root of $(\mathbb{Z}_n, +_n)$ and 3 is a primitive root of $(\mathbb{Z}_7^*, \times_7)$. Not all groups have primitive roots, and the groups for which a primitive root exists are also called *cyclic groups*.

    For the additive groups of the residue classes modulo n the neut-   *When is a multiplic-* ral element in respect to the multiplication 1 is always the primit-   *ative group* $(\mathbb{Z}_n^*, \times_n)$ ive root. A generator does not always exist for multiplicative groups   *considered cyclic?* $(\mathbb{Z}_n^*, \times_n)$. This raises the question of which circumstances make a multiplicative group $(\mathbb{Z}_n^*, \times_n)$ cyclic.

    The following theorem gives the answer to this question. However, in contrast to the results discussed in the preceding sections for which it was relatively easy to provide proof, this theorem as well as others in this section do not lend themselves to brief coverage. Complete explanations will therefore no longer be provided and the reader is instead referred to the appropriate literature.

Theorem 4.6 *Group* $(\mathbb{Z}_n^*, \times_n)$ *precisely has a primitive root when*   *Existence of a* $n \in \{2, 4, p, 2 \times p^e\}$, *with* p *being an odd prime and* $e \in \mathbb{Z}^+$.   *primitive root*

This result, the proof of which can be looked up in [NZ80], gives a necessary and sufficient criterion for the existence of a primitive root for group $(\mathbb{Z}_n^*, \times_n)$.

    The question that still remains is how to find such primitive   *How can primitive* roots efficiently without first trying out all possibilities. There is no   *roots be found* way to give a general response to this question. However, it is pos-   *efficiently?* sible to construct a group $(\mathbb{Z}_n^*, \times_n)$ using a clever choice of n so that a primitive root can be calculated at the same time. Before an appropriate scheme is specified, we first have to highlight some background information and familiarise ourselves with other results.

Theorem 4.7 *If $(S, \circ)$ is a group and $b \in S$, then $(S', \circ)$ with $S' := \{b^a \mid a \in \mathbb{Z}^+\}$ is also a group.*

The proof of this theorem can be read in [CLR01, Section 33.3]. As $S' \subseteq S$, $(S', \circ)$ is also called a *subgroup* of $(S, \circ)$. If b is a primitive root of $(S, \circ)$, then it holds that $S' = S$.

Order of a group and an element

Definition 4.6 *(Order of a group and an element) Let $(S, \circ)$ be a group, e the neutral element of this group and $b \in S$ an arbitrary element of the group. Also let $c \in \mathbb{Z}^+$ be the smallest number so that $b^c = e$, if such a c exists, and if not, let $c := \infty$. Then $|S|$ is called the **order of the group** $(S, \circ)$ and c is called the **order of the element** b.*

A relationship exists between the order of a group and that of one of its subgroups, as recorded in the following theorem:

Theorem 4.8 *(Lagrange) If $(G, \circ)$ is a finite group and $(H, \circ)$ is a subgroup of $(G, \circ)$, then the order of H divides the order of G.*

What particularly applies to all elements $b \in G$ is that the order of b divides the order of G. Another statement about the number of elements of a certain order can be made in respect to finite cyclic groups and is gives in the following theorem:

Theorem 4.9 *If $(G, \circ)$ is a finite cyclic group of the order n and d is a divisor of n, then G has exactly $\Phi(d)$ elements of the order d. In particular, G therefore has $\Phi(n)$ elements of the order n (primitive roots).*

Construction of cyclic groups and choice of primitive root

Theorems 4.6, 4.8 and 4.9 form the basis for the following algorithm that can be used to construct a cyclic group and a primitive root for this group:

- Choose a large prime number q so that $p := 2 \times q + 1$ is also a prime number.
- As p is a prime number, it follows with Theorem 4.6 that $(\mathbb{Z}_p^*, \times_p)$ is a cyclic group.
- The order of $\mathbb{Z}_p^*$ is $2 \times q$ and it holds that $\Phi(2 \times q) = \Phi(2) \times \Phi(q) = q - 1$ as q is a prime number.
- Therefore, according to Theorem 4.9, the probability of selecting a primitive root by randomly choosing an element of $\mathbb{Z}_p^*$ is $(q - 1)/(2 \times q) \approx 1/2$.
- An efficient test can be executed with Theorem 4.8 to determine whether a randomly chosen g is a primitive root because the only thing that needs to be checked is whether

$g^2 \equiv 1 \pmod{p}$ or $g^q \equiv 1 \pmod{p}$. If not, then the order has to be of $g = |\mathbb{Z}_p^*|$ since the order of g must be a divisor of the order of $\mathbb{Z}_p^*$ according to Theorem 4.8.

■ The generator of the subgroup with two elements is always $p - 1$, for $(p - 1)^2 \equiv p^2 - 2p + 1 \equiv 1 \pmod{p}$. Practically, it is therefore even sufficient to choose any number g with $1 < g < p - 1$, for all of these numbers create either the whole group or a subgroup that contains $p - 1/2$ elements, which should still be very large. Numbers p with this property are also called *safe primes*.

These results give us the mathematical background we need to deal with the problem of the discrete logarithm and its cryptographic applications.

Definition 4.7 *(Discrete logarithm) Let p be a prime number, g a primitive root of $(\mathbb{Z}_p^*, \times_p)$ and $c \in \mathbb{Z}_p^*$ any element. Then a number $z \in \mathbb{Z}^+$ exists so that $g^z \equiv c \pmod{p}$. The number z is called the* **discrete logarithm of c modulo p to the base g**.

Discrete logarithm

For example, 6 is the discrete logarithm of 1 modulo 7 to the base 3 since $3^6 \equiv 1 \pmod{7}$.

Calculating the discrete logarithm z for given numbers g, c and p is a computationally difficult problem and the asymptotic runtime of the best known algorithms is superpolynomial to the bit length of prime number p.

Computation of discrete logarithms requires exponential runtime

The problem consequently presents a promising candidate for the design of asymmetric cryptographic schemes. Actually, a number of algorithms have already been proposed and the two of the most common ones are discussed in the following sections.

4.5 The Diffie–Hellman Key Exchange Algorithm

The Diffie–Hellman key exchange algorithm was published for the first time in May 1976 [DH76]. The paper also introduced the general basic principles of asymmetric cryptography, thus giving fundamental significance to the development of this discipline. Even though the algorithm is not essentially an asymmetric cryptographic scheme, it is nevertheless an important algorithm that is currently being used in numerous cryptographic protocols, not least because it is the only secure scheme of its specific type.

Agreeing a secret
over an authentic
but not confid-
ential channel
In its original form, the algorithm enables two entities A ('Alice') and B ('Bob') to agree a shared secret over a public channel. In this context a public channel is a communication medium that is not secure from eavesdropping. This means that an attacker E ('Eve', based on the word 'eavesdrop') can obtain all messages exchanged between A and B.

It is important for A and B to have the assurance that messages sent through the communication channel cannot be modified because of the threat of 'man-in-the-middle' attacks — more on this later.

The mathematical foundation of the algorithm is the problem of the discrete logarithm in finite cyclic groups introduced in the last section. If A and B want to agree on a shared secret and a public channel is the only communication medium available to them, then they can proceed as follows:

- A chooses a prime number p, a primitive root g of $\mathbb{Z}_p^*$ and a random number $q \in \mathbb{Z}_p^*$. A and B can either agree on values for p and g before the first protocol run or A can send these values with her first message to B.

  A now computes $v = g^q \bmod p$ and sends to B: (p, g, v)
- B also selects a random number r, computes $w = g^r \bmod p$ and sends w to A.
- A computes $s = w^q \bmod p$.
- B computes $s' = v^r \bmod p$.

Since $g^{(q \times r)} \bmod p = g^{(r \times q)} \bmod p$, it holds $s = s'$ so that A and B have agreed on the same number. An attacker E who is eavesdropping on the public channel cannot easily figure out the number s computed by A and B. The fundamental problem that needs to be solved by E is called Diffie–Hellman problem. It is assumed that the calculation of s implies that E needs to calculate the discrete logarithm modulo p to the base g from one of the two numbers v or w. The prime number p chosen by A and B needs to be large enough so that an attacker cannot discover their shared secret by computation of the discrete logarithm.

In practice it is not mandatory that g be a primitive root of $(\mathbb{Z}_p^*, \times_p)$, and it suffices if g creates a sufficiently large subgroup of $(\mathbb{Z}_p^*, \times_p)$.

If a potential attacker E is able to modify messages on the path between A and B, she can execute what is called a *man-in-the-middle attack*:

- E randomly selects two numbers q', r' and computes:

$$v' = g^{q'} \bmod p \quad \text{and} \quad w' = g^{r'} \bmod p$$

- The message (p, g, v) sent by A is intercepted by E who instead sends message (p, g, v') to B.
- E also intercepts message (w) sent by B and instead sends (w') to A.
- A computation of the supposed shared secret now produces the following situation:
  - A computes $s_1 = w'^q \bmod p = v^{r'} \bmod p$, with the last computation being one executed by E.
  - B computes $s_2 = v'^r \bmod p = w^{q'} \bmod p$, with the last computation again being one executed by E.

  In essence, A and E have agreed on a shared secret s_1, but E and B have agreed on a different secret s_2.

If A and B use their respective supposed secret to encrypt messages they exchange over a public channel, E can intercept these messages, decrypt them and then send them newly encrypted to the actual receiver. From this point onwards E actually has to manipulate all message traffic secured through a 'shared secret' between A and B if he or she wants to avoid discovery.

An attacker can subsequently control the communication

This example demonstrates the importance of being 'certain' about a person with whom one has negotiated a key, that is, the authenticity of key-exchange messages is vital. We will take another look at this aspect in Chapter 7.

Authenticity of key-exchange messages is vital!

4.6 The ElGamal Algorithm

The ElGamal algorithm was published in 1985 [ElG85]. The algorithm can be used either for digital signatures or for encrypting data although, unlike RSA, the two computation variants differ from one another. Like the Diffie–Hellman key-exchange scheme, it is based on the problem to solve the discrete logarithm. However, as it uses additive as well as multiplicative operations, it is computed in finite fields rather than in finite groups like Diffie–Hellman. However, the group $(\mathbb{Z}_p^*, \times_p)$ often used for Diffie–Hellman meets the requirements of a field if 0 and the operation $+_p$ are added, so in practice there is actually little difference between the two mathematical structures.

Calculating a key pair   The following steps are necessary to calculate a key pair for the ElGamal algorithm:

- Choose a large prime number p, a primitive root g of the multiplicative group $(\mathbb{Z}_p^*, \times_p)$ and a random number v so that $1 \leq v \leq p - 2$.
- Compute: $y = g^v \bmod p$.
- The public key is: (y, g, p).
- The private key is: (v, g, p).

ElGamal signatures   The following scheme is used to sign a message $m < p$:

- Choose a large random number k so that k is relatively prime to $p - 1$.
- Compute: $r = g^k \bmod p$.
- Use the extended Euclidean algorithm to calculate k^{-1}, the inverse element to $k \pmod{p - 1}$.
- Compute: $s = k^{-1} \times (m - v \times r) \bmod (p - 1)$.
- The signature of the message m is (r, s).

Signature check   Checking whether $y^r \times r^s \equiv g^m \pmod{p}$ is all that is needed to verify a signature. The following lemma is helpful for proofing the correctness of this scheme:

Lemma 4.3 *Let p be a prime number and g a generator of $(\mathbb{Z}_p^*, \times_p)$, it then holds that:*

$$i \equiv j \pmod{p - 1} \Rightarrow g^i \equiv g^j \pmod{p}$$

For proof of this lemma one has to be sure that

- $i \equiv j \pmod{p - 1} \Rightarrow \exists\, k \in \mathbb{Z}^+ : (i - j) = (p - 1) \times k$
- Therefore, according to Theorem 4.4 (Euler):

$$g^{(i-j)} \equiv g^{(p-1) \times k} \equiv 1^k \equiv 1 \pmod{p}$$

$$\Rightarrow g^i \equiv g^j \pmod{p} \quad \square$$

Correctness of ElGamal signature check   The following calculation proves the correctness of the ElGamal signature check:

$$s \equiv k^{-1} \times (m - v \times r) \pmod{p - 1}$$
$$\Leftrightarrow \quad k \times s \equiv m - v \times r \pmod{p - 1}$$
$$\Leftrightarrow \quad m \equiv v \times r + k \times s \pmod{p - 1}$$
$$\Rightarrow \quad g^m \equiv g^{(v \times r + k \times s)} \pmod{p} \qquad \text{(Lemma 4.3)}$$
$$\Leftrightarrow \quad g^m \equiv g^{(v \times r)} \times g^{(k \times s)} \pmod{p}$$
$$\Leftrightarrow \quad g^m \equiv y^r \times r^s \pmod{p} \quad \square$$

The security of ElGamal signatures is based on the fact that an *Security of ElGamal* attacker needs the private key v to compute value s. Therefore, the *signatures* attacker must compute the discrete logarithm of y modulo p to the base g in order to forge signatures.

It is vital for the security of ElGamal signatures that a new random number k is chosen for each signature. Otherwise an attacker will be able to compute v from two different messages and their signatures, formed using the same k [MOV97, Note 11.66.ii].

An alternative to a truly random choice of k is the usage of a cryptographic hash function (see Chapter 5) to derive a unique k for each message and the private key. In this way messages can be signed without the need of secure randomness and without the possibility to reuse the same k for different private keys or messages.

Anyway, with the ElGamal scheme messages should not be signed directly and instead a *cryptographic hash value* should be computed that is then signed using an ElGamal algorithm. If messages are signed directly with an ElGamal algorithm, an attacker may be able to construct a message with a valid signature in certain circumstances [MOV97, Note 11.66.iii].

A secure variation of ElGamal, which also signs cryptographic hash values, has been standardised by NIST under the name *Digital Signature Algorithm* (DSA) [NIS13].

The encryption of a message m with $m < p$ can be realised using *ElGamal encryption* the ElGamal scheme as follows:

- Choose a random number $k \in \mathbb{Z}^+$ with $k \leq p - 1$.
- Compute: $r = g^k \bmod p$.
- Compute: $s = m \times y^k \bmod p$.
- The ciphertext is (r, s). Note that the ciphertext is twice as long as the original message m.

The following two steps are needed to decrypt a message: *ElGamal decryption*

- The private key v is first used to compute $r^{(p-1-v)} \bmod p = r^{-v} \bmod p$ (again Theorem 4.4 is adopted).
- r^{-v} can then be used to compute m, since:

$$m = r^{-v} \times s \bmod p$$

The following congruence is used to prove the correctness of El- *Correctness of* Gamal decryption: *ElGamal decryption*

$$r^{-v} \times s \equiv r^{-v} \times m \times y^k$$
$$\equiv g^{(-v \times k)} \times m \times y^k$$

$$\equiv g^{(-v \times k)} \times m \times g^{(v \times k)}$$

$$\equiv m \qquad\qquad (\text{mod } p) \quad \square$$

Security of ElGamal encryption

The security of ElGamal encryption is based on the fact that an attacker must solve the discrete logarithm to obtain v in order to decipher an encrypted message.

As with ElGamal signatures, it is vital for the security of El-Gamal encryption that a new random number k is chosen for each message because an attacker is otherwise able to compute v [MOV97, Note 8.23.ii].

4.7   Security of Conventional Asymmetric Cryptographic Schemes

Generalisation to other mathematical groups and fields

The algorithms presented in this chapter were invented for the multiplicative groups $(\mathbb{Z}_p^*, \times_p)$ and the fields $(\mathbb{Z}_p, +_p, \times_p)$. During the 1980s it was shown that these algorithms could be generalised and also used with other groups or fields. The main motivation for this generalisation lies in the security sought for these algorithms, which until now has been directly related to key length.

Success in the field of prime number tests and factorisation

Since the invention of the RSA algorithm there has been considerable success in mathematical research in the fields of prime number tests, prime factor analysis [CP05] and the computation of the discrete logarithm. Not least this success can be attributed to the importance of these results for the security of the algorithms based on these problems:

- When the *RSA-129 challenge*, the factorisation of a 129-digit (≈ 428 bit) long number, was published in 1977, it was estimated that it would take around 40 quadrillion years to solve the problem. In actual fact, it took less than 20 years; in 1994 it took only eight months for a network of computers communicating over the Internet with a computing time equivalent to around 5000 MIPS-years to solve the task. One MIPS-year corresponds to the processing time that a computer capable of executing one million instructions per second can provide in one year. An Intel i7 processor has a computing capacity of 80,000 MIPS.

  However, the reason why the original estimate was refuted was not because of a false calculation in 1977 but because the estimate was based on other assumptions. The estimate may have been totally correct in respect of the algorithms for prime factor factorisation known in 1977, but what happened is that advances in mathematics in the following 17 years enabled the same tasks to be completed with considerably less processing time.

■ Then only two years later, in 1996, a new algorithm was used successfully in factorising a 130-digit (≈ 431 bit) long number with a computational effort of about 500 MIPS-years. A problem that was eight-times larger was thus solved with a tenth of the computational effort.

■ In 2009 researchers were able to factorise a number with 232 digits (768 bit) in about 1500 AMD64 years [KAF⁺10]. Therefore, the factorisation of at least some keys with a length of 1024 bits will likely be possible within the next few years.

These examples show the risks to the security of asymmetric cryptographic algorithms that result from mathematical progress. As a consequence, the minimal requirements for key length have to be corrected upward at regular intervals. This is currently at about 2048 bits.

Risks due to mathematical progress

The longer key lengths indeed increase the level of security but, on the downside, they result in a reduction in processing speed. The reason is the required exponentiation of individual key values during the execution of the algorithms, and this operation involving such long keys is relatively time-consuming. The speed-up that is caused by more modern processors also makes attacks faster. Thus, users must reckon that longer keys lead to a truly longer processing time in future.

Performance loss due to increased key length

The most efficient factorisation algorithms are based on specific properties of $(\mathbb{Z}_p^*, \times p)$ and $(\mathbb{Z}_p, +_p, \times_p)$. Therefore, a number of mathematicians have tried to generalise these algorithms to other mathematical structures that are not as receptive to optimised factorisation algorithms or to algorithms used to compute the discrete logarithm.

4.8 Principles of Cryptography Based on Elliptic Curves

The basic idea of using other groups for realising asymmetric cryptography is to accept more complex basic operations on the group elements in return for assurance that a shorter key length can offer a comparable degree of security. In this way the overall computational overhead for the algorithms can be reduced without

Fields with more complex design are intended to enable shorter key lengths

compromising security. The mathematical structure that has proved to be very promising for this purpose is the *group of points on an elliptic curve over a finite field*, referred to as *Elliptic Curve Cryptography* (ECC).

The elements of these fields consist of the points (x, y) whose coordinates comply with the Weierstrass equation $y^2 = x^3 ax + b$ for two fixed parameters a and b, and a special point $\mathcal{O}$, referred to as point at infinity. The coordinates of the points are themselves elements of an underlying field, such as $\mathbb{R}$, $\mathbb{Z}_p$, or with similar equations also $GF(2^n)$. Although coordinates with real numbers are not used in cryptography, the basic group operations can be explained relatively comprehensibly through elliptically curves over $\mathbb{R}$. We will therefore describe these initially.

4.8.1   Elliptic Curves over $\mathbb{R}$

Already when real-valued coordinates are taken as a basis, the parameters a and b strongly influence the appearance of an elliptic curve. Figure 4.3 shows two elliptic curves with slightly different parameters. Due to the structure of the Weierstrass equation, both curves are symmetric to the x-axis. Notwithstanding their different appearance, they have another common characteristic: for almost any pair of points on the curves another point can be found that lies on the straight line defined by the two points. It is precisely this characteristic that is required for the definition of the group arithmetic.

Geometrical addition of points on elliptic curves via $\mathbb{R}$

The group operation on elliptic curves links two points on the curve or point $\mathcal{O}$ with each other and a third point on the curve. This logic operation is referred to as point addition. For elliptic curves

Figure 4.3
Two elliptic curves over $\mathbb{R}$

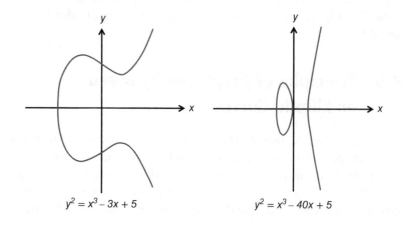

$$y^2 = x^3 - 3x + 5 \qquad\qquad y^2 = x^3 - 40x + 5$$

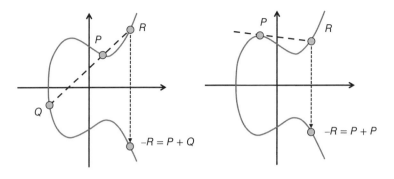

Figure 4.4

*Addition of two points
in general position
(left) and addition of
identical points (right)*

over $\mathbb{R}$ the following geometrical interpretation applies: As shown in Figure 4.4, the result corresponds to the point addition of two points P and Q in the general location of the mirror image of the third point, which is determined by the straight line through P and Q. In addition there are a number of special cases:

- If P and Q are identical, the third point is determined by the intersection of the tangent that touches the elliptic curve at point P.
- If $P = (x, y)$ and $Q = (x, -y)$, i.e. if the points are mirrored along the x-axis, the straight line does not intersect the curve a third time. In this case the result of the addition is the special point $\mathcal{O}$, which does not lie on the curve and because of this property is referred to as point at infinity. It represents the identity element with regard to the point addition, so that in this case P and Q are inverse to each other.
- If $\mathcal{O}$ is added to a point P, by definition the result is P. In particular, $\mathcal{O} + \mathcal{O} = \mathcal{O}$ applies, so that $\mathcal{O}$ is inverse to itself.

This definition also determines key properties of an Abelian group. For example, an identity element exists with $\mathcal{O}$, each element has an inverse element and the result of several consecutive additions does not depend on the order. Furthermore, the point addition is commutative.

Obviously, for computer-aided realisation of the point addition the elliptic curves are not drawn, but determined through calculation of the points. If one of the points is $\mathcal{O}$, the result is the respective other point. In the event that the points are inverse to each other, $\mathcal{O}$ can be assumed as the result. For general positions, or if the points P and Q are identical, one can determine the slope α of the straight line in the first instance. For the general case this is the difference quotient of the point coordinates. In the case of the tangent construct the slope can be determined from the derivative

*Algebraic point
addition on elliptic
curves over $\mathbb{R}$*

of the equation for the elliptic curve, so that the following applies:

$$\alpha = \begin{cases} \dfrac{y_Q - y_P}{x_Q - x_P} & \text{if } P \neq Q \wedge P \neq -Q \\[2ex] \dfrac{3x_P^2 + a}{2y_P} & \text{if } P = Q \wedge y_P \neq 0 \end{cases}$$

The slope of the straight line can then be used to determine the sum of P and Q:

$$x_{Q+P} = \alpha^2 - x_P - x_Q$$

$$y_{Q+P} = \alpha(x_P - x_{Q+P}) - y_P$$

Multiplication of natural number and point   The generally defined addition of any two points naturally also explains sums such as $P+P+P$ or $P+P+P+P$, i.e. the multiple sum of the same point. It is precisely this technique that corresponds to the scalar multiplication of a natural number x and a point on a curve P. To calculate the product quickly it makes sense to use an algorithm similar to the Square and Multiply algorithm. The difference between g^x and xP essentially only results from different notations for the operators. What this means is that first $P + P = 2P$ is calculated, then $2P + 2P = 4P$ etc. until the point xP can be formed through addition of the partial results. The algorithm sketched out here has a logarithmic runtime and can of course only be used if x is known. Although determining an x such that for a fixed P and Q the equation $xP = Q$ applies is still possible for elliptic curves over $\mathbb{R}$, for other groups this would be very complex. This problem is referred to as the solution of the *discrete logarithm for elliptic curves* and corresponds to the discrete logarithm in conventional asymmetric cryptography techniques. Notwithstanding the same name, the logarithm thus refers to the multiple addition of a point to itself. The multiplication of a point with itself is not required, and it is generally not defined how two points are multiplied with each other. In the following sections multiplication for elliptic curves will always refer to scalar multiplication of a natural number with a point.

The discrete logarithm for elliptic curves

4.8.2   Elliptic Curves over $\mathbb{Z}_p$

If the coordinates on an elliptic curve are selected in relation to $\mathbb{Z}_p$, the elliptic curve becomes a finite number of points. The example in Figure 4.5 shows the points of the curve $y^2 \equiv x^3 - 3x + 5 \pmod{19}$. Similar to the curves over $\mathbb{R}$, each point (x, y) has an inverse point $(x, p - y)$. The characteristic referred to above, i.e. the fact that generally there are always three points that lie on a straight line,

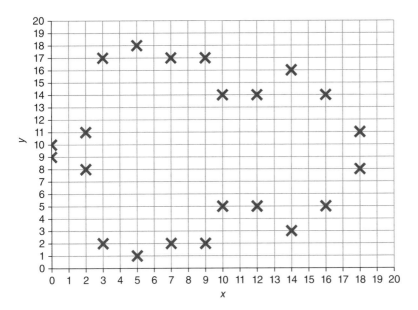

Figure 4.5
Points of the elliptic
curve $y^2 \equiv x^3 - 3x + 5$
(mod 19)

is no longer that obvious, not least in view of the fact that not all
x values have corresponding points.

Another somewhat more complex aspect than for curves over $\mathbb{R}$ *Calculation of a point*
is the calculation of a y coordinate of a point for a given x. Because *for a given x*
of the calculation in $\mathbb{Z}_p$ it is not possible to simply determine the
square root of $x^3 + ax + b$. Therefore, it is common practice to use
a mathematical 'trick' that becomes possible if the prime number
$p \equiv 3 \pmod 4$ is selected. In this case the two possible values are
$y_{1,2} = \pm(x^3 + ax + b)^{\frac{p+1}{4}}$. The derivation of this relationship is comparatively simple. According to the Euler criterion [MOV97, 4.14],
$f(x)^{\frac{p-1}{2}} \equiv 1 \pmod p$ applies if $y^2 = f(x) \pmod p$ has a solution y.
Since $p + 1$ is divisible by 4 as premised, the following transformation becomes permissible:

$$f(x)^{\frac{p-1}{2}} \equiv 1 \pmod p \qquad\qquad |\times f(x)$$
$$f(x)^{\frac{p+1}{2}} \equiv f(x) \equiv y^2 \pmod p \qquad\qquad |\sqrt{}$$
$$\pm f(x)^{\frac{p+1}{4}} \equiv y \pmod p \qquad \square$$

Note that the formula can also be calculated for x values that do
not meet the Euler criterion. However, the calculated points would
not be elements of the group, so that the Euler criterion has to be
additionally verified during point construction.

The algebraic operations on an elliptic curve over $\mathbb{Z}_p$ are ana- *Algebraic point*
logous to curves over $\mathbb{R}$. If the two points to be added are inverse to *arithmetic on elliptic*
each other, the point $\mathcal{O}$ is returned. If one of the points to be added *curves over $\mathbb{Z}_p$*

is $\mathcal{O}$, the result of the addition is the respective other point. In the two other cases the x and y coordinates of the sum are determined on a modulo p basis. Although a division is required to determine the 'slope' of the straight line based on the formulas already introduced for elliptic curves over $\mathbb{R}$, it is possible to use multiplication with the inverse element in $\mathbb{Z}_p$. The extended Euclidean algorithm can be used to determine the inverse element, as already applied in Section 4.6 for conventional asymmetric cryptography. The scalar multiplication can also be realised for curves over $\mathbb{Z}_p$ through repeated addition. The difficulty of the problem to calculate the discrete logarithm is that a number x has to be determined for two known points P and Q so that $xP = Q$ applies.

Number of points on an elliptic curve over $\mathbb{Z}_p$ Since the security of cryptographic algorithms is essentially based on the degree of difficulty in solving the discrete logarithm, it is necessary to be able to generate as many elements as possible through multiple addition of a point. Compared with conventional cryptography over $\mathbb{Z}_p$, the order of these subgroups is no longer $p-1$. For example, the curve $y^2 \equiv x^3 - 3x + 5 \pmod{19}$ contains 22 points, in addition to point $\mathcal{O}$. An estimation of the size of the generated group n can be obtained through Hasse's theorem on elliptic curves. Accordingly, the order n is between:

$$p + 1 - 2\sqrt{p} \leq n \leq p + 1 + 2\sqrt{p}$$

If the number of elements has to be determined exactly, this can be done in logarithmic runtime with the aid of Schoof's algorithm [Sch85]. The mathematical details would far exceed the scope of this book, which is limited to basic mathematical principles. In any case, the group should be large enough to make it difficult for attackers to try out all possible points.

4.8.3 Elliptic Curves over $GF(2^n)$

In addition to operations over $\mathbb{Z}_p$, elliptic curves can also be used for cryptographic purposes via the so-called Galois fields, which are named after Évariste Galois. Essentially this is an extension of $\mathbb{Z}_p$, since in a $GF(x^n)$ the addition and multiplication operations are defined via polynomials of degree $n - 1$. The coefficients of the polynomials are elements from $\mathbb{Z}_x$. The field $GF(p)$ thus exactly matches the special case $\mathbb{Z}_p$. For cryptographic purposes $GF(2^n)$ is often used. In this case only two values (0 and 1) exist for the n coefficients a_0 to a_{n-1}. Since the coefficients can be expressed through n bits, it is common practice to specify only the corresponding numbers in hexadecimal notation. For example: $x^4 + x^2 + x^1 \hat{=} 2^4 + 2^2 + 2^1 = 16h$.

The addition in a field $GF(2^n)$ corresponds to the addition of the individual coefficients of the terms with the special case of the addition of two 1 values. In this case the result is 0 by definition. For example: $x^3 + x + 1 \oplus x^2 + x = x^3 + x^2 + 1$. The addition therefore corresponds to a simple XOR operation on the coefficients and can quickly be implemented in hardware and software.

Addition of two $GF(2^n)$ elements

The multiplication in $GF(2^n)$ corresponds to a polynomial multiplication with subsequent modulo division through an irreducible polynomial of degree n. Irreducible polynomials are similar to the prime numbers of natural numbers. They are only divisible through themselves and 1 without remainder. The multiplication can also be calculated very quickly in hardware through shift and XOR operations. Newer Intel processors have a separate CLMUL command for $GF(2^n)$ multiplication, so that the multiplication can also be implemented quickly through software.

$GF(2^n)$ multiplication

Similar to $\mathbb{Z}_p$, generators also exist with regard to multiplication in field $GF(2^n)$. For example, the result for the term x with regard to the irreducible polynomial $x^4 + x + 1$ generates all elements of the field: x, x^2, x^3, $x + 1$, $x^2 + x$, $x^3 + x^2$, $x^3 + x + 1$, $x^2 + 1$, $x^3 + x$, $x^2 + x + 1$, $x^3 + x^2 + x$, $x^3 + x^2 + x + 1$, $x^3 + x^2 + 1$, $x^3 + 1$, 1, x, ... The other concepts of finite fields are also applicable: with regard to addition and multiplication, each term in $GF(2^n)$ has a corresponding term resulting in 1. In the example the term $x^3 + 1$ is inverse to x with regard to multiplication with reduction through the irreducible polynomial $x^4 + x + 1$, since $x^3 + 1 \odot x = 1$. The multiplicative inverse of a given element can be determined through an adjusted version of the extended Euclidean algorithm.

Generators and inverse elements in $GF(2^n)$

In addition to the elliptic curves over $\mathbb{Z}_p$ described above, elliptic curves can also be defined over $GF(2^n)$. In this case the 'curve' also consists of a set of points. However, for defining the points it is no longer possible to use functions of the form $y^2 = x^3 + ax + b$. As described in Section 4.8.1, in this case the formal derivative α of the curve at a point $P(x, y)$ would correspond to

Properties of elliptic curves over $GF(2^n)$

$$\alpha = \frac{3x^2 + a}{2y}$$

However, in $GF(2^n)$ $2y$ is always 0, since each element of the field is inverse to itself with regard to addition. As in $\mathbb{R}$, division through 0 is not possible in $GF(2^n)$. For this reason it is common to use curves of the form $y^2 + xy = x^3 + ax^2 + b$.

Because of the modified definition of the curve, the point operations are slightly different. Although the point $\mathcal{O}$ still exists and the respective addition operations still match, the sum $P + Q$ is generally defined as follows:

$$x_{Q+P} = \alpha^2 + \alpha + x_P + x_Q + a$$

$$y_{Q+P} = \alpha(x_{Q+P} + x_P) + x_{Q+P} + y_P$$

The inverse point $-P$ with regard to the point addition is defined as $(x, x + y)$.

The other conceptual differences compared with elliptic curves over $\mathbb{Z}_p$ are minor, so that further details for curves over $GF(2^n)$ are not provided here. Interested readers will find further information on the implementation of arithmetic operations in these groups in [IEE00], for example.

4.8.4   Cryptographic Protocols Based on Elliptic Curves

Elliptic curves over $\mathbb{Z}_p$ or $GF(2^n)$ can be used for realisation of encryption and signature procedures, as described above. As for other cryptographic functions, the latter offer speed benefits if the procedures are realised in hardware. According to current knowledge, the security properties are comparable. Based on a suitable curve, both the *Diffie–Hellman key exchange* and the *ElGamal algorithm* can be implemented securely with shorter key lengths.

Diffie–Hellman key exchange on elliptic curves   The idea of Diffie–Hellman key exchange can easily be transferred to elliptic curves. The technique is generally referred to as *Elliptic Curve Diffie–Hellman (ECDH)* and works as follows: The two involved instances A ('Alice') and B ('Bob') first agree on an elliptic curve and a point P on this curve. P must differ from $\mathcal{O}$, since the point serves as generator. A then selects a random number q, calculates $Q = qP$ and transfers Q to B. Party B proceeds accordingly, i.e. it generates a random number r, calculates $R = rP$ and transfers R to A. Both parties can then calculate a shared secret. A generates the point $S = qR$ and B the point $S' = rQ$. Since $qR = qrP = rqP = rQ$, the determined points S and S' must be identical. A passive attacker that monitors the communication cannot deduce the secret without solving the Diffie–Hellman problem for elliptic curves, which is assumed to be as difficult as determining r or q through solving the discrete logarithm. The communicating parties therefore use the point S to protect further communication through a symmetric technique, for example. To derive the key a *cryptographic hash value* (see also Chapter 5) for the coordinates of point S can be used, for example.

As already mentioned, it is also possible to use the ElGamal *ElGamal encryption* algorithm on elliptic curves. To this end it is first necessary to gen- *on elliptic curves* erate a key pair for an elliptic curve E to be determined with a generator point G, also to be determined. The private key is then a random number $v \in \mathbb{N}$, whereby $1 < v < n$ should apply with the number of points on curve n. The public key consists of the triple (Y, G, E). In addition to the point G and the curve E, the point $Y = vG$ is also published. The security of this scheme is again based on the fact that it is not possible to derive the private key from the public key due to the difficulty of calculating the discrete logarithm on elliptic curves.

In order to encrypt a message with the public key, first a further random number $k \in \mathbb{N}$ with $1 < k < n$ is generated and used to cal- culate a point $R = kG$. The message then also has to be converted into a point M, in order to determine a further point $S = M + kY$. The points R and S form the encrypted text and can be transferred securely. The length of the message approximately corresponds to twice the key length, since the points are transferred in so-called *compressed form*. For each point this only comprises the x value and a further bit that indicates whether the larger or smaller cor- responding y coordinate should be used.

A challenge for the encryption is coding of the message in a valid *Coding of message* point on curve E. A naïve approach would be to interpret the mes- *texts in points* sage text as the x coordinate and calculate a valid y coordinate. However, as indicated in Section 4.8.2, not every x coordinate can be assigned a point, which means that not every message could be encrypted. In order to overcome this limitation it is necessary to use a suitable coding technique, as suggested in [Kob87b], for example. First, a sufficiently large constant c is selected, depending on the curve. Then a check is carried out for the message m to ascertain whether $c \times m$ represents a possible x value for a point M on the curve. If this is not the case, further values $cm + 1$, $cm + 2$, ... are checked until a suitable coordinate is found. If the value selected for c is too small, it may not be possible to find a suitable point, since the values from $cm + c$ are reserved for the next message text. The recipient can reverse the coding by dividing the x coordinate of a point through c based on integer division.

To decrypt the message the recipient can calculate the point M *Decryption in* through $S - vR$ that corresponds to message m. The subtraction *the ECC version* refers to the addition of the inverse point. The derivation of the *of ElGamal* relationship can be based on simple application of the formulas for forming S and R:

$$S - vR =$$

$$M + kY - vR =$$

$$M + (kvG - vkG) =$$

$$M + \mathcal{O} = M$$

Signatures based on elliptic curves   Signing is much more similar to the conventional ElGamal technique. To this end the sender initially selects a random number $k \in \mathbb{N} < n - 1$ and calculates the point $R = kG$. Then the x coordinate of point R, referred to as r below, is used to calculate the value $s = k^{-1}(m + rv) \pmod{n}$. Once again, n is the size of the group over the elliptic curve, while k^{-1} is the inverse value to k with regard to $\mathbb{Z}_n$. Similar to the conventional technique, the signature consists of (r, s) and also has approximately twice the length of the key material used. As in the conventional ElGamal technique, security considerations necessitate that a k is never used repeatedly for different messages.

Verification of ECC signatures   To verify a signature all the recipient of a message has to do is check whether the point $ms^{-1}G + rs^{-1}Y$ has the x coordinate r. Here too a derivation is comparatively straightforward by checking:

$$ms^{-1}G + rs^{-1}Y =$$

$$ms^{-1}G + rs^{-1}vG =$$

$$(m + rv)(s^{-1})G =$$

$$(ks)(s^{-1})G =$$

$$kG = R$$

However, in an implementation it is necessary to check additional parameters in order to ensure security. For example, attackers must be prevented from using the point $\mathcal{O}$ as generator G. A complete list of criteria that must be checked can be found in [NIS13], for example.

4.8.5 Security of cryptographic techniques over elliptic curves

The mathematical operations on the fields described above can be implemented efficiently both in hardware and in software. The best currently known algorithms for calculating the discrete logarithm are far less efficient than those for the field $(\mathbb{Z}_p, +_p, \times_p)$.

Symmetric algorithms	RSA	ECC-based algorithms
112 bit	2048 bit	224-255 bit
128 bit	3072 bit	256-383 bit
192 bit	7680 bit	384-511 bit
256 bit	15360 bit	$\geq$ 512 bit

Table 4.2
Key lengths for different techniques with comparable security level

Recommended key lengths based on the current state of research are regularly published by NIST, for example [NIS12]. Table 4.2 summarises comparable key lengths for the individual techniques. Even though these numbers should be treated with caution, they nevertheless show impressively that a conventional RSA technique cannot meaningfully be combined with AES and 256 bit keys because of the very long keys.

However, the security of cryptographic techniques over elliptic curves depends not only on the key length. Weak points that were made public in the past nearly always relate to the implementations or certain subgroups of elliptic curves. For example, A. Menezes found sub-exponential algorithms for the computation of the discrete logarithm for the special case of what is called *super-singular elliptic curves*, although these solutions are not appropriate for use in general cases [Men93]. A more thorough introduction into cryptanalysis with elliptic curves would exceed the mathematical scope of this book. We therefore refer the reader to other literature available on this topic [Kob87a, Men93].

Security of certain ellipsoidal curves

In general, except perhaps for professional cryptographers, it therefore makes sense to use predefined curves, such as [LM10, BSI12] or [NIS13], and recognised standards such as ECDSA or ECGDSA. Some publications show that all parameters such as a and b were selected at random when the standards were created. Generally for each constant k a value x is published so that the following applies for a recognised function h that cannot easily be inverted: $h(x) = k$. In addition, the fact that x was not determined through trial and error must be verifiable. In this context this means selecting the first decimal places of π, for example. This process is a serious indication that the defined curves do not contain a *cryptographic trap door*, that is, no security flaw that is only known to the authors.

Application of recognised standards

In addition to potential problems relating to the selection of the elliptic curves used, in many cases the actual implementation

Implementation security

is also susceptible to attacks, as already indicated. Because of the large number of case differentiations for ECC operations, such as the special handling of point $\mathcal{O}$, there is a risk that attackers can measure them outside a trustworthy environment, for example through different response times or varying electricity consumption. These so-called side channel attacks can then allow conclusions to be drawn about the key space. For example, there was a problem in the widely used library OpenSSL 0.9.8o, which allowed conclusions to be drawn regarding the size of k during the calculation of kP [BT11]. The cause was very simple: The loop for executing the multiplication was terminated as soon as all bits of k were processed. Depending on the size of k, there were more or fewer point duplications. This measurable quantity alone can significantly reduce the search space for an attacker. The same software library contained a further fault [BBP$^+$12] that enabled the whole private key to be determined with a few queries. This was caused by the fact that points were not checked correctly, thereby giving the attacker the opportunity to reduce the search space further and further. Because of the wide range of opportunities to make subtle, yet security-critical, errors in the implementation of an ECC system, up-to-date standard solutions should generally be used wherever possible.

4.8.6   Current Developments in EC Cryptography

Compared with conventional asymmetric cryptography, EC cryptography is still a very active research field, so that interesting further developments with effects on systems used in practice are to be expected over the coming years. Because this area is comparatively new, it is definitely advisable to check the patent situation before implementation in commercial products. For some techniques and implementation options it is known that patent protection has not yet expired.

Use of bilinear pairings   With regard to other developments, the so-called *bilinear pairings* are particularly noteworthy. They enable two additives groups G_1 and G_2 to be mapped on a multiplicative group G_3 so that certain properties are achieved. For example, the following applies for a bilinear transformation: $e : G_1 \times G_2 \rightarrow G_3 : e(aP, bQ) = e(P, Q)^{ab}$. This calculation scheme can be used to develop cryptographic protocols with innovative properties, such as the following:

- *Secret handshakes* [SM09] enable exchange of keys between parties, if they have certain properties, for example if they belong to the same organisation. If the properties do not match, the key exchange fails, and none of the parties knows the identity of its counterpart.

■ With *identity-based encryption*, public keys do not have to have a certain form, e.g. an e-mail address can simultaneously be used as public key. Further details on identity-based encryption can be found in [BF03], for example.

In addition to further fields of application, research also focuses on suitable groups for cryptographic applications. In this context the so-called *Edwards curves* have been mentioned [BLR08], for example, since they could be more robust against side-channel attacks.

4.9 Summary

Asymmetric cryptography enables two matching but distinct keys to be used for encryption and decryption or for signing and signature checking.

Basic idea of asymmetric cryptography

The algorithms that are still considered secure today and have also proven effective in practice are:

■ *RSA algorithm*, based on the difficulty of factorising large integers

■ *Diffie–Hellman key exchange* (not actually an asymmetric scheme), based on the difficulty of calculating the discrete logarithm of the number y modulo of a prime number p to a given base g in finite fields

■ *ElGamal algorithm*, which is also based on the problem of the discrete logarithm

Because the security of these algorithms relies on the complexity of the mathematical problems named, advances in the field of mathematical algorithms represent the greatest threat to these schemes. One should always bear in mind that, unlike forecasting technological progress in the field of processor construction, estimating the impact of algorithmic advances is very difficult, if not impossible.

Security of asymmetric algorithms

The following practical considerations in particular have to be taken into account with the use of asymmetric cryptographic algorithms:

Practical considerations

■ Asymmetric cryptographic operations are magnitudes (around a factor of 100 to 1000) slower than symmetric schemes.

■ Consequently, they are seldom used for encrypting or signing bulk data. Instead symmetric encryption schemes or cryptographic hash functions (see also Chapter 5) are used for this purpose, and asymmetric schemes are reserved for the encryption of so-called session keys or for the signing of cryptographic hash values.

4.10 Supplemental Reading

[Bre89] offers a good introduction to the mathematical background of prime number tests and factorisation, whereas [NZ80, Kob87a] provides a general introduction to number theory, with the latter book also highlighting cryptographic applications. Cryptography with elliptic curves is discussed in detail in [Men93]. An easy-to-understand introduction into the subject with emphasis on the implementation and computing time of algorithms can also be found in [CLR01, Chapter 33]. The subject is also covered in detail in [MOV97]. We also highly recommend a study of the three main original articles [DH76, RSA78, ElG85].

[Bre89]   BRESSOUD, D. M.: *Factorization and Primality Testing*. Springer, 1989

[CLR01]   CORMEN, T. H.; LEISERSON, C. E.; RIVEST, R. L.: *Introduction to Algorithms*. B&T, 2001
           A well-known standard reference for algorithms that assumes that mathematical operations are performed in $\mathcal{O}(1)$. For operations with very large numbers this assumption is no longer true, therefore runtime estimates must be carried over with care.

[CP05]   CRANDALL, R.; POMERANCE, C.: *Prime numbers: A computational perspective*. Springer Press, 2005

[DH76]   DIFFIE, W.; HELLMAN, M. E.: *New Directions in Cryptography*. In: *Trans. IEEE Inform. Theory, IT-22*, 1976, pp. 644–654

[ElG85]   ELGAMAL, T.: A Public Key Cryptosystem and a Signature Scheme Based on Discrete Logarithms. In: *IEEE Transactions on Information Theory* 31, July 1985, No. 4, pp. 469–472

[Kob87a]   KOBLITZ, N.: *A Course in Number Theory and Cryptography*. Springer, 1987

[Men93]   MENEZES, A. J.: *Elliptic Curve Public Key Cryptosystems*. Kluwer Academic Publishers, 1993

[MOV97] MENEZES, A.; OORSCHOT, P. van; VANSTONE, S.: *Handbook of Applied Cryptography*. CRC Press LLC, 1997

[NIS13] NIST (NATIONAL INSTITUTE OF STANDARDS AND TECHNOLOGY): *Digital Signature Standard (DSS)*. 2013. – FIPS PUB 186-4 - Federal Information Processing Standards Publication

[NZ80] NIVEN, I.; ZUCKERMAN, H.: *An Introduction to the Theory of Numbers*. 4th edition, John Wiley & Sons, 1980

[RSA78] RIVEST, R.; SHAMIR, A.; ADLEMAN, L.: A Method for Obtaining Digital Signatures and Public Key Cryptosystems. In: *Communications of the ACM*, February 1978

4.11 Questions

1. Which properties must a practical asymmetric cryptographic scheme have?
2. Why is it important for the sender of an asymmetrically encrypted message to check the authenticity of the public key of the receiver?
3. Using the extended Euclidean algorithm, compute the greatest common divisor of 210 and 126 as well as the two coefficients of the corresponding linear combination.
4. Using Theorem 4.2, show that $\sqrt{2}$ is not a rational number.
5. Compute $\Phi(21)$.
6. Explain how the RSA algorithm functions.
7. The following requirement of the RSA key appears in the 1988 version of International Standard X.509: '*It must be ensured that $e > log_2(n)$ to prevent attack by taking the e-th root modulo n to disclose the plaintext.*'

    Although the condition required is correct, the reasoning given is not right. Explain the error in the reasoning and give the right reasoning for this requirement.
8. Why would the RSA algorithm be insecure, if an algorithm was found to quickly solve the discrete logarithm problem?
9. Find a primitive root of $(\mathbb{Z}_{11}^*, \times_{11})$.
10. Compute the discrete logarithm of 1 modulo 5 to base 3 and of 1 modulo 11 to base 3.
11. How does a man-in-the-middle attack work on Diffie–Hellman key exchange and how can it be prevented or detected?

12. Is a primitive root of group $(\mathbb{Z}_p^*, \times_p)$ really needed with the ElGamal algorithm or is it enough if g produces a sufficiently large subgroup of $(\mathbb{Z}_p^*, \times_p)$?

13. What is the practical disadvantage of transmitting messages encrypted with the ElGamal algorithm compared to RSA-encrypted messages?

14. The idea of the RSA algorithm can be transferred to an approach that uses ECC over $\mathbb{Z}_p$ (e.g. see [Dem93]). To do so the message is converted to a point M. The ciphertext C is derived by $e \times M$ and can be transformed to the original message by calculating $d \times C = d \times e \times M = M$. The used elliptic curve is constructed such that d can only be derived by factorising a large integer into two prime factors. Find arguments why the usage of ECC does not result in a security advantage and why the key length may not be safely reduced in comparison to the conventional RSA algorithm.

5 Cryptographic Check Values

This chapter looks at how a check value can be added to data so that the data can be verified at a later point in time to determine whether it has been accidentally or intentionally modified. In the first section, the *cryptographic check values* developed for this purpose are delineated from *error checksums* familiar from data communications. The requirements of these check values are discussed and the two principal categories of cryptographic check values, *modification detection codes* and *message authentication codes*, are introduced. The two sections that follow discuss both categories in detail and Section 5.5 concludes with a description of schemes that calculate authentication codes and encrypt data at the same time.

5.1 Requirements and Classification

In data communications it is common to calculate an error check-sum for transmitted data units. This checksum enables a receiver to check whether the message was altered during transmission. The computation of *parity bits*, or the variant *bit-interleaved parity*, and the *Cyclic Redundancy Check (CRC)* are two well-known schemes for this task [PD00, Section 2.4].

Error checksums

The usefulness of these schemes motivates an interest in computing comparable checksums that enable the checking of data after transmission (or loading storage, etc.) to determine whether it has been modified. However, one has to take into account that it makes a big difference whether data is altered due to *accidental error* or *intentional modification*.

Security in Fixed and Wireless Networks, Second Edition.
Guenter Schaefer and Michael Rossberg.

CRC is not suitable as
a cryptographic check
value

For example, if an attacker wants to modify a protocol data unit that is protected from error by a CRC-checksum, he or she must only ensure that the forged data unit has a valid CRC-checksum. This scheme is no more effective at protecting against intentional modification than other error-detection values because an attacker simply has to compute a new CRC-checksum for the modified data unit.

One could of course be naïve and decide to encipher the CRC-checksum of the original message using a previously negotiated session key before transmission to prevent an attacker from simply computing a new encrypted CRC. In fact, this approach was pursued during the standardisation of the wireless local area network standard IEEE 802.11. Unfortunately, it does not offer adequate protection from intentional modification, as we will see in Chapter 15.

This is due to the fact that a cryptographic check value must satisfy a number of requirements that make it impossible for an attacker to forge such a check value and that cannot be provided by a common error checksum.

Principle categories

Two principal categories of cryptographic check values can be distinguished at a higher level of consideration:

- *Modification Detection Codes (MDC)* that in a certain way implement 'cryptographic fingerprints' of messages.
- *Message Authentication Codes (MAC)* that also include a previously negotiated 'secret', i.e. a session key into the computation, thereby enabling a direct verification of the authenticity of a message.

Main application
and design goals

The main application of these schemes is in checking the authenticity of a message although the concrete design goals of both categories differ:

- An MDC represents the digital fingerprint of a message that can be signed with an asymmetric cryptographic scheme such as RSA or ElGamal. Because it is only the 'fingerprint' that is being signed, it should not be computationally feasible for an attacker to construct two messages that are mapped to the same MDC. This would enable an attacker to use a signed MDC for a different message.
- A MAC, on the other hand, allows verification that the creator of a message knows the secret key K that was used in the computation of the MAC of this message, and consequently the message cannot be meaningfully modified without knowledge of the key.

In addition to the main application just described, other applications of cryptographic check values are possible, for example:

Other applications

- verification of knowledge of a particular data value;
- generation of sessions keys;
- generation of pseudo-random numbers (see also Chapter 6).

Depending on the application, cryptographic check values must sometimes satisfy other requirements. The following section takes a detailed look at both categories of cryptographic check values, with the main emphasis on how they function and how they are used to detect modifications.

5.2   Modification Detection Codes

Modification detection codes are computed using *cryptographic hash functions*. These hash functions are distinguished from conventional hash functions:

Definition 5.1   *A **hash function** is a function h that has the two following properties:*

Hash function

- **Compression:** *The function h maps input values of an arbitrary finite bit length to output values of a fixed bit length which is specific for h.*
- **Ease of computation:** *If h and an input value x are given, then it is easy to compute h(x).*

In comparison, cryptographic hash functions must satisfy yet other requirements:

Definition 5.2   *A **cryptographic hash function** is a hash function h that additionally has the following properties:*

Cryptographic hash function

- **Pre-image resistance:** *This property requires that it should not be computationally feasible to calculate an pre-image x for a given value y so that $h(x) = y$.*
- **2nd pre-image resistance:** *This property requires that for a given value x it should not be computationally feasible to find a second value x' that is mapped to the same value $h(x) = h(x')$.*
- **Collision resistance:** *This property requires that it should not be computationally feasible to calculate two pre-images $x_1 \neq x_2$ that are mapped to the same value $h(x_1) = h(x_2)$.*

Other potential
requirements

Depending on the intended application, cryptographic hash functions may sometimes have to meet further requirements, for example *partial pre-image resistance*. This means that if only t bits of the image are not known, an average of 2^{t-1} computing steps are needed to calculate the remaining t bits.

In the next section a discussion on potential attacks on modification detection codes is given, which also provides a justification for the properties listed above. Following that, the general structure of some common cryptographic hash functions, along with important representatives of this class of functions, will be explained.

5.2.1   Attacks on Modification Detection Codes

A modification detection code should represent a tamper-proof 'digital fingerprint' of a message and allow it to be signed using an asymmetric cryptographic scheme to verify the authenticity of the message. It is vital that it is not computationally feasible for two messages $x_1 \neq x_2$ to be created with the same modification detection code $MDC(x_1) = MDC(x_2)$. Otherwise, an attacker E could try to recover a digital signature for a 'harmless' message x_1 from an entity A and use it for a 'not so harmless' message x_2, an electronic order for goods or services, for example.

The collision resistance of the cryptographic hash function used for digital signatures is therefore particularly important. This aspect will be examined closely below.

Birthday phenomenon

For this purpose we will first take a look at what is called the *birthday phenomenon*, which is directly responsible for the minimum length requirement for the output of cryptographic hash functions.

In its basic form the birthday phenomenon supplies an answer to the question of 'how many people have to be in a room so that the probability of two people having the same birthday is at least 50%'. For reasons of simple computation, we leave leap years out of the equation and assume that each birthday has the same probability.

$P(n, k) \approx$ at least
one duplication

First we define $P(n, k)$ as the probability that at least one duplication will occur with k randomly selected variables each capable of assuming an equally probable value between 1 and n. This corresponds to the random experiment of having a box of n different balls and pulling out a ball k times with the respective ball being put back in the box each time.

$Q(n, k) \approx$ no
duplication

We also define $Q(n, k)$ as the probability that no duplication will occur with the experiment described. If a ball should be pulled out more than once, we can therefore select the first ball from n possible balls, the second ball from $n-1$ possible balls and so forth. Thus the number of different possibilities of pulling out k balls from n different balls without duplication is on the order of:

$$N = n \times (n-1) \times \ldots \times (n-k+1) = \frac{n!}{(n-k)!}$$

The number of different possibilities of pulling out k balls from n possible balls and returning them to the box is n^k. Therefore:

$$Q(n,k) = \frac{N}{n^k} = \frac{n!}{(n-k)! \times n^k}$$

So it holds that:

Computing $P(n,k)$

$$P(n,k) = 1 - Q(n,k)$$

$$= 1 - \frac{n!}{(n-k)! \times n^k}$$

$$= 1 - \frac{n \times (n-1) \times \ldots \times (n-k+1)}{n^k}$$

$$= 1 - \left[\frac{n-1}{n} \times \frac{n-2}{n} \times \ldots \times \frac{n-k+1}{n} \right]$$

$$= 1 - \left[\left(1 - \frac{1}{n}\right) \times \left(1 - \frac{2}{n}\right) \times \ldots \times \left(1 - \frac{k-1}{n}\right) \right]$$

Using the inequation $\forall\, x \geq 0: (1-x) \leq e^{-x}$ we then have:

$$P(n,k) > 1 - \left[\left(e^{\frac{-1}{n}}\right) \times \left(e^{\frac{-2}{n}}\right) \times \ldots \times \left(e^{\frac{-(k-1)}{n}}\right) \right]$$

$$= 1 - e^{-\left[\frac{1}{n} + \frac{2}{n} + \ldots + \frac{k-1}{n}\right]}$$

$$= 1 - e^{-\frac{k \times (k-1)}{2 \times n}}$$

The following equation was used in the last step:

$$1 + 2 + \ldots + (k-1) = \frac{(k^2 - k)}{2}$$

Returning to the original question of how many people would have to be together in a room so that the probability that at least two of these people have the same birthday is greater than or the equal to 0.5, we have to solve the following equation:

$$\frac{1}{2} = 1 - e^{-\frac{k \times (k-1)}{2 \times n}}$$

$$\Leftrightarrow \quad 2 = e^{\frac{k \times (k-1)}{2 \times n}}$$

$$\Leftrightarrow \quad ln(2) = \frac{k \times (k-1)}{2 \times n}$$

Estimating for large k   For large k we can estimate $k \times (k - 1)$ through k^2 and arrive at:

$$k \approx \sqrt{2 \times ln(2) \times n} \approx 1.18 \times \sqrt{n}$$

For $n = 365$ the result with $k \approx 22.54$ is quite close to the actual value $k = 23$.

We have therefore shown that the quantity k of the values that have to be selected from n possible values in order to arrive at two identical values with a probability greater than or equal to 0.5 is of the magnitude of $\sqrt{n}$.

Use for attacks   This fact can be exploited for attacks on modification detection codes [Yuv79]:

- Assume that E wants to induce A to sign a message m_1 that A normally would not sign, e.g. an electronic order. E knows that A signs her message by first computing a modification detection code $MDC(m)$ of length r bits and then signs it with her private key.

- Because E also knows that A would not sign message m_1, she will not present it to her directly for signing. If she tried to construct a second harmless message m_2, which is mapped to the same modification detection code $MDC(m_2) = MDC(m_1)$, the average computational effort required would be of the magnitude of 2^{r-1} because on average she would have to search through half the search space.

- Instead E takes advantage of the birthday phenomenon and, using the two messages m_1 and m_2 as a basis, starts to construct variations of these messages m_1' and m_2' until she finds a combination that is mapped to the same modification detection code $MDC(m_1') = MDC(m_2')$. For example, E can use character combinations in the form of '<space>, <backspace>' or replace individual words with synonyms to create messages that are semantically identical but have different coding.

- As we know from the birthday phenomenon, on average E requires $\sqrt{2^r} = 2^{r/2}$ variations of both messages to ensure that the probability of a successful collision with $MDC(m_1') = MDC(m_2')$ is greater than or equal to 0.5.

- Because E has to create and store the variations of the messages, the storage and computation effort is of the magnitude of $2^{r/2}$.

- After E has found two suitable messages m_1' and m_2', she presents message m_2' to A for signing. The signature generated by Alice likewise represents a valid signature of message m_1' so that E can subsequently make the claim that A signed message m_1'.

Attacks that follow this pattern are called *birthday attacks*. Accord- ing to current estimates, a cryptographic hash function should have an output value of a 160-bit minimum length to make it secure from this attack technique as an average effort of 2^{80} is not considered feasible.

Birthday attacks

Let us assume that A uses a cryptographic hash function that produces a 96-bit length output and then signs it with a 2048-bit long RSA key. Because it is not feasible to break a 2048-bit long RSA key with the algorithms currently known, one would assume that the security a signature with such a key offers could not be com- promised. However, adequate security is not provided due to the possibility of a birthday attack, the average effort of which in this case is of the magnitude of 2^{48}. This example shows the importance of evaluating all known attack techniques on distinct cryptographic algorithms used as well as on task-specific combinations when as- sessing the security of a cryptographic solution. One can make an analogy to a chain that is known only to be as strong as its weak- est link.

With cryptographic 'solutions' it is always necessary to evaluate concrete combinations of different schemes

5.2.2 General Structure of Cryptographic Hash Functions

Comparable to the development of symmetric encryption al- gorithms that make use of certain established structures, such as the Feistel network, the design of the most commonly used cryp- tographic hash functions today is based on the underlying general structure shown in Figure 5.1 – the so called Merkle-Dåmgard structure.

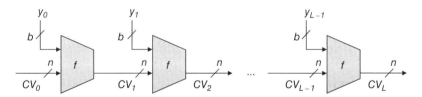

Figure 5.1 Merkle-Dåmgard structure of crypto- graphic hash functions

A length field is appended to an arbitrary message y and the mes- sage is padded to an integer multiple of the block size b of the cryp- tographic hash function. Let $(y_0 \,\|\, y_1 \,\|\, \dots \,\|\, y_{L-1})$ be the resulting message that is structured into L blocks of block size b. Again '$\|$' denotes the concatenation of blocks.

Padding and appending of length field

In order to compute the hash value $h(y_0 \,\|\, y_1 \,\|\, \dots \,\|\, y_{L-1})$, the message is processed block by block, and in each step a so-called *chaining value* CV_{i+1} of length n bits is computed from the message

Chaining with a chaining value

block y_i and the chaining value CV_i using a *compression function* f that maps $(n + b)$ bits to n bits: $CV_{i+1} := f(CV_i, y_i)$.

Initialisation vector   The first chaining value CV_0 requires an initialisation vector IV that is normally defined by the cryptographic hash function. The cryptographic hash value of the message is then the value of the chaining value after the last iteration step: $h(y_0 \,\|\, y_1 \,\|\, \cdots \,\|\, y_{L-1}) := CV_L$.

The functioning of such a cryptographic hash function can be summarised as follows:

$$CV_0 := IV$$
$$CV_i := f(CV_{i-1}, y_{i-1}) \qquad 1 \leq i \leq L$$
$$H(y) := CV_L$$

It has been proved that the collision resistance of compression function f for this structure also ensures the collision resistance of the resulting cryptographic hash function h [Mer89].

The cryptanalysis of cryptographic hash functions concentrates on the compression function   Consequently, the analysis of cryptographic hash functions normally concentrates on the internal structure of the compression function f and tries to find efficient techniques for creating collisions for a single execution of function f.

The minimum bit length required by hash value $h(x)$ today is normally 160 bits. This requirement was established due to the threat of the already discussed *birthday attacks*. With a block length of 160 bits, such an attack requires an average effort of the magnitude of 2^{80}, which according to today's knowledge is considered impractical.

The three of the currently most widely known cryptographic hash functions, *MD5*, *SHA-1* and *SHA-2*, which all follow the general structure just outlined, are explained in the following sections. Subsequently, the novel *SHA-3* is covered, which is based on a different principle, the so-called *cryptographic sponge functions*.

5.2.3   MD5

The cryptographic hash function *Message Digest 5 (MD5)* [Riv92] was designed by Rivest as a successor to the insecure function *Message Digest 4 (MD4)* [Riv91].

Padding and addition of length field   MD5 is constructed according to the structure described above. First one '1' bit and so many '0' bits are added to message y that the length of the resulting message is congruent to 448 modulo 512. Then the length of the original message is appended as a 64-bit long length field so that the length of the resulting message is an integer multiple of 512. This message is then divided into blocks y_i of length $b = 512$ bits.

The length of the chaining value is $n = 128$ bits and the value is *Chaining value and* structured into four 32-bit long registers A, B, C, D. The following *initialisation vector* predefined initialisation vectors are written into the register for the initialisation:

$$A := 0x\ 01\ 23\ 45\ 67 \qquad\qquad B := 0x\ 89\ AB\ CD\ EF$$

$$C := 0x\ FE\ DC\ BA\ 98 \qquad\qquad D := 0x\ 76\ 54\ 32\ 10$$

This initialisation vector is given in the so-called Little-Endian format, i.e., the lower-valued bytes are noted at the beginning.

Each block y_i of the message is then mixed with chaining value *Compression function* CV_i through function f, which is realised internally through four rounds, each with 16 steps. Each round is based on a similar structure and uses a table containing 64 constant values each 32 bits long. In addition, a round-specific logical function g is used in each round. Figure 5.2 shows a block diagram of an individual step.

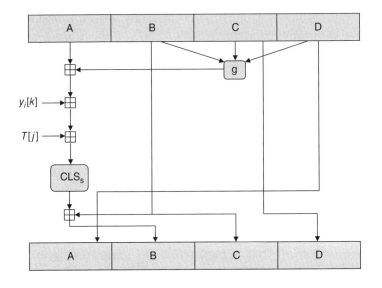

Figure 5.2
An iteration of the
MD5 function

In each step the contents of registers B, C and D are linked to the *Iteration step process* round-specific function g and the function value is added (modulo 2^{32}, represented by the character ⊞) to the contents of register A. The resulting value is then added to $y_i[k]$, the kth 32-bit word of the ith message block, and then added again to $T[j]$, the jth table entry, with j incremented modulo 64 with each step. The result is then cyclically left shifted by s bits (Cyclical Left Shift, CLS) before it is written into register B for the next step. The quantity s by which each shift takes place is fixed for each round (the exact specification will not be dealt with here). Furthermore, the contents of register D are written into A, those of register B into C and those of register C into D. The MD5 value of message y is then the contents of the registers after the last data block y_i has been processed.

Security of MD5   Concerning MD5's security, it should be noted that each bit of the 128-bit long output depends on each bit of input message y. However, already the length of the output with 128 bits is generally already judged to be too short (also see Section 5.2.1).

Cryptanalysis of MD5   Important advances in the analysis of MD5 were made between 1992 and 1996. In 1996 Dobbertin published an attack that produced a collision for the function f of MD5. Even if this attack was not expanded to a collision for the full MD5 function, it created considerable concern for the security of MD5. Nevertheless, it was not until 2004 that cryptanalysts published a genuine MD5 collision [WFL+04]. Meanwhile, progress has been such that collisions can be calculated within seconds on standard PCs [Kli06]. As a result, MD5 may no longer be used in cases where collision resistance in any form is required. Unfortunately, in many cases the need for this feature is not immediately obvious. However, there are a number of examples that can provide an idea:

- In [LD05] a procedure was published that can generate two PostScript documents with freely chosen different content and identical MD5 test value, based on a single known collision.
- In [LWW05] the authors describe how certificates with identical checksum but different rights can be generated. Because of the collision the signature generated by a private key continues to apply.
- The so-called *Nostradamus* attack [KK06] describes freely selectable message extensions based on collisions.

In cases where all that is required is pre-image resistance, MD5 can still be regarded as relatively secure: The best published attack requires around $\mathcal{O}(2^{123.4})$ calculations [SA09].

5.2.4   SHA-1

The function *Secure Hash Algorithm 1 (SHA-1)* was developed by the National Security Agency (NSA). The NSA designed SHA-1 according to the structure of the MD4 function, so that SHA-1 also follows the general Merkle-Dåmgard structure described above.

SHA-1 works on block lengths of 512 bits and produces an output value of length 160 bits. Its procedure for preparing a message y and separating it into blocks y_i is identical to that of MD5.

Padding and addition of length field

The chaining value of SHA-1 is the 32-bit longer output divided into five registers of length 32 bits. For initialisation these registers are filled with the following constants:

Chaining value and initialisation vector

$$A := 0x\,67\,45\,23\,01 \qquad\qquad B := 0x\,EF\,CD\,AB\,89$$

$$C := 0x\,98\,BA\,DC\,FE \qquad\qquad D := 0x\,10\,32\,54\,76$$

$$E := 0x\,C3\,D2\,E1\,F0$$

For the first four registers this value corresponds to that of MD5. However, in contrast to MD5, the definition of SHA-1 is given for a Big-Endian architecture in which the octets are in opposite order so that the construction looks different at first glance.

Each message block y_i is mixed with the content of chaining value CV_i through application of function f, resulting in the new chaining value CV_{i+1}. The function f is implemented in four rounds with 20 steps each. The rounds all have the same structure but a specific logical function f_1, f_2, f_3 or f_4 is used per round. In addition, each step makes use of a fixed additive constant K_t that remains unchanged during a round.

Compression function

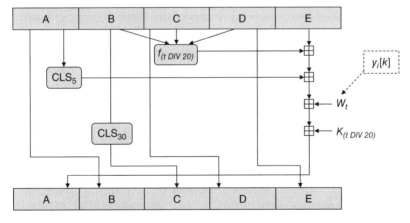

Figure 5.3

An iteration of the SHA-1 function

Figure 5.3 shows a block diagram of the internal structure of a step. The current message block y_i is logically integrated into the processing through value W_t, which is defined according to the following recursive relationship:

$$t \in \{0, \dots, 15\} \quad \Rightarrow W_t := y_i[t]$$

$$t \in \{16, \dots, 79\} \quad \Rightarrow W_t := CLS_1(W_{t-16} \oplus W_{t-14} \oplus W_{t-8} \oplus W_{t-3})$$

After the 79th step each one of registers A, B, C, D and E is added modulo 2^{32} to the content of the corresponding register before the 0th step, and the result is written into the relevant register for processing the next message block.

As with MD5, the SHA-1 value of message y is the content of the register after the last data block y_i has been processed.

Comparison with MD5   In terms of security, it should be noted that SHA-1 offers better protection against brute-force and birthday attacks (see below) than MD5 does because of its longer output value. A further comparison shows that SHA-1 is around 25% slower in processing than MD5, which is a direct consequence of the processing effort required for the 25% longer chaining value. Both algorithms are simple to define and implement, and do not require any extensive programmes or substitution tables. Concerning the design for Little-Endian or Big-Endian architecture (selected as indicated above), there is no particular advantage to choosing one function over the other.

Security of SHA-1   In terms of collision resistance SHA-1 is only slightly more secure than MD5. Although no practical collisions are known at this stage, in 2005 a theoretical attack with a complexity of 2^{69} was published, which was later improved to 2^{63} [WYY05]. Currently further progress has been reported [Man11], so that it is quite likely that the collision resistance of SHA-1 might be broken over the coming years. Furthermore, the weaknesses of the Merkle-Dåmgard structure, which were already referred to in the context of MD5, are also present in SHA-1. In the event of collisions becoming known, they would enable attacks such as the Nostradamus attack [KK06].

5.2.5 The SHA-2 Family

The reservations of cryptographers with regard to the security of SHA-1 have led to the revision of the SHA standard by the NSA. As a result, document FIPS PUB 180-2 [NIS02] was published for the first time in 2001. It defines a number of very similar hash functions: the so-called SHA-2 family. The representatives SHA-224, SHA-256, SHA-384 and SHA-512 differ mainly in terms of their output lengths, which are between 224 and 512 bits. As in the previous standards, all functions are Merkle-Dåmgard constructions. SHA-224 and SHA-384 are merely shortened versions of SHA-256 and SHA-512 functions with different initialisation constants. The internally processed block size is 512 bits for SHA-256 and 1024 bits for SHA-512. The blocks are subdivided into eight registers. The size of the individual registers is therefore 32 bits for SHA-256

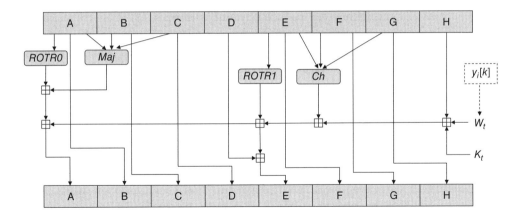

and 64 bits for SHA-512. Because of the larger state a higher number of rounds is required for the longer version of the hash function, in order to ensure good 'mixing', so that the number of rounds is increased to 80, compared with 64 rounds for SHA-256.

As shown in Figure 5.4, in the individual SHA-2 rounds several non-linear logical functions for compressing the input y_i are executed. In the first 16 rounds the value W_t corresponds to the input blocks. Subsequently it is determined by the function $W_t := W_{t-16} \boxplus \sigma_0(W_{t-15}) \boxplus W_{t-7} \boxplus \sigma_1(W_{t-2})$, with $\boxplus$ once again representing addition truncated to the block size, and the σ functions representing XOR combinations of shifted input values. The constants K_t are presumably intended to ensure a balanced ratio between set and non-set bits, if very long 0 or 1 series are part of the input. The actual values of K_t are chosen in a reproducible manner and represent the cube root of the tth prime number, so it is safe to assume that there is no cryptographic back door at this point. The functions Maj and Ch exactly match the non-linear functions f_1 and f_3 used in SHA-1.

Overall the design of the SHA-2 functions is therefore relatively similar to SHA-1. However, because of the larger block size and the more complex rounds function, the technique is around 30–50% slower. Nevertheless, it should be noted that, thanks to the use of 64-bit operations, on 64-bit processors SHA-512 and SHA-384 may be faster than the shorter SHA-2 versions. The larger block sizes and the more complex structure of the SHA-2 functions make attacks significantly more difficult compared with SHA-1 and MD5. Still, there are some theoretical problems. For example, as early as 2004 it was shown that a modified rounds function, which uses XOR operations instead of additions and symmetric constants, generates highly correlated outputs [GH04]. In addition, for SHA-2

Figure 5.4
Configuration of the rounds function in SHA-2

Security of SHA-2

versions with reduced round numbers attacks are conceivable which, although not likely in practice, are more efficient than a brute-force search (e.g. [AGM$^+$09]). Therefore, although currently SHA-2 can be regarded as secure in practice, some fundamental reservations remain regarding the Merkle-Dåmgard structure.

5.2.6   SHA-3

Security concerns with regard to SHA-2 have led to a new standardisation procedure

In 2007 the fundamental security concerns relating to SHA-1 and SHA-2 resulted in NIST announcing a new open competition. The aim was for a secure hash function based on open design criteria to become the SHA-3 standard. In 2011 five finalists were announced, which showed no significant weaknesses in the process. In October 2012 NIST chose the submission by four Europeans under the name of 'Keccak' [BDP$^+$11b] as the official winner. Interestingly, one of the inventors of Keccak is Joan Daemen, who was also involved in the development of AES. In early 2013 NIST announced an intention to make substantial changes in the algorithm for SHA-3 in order to increase the speed, but this was dropped after protests by renowned cryptographers. In this book SHA-3 and Keccak are therefore used synonymously. Even without the changes envisaged by NIST, the algorithm is characterised by high execution speed. This applies in particular to hardware implementations. The technique is very well documented and is based on clearly defined design criteria.

Cryptographic sponge functions

In view of the substantial doubt emerging concerning the security of the Merkle-Dåmgard structure, SHA-3 uses an alternative construct: so-called *cryptographic sponge functions*. These function family can be used to realise virtually all symmetric cryptographic techniques. However, only the use as a hash function is part of the SHA-3 standard. The sponge functions work in two phases. First the input data are 'absorbed' into an internal state. Then outputs of any length are generated from the internal state. Figuratively speaking, the state of the sponge function is 'pressed out'. In the SHA-3 standard, only output lengths of 224, 256, 384 and 512 bits are allowed.

Figure 5.5 shows the schematic sequence of the two phases. The internal state is subdivided into two registers, which are both initialised with 0. A register of size r is regarded as public. The input data is linked with the content via an XOR operation. The second register of size c remains private, that is, it is never read or modified from outside the hash function. In the case of SHA-3 the register sizes are chosen in such a way that the total size

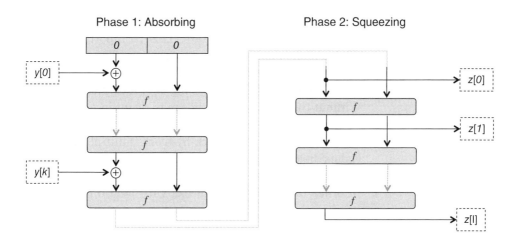

Phase 1: Absorbing Phase 2: Squeezing

is 1600 bits. During the 'absorption' the public register is always linked with r bits of the input via an XOR operation. Both registers are then recalculated via a function f. In contrast to the Merkle-Dåmgard structure, this is a relatively complex function with several rounds. It is comparable to a kind of block cipher with very large block size. The 'squeezing' phase begins once all input blocks have been added to the internal state in this way. The content of the public register is output each round until the required output length has been reached. Between two rounds the content of the register is modified through f, so that information from the private register gradually migrates into the output. If there was a collision in the private register, i.e. if there were two inputs that generate the same value, it would result in the same output. In SHA-3 the size c of the private register is therefore always twice the output length of the hash function. The effort required to generate an internal collision therefore approximately corresponds to that of a preimage attack.

Figure 5.5
Hashing with cryptographic sponge functions

The security of a sponge function heavily depends on the security of the function f. In particular, it must achieve secure cryptographic mixing of the contents of the two registers. To this end SHA-3 uses five subfunctions (θ, ρ, π, χ, ι), which are executed consecutively in 24 rounds. All functions operate on a three-dimensional bit matrix of size $5 \times 5 \times w$, while w is chosen depending on the size of the two registers. In the case of the standardised variant of Keccak, $w = 64$, resulting in an overall size of 1600 bits. The subfunctions change some bits individually, or based on columns or blocks. The executed operations are often represented through $GF(2^n)$ operations. Each individual subfunction has a clearly defined purpose:

Function f in SHA-3

- The functions θ and ρ ensure that the values of individual bits quickly affect the whole state. This is important for a good mixing of the public and private registers. These functions are therefore always executed before all others.

- π results in long-term scattering of values through the state. Without this function, changes may result in periodically correlating outputs.

- The function χ uses block-by-block multiplication in the Galois field in order to prevent f becoming linear, which would make it easy to analyse.

- In order to prevent data blocks with long 0 or 1 sequences resulting in very similar outputs, ι executes an XOR operation with constants that have uniformly distributed 0 and 1 bits.

Security of SHA-3   The very clear design of SHA-3 and the long public selection process are good indicators of its security. Currently there are no known serious weaknesses in SHA-3: the best published attack for generating preimages only works with a version of the function f that was reduced to eight rounds. The authors of SHA-3 assume that a version with 11 rounds would provide adequate protection against collision attacks. Compared with the other hash functions described above, SHA-3 offers a further benefit: The internal state is significantly larger than the block size. This enables a further security characteristic of hash functions to be met more reliably, namely resistance against appending of additional information. This characteristic, referred to as *Chosen Target Forced Prefix (CTFP) Preimage Resistance* [KK06], indicates that it should not be possible to construct a message $m = P||S$ and $H(m) = y$ for a fixed character string P and a variable character string S. For Merkle-Dåmgard constructions this is only as difficult as finding a collision. With cryptographic sponge functions, this is exponentially more difficult in relation to the length of the internal register. In addition, in contrast to Merkle-Dåmgard constructions, SHA-3 offers no known possibility for quickly generating multi-collisions [Jou06].

5.3 Message Authentication Codes

Definition 5.3 *An* **algorithm for computing message authentication codes** *is a family of functions h_K that is parameterised through a secret key K and has the following properties:*

- **Compression:** *The functions h_K map input values of an arbitrarily finite bit length to an output value of a bit length fixed* for h_K. This is also called a **Message Authentication Code (MAC)**.

■ **Simplicity of computation:** *If a family of functions h_K, the key K and an input value x exist, then $h_K(x)$ can be computed with little effort.*

■ **Computation resistance of MACs to new messages:** *This property means that a valid MAC $h_K(x)$ cannot be computed from a range of known pairs $(x_i, h_K(x_i))$ for a new message $x \neq x_i \: \forall i$ unless the key K is known.*

At this juncture it should be mentioned that the latter property, computation resistance of message authentication codes, implies that it should not be possible to calculate key K from a range of pairs $(x_i, h_K(x_i))$ ('key non-recovery'). However, a reverse conclusion cannot be reached because, depending on the structure of the MAC algorithm, knowledge of key K is not required to forge a valid MAC for a message from a range of known pairs of messages and corresponding MACs.

Calculation of key K not always necessary for forging a MAC

We will use the following definition of an insecure message authentication scheme to present an instructional example:

Example of an insecure MAC

■ Input: Message $m = (x_1 \| x_2 \| \: \dots \: \| x_n)$ in which each x_i represents a 64-bit long message block and key K.

■ Compute: $\Delta(m) := x_1 \oplus x_2 \oplus \dots \oplus x_n$, with '$\oplus$' denoting the bit-wise XOR operation.

■ Ouput: MAC $C_K(m) := E(K, \Delta(m))$, with $E(K, x)$ denoting encryption with the DES algorithm.

Because the key length of the DES algorithm is 56 bits and its block size is 64 bits, one would assume that an attacker has to apply an effort of a magnitude of around 2^{55} to discover key K and thus break the MAC, that is, be in a position to compute valid MACs for new messages.

Security expectations

Unfortunately, the scheme is insecure because it allows attackers who do not know key k to compute valid MACs to specifically constructed messages. Let us assume that an attacker called Eve has recorded a message $(m, C_K(m))$ from Alice to Bob and that this message is 'secured' with a secret key K known only to Alice and Bob. Eve can use this message to construct a new message m' that is mapped to the same MAC:

The scheme is actually insecure!

■ Let $y_1 \| y_2 \| \: \dots \: \| y_{n-1}$ be a message of $n-1$ arbitrary 64-bit blocks.

■ Eve computes the following for these values:

$$y_n := y_1 \oplus y_2 \oplus \ldots \oplus y_{n-1} \oplus \Delta(m)$$

■ The new message m' is: $m' := (y_1 \| y_2 \| \ldots \| y_n)$
■ When Bob receives and checks the message $(m', C_K(m))$, he concludes that the contained MAC is correct and therefore accepts the message as an authentic message from Alice.

5.3.1 Schemes for the Computation of Message Authentication Codes

The two most frequently used schemes for computing message authentication codes break down into the following two categories:

■ *Cipher block chaining-MACs (CBC-MACs)* use a block cipher in CBC mode and take the last ciphertext block as the message authentication code.
■ *Message authentication codes based on MDCs* are used frequently because they are efficient, but cryptographically they should be viewed with some caution. This concerns some implicit though not yet proven assumptions about certain properties of the underlying MDC (also see Section 5.4).

Little difference between computation of a CBC-MAC and CBC encryption

Figure 5.6 illustrates the general structure of a CBC-MAC. A CBC-MAC differs little from CBC encryption except that it only requires the last block of the ciphertext even though it does not always use all of it. Because secret key K is already included in the computation of a MAC, it does not have to be encrypted again and can be used directly to prove the authenticity of a message.

Figure 5.6
General structure of a CBC-MAC

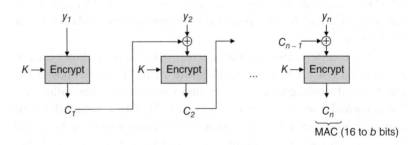

MACs on their own cannot realise digital signatures

However, the same key K must also be known to the checking entity. A MAC in principle therefore cannot be used to realise digital signatures that can be checked by independent third parties unless it deploys an additional asymmetric cryptographic algorithm.

5.3.2 Security of CBC-based Algorithms

Regarding the security of message authentication codes based on block ciphers in CBC mode, note that attackers must obtain knowledge of pairs of form $(m_i, MAC(x_i))$ because without knowing key K they will not be able to compute a valid pair $(m, h_K(m))$. This condition means that the MACs used can be shorter than MDCs without causing any reduction in security.

Another approach that can be used to make CBC-MAC more secure is triple encryption (e.g. 3DES) with different keys on the last ciphertext block. It takes only two additional encryption operations to triple the effective key length, thus merely an additive constant increase of computational effort.

Multiple encryption increases security effectively

However, this strengthening of the technique is unable to eliminate certain 'unpleasant' characteristics. For example, the method maps the message blocks 0xFF and 0xFF00 to the same authentication value if the two blocks are at the end of a message and blocks are filled with zeros.

There is no simple way to carry out a birthday attack on an MAC without knowing the key K. As already mentioned, it is highly unlikely that valid combinations of the form $(m, h_K(m))$ can be generated without the correct key. With a simple CBC-MAC it is nevertheless possible for attackers to utilise the birthday paradox [PO95]. During authentication of messages consisting of several blocks, an internal state is calculated for each block. In cases where large data quantities are processed over the lifetime of a key, a collision of these internal states may occur. Attackers – if they were able to detect such a case – could exchange the openings of the messages that led to the collision, thereby generating two new, valid packets.

Birthday attacks on MACs

The birthday attack described here might initially appear very theoretical, but it may have real effects in certain circumstances. If messages of different lengths can be protected with CBC-MACs, an attacker can easily assemble new messages from legitimate packets. To this end attackers could record two packets from blocks $y_0, \ldots, y_{n-1}$ and $y'_0, \ldots, y'_{m-1}$ with MACs t and t'. They could then send the packet $y_0, \ldots, y_{n-1}, t \oplus y'_0, \ldots, y'_{m-1}$ with the valid MAC t'. This attack has to be counteracted at the protocol level, for example through authentication of the overall packet length.

Further attacks on CBC-MACs with variable message lengths

5.3.3   The CMAC Method

Weaknesses of the CBC-MAC method triggered the development of a number of alternatives at the beginning of the last decade. The *Cipher-based MAC* (CMAC) is a method recommended by NIST [Dwo05] that has similar characteristics to CBC-MAC, but not its weakness with variable message lengths.

Derivation of MAC keys   With this method the first step is to derive two keys K_1 and K_2 from key K by multiplying $E_K(0^b)$ with the polynomials x and x^2 in $GF(2^b)$. The irreducible polynomial of the Galois field depends on the block size b and is defined in the standard. The derived keys can be used for several messages and therefore only have to be generated once per key K.

Functionality of CMAC   A message authentication value is now formed in the same way as with the CBC-MAC method, except that the last plain text block is linked with a derived key via an XOR operation before the encryption. This linking prevents concatenation of two legitimate messages, since the derived keys are unknown to attackers.

Filling the last block   Which key is selected depends on the length of the block: if the block is complete K_1 is used, otherwise K_2 is used. In order to prevent extensions within the last block in the latter case, incomplete blocks with missing j bits are filled with the series 10^{j-1}. The use of different keys prevents attackers from using this filling pattern as a legitimate extension in cases where the last block is incomplete.

In this way CMAC prevents known attacks on CBC-MAC, so that ultimately the only disadvantage is the comparatively high computational overhead of the CBC method. If additionally a cipher with a block size of at least 128 bits is used, the probability for internal collisions during the calculation of the MAC is sufficiently low.

5.4   Message Authentication Codes Based on MDCs

MDCs as MACs   The effort of using cryptographic hash functions to compute message authentication codes is mainly motivated by the fact that cryptographic hash functions require less computation. Furthermore, products that only contain cryptographic hash functions and no encryption algorithms are often excluded from export restrictions, which is a further advantage.

Basic idea   The basic idea behind the construction of MACs based on MDCs is that a shared secret is 'mixed' with a message in such a way that an attacker is not able to construct an appropriate MDC-MAC for a new message m' by eavesdropping on MDC-MACs $h(m_i)$ for a range of messages m_i.

The assumption that an attacker must have knowledge of secret K in order to construct a valid MDC-MAC into a new message m' raises some concerns when Merkle-Dåmgard functions are used naïvely:

Security concerns for Merkle-Dåmgard functions

- It has been shown that the construction $h(K \parallel m)$ is not secure if h is a Merkle-Dåmgard function because an attacker can lengthen eavesdropped messages and then give these modified messages a valid MDC-MAC without knowledge of key K [MOV97, Note 9.64].
- The construction $h(m \parallel K)$ can be broken with an expected effort of only $2^{n/2}$, as it is sufficient to find a collision [MOV97, Note 9.65].
- The construction $h(K \parallel m \parallel K)$, sometimes also called *prefix-suffix mode*, also does not offer adequate security [MOV97, Note 9.66].

Note that cryptographic sponge functions are not vulnerable to these weaknesses. Attackers simply do not obtain knowledge about the state of the internal register in this case, which also provides resistance against collisions.

The following construction has established itself as the most popular scheme:

HMAC

$$MDC\text{-}MAC(K,m) := h(K \oplus p_1 \parallel h(K \oplus p_2 \parallel m))$$

Here, the key material is first filled with '0' bits to the block size of h. Subsequently, the extended key is XORed with two different patterns p_1 and p_2 to change it in two different calls of the hash function. Even when Merkle-Dåmgard functions are used, there are no known effective attacks against this scheme, so it is currently regarded as secure [MOV97, Note 9.67] for suitable hash functions. Nonetheless, the use of the MD5 function should be avoided for its known weaknesses. The scheme was standardised in RFC 2104 ('Request for Comments') [KBC97] by the *Internet Engineering Task Force (IETF)* and is generally referred to as the *Hashed Message Authentication Code (HMAC)*

5.5 Authenticated Encryption

The application of independent methods for encryption and authentication of message blocks results in slow processing, particularly

Separate processing too slow

if a block cipher is also used for authentication. Therefore, various ways of combining these mechanisms have been considered in order to offer more efficient protection. During the last 10 years this has led to the development of a wide range of algorithms for *authenticated encryption*. These are referred to as *Authenticated Encryption with Associated Data (AEAD)* since, in addition to the actual encrypted data, further data can be authenticated. For example, it is possible to additionally authenticate the packet headers and initialisation vectors, even if these cannot be encrypted.

AEAD methods combine encryption and message authentication

The best-known AEAD methods include:

- the Galois/Counter Mode (GCM);
- the Counter with CBC-MAC (CCM) Mode;
- the Offset Codebook Mode (OCM).

In this textbook we will only explain the widely used Galois/Counter Mode in more detail. In addition we will show an interesting construction that uses cryptographic sponge functions such as SHA-3 to construct an AEAD method. The CCM Mode is used almost exclusively in WiFi applications and is therefore briefly introduced in this context in Section 15.4.2.

5.5.1   The Galois/Counter Mode (GCM)

The Galois/Counter Mode (GCM) is probably the best-known AEAD mode and has found its way into a wide range of network security protocols. It is used in the security protocols IEEE 802.1AE, IPsec, TLS and SSH, for example, which are described in Chapters 11 to 13. Its importance is no doubt related to the fact that GCM was one of the first known AEAD modes and that a NIST recommendation exists [Dwo07]. In addition, it is not subject to patents, and calculation, particularly in hardware, is efficient through the application of Galois field arithmetics. In recent x86 processors there is even provision for special commands to realise the required operations. Furthermore, the computing-intensive steps can be pre-calculated and parallelised. As with OFB and the CFB mode, the ciphertext does not have to be extended to match the block size, so that the message size does not grow unnecessarily.

GCM operation sequence

Figure 5.7 shows the sequence of an encryption based on an initialisation vector with a length of 96 bits. If other lengths are to be used for the initialisation vectors, additional calculations have to performed, which are not explained in detail here. GCM uses a single cipher with a block size of 128 bits for authentication and encryption, such as AES. With GCM, authentication of the blocks

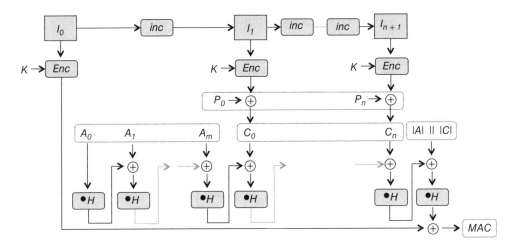

$A_0, \ldots, A_m$ and the additional encryption of the blocks $P_0, \ldots, P_n$ only requires a total of $n+1$ calls of the block cipher for each packet. In GCM, the input for the cipher is a 128-bit counter I_0, which is initially set to the initialisation vector with a length of 96 bits concatenated with a 32-bit counter of value 0. Thanks to the independence of the plain text these encryptions can be pre-calculated efficiently and/or parallelised. The first encrypted value is used for securing the MAC, all other cipher outputs are used for encryption of the blocks $P_0, \ldots, P_n$ through a simple XOR operation. In order to calculate the MAC, all transferred data, that is, $A_0, \ldots, A_m$ and the ciphertext $C_0, \ldots, C_n$, and their lengths are 'scattered' over a $GF(2^{128})$ through alternate multiplications and additions. The individual input blocks are multiplied with a value H in $GF(2^{128})$ over the irreducible polynomial $x^{128} + x^7 + x^2 + x + 1$ and linked with the next input block via an XOR operation. H corresponds to $E_K(0^{128})$, that is, a block of 0 bits that was encrypted with the key K. Since the value H does not depend on the initialisation vector, it does not have to be recalculated for each packet. However, in order to ensure the security of the GCM, H must remain secret.

Figure 5.7
Simplified Galois/Counter Mode sequence

Calculation of the GCM is very fast, particularly compared with having to carry out two block cipher operations for authentication and encryption. However, certain basic conditions have to be met in order to ensure that the application is secure. This is because the construction appears fragile, despite the fact that the method's security has been proved under certain conditions, for example the block cipher is indistinguishable from random bit sequences. On no account may initialisation vectors be used twice. Otherwise, not only can the XOR value of the plain texts be calculated, but also the

Security of GCM

value H. An attacker might then be able to modify packets without being detected.

Problems with short MAC lengths

Another method for attackers to draw conclusions on H would be to generate packets and check whether they are regarded as authentic [Dwo07]. The problem might occur, for example, if an administrator regards a MAC length of 32 bits as sufficient because a video stream is transmitted, in which individual forged packets hardly have any effect for the user. However, if attackers additionally had the opportunity to check whether their attempt was successful, they could gradually reduce the search space for H. The chances for attackers to obtain positive feedback are sufficiently small for normal MAC lengths of around 96 bits.

H can create small subgroups

Another possible problem is weak values for H. This problem becomes obvious if the key K generates a value H that only consists of 0 bits. In this case the MAC would always be the same. To a lesser extent the problem can also occur for other H, since the suggested $GF(2^{128})$ also contains subgroups of order 3, for example [Saa11]. If the probability that such a weak key is selected is not acceptable, an implementation could test for such weak keys and reject them.

Achieved level of forging security

Because of the way in which MACs are shortened in GCM, in order to forge a message consisting of 2^k blocks with a MAC length of t an attacker would not need $\mathcal{O}(2^t)$ operations, but only $\mathcal{O}(2^{t-k})$ [Fer05]. However, provided the MAC is sufficiently long, this potential weak spot should not be a problem in practice either.

5.5.2   The SpongeWrap Method

Another option for implementing an AEAD method that is currently under discussion is offered by cryptographic sponge functions. The authors of Keccak have suggested a very simple and easy to understand construction referred to as SpongeWrap, for which they have proven basic security properties [BDP+11a]. In this procedure, data are alternately entered into, and read from, the structure, rather than using inputs first to fill the sponge function, then generating outputs afterwards. This so-called *duplex mode* has been proved to offer the same level of security as the 'normal' operating mode.

SpongeWrap functionality

Figure 5.8 shows a simplified sequence of cryptographic protection based on SpongeWrap. For the purpose of this textbook we have assumed that the key length and the MAC length are definitely smaller than the processed block size, tha is, the size of the public register. As for the standardised SHA-3 method, with Sponge-Wrap data are only written into the sponge structure at first. In

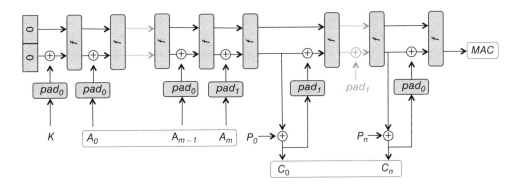

Figure 5.8
Simplified sequence
of the SpongeWrap
method

addition to the key, this includes all data that are to be authenticated. In order to achieve a clear distinction of input block types,
all data are filled with at least one bit, which for the last block
of a type always alternates between 0 or 1. In the last key block
this bit is 0. In the last block of authenticated data it changes to 1.
Further data is then encrypted in duplex mode. To this end one
block at a time is read from the public register and linked with the
plaintext via an XOR operation. The ciphertext is output and at
the same time written into the public register again, together with
filler bits. The MAC is then formed through reading of the sponge
function.

Properties of
SpongeWrap

Although the structure of SpongeWrap enables the generation
of ciphertexts with the length of the plain texts, some other functional properties are not met, which were design criteria for most
other AEAD modes. For example, the calculation cannot be parallelised or pre-processed. As the method is very recent, it is impossible
to guarantee its security at the present time. Nonetheless, certain
security aspects of the method have already been demonstrated,
provided SHA-3 remains secure. One interesting feature, which is
a clear indication of the method's robustness, is the fact that attackers can only reconstruct one new data block, even if the authenticated data contains no initialisation vector or an initialisation vector
is used twice.

5.6   Summary

Delineating error
checksums

Cryptographic check values enable messages to be checked to ensure that they have not been intentionally modified after a check
value has been created. In contrast to error checksums, such as the
Cyclic Redundancy Check (CRC), the effectiveness of cryptographic
check values is not based on the non-applicable assumption that

modifications to a message can only occur as the result of random events.

Categories   There are two principal categories of cryptographic check values: *modification detection codes (MDCs)*, which only receive the protected message as input and merely compute a 'digital fingerprint' of the message, and *message authentication codes (MACs)*, which are additionally parameterised with a secret key such that they can be directly used to verify the authenticity of the message.

MDCs   MDCs are computed with *cryptographic hash functions* and the two most commonly used algorithms are *SHA-1* and *SHA-2*. Because of the inadequate length of the output value of MD5 (128 bits) and a weakness in its internal compression function, MD5 should not be used for applications that require *collision resistance*. Collision resistance implies that it should not be possible to find two arbitrary messages that are mapped to the same modification detection code. This requirement together with an adaptation of the *birthday phenomenon* (only 23 people have to be in a room so that the probability of at least two people having the same birthday is 50%) accounts for the minimum length of the output value of cryptographic hash functions, which is currently estimated at 160 bits.

MACs   To compute message authentication codes the *HMAC construction* has established itself as a popular algorithm. It is widely recognised as a viable scheme because it can be computed efficiently and is one of the few schemes considered secure.

AEAD schemes   Besides schemes that only secure in terms of integrity or authentication, novel schemes for authenticated encryption have been developed over the last few years. The most widely used of these so-called AEAD schemes is the Galois/Counter Mode (GCM), which uses efficient Galois field multiplications to calculate authentication values. The secure usage of GCM requires a strict obedience of several conditions, for example a sufficient MAC length and the unique usage of initialisation vectors.

5.7   Supplemental Reading

[KBC97]   Krawczyk, H.; Bellare, M.; Canetti, R.: *HMAC: Keyed-Hashing for Message Authentication.* February 1997. – RFC 2104, IETF, Status: Informational
https://tools.ietf.org/html/rfc2104

[MOV97]   MENEZES, A.; OORSCHOT, P. van; VANSTONE, S.:
           Handbook of Applied Cryptography. CRC Press LLC,
           1997
[Riv92]   RIVEST, R. L.: *The MD5 Message Digest Algorithm*,
           April 1992. RFC 1321
[NIS02]   NIST (NATIONAL INSTITUTE OF STANDARDS AND
           TECHNOLOGY): *Secure Hash Standard*. FIPS (Federal
           Information Processing Standard) Publication 180–2,
           2002
[BDP+11a] BERTONI, G.; DAEMEN, J.; PEETERS, M.; ASSCHE,
           G. V.: *Cryptographic sponge functions*. Research
           report. Version 0.1, 2011
[BDP+11b] BERTONI, G.; DAEMEN, J.; PEETERS, M.; ASSCHE,
           G. V.: *The Keccak reference*. Research report. Version
           3.0, 2011
[Dwo07]   DWORKIN, M.: *Recommendation for Block Cipher
           Modes of Operation: Galois/Counter Mode (GCM)
           and GMAC*. NIST Special Publication 800-38D, 2007
[Yuv79]   YUVAL, G.: How to Swindle Rabin. In: *Cryptologia*
           July 1979

5.8 Questions

1. Delineate cryptographic check values from error checksums. Can cryptographic check values be used as error checksums?
2. Explain the difference between modification detection codes and message authentication codes.
3. Describe the generic structure of the two functions MD5 and SHA-1.
4. Explain the connection between the birthday phenomenon and cryptographic hash functions.
5. For SHA-1 give the value of W_{19}, processing the first message block.
6. Formulate the MD5 algorithm in programming language pseudo-code.
7. Why are message authentication codes not vulnerable to attacks based on the birthday phenomenon?
8. Why is the usage of the HMAC scheme often not required when SHA-3 is deployed?
9. Name disadvantages of the SpongeWrap scheme.

6 Random Number Generation

Generating random numbers for cryptographic algorithms is a subject that has appeared frequently in previous chapters (e.g. Sections 4.3, 4.5 and 4.6). This chapter looks at how such 'random' calculations of numbers can be realised using deterministic algorithms.

6.1 Random Numbers and Pseudo-Random Numbers

Even though computers are excellent for all sorts of computation in a diverse range of application scenarios, in principle they are not really designed to generate 'truly random' results. Therefore, the seemingly trivial task of generating random numbers is more of an effort for a computer than one would think.

This is because algorithms and the hardware on which they are executed basically work in a deterministic way, and in reality random results cannot be generated through entirely deterministic means.

In principle hardware and software work in a deterministic way

Consequently, the usual approach is to generate a large set of 'pseudo-random' information from a relatively small set of 'truly random' information. Before concrete methods are introduced to address this task, some concrete definitions are used to explain the exact difference between 'random' and 'pseudo-random'.

Definition 6.1 *A **random bit generator** (RBG) is a device or a scheme that outputs a sequence of statistically independent and uniformly distributed bits.*

Random bit generator

A random bit generator can be used to generate uniformly distributed random numbers in a given interval $[0, n]$. First a random bit

Security in Fixed and Wireless Networks, Second Edition.
Guenter Schaefer and Michael Rossberg.
Copyright © 2014 by dpunkt.verlag GmbH, Heidelberg, Germany.
Title of the German original: Netzsicherheit   ISBN 978-3-86490-115-7
Translation Copyright © 2016 by John Wiley & Sons, Ltd., All rights reserved

sequence of length $\lfloor lg_2(n) \rfloor + 1$ is generated and converted into a non-negative integer. If the recovered number is greater than n, it is discarded and the process is repeated until a random number $\leq n$ is produced.

Pseudo-random bit generator

Definition 6.2 *A* **pseudo-random bit generator** *(PRBG) or pseudo-random number generator (PRNG) is a deterministic algorithm that receives as input a truly random binary sequence of length k and produces as output a binary sequence of length m, which appears to be random and is distinctly longer than the input binary sequence. This input is referred to as* **seed** *and the established term for the output is* **pseudo-random bit sequence**.

The output of a pseudo-random bit generator is not really random. In actual fact, only a small number of 2^k outputs are generated out of a total of 2^m possible bit sequences because a generator always produces the same output for each fixed seed.

'True' randomness is time-consuming to produce

The motivation for using pseudo-random bit generators is that it can be too time-consuming to produce truly random number sequences of length m. Sometimes the only method available is manual-like non-deterministic mouse moves or keyboard inputs, and yet some systems (e.g. web servers that are supposed to support secure connections using TLS, see Chapter 13) require a large number of random numbers. Consequently, to an extent, a pseudo-random bit generator is used as a 'cost-efficient' extension of the 'expensive' truly random numbers used to initialise it.

Example of a PRBG

A simple example of a PRBG is the generator below, which generates a random bit sequence $y_1, y_2, \ldots$ according to the following linear recursion equation, which is parameterised with three values a, b, q and initialised with a seed y_0:

$$y_i = a \times y_{i-1} + b \bmod q$$

6.2 Cryptographically Secure Random Numbers

The PRBG discussed above has a drawback that makes it unsuitable for cryptographic applications: even without knowledge of the values of a, b, q and y_0, attackers can use the observed values $\{y_i, y_{i+1}, \ldots, y_{i+j}\}$ to predict the other values $\{y_{i+j+1}, y_{i+j+2}, \ldots\}$ produced by a generator.

This section therefore defines the criteria for preventing this kind of undesirable prediction and for evaluating cryptographically secure random numbers.

The following requirements normally apply to pseudo-random bit generators that are used in cryptographic applications:

- The length k of the seed for a PRBG should be large enough so that a complete search of all possible seeds is not practical for an attacker using the resources available in our universe.
- Statistically it should not be possible to distinguish the output of a PRBG from truly random bit sequences (see Section 6.3).
- An attacker with limited resources should not be able to predict the output bits of a PRBG if he or she does not know the seed.

Requirements of cryptographic applications

The last requirement mentioned, non-predictability of a pseudo-random bit sequence, is stated somewhat more formally in the following definition:

Definition 6.3 *A PRBG is acknowledged as having passed all statistical polynomial-time tests if no algorithm with polynomial-time exists that can correctly distinguish between an output sequence of the PRBG and a truly random bit sequence of the same length with probability significantly greater than* 0.5.

'All polynomial tests' criterion

Polynomial-time in this case means that the runtime of the algorithm in a deterministic calculation model is bound by a polynomial of length m of the bit sequence. Algorithms where the property mentioned can be proven obviously satisfy the security requirements introduced above. In practice, however, proof of this criterion turns out to be rather difficult.

The following criterion has proven to be much more manageable:

Definition 6.4 *A PRBG is acknowledged as having passed the next-bit test if there is no polynomial-time algorithm that upon input of the first m bits of the bits generated by the PRBG can predict the $(m + 1)th$ bit of the output sequence with probability significantly greater than* 0.5.

Next-bit test

Although this definition clearly limits the set of algorithms that have to be considered compared to the first definition, it does show that both definitions describe the same PRBG (refer to [Sti06, Section 8.2] for the proof):

Theorem 6.1 *(Universality of the next-bit test) A PRBG passes the next-bit test when it passes all statistical polynomial-time tests.*

This background enables us to formulate the conditions under which a PRBG is considered secure for cryptographic applications:

CSPRBG **Definition 6.5** *A PRBG that passes the next-bit test — possibly under some plausible but unproven mathematical assumption, such as the intractability of the factoring problem for large integers — is* called a **cryptographically secure pseudo-random bit generator** *(CSPRBG) or* **cryptographically secure pseudo-random number generator** *(CSPRNG).*

6.3   Statistical Tests for Random Numbers

It is recommended that several statistical tests be conducted on the output of a random bit generator so that a certain confidence can be gained in the randomness of the generated bit sequences before the generator is used. A selection of different tests are listed below with a brief description:

Monobit test
- The *monobit test* verifies whether a bit sequence contains the same number of '1' bits as '0' bits.

Serial test
- The *serial test*, sometimes also called *two-bit test*, extends the idea of the monobit test to pairs of bits and checks whether a bit sequence contains an equal number of '00', '01', '10' and '11' pairs.

Poker test
- The *poker test* examines the number of sequences n_i of length q that contain the same value, with the parameter q of this test selected according to the length m of the analysed bit sequence such that $\lfloor m/q \rfloor \geq 5 \times 2^q$. Here too, random bit sequences should always produce equally distributed values.

Runs test
- The *runs test* checks whether the number of sequences containing either only '1' bits or only '0' bits ('runs') and being analysed for a range of differently specified sequence lengths fall within the numbers of 'runs' one would expect for truly random bit sequences.

Autocorrelation test
- The *autocorrelation test* checks a bit sequence to verify whether correlations exist between the bit sequence and non-cyclically shifted (by a certain number of bits) versions of the bit sequence.

Maurer's universal test
- The *universal test from Maurer* checks whether bit sequences generated by a random bit generator can be compressed since compression of truly random bit sequences is usually impossible.

The descriptions given here only highlight the basic idea of each test. The reader is referred to [MOV97, Sections 5.4.4 and 5.4.5] for a detailed and mathematically thorough description of the tests.

6.4 Generation of Random Numbers

Hardware- and software-based schemes, some outlined briefly below, are proposed for introducing true randomness into the process of key creation.

Hardware-based random bit generators are normally based on the non-exact reproducibility of certain physical phenomena. Examples include:

Hardware-based random bit generators

- observing the elapsed time between the emission of particles during radioactive decay [Gud85, Gud87];
- measuring thermal noise [Ric92];
- measuring the charge difference between two closely adjacent semiconductors [Agn88];
- observing frequency fluctuations due to the instability of a freely running oscillator [AT&86];
- measuring the amount by which a semiconductor can be charged during a fixed period of time;
- the measurement of the state of an odd number of NOT gates that are circularly connected;
- observing the fluctuation in access times due to air turbulence in sealed disk drives;
- recording sound using a microphone or video input from a camera, e.g. at a busy intersection.

Manually throwing dice has also been recommended as a secure method for generating what are called *master keys* in key hierarchies [MM78]. Because of the increase in the number of random numbers that need to be generated, this method is considered too time-consuming and therefore no longer up-to-date.

A hardware-based random bit generator should ideally also be implemented in a tamper-proof module to shield it from potential attackers.

Software-based random bit generators could be based on the following ideas:

Software-based random bit generators

- determining the current system time;
- measurement of elapsed time between keystrokes or mouse movements;

- reading the content of input and output buffers;
- use of user input;
- calculation of current values of an operating system, such as system load or statistics for hard disk accesses.

Combination of multiple random sources

Ideally, multiple random sources should be mixed together by concatenating their values and computing a cryptographic hash value to prevent attackers from being able to guess the random value. If the current system time is the only random source, then attackers can calculate the pseudo-random bit sequence that was computed on the basis of the seed if they have an approximate idea of when the pseudo-random bit generator was initialised.

Eliminating uneven distribution

In case a random bit generator produces an uncorrelated but not uniformly distributed bit sequence, that is, it produces '1' bits with the probability $p \neq 0.5$ and '0' bits with the probability $1 - p$, with p not necessarily a known but a fixed parameter, the following method can be used to eliminate the uneven distribution of '0' and '1' bits:

- the bit sequence is divided into pairs;
- all '00' and '11' pairs are discarded;
- the output is a '1' for each '10' pair and a '0' for each '01' pair.

On the assumption that the original bit sequence has no correlations, this scheme produces uncorrelated bit sequences in which '0' and '1' bits occur with the same frequency. However, at least 75% of the created random bits are discarded.

Eliminating uneven distribution using cryptographic hash functions

An alternative practical method for eliminating uneven distribution or even correlations is the application of a cryptographic hash function to the output of the random bit generator. Even if the correctness of this method cannot be proven, it has been successfully used in practice and no fundamental security flaws have yet been found.

6.5 Generating Secure Pseudo-Random Numbers

A number of different methods that use cryptographic hash functions or encryption algorithms have been proposed for generating cryptographically secure pseudo-random numbers. Although the security of these methods cannot be proven, they appear to offer sufficient security for most practical applications, and so far no security flaws have been discovered.

One representative of this class of methods is the generator *ANSI X9.17* that was standardised by the American Standardization Institute (ANSI) (see Figure 6.1).

```
// Algorithm: RandomX917
// Input:    a 64-bit long seed s,
//           a natural number m,
//           a 3DES key k
// Output:   an m block long random bit sequence

uint64* RandomX917(unit64 s, uint m, DES3_Key k) {
  uint64* x = malloc(m * sizeof(uint64));
  uint64  q = DES3(k, DateTime());
  for(int i = 0; i < m; i++) {
    x[i] = DES3(k, q xor s);
    s = DES3(k, x[i] xor q);
  }
  return x;
}
```

Figure 6.1
The random generator
ANSI X9.17

The ANSI X9.17 generator was certified for the pseudo-random generation of keys and initialisation vectors for use with DES and standardised as the US Federal Information Processing Standard (FIPS).

Further random bit generators that are based on cryptographic hash functions or encryption algorithms and which work on similar principles can be found in [BK12].

As mentioned above, it has not been proven that this class of random number generators is secure in the sense of Definition 6.5. Therefore, two schemes are presented below where this can be proven under the assumption that the factorisation of large integers and the calculation of discrete logarithm are infeasible.

The first of these two schemes is the *RSA generator*, which, as its name suggests, is based on the RSA algorithm. The security of this generator stems from the difficulty of the factorisation problem.

RSA generator

- Output: a pseudo-random bit sequence $z_1, z_2, \ldots, z_k$ of length k.
- Initialisation:
  - generate two secret prime numbers p and q that are suitable for the RSA algorithm
  - compute $n = p \times q$ and $\Phi = (p-1) \times (q-1)$

- choose a number e so that $1 < e < \Phi$ and $\gcd(e, \Phi) = 1$
- choose a random integer y_0 so that $y_0 \in [1, n]$.

■ Generation of k random bits $z_1, \ldots, z_k$:

```
for(i = 1; i <= k; i++) {
    yᵢ = (yᵢ₋₁)ᵉ   mod   n
    zᵢ = yᵢ & 1 // select lowest bit
}
```

Improving efficiency The efficiency of this generator can be slightly improved if j lower-valued bits of each number y_i are chosen, with $j = c \times lg(lg(n))$ guaranteed for a certain constant c that depends on the bit length m of the number n. However, so far it has not been possible to make a general calculation of the value of this constant for arbitrary m in such a way that the condition can be proven in Definition 6.5 (nevertheless for $j = 1$ the condition is met).

The computational effort a generator requires to calculate one or j pseudo-random bits is considerable because an exponentiation with the number e modulo n has to be executed each time.

Blum-Blum- The *Blum-Blum-Shub generator*, named after its inventors, is a
Shub generator slight improvement in this respect. This generator replaces the exponentiation with e through squaring and its security is also based on the difficulty of the factorisation problem.

■ Output: a pseudo-random bit sequence $z_1, z_2, \ldots, z_k$ of length k.
■ Initialisation:
  - generate two secret prime numbers p and q so that p as well as q are each congruent to 3 modulo 4
  - compute $n = p \times q$
  - choose a number $s \in [1, n-1]$ so that $\gcd(s, n) = 1$
  - compute $y_0 = s^2 \bmod n$.
■ Generation of k random bits:

```
for(i = 1; i <= k; i++) {
    yᵢ = (yᵢ₋₁)²   mod   n
    zᵢ = yᵢ & 1 // select lowest bit
}
```

Improving efficiency The efficiency of the Blum-Blum-Shub generator can be minimally increased in a similar way to the RSA generator if not one but j bits are chosen in each step, with similar conditions existing for the maximum number of bits allowed.

In 2007 NIST presented the Dual Elliptic Curve Deterministic Random Bit Generator – Dual EC DRBG in short – as an alternative to the very slow methods described above [BK12]. It is based on the problem of calculating the discrete logarithm on elliptic curves. Figure 6.2 shows the general sequence. The generator has an internal state t, which first has to be initialised with a start value. In order to generate random bits, t is multiplied with a point P. The x coordinate of the resulting point is then the new internal state. At the same time the x coordinate is multiplied with a further point Q. From the result of this second multiplication, r bits are returned as pseudo-random values. The number of bits depends on the curve used and varies between 240 and 504.

The Dual Elliptic Curve Deterministic Random Bit Generator

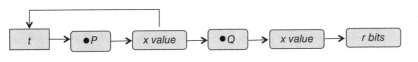

The Dual EC DRBG method attracted a good deal of attention with regard to security [SF07]. The main problem is that the standard defines the points P and Q, but the way in which they were generated by the NIST was not shown. If P were to be selected such that $P = eQ$ for a constant e, then the authors of the standard would be able to determine e^{-1} and then draw conclusions on the internal state from the random bits. This would make the pseudo-random number generator predictable for a certain group of people. If the method is to be used, one should always select self-generated values for P and Q at the same time. In addition it should also be considered that there is no proof of security for Dual EC DRBG, and the number of output bits per round should be selected as conservatively as possible. Newer versions of the NIST standards will no longer include Dual EC DRBG [BK14].

Figure 6.2
Dual Elliptic Curve Deterministic Random Bit Generator sequence

Cryptographic back door

6.6 Implementation Security

Over recent years it has became apparent that in many cases the security of cryptographic protocols was not weakened through attacks on the principle of pseudo-random number generators. Rather, security problems seem to have been caused repeatedly by implementation errors.

Probably the best-known error of this type was discovered in May 2008. As it turned out, a maintainer of the Debian Linux distribution made a subtle change in the OpenSSL implementation

Weakness of CSPRBG in Debian

in September 2006. In order to eliminate warnings that were issued by a tool for identifying memory errors, he commented out a somewhat counter-intuitive line in the code. As a result, the start value of the OpenSSL CSPRBG depended exclusively on the process ID number, so that in a whole range of cryptographic applications only 32,768 different pseudo-random data streams could be generated. This event is noteworthy primarily for two reasons. On the one hand, it would appear that this blatant weakness remained unnoticed for more than 1.5 years. On the other hand, the cryptographic library that is probably most widely used will, in normal configuration, generate alleged memory errors. Although these errors are harmless at this point, they make fault finding considerably more difficult/problematic in applications where security is crucial.

Study on the effect
of weaknesses
in CSPRBG

In 2012 an interesting study on the security of asymmetric keys was published [HDW+12]. The authors of the publication established cryptographic connections to 23 million computers and examined the public keys used for anomalies. They found that 0.34% of the machines used identical keys. The authors ascribed this to insufficient entropy in the pseudo-random number generators. In addition, the authors were able to compromise around 1.0% of the DSA keys and 0.5% of the RSA keys due to lack of sufficiently random elements. One of the problems identified was the low entropy of pseudo-random number generators after the initial system startup. If asymmetric key pairs are generated at this stage, they may not be secure.

CSPRBG should therefore be continually monitored for functional errors due to problems already encountered. Whenever pseudo-random number generators are used, it is essential to ensure adequate entropy and regular renewal of seeds. If entropy is found to be inadequate, no further cryptographic operations should be carried out. For example, under Linux reading of `/dev/random` is blocked, while reading of `/dev/urandom` is still possible even if entropy is inadequate, which may lead to problems.

6.7   Summary

Generating random numbers is a requirement of many cryptographic protocols and therefore constitutes an important aspect of basic cryptographic knowledge. As only a small number of truly random bits can usually be introduced into this process, *pseudo-random bit generators* that generate long pseudo-random bit sequences from a truly random seed are normally used. It should not be possible to distinguish generated pseudo-random bit sequences from truly random bit sequences.

Note that not all pseudo-random bit generators are appropriate for cryptographic purposes as they also must satisfy the requirement of *non-predictability* if they are used for cryptographic applications. One way of proving that this prerequisite has been met is by showing that no algorithm with a polynomial time requirement can be constructed that can predict the $(m+1)$th output bit with probability greater than 0.5 when the first m output bits of the generator are known *(next-bit test)*.

Prerequisites for cryptographic purposes

Various hardware- and software-based methods are recommended for the generation of truly random bits. However, before such methods are used, a series of statistical tests should be conducted on their output so that a certain confidence can be gained in the randomness of their output.

Random bit generators

In practice schemes based on cryptographic hash functions or encryption algorithms are a particularly efficient way of generating pseudo-random bit sequences. Although no theoretical proof of the security of these schemes exists, no serious security flaws have been discovered with them so far. The *RSA generator* and the *Blum-Blum-Shub generator* have been proven to be secure schemes for generating pseudo-random bit sequences but are relatively inefficient. The unproven but more efficient *Dual EC DRBG* should be avoided — at least with the predetermined constants.

Pseudo-random bit generators

A summary of practical thoughts and rules for secure operation of random number generators, which is worth reading for administrators and programmers, can be found in [ESC05].

6.8 Supplemental Reading

[BK12]   BARKER, E.; KELSEY, J.: *Recommendation for Random Number Generation Using Deterministic Random Bit Generators*. NIST Special Publication 800-90A, 2012

[ESC05]   EASTLAKE 3RD, D.; SCHILLER, J.; CROCKER, S.: *Randomness Requirements for Security*. 2005. – RFC 4086, IETF, Status: Best Current Practice, `https://tools.ietf.org/html/rfc4086`

[MOV97]   MENEZES, A.; OORSCHOT, P. van; VANSTONE, S.: *Handbook of Applied Cryptography*. CRC Press LLC, 1997

Chapter 5 deals with generating cryptographically secure random numbers.

[Sti06]   STINSON, D. R.: *Cryptography: Theory and Practice (Discrete Mathematics and Its Applications).* CRC Press, 2006
Section 8.2 contains proof of the universality of the Next-Bit-Test (Theorem 6.1).

6.9   Questions

1.   Explain the differences between random numbers, pseudo-random numbers and cryptographically secure pseudo-random numbers.

2.   Why is initialisation of a pseudo-random bit generator with only current system time questionable from a security standpoint if it is to generate random numbers for use in (interactive) cryptographic protocols?

3.   Assume that you should be checking the output of a pseudo-random bit generator with the monobit test and the serial test. Write pseudocode for the two appropriate functions, making the assumption that the preceding generated random bit sequence is stored in a field $r[1, n]$ of data type 'bit'. How do you have to change your procedures if the field is of data type 'octet'?

4.   Write pseudocode for a procedure that removes inequality distributions of '0' and '1' bits from a pseudo-random bit sequence stored in the array $r[1, n]$. To which length does the generated pseudo-random bit sequence then shrink in the worst case?

5.   Does multiple recursive use of the procedure described for reducing uneven distributions of '0' and '1' bits make sense?

6.   Assume that you are basically processing each generated random bit sequence using the procedure to reduce uneven distribution. By how much does a generated random bit sequence shrink in an average case if the random bit generator supplies truly random bits?

7 Cryptographic Protocols

There was a brief mention in Section 2.1 that cryptographic protocols represent the applications of cryptographic algorithms. We start this chapter by introducing the basic properties of cryptographic protocols and follow that with a close analysis of their two main fields of application for network security: authentication and key management.

7.1 Properties and Notation of Cryptographic Protocols

Definition 7.1 *A **cryptographic protocol** is defined as a series of steps and message exchanges between multiple entities in order to achieve a specific set of security objectives.*

Similar to general communication protocols, cryptographic protocols must incorporate a number of properties to qualify as protocols:

Basic properties of protocols

- Each entity involved in a protocol run must know the protocol as well as all required steps and message formats in advance.
- Each entity involved in a protocol run must be in agreement with executing the protocol in accordance with the definition.
- The protocol must be unambiguous, i.e. all steps must be well defined and there should be no possibility of misunderstanding the protocol run.
- The protocol must be complete and, in particular, a specific action must be given for each possible situation.

Security in Fixed and Wireless Networks, Second Edition.
Guenter Schaefer and Michael Rossberg.
Copyright © 2014 by dpunkt.verlag GmbH, Heidelberg, Germany.
Title of the German original: Netzsicherheit ISBN 978-3-86490-115-7
Translation Copyright © 2016 by John Wiley & Sons, Ltd., All rights reserved

Additional require- Cryptographic protocols must fulfil an additional requirement in
ment order to achieve their purpose:

- It should not be possible to do or learn anything other than what is specified in the protocol.

Applications A multitude of different cryptographic protocols are available and implement a variety of applications:

- *Key exchange:* The Diffie–Hellman scheme for key exchange presented in Section 4.5 is an example of a pure key exchange protocol that allows no conclusion about the authenticity of the partners involved in the exchange.
- *Authentication:* This proves the identity of the sender of a message *(data origin authentication / data integrity)* or of a communication partner *(entity authentication)*. The latter security service also requires a guarantee of the freshness of message exchanges (see below).
- *Combined authentication and key exchange:* Many authentication protocols sometimes integrate optional key exchange into the authentication process.
- *Secret splitting:* If information is to be distributed over multiple entities in such a way that only all entities together can reconstruct and read the information, then a protocol of this class can be used to securely distribute keying information. This is called *secret splitting*. One conceivable application for this would be dividing a code sequence to open a safe.
  In a general case, information can even be divided up among n entities in such a way that a minimum of $m \leq n$ entities is required to read the information. Cryptographic protocols with this property are also referred to as *secret sharing*.
- *Time stamping:* It is often important to be able to prove that a particular message was created or sent at a specific time. This task can be performed with a time stamp using a recognised and trustworthy entity (e.g. a notary). The message is presented in plaintext to the trustworthy entity, which stamps the time and signs it.
- *Blind signatures:* In some circumstances it is not desirable to notify a third party of the content of a message even though secure confirmation is needed of the exact time that the message was created. Protocols for creating *blind signatures* are available for this situation.
- *Key escrow for third parties:* Protocols in this category ensure that not only users but also certain authorised entities (e.g.

prosecution authorities) can learn the key used to secure a communication. Note that the demand for access to keys is controversial and that a great deal of doubt exists about the security of such protocols from a technical view.

- *Proof of knowledge without revealing information:* If an entity A wants to prove to another entity B that it has certain information without revealing the actual information, it can execute a protocol with B to provide *zero knowledge proof*. The protocol also guarantees that A can only execute the protocol correctly if it really has the information concerned.
- *Secure digital elections:* This set of protocols aims to enable electronic elections while ensuring that attempted fraud will not remain unnoticed.
- *Electronic payments:* This is a particularly interesting applications field for cryptographic protocols because of its importance as the basis for future *e-commerce* applications although it is an area where the potential for abuse is especially high.

The list above shows that the versions and applications of cryptographic protocols are as diverse as the security needs that exist in the real world. Two of the categories mentioned have special relevance for network security: *authentication* and *key distribution*. Both categories will be covered in detail in this chapter. Readers who are interested in specific protocols for the other categories listed may refer to the extensive specialist literature available [MOV97, BSW10, CJR⁺10].

Authentication and key distribution are particularly relevant for network security

7.2   Data Origin and Entity Authentication

Definition 7.2   Data origin authentication *is the security service that enables verification of the originator and the validity of a message. Verification is therefore possible at a later time to check whether the content of a message or, more generally, data is still exactly the same as created by its originator. A synonymous term for this is* **data integrity**.

Data origin authentication and data integrity

Data origin authentication and data integrity are sometimes introduced as two different security services, with the first one guaranteeing the secure identification of the originator of a message and the second one the validity of the message itself. However, this artificial split makes little sense. Without the identity of the originator of messages, data integrity is meaningless in security terms because all non-inherently faulty dates (thus unreasonable dates like February 30th, a PDU with an erroneous CRC checksum, etc.) are *a priori* 'integer'. What is of more interest is whether the date being checked was sent by an attacker or by the expected originator. A simple thought may help to envision this fact more plastically: Assume you receive a message that is 'authentic', that is, from the correct sender, but no longer 'integer', that is, an attacker modified it. Are the data in this message trustworthy? Of course not, as they are not in their original state. However, if you receive a message that is 'integer', that is, not modified, but not 'authentic', that is, created by an attacker, it must not be trusted either.

The relationship of the data integrity service to cryptographic protocols is twofold:

- Some cryptographic protocols implement the data integrity service. Normally, they consist of one protocol step and therefore are not particularly interesting from a technical view. For example, Alice could prove the integrity of her messages by encrypting them with her private key. Every other entity that knows Alice's public key and has the assurance that it really is Alice's public key can check the integrity of her messages by decrypting the encrypted message using Alice's public key and checking the plausibility of the received message. If a significant number of possible messages are known to be invalid, the receiver may conclude that an encrypted, valid message is also integer. However, there are a few things to be kept in mind. Details can be found in Section 13.1.5.
  A better way to verify the message integrity is to compute a modification detection code (see also Chapter 5) for all messages and then sign them with a suitable private key.
- Data integrity of messages exchanged in cryptographic protocols is often an important property, so to an extent it represents a basic building block of cryptographic protocols.

Entity authentication   **Definition 7.3   (Entity authentication)** *is the security service that enables communication partners to carry out a forgery-proof verification of the identity of their peer entities.*

Entity authentication is actually the most fundamental security service as all other security services are based on forgery-proof identification of the entities in a system and therefore build on this security service.

Implementation possibilities   In general, different means are available to implement entity authentication:

- *knowledge*, such as passwords, touch gestures, etc.;
- *ownership*, for example physical keys or access cards;
- *immutable properties*, thus biometric properties such as fingerprints, physical unclonable functions (PUFs), etc.;
- *location area* of an entity, for instance customers rarely check the authenticity of tellers in the branches of a bank;
- *delegation of authentication check*, where the verifying entity accepts that another entity it trusts has already established authentication.

Because it is difficult or insecure to use the means listed here to make direct verification in communication networks, cryptographic protocols are needed for this purpose. These will be examined in detail during the course of this chapter.

First we will examine the general difference between data origin and entity authentication because the latter requires more than just an exchange of authentic messages. This is because when entity B receives authentic messages from another entity A, it cannot be sure whether A really sent the messages at this specific moment or whether an attacker E is replaying old, recorded messages from A. The freshness of messages is therefore especially important in cryptographic protocols, specifically in applications where authentication verification only takes place once at the beginning of a communication, for example through the transmission of a PIN at connection set-up.

Difference between data origin and entity authentication

There are two principal means for checking the freshness of a message:

Freshness check

- *time stamps* require clocks or index numbers that are synchronised with predetermined accuracy;
- uniquely used *random numbers* — so-called *nonces* — that are exchanged in challenge response dialogues (nonce is an abbreviation for '*n*umber used only *once*').

Most of the authentication protocols covered in this chapter also simultaneously exchange session keys to secure the communication relationship that follows authentication. With some of these schemes there is no proof of authenticity until the session key is used.

In terms of a general approach, two main categories of protocols for entity authentication are distinguished:

Main categories of entity authentication

1. With *arbitrated authentication* an arbiter, or *trusted third party* (TTP), is involved in the authentication dialogue. This

is particularly important when proof that authentication actually took place is required at a later date. Another reason for including a trusted third party is the possibility of using symmetric cryptology to implement services that permit authentication between entities that have not yet agreed a secret key with each other. Examples include the method by *Needham–Schroeder* [NS78] or the more secure *Otway-Rees scheme* [OR87] and the *Kerberos* authentication and authorisation protocol for workstation computer clusters [Bry88, NYH+05].

2. *Direct authentication* of two partners is carried out without including an independent entity and therefore provides no proof to third parties that authentication actually took place. Nevertheless, each entity participating in the communication can recognise the respective peer entity to be authentic with extremely high probability. Examples of this are the three modular authentication protocols of International Standard X.509 [IT93].

Advantages of an authentication entity

The following advantages can result from the use of an arbitrated authentication entity:

1. If subsequent conflicts occur, only an independent entity can prove to third parties that authentication actually took place.
2. With the application of symmetric cryptographic schemes an authentication entity can be used to reduce the number of keys needed in a network. If n possible communication partners should authenticate each other in arbitrary pair combinations using a symmetric encryption scheme, this will require $n(n-1)/2$ secret keys because each possible pair has to share one secret key. When an authentication entity is introduced, agreement of n secret keys between the communication partners and the authentication entity is sufficient.
3. When a large number of authenticating entities exist, it may still be necessary to include independent entities in the process, even if the authentication scheme is based on asymmetric cryptography. The problem in such cases is the authenticity of the public key. An attacker M should therefore be prevented from tricking other entities into accepting 'his' key as the key of another entity A. Use of a trusted certification authority that can confirm the authenticity of keys through a signature with its own private key is recommended.

    The advantage is that the certification authority only has to confirm the authenticity of the corresponding public key and sign the certificate once for each entity and is, therefore, not actively involved in each authentication process. Consequently, authentication protocols of this type are often classified in the category of direct authentication.

Direct schemes based on symmetric cryptographic algorithms prove to be unsuitable when a large number of authenticating entities are involved. Because of the number of keys that have to be kept secret, secure distribution of the keys is no longer practical when authentication relationships between arbitrary pairs are to be established by entities. With methods based on symmetric cryptography and trusted entities a bottleneck tends to develop as the number of authenticating entities increases because of the active involvement of the TTP in each authentication process. The trusted entity also can monitor all authentication activities, which in some circumstances can be undesirable.

Authentication based on symmetric cryptography is not suitable for very large populations

Even authentication schemes based on asymmetric encryption require additional certification of public keys by a trusted entity when a large number of authenticating entities are involved. This is the only practical way of implementing authentication and key management.

Requirements of key certification

The key representatives of both categories, the Needham–Schroeder protocol, the Otway–Rees protocol, Kerberos and International Standard X.509, are explained in the following sections. The notation used in the course of this discussion is summarised in Table 7.1.

7.3 Needham–Schroeder Protocol

The Needham–Schroeder protocol [NS78] enables two entities Alice (A) and Bob (B) to authenticate each other, making use of a TTP entity and to negotiate a session key at the same time.

For this purpose the protocol uses a symmetric encryption algorithm as the fundamental cryptographic primitive. The trusted entity has a database with all users U that want to use the authentication service offered by the entity, as well as a secret key $K_{U,TTP}$ for each user.

The objective of the protocol is to enable two users, A and B, to obtain secure verification of each other's identity and, at the same time, to negotiate a session key for securing the communication that directly follows. The protocol consists of the following steps:

Protocol objectives

Table 7.1

Notation of cryptographic protocols

Notation	Meaning
A	Name of A, analogous for B, TTP and CA
CA_A	Certification authority of A
r_A	Random number chosen by A
t_A	Time stamp generated by A
$(m_1, \cdots, m_n)$	Concatenation of messages m_1 to m_n
$A \rightarrow B : m$	A sends message m to B
$K_{A,B}$	Secret key only known to A and B
$+K_A$	Public key of A
$-K_A$	Private key of A
$\{m\}_K$	Message m encrypted with key K
$H(m)$	MDC over message m
$A[m]$	Shorthand notation of $(m, \{H(m)\}_{-K_A})$
$Certificate_{-K_{CA}}(+K_A)$	Certificate for $+K_A$ issued by CA
$CA \ll A \gg$	Shorthand notation for $Certificate_{-K_{CA}}(+K_A)$

1. Alice chooses a random number r_A, creates a message that contains her name A, Bob's name B and the random number, and then sends this message to the trusted entity TTP:

$$A \rightarrow TTP: \quad (A, B, r_A)$$

2. The trusted entity TTP generates a session key $K_{A,B}$ to secure the communication between A and B, encrypts this key together with the name of A using key $K_{B,TTP}$, which is agreed with B, and sends the following message encrypted with key $K_{A,TTP}$ to Alice:

$$TTP \rightarrow A: \quad \{r_A, B, K_{A,B}, \{K_{A,B}, A\}_{K_{B,TTP}}\}_{K_{A,TTP}}$$

3. Alice decrypts this message, verifies that the random number r_A contained is the same one as in her first message and then sends the following message to Bob:

$$A \rightarrow B: \quad \{K_{A,B}, A\}_{K_{B,TTP}}$$

4. Upon receipt and decryption of this message, Bob generates a random number r_B, encrypts it with $K_{A,B}$ and sends

it to Alice:

$$B \rightarrow A: \quad \{r_B\}_{K_{A,B}}$$

5. Alice decrypts the message with $K_{A,B}$, computes $r_B - 1$, encrypts the result with $K_{A,B}$ and sends it back to Bob:

$$A \rightarrow B: \quad \{r_B - 1\}_{K_{A,B}}$$

6. Bob decrypts the received message and verifies that it contains $r_B - 1$. If it does, Bob assumes that he is really communicating with Alice.

The purpose of the last two messages is to allow Alice to prove to Bob that she really holds key $K_{A,B}$. Without knowledge of this key she would not be able to compute the response $\{r_B - 1\}_{K_{A,B}}$ (implicitly the properties of a block cipher are assumed here). As Bob knows that TTP also encrypted the session key $K_{A,B}$ in his message using Alice's key $K_{A,TTP}$, he concludes that Alice knows key $K_{A,TTP}$ and is therefore his authentic communication partner. *Argumentation about the functioning of the protocol*

However, this argumentation contains an error that can be exploited by attacker Eve (E) if she can discover a valid session key $K_{A,B}$ [DS81]. As the protocol offers no possibility of recognising an old session key of an earlier session, attacker Eve can impersonate as Alice to Bob if she has knowledge of an old session key $K_{A,B}$ and of the third message in the relevant protocol run: *Weakness of the protocol*

1. Eve sends the recorded message:

$$E \rightarrow B: \quad \{K_{A,B}, A\}_{K_{B,TTP}}$$

2. Upon receipt and decryption of this message, Bob generates a random number r_B, encrypts it with $K_{A,B}$ and sends it to Alice:

$$B \rightarrow A: \quad \{r_B\}_{K_{A,B}}$$

3. This message is intercepted by Eve who decrypts it with $K_{A,B}$. Eve then computes $r_B - 1$, encrypts the result with $K_{A,B}$ and sends it to Bob:

$$E \rightarrow B: \quad \{r_B - 1\}_{K_{A,B}}$$

4. Bob decrypts the received message and verifies that it contains $r_B - 1$. If it does, Bob assumes that he is really communicating with Alice, in which case Eve has successfully impersonated Alice.

Intended vs achieved
protocol objectives
Note that the protocol should actually be ensuring that only one entity with knowledge of key $K_{A,TTP}$ can impersonate Alice. However, due to the protocol flaw described, it is sufficient to have knowledge of a session key $K_{A,B}$ and the third message of the associated protocol in order to pass oneself off as Alice to user B. Since key $K_{A,B}$ could be used to encrypt a large quantity of data after a protocol run, it is potentially more open to cryptanalysis than key $K_{A,TTP}$. In summary, the Needham–Schroeder protocol provides less security than originally intended.

A number of cryptographers submitted proposals for improvements that would help the protocol meet its original objectives.

Otway–Rees protocol   In principle, the solution worked out by Needham and Schroeder themselves [NS87] is the same one as the *Otway–Rees protocol* [OR87] that appeared in the same journal:

1. Alice creates a message with an index number i_A, her name A, Bob's name B and the same information plus a random number r_A, encrypted with the key $K_{A,TTP}$ that she agreed with the trusted entity TTP, and sends this message to Bob:

$$A \rightarrow B: \ (i_A, A, B, \{r_A, i_A, A, B\}_{K_{A,TTP}})$$

2. Bob generates a random number r_B, encrypts it and i_A, A together with B using key $K_{B,TTP}$ that he agreed with TTP and sends the following message to TTP:

$$B \rightarrow TTP: \ (i_A, A, B, \{r_A, i_A, A, B\}_{K_{A,TTP}},$$
$$\{r_B, i_A, A, B\}_{K_{B,TTP}})$$

3. Upon receipt of this message TTP decrypts the two message parts contained, generates a new session key $K_{A,B}$ and two encrypted messages, one for Alice and one for Bob, and sends both to Bob:

$$TTP \rightarrow B: \ (i_A, \{r_A, K_{A,B}\}_{K_{A,TTP}}, \{r_B, K_{A,B}\}_{K_{B,TTP}})$$

4. Bob decrypts his part of the message using key $K_{B,TTP}$, verifies that the random number r_B contained matches the one he sent in his previous message and then sends Alice her part of the message:

$$B \rightarrow A: \ (i_A, \{r_A, K_{A,B}\}_{K_{A,TTP}})$$

5. Alice decrypts this message using key $K_{A,TTP}$ and compares the contained random number r_A with the number generated in the first protocol step. Now when she uses session key

$K_{A,B}$ for encrypted communication with Bob she can be sure that she is communicating with Bob because only TTP would have been able to create message part $\{r_A, K_{A,B}\}_{K_{A,TTP}}$. A potential attacker Eve is not able to modify message part $\{r_A, i_A, A, B\}_{K_{A,TTP}}$ that was created in the first protocol step.

Using the same argument, Bob can conclude that he is communicating with Alice when he receives interpretable messages from her that are encrypted with the session key $K_{A,B}$.

It goes without saying that Alice as well as Bob must be able to rely completely on the correct role and honesty of the trusted entity TTP.

7.4   Kerberos

The *Kerberos* authentication protocol was invented during the late 1980s at the *Massachusetts Institute of Technology (MIT)* in Boston as part of Project *Athena*. It is still under active development however, and with the publication of Kerberos 5 there has been a major revision in 2005 [NYH$^+$05]. The system serves as an authentication and access control service for workstation clusters. The main objectives in the design of Kerberos were:

Main objectives of Kerberos

- ▪ *Security:* Neither passive nor active attackers should be able to impersonate someone else when accessing a service or be able to eavesdrop on the information needed to do so.
- ▪ *Reliability:* Because each use of a service requires prior authentication, the Kerberos service itself must be designed to be particularly reliable and always available.
- ▪ *Transparency:* Beyond the requirement of entering a password at the beginning of a session, the authentication process should be largely transparent to the user.
- ▪ *Scalability:* Kerberos must have the ability to support a large number of users, workstations, services and servers.

The fundamental usage scenario of Kerberos is a user Alice who wants to use one or more services that are provided by different servers $S1$, $S2$, … connected over an insecure network. Kerberos covers the following security aspects of the scenario:

Usage scenario and security aspects

- ▪ *Authentication:* Alice first authenticates herself to an authentication server (AS) that issues her with a temporary permit to request access to services. This permit is called a *ticket-granting ticket (TGT)* and is comparable to a passport with a limited duration of validity (lifetime).

■ *Access control:* Alice uses the *TGT* in a second step to receive service-specific access authorisation, e.g. for access to server *S*1 that offers printing and file services. The *TGS* verifies that Alice is authorised to have access to the service requested and if so responds with a *service-granting ticket (SGT)* for server *S*1.

■ *Key negotiation:* The authentication server generates a session key for the communication between Alice and *TGS* and the Ticket-Granting Server generates a corresponding session key for the communication between Alice and the service-specific servers. As with the Needham–Schroeder and Otway–Rees protocols, this key is also used for authentication purposes.

Figure 7.1
Overview of the
Kerberos protocol

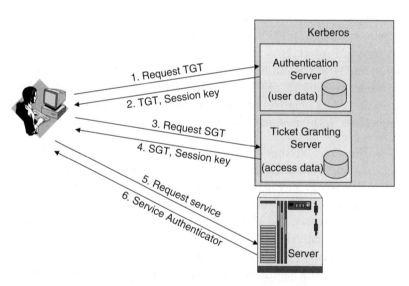

Protocol run   Figure 7.1 presents an overview the involved instance and protocol run in the widely spread versions 4 and 5 of Kerberos. However, the following section will concentrate Kerberos version 4 initially.

Initiation   1. User Alice logs onto her workstation and requests access to a particular service. From now on Alice is represented by the workstation in the Kerberos protocol. The workstation sends the first message with Alice's name A, the name of an appropriate Ticket-Granting Server TGS and a time stamp t_A to the authentication server:

$$A \rightarrow AS \colon (A, TGS, t_A)$$

2. The authentication server AS verifies in its user database that it knows Alice and from Alice's password, which is also stored in the user database, generates a key K_A. It then extracts the network address of Alice's workstation $Addr_A$ from the protocol data unit received from Alice, creates a ticket-granting ticket $Ticket_{TGS}$ and a session key $K_{A,TGS}$ and sends the following message to Alice:

Output of TGT

$$AS \rightarrow A: \ \{K_{A,TGS}, TGS, t_{AS}, LifetimeTicket_{TGS},$$
$$Ticket_{TGS}\}_{K_A}$$

LifetimeTicket$_{TGS}$ refers to the maximum time period the ticket is valid and *Ticket$_{TGS}$* is defined as follows:

$$Ticket_{TGS} = \{K_{A,TGS}, A, Addr_A, TGS, t_{AS},$$
$$LifetimeTicket_{TGS}\}_{K_{AS,TGS}}$$

3. Upon receipt of this message, the workstation asks Alice to enter her Kerberos password, which it uses to compute key K_A. This key enables the workstation to decrypt the message. If Alice does not enter the correct (authentic) password, the key K_A is not computed correctly and consequently the decrypted message does not produce interpretable plaintext. The remaining steps of the Kerberos protocol then fail.

User authentication and request for a SGT

   Alice (thus the workstation) generates an *authenticator* and sends it together with her ticket-granting ticket and the name of desired server $S1$ to Ticket-Granting Server TGS:

$$A \rightarrow TGS: \ (S1, Ticket_{TGS}, Authenticator_{A,TGS})$$

The *Authenticator$_{A,TGS}$* is defined as follows:

$$Authenticator_{A,TGS} = \{A, Addr_A, t'_A\}_{K_{A,TGS}}$$

4. The Ticket-Granting Server TGS decrypts $Ticket_{TGS}$, extracts key $K_{A,TGS}$ from the resulting plaintext and uses it to decrypt $Authenticator_{A,TGS}$. If the name and address of the authenticator and the tickets match and the time stamp is still sufficiently fresh, it verifies that Alice is allowed access to server $S1$, produces a time stamp t_{TGS}, a session key $K_{A,S1}$, a ticket $Ticket_{S1}$ for access to server $S1$ and sends the following message to Alice:

Authorisation check and output of SGT

$$TGS \rightarrow A: \ \{K_{A,S1}, S1, t_{TGS}, Ticket_{S1}\}_{K_{A,TGS}}$$

in which $Ticket_{S1}$ is defined as follows:

$$Ticket_{S1} = \{K_{A,S1}, A, Addr_A, S1, t_{AS}, Lifetime\,Ticket_{S1}\}_{K_{TGS,S1}}$$

Authentica-
tion to server

5. Alice decrypts this message and now holds a session key for secure communication with server $S1$. She generates a new authenticator and sends it together with her ticket to $S1$:

$$A \rightarrow S1:\ \ (Ticket_{S1}, Authenticator_{A,S1})$$

with $Authenticator_{A,S1}$ in turn defined as:

$$Authenticator_{A,S1} = \{A, Addr_A, t'_A\}_{K_{A,S1}}$$

Authentication
check by server

6. Server $S1$ decrypts the received ticket using key $K_{TGS,S1}$ that was agreed between it and the Ticket-Granting Server and thus obtains session key $K_{A,S1}$. It uses this key to verify the authenticator and then responds to Alice:

$$S1 \rightarrow A:\ \ \{t'_A + 1\}_{K_{A,S1}}$$

Verifying server
authenticity

7. Alice decrypts this message and checks the contained time stamp incremented by one. If this verification is successful, Alice assumes she is communicating with server $S1$ because except for TGS, only $S1$ knows key $K_{TGS,S1}$ and can use it to decrypt $Ticket_{S1}$, which contains session key $K_{A,S1}$. Therefore, only $S1$ is able to decrypt $Authenticator_{A,S1}$ and to respond with the incremented time stamp $t'_A + 1$ encrypted with key $K_{A,S1}$.

Inter-realm
authentication

This fundamental authentication dialogue can be extended to a protocol for *inter-realm authentication*. Let us look at an organisation that operates workstation computer clusters at two different locations. We will assume that user A at the first location wants to access the service of a server at the second location. If autonomous Kerberos servers and user databases are being operated at both locations, this means that actually two distinct domains exist, in Kerberos terminology also called *realms*. Kerberos enables inter-realm authentication to avoid a user A having to be registered in both domains. Figure 7.2 shows the entities involved and an overview of the protocol run.

Secret key required

Inter-realm authentication requires that the two Ticket-Granting Servers of both domains have together agreed upon a secret key $K_{TGS1,TGS2}$. The basic idea is that the local Ticket-Granting Server views the remote Ticket-Granting Server as a 'normal' server and therefore can issue a ticket for it. After Alice obtains a ticket-granting ticket (TGT_{rem}) for the remote domain, she sends a request to the remote Ticket-Granting Server

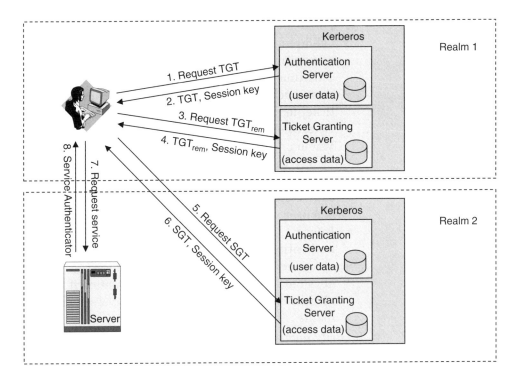

Figure 7.2

The Inter-Realm Kerberos Protocol

to issue her with a service-granting ticket for requested server $S2$. With inter-realm Kerberos authentication it is crucial that the remote domain trusts the authentication server of the local domain as it does not carry out its own authentication check of 'visiting' users.

The discussion so far has described Version 4 of the Kerberos protocol. A number of shortcomings were found in this version that can be classified into two categories:

Shortcomings of Kerberos Version 4

■ *Technical shortcomings*: Because Kerberos Version 4 was developed as part of Project Athena and with regard to the special requirements of this project, it is not orientated towards general usability. Consequently, the following shortcomings are evident:

Technical shortcomings

● Dependence on a concrete encryption algorithm: Version 4 of the Kerberos protocol stipulates use of the DES algorithm.

DES

● Dependence on a concrete communication protocol: The format of the address field $Addr_A$ is defined so that it can only accept a single IPv4 address.

Only IPv4-based

● Encoding of messages: The protocol uses a non-generic, inextensible method to encode the exchanged messages.

Message encoding

● Period of ticket validity: Because the period of ticket validity is specified in an octet in units of 5 minutes, the maximum validity of a ticket is little more than 21 hours. This time span is not sufficient for a variety of applications, such as extensive simulations, which need a valid ticket for the duration of their computation.

● Delegation of authentication/authorisation: Kerberos Version 4 does not support delegating authorisation, a facility that can be very useful in some circumstances. For instance, if delegation is allowed, a printing service can be given the right to access a certain file on behalf of a user who wants to print the file.

● Inter-realm authentication: The method of inter-realm authentication does not scale well for large numbers N of connected domains because basically $N(N-1)/2$ secret keys have to be generated and distributed if users from all domains should have access to servers of all other domains.

■ *Security flaws*: In addition to the technical shortcomings described, Kerberos protocol Version 4 also has some cryptographic flaws:

● Encryption in PCBC mode: The non-standardised operating mode *Propagating Cipher Block Chaining (PCBC)* was specified for encryption with DES. The intention was to implement confidentiality and data integrity in one step without the need to compute a modification detection code. Unfortunately, attack techniques against PCBC mode enabling the substitution of ciphertext blocks were discovered and therefore it does not provide adequate data integrity protection [Koh89].

● Session key: Each ticket contains a session key that the user utilises to encrypt an authenticator. However, the same key is also used to secure the communication between workstation and server that immediately follows. The fact that a user can use a ticket for multiple independent service uses means that successive communication relationships are vulnerable to replay attacks. A better approach would be to have a strict separation between keys that are used for authentication and session keys that protect exchanged data units and always to negotiate new keys for the second use.

● Attacks on passwords: Because the actual authentication key K_A of a user A is generated directly from the password of the user, Kerberos is vulnerable to password guessing attacks where attackers systematically try out different passwords. Another problem with Kerberos Version 4 is that the authentication server responds to the first unprotected message of a user with a message encrypted with key K_A. The general structure of this message is known and furthermore the user has contributed the content of it. Consequently, an attacker can easily find an encrypted message where he knows some of the parts and can use it for a systematic search for the key by trying out frequently selected passwords. This problem and possible solutions will be discussed further in Section 7.7.

- Double encryption: The double encryption of the tickets in the second and fourth protocol steps does not increase security and therefore is a waste of computing resources.

Double encryption

In response to the deficiencies that had come to light a new version of the Kerberos protocol was specified, which eliminates the criticisms described above [KNT94, NYH⁺05]. The basic procedure and the instances involved were retained. Only the format of the exchanged messages was adjusted. Kerberos now uses a more uniform format and ASN.1 coding to minimise the risk of errors pertaining to security and to make the protocol and implementations extensible. In addition, all cryptographic methods are flexibly interchangeable.

Kerberos Version 5

Version 5 of the Kerberos protocol standardises the simple dialogue as well as a range of advanced methods, such as client–client authentication, pre-authentication and re-authentication of tickets or cross-domain authentication. In the simplest case the dialogue sequence is as follows:

1. User Alice first logs into the Authentication Server, as in Version 4:

Initiation

$$A \rightarrow AS: \ (A, TGS, t_{start}, t_{end}, n, Addr_A, \dots)$$

In contrast to the previous version, it is now possible to specify explicit times for which the new ticket is to be valid (from t_{start} to t_{end}). Thanks to the explicit transfer of Alice's addresses ($Addr_A$), several addresses can be authenticated simultaneously. Furthermore, a nonce n is sent that prevents replaying of messages, even if clock synchronisation were to fail.

TGT output　2. In addition to the ticket, which serves as proof of authentication vis-à-vis other servers, the response to Alice contains encrypted information for Alice. The information is encrypted with Alice's password or a comparable secret. This information includes the key for the Ticket-Granting Server, the date of the last authentication, the nonce n, various time stamps relating to the lifetime of the ticket, and the values sent by Alice for creating the ticket:

$$AS \rightarrow A: \ (A, Ticket_{TGS}, \{K_{A,TGS}, t_{lastRequest}, n, t_{expire}, t_{AS},$$
$$t_{start}, t_{end}, t_{renew}, TGS, Addr_A\}_{K_A})$$

Alice checks the nonce n and the specified addresses for correctness and can be sure to have received a valid ticket. In Kerberos Version 5 this ticket is always transferred in plaintext, since it is only valid with a current authenticator. The TGT is structured as follows:

$$Ticket_{TGS} = (TGS, \{K_{A,TGS}, A, transited, t_{AS}, t_{start}, t_{end},$$
$$t_{renew}, Addr_A, restrictions\}_{K_{AS,TGS}})$$

It consists mainly of encrypted information for the TGS, with some additional information compared with Kerberos Version 4. The field *transited* contains information relating to the authentication chain in environments with several domains. The lifetime information has become more complex, in order to enable tickets to be pre-issued, and it is now possible to pass on additional limitations to the server (*restrictions* field).

SGT request　3. In order to obtain an SGT, Alice initiates a procedure similar to step 1, the only difference being that the TGT and an authenticator are transferred as well:

$$A \rightarrow TGS: \ (A, S1, t_{start}, t_{end}, n', Addr_A,$$
$$Authenticator_{A,TGS}, Tickets, \ldots)$$

The authenticator serves as proof that Alice is, in fact, currently authorised to use the TGT. In addition to a current time stamp, it contains an explicit cryptographic checksum, so that modification of messages no longer represents a serious threat. It is also possible to add an explicit sequence number to prevent replay attacks:

$$Authenticator_{A,TGS} = \{A, CheckSum, t'_A, K'_{A,TGS},$$
$$Seq\#, \ldots\}_{K_{A,TGS}}$$

Another special feature is the option to replace the key $K_{A,TGS}$ with a temporary key $K'_{A,TGS}$.

4. The SGT is issued in exactly the same way as step 2: *Issuing the SGT*

$$TGS \rightarrow A: \quad (A, Ticket_{S1}, \{K_{A,S1}, t_{lastRequest}, n', t_{expire}, t_{TGS},$$
$$t_{start}, t_{end}, t_{renew}, S1, Addr_A\}_{K_{A,TGS}})$$

5. Using the SGT, Alice can now initiate an authentication with the actual server $S1$: *Key negotiation with server S1*

$$A \rightarrow S1: \quad (Ticket_{S1}, Authenticator_{A,S1})$$

Here too, the authenticator has a similar structure to the previous dialogue:

$$Authenticator_{A,S1} = \{A, CheckSum, t'_A, K'_{A,S1},$$
$$Seq\#, \dots \}_{K_{A,S1}}$$

In particular, the key can be changed.

6. After checking the specified values, S1 can confirm the change:

$$S1 \rightarrow A: \quad \{t_{S1}, K'_{A,S1}, Seq\#, \dots \}_{K_{A,S1}}$$

The Kerberos protocol implemented in Version 5 offers significant improvements with regard to technical weaknesses and security properties. Nevertheless, some potential problems remain: *Assessment of improvements in Kerberos Version 5*

- Comparatively good clock synchronisation is required, particularly between the servers, even though the accuracy requirements have been reduced by the introduction of sequence numbers.
- The availability of the Authentication and Ticket-Granting Servers remains critical.
- The password-guessing attacks of the type referred to above are still possible in principle, even though such attacks can be slowed down considerably through hash functions that are very complex to calculate [Rae05].

7.5 International Standard X.509

In 1988 Recommendation X.509 [IT93] was standardised by the *International Telecommunications Union* (ITU) as part of the X.500 recommendations for the provision of directory services. Use of the X.500 Directory Service for the realisation of authentication services is described in this recommendation, and relevant procedures and data formats are specified. In terms of content, the recommendation makes a distinction between two independent parts:

Key certification
1. As an important prerequisite for the practical application of asymmetric cryptographic algorithms for the realisation of security services, the recommendation describes methods for a worldwide and secure distribution of public keys. This includes the definition of *certificates* for public keys to prove their authenticity and methods for hierarchical certification. For the usage in network protocols this part of the X.509 standard is updated and normatively extended in [Sch05].

Authentica-tion protocols
2. The recommendation also contains various schemes for authenticating entities. These range from 'simple' authentication based on passwords to 'strong' *authentication protocols*.

The concepts of the certificates based on X.509 are introduced briefly below. The section that follows describes the authentication protocols of the recommendation.

7.5.1   X.509 Key Certificates

Certificates are issued by a *certification authority* – in its function comparable to an identification card authority – and essentially contain the unique name of the 'holder', his or her public key, the period of validity and a digital signature. Figure 7.3 shows the structure of an X.509 certificate.

For clarity, the following notation will be used in the following explanations:

$$A[I] := (I, \{H(I)\}_{-K_A})$$

In the notation $-K_A$ denotes the private key of entity A, I arbitrary information for signing, H a cryptographic hash function and $\{x\}_{-K_A}$ the value of x encrypted with A's private key. In X.509 notation, a certificate issued by certification authority CA for the public key of entity A is structured as follows:

$$CA \ll A \gg := CA[V, SN, AI, CA, T_A, A, +K_A]$$

Components of X.509 certificates
It contains the version number V of the X.509 standard, one unique serial number SN per certification authority, the name and the

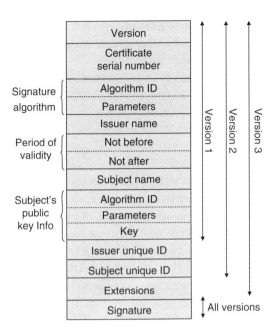

Figure 7.3

Structure of X.509 certificates

parameters of the signature scheme AI used, the name of the certification authority CA, the period of validity of certificate T_A and the name of the entity being certified A along with its public key $+K_A$ (also see Figure 7.3). CA signs this information with its private key $-K_{CA}$.

If the entities that want to authenticate each other know the public key $+K_{CA}$ of the certification authority, they can use the certificate for verification of each other's public key.

If the number of users requiring authentication is extensive or users are separated by large geographical distances, it is not practical for one central certification authority to sign all public keys. Consequently, X.509 provides for the formation of a *certification hierarchy*. In such a hierarchy additional certificates are used to link together multiple certification authorities. Certificate hierarchies and all involved systems are usually referred to by the term

Certification hierarchy

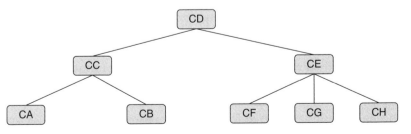

Figure 7.4

Example of an X.509 certification hierarchy

public key infrastructure (PKI). Figure 7.4 shows a hypothetical X.509 certification hierarchy (this illustration only shows certification authorities and no users).

In this example an entity A that trusts certification authority CA can check the public key of entity H, whose key is certified by certification authority CH through a *chain of certificates*. In X.509 notation a certificate chain is structured as follows:

$$X_1 \ll X_2 \gg X_2 \ll B \gg$$

In this chain, certification authority X_2 is certifying entity B. X_2 in turn is certified by certification authority X_1. So that the chain can also be formed in the opposite direction, X_2 also has to certify X_1. In X.509 the length of certification chains is not limited. If entity A in the example shown in Figure 7.4 wants to verify the public key of entity H, she will need the following certification chain:

$$CA \ll CC \gg CC \ll CD \gg CD \ll CE \gg CE \ll CH \gg CH \ll H \gg$$

A drawback of this approach is the dependence on the integrity of all certificates in the chain. If a single private key was compromised, no security objectives would be guaranteed any more. Therefore, at least for some systems developers and administrators tend to introduce cross-certifications to allow for verification over different paths or to at least reduce the number of intermediate steps.

Storage in public directories
Because the certificates cannot be forged if the certification authorities are operated securely, they can be stored in a public directory. X.509 provides for the X.500 Directory Service that contains the appropriate ASN.1 definitions of the required data formats.

Reasons for premature invalidation
As a rule, a new certificate is issued in time before the currently valid certificate expires. In some circumstances it may be necessary to invalidate a certificate even before it expires:

- There is a suspicion that the private key of an entity has become known.
- The issuing certification authority is no longer certifying a particular entity.
- There is a suspicion that the private key of a certification authority has become known. If this is the case, all certificates signed with this key must be invalidated.

Certificate revocation list
Therefore, in addition to certificates, the X.500 directory also stores what are called *certificate revocation lists* (CRLs) that contain all invalidated certificates. The verification of a certificate also has to check whether it has already been invalidated. The directory service is normally consulted for this information.

7.5.2 Direct Authentication Protocols Based on X.509

In addition to password-based and so-called 'simple' authentication, the X.509 recommendation defines three cryptographic authentication protocols that are referred to as 'strong' and build on one another. These are defined as follows:

1. If entity A is merely being authenticated to entity B, then A *One-way authentica-* sends the following message to B *(one-way authentication):* *tion*

$$A \to B: \ (A[t_A, r_A, B, sgnData, \{K_{A,B}\}_{+K_B}], CA \ll A \gg)$$

This entity receives a message signed by A and the certificate $CA \ll A \gg$. The signed message contains a time stamp t_A, a unique and random value r_A within the period of validity of the time stamp, the name of B, optional user data $sgnData$ and a likewise optional session key $K_{A,B}$, which is encrypted with the public key $+K_B$ of B.

2. On receipt of this message, B checks the respective certificate with $+K_{CA}$ and extracts the public key $+K_A$ of A. To check the authenticity of the key, B may have to request other certificates from the public directory and verify a certification chain from its own certification authority all the way to the public key of A. Then B uses key $+K_A$ to verify the message computed by A through the received message. Based on the values t_A, r_A and B, B either accepts the authentication or declines it. The scheme requires that all participants have synchronised clocks. The value r_A of B is stored until the validity of time stamp t_A has expired so that the tolerated clock difference selected does not have to be too small. Within this time span B accepts no authentication messages with the same r_A from A.

3. If mutual authentication is desired, then B sends a similar *Two-way authentica-* message to A *(two-way authentication):* *tion*

$$B \to A: \ (B[t_B, r_B, A, r_A, sgnData, \{K_{B,A}\}_{+K_A}], CA \ll B \gg)$$

The time stamp contained in the message is not necessarily required as A can check whether the value r_A matches both the value sent by her earlier and the value generated for the current dialogue.

4. If no synchronised clocks are available, *three-way authentic-* *Three-way* *ation* can take place. For this kind of authentication A addi- *authentication* tionally sends the following message to B:

$$A \to B: \ \{A[r_B]\}$$

In this instance A is authenticating herself to B by being able to sign the random number generated by r_B in the current dialogue.

The protocols can also be used with symmetric cryptography

Recommendation X.509 designates the use of asymmetric encryption algorithms for the digital signatures of messages. However, the authentication protocols described above can just as easily be executed with a signing scheme based on symmetric cryptography. In this case A and B must agree a secret authentication key $AK_{A,B}$ beforehand, in which case conveying and verifying certificates becomes superfluous.

7.6   Security of Negotiated Session Keys

The cryptographic protocols discussed so far in this chapter carry out entity authentication, simultaneously negotiating a session key for the communication relationship that immediately follows. More precisely, 'negotiation' of the key always involves one entity specifying a key and distributing it to the other entity or entities.

Lack of authentication with Diffie–Hellman

The Diffie–Hellman scheme for key negotiation was presented in Section 4.5 with an explanation that it does not offer its own authentication mechanism for message exchanges. This means that, without additional cryptographic measures, neither of the two entities can be certain about which entity it has exchanged a session key with. This circumstance suggests linking Diffie–Hellman key exchange to supplementary data origin authentication. For example, after or during key negotiation, each entity computes a signature over all the message elements it transmits and then sends it to the peer entity.

However, this requires access to an authentication key that both parties already have or to certified public keys. The question thus arises about the added benefit of using the Diffie–Hellman scheme if its security has to rely on other keys. After all, these authentication keys can just as easily be deployed directly to distribute a session key.

Advantages of key negotiation with Diffie–Hellman

Depending on the security requirements demanded of the key distribution, use of the Diffie–Hellman scheme is advantageous or necessary because it guarantees a security feature that cannot be provided when session keys are distributed directly. This is called *Perfect Forward Secrecy*.

Perfect Forward Secrecy

Definition 7.4 *A cryptographic protocol for key negotiation guarantees the property of* **Perfect Forward Secrecy** *when a possible* *compromising of a key $K1$ in the future will have no effect on the security of exchanged or stored data protected with a session key $K2$ that was negotiated with the help of key $K1$ before $K1$ was compromised.*

The cryptographic protocols presented in this chapter cannot guarantee Perfect Forward Secrecy. For example, with Kerberos authentication and key distribution, if the authentication key K_A becomes known at a later time, an attacker can subsequently decrypt all recorded messages by first computing session key $K_{A,TGS}$ from the response message of the authentication server to A and then use this key to ascertain session key $K_{A,S1}$ from the response message of the Ticket-Granting Server to A.

If, however, two entities A and B negotiate a session key $SK_{A,B}$ using the Diffie–Hellman scheme and authenticate their messages with a secret authentication key $AK_{A,B}$, an attacker cannot subsequently use the authentication key to ascertain the session key. The attacker would still need to solve the Diffie–Hellman problem, which is assumed to involve the calculation of a discrete logarithm, as previously discussed. The attacker also cannot actively attack the Diffie–Hellman scheme afterwards using a man-in-the-middle approach as the dialogue has already taken place and therefore can no longer be manipulated. Consequently, Diffie–Hellman is used for key negotiation in several network security protocols. These protocols are covered extensively in Part 2.

Perfect Forward Secrecy can be achieved with the Diffie–Hellman scheme

7.7 Advanced Password Authentication Methods

All methods offering authentication based on passwords and described previously in this chapter, such as Kerberos and the Otway–Rees protocol, have a common weakness: passive attackers can read the exchanged messages and then systematically check potential passwords. In the Otway–Rees protocol, for example, this approach can even succeed with the first message. Attackers can attempt to decrypt the term $\{r_A, i_A, A, B\}_{K_{A,TTP}}$ and will know that they have determined $K_{A,TTP}$ as soon as valid values for A, B and i_a are obtained. Even if password authentication is secured through a Diffie–Hellman exchange, attackers can use a man-in-the-middle attack to obtain cryptographic values that enable them to try out passwords without having to exchange messages. Because of the high processing speed of modern systems (particularly GPUs and

The systematic trying of passwords is a significant problem for widely used authentication protocols

cloud resources), such systematic trials quickly start to necessitate passwords with such a high complexity that they would no longer be manageable for humans.

Key derivation functions can linearly increase the effort for attackers

An initial way out is offered by so-called *key derivation functions (KDF)*, which can convert passwords into the actual key through complex arithmetic operations. Consequently attackers also have to acquire more processing power in their attempts to break passwords by trial and error. However, it should be noted that this is of only limited benefit, since in many cases attackers have access to high-performance systems, and longer calculation time for the KDF only results in a linear benefit, while the effort for attackers increases exponentially with the password length.

PAKE schemes use asymmetric cryptography to hamper offline attacks

A better option is offered by so-called PAKE protocols (*password-authenticated key exchange*). The core idea here is to use asymmetric cryptography to achieve a key exchange, authenticated by the password. In contrast to simple Diffie–Hellman-based authentication, in the event of an invalid password none of the two parties should be able (with acceptable computing effort) to infer anything, except for the fact that this one password was obviously invalid. These methods therefore belong to the so-called *zero-knowledge protocols*.

Initial PAKE scheme

An initial, very simple protocol that is part of the PAKE scheme category is *Encrypted Key Exchange (EKE)* [BM92]. Here, two parties A and B want to negotiate a shared symmetric key K_r and authenticate it based on a shared password $K_{A,B}$.

1. In the first step, A chooses a temporary public key $+K_{ar}$ and sends it encrypted to B protected with the shared secret:

$$A \rightarrow B: \ A, \{+K_{ar}\}_{K_{A,B}}$$

2. After receipt of the message, B can decipher the public key $+K_{ar}$ and generate a random shared session key K_r with high entropy. This key is encrypted through $+K_{ar}$ as well as $K_{A,B}$ and sent back to A:

$$B \rightarrow A: \ \{\{K_r\}_{+K_{ar}}\}_{K_{A,B}}$$

3. A and B then have the same secret K_r and can verify that they are in possession of the same session key by exchanging the nonces r_A and r_B:

$$A \rightarrow B: \ \{r_A\}_{K_r}$$
$$B \rightarrow A: \ \{r_A, r_B\}_{K_r}$$
$$A \rightarrow B: \ \{r_B\}_{K_r}$$

At this point it is implicitly clear that both parties knew $K_{A,B}$ and that no man-in-the-middle attack took place.

A prerequisite for the security of EKE is that the value $+K_{ar}$ is indistinguishable from a random number. Otherwise the attacker could draw conclusions about $K_{A,B}$ from the first message. Implementations must take this into account. The authors of EKE therefore suggest that e but not n is encrytped when RSA is used, since n is characterised by the fact that it has no small prime factors. The prerequisite that the encrypted term must be indistinguishable from a random series also applies to the second message $K_{A,B}$, in order to prevent attackers systematically trying values for $K_{A,B}$. Thanks to the double encryption of K_r in the second step, it is subsequently impossible for attackers to make a direct connection between K_r and $K_{A,B}$.

Prerequisite for the security of EKE

However, in conjunction with RSA the EKE introduced here is insecure, as the following scenario shows [Pat97]. In the first step of the procedure, an active attacker can simply select $n = pq$ such that $(p-1)$ and $(q-1)$ are divisible by 3. This n is then sent to B, together with a number X, so that B believes X is the encrypted public key. B 'decrypts' X and obtains random number e', which with a probability of $1/3$ is itself divisible by 3. In the second step B sends $\{K_r^{3k} \bmod n\}_{K_{A,B}} = Y$ to the attacker. The attacker can now use different passwords P' to test whether $D(P',Y)^{\frac{p-1}{3}} \bmod p = D(P',Y)^{\frac{q-1}{3}} \bmod q = 1$. For the real password both terms must be 1, since:

EKE in conjunction with RSA is insecure

$$(K_r^{3k} \bmod n)^{\frac{p-1}{3}} \bmod p \equiv$$
$$(K_r^{3k})^{\frac{p-1}{3}} \bmod p =$$
$$(K_r^k)^{p-1} \bmod p =$$
$$(K_r^k)^{\Phi(p)} \bmod p = 1 \qquad \text{(according to Theorem 4.4)}$$

The derivation for q is analogous. Compliance with the equation does not necessarily mean that the password is correct, since in $1/9$ of cases the result could randomly be 1 for both terms. However, the real password can quickly be isolated through multiple application of the procedure with random X values.

In addition to this security issue, there is a further problem with the first EKE protocol: It offers no perfect forward secrecy. The authors have therefore presented a second protocol, referred to as *DH-EKE* below, in order to distinguish it from the first one. The

DH-EKE offers perfect forward secrecy

procedure is essentially a cleverly authenticated Diffie–Hellman exchange:

1. $A \rightarrow B$: $A, \{g^{r_a} \bmod p\}_{K_{A,B}}$

2. $B \rightarrow A$: $B, \{g^{r_b} \bmod p\}_{K_{A,B}}, \{c_b\}_{K_s}$

3. $A \rightarrow B$: $B, \{c_a \,\|\, c_b\}_{K_s}$

4. $B \rightarrow A$: $B, \{c_a\}_{K_s}$

The session key K_s corresponds to the Diffie–Hellman secret $g^{r_a r_b} \bmod p$, whereby the strength of the method is no longer independent of the asymmetric cryptosystem. Implicitly it is assumed that the Diffie–Hellman presumption is true. As in the EKE method described above, values that are secured with $K_{A,B}$ must be indistinguishable from random values. To this end p must be chosen such that the number of invalid values for the block size of the symmetric cipher is as small as possible. If, for example, a p with length of 1023 bits was chosen and the block limit was 1024 bits, it would be possible to try different values for $K_{A,B}$. Whenever a resulting number is greater than p, the value can be ruled out.

Patent protection issues led to the development of alternative PAKE schemes

Both EKE methods have two fundamental problems. For a long time they were protected by a very generally formulated patent [BM93], and the server must store passwords in plaintext. Particularly for the first reason a whole range of alternative methods were developed, a full discussion of which would exceed the scope of this book. The so-called *Dragonfly* protocol will be discussed in the context of WiFi security in Section 15.2.2. In the following section we describe the *Secure Remote Password (SRP)* method, which is the method that has been most widely used to date.

Secure Remote Password protocol

The SRP protocol exists in a number of slight variations in different publications and standards. The SRP-3 protocol, for example, was published in 2000 in RFC 2945 [Wu00]. The latest version is SRP-6a [Wu02], which is described below.

Initialisation of the method

Server B initially determines a random value $s_{A,B}$, which is secured through a cryptographic hash function, together with a user name and password. $s_{A,B}$ is referred to as a *salt value*, which is intended to hamper dictionary attacks — in the case of a compromise — based on the fact that individual hash values have to be calculated for each user. The result of the hashing is $x = H(s_{A,B} \,\|\, username \,\|\, password)$ and this is used to calculate a so-called verifier $v = g^x \bmod p$. The latter is stored in the server, together with the user name and salt value.

The actual authentication protocol uses four messages: *Exchange sequence*

1. In the first step A only sends the user name, since the salt value is not yet known, and the password can therefore not be processed:

$$A \to B: \ A$$

2. Server B responds with the values p, g and $s_{A,B}$ in plain text. The prime number and the generator are already included in the calculation of the verifier and therefore have to be specified by the server. The message also contains the first part of a Diffie–Hellman exchange, in which a multiple of the verifier v was added to g^{r_b}:

$$B \to A: \ p, g, s_{A,B}, \overbrace{(\underbrace{H(g \parallel p)}_{k} \times v + g^{r_b}) \bmod p}^{Y_B}$$

3. A now calculates its part of the Diffie–Hellman exchange $Y_A = g^{r_a} \bmod p$, a cryptographic check value over the Diffie–Hellman values $u = H(Y_A, Y_B) \bmod p$ and the shared secret $S = (Y_B - k \times g^x)^{r_a + ux} \bmod p$. The check value u ensures that the secret can only be calculated correctly if no man-in-the-middle attack has taken place. The response contains Y_A and also proof that A was able to calculate the secret S:

$$A \to B: \ \overbrace{g^{r_a} \bmod p}^{Y_A}, H(Y_A, Y_B, S)$$

4. B also calculates the secret $S' = (Y_A v^u)^{r_b} \bmod p$, which, without a man-in-the-middle attack, corresponds to S and demonstrates knowledge of A:

$$B \to A: \ H(Y_A, H(Y_A, Y_B, S), S)$$

After the successful exchange, both parties can derive a session key $K_s = H(S)$.

In terms of security SRP is a so-called *augmented PAKE scheme*, *Security of SRP* which means that, even if an attacker takes over a server, the passwords are not immediately accessible. Instead, each password has to be found by trial and error, and the verifier v cannot be used for authentication as client vis-à-vis other servers. This even applies if they use the same salt value, for example in cases where they use the same password database, since the value x is required for the calculation on the client side. However, a basic assumption of SRP is that passwords with low entropy can be used, so that the security gain through the salt method is generally likely to be comparatively small. In particular, calculation of the verifier does not offer protection from a scenario whereby an attacker pretends to be a server with the same password after the authentication database has been compromised. Another factor is that SRP uses calculations based on a number field and not based on a group, so it does not work with cryptography based on elliptic curves. Like EKE, SRP is protected by patents, although free use of the method is guaranteed.

7.8   Formal Validation of Cryptographic Protocols

In the literature there are a number of known examples in which a cryptographic protocol contains flaws that enable attackers to influence the protocol without requiring the appropriate key, or where the cryptographic algorithms used by the protocol have to be broken [Mea95]. One example is the *Needham–Schroeder protocol* [NS78], which allows attackers to specify a potentially compromised key as the new session key (see also Section 7.3) [DS81]. Other examples are the authentication protocol of the draft version of International Standard X.509 [IT87], which contains a similar flaw [BAN90], and the *licensing system for software by Purdy, Simmons and Studier* [PSS82], which an attacker was able to circumvent by combining recorded messages [Sim85].

These examples motivate the need for a formal validation of cryptographic protocols because informal methods are not adequately able to analyse security flaws in protocols. An overview of popular approaches in this field is therefore given followed by a detailed description of a particularly easy-to-handle and successful approach, *GNY logic*.

7.8.1   Classification of Formal Validation Methods

A number of approaches were developed for the formal validation of cryptographic protocols. These can be divided into the following four categories [Mea92]:

General approaches   1. *General approaches to prove certain protocol properties:* Approaches in this category consider cryptographic protocols as conventional programmes and analyse them using the usual methods of software verification, such as automaton-based approaches [Sid86, Var89] or predicate logic [Kem89]. Alternatively, they use special specification languages to describe and analyse protocols [Var90]. In its requirements, proof of the security of a cryptographic protocol differs considerably from proof of the correctness of a protocol because malicious manipulation normally does not need to be considered in the latter proof. The approaches in this category are therefore not particularly suitable for analysing attacks on cryptographic protocols.

2. *Expert system-based approaches:* Approaches of this type use the knowledge of human experts formalised with deductive rules, thereby enabling an automated and possibly interactive analysis of cryptographic protocols [LR92, MCF87]. Although this procedure lends itself well to the analysis of protocols with known attack patterns, it is less appropriate for tracking down loopholes based on unknown attack patterns [Sch96, p. 66].

   Expert system based approaches

3. *Algebraic approaches:* Approaches in this category model cryptographic protocols as algebraic systems. In addition to the protocol steps, the model records the knowledge and beliefs obtained by peer entities during an authentication dialogue and analyses the resulting model using algebraic operations. Examples of approaches in this category are provided by [Mer83, Tou91, Tou92a, Tou92b, WL93].

   Algebraic approaches

4. *Special logic-based approaches:* This category was established as a result of the approach *BAN logic*, named after its inventors Burrows, Abadi and Needham [BAN90]. Since its introduction, it has maintained its reputation as a particular easy-to-use strategy for a formal analysis of cryptographic protocols. Approaches of this type define a series of predicates, together with mapping instructions for converting message exchanges into formulas, thereby enabling an analysis of the *knowledge* and *beliefs* that peer entities obtain during an authentication dialogue as part of the protocol run. Numerous improvements have been proposed for BAN logic and for extended approaches based on the same idea [GS91, GNY90, KW94, MB93, Oor93, Sne91]. Other logic-based approaches include [BKY93, Bie90, Mos89, Ran88, Syv90, Syv91, Syv93a, Syv93b, SO94].

   Logic-based approaches

   GNY logic [GNY90] is one of the most widely used of these approaches and because of its easy handling will be presented in detail. However, this specialised section may also be skipped without impairing the understanding of the rest of the book.

7.8.2 GNY Logic*

GNY logic was named after its inventors *Gong, Needham* and *Yahalom* and published for the first time in 1990 [GNY90]. Analyses using this logic focus on systematically deducing the *knowledge* and *beliefs* obtained by the peer entities of a cryptographic protocol during a dialogue from previously specified conditions and message exchanges.

Knowledge and belief   In this context, *knowledge* is knowing certain data values that are exchanged or negotiated during a dialogue (e.g. keys), whereas *beliefs* assess the exchanged data. Examples of beliefs include assumptions that a message was sent by a specific communication partner (and therefore not by an attacker), that a reported value is appropriate for use as a session key, or that a certain message is not a repetition of a message sent earlier.

Protocol model   The cryptographic protocol is assumed to be a distributed *for GNY logic* algorithm implemented by communicating state automatons. Message exchanges between automatons can be arbitrarily delayed, replayed, deleted or modified by attackers or even invented and inserted by them during transmission. It is also assumed that attackers cannot break the cryptographic algorithms used to secure message exchanges. Each partner of a cryptographic protocol manages two disjunctive quantities:

Knowledge   1. *knowledge*, the set of data values he or she holds or obtains during a dialogue;

Belief   2. *belief*, the set of his or her beliefs about these data values.

Before a protocol run, these sets receive initial elements that are obtained from the preconditions of the authentication protocol. During the protocol new elements can be obtained for these sets from messages received. The following means of expression can be used for the notation of these elements:

Formulas   ■ *Formulas* are used as names for variables that can contain arbitrary bit patterns. In the notation of GNY logic, X and Y refer to arbitrary data values, whereas K and S are used for keys and shared secrets. With X and Y, the union of these values (X, Y) is also a formula, with the union in the logic treated as a quantity with the properties associativity and commutativity.

In addition, $\{X\}_K$ denotes the value X symmetrically encrypted with key K and $\{X\}_K^{-1}$ denotes the plaintext associated with X and key K after encryption with a symmetric scheme. It therefore holds that $\{\{X\}_K\}_K^{-1} = X$.

$\{X\}_{+K}$ and $\{X\}_{-K}$ are used for the notation of asymmetric schemes and it holds that $\{\{X\}_{+K}\}_{-K} = X$.

$H(X)$ denotes the value that results from the application of a cryptographic hash function to the value X. Lastly, $F(X)$ denotes a function that can be reversed efficiently, such as the XOR function.

■ *Statements C* describe the knowledge and the beliefs of the peer entities of a protocol about certain formulas. Let P and Q be possible peer entities of a protocol and X, S and $+K$ be formulas. The following statements can then be formed:

- $P \triangleleft X$: Entity P receives message X. Message X can be extracted from the received message either directly or by using a computation algorithm known to the communication partners.

- $P \ni X$: Entity P possesses formula X. An entity possesses all initial elements of the quantity knowledge as well as all formulas that it obtains during a protocol run. In addition, it possesses all formulas that it can compute from existing formulas.

- $P \mid\sim X$: Entity P has transmitted X. Formula X can be directly transmitted in a message or computed from a message transmitted by P.

- $P \mid\equiv \#(X)$: Entity P has the belief that formula X is *new*, meaning that this formula was never used in earlier protocol dialogues. This property can be guaranteed by the fact that formula X was generated with a random generator.

- $P \mid\equiv \phi(X)$: Entity P has the belief that it recognises formula X. It is possible that P has certain knowledge about the structure of formula X before it receives the formula. It is also possible that P recognises a specific value in the formula or that the formula contains a certain redundancy. This property is needed if an entity should be prevented from accepting a randomly generated value as a formula.

- $P \mid\equiv P \xrightarrow{S} Q$: Entity P believes that value S is an appropriate secret for securing message exchanges between P and Q. This secret can be a symmetric encryption key or a value for the computation of message

Statements

Receipt of a message

Possessing a formula

Transmitting a formula

Freshness of a formula

Recognisability of a formula

Confidentiality of a formula

authentication codes. The notation is symmetric, which means $P \xleftrightarrow{S} Q$ and $Q \xleftrightarrow{S} P$ can be used synonymously.

Authenticity of public keys

- $P \mathbin{|\equiv} \xrightarrow{+K} Q$: Entity P has the belief that value $+K$ is the public key of Q and that the corresponding private key $-K$ is only known to Q.

C_1 and C_2 can also be used to form other statements:

Union of statements

- C_1, C_2: In GNY logic a union of statements is handled as a union of quantities with the properties associativity and commutativity.

Beliefs about statements

- $P \mathbin{|\equiv} C_1$: Entity P has the belief that statement C_1 is true.

Competence

- $P \mathbin{|\Longrightarrow} C1$: Entity P is competent to evaluate statement $C1$.

Furthermore, an X formula can have a '$\star$' prefix attached to it. In this case, entity P, which possesses the formula, knows that it has not produced and transmitted formula X in the current protocol dialogue itself. The statement $P \triangleleft \star X$ is an example of the use of this prefix. It is required in the analysis of cryptographic protocols to ensure that certain formulas cannot be *reflected* by an attacker, meaning that they are sent back to the actual sender of a message.

In GNY logic the symbol '$\star$' is also used in another connection. The statement $P \mathbin{|\Longrightarrow} P \mathbin{|\equiv} \star$ means that P has the jurisdiction to judge all its beliefs.

In conclusion, a condition C can be attached to a formula X to express that an entity should only transmit formula X to a peer entity if the statement C is true. This fact is expressed in GNY logic by attaching symbol $\rightsquigarrow$ followed by statement C to a formula X: $(X \rightsquigarrow C)$.

Transforming a protocol into statements

In analyses with GNY logic, cryptographic protocols are first conveyed through syntactical analysis into statements of the form described above:

- Two lines $P \mathbin{|\sim} X$ followed by $Q \triangleleft X$ are created for each line of the form $P \rightarrow Q: X$. The assumption is that the transmission service is reliable and that no errors that cannot be attributed to intentional manipulation will occur.
- After all messages of a protocol are processed, all lines of the form $P \mathbin{|\sim} X$ and $P \triangleleft Z$ are analysed in the sequence of their occurrence for each partner P of the protocol. Each partial formula Y of a formula Z is checked in a statement $P \triangleleft Z$ to verify whether it occurred previously in a formula X of a statement $P \mathbin{|\sim} X$. If this is not the case, then it means that P did not

transmit the message itself and a '$\star$' prefix is attached to the beginning of partial formula Y. Once this step is completed, it is possible at a syntactical level to recognise whether a specific formula Y can possibly be reflected by an attacker. After this step all lines of form $P|\sim X$ are deleted.

- In a final step formulas of the form $\{\{X\}_K\}_K^{-1}$ are reduced to X. A corresponding reduction is made for asymmetrically encrypted values.

The actual analysis of the protocol takes place after these preparatory steps have been completed. An attempt is made to use the deductive rules of GNY logic to deduce new formulas from the given formulas and those obtained during the dialogue until the objectives of the cryptographic protocol are derived.

Common objectives of cryptographic protocols are that all peer entities (e.g. P and Q) possess a specific key K after a dialogue is completed and believe in the secretness of this key: $P \ni K$, $Q \ni K$, $P |\equiv P \xleftrightarrow{K} Q$ and $Q|\equiv P \xleftrightarrow{K} Q$. Another objective is that all peer entities believe that the other peer entities also believe in the secretness of the key: $P |\equiv Q|\equiv P \xleftrightarrow{K} Q$ and $Q|\equiv P |\equiv P \xleftrightarrow{K} Q$. *Protocol objectives*

GNY logic provides a set of rules of deduction to deduce these objectives from the initial conditions and the formulas added during a protocol run. Some of these rules are listed below with an identifier chosen by the inventors of GNY logic indicated in parentheses: *Rules of deduction of GNY logic*

- Receipt of formula X, in particular, can be inferred from the receipt of a formula $\star X$ that was not sent by P itself (Rule T1, 'T' denotes the 'being-told' rules on the receipt of formulas): *T1*

$$\frac{P \lhd \star X}{P \lhd X}$$

- Receipt of each of its partial formulas can be inferred from the receipt of a combined formula (T2): *T2*

$$\frac{P \lhd (X, Y)}{P \lhd X}$$

- If P receives a formula $\{X\}_K$ that is encrypted with key K and if P is in possession of key K, then this can be used to infer the receipt of formula X (T3): *T3*

$$\frac{P \lhd \{X\}_K, P \ni K}{P \lhd X}$$

P1 ■ If P receives a formula X, then it can be concluded that P is in possession of formula X (P1, 'P' generally identifies 'possession' formulas):

$$\frac{P \lhd X}{P \ni X}$$

F1 ■ If P believes the freshness of a formula X, then P is also of the view that each formula that has X as a partial formula is fresh and that each function value $F(X)$ computable with a feasible effort is fresh (F1, 'F' denotes 'freshness' rules on the currentness of formulas):

$$\frac{P \mid\equiv \#(X)}{P \mid\equiv \#(X, Y), \ P \mid\equiv \#(F(X))}$$

R1 ■ If P believes in the recognisability of a formula X, then it can be concluded that P also believes in the recognisability of each combined formula containing X as a partial formula and that P is convinced of the recognisability of a computationally feasible function $F(X)$ (R1, 'R' denotes 'recognisability' rules for formulas):

$$\frac{P \mid\equiv \phi(X)}{P \mid\equiv \phi(X, Y), \ P \mid\equiv \phi(F(X))}$$

I1 ■ Let us say P receives a formula $\{X\}_K$ encrypted with key K that it did not create itself and P possesses key K and considers it an appropriate key to secure communication with Q. If P also believes that message X is recognisable and X or K is current, then it can be interpreted that P believes Q conveyed messages X and $\{X\}_K$ and possesses key K (I1, 'I' denotes rules on the 'interpretation' of formulas).

$$\frac{P \lhd \star \{X\}_K, \ P \ni K, \ P \mid\equiv P \xrightarrow{K} Q, \ P \mid\equiv \phi(X), \ P \mid\equiv \#(X, K)}{P \mid\equiv Q \mid \sim X, \ P \mid\equiv Q \mid \sim \{X\}_K, \ P \mid\equiv Q \ni K}$$

J1 ■ If P believes that Q has jurisdiction over statement C and if P holds the view that Q believes in the correctness of statement C, it can be deduced that P also believes in the correctness of statement C (J1, 'J' denotes 'jurisdiction' rules):

$$\frac{P \mid\equiv Q \mid\Longrightarrow C, \ P \mid\equiv Q \mid\equiv C}{P \mid\equiv C}$$

J2 ■ If P holds the view that Q is honest and competent in respect of all its beliefs ($P \mid\equiv Q \mid\Longrightarrow Q \mid\equiv \star$) and if P holds the view that Q sent message X on the condition C and that message X is fresh, it can be concluded that P holds the view that Q believes in the correctness of statement C (J2):

$$\frac{P\mid\equiv Q\mid\Longrightarrow Q\mid\equiv \star,\ P\mid\equiv Q\mid\sim (X\rightsquigarrow C),\ P\mid\equiv \#(X)}{P\mid\equiv Q\mid\equiv C}$$

The reader is referred to [GNY90] for a comprehensive introduction to GNY logic and a complete list of all its rules. The use of the logic is clarified below using an analysis of the Needham–Schroeder protocol.

7.8.3 An Example of GNY Logic*

The Needham–Schroeder protocol, introduced in Section 7.3, will be examined again to illustrate analysis based on GNY logic. In summary it consists of the following messages:

1. $A \rightarrow TTP$: (A, B, r_A) *Protocol definition*
2. $TTP \rightarrow A$: $\{r_A, B, K_{A,B}, \{K_{A,B}, A\}_{K_{B,TTP}}\}_{K_{A,TTP}}$
3. $A \rightarrow B$: $\{K_{A,B}, A\}_{K_{B,TTP}}$
4. $B \rightarrow A$: $\{r_B\}_{K_{A,B}}$
5. $A \rightarrow B$: $\{r_B - 1\}_{K_{A,B}}$

In the following syntactical analysis only those message parts of each entity are listed that are of interest in this context. Therefore, the partial message encrypted with $K_{B,TTP}$ is not given for A in the second step because A cannot decrypt it and thus cannot make any further inferences from it. The following formulas are derived:

1. $TTP \triangleleft \star A, \star B, \star r_A$ *Syntactical analysis*
2. $A \triangleleft \star \{r_A, B, \star K_{A,B} \rightsquigarrow TTP\mid\equiv A \overset{K_{A,B}}{\longleftrightarrow} B\}_{K_{A,TTP}}$
   $\rightsquigarrow TTP\mid\equiv A \overset{K_{A,B}}{\longleftrightarrow} B$
3. $B \triangleleft \star \{\star K_{A,B}, \star A\}_{K_{B,TTP}} \rightsquigarrow TTP\mid\equiv A \overset{K_{A,B}}{\longleftrightarrow} B$
4. $A \triangleleft \star \{\star r_B\}_{K_{A,B}}$
5. $B \triangleleft \star \{\star F(r_B)\}_{K_{A,B}} \rightsquigarrow A\mid\equiv A \overset{K_{A,B}}{\longleftrightarrow} B$

A formalisation of the initial conditions leads to the following formulas: *Conditions*

- The two entities A and B possess their own authentication key $K_{A,TTP}$ or $K_{B,TTP}$ and believe in the appropriateness of this key:

$$A \ni K_{A,TTP}; \qquad A \mid\equiv A \stackrel{K_{A,TTP}}{\longleftrightarrow} TTP$$

$$B \ni K_{B,TTP}; \qquad B \mid\equiv B \stackrel{K_{B,TTP}}{\longleftrightarrow} TTP$$

Furthermore, A and B have random numbers and believe in their freshness. A believes that the name of B is recognisable and B believes that the random number r_B is recognisable:

$$A \ni r_A; \qquad A \mid\equiv \#(r_A); \qquad A \mid\equiv \phi(B)$$

$$B \ni r_B; \qquad B \mid\equiv \#(r_B); \qquad B \mid\equiv \phi(r_B)$$

Finally, both A and B believe in the honesty of trusted entity TTP and that TTP can generate an appropriate session key for secure communication between A and B:

$$A \mid\equiv TTP \mid\Longrightarrow TTP \mid\equiv \star; \qquad A \mid\equiv TTP \mid\Longrightarrow (A \stackrel{K_{A,B}}{\longleftrightarrow} B)$$

$$B \mid\equiv TTP \mid\Longrightarrow TTP \mid\equiv \star; \qquad B \mid\equiv TTP \mid\Longrightarrow (A \stackrel{K_{A,B}}{\longleftrightarrow} B)$$

- The trusted entity possesses the necessary keys $K_{A,TTP}$, $K_{B,TTP}$ and $K_{A,B}$, and believes in their respective secretness:

$$TTP \ni K_{A,TTP}; \qquad TTP \mid\equiv A \stackrel{K_{A,TTP}}{\longleftrightarrow} TTP$$

$$TTP \ni K_{B,TTP}; \qquad TTP \mid\equiv B \stackrel{K_{B,TTP}}{\longleftrightarrow} TTP$$

$$TTP \ni K_{A,B}; \qquad TTP \mid\equiv A \stackrel{K_{A,B}}{\longleftrightarrow} B$$

The rules of GNY logic can be used to make the following inferences for each protocol run:

TTP possesses formulas A, B and r_A

1. With rules T1 and P1 it can be deduced from *Message 1* that the trusted entity knows formulas A, B and r_A: $TTP \ni A, B, r_A$.

A possesses the session key and believes in its secrecy

2. With *Message 2* it should be noted that extension $\leadsto TTP \mid\equiv A \stackrel{K_{A,B}}{\longleftrightarrow} B$ of the formulas is correct as it directly follows from the initial conditions. It can also be assumed that receiver A of this message cannot mistakenly use key $K_{A,B}$ for a different communication partner than B as the name of entity B is contained in the message.
Through rules T1, T3 and P1 it can now be inferred that A knows the contents of the message: $A \ni (r_A, B, K_{A,B},$

$\{K_{A,B}, A\}_{K_{B,TTP}}$). In particular, using rule T2, A knows the session key: $A \ni K_{A,B}$.

With rule F1 it can also be inferred that A believes in the freshness of this message, i.e. $A \mid\equiv \#(r_A, B, K_{A,B}, \{K_{A,B}, A\}_{K_{B,TTP}})$.

Likewise, through rule R1 it is inferred that A believes in the recognisability of this message, i.e. $A \mid\equiv \phi(r_A, B, K_{A,B}, \{K_{A,B}, A\}_{K_{B,TTP}})$.

Through rule I1 it can now be concluded that A believes that trusted entity TTP created the message, thus $A \mid\equiv TTP \mid\sim (r_A, B, K_{A,B}, \{K_{A,B}, A\}_{K_{B,TTP}})$.

Using rule J2 we find that A believes that TTP considers the session key to be secret: $A \mid\equiv TTP \mid\equiv B \overset{K_{B,TTP}}{\longleftrightarrow} TTP$.

Therefore, through rule J1 it can be inferred that A also believes the session key is secret: $A \mid\equiv B \overset{K_{B,TTP}}{\longleftrightarrow} TTP$.

3. Regarding *Message 3* it should be noted that the extension $\leadsto TTP \mid\equiv A \overset{K_{A,B}}{\longleftrightarrow} B$ is inferred from the conditions and is therefore correct. With rules T1, T3 and P1 it can be inferred that B possesses the session key, i.e. $B \ni K_{A,B}$. *(B possesses the session key)*

At this juncture no other useful conclusions can be reached using the rules of GNY logic. The reason for this is that one cannot infer that B believes in the freshness of the message received from A. In fact, this message could also turn out to be a replay of a previously recorded message.

4. Through rules T1, T3 and P1, it can be concluded from *Message 4* that A knows random number r_B, thus $A \ni r_B$. However, other conclusions cannot be reached. The reason for this is that A is unable to recognise the contents of Message 4 because even without knowing key $K_{A,B}$ an attacker can send a ciphertext that when decrypted provides a bit pattern that could be interpreted by A as a random number. The attacker in this case would not know the random number assumed by A, but this would be unnecessary anyway at this point in the protocol. *(A possesses r_B)*

5. No further useful inferences can be made from *Message 5* for achieving the objectives of the protocol. This is because B has been unable to arrive at any beliefs about the session key $K_{A,B}$. *(B believes neither in the freshness nor in the secrecy of the session key)*

Overall this means that the protocol provides no useful new beliefs after the third message; therefore, Messages 4 and 5 can just as well be eliminated without causing any change to the result of a protocol run. A possesses the session key and believes in its secrecy, whereas B only possesses the session key but associates no further beliefs with it.

The introduction to GNY logic [GNY90] mentioned earlier also explains how the approach can be used to prove how the intended protocol objectives for a modified version of the Needham–Schroeder protocol can be achieved. For reasons of space we will not present these explanations because our primary aim in this section is to provide an initial idea of the formal analysis of cryptographic protocols.

7.9 Summary

Definition of cryptographic protocols

Cryptographic protocols are defined through a series of processing steps and message exchanges between multiple entities with the purpose of achieving a specific security objective. Numerous different cryptographic protocols are available for implementing diverse applications, with authentication and key management representing the most important applications for network security.

Categories

The cryptographic protocols for entity authentication can be divided into the two principal categories of *protocols with trusted entity* and *direct authentication protocols*.

Needham–Schroeder, Kerberos

Representatives of the first category include the insecure *Needham–Schroeder protocol*, the (secure) *Otway–Rees protocol* as well as the *Kerberos* authentication and authorisation system for workstation computer clusters.

X.509

The International Standard X.509 defines data formats and techniques for the certification of public keys and three modular direct authentication protocols that can be implemented with either asymmetric or symmetric cryptographic algorithms.

A low password entropy may form a significant problem

A frequent problem in the context of cryptographic protocols is the low entropy of passwords. This allows not only for an efficient retrieval of passwords from compromised password databases, but also for a systematic testing. Redress is provided by so-called PAKE schemes, which use asymmetric cryptography to exchange session keys and authenticate them using zero knowledge proofs. Patent issues led to a development of several of such protocols. This book particularly presented the EKE and SRP schemes.

Formal validation

Because the definition of secure cryptographic protocols has proven to be error-prone in the past, formal validation of new cryptographic protocols is highly advisable. A number of different approaches are available for this purpose, with logic-based approaches such as GNY logic proving to be particularly simple to use for detecting some classes of security flaws.

7.10   Supplemental Reading

[BM92]   BELLOVIN, S.; MERRITT, M.: Encrypted Key Exchange: Password-Based Protocols Secure Against Dictionary Attacks. In: *IEEE Computer Society Symposium on Research in Security and Privacy*, 1992, pp. 72–84

[Bry88]   BRYANT, R.: *Designing an Authentication System: A Dialogue in Four Scenes.* 1988. – Project Athena, Massachusetts Institute of Technology, Cambridge, USA

[GNY90]   GONG, L.; NEEDHAM, R. M.; YAHALOM, R.: Reasoning About Belief in Cryptographic Protocols. In: *Symposium on Research in Security and Privacy* IEEE Computer Society, IEEE Computer Society Press, May 1990, pp. 234–248

[KNT94]   KOHL, J.; NEUMAN, B.; TS'O, T.: The Evolution of the Kerberos Authentication Service. In: BRAZIER, F.; JOHANSEN, D. (Eds): *Distributed Open Systems*, IEEE Computer Society Press, 1994

[NS78]   NEEDHAM, R. M.; SCHROEDER, M. D.: Using Encryption for Authentication in Large Networks of Computers. In: *Communications of the ACM 21*, December 1978, No. 12, pp. 993–999

[NS87]   NEEDHAM, R.; SCHROEDER, M.: Authentication Revisited. In: *Operating Systems Review 21*, 1987

[OR87]   OTWAY, D.; REES, O.: Efficient and Timely Mutual Authentication. In: *Operating Systems Review 21*, 1987

[Pat97]   PATEL, S.: Number Theoretic Attacks On Secure Password Schemes. In: *IEEE Symposium on Security and Privacy*, 1997, S. 236–247
           Interesting cryptanalytic considerations to EKE.

[Sti09]   STINSON, D. R.: *Cryptography: Theory and Practice (Discrete Mathematics and Its Applications).* CRC Press, 2006
           Sections 9 to 12 contain substantial elucidations about numerous cryptographic protocols.

7.11   Questions

1. Does it make sense to talk about message integrity without also considering data origin authentication? What is the opposite situation?

2. Why is merely exchanging authentic messages not sufficient for implementing entity authentication?

3. Must a trusted entity always be directly incorporated into a cryptographic protocol?

4. Name the typical tasks of a trusted entity and list as many examples of protocols as possible where a trusted entity is either directly or indirectly involved.

5. Which problems need to be expected if RC4 was used in conjunction with the Needham–Schroeder protocol? Discuss the integrity check of the last message.

6. Explain why Kerberos makes a distinction between ticket-granting and service-granting tickets.

7. Why does Kerberos Version 5 require synchronised clocks, even though sequence numbers were introduced?

8. What are the complexity requirements of passwords in a Kerberos domain?

9. Why are certificates only valid for a limited period of time?

10. Can you execute an authentication test completely 'offline' on the basis of certified keys?

11. Why are two message exchanges not sufficient for mutual authentication without synchronised clocks?

12. Can the property of Perfect Forward Secrecy be guaranteed with a session key exchange based on RSA encryption? Would this be possible with ElGamal encryption?

13. List the typical objectives of an authentication protocol with integrated key negotiation.

14. What makes dictionary attacks a significant problem?

15. Give three reasons why choosing $p = 193$ would lead to security issues in DH-EKE.

16. Discuss why DH-EKE cannot easily be used with elliptic curves.

17. Which mathematical requirement prohibits the usage of SRP with elliptic curves?

8 Secure Group Communication*

The protocols and methods described in the previous chapter are used to protect the communication between two end points. However, in many cases data has to be sent to several recipients simultaneously. This form of communication poses certain challenges, which in almost all cases can be broken down to two factors:

- Because groups may be large, even the process of agreeing on a key involves significant effort, resulting in potential *scalability problems*.
- *Symmetric message authentication values are only of limited benefit*, since the key must be known to a larger group, which means that it is no longer possible to distinguish between 'originator' and 'verifiers' of message authentication values without additional measures.

In the context of this complex topic, a wide range of protocols for protecting group communication processes have been developed [HD03, RH03, ZRM05]. This chapter will first examine some specific requirements for such processes before describing special methods for protecting confidentiality and source authentication.

8.1 Specific Requirements for Secure Group Communication

Depending on the number of sources, in broadcast or multicast systems a distinction can be made between *individual* and *multi-source scenarios*. The former are generally used for video

Individual and multi-source scenarios

---

and audio streaming, for example, while video conferences and file-sharing services usually involve several actors as senders. This has significant consequences for the architecture of systems for *group key management (GKM)*. Whilst for individual sources it may be acceptable to organise the GKM centrally, for distributed senders such a limitation is not acceptable in many cases for reasons of availability.

Non-functional requirements   In any case, a method for securing group communication should be able to forward data for upper network layers transparently, introduce only little additional latency, and only use few computing, memory and network resources for management tasks.

Security goals in group communication   With regard to the five general security goals (Definition 1.2), in some group communication situations a distinction can be made between further subgoals:

- **Confidentiality:** No member joining a group should be able to decrypt previously exchanged messages (*backward secrecy*). At the same time no member that has left the group should be able to decrypt traffic that is subsequently exchanged within the group (*forward secrecy*). This is also the reason why key independence and perfect forward secrecy is stipulated in some cases. The latter was introduced in Section 7.6. If key independence is ensured, the keys used do not build on each other, so that not only former group members, but also external attackers, who may have compromised individual keys in the past, are excluded from the system. An additional requirement may be traceabilty for each group member that has contributed keying material to the session key.

- **Accountability:** Depending on the security level required, it may be sufficient to verify that messages were sent by a group member. However, it is advisable to carry out *source authentication* in individual source scenarios or in cases where individual devices may have been compromised.

- **Controlled access:** Both sending and receiving of group packets should only be possible for legitimised devices otherwise there is a risk of availability problems because the group communication scheme reaches a high number recipients when individual messages are sent.

- **Availability:** Protection of the group communication should not result in additional exposed points of failure, such as key servers. In addition, in many cases there is a requirement for *graceful degradation*, which means that, in the event of one or more components being compromised, the security procedure should continue to function, albeit in weakened form.

8.2 Negotiation of Group Keys

In the simplest case confidential communication within a group can
be ensured by means of asymmetric cryptography. To this end the n
members of the group publish their public keys $+K_1, \ldots, +K_n$, and
a member m_i of the group sends a message m to the members as
follows:

A simple encryption scheme with high effort

$$m_i \rightarrow * : \ (\{K\}_{+K_1}, \ \ldots \ \{K\}_{+K_{i-1}}, \{K\}_{+K_{i+1}}, \ \ldots \ \{K\}_{+K_n}, \{m\}_K)$$

It means that the content of each message is secured through a
temporary symmetric key K, which itself is transmitted securely
through the individual public keys. The method is secure, although
it involves very high effort, even for very small groups and small
quantities of transferred data, both in terms of computing and network resources.

For this reason GKM methods usually negotiate symmetric
group keys, in order to ensure confidentiality. Usually a distinction
is made between two different keys: The so-called *traffic encryption key* (TEK) is used to encrypt the user data, the so-called *key
encryption key* (KEK) is used to secure the GKM and therefore also
the exchanged TEKs.

Solution: application of symmetric group keys

In the simplest case, centralised methods can be used for key
distribution. For reasons of scalability and availability, several
servers can be used, thereby decentralising key management. A
distributed management approach may be used in conferencing applications, for example, when participant numbers are usually limited, and so a group key can be agreed by contributions from each
participant. Representative methods for each of these strategies are
presented below.

Centralised, decentral- ised and distributed GKM

8.2.1 Centralised Key Management

In the simplest case, group keys are distributed via pairwise
communication relationships between the group members and
a single central key server, the so-called *Group Controller* (GC).
An example for such a protocol is the Group Key Management
Protocol (GKMP) [HM97b, HM97a], which was standardised by
the IETF. The protocol requires sending and receiving group
members to register at a central GC, which issues a shared key
to all authorised group members and in addition initiates regular
key changes. A disadvantage of this simple method is the poor
scalability, particularly if forward and backward secrecy are
required. Although keys can be changed through an individual

Pairwise key with a Group Controller

group message if new members join the group, the situation is different when individual members leave the group. Then the remaining group members have to each be issued with a new key to maintain forward secrecy. Each size reduction of a group with n members therefore necessitates $\mathcal{O}(n)$ encryptions and messages.

Use of Secure Locks An option for reducing the communication effort was suggested in [CC89]. In this case the central GC uses the Chinese remainder theorem (see Section 4.2) in order to enable the redistribution of keys through an individual packet. As a preparatory measure, on joining the group, each member m_i is assigned a number N_i. These numbers are relatively prime to each other, that is $ggT(N_i, N_j) = 1 \Leftrightarrow i \neq j$. To distribute a new key K, GC first encrypts it with the keys of the members. The result is the tuple $(\{K\}_{K_1}, \ldots, \{K\}_{K_n})$, which can be used to solve the following system of equations, based on the Chinese remainder theorem:

$$L \equiv \{K\}_{K_1} \pmod{N_1}$$
$$L \equiv \{K\}_{K_2} \pmod{N_2}$$
$$\cdots$$
$$L \equiv \{K\}_{K_n} \pmod{N_n}$$

GC sends the value L to all group members in a message that contains the shared key K, based on calculation of $D(K_i, L \bmod N_i)$. However, despite the coding this approach does not resolve the scalability problem: $\mathcal{O}(n)$ encryptions are still required, the calculation based on the Chinese remainder theorem becomes more complex with increasing group size and the size of L also grows.

Logical Key Hierarchy In order to make the distribution of new keys for excluding group members more efficient, a number of tree-based methods were developed at the end of the 1990s. The best-known among these methods is the *Logical Key Hierarchy* (LKH) [HH99, WHA99]. The core idea of the LKH is to allocate the n group members not one or two keys, but $\log_2 n$ keys, which are in hierarchical order relative to one another. Commonly a balanced binary tree is assumed, whereby the method neither requires strict balancing nor is it limited to two child nodes, but the required efforts change accordingly. Based on this hierarchy, in an average case the logarithmic number of keys is changed with only logarithmic effort when a group member is removed or added.

Operating principle of LKH based on an example Figure 8.1 shows an example hierarchy for seven group members $m_0, \ldots, m_6$. The members have individually shared keys with the GC, which represent the leaf nodes $K_0, \ldots, K_6$. In addition they know all keys on the path between their individual key and the

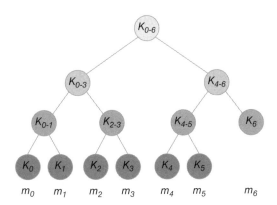

Figure 8.1

Example of a Logical Key Hierarchy for seven group members

root node, which is known to all group members. If a new member m_7 were to join the group, instead of K_6 a new subtree with the keys K_{6-7}, K_6 and K_7 is added. In addition, the key K_{4-6} is replaced with a new key K_{4-7}, and analogously K_{0-6} with K_{0-7}. In order to notify the group members, only three different subgroups $((m_0, \ldots, m_3), (m_4, m_5), (m_6))$ have to be supplied with different key material. Provided network multicast is available and the group are not unreasonably large, this can be done with a single group message, for example by transferring

$$GC \to *: \quad (m_7 \text{ added}, Seq\#, \{K_{0\text{-}7}\}_{K_{0\text{-}6}},$$

$$\{K_{4\text{-}7}\}_{K_{4\text{-}6}}, \{K_{6\text{-}7}\}_{K_6}, \{K_{6\text{-}7}\}_{K_7}, Sig)$$

with a digital signature Sig and sequence number $Seq\#$. Similarly, group members can be excluded.

Although LKH and similar methods can significantly improve the scalability problems of secure group communication processes, some fundamental problems of central methods remain:

Disadvantages of central GKM methods

- If forward secrecy and backward secrecy need to be assured, all other group members have to receive a new symmetric group key within a short space of time. For large groups this results in significant overhead, which can only be managed through periodic key changes, i.e. a weakened form of forward and backward secrecy.
- The GC always represents an exposed point for attackers, so that availability is difficult to guarantee. Some systems resolve this problem through redundant GCs, in which case there is the problem of secure synchronisation between the GCs.

■ The GC must be absolutely trustworthy. If the GC were to be compromised, it is impossible to restore secure group communication without external manual intervention, thus these approaches do not meet the graceful degradation property.

8.2.2   Decentralised Key Management

The disadvantages referred to above can only be eliminated if several physically separate instances carry out an independent GKM for different subgroups. Such methods are referred to as decentralised methods, since no individual single point of failure has to exist, and the subgroups can tolerate the failure of another subgroup.

Iolus as an example for decentralised GKM

Perhaps best-known method with such properties is *Iolus* [Mit97]. It involves the introduction of so-called *Group Security Intermediaries* (GSIs), which take on the role of the central GC for their respective subgroups and are located at physical network transition points. Ideally these GSI processes would work on the gateways of the networks that supply them with multicast. Iolus stipulates that the GSIs form a tree structure, including a special root node. This so-called *Group Security Controller* (GSC) serves as GC for the GSIs of the first level and ensures that all GSIs of this level have a shared group key. An example scenario for an Iolus infrastructure is shown in Figure 8.2. A server distributes data which is initially sent to the corresponding GSI 4 for so-called 'GSA assisted multicasting'. GSA stands for *Group Security Agent* and is a collective term for GSI and GSC. GSI 4 then transfers the data

Figure 8.2
Iolus scenario with GSI on two hierarchy levels

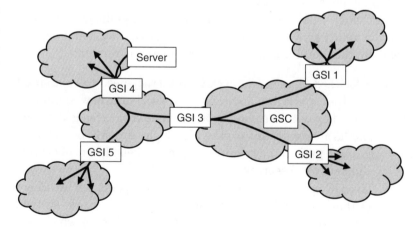

in encrypted form to the directly adjacent GSI 3 and GSI 5, with which it shares a group key, specified by GSI 3. GSI 3 transfers the received data to the remaining GSI 1 and GSI 2, using the group key distributed by the GSC. This process is referred to as re-encryption. In order to avoid the process becoming too computationally intens- *Re-encryption of the* ive, the developers of Iolus suggest securing each packet by a new *data packets* symmetric key and transferring that key securely with the respect- ive group key. The effort is thus limited to re-encryption of the key.

Thanks to the decentralised architecture, the effects of a GSI *Advantages compared* failure in Iolus are limited to the corresponding subnets. Also, *with centralistic* adding and removing of individual members only results in key *approaches* changes within the subgroups managed by the GSI. The GSI them- selves should be comparatively static, so that the load in the GSC should be low. The downside is that naturally the GSC represents a further exposed point. One way to avoid this is for the GSI to oper- ate another GKM among them that does not require a server. Such GKM types are described in more detail in the next section.

8.2.3 Distributed Key Management

In the simplest form of distributed key negotiation the group mem- bers elect a coordinator and agree on a member, who then serves as GC and deals with the distribution of group keys.

A more elegant and also potentially more robust option involves extending the Diffie–Hellman key exchange described in Section 4.5 for groups. In addition to ensuring perfect forward secrecy, this approach has the safety-related advantage that each group member can verify that it has contributed to the shared key. The method is therefore referred to as *contributory key exchange*.

Group Diffie–Hellman

A number of options exist for group-based implementation of the *Diffie–Hellman for* Diffie–Hellman exchange. A comparatively comprehensible and *group keys can be* also – relatively – efficient method is described in [STW00] under *implemented in* the name IKA.2. The aim of this protocol is for the group members *various ways* $m_0, \ldots, m_n$ to calculate a shared secret $g^{s_0 s_1 \cdots s_n} \bmod p$, whereby $s_0, \ldots, s_n$ are the respective secret values of the group members.

The protocol assumes a total order among the group members *Example of a Diffie–* and has four phases. In the first phase, referred to as *upflow*, *Hellman protocol for* member m_0 initiates the method and members $m_0, \ldots, m_{n-1}$ *groups* accumulate $g^{s_0 s_1 \cdots s_{n-1}} \bmod p$:

$$m_0 \rightarrow m_1: \ (g^{s_0} \bmod p)$$
$$m_1 \rightarrow m_2: \ (g^{s_0 s_1} \bmod p)$$
$$\vdots$$
$$m_{n-2} \rightarrow m_{n-1}: \ (g^{s_0 s_1 \cdots s_{n-2}} \bmod p)$$

m_{n-1} then announces the result to all other members in a *broadcast* phase:

$$m_{n-1} \rightarrow m_*: \ (g^{s_0 s_1 \cdots s_{n-1}} \bmod p)$$

In the third phase, referred to as *response*, the individual members send member m_n the previous result after computationally eliminating their own secret by using the inverse, which can easily be found via the extended Euclidean algorithm:

$$m_0 \rightarrow m_n: \ (g^{s_1 s_2 \cdots s_{n-1}} \bmod p)$$
$$m_1 \rightarrow m_n: \ (g^{s_0 s_2 \cdots s_{n-1}} \bmod p)$$
$$\vdots$$
$$m_{n-1} \rightarrow m_n: \ (g^{s_0 s_1 \cdots s_{n-2}} \bmod p)$$

Member m_n now contributes its own secret s_n to the individual results and responds to each member in a last *broadcast* phase:

$$m_n \rightarrow m_0: \ (g^{s_1 s_2 \cdots s_{n-1} s_n} \bmod p)$$
$$m_n \rightarrow m_1: \ (g^{s_0 s_2 \cdots s_{n-1} s_n} \bmod p)$$
$$\vdots$$
$$m_n \rightarrow m_{n-1}: \ (g^{s_0 s_1 \cdots s_{n-2} s_n} \bmod p)$$

Each member can then calculate the shared key $g^{s_0 s_1 \cdots s_n} \bmod p$, without anyone needing to transmit it directly.

Joining of new members   An interesting feature of the protocol is a 'trick' that enables a new member m_{n+1} to be added quickly. To this end member m_n initiates a renegotiation, which starts directly in the second phase. At this point the old value $g^{s_0 s_1 \cdots s_n} \bmod p$ must not be transmitted, since it was already used as key. m_n therefore chooses an additional new secret s_n' and starts the second phase by sending:

$$m_n \rightarrow m_*: \ (g^{s_0 s_1 \cdots s_{n-1} s_n s_n'} \bmod p)$$

If a member leaves the group, the same 'trick' can be used. A distinction is made between two cases: If the member with the highest index m_n is to be removed, the protocol starts in phase 2 again, initiated by member m_{n-1}. Here too the transmitted value must be modified through an additional secret s'_{n-1}, so that the following message is sent:

Removing members

$$m_{n-1} \rightarrow m_* : \quad (g^{s_0 s_1 \cdots s_{n-1} s'_{n-1}} \bmod p)$$

If another member m_d with $d \neq n$ is to be removed, m_n becomes active and adds a further secret s'_n to the messages received in phase 3. It is sent to all group members except m_d. Since m_d does not receive the value without its secret, the member is unable to calculate the new key $g^{s_0 s_1 \cdots s_{n-1} s_n s'_n} \bmod p$. The fact that the value s_d is still part of the new key is therefore irrelevant.

    If the values g, p and $s_0, \ldots, s_n$ selected are large enough, it can be assumed that the presented group-based Diffie–Hellman method – similar to the original method – is secure with regard to passive attacks, as long as the discrete logarithm cannot be calculated efficiently. However, the exchanged messages must be authenticated in order to prevent active attacks. A significant disadvantage is the considerable communication and computational overhead, which increases linearly with the group size.

Properties of the Group Diffie–Hellman

Tree-Based Group Diffie–Hellman

In order to increase the efficiency of the calculation, a method referred to as *Tree-Based Group Diffie–Hellman (TGDH)*, in which members establish a tree structure based on the keys, was published in [KPT04]. As in the LKH method described above, here too the root represents the shared group key, and each group member knows the keys on the path from a corresponding leaf node to the root node. However, in contrast to LKH, TGDH uses only binary trees. In addition, the keys for the individual levels are not independent of each other, but are calculated from the keys of the two respective child nodes. For each key of an inner node $K = g^{K_l K_r} \bmod p$ applies, where K_l and K_r are the keys of the left and right child node. The keys of the leaf nodes are the respective secrets s_i of the individual members. Figure 8.3 shows an example hierarchy for the keys of a scenario with seven group members.

TGDH establishes a key hierarchy in order to increase the efficiency

    In contrast to LKH, TGDH is a distributed method, that is, there is no central GC. Instead, each participant knows the tree structure, all keys from their own leaf node to the root and the corresponding so-called *blinded keys* for all keys. This concealment

Distributed provision of the key hierarchy

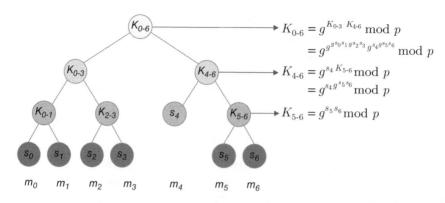

$$K_{0\text{-}6} = g^{K_{0\text{-}3}\ K_{4\text{-}6}} \bmod p$$
$$= g^{g^{g^{s_0 s_1} g^{s_2 s_3}} g^{s_4 g^{s_5 s_6}}} \bmod p$$

$$K_{4\text{-}6} = g^{s_4\ K_{5\text{-}6}} \bmod p$$
$$= g^{s_4 g^{s_5 s_6}} \bmod p$$

$$K_{5\text{-}6} = g^{s_5 s_6} \bmod p$$

Figure 8.3

Example of a TGDH key hierarchy

represents an exponentiation with base g, that is, the concealed key BK that corresponds to key K is $g^K \bmod p$. Because of the presumption that the discrete logarithm is difficult to calculate, the concealed keys can be known to all participants.

The hierarchy is configured iteratively, that is, the participants add themselves one by one. To this end the joining node m_{n+1} first sends a message to all participants, which contains its concealed key BK_{n+1}:

$$m_{n+1} \rightarrow m_* : \quad (g^{s_{n+1}} \bmod p)$$

Joining of nodes

All other participants can now calculate the optimum insertion position in order to keep the key tree as balanced as possible. The construction rule means that in each case an existing participant has to give up its position and form a new node with the new participant. This existing participant then takes on additional tasks and is therefore referred to as the *sponsor* in the literature. In the example hierarchy this sponsor would be m_4, resulting in a fully balanced tree. Using BK_{n+1} and its own key s_i, the sponsor m_i can now calculate the newly created inner key $g^{s_{n+1} s_i} \bmod p$. In the same way it can calculate the new keys for the higher levels from a key and a concealed key. The result of these calculations is saved, and the respective keys are concealed through additional exponentiation. These new concealed keys are now announced to the group, thereby completing the insertion process:

$$m_i \rightarrow m_* : \quad \left(g^{g^{s_{n+1} s_0}} \bmod p \ldots \right)$$

In the simplest case – with two participants – this procedure corresponds exactly to the calculation of the Diffie–Hellman secret for two parties.

Removing group member

The procedure for removing group members is similar. A distinction has to be made between two cases. In the simpler case the sibling node of the leaf to be removed is also a leaf node. In this case the inner node linking the nodes is deleted, and the remaining leaf is raised one level. The corresponding group member becomes the sponsor, calculates all new keys up to the root and notifies the other nodes. If the sibling node contains a whole subtree, the participant whose leaf node is furthest to the right becomes the sponsor. In addition to the leaf node to be removed, it also removes the directly connected inner node, so that the whole subtree is raised one level. If, for example, in the scenario shown in Figure 8.3 member m_4 were to leave the group, m_6 would become the sponsor and remove nodes s_4 and $K_{4\text{-}6}$.

Overall TGDH is significantly more efficient than the GDH method described above. In particular, the number of exponentiations that have to be carried out when members join or leave a group is limited to logarithmic values. However, it is nonetheless unsuitable for implementation with large groups since, on the one hand, the communication effort is too great, and on the other hand the protocol described here is insufficiently robust against simultaneous failures and transients errors. More robust options are described in [BBM09], for instance. Still, it has been shown that Diffie–Hellman-based protocols are suitable for negotiating keys in small or relatively static groups, without using exposed GC.

Properties of TGDH

8.3   Source Authentication

The previous sections focused on protecting confidentiality during group communication. Secure communication requires additional keys for authentication. In the simplest case a symmetric group key is used, which is generated in a similar way to the key for the protecting confidentiality. However, in this case a message authentication value can only be used to verify that a message was sent by a group member. In contrast to pairwise keys it is no longer possible to distinguish individual instances. During transmission of a media stream for a TV programme, for example, it may be expedient to differentiate between legitimate senders and receivers. In this case the term *source authentication* is used.

Use of symmetric group keys for authentication

In the simplest case source authentication can be realised through application of asymmetric cryptography, if each message is digitally signed by the sender. This signature is then checked by the receivers. However, this 'naïve' method requires enormous effort in terms of both calculations and the requisite bandwidth. Although for both aspects the effort can be limited by using elliptic

A naïve method

curve cryptography, there is still room for improvement. In the following sections we give examples of methods which limit the effort for asymmetric cryptography or do not use asymmetric cryptography at all. Instead they differentiate senders and receivers by other means.

8.3.1   Block-by-block Authentication

Naïve block-by-block authentication

One possible approach for saving computing time and bandwidth for asymmetric cryptography is to consolidate several messages to a block and sign them simultaneously. The authentication takes place analogously, as soon as all messages and the signature have been received. However, in packet-oriented networks such as the Internet, this has a serious disadvantage: if individual messages are lost, it is not possible to restore the whole block. This can lead to significant issues depending on which transport or application protocol is used.

Block authentication with erasure codes

A more complex method is therefore proposed in [PM03], which uses so-called *erasure codes* to restore lost packets. For the purpose of this discussion, the precise functionality of erasure codes is irrelevant. Suffice it to say that the transferred data volume is slightly increased, due to the coding, but it benefits from full restoration of the information, in the event of some transmission losses.

Figure 8.4
Block diagram showing block-by-block authentication according to [PM03]

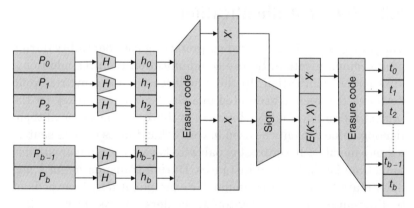

Figure 8.4 shows a schematic diagram of the sequence in the sender. First the message blocks $P_0, \ldots, P_b$ are compressed through a cryptographic hash function H, and any existing structure information is destroyed. Then the resulting values $h_0, \ldots, h_b$ are concatenated and protected with an erasure code, where two values X and X' are calculated. The first value is identical to the input when an erasure

code is used. The second value X' contains the actual redundancy information. Therefore, since the value X represents the hash values of the plaintexts, signing it with $E(K^-, X)$ is then sufficient to authenticate the plaintexts securely. In addition to the signature, the value X' has to be transferred to the receivers. This ensures that authentication can take place, even if some plaintexts are lost and X is incomplete on the receiver side. However, additional data cannot be transmitted through new packets, since these may also be lost, in which case the whole block would have to be discarded. The additional information is therefore split into b smaller parts, so-called *tags*, which are appended to the packets. It is also protected by an erasure code, to enable restoration of the signature and X' in the event of a packet loss.

At the receiver end the sequence is basically reversed: the signature and the redundancy information X' are calculated from the received tags. At the same time the hash values of the received plaintexts can be determined, and X' can be used to reconstruct the hash values of any lost messages. The signature is then checked, and the messages can be delivered to the higher layers.

The method thus limits the computational effort and the transmission effort compared with individual signatures. At the same time, the method can cope with the loss of some messages without having to discard the whole block. However, two problems remain with block-by-block authentication. On the one hand, data has to be buffered both in the sender and in the receiver, resulting in possibly significant delays. On the other hand, attackers could significantly disrupt the method with forged packets, since individual invalid tags mean that the whole block would have to be discarded.

The more efficient method requires buffering of the data

8.3.2   Combinatorial Selection of Symmetric MACs

As already indicated, symmetric MACs can be used as an alternative for source authentication. However, in this case the asymmetric knowledge has to be generated by other means, for example where each group participant can only check part of the message authentication value.

In [CGI$^+$99] calculating a range of conventional, symmetric message authentication values was suggested with independent keys for each message, 760 being used as an example. The first bit of the respective message authentication values is appended to the message, so that the length of the resulting MAC is 760 bits. Each group participant now checks the part of the MAC for which they have keys. In the original description, each participant is assumed

Construction of a MAC from many conventional message authentication values

to know around $1/10$ of the key space, thus affording adequate protection against simply guessing a valid combination (average effort 2^{75}). If an attacker controls one or several group members, they are able to learn more about the key space and can reduce the average guessing effort accordingly. The effort for the attacker and the legitimate users can be controlled via the MAC length and the proportion of keys known to each node. It is also possible to configure the key space so that a certain minimum number of group members would have to be compromised to be able to send invalid messages to a certain participant [CPS03].

Compared with block-by-block authentication this method does not result in significant delays, and attackers cannot use it to discard legitimate messages. Compared with individual signing based on conventional asymmetric cryptography (RSA and ElGamal), it generates shorter signatures and saves computing resources in the source. However, an expedient choice of the public exponent (for example 65,537) makes verification of RSA signatures faster than combinatorial MACs, without causing security issues in the event of compromised group members. The method is therefore only sensible in small groups, since the benefit is further reduced, compared to cryptography with elliptic curves, and also because in larger scenarios internal attackers can significantly increase their chances of convincing a group participant by compromising some nodes.

8.3.3   TESLA

Basic idea: knowledge asymmetry through subsequent disclosure of the key

Another option for realising a knowledge asymmetry is used by the protocol for Timed Efficient Stream Loss-tolerant Authentication (TESLA) [PSC+05]. In this protocol the source furnishes messages with a conventional, symmetric MAC, although the keys used for the process are not disclosed until later – by which time they may no longer be used for issuing new MACs. Figure 8.5 shows the basic approach. The time is divided into periods of identical length, and within each period the source uses a key for calculating symmetric message authentication values. The source discloses the key it used after δ time steps, and buffered messages are then checked in the receivers.

Use of hash chains

In reality the approach is somewhat more complex, in order to enable authentication of the published keys themselves. To this end the sender initially chooses a natural number n and a random key K_n. In real systems n could be 10^6, for example. The sender then uses a cryptographic hash function H to calculate the key

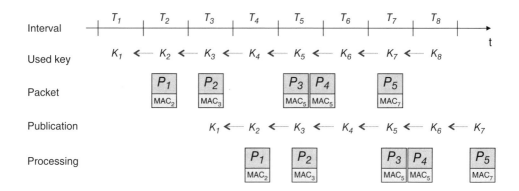

Figure 8.5
Time sequence of authentication with TESLA

K_0 through n times recursive insertion in $K_{i-1} = H(K_i)$. The key K_0 is then transmitted to all receivers in an authentic manner, for example by using a conventional digital signature and saving the value permanently in the devices or through pairwise protection and transmission (μTESLA, [PST$^+$02]). The method starts at time step T_1, when the sender uses the key K_1. If δ is 2, for example, at time T_3 the key K_1 is published through a broadcast without further protection. The recipients now check whether the key is authentic by checking $H(K_1) = K_0$. The data packets held in the buffer are then checked and delivered, as required. If the disclosure message fails to reach all recipients, then all they have to do to re-synchronise themselves is to use the hash function twice at the time of the next publication.

On account of its low computing and transmission effort, TESLA is particularly useful in scenarios where large data quantities are sent continuously. However, this method inherently also leads to a non-negligible processing delay. In addition, a more or less loose time synchronisation is required. Depending on the application scenario this may be relatively difficult to achieve if attackers can delay messages selectively.

8.4 Summary

In this chapter we have described some aspects of group security and provided a short introduction to this rather complex topic. This complexity is due to the group sizes, which make key management difficult simply for scalability and efficiency reasons. On the other hand, the associated frequent fluctuations are problematic if *backward* and *forward secrecy* are required.

Challenges of safe group communication

The fact that the requirements are difficult to meet has led to a wide range of solutions for negotiating symmetric group keys.

Negotiation of symmetric group keys

Particularly noteworthy are the centralised, simple *Group Key Management Protocol* (GKMP) and also the centrally organised *Logical Key Hierarchy* (LKH), although the latter achieves significantly better scaling. Since central *group controllers* always represent potential points of failure, decentralised methods such as Iolus may be more suitable for large groups. Fully distributed methods, such as the *GDH* or *TGDH* methods presented in this chapter, also have no exposed instances. However, due to their high calculation and communication effort they are only suitable to a limited extent for large groups or scenarios with high participant dynamics.

Efficient source authentication

In addition to confidentiality, we also discussed the issue of securing the message authentication for individual sources. Since simple signing of each message with asymmetric methods is generally too complex, a range of possible alternatives has been developed. However, these alternatives have various disadvantages and they lead to considerable delays for *block-by-block authentication* and also *TESLA*. Selective verification of combinatorial message authentication values (see Section 8.3.2) offers hardly any benefits yet leads to poorer security if the attacker controls several participants.

On the whole, there is no satisfactory, generally applicable solution for secure group communication. Each individual method has to be adapted to the specific application scenario and the security requirements.

8.5 Supplemental Reading

[HD03]   HARDJONO, T.; DONDETI, L. R.: *Multicast and Group Security*. Artech House, 2003
[RH03]   RAFAELI, S.; HUTCHISON, D.: A Survey of Key Management for Secure Group Communication. In: *ACM Computing Surveys* 35 (2003), No. 3, pp. 309–329
[ZRM05]   ZOU, X.; RAMAMURTHY, B.; MAGLIVERAS, S.: *Secure Group Communications Over Data Networks*. Springer, 2005

8.6 Questions

1.   What are the differences between groups and individual communication with regard to security?

2. List the advantages and disadvantages of using a binary tree instead of a tree with any number of child nodes per inner node for LKH.
3. What are the problems with Iolus with regard to scalability?
4. Is there a possibility that the key trees are not balanced in the TGDH protocol presented in this chapter? If yes, how?
5. How high is the computational effort for the sponsor and for all other participants associated with addition to a TGDH group?
6. In scenarios where unicast packets are to be secured with group keys, what effect does simple block authentication have on the network layer, which signs and authenticates 100 IP packets at a time, and on the effectiveness of the TCP acting in the transport layer above?
7. Consider a scenario where a combinatorial MAC is to be formed, and for each participant a guaranteed security level of 96 bits is to be offered, even in a situation where any number of other nodes are compromised. What is the maximum number of participants for which this symmetric method offers an advantage with regard to the bandwidth compared with 2048-bit long RSA signatures?
8. Why is a high fluctuation of the delay times in the network problematic for TESLA?

9 Access Control

Previous chapters have dealt with a range of algorithms and schemes that all play a specific part in guaranteeing that data and resources in information-processing systems are protected against unauthorised eavesdropping, and are available to legitimate users. Important prerequisites include that the entities of a system can be clearly and securely identified, that data is protected against eavesdropping and modification by cryptographic schemes, and that events that have taken place can subsequently be proven to third parties.

This chapter expands on the issue of how decisions are made and implemented in a system in order to determine which entities are authorised access to certain services and information. We start by introducing some central terms and concepts. The section that follows provides an explanation of 'security labels' that are integrated in some classic multi-user operating systems. The next section addresses the specification of access control guidelines. The chapter concludes with a general overview of the basic categories of access control mechanisms.

9.1 Definition of Terms and Concepts

Definition 9.1 *The term* **access control** *describes the process of mediation between the requests of the* **subjects** *of a system to perform certain* **actions** *on specific* **objects***. The main task of access control is to decide, based on a defined* **security policy***, whether or not a specific access can be permitted and to enforce this decision.*

Access control

Figure 9.1

The concept of a
reference monitor

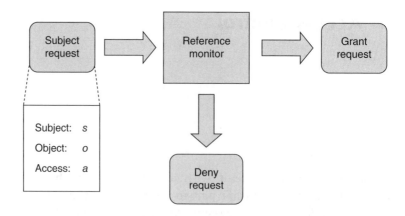

The concept of the *reference monitor*, illustrated in Figure 9.1, is a central model of access control. A reference monitor is an imaginary entity within a system. All access requests are directed to the reference monitor for verification and, based on the security policies *A reference monitor* defined in the system, it decides whether access should be permit-*is often only a* ted. In real systems this concept is normally not implemented as a *conceptual entity* special system entity and the functionality of the reference monitor is distributed over a number of system functions. It is, therefore, often more a conceptual rather than an actual entity.

Security policy   **Definition 9.2** *The* **security policy** *of a system defines the conditions under which access requests by subjects that want to access specific objects by performing certain actions on them are mediated and enforced by the reference monitor functionality of a system.*

The term 'security policy' is often also interpreted in a wider sense that encompasses all security aspects of a system, including threats, risks, security objectives, possible countermeasures, etc. *Access control policy* In this book we sometimes use the wording *access control policy* when we want to clarify that a security policy primarily refers to the definition of access rights.

The definitions introduced to this point are normally given in the context of the security of computers and operating systems. In this connection subjects and objects are defined as follows:

Subject, object   **Definition 9.3** *A* **subject** *is an active entity that can initiate requests in order to access certain resources and then uses these resources to complete specific tasks. An* **object** *is a passive repository used to store information.*

Examples of objects based on this definition include files, directories, etc., whereas subjects are realised through processes in the
sense of operating systems.

However, in the context of communication systems it is not al-   *Relationship*
ways easy to make a clean separation between subjects and objects.   *to communica-*
For instance, when an entity sends a message to another entity, it   *tion systems*
is not necessarily clear whether the receiving entity should be considered as an object or a subject.

Furthermore, an understanding is needed in this context about   *Type of access*
what 'access' is in a communication system, and what types of
access exist. In classic operating system tutorials a distinction is
made between the access types 'read', 'write' and 'execute,' whereas
in the context of object-oriented programming each method offered
by an object interface is defined as its own access type.

For example, an initial naïve approach would be to define the
two access types 'send' and 'receive' for communication systems. As
we will see in Chapter 21, intermediate systems only transmit data
streams and so this distinction proves to be of little help when implementing an access control policy for networks. In fact, communication flows in networks are usually symmetric.

9.2 Security Labels

We have seen that a direct transfer of access control concepts from
operating systems to communication systems is not always obvious.
Nevertheless, we will discuss these concepts further in this chapter
because some of them have found acceptance, in one form or another, in the implementation of access control in communication
networks. This section therefore introduces the concept of *security
labels*.

Definition 9.4 *A **security level** is defined as an hierarchical at-*   *Security level*
tribute that indicates the level of sensitivity of the subjects and ob-
jects of a system.

The term 'hierarchical attribute' is often used to express that the
level in each case can be brought into a strict order ('<'). An example of security levels in the military is the categorisation of information as 'unclassified' < 'confidential' < 'secret' < 'top secret'.
The commercial sector tends to use the labels 'public' < 'sensitive'
< 'proprietary' < 'restricted'. There is no major difference between
them, as what is essential in both classifications is the strict order
that exists regardless of the respective names given to the levels.

Security category   **Definition 9.5** *A **security category** is a non-hierarchical group-*
ing of subjects or objects that simplifies the process of indicating the
level of their sensitivity.

Security categories combine subjects or objects that are awarded
the same access capabilities. This leads to the use of the 'need to
'Need to know'   know' principle, which requires that an entity should only access
principle   the information it needs to complete its tasks. In the military, for
example, a general in the army is not necessarily able to access
confidential information from the air force, even if he is authorised
to access information classified as 'top secret' for the armed forces.
An example from the commercial sector would be the separation of
an organisation's important information into diverse product areas
and management.

Security label   **Definition 9.6** *A **security label** is an attribute that is associated*
with the entities (subjects, objects) that exist in a system and indic-
ates their hierarchical level of sensitivity and their security category.
Formally this is expressed as follows:

$$Labels = Levels \times \mathcal{P}(Categories)$$

Here $\mathcal{P}(S)$ refers to the *powerset* of the set S, that is, the set of all
subsets of S.

Binary relations on the set of security labels constitute an important concept for specifying security policies based on security
labels. A binary relation on a quantity S is a subset of the cross
Dominates relation   product $S \times S$. An example is the *dominates relation* that enables a
comparison between two security labels:

$$Dominates : Labels \times Labels$$

$$Dominates = \{(b_1, b_2) \mid b_1, b_2 \in Labels \wedge$$

$$level(b_1) \geq level(b_2) \wedge$$

$$categories(b_2) \subseteq categories(b_1)\}$$

This relation implies that a security label b_1 dominates another
label b_2 if its level of sensitivity is greater than or equal to that
of the dominated label and if the set of security categories of the
dominated label b_2 is a subset of the set of the dominating label b_1.
This relation can be generalised such that arbitrary *partial orders*
can be used [Den76].

9.3   Specification of Access Control Policies

Formal notation is often used in the specification of access control policies. Before introducing this notation, let us consider the following mappings:

$$allow :\ Subjects \times Accesses \times Objects \rightarrow Boolean$$

$$own :\ Subjects \times Objects \rightarrow Boolean$$

$$admin :\ Subjects \rightarrow Boolean$$

$$dominates :\ Labels \times Labels \rightarrow Boolean$$

These mappings always produce a Boolean output value, that is, 'true' or 'false', depending on whether or not the statement of facts suggested by the name of the mapping has been fulfilled. Thus, for example, the 'allow' mapping produces the value 'true' for precisely all tuples (s, a, o) where the subject s has authorisation to use action a to access object o. The mapping 'own' enables us to express whether an object is owned by a specific subject, and 'admin' indicates whether a subject is a member of the set of system administrators. The mapping 'dominates' supplies the value 'true' precisely for all tuples (b_1, b_2) for which $(b_1, b_2) \in Dominates$ holds.

A number of general access control policies can be defined on the basis of these structures:

General access control policies

$$ownership :\ \forall\, s \in Subjects, o \in Objects, a \in Accesses :$$
$$allow(s, o, a) \Leftrightarrow own(s, o)$$

$$own\_admin :\ \forall\, s \in Subjects, o \in Objects, a \in Accesses :$$
$$allow(s, o, a) \Leftrightarrow own(s, o) \vee admin(s)$$

$$dom :\ \forall s \in Subjects, o \in Objects, a \in Accesses :$$
$$allow(s, o, a) \Leftrightarrow dominates(label(s), label(o))$$

The last *'dom' policy* listed requires that a system stores and processes security labels for the entities (subjects, objects) that exist in the system. Its advantage over other policies is that it enables complex access control policies to be implemented.

9.4   Categories of Access Control Mechanisms

Concrete mechanisms are required to implement the concepts described so far in real systems. This section presents a general classification of the proposed mechanisms.

Access control
mechanism

Definition 9.7 *The concept of a reference monitor is implemented in real systems through an* **access control mechanism**.

The access control mechanisms proposed in the literature are normally divided into the following categories [SC01]:

Discretionary access
control

- *Discretionary access control* comprises the procedures and mechanisms that mediate access requests at the discretion of individual users. An example of this category of access control mechanisms is commonly used administration of access rights for files in the Windows operating system, where users can independently define the access rights for files created by them.

Mandatory
access control

- *Mandatory access control* refers to the procedures and mechanisms that enforce the mediation of access requests by means of a uniform set of rules specified by a central entity.

Role-based
access control

- *Role-based access control* is a more recent development that was particularly popular during the 1990s and which also underwent further development at that time. Conceptually, it supplements the two classic approaches listed above. The key innovation compared with classic approaches is its approach to access. It states that the decision as to whether a subject may use a specific method to access a certain object should not depend on the identity of the subject or on a general policy, but be determined by the concrete role in which the subject perceives his task. This simplifies the rights administration process [SCF$^+$96].

What also applies is that the two classic approaches can be combined, with the mandatory access control decisions normally overriding the discretionary access of the user. An example is the use of discretionary access control on single computers combined with mandatory access control in dedicated intermediate systems of a communication network (also see Chapter 21 on Internet firewalls).

Access matrix

The *access matrix*, in which the rows in a system represent existing subjects and the columns the objects, has proven to be a useful concept for defining access control mechanisms [Amo94].

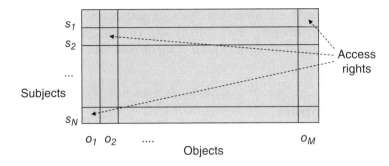

Figure 9.2

*The conceptual
access control matrix*

Each cell in the matrix contains the access rights of the subject addressed by the row to the object addressed by the column (also see Figure 9.2).

Because most entries in this conceptual matrix will be empty in real systems, direct implementation of the matrix is not very efficient in terms of storage consumption. Consequently, various other implementation designs have established themselves: *Implementation of access matrix*

- ■ For each object in a system, *access control lists (ACLs)* store *Access control lists* lists of the subjects that are permitted access to the object, sometimes in conjunction with the specific access rights of each individual subject. Access control lists are normally used together with discretionary access control because the quantity of ACLs makes them difficult to be maintained by a central administrative facility.
- ■ To an extent, *capabilities* are a complementary concept to *Capabilities* ACLs because a list is stored for each subject containing the objects and the specific access types that the subject can use to access a specific object. The advantage, and possibly the danger, of capabilities lie in the fact that they make it viable for rights to be delegated between subjects. Consequently, they are normally used in conjunction with discretionary access control.
- ■ *Security labels* are mostly combined with mandatory access *Security labels* control because the generation and administration of security labels can easily be automated through by centrally specified system policies.

What is common to all implementation alternatives for the administration of access rights mentioned above is that the integrity of the respective data structures is an essential prerequisite for the security achievable by the scheme. If these data structures *Integrity of access data structures is crucial!*

cannot be effectively protected from unauthorised manipulation by individual subjects, then all access control procedures are doomed to fail in their task of protecting objects from unauthorised access.

9.5   Summary

Tasks of access control

Access control encompasses the administration and implementation of access rights that regulate under which conditions and with which actions the subjects of a system can access the objects of the system.

Allocation of rights

Depending on the access control mechanisms used, these rights can be allocated either on the basis of discretionary access control or mandatory access control. A simpler form of access rights administration involves a definition of roles where specific access rights are allocated in a second step. The rights for specific subjects can be defined on the basis of a possibly dynamic allocation of subjects to certain roles (role-based access control). In practice the fundamental approaches are often combined.

Reference to Internet firewalls and IEEE 802.1Q

Even though there may not always be an obvious reason for transferring the fundamentals presented in this chapter to situations that exist in communication networks, they do represent central concepts for understanding access control issues in networks. This topic will be dealt with again in Chapter 21 on Internet firewalls and in Section 11.1 with regard to the standard IEEE 802.1Q.

9.6   Supplemental Reading

[Amo94]   AMOROSO, E. G.: *Fundamentals of Computer Security Technology*. Prentice Hall, 1994
               Chapter 22 deals with access control mechanisms; other basic concepts related to access control are introduced in Chapters 6 to 13.

[SC01]   SAMARATI, P.; CAPITANIDI VIMERCATI, S. de: Access Control: Policies, Models, and Mechanisms. In: FOCARDI, R.; GORRIERI, R. (Eds): *Foundations of Security Analysis and Design; Lecture Notes in Computer Science* Vol. 2171, Springer, 2001, pp. 137–196.

[SCF$^+$96]   SANDHU, R.; COYNE, E.; FEINSTEIN, H.; YOUMAN, C.:
Role-Based Access Control Models. In: *IEEE
Computer* 29 (1996), No. 2, pp. 38–47.

9.7   Questions

1.   What does the term 'reference monitor' mean?
2.   How are the terms 'security level', 'security category' and 'security label' connected?
3.   Which of the access control policies *ownership, own_admin* or *dom* is normally used for the file system of the Unix operating system?
4.   To which of the three categories of access control mechanisms – discretionary, mandatory or role-based – would you allocate rights assignments to files common in Unix?
5.   Do access control lists support delegating rights between subjects?
6.   The *dominates* relation is transitive, that is, a subject that is 'larger' in the partial order has at least equivalent rights. Does it make sense in computer networks to let the right to communicate also be transitive? Discuss the consequences if you need to consider that connections in computer networks commonly need to be bidirectional.

Part II

Network Security

Part II

Network Security

10 Integration of Security Services in Communication Architectures

The fundamentals of data security technology introduced in Part I of this book will be discussed in the following chapters from the perspective of their use in architectures and protocols of network security. The first chapter discusses basic issues and each of the three chapters that follow introduces and explains the network security protocols of layers 2, 3 and 4.

The first section of this chapter starts with the motivation for the basic design issues that are raised with the integration of security services into communication architectures. Section 10.2 presents a pragmatic model for secure networked systems. Using this model as the basis, the three remaining sections examine general and specific issues concerning placing security services in layered communication architectures.

10.1 Motivation

Analogous to the structured approach for conducting a security analysis for a given communication architecture (also see Section 1.3), the issues that arise in conjunction with the integration of security services into communication systems can also be categorised according to two dimensions. Along a horizontal orientation, there is the question of which security services should be implemented *into which systems* of a communication network (also see Figure 10.1). Individual security services can conceivably be provided in end systems or intermediate systems. Regarding integration into intermediate systems, a further differentiation

Two dimensions guide the categorisation of design decisions

Security in Fixed and Wireless Networks, Second Edition.
Guenter Schaefer and Michael Rossberg.
Copyright © 2014 by dpunkt.verlag GmbH, Heidelberg, Germany.
Title of the German original: Netzsicherheit   ISBN 978-3-86490-115-7
Translation Copyright © 2016 by John Wiley & Sons, Ltd., All rights reserved

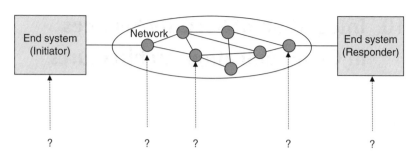

can be made as to which security services should be embedded into which intermediate systems, for example whether these services should be integrated solely on the 'boundary nodes' of a network or also generally within the network.

On one hand it could be argued that security services should basically be supplied in end systems because it is only there that users have total control over them and can be sure that their data will have the desired protection. However, on the other hand, the opposite approach can be taken with the argument that the user's control over security services is what actually leads to the source of insecurity (refer also to the principles of 'discretionary' and 'mandatory access control' in Chapter 9). However, as this chapter will show, the requirements that come to light and the constraints needing consideration are of a very diverse nature.

On the other hand, design decisions are also needed along a vertical orientation to identify the *layers* into which specific security services should be integrated (see Figure 10.2). Here again it is

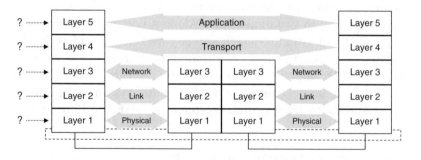

possible to take one or the other extreme position, dictating that security services should basically be supplied in the application layer because only applications have a complete knowledge of the semantics and thus the sensitivity of potentially protected data. It is just as easy to argue that basically all data, including the protocol information of the deeper layers, requires equal protection to ensure that the best possible security is achieved. This would mean that security services should be extended to the deepest protocol layer possible. Even if both arguments have certain validity, the aspects of real networks concern so many layers that the issue of security cannot be resolved satisfactorily using a simple 'wholesale solution'.

'One size does not fit all!'

In this chapter we will take a close look at these aspects from a general perspective. The simple, pragmatic model of secure networked systems in the next section provides a useful orientation for our discussion.

10.2 A Pragmatic Model

Ultimately, the basic objective in setting up communication networks and distributed systems is to make certain applications available to the users of these systems. Based on this consideration, Figure 10.3 shows a pragmatic model for secure networked systems [For94].

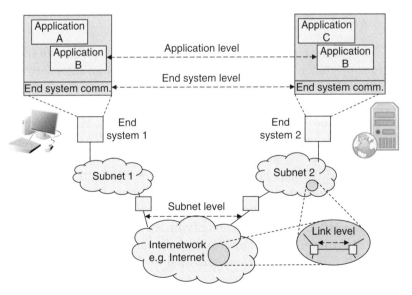

Figure 10.3
A pragmatic model for secure networked systems

In the model, a distinction is made between four principal *levels* where specific security requirements and measures can be embedded:

Application level
- The *application level* relates to requirements that have to be met for specific applications and the relevant measures that are provided directly in the applications themselves. Applications are software systems that handle certain tasks, such as the handling of e-mail, web services, word processing, data storage, process control, etc.

End system level
- The *end system level* relates to requirements and measures that should be addressed uniformly between end systems. End systems are devices ranging from personal computers through servers to mainframes, but also including mobile phones, for example. The security policy of an end system is normally more or less uniformly specified by an entity, also called a *policy authority*, for the entire end system.

Subnetwork level
- At the *subnetwork level* requirements and measures for communication facilities that fall under the control of an administrative organisation (e.g. department, company) should be dealt with on a uniform basis. The main idea is to ensure that communication between certain subnetworks over potentially untrustworthy networks (e.g. the Internet) is uniformly secure. The security policies for the subnetworks are normally specified uniformly for all systems in a subnetwork.

Link level
- The *link level* relates to the security between the separate nodes of a communication network that are directly linked over a physical medium ('link').

Delineating the terms internetwork and subnetwork
The term *internetwork* contained in Figure 10.3 refers to a set of interconnected subnetworks. What distinguishes an internetwork from a subnetwork, which can actually also consist of a series of interconnected networks (e.g. LANs) and is guided by a security policy that has been allocated by a policy authority, is that no uniform security policy exists for an internetwork. Consequently, an internetwork is normally not categorised as a trusted network.

Relationship between requirement levels and protocol layers
Comparing the layer model for communication systems commonly used today, we can see that the levels shown in Figure 10.3 cannot be aligned one-to-one with the protocol layers. As Figure 10.4 illustrates, the only direct association is from the application level to the application layer as the security services supplied in this level are implemented in the application layer or directly in the application itself.

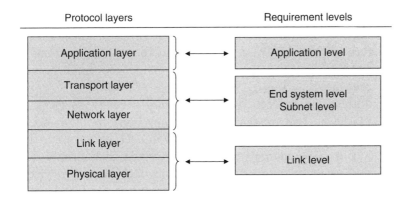

Protocol layers   Requirement levels

Figure 10.4

*Mapping between
protocol layers and
requirement levels is
not one-to-one*

Security measures to meet the requirements of the end system and subnetwork levels can be implemented in the transport layer as well as in the network layer. Likewise, requirements at the link level can be implemented in the data link layer and the physical layer.

10.3   General Considerations for the Placement of Security Services

The following general considerations should be included in decisions on the placement of security services.

- *Mixing different data streams:* As a result of multiplexing in communication systems there is a tendency in the lower levels or layers for data streams with different sources and sinks and from different applications to exist as mixed data streams. Normally, the security service for a specific level or layer will homogeneously handle the data traffic processed in this level or layer. However, this can lead to inadequate control of the security mechanisms being used on certain data. For example, if a security policy demands that traffic be handled specifically to deal with particular applications or users, this would be better implemented at a higher level.   *Mixing data streams*

- *Routing knowledge:* The lower levels usually have more knowledge about the security characteristics of different communication paths, e.g. routes or links. In environments where these characteristics vary significantly, placement of coordinated security mechanisms in the lower levels can provide considerable benefits in terms of effectiveness and efficiency. Communication paths that are particularly at risk   *Routing knowledge* (e.g. wireless links or routes traversing public networks between two interconnected local area networks) can therefore be specifically secured without those other parts of the network that are less at risk requiring additional security measures.

Number of protection points

■ *Number of protection points:* When security services are placed on the application level, they must be implemented in every sensitive application and in each end system. This also requires management of the involved cryptographic keys and security relevant configuration data in each device. A similar situation occurs with placement on the link level, as all devices terminating untrustworthy connections must implement security services. Placement of security services in the 'middle' of an architecture tends to reduce the number of points providing protective measures.

Protection of protocol information

■ *Protection of protocol information:* By nature the security measures of the higher protocol layers cannot protect the protocol fields of the layers below them. This is a point that should not be ignored, particularly as not only user data but also the network infrastructure itself has to be protected.

Source and sink binding

■ *Source and sink binding:* Some security services, such as data origin authentication and non-repudiation, are based on a relationship between data and its sender and partly its receiver. This relationship can be established more effectively at the higher levels, particularly at the application level.

Beyond the general considerations listed, the following more level-specific observations also help to provide useful arguments for determining the most appropriate placement of individual security services for a specific network configuration.

Application level

In some cases, the *application level* is the only sensible level where certain security services can be implemented. An applications-specific security service, such as access control for a distributed file service, can only be implemented completely at the application level. It may also be necessary for a security service to be effective beyond certain application gateways. An example would be confidentiality and data origin authentication for e-mails, which may be transported over multiple e-mail gateways before they are delivered to the receiver. Furthermore, the semantics of certain data elements may also require special security. For example, with the non-repudiation security service sufficient knowledge of the semantics of certain data elements exists only in the application itself. Lastly, the programmers of an application sometimes have no other choice but to integrate certain security services into the application level because the security mechanisms at the lower levels cannot be influenced by them.

The *end system level* is particularly suitable when end systems are categorised as trusted but the network in between is not trusted. Also, it is often advantageous if security services can be implemented transparently in relation to applications and if the configuration and management of security services can be transferred to a designated system administrator.

End system level

The *subnetwork level* should not be confused with the end system level, even if the security services are sometimes implemented in the same protocol layer. When security measures are implemented at the subnetwork level, the same protection is normally awarded to all end systems of the subnetwork concerned. The assumption is that a subnetwork connected directly to an end system is just as trustworthy as the end system itself. The basis for this assumption is that the end system and the subnetwork are sited at the same location and configured and administered by the same staff. The advantage of implementing security measures at the subnetwork level is that there are normally far fewer subnetwork gateways than there are end systems, and security measures are therefore needed for fewer systems.

Subnetwork level

The *link level* is especially recommended for the implementation of security measures when relatively few untrustworthy communication links exist. It is therefore easier and more cost-effective to secure only those links that are categorised to be insecure. Depending on the underlying technology, the link level also enables the use of specific protection mechanisms such as spread spectrum transmission or key-dependent switching between different transmission frequencies (frequency hopping). The link level is also the level where protection from *traffic flow analysis* can be realised most effectively as many traffic flows are mixed here.

Link level

Another aspect in connection with security measures is the potential user interaction that cannot elegantly be integrated into the current model because users are outside the communication systems. For example, authentication in particular requires interaction with a user. The following design alternatives are available:

Interaction with the user

■ *Local authentication:* In this case the users authenticate themselves to an end system. The end system in turn

Local authentication

authenticates itself to the remote system and at the same time names the identity of the user. With this version, the remote end system must have confidence that the local end system correctly handled the authentication verification. This variant is realised by the *Network File System (NFS)*, for example.

Specific protocol elements
- ■ *Use of specific protocol elements at the application level:* A user supplies the local system with certain authentication information that the local system securely forwards to the remote system using specific protocol elements. In this case the remote system verifies the authentication itself. A representative for this kind of authentication is the *Server Message Block* (SMB) protocol.

Combined techniques
- ■ *A combination of these techniques:* The Kerberos system presented in Section 7.4 can be used as an example that combines local and remote authentication as it undertakes both local and remote authentication.

10.4   Integration in Lower Protocol Layers vs Applications

This section supplements the discussion with additional considerations that support the integration of security services, particularly in the lower protocol layers:

Security
- ■ *Security:* This can motivate the integration of security measures in lower protocol layers in two ways. Firstly, the network infrastructure itself must be protected so that it can guarantee its availability and ensure that it is functioning correctly, including its ability to provide an accurate and verifiable accounting of service usage. Secondly, security measures implemented in network elements are often more difficult to attack than those in end systems, as end systems generally have a more complex and more flexible software configuration and therefore more weaknesses. Furthermore, network elements are not as exposed to incautious users. This is particularly the case when measures are realised in tamper-resistant hardware and cannot be deactivated or bypassed.

Application independence
- ■ *Application independence:* Fundamental security services can be implemented once in the lower layers for all applications and do not have to be integrated into each individual application.

- *Quality of service:* Data streams that make special demands *Quality of service*
on the quality of a transmission service (minimal delay, delay
fluctuation, etc.) can profit from being integrated into the
lower protocol layers, where it is easier to combine the quality of service-orientated scheduling of a communication system with the scheduling of cryptographic operations. Take
an example in which multiple data streams with different
requirements and traffic characteristics (e.g. voice transmission and file transfer) are encoded by a hardware encryption module and then transmitted. In this case the quality
of service-orientated scheduling of both operations can be integrated more effectively if encryption is executed directly on
the communication adapter before transmission. *Asynchron-
ous Transfer Mode (ATM)*, which is the basis of *broadband
ISDN*, is a somewhat aged but well-suited example of a communication architecture that can support such an integration,
even securing end system to end system [ATM97b, ATM97a,
ESS⁺98, Sch98, SHB95, Sta95, Sta98, SR97].
- *Efficiency:* Because of the improved possibilities for integ- *Efficiency*
rating hardware support directly onto a communications
adapter, cryptographic operations can be executed more
efficiently when integration is in the lower protocol layers.
Although an application might use a special hardware
device to carry out an efficient computation of cryptographic
operations by calling up the appropriate functions, it has to
be considered that this may involve additional data transport
over the system bus, which inevitably affects performance.

10.5 Integration into End Systems or Intermediate Systems

Aside from identifying the layer where certain security services are
to be implemented, it is also important to establish whether particular security services should be integrated into end systems or into
intermediate systems.

In respect to integration into end systems, it should be noted *Integration into*
that this could generally take place at the applications level as well *end systems usually*
as at the end system level. In some circumstances it can make sense *addresses require-*
to incorporate security also at the link level, for instance when a *ments of the applic-*
public phone line is used to connect an end system to a dedicated *ations or end system*
system. This would be the case if remote maintenance access exists *level*
for a switching system.

Integration into intermediate systems tends to address requirements of the subnetwork or link level better

Integration into intermediate systems can take place at all four levels. Depending on the level, there is a tendency, however, for different security objectives to be pursued. Therefore, if security is integrated at the applications or end system level, it tends to secure management interfaces of the intermediate systems rather than the actually transported data. The latter is more apt to occur at the subnetwork or link level.

Depending on the intended security objectives, integration into either end systems or intermediate systems can make sense. In practice both forms are often found.

Figure 10.5
Authentication relationships in internetworks

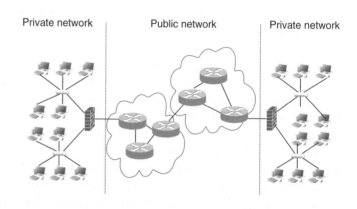

Authentication relation			Application for securing
End system	⟷	End system	User channels
End system	⟷	Intermediate system	Management interfaces Accounting
Intermediate	⟷	Intermediate system	Network operation: Signalling, Routing, Accounting, ...

Authentication relationships in internetworks

Figure 10.5 presents an overview of authentication relationships in internetworks [Sch98]. As can be gleaned from this figure, authentication relationships in internetworks are needed between arbitrary combinations of different end and intermediate systems while at the same time pursuing completely different security objectives. Authentication between end systems (or the applications run in them) generally aims to secure actual data traffic. Authentication between end and intermediate systems, on the other hand, is aimed more towards securing management interfaces and producing a verifiable accounting of service usage. Authentication between intermediate systems is mainly designed to secure network operations, signalling, the exchange of routing information and, in some cases, provide an important basis for the verifiable accounting of data transmitted between network gateways.

10.6 Summary

The integration of security services and mechanisms into communication architectures is guided by the consideration of which security services should be implemented in which nodes and which security services should be realised in which layer.

A simple pragmatic model for secured networked systems that distinguishes between four different levels with different security requirements and where security measures can be taken is useful for design decisions.

Pragmatic model

As a number of arguments exist for and against each of these levels, there is no single correct solution to this design problem. A wholesale solution would not be sensible anyway, as different solutions have to be found based on the respective security objectives being pursued and this also means that different trade-offs have to be taken into account. The security measures that result often present a compromise in terms of achievable security, performance, flexibility, etc.

A 'wholesale solution' does not exist

The remaining chapters in this part of the book closely examine numerous examples of network security protocols and architectures, thus enabling us to learn how to make a better assessment of the consequences of respective design decisions.

10.7 Supplemental Reading

[For94]   FORD, W.: *Computer Communications Security – Principles, Standard Protocols and Techniques*. Prentice Hall, 1994
Chapter 3 introduces the integration of security measures in communication architectures and also describes the pragmatic model presented in this chapter.

10.8 Questions

The intention of the questions below is to integrate the knowledge presented in the whole of Part II. We therefore recommend that you continue with the following chapters and read this chapter again later before responding to questions that seem too difficult at this point.

1. Name the security objectives that particularly require that measures be integrated in nodes on the 'boundary' of a network.

2. Name a security protocol treated in this book that can be used either at the end system or at the subnetwork level.

3. Which of the security protocols discussed are particularly appropriate for exploiting knowledge about the security characteristics of certain data paths?

4. List the attacks from which a network infrastructure should be protected in particular, and the security objectives that have to be ensured in this context.

5. Assume that you could configure an e-mail gateway so that e-mails exchanged between two company locations are basically signed and encrypted between the two e-mail gateways. To which of the levels described would you allocate such a security measure?

6. Explain the advantages and disadvantages of the strategy presented in the previous question and discuss alternative concepts.

7. Which security protocols discussed in this book can implement security measures at the end system level?

8. At which layer would you protect a voice over IP system if you want to keep traffic flows secret, i.e. who calls whom?

9. Are there difficulties with an encryption on application layer? Discuss the problems arising with spam and virus protection.

11 Link Layer Security Protocols

According to the classic OSI model for open communication systems, the link layer (the second layer in the model) provides a reliable data transmission service between two peer entities that are directly connected over a shared medium (e.g. cable or radio transmission link). Its main tasks thus encompass *framing, error detection* and *correction* as well as the control of joint access to shared mediums (e.g. Ethernet or radio link). The latter task is also referred to as *Medium Access Control (MAC)*. However, this term should not be confused with the description of access control given in Chapter 9. Likewise, use of the abbreviation MAC should make a distinction between its double meanings 'Medium Access Control' and 'Message Authentication Code'.

OSI layer 2 tasks

Not all current communication protocols and technologies fit nicely into this model. For instance, wireless connections to a WLAN access point have characteristics that extend beyond those of the link layer, and some protocols for realising *virtual private networks (VPN)* perform additional tasks than those assigned by the OSI model to layer 2.

Fitting protocols into the OSI model is not always easy

As a result, a concise paraphrasing of the term *security protocols of the link layer*, which interprets these as security protocols of the second OSI layer, does not appropriately reflect the reality of current communication architectures. In this book we therefore settle for the following more intuitive definition:

Definition 11.1 *The objective of a* **link layer security protocol** *consists of guaranteeing certain security properties of the protocol data units of the link layer, which means the protocol data units that transport the protocol data units of the network layer, e.g. IP packets.*

Security in Fixed and Wireless Networks, Second Edition.
Guenter Schaefer and Michael Rossberg.
Copyright © 2014 by dpunkt.verlag GmbH, Heidelberg, Germany.
Title of the German original: Netzsicherheit ISBN 978-3-86490-115-7
Translation Copyright © 2016 by John Wiley & Sons, Ltd., All rights reserved

The following sections present approaches for securing access to local area networks that are based on the standards of the IEEE 802 series. This is followed by a definition of the Point-to-Point Protocol, which is the protocol most frequently used over dial-up or DSL connections for access to the Internet and incorporates some fundamental security functions. Building on this discussion, Section 11.5 presents the Point-to-Point Tunneling Protocol that enables the usage of PPP to be extended over the entire Internet. Section 11.6 concludes the chapter with comments on virtual private networks.

11.1   Virtual Separation of Data Traffic with IEEE 802.1Q

The *802-LAN/MAN Standardisation Committee* of the *Institute of Electrical and Electronics Engineers (IEEE)* develops standards for local networks (local area networks, LANs) and regional networks (metropolitan area networks, MANs). The standards most widely used are those of the Ethernet family (IEEE 802.3), the 802.11 series for wireless local area networks (wireless LANs, WLANs) and the Worldwide Interoperability for Microwave Access standard (WIMAX, 802.16).

The IEEE 802 protocol family

In order to separate data traffic from different domains in IEEE 802 networks, the *IEEE-802.1Q* Working Group has defined a method that network devices can use to mark messages and limit delivery to certain end points, based on the tagging. Devices that are assigned the same tagging can only communicate with each other. They form a so-called *virtual local area network (VLAN)*. This enables, for instance, mobile terminal devices belonging to guests to use the Internet within a dedicated VLAN that is separated from critical servers, without having to establish a further physical infrastructure. Even though the standard [IEE11a] is not a security protocol in the proper sense, the method is often used to implement controlled access to the data link layer, which is why it is described here.

Use of virtual LANs

As already indicated, a switch or terminal device assigns a so-called *VLAN tag* to each packet, which includes a 12-bit long VLAN identification number (VLAN-ID). The active network components (e.g. switches) use this ID to limit message forwarding to certain ports. Since the VLAN-ID is in no way cryptographically protected, it is essential that VLANs are only used

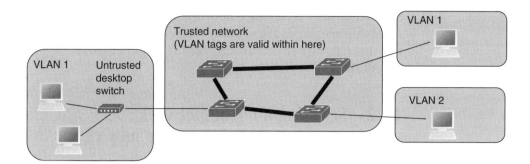

in fundamentally trustworthy environments, where active attacks can be ruled out on messages exchanged via communication paths and manipulations of network elements. As shown in Figure 11.1, in practice VLAN IDs therefore only tend to be used within trustworthy parts of the network. VLAN tags are generally allocated on the first physically secured switch and removed by the last trustworthy switch, so that the method is transparent for the terminal devices. In most cases the allocation of messages to VLANs is static, that is, all messages on a network port are assigned to a certain VLAN. VLANs are generally coupled via routers, which are connected to several ports of different VLANs. Alternatively, it is possible for the routers to allocate VLAN tags to their packets themselves, although for security reasons it is often necessary to have this allocation checked in the switches. VLAN technology has been subject to further developments over recent years and now offers a range of additional options. For example, the priority of individual VLANs can be increased so that voice messages reach their destination faster. VLAN tags can also be nested, in order to map trust hierarchies.

Figure 11.1
Structure of a physical local area network with VLANs
VLAN tags should only be used in trustworthy situations

Because of the lack of cryptographic authentication for the VLAN tags, the secure separation of VLANs depends on the correct function of each component of the trustworthy network area. This not only means that switches and cables must be protected from manipulation by attackers, it also means that not even a single switch must forward messages with VLAN tags from untrustworthy ports. Furthermore, in many cases interactions between VLANs cannot be ruled out. For example, an attacker may generate a large amount of traffic in a VLAN and in this way cause disturbance in another VLAN, even without direct access.

Security of VLANs

In situations where VLANs are used for tasks relevant to security, there may be additional side effects that are not immediately apparent. If, for example, a router connects two different VLANs

Side effects of VLANs must be taken into account

to the Internet via the same network interface, it should be kept in mind that messages are not only relayed to and from the Internet, but that this router can also be used to send packets between the two VLANs.

11.2   Securing a Local Network Infrastructure Using IEEE 802.1X

The usage of not further secured VLAN tags already shows that devices within local infrastructures are usually rather heavily trusted. This trust induces that attackers must not be able to attach their own devices to these local networks.

Hence, for the security of access to local networks a subgroup of the 802 committee has released a standard labelled *IEEE 802.1X* [IEE10] that aims to restrict access to LAN services to legitimate users and devices. This standard, like other standards of the 802.1 family, can in principle be used with other technologies of the 802 series.

Port-based access control   The basic characteristic of the standard is *port-based access control*, which is used to perform authentication and authorisation of devices connected to LAN ports. A LAN port is a logical (often also physical) access point with point-to-point connection characteristics. It could be the access port of an Ethernet switch or the logical access point of a WLAN base station.

The IEEE 802.1X standard conceptually distinguishes between two logical ports (also see Figure 11.2): an *uncontrolled port*, which enables a device to prove its identity through an authentication exchange, and a *controlled port*, which allows proven authenticated

Figure 11.2
Controlled and uncontrolled ports with IEEE 802.1X

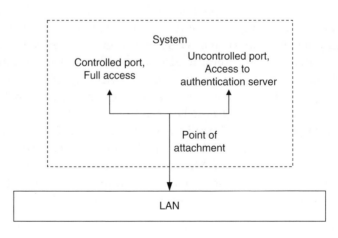

devices to access the general data transmission service of the local area network.

Three principal roles are distinguished in the authenticity verification of connected devices:

Roles of IEEE 802.1X

- A device that wants access to the data transmission service of the LAN finds itself in the role of *supplicant* when it is providing and proving its identity during the authentication exchange.

  Supplicant

- The access point of the LAN infrastructure, such as an Ethernet-Switch, functions as an *authenticator*, demanding that a device provide and prove its identity.

  Authenticator

- The authenticator does not itself verify the credentials provided by a supplicant during the authentication exchange. Instead, it forwards them to an *authentication server* that then notifies it of the results of the authentication verification.

  Authentication server

The explicit distinction between the roles of an authenticator and an authentication server allows for scalable and easy management of authentication data even in very large installations, like the wireless access points of a whole university. Otherwise, each of the access points would have to keep current records of the authentication data of all possible users.

Prior to a device's successful authentication of itself to the authenticator of a LAN, it only has access to an uncontrolled port. This port is uncontrolled in the sense that it can be accessed even before authentication has been successfully performed. However, it only allows authentication message exchange and cannot be used for the transmission of arbitrary data units.

Access prior to authentication is only possible to the uncontrolled port

An authentication exchange can be initiated by a supplicant as well as by an authenticator. The controlled port is opened as soon as the exchange is successfully completed.

The IEEE 802.1X standard does not define any authentication protocols of its own but instead recommends the use of existing protocols, such as the *Extensible Authentication Protocol (EAP)* [ABV+04] for basic authentication without key agreement or the *PPP EAP TLS Authentication Protocol* standardised in RFC 5216 [SAH08], which also enables session keys to be negotiated during an authentication exchange. IEEE 802.1X also recommends that the authentication server is implemented in accordance with the IETF specification for a *Remote Authentication Dial In User Service (RADIUS)* [RWR+00].

IEEE 802.1X does not define its own authentication protocols

EAP over LANs   For the exchange of EAP protocol data units IEEE 802.1X spe-
(EAPOL)   cifies the protocol *EAP over LANs (EAPOL)*, which mainly defines
techniques for the encapsulation of EAP-PDUs into the payload
of transmission frames of the 802 protocol suite. The encapsulated PDUs are then exchanged between the *port access entities
(PAE)* of the supplicant and the authenticator. Conventional RA-
DIUS messages can be used between the authenticator and the authentication server. Figure 11.3 presents an overview of the sample
authentication of a device. Details of the EAP authentication protocol are given in Section 11.4.2 as EAP was initially specified in
the context of the Point-to-Point Tunneling Protocol.

Figure 11.3
Protocol run of
EAPOL protocol

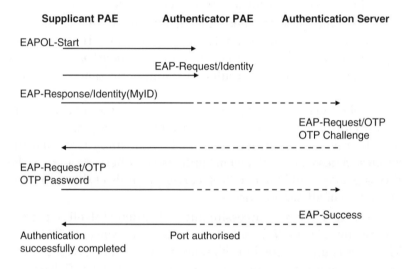

IEEE 802.1X   In summary it should be noted that IEEE 802.1X primarily
provides access   provides access control for the transmission services offered by local
control for LANs   area networks. However, the standard does not define how to secure
actual data transmission from passive or active attacks and addi-
tional security protocols are therefore required.

11.3   Encryption of Data Traffic with IEEE 802.1AE

A further security service is required to protect the actual data
traffic, since 802.1X can only be used to authenticate devices.
The purpose of the relatively new IEEE-802.1AE method [IEE06,
IEE11b], also referred to as *MAC security (MACsec)*, is to close this
loophole by enabling protection of the traffic between two active

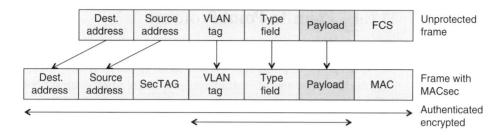

| Dest. address | Source address | VLAN tag | Type field | Payload | FCS | Unprotected frame |

| Dest. address | Source address | SecTAG | VLAN tag | Type field | Payload | MAC | Frame with MACsec |

Authenticated
encrypted

network components in the LAN by cryptographic measures. In this way, attackers who may, for example, eavesdrop on Ethernet cables, are prevented from drawing inferences about the transferred data. The standard makes provision for combination with any 802 standards without dedicated security protocol. As a consequence it is mainly relevant for the 802.3 sector. Compromised devices would, however, pose a real problem as protection is only provided for transfer via links.

Figure 11.4
Protecting a 802.3 frame with MACsec

Technically IEEE 802.1AE is designed as an extension to IEEE 802.1X, that is, in the first instance devices mutually authenticate themselves via IEEE 802.1X and negotiate a cryptographic key during this process. This key is then used to encrypt the actual user data and to authenticate it at the same time. AES in Galois/Counter Mode (GCM, see Section 5.5.1) is used for this purpose. Support of AES with 128-bit keys is a requirement for MACsec. Optionally, 256-bit long keys may be used.

Deriving of key material through 802.1X

Figure 11.4 shows the operating principle of MACsec based on the treatment of an Ethernet frame. First, a new field is added after the source address, which is referred to as *SecTAG*. This tag always starts with the reserved sequence 0x88e5, which makes it possible to distinguish cryptographically protected packets from unsecured packets. In addition, the tag may contain, for instance, a packet number to prevent attackers replaying packets. The SecTAG is followed by further 802.3 protocol data and the actual user data. All these fields are linked with the keystream via an XOR operation based on the GCM method, so that an attacker is also unable to read the VLAN tag, for example. The whole frame is authenticated by appending the message authentication value, without using the CRC checksum, which, in any case, is not secure. In the context of MACsec the latter is also referred to as integrity check value (ICV).

Overview of the protocol sequence

With regard to the security of the method it should once again be noted that MACsec only protects the communication path, i.e. data transferred between two buildings, for instance. The devices themselves continue to have access to the data and have to be protected physically and by other means.

11.4   Point-to-Point Protocol

The Internet is implemented, besides the discussed local networks, through point-to-point connections in large parts. Examples include connections between Internet routers established over WANs, and dial-up connections used by hosts to gain access to an Internet service provider over the telephone network.

Point-to-Point   A typical protocol in this context is the *Point-to-Point Protocol*
Protocol   *(PPP)*, [Sim94b, Sim94c], which enables IP packets to be transmitted over serial lines.

Figure 11.5
Classical usage
scenario for PPP

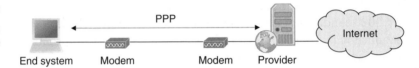

Figure 11.5 shows a classical usage scenario for PPP in which a computer using a modem over a telephone connection dials up a network provider that functions as a gateway to the Internet. A subtype of PPP that is encapsulated in Ethernet frames – called PPPoE [MLE+99] – is also used for connection control in modern DSL scenarios.

11.4.1   Structure and Frame Formats

PPP components   The main components of PPP are:

- Layer 2 frame format for frame delineation and error detection;
- *Link Control Protocol*   the *Link Control Protocol (LCP)*, the main task of which is connection control (thus connection setup, test and release as well as parameter negotiation);
- *Network Control*   a range of *Network Control Protocols (NCP)* that are specifically tailored to the needs of the respective network layer protocols to be transported in PPP frames (IP, IPX, NetBEUI, AppleTalk, etc.).

Layer 2 frame format   Figure 11.6 shows the layer 2 frame format of PPP. The protocol uses character-oriented transmission, that is, the transmission frames are aligned to octet boundaries and character stuffing is used to achieve code transparency. With respect to layer 2 functions PPP basically realises the popular HDLC protocol. Transmission frames therefore always begin with the bit pattern '01111110',

			1 or 2	variable	2 or 4	1	Octets
Flag 01111110	Address 11111111	Control 00000011	Protocol	Payload	Checksum	Flag 01111110	

Figure 11.6
Frame format of PPP

followed by the address and the control fields. The protocol field indicates which frame type is being transported in the payload. For error detection a CRC value is computed and transmitted in the checksum field. The frame also closes with the characteristic bit pattern '01111110'.

As Figure 11.6 shows, unnumbered frames are usually transmitted. However, in usage scenarios with high error probability, a reliable transmission mode with sequence numbers and retransmission can also be negotiated. Unless a different size has been negotiated, the maximum payload size is 1500 octets.

A classical usage scenario for PPP is a personal computer (PC) accessing the Internet via a modem and dial-up connection over the telephone network:

Usage scenario 'Internet access' via modem

- The modem of the user dials the telephone number of an Internet service provider (ISP) and sets up a 'physical' connection to the access computer of the ISP over the telephone network.
- The calling PC sends multiple LCP packets, which are always transmitted in PPP layer 2 frames, in order to negotiate the desired PPP parameters.
- Optionally, a security-specific negotiation subsequently takes place (details follow).
- The network layer is then configured through an exchange of NCP packets. In this connection the *Dynamic Host Configuration Protocol (DHCP)* optionally arranges for the dynamic allocation of an IP address.
- Once the connection is completely configured, the actual usage phase begins, during which arbitrary IP packets can be exchanged between the PC and any other computers in the Internet. The IP packets are transmitted in PPP packets from the PC to the access gateway, which decapsulates and sends them to the next Internet router. Similarly, the IP packets destined for the PC from the access gateway are encapsulated into PPP packets and transmitted to the PC.
- During the connection termination phase the IP address reserved for the PC is released.
- Lastly, the layer 2 connection is terminated using the LCP protocol and the modem closes down the 'physical' connection to the ISP access computer.

Figure 11.7

Frame format of PPP

link control protocol

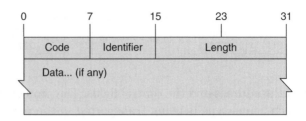

LCP frame format Figure 11.7 shows the frame format for the LCP. The significance of the fields contained is as follows:

- The *code* field indicates the requested service primitive. The key primitives are Configure-Request, Configure-Ack, Configure-Nack and Configure-Reject for the request or confirmation of configuration commands; Terminate-Request and -Reject for the termination of a connection; Code-Reject and Protocol-Reject for the rejection of non-supported options; Echo-Request and -Reply and Discard-Request.
- The *identifier* field is used to map replies to previous requests.
- The *length* field indicates the length of the LCP packet, including the LCP header (code, etc.).
- The *data* field is optional and contains command-specific information.

The configure primitives enable the agreement of layer 2-specific configuration details, such as the maximum size of the payload field in layer 2 frames, data compression and peer entity authentication.

PPP security services The PPP specification recommends the optional execution of an authentication exchange after the setup of a layer 2 connection. One of the two peer entities requests this exchange by signalling the appropriate configure-request commands. Furthermore, encryption of user data can be negotiated after successful authentication. The respective security protocols are explained in detail in the sections below.

11.4.2   PPP Authentication Protocols

Two authentication protocols were defined for the first version of PPP [LS92]: *Password Authentication Protocol (PAP)* and *Challenge Handshake Authentication Protocol (CHAP)*. As time went by these protocols were supplemented by an extensible protocol called *Extensible Authentication Protocol (EAP)* [ABV+04], which was then extended several by other variants, for example by the *EAP Transport Layer Security Protocol (EAP-TLS)* [SAH08].

The password authentication protocol (PAP) was defined in RFC 1334 [LS92] in 1992. It is a very simple protocol with the prerequisite that the authenticator knows a password of the peer entity. After successful setup of a layer 2 connection, the authenticator requests that the peer entity use PAP to authenticate itself. The latter entity then sends an Authenticate-Request packet with its identity and a password. The authenticator verifies whether it knows the identity provided and whether the password is correct. If verification is successful, it replies with an Authenticate-Ack message, whereas if the authentication is faulty, it sends an Authenticate-Nack message. The protocol is insecure because it does not provide for any cryptographic protection of the password. It is therefore no longer mentioned in the more recent RFCs for PPP authentication [Sim96].

Password authentication protocol

The Challenge Handshake Authentication Protocol (CHAP) was also specified in RFC 1334. It is a simple challenge-response protocol. Both peer entities must know a shared secret (thus an authentication key) they can use to perform the following authentication exchange [Sim96]:

Challenge Handshake Authentication Protocol

- After the setup of a layer 2 connection, one of the two entities (A) sends a challenge that consists of an identification *identifier*, a random number r_A and the name of A:

$$A \rightarrow B: \quad (1, identifier, r_A, A)$$

- The peer entity B computes the value of a cryptographic hash function over its name, the shared secret $K_{A,B}$ and the random number r_A. It sends this value along with the identification of the protocol run and its name to A:

$$B \rightarrow A: \quad (2, identifier, H(B, K_{A,B}, r_A), B)$$

- Upon receipt of this message, A itself computes the hash value and compares it with the value received. If both values match, A responds with a success message.

The still up-to-date version of the protocol specification, RFC 1994, specifies that MD5 must be supported as a cryptographic hash function and that the use of any other hash functions can be negotiated.

Figure 11.8 presents the frame format of the CHAP messages *Challenge* (Code 1) and *Response* (Code 2). The identifier is an octet that has to be changed with each challenge and is used to enable a simple mapping of responses to challenges. The length field indicates the total length of a message and 'value size' gives the length

Figure 11.8
Frame format of PPP
Challenge Handshake
Protocol (1)

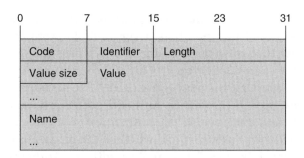

of the contained value (random number r_A or hash value according to description above). The last field, the name field, contains the identity of the sending entity. Its length is not explicitly transmitted and instead is computed by subtracting the length of the other fields from the total message length.

Figure 11.9
Frame format of PPP
Challenge Handshake
Protocol (2)

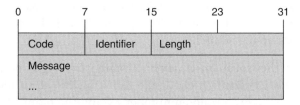

Figure 11.9 presents the format of the CHAP messages *Success* (Code 3) and *Failure* (Code 4). Compared with the messages explained above, these messages only contain an optional message element to indicate status messages or error situations. These messages are implementation dependent and are not interpreted by the protocol entities but solely indicated to the user.

Extensible Authentication Protocol   The *Extensible Authentication Protocol (EAP)* is a generic protocol that supports a range of diverse authentication methods that can also be more complex in nature than just 'a challenge plus a response.'

The protocol provides a series of basic commands:

- *Request, Response* are supplemented by a type field and type-specific data fields.
- *Success, Failure* are used to indicate the results of an authentication exchange.

Examples of type fields are *Identity, Notify, Nak* (only used in responses to indicate non-supported requests), *MD5 Challenge* (same as CHAP), *One-Time Password, Generic Token Card* and *EAP-TLS*.

The basic idea behind the *One-Time Password (OTP)* protocol consists of transmitting a 'password' that can only be used for one run. This prevents a potential attacker who is eavesdropping on such a password from using it in future authentication attempts. No exact procedure is defined in the context of EAP, how to run an authentication dialogue, however it is referred to [HMN+98]. In this case, prior to the initial protocol run, both peer entities A and B must perform an initialisation and agree on a shared starting value. The authenticator A chooses a random number r_A and sends it to supplicant B, who applies a hash function n times to compute a hash value over the random number and a personal secret value $Password_B$. The resulting value is the initial 'one-time' password of B: $PW_n = H^n(r_A, Password_B)$. The tuple (n, PW_n) must be transmitted to A in a 'secure' way (= authentically) and stored for later usage there.

One-Time Password

The actual authentication exchange then consists of the following steps:

OTP protocol exchange

1. The authenticator sends the number $n-1$ to B:

$$A \to B: \quad n - 1$$

2. B then computes a new one-time password $PW_{n-1} := H^{n-1}(r_A, Password_B)$ and sends it to A:

$$B \to A: \quad PW_{n-1}$$

3. The authenticator now computes $H(PW_{n-1})$ and compares the result with PW_n. If both values match, A assumes that B is authentic and stores the tuple $(n-1, PW_{n-1})$ for the next authentication process. This exchange can be executed $(n-1)$ times before the procedure needs to be initialised again.

The security of this procedure is based on the fact that an attacker who eavesdrops on one of the one-time passwords PW_i will not be able to compute the value $H^{-1}(PW_i)$ that is necessary for the next authentication exchange. It is important that there is no active attack, for example a man-in-the-middle attack, as the presented OTP protocol does not offer any protection in this case. Another postulate is that legitimate users are always able to transmit their password 'faster', that is, an attacker must not be able to eavesdrop and use a password before the original transmission reaches its destination.

The *generic token card* method performs a simple challenge-response exchange. However, unlike CHAP, the user is also

Generic token card

included in the exchange in which the random number selected by the authenticator is indicated to him or her. To compute the response, the user uses a small device the size of a credit card, called a *generic token card*. The user enters the random number onto the card and the card computes the appropriate response, which the user then has to transfer manually to the computer. The advantages of this method are that users have better control over when they actually perform authentication and the card is more manipulation safe than a full-fledged computer, as it does not have its own network connectivity and no complex software is installed on it.

EAP-TLS   The *EAP-TLS* method uses the authentication exchange of the *Transport Layer Security* protocol, whose most current version is specified in RFC 5246 [DR08]. As the TLS protocol operates in or above the transport layer, it is explained in Chapter 13.

Other EAP methods   In addition to the EAP extensions described here, a wide range of other proprietary and standardised methods are available. Particularly noteworthy methods from the first category are the CHAP-based, cryptographically weak Lightweight Extensible Authentication Protocol (LEAP), which was occasionally used in WLAN applications, and EAP Tunneled Transport Layer Security (EAP-TTLS) [FB08], which is also based on TLS protection but enables clients to authenticate themselves via user name and password. The second category includes a range of password-based methods such as EAP-PSK, EAP-PWD and EAP-EKE, which each have different advantages and disadvantages with regard to cryptographic security, computational overhead and flexibility. EAP-EKE [SZT$^+$11] uses the DH-EKE method described in Section 7.7, although it is not widely used due to the patent situation.

11.4.3   PPP Encryption

Once a PPP connection has been successfully authenticated, the *Encryption Control Protocol* encryption of the transmitted user data can be negotiated. The *Encryption Control Protocol (ECP)* [Mey96] defined in RFC 1968 is used to negotiate the method used and its parameters. ECP uses the same frame format as the link control protocol (LCP) and introduces two additional service primitives: *Reset-Request* and *Reset-Ack*. With the help of these primitives decryption errors can be indicated and acknowledged allowing for cryptographic resynchronisation (also see Section 2.5).

The configure primitive is used to negotiate a specific cryptographic scheme with the desired scheme defined as the parameter.

The values *DESE* and *3DESE* are predefined for simple or triple DES encryption and *proprietary* for the negotiation of proprietary schemes. Proprietary schemes are uniquely identified through a registered *Organisational Unit Identifier (OUI)* that identifies the vendor plus a vendor-specific value for the identification of a specified scheme.

Exactly one ECP packet can be transported in the PPP data field. Two values are defined for identifying ECP packets in the PPP protocol field: 0x8053 for standard mode and 0x8055 for the separate encryption of individual link layer connections when several such connections exist to the same destination, for example with the simultaneous use of multiple ISDN connections to the same peer entity.

A PPP frame can transport exactly one ECP packet

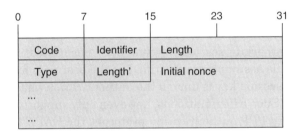

Figure 11.10
Frame format of PPP Encryption Control Protocol

Figure 11.10 illustrates the frame format of an ECP message requesting a DESE encryption protocol. Similar to LCP, the request is made using a configure-request primitive (Code 1). The *type* field contains the value 3 when it requests DESEv2 (DESEv2 is an updated version which replaced the first version of the protocol). The *length* field that follows indicates the total length of this configuration option (10 with DESEv2). The parameter *Initial nonce* contains an eight octet long initialisation vector for DES in CBC mode (also see Section 3.1).

The format of PPP packets encrypted in accordance with the DESEv2 protocol [SM98b] is illustrated in Figure 11.11 and includes the link layer header for the encapsulation into HDLC frames. The address field contains the value '11111111' and the control field the value '00000011'. The value 0x0053 in the *protocol ID* field identifies the DESE protocol. The sequence number field that follows is initially assigned the value 0 and incremented by 1 with each packet transmitted by the sending peer entity. The length of the actual user data is padded to an integer multiple of eight octets prior to encryption and then encrypted with the DES algorithm in CBC mode.

DESEv2

Figure 11.11
Format of encrypted
PPP packets
(DESEv2)

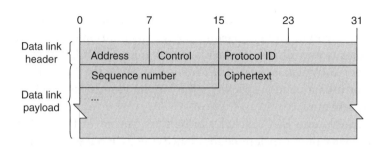

Figure 11.11
Format of encrypted PPP packets (DESEv2)

3DESE The 3DESE protocol, which can be negotiated with the ECP protocol per configure-request with the type field set at value `0x02` and is very similar to the DESEv2 protocol, can be used as an alternative to DESEv2 [Kum98]. The only difference between the two protocols is that 3DESE involves triple DES encryption with three different keys.

Session keys are a All encryption protocols for PPP are based on the assumption
prerequisite of PPP that an appropriate session key has been negotiated prior to en-
encryption protocols cryption. This assumption is justified as the best time for the negotiation of a session key is during the authentication phase of a PPP connection. Such a negotiation is, however, only supported by one of the described PPP authentication protocols, the EAP-TLS protocol (see Section 13.1.3).

11.5 Point-to-Point Tunneling Protocol

The PPP protocol was originally only designed to be run directly between peer entities sharing a layer 2 connection. An example is a PC that is connected over a telephone connection to the ac-
Basic idea of PPTP cess computer of an ISP. The basic idea behind the design of the *Point-to-Point Tunneling Protocol (PPTP)* was to extend the reach of PPP over the entire Internet by defining a method for transporting PPP packets as the payload of IP packets. This allows for PPTP being able to establish 'logical layer 2 connectivity' over which arbitrary layer 3 protocols such as IPv4, IPv6, IPX, Net-BEUI, AppleTalk, etc. can operate. Furthermore, it is possible to authenticate connections and match them with a user account.

Content and transport The payloads of PPTP packets are therefore PPP packets
of PPTP packets without layer 2-specific protocol fields such as HDLC information fields, the insertion of additional characters to achieve code transparency, CRC checksums, etc. For transport in the Internet the PPP packets are encapsulated into the payload of packets of the *Generic Routing Encapsulation Protocol (GRE)*, which are then

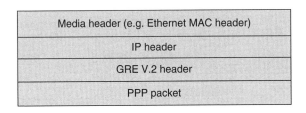

Figure 11.12
Structure of PPTP
packets

encapsulated into the payload of IP packets. Figure 11.12 shows the structure of the resulting PPTP packets.

11.5.1 Basic Versions of PPTP Packet Encapsulation

Based on the encapsulation described, PPTP in a way creates a *tunnel* through the Internet in which PPP packets are transported. Such a tunnel can be realised between diverse entities with the following two types highlighting the kinds of differences that exist:

- Between a user PC and a *PPTP remote access server (RAS)*: With this version the user PC encapsulates the PPP packets itself and sends the resulting IP packets to the RAS server of the network where logical layer 2 connectivity should be available. As the encapsulation takes place with the active involvement of the user PC, this version is also called *voluntary tunneling*. The RAS server acts as the tunnel end point for the user PC in the destination network.

  Voluntary tunneling

- Between the local access node *(Point of Presence, POP)* of an ISP and a PPTP remote access server: This version does not involve the user PC in the decision about whether packets should be tunnelled with PPTP. It is therefore also called *compulsory tunneling*. In this instance, the dial-up node of the ISP functions as a *proxy client* of the user PC *vis-à-vis* the RAS server. Although security can be realised at the subnetwork level with this version, true end-to-end security between the user PC and the RAS service cannot be achieved this way because the dial-up node of the ISP is the cryptographic peer entity of the RAS server. Consequently, for security reasons preference may be given to voluntary encapsulation, if possible.

  Compulsory tunneling

  The dial-up node functions as a proxy

Figure 11.13 shows the frame structure on the different network segments when a user PC (client) accesses an application server that is located in an Intranet to which the client is attached through compulsory PPTP tunnelling.

Compulsory tunneling

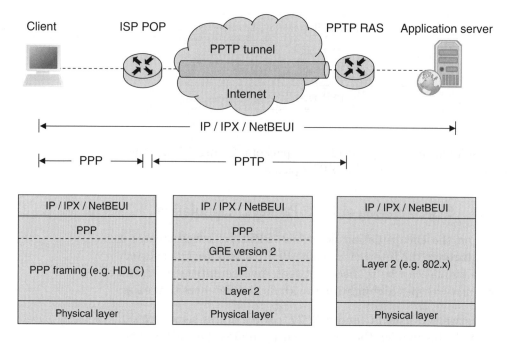

Figure 11.13
Compulsory tunneling with PPTP

The client PC exchanges layer 3 frames (IPv4, IPv6, IPX, NetBEUI, etc.) that are conventionally encapsulated in PPP frames with the dial-up node. The dial-up node encapsulates the received layer 3 frames in new PPP frames that themselves are encapsulated in GRE frames. These are in turn encapsulated in IP packets and sent to the RAS server. The RAS server decapsulates these packets and routes the contained layer 3 frames of the client PC to the local sub-network. layer 3 frames from the opposite direction are routed in a similar way to the client PC.

Voluntary tunneling

Voluntary tunneling by the client PC creates a complex frame structure on the network segment between the client PC and the dial-up node of the ISP, as shown in Figure 11.14.

Direct PPTP tunnel between PC and RAS server

In this case, a PPTP tunnel is created directly between the client PC and the RAS server. The IP packets being transported for this purpose are again encapsulated in PPP frames between the client PC and the dial-up node of the ISP. The dial-up node extracts the IP packets from the PPP frames and routes them without any further processing to the RAS server. The PPTP tunnel is not visible to the dial-up node because the IP packets of the client PC are not analysed by it.

Frame construction in client PC

Figure 11.15 illustrates the construction of the frame structure in the client PC for TCP or UDP-oriented transmission with voluntary tunneling. First an application process generates user

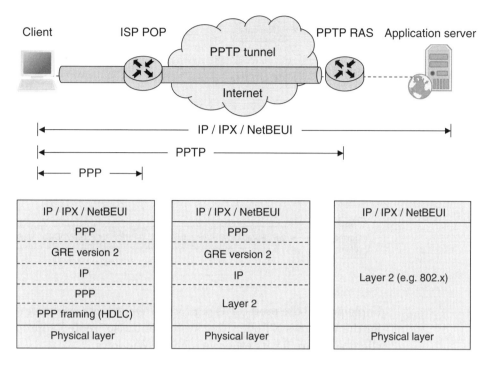

data and sends it with the appropriate system call to the protocol processing interface of the operating system (this normally involves using a *socket interface*). The TCP/IP module then prepares an appropriate TCP or UDP frame and places an IP header in front of it. The PPTP software active in the computer encapsulates this IP packet into a PPP and a GRE frame and arranges for this data to be sent in an IP packet. The IP packet itself is prepared by the TCP/IP module and the appropriate system function is invoked to send the packet. The PPP device driver active in the system encapsulates the IP packet into a PPP frame and sends this frame over the modem connected to the computer to the dial-up node of the ISP. This process is run in 'reverse order' for incoming data with the different protocol headers being processed successively and stripped until the user data can be delivered to the addressed application process.

Figure 11.14
Voluntary tunneling with PPTP

11.5.2 Development of PPTP and Alternative Approaches

As a result of Microsoft's support of the protocol in its operating systems, PPTP has enjoyed widespread use during recent years. In fact, Microsoft was heavily involved in the development of the protocol and the corresponding RFC 2637 [HPV$^+$99]. Microsoft

Widespread use due to Microsoft's support in its operating systems

Figure 11.15
Frame construction
with voluntary
PPTP tunnelling

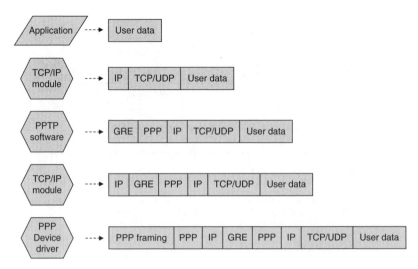

implemented the protocol as part of its *Remote Access Service (RAS)* for the Windows NT operating system and also created appropriate client software for its other versions of Windows.

Proprietary extensions   In addition, Microsoft specified proprietary extensions for the PPP protocol, in particular *Microsoft PPP CHAP Extensions* [ZC98] and *Microsoft Point-to-Point Encryption Protocol (MPPE)* [PZ01].

No genuine PPTP *security measures*   PPTP does not define any security measures of its own and instead only uses the appropriate protocol mechanisms of the PPP standard or the above extensions proposed by Microsoft. However, not least also because the network-topological usage scenarios were changed from those in PPP, a number of deficiencies were discovered in Microsoft's extensions and in PPTP Version 1 as well as in the improved Version 2 [SM98a, SMW99]. Currently it is possible to reconstruct passwords of arbitrary complexity from MS CHAP dialogues within a few hours [MHR12]. Therefore, even Microsoft recommends avoiding the usage of MS CHAP. Instead MS CHAP authentication messages should be encapsulated with EAP and protected by TLS, which will be described in Section 13.2.

Other developments   At about the same time that PPTP was being developed, Cisco, a company that mainly specialises in network technology, presented a proposal for a competing protocol, the *Layer 2 Forwarding protocol (L2F)* [VLK98]. The IETF working group therefore could not reach a general consensus on adopting PPTP as a standard protocol. As a result, a compromise was reached in which the advantages of both protocols were merged into a single protocol, the *Layer 2 Tunneling Protocol (L2TP)* [TVR$^+$99, LTG05].

The two protocols (PPTP and L2TP) have the following similar-   *Comparison of PPTP*
ities and differences: *and L2TP*

- Both protocols use PPP for the initial encapsulation of layer 3
  frames (IP, IPX, NetBEUI, AppleTalk, etc.). They also extend
  the PPP model by allowing layer 2 end points to reside on
  other systems than the PPP end points. Both protocols also
  support voluntary and compulsory tunneling.

- Both protocols offer optional protocol header compression,
  with L2TP operating with a minimum overhead of four octets compared with six octets for PPTP.

- For the communication protocols between the two tunnel end
  points PPTP requires the transport of GRE-PDUs in IP packets, whereas L2TP supports a range of different technologies,
  such as IP (with UDP), Frame Relay, X.25 or ATM.

- PPTP only supports one tunnel between two tunnel end points
  (host or gateway system), whereas L2TP allows multiple tunnels simultaneously, therefore enabling separate tunnels to
  be created for different quality of service requirements of the
  transmission service.

- L2TP contains no own mechanisms to secure the confidentiality or authentication and integrity of the transported data.
  Only control messages may be protected in terms of integrity
  and authentication by an HMAC MD5 authentication code.
  The security must be provided either by the encapsulated
  protocol – like PPP – or the L2TP frames themselves must be
  completely encapsulated by a different protocol, for example
  IPsec, which is presented in the next chapter. The latter solution is more secure and also more widely used.

PPTP as well as L2TP enable *virtual layer 2 connectivity* between   *Virtual layer*
systems that are only able to communicate with each other over a   *2 connectivity*
switching network (with layer 3 involvement). The advantages of
virtual layer 2 connectivity are that the respective systems can use
any layer 3 protocol (IP, IPX, NetBEUI, AppleTalk, etc.) to communicate with each other and systems can also be users of the same
layer 3 subnetwork no matter what their actual location is. To a
certain extent, this makes it possible to implement *virtual layer 3
subnetworks*. This idea is considered more fully in the following section, which presents different definitions and implementations for
virtual private networks (VPN).

11.6   Virtual Private Networks

Various definitions   A number of different definitions exist for the term *virtual private networks (VPN)*. Three of the most common definitions are as follows [FH98]:

- A virtual private network is a private network that is set up within a public network infrastructure (such as the Internet).
- A virtual private network is a communications environment in which access to communication services is controlled to permit connections only within a well-defined group of entities. This communications environment is formed through a partitioning of the common underlying communication medium with the communication medium providing its services to the virtual network on a non-exclusive basis.
- A virtual private network is a logical computer network with restricted usage that is constructed from the system resources of a relatively public physical network (such as the Internet) with encryption often used and tunnelling links created by the virtual network across the public network.

The last two definitions explicitly incorporate certain security properties such as *controlled access* and *encryption*, whereas the first definition makes no mention of this. In reality, several techniques exist for building virtual private networks that provide only minimal security against external attacks. The primary intention with this type of virtual private network lies more in providing uniform logical addressing than incorporating security measures.

A number of different techniques exist for building virtual private networks:

Dedicated connections   ■ *Based on dedicated connections*: A VPN is established through dedicated layer 2 connections, for example using ATM or Frame-Relay connections, Multi-Protocol over ATM (MPOA) or Multi-Protocol Label Switching (MPLS). Depending on the protocol architecture of the underlying connection technology, the security mechanisms for VPNs in this category can be provided efficiently by the protocols used on the links. An example of this would be using the *ATM security specification* to secure a VPN [ATM99]. There are, however, no commercial systems available to do this.

Route filtering   ■ *Per route filtering and controlled route propagation*: The basic idea behind this approach is to control the propagation of routing information so that only certain network nodes or subnetworks receive routing information for the other subnetworks of a VPN. At least for neighbouring networks, the level of security that can be achieved with this approach relies only on the secrecy of certain routing information. It should therefore be classified in the category *'Security by Obscurity'* and be avoided because it is based on attackers not gaining knowledge about the network topology of such a VPN.

- *By building tunnels through the Internet*: Approaches in this category use the protocols GRE, PPP, PPTP and L2TP discussed in this chapter. The *security architecture for the Internet protocol IPsec*, which supplies security services directly in the network layer IP and is discussed in detail in the following chapter, should also be allocated to this category.

Tunnel building

In this book virtual private networks are mainly of interest because of the level of security they can provide. Consequently, approaches based on route filtering and controlled route propagation are not given any further attention. Not least because of space, this book mainly focuses on the prevalent Internet protocol suite, and approaches based on dedicated connections are therefore not examined. However, interested readers are particularly advised to compare the security protocols handled in this book with the ATM security specification [ATM99]. The connection-orientated communication model available with ATM offers some advantages for the efficient implementation of security measures compared with connectionless Internet technology.

Irrespective of the degree of security possible in a VPN, other external influences (e.g. quality of service) mentioned in this book cannot be excluded in the case of VPNs that are mainly implemented through tunnel-building in the Internet. The Internet publication *Wired* wrote the following fitting comments in its February 1998 issue: *'Sure, it's a lot cheaper than using your own frame relay connections, but it works about as well as sticking cotton in your ears in Times Square and pretending nobody else is around.'*

External influence on quality of service, etc.

11.7 Summary

According to the OSI model, the main task of the link layer is to provide reliable data transmission between systems that are directly connected over a medium. The responsibility for providing security from intentional manipulation is usually not one of its core services. As a result, the security protocols of the link layer should be interpreted in the sense that they secure the protocol data units of the communication layer that is transporting the protocol data units of the network layer.

IEEE 802.1.1Q,
802.1X and 802.1AE

In local area networks (LANs), such as Ethernet, and to some extend also wireless LANs (WLANs) or WIMAX, that are based on IEEE 802 standards, *IEEE 802.1Q, IEEE 802.1X* and *IEEE 802.1AE* allow for the realisation of security services. IEEE 802.1Q may be used to separate traffic and to organise so-called virtual LANs (VLANs). A premise is, however, the protection of the attached VLAN tags by physical or cryptographic means. The latter may be realised by the two other standards, whereas IEEE 802.1X restricts access to the data transmission service of LANs to authenticated and authorised hosts only. For this purpose the standard introduces the basic property of *port-based access control*, which only allows systems attached to a LAN port access to the data transmission service of the LAN if a prior successful authentication and authorisation check has been performed. A further specification for securing data transmission in LANs from eavesdropping or the modification of transmitted data units is included in 802.1AE. The described mechanism, also called MACsec, protects PDUs by making use of AES-GCM.

PPP

In addition to normal layer 2 protocol functions, the *Point-to-Point Protocol (PPP)* that was designed for the exchange of layer 3 protocol data units over direct connections (e.g. dedicated lines, telephone connections) also contains optional protocol mechanisms for authenticating peer entities and protecting transmission from eavesdropping. This involves performing an authentication exchange and using an encryption protocol after the establishment of a layer 2 connection. The protocol does not, however, provide for cryptographic security against intentional manipulation or measures against replaying data units.

PPTP

The *Point-to-Point Tunneling Protocol (PPTP)* enables PPP to be used between systems that do not share a serial connection by performing an encapsulation of PPP data units in IP packets. This allows separate systems even from remote network areas to operate in a particular layer 3 subnetwork. PPTP does not define any new security measures of its own but instead uses the protocol functions that already exist in PPP. The *Layer 2 Tunneling Protocol (L2TP)* that was developed during Internet standardisation combines the advantages of PPTP, which was heavily influenced by Microsoft, and the protocol *Layer 2 Forwarding (L2F)*, which was specified by Cisco. None of these protocols provides an adequate cryptographic protection. Instead, the companies distributing products involving the protocols recommend the usage of L2TP and an encapsulation with IPsec, which will be presented in the next chapter.

The approaches mentioned above enable *virtual private networks (VPN)* to be constructed through tunnel building through the Internet. Other techniques for building VPNs include the use of *dedicated layer 2 connections* and *route filtering*, although the latter is not actually a security measure since its 'security' depends on the secrecy of the routing information. An alternative approach, also based on tunnel building, is the *IPsec security architecture* discussed in the next chapter.

Virtual private networks

11.8 Supplemental Reading

[ATM99]   ATM FORUM: *ATM Security Specification Version 1.0.* February 1999. – AF-SEC- 0100.000

[HPV+99] HAMZEH, K.; PALL, G.; VERTHEIN, W.; TAARUD, J.; LITTLE, W.; ZORN, G.: *Point-to-Point Tunneling Protocol.* July 1999. – RFC 2637, IETF, Status: Informational,
          https://tools.ietf.org/html/rfc2637

[IEE06]   IEEE (INSTITUTE OF ELECTRICAL AND ELECTRONICS ENGINEERS): *Standards for Local and Metropolitan Area Networks – Security.* The Institute of Electrical and Electronics Engineers (IEEE), IEEE Std 802.1AE-2006, 2006

[IEE10]   IEEE (INSTITUTE OF ELECTRICAL AND ELECTRONICS ENGINEERS): *Standards for Local and Metropolitan Area Networks – Port Based Network Access Control.* The Institute of Electrical and Electronics Engineers (IEEE), IEEE Std 802.1X-2010, 2010

[IEE11a] IEEE (INSTITUTE OF ELECTRICAL AND ELECTRONICS ENGINEERS): IEEE *Standard for Local and metropolitan area networks – Media Access Control (MAC) Bridges and Virtual Bridged Local Area Networks.* The Institute of Electrical and Electronics Engineers (IEEE), IEEE Std 802.1Q-2011, 2011

[LTG05]   LAU, J.; TOWNSLEY, M.; GOYRET, I.: *Layer Two Tunneling Protocol – Version 3 (L2TPv3).* March 2005. – RFC 3931, IETF, Status: Proposed Standard,
          https://tools.ietf.org/html/rfc3931

[Mey96]   MEYER, G.: *The PPP Encryption Control Protocol (ECP).* Juni 1996. – RFC 1968 , IETF, Status:

Proposed Standard,
https://tools.ietf.org/html/rfc1968

[SM98a]   SCHNEIER, B.; MUDGE: Cryptanalysis of Microsoft's
Point-to-Point Tunneling Protocol (PPTP). In: *ACM
Conference on Computer and Communications
Security*, 1998, pp. 132–141

[SMW99]   SCHNEIER, B.; MUDGE; WAGNER, D.: Cryptanalysis of
Microsoft's PPTP Authentication Extensions
(MS-CHAPv2). In: *International Exhibition and
Congress on Secure Networking – CQRE [Secure]*, 1999

[SZT+11]   SHEFFER, Y.; ZORN, G.; TSCHOFENIG, H.; FLUHRER, S.:
*An EAP Authentication Method Based on the
Encrypted Key Exchange (EKE) Protocol*. February
2011. – RFC 6124, IETF, Status: Informational,
https://tools.ietf.org/html/rfc6124

[TVR+99]   TOWNSLEY, W.; VALENCIA, A.; RUBENS, A.; PALL, G.;
ZORN, G.; PALTER, B.: *Layer Two Tunneling Protocol
(L2TP)*. August 1999. – RFC 2661, IETF, Status:
Draft standard,
https://tools.ietf.org/html/rfc2661

[ZC98]   ZORN, G.; COBB, S.: *Microsoft PPP CHAP Extensions*.
October 1998. – RFC 2433, IETF, Status:
Informational,
https://tools.ietf.org/html/rfc2433

11.9   Questions

1. Can IEEE 802.1X be used to protect the integrity and confidentiality of user data exchanged in a local area network?

2. Compare the concept of security labels, introduced in Chapter 9, with the tags used in IEEE 802.1Q.

3. Is a VLAN separation according to IEEE 802.1Q effective, if an administrator needs to assume that attackers may have physical access to some switches? What would happen if a protection according to 802.1AE was used at the same time?

4. Why may an 802.1AE encryption not make direct use of a statically shared secret between two or more switches?

5. What is the advantage of using the standard IEEE 802.1X to secure local area networks considering that authentication verification is divided between the authenticator and the authentication server? What are the disadvantages from a security perspective?

6. Why is it that with PPP neither DESEv2 nor 3DESE can be used to secure the Password Authentication Protocol?

7. Which packet sizes result in a severer impact of the protocol overhead created by PPTP: small or large IP packets?

8. Why are two PPP packet headers needed for PPTP with voluntary tunneling?

9. Which of the protocols PPP, PPTP and L2TP protect the data integrity of transmitted user data?

10. Among other configurations the EAP-EKE protocol may be used with $\mathbb{Z}_p$ for $p = 2^{1024} - 2^{960} - 1 + 2^{64} \times (2^{894}\pi + 129093)$. This number starts with 66 '1' bits. Does this lead to security implications for DH-EKE?

11. What are the advantages of virtual private networks?

12 IPsec Security Architecture

The *IPsec security architecture* comprises a range of protocols and a framework architecture that are used to secure the protocol data units of the *Internet Protocol (IP)*. After a brief review of the basic background of the IP, this chapter presents an overview of the main components of the IPsec architecture with detailed discussions appearing in the subsequent sections.

12.1 Short Introduction to the Internet Protocol Suite

As a network layer protocol, the IP has the task of enabling communication between systems that are not directly connected to one another over a shared medium. IP thus offers a connectionless datagram service with no guarantee of packet delivery and is therefore characterised as 'unreliable.' However, this characterisation of IP as being unreliable should not suggest that IP packets are frequently not delivered correctly when the traffic load in the Internet is at a 'normal' level. It only means that the protocol does not provide explicit mechanisms to guarantee correct delivery or any other assurances for quality of service (e.g. end-to-end delay or jitter). The IP service is therefore referred to as *'best effort'*. *'Best effort' service*

Figure 12.1 shows how IP is embedded in the *TCP/IP protocol suite*. The TCP/IP suite organises the distributed information

Unreliable datagram service

'Best effort' service
TCP/IP protocol suite

Figure 12.1

*Distributed informa-
tion processing based
on TCP/IP protocol
suite*

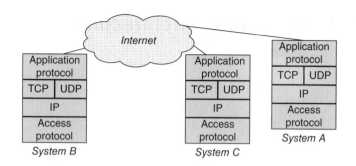

processing in systems connected over a compound network like the
Internet, that is, a 'network of networks', into four protocol layers:

Access protocols
- A series of *access protocols* that perform functions up to and
  including the second OSI layer and which, in practice, are
  often realised through a LAN protocol, such as Ethernet,
  WLAN or, with point-to-point connections, through PPP.

Internet Protocol
- The *IP*, which provides an unreliable connectionless datagram service.

*Transmission
Control Protocol*
- The *Transmission Control Protocol (TCP)*, which provides a
  reliable connection-oriented transport service realised over
  IP.

*User Datagram
Protocol*
- The *User Datagram Protocol (UDP)*, which offers an unreliable and connectionless transport service and is therefore
  basically only an application interface to IP with application
  process addressing.

Application protocols
- A range of *application protocols*, including *Simple Mail Transfer Protocol (SMTP)* for the delivery of e-mail and *Hypertext
  Transfer Protocol (HTTP)* for transmission of web page structures, to name just two of the currently most important ones.

Figure 12.2
*Format of an
IPv4 packet*

Ver.	IHL	ToS		Length	
IP identification			Flags	Fragment offset	
TTL		Protocol		IP checksum	
Source address					
Destination address					
IP options (if any)					
TCP / UDP / ... Payload					

Figure 12.2 shows the structure of an IP packet in version 4 (IPv4).
The fields contained in the protocol header have the following significance:

- *Version (Ver.):* This 4-bit field gives the protocol version. Most systems are still using version 4 of the protocol although specifications for its successor, version 6, have been available for some time. Version 5 was used for an interim version with an incomplete specification. *Version*

- *IP header length (IHL):* This 4-bit field gives the length of the IP header in 32-bit words. *IP header length*

- *Type of service (ToS):* The original purpose of this 8-bit field was to express specific quality of service requirements for packets in the form of prioritisation. Currently 6 bits are used to mark IP flows in scenarios where quality-of-service (QoS) guarantees are given. The remaining 2 bits are used for congestion control (Explicit Congestion Notification, ECN). *Type of service*

- *Length:* The overall length of a packet, including packet header and user data, is indicated in octets in this 16-bit field. Like all other protocol fields in the TCP/IP protocol suite, this field is coded in 'big endian' representation. *Length*

- *IP identification:* This field 'uniquely' identifies IP packets and is very important for the segmentation and reassembling of fragmented IP packets. *IP identification*

- *Flags:* The flag field contains 3 bits to indicate whether an IP packet can be fragmented or whether an IP packet is the last fragment of a larger packet, and 1 bit that is reserved for future applications. *Flags*

- *Fragment offset:* This 13-bit field contains the position of a fragment within a fragmented IP packet. *Fragment offset*

- *Time to Live (TTL):* At every IP-processing network node this 8-bit field is decremented by one. When the TTL field reaches 0, the packet is discarded before the packet is forwarded to the next node, thereby preventing packet looping in the case of inconsistent routing information. *Time to Live*

- *Protocol:* This 8-bit field shows the (transport) protocol of the payload and is therefore used by hosts to identify the correct protocol entity (TCP, UDP, etc.) for the user data. *Protocol*

- *IP checksum:* The 16-bit checksum contained in this field is used to detect errors in the protocol header. As it is not a cryptographic checksum, it can easily be forged. *IP checksum*

- *Source address:* This field contains the 32-bit long source address of the sending system. *Source address*

- *Destination address:* This is also a 32-bit long field and it contains the destination address of the intended receiver of an IP packet. *Destination address*

■ *IP options:* An IP packet header can optionally carry variable-length information. As options are not of high importance to IPsec, they will not be discussed further.

Ver.	Traffic Class	Flow Label	
Payload Length		Next Header	Hop Limit
Source Address			
Destination Address			
IP Options (if any, like higher level protocols)			
TCP / UDP / ... Payload			

Figure 12.3 shows the typical structure of headers when IP version 6 (IPv6) is used. Note that the header is greatly simplified. Only the following fields are used, in addition to the version number:

■ *Traffic Class:* This 8-bit long field is used to prioritise certain traffic flows. It is comparable to the ToS field in IPv4.

■ *Flow Label:* This 20-bit long field can be used to mark related IP packets so that they are processed in the same way in the routers. This field is similar to the Traffic Class field and is used for implementing QoS.

■ *Payload Length:* In contrast to IPv4, only the data length (without header) is stored in this 16-bit long field, including the length of any options.

■ *Next Header:* This 8-bit long field is similar to the protocol field in IPv4. If IP options are used, the value of the next option is stored here.

■ *Hop Limit:* The purpose of this field is identical to the TTL field in IPv4. The new name is intended to indicate that there is no temporal limit.

■ *Source Address:* This field contains the 128-bit long source address of the sender.

■ *Destination Address:* The destination address field is also 128 bits long and generally concludes the IP header.

■ *IP Options:* As in IPv4, an IPv6 packet header can contain optional information of variable length. For example, packet fragmentation is resolved through an option field. However, the options have to be interpreted as further encapsulated protocols. In many cases their behaviour is more or less transparent for the IPsec security architecture. Some option fields, such as those that affect the routing, should be treated with caution in environments where security is crucial.

The original IP has some fundamental security deficiencies because security aspects were not included in the requirements for the protocol during its development. However, IP version 6 can normally be used without further security precautions. In both cases, there are no assurances regarding the following security properties when an entity is receiving an IP packet:

Security problems with IP protocol

- *Data origin authentication and data integrity:* Was the packet actually sent by the entity indicated as the sender in the protocol header, and does the packet contain the exact content placed in it by the sender, or was the content of the packet modified while in transit to the receiver? Is the destination address given in the packet header actually the address the sender of the packet specified as the original receiving entity?

  Data origin authentication and data integrity

- *Replay protection:* Is this packet the fresh packet sent by the indicated sender or an intentional replay of an old packet by an attacker?

  Packet replaying

- *Confidentiality:* Was the packet spied on by an unauthorised third party while in transit from sender to receiver?

  Confidentiality

12.2 Overview of the IPsec Architecture

The objective of the IPsec security architecture is to eliminate the security problems listed above. Its security objectives are therefore as follows:

IPsec security objectives

- *Data origin authentication and data integrity:* It should not be possible to send an IP packet with a forged source address or to modify the destination address of an IP packet without detection by the receiver. It also should not be possible for the content of a packet to be modified without detection by the receiver.

- *Replay protection:* It should not be possible for a packet to be replayed at a later time without detection by the receiver.

- *Confidentiality:* It should not be possible to read the content of transmitted IP packets. Furthermore, IPsec should provide limited protection from traffic flow analyses.

Another important objective of the IPsec architecture is to give sender, receiver and all intermediate gateway nodes the option of

Security policy

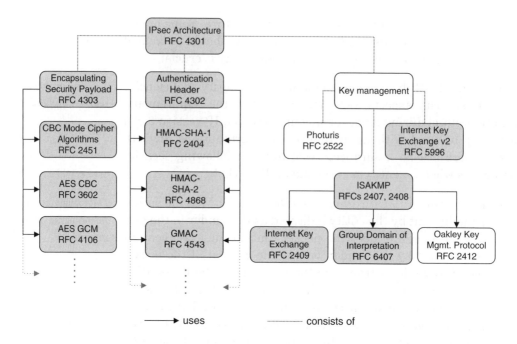

Figure 12.4
Overview of
IPsec Standards

Main concepts
and components

deciding which security requirements they want to apply to specific IP traffic flows according to the local *security policy*. The sending entities (host and gateway systems) secure IP packets according to a local security policy and receiving entities discard packets that have inadequate protection because they lack confidence in these packets.

An overview of the key components of the IPsec architecture is presented in Figure 12.4. The main concepts of the architecture are defined in RFC 4301 [KS05]. These include the concept of *Security Association (SA)*, the conceptual *Security Associations Database (SADB)*, the *Security Policy* and the conceptual *Security Policy Database (SPD)*. RFC 4301 also gives an overview of the two fundamental security protocols of the architecture, *Authentication Header (AH)* and *Encapsulating Security Payload (ESP)*, both of which are specified in separate RFCs. Both protocols can be operated in one of two possible operation modes, *transport mode* or *tunnel mode*. Other RFCs specify details on the use of specific cryptographic operations with AH and ESP:

- Triple-DES, AES and other block ciphers in cipher block chaining (CBC) mode are provided for encryption. AES may also be used in counter mode. Despite some efforts there is no standard for using streaming ciphers, like RC4, with IPsec.

■ Data origin authentication and integrity protection for IP packets is often realised using an HMAC construction, with MD5 [MG98a], SHA-1 [MG98b], SHA-2 [KF07] and RIPEMD-160 [KP00] currently provided as cryptographic hash functions. Furthermore, it is possible to use AES in GMAC [MV06], CMAC [SPL06] or XCBC mode [FH03].

■ IPsec also offers two mechanisms for authenticated encryption. Besides the use of the Counter with CBC-MAC (CCM) mode [Hou05], it is possible to deploy GCM [VM05], which has already been discussed in Section 5.5.1. Details regarding CCM will be given in Section 15.4.2 in the context of WLANs. In any case the usage of the block cipher AES is recommended.

The *Internet Key Exchange Protocol (IKE)* in version 1 or 2 is used to negotiate the keys needed for the cryptographic operations above and perform entity authentication.

In this context a security association (SA) can be interpreted *Security association* as a type of 'simplex connection' that provides specific security services to the traffic it carries. The term 'connection' is used with quotation marks because the IP realises a *connectionless* and thus a *stateless* service for all participating entities. However, the respective peer entities require certain state knowledge to implement the security services, for example in respect of the security mechanisms and keys used. This state is administered through SAs established, deployed and dissolved between peer entities. As an SA is basically only used for one communication direction, two SAs are always needed for the usual bidirectional communication.

The security services negotiated for an SA are supplied by one *Identification of SAs* of the two security protocols: *Authentication Header (AH)* or *Encapsulating Security Payload (ESP)*. A triple, which consists of a *Security Parameter Index (SPI)*, an IP destination address and the identifier of one of the two security protocols (AH or ESP), provides the unique SA identification for each system.

An SA can basically be established between the following *Peer entities of SAs* entities:

■ host ↔ host;
■ host ↔ gateway;
■ gateway ↔ gateway.

Two conceptual databases should exist in each system for the administration and specification of SAs. The *Security Association Database (SADB)* contains the SAs active in a system at any given *Administration and specification of SAs and their parameters* time, and the *Security Policy Database (SPD)* defines which security services are being applied to which IP packets and how this application should be executed. The SPD therefore identifies which SAs need to be established between which peer entities for which data streams and specifies the parameters to be negotiated for these associations. These databases are thus called 'conceptual databases' since no 'real' database technology is required, e.g. a relational database with general query language like SQL. The security architecture does not define how the databases are implemented, but they are normally simpler than the general concepts of database management systems.

Figure 12.5
Packet formats
for transport and
tunnel modes

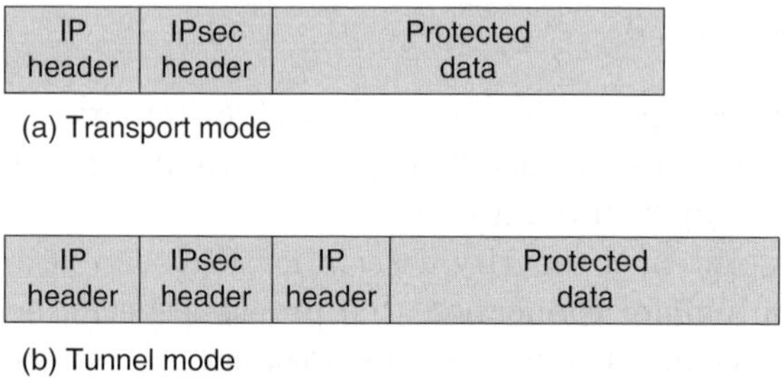

IP header	IPsec header	Protected data

(a) Transport mode

IP header	IPsec header	IP header	Protected data

(b) Tunnel mode

Protocol modes   An SA is basically operated in one of the following two modes:

Transport mode
- *Transport mode* can only be used between the end points of a communication relationship, i.e. between two hosts, or — if a data stream is destined directly for a gateway system, e.g. in the case of network management applications — between a host and a gateway system.

Tunnel mode
- *Tunnel mode* can be used between any systems.

The difference between the two protocol modes is that transport mode only adds a security-specific protocol header (and possibly a trailer) whereas tunnel mode totally encapsulates the protected IP packets (see also Figure 12.5). This encapsulation of IP packets enables gateway systems to protect certain data streams on behalf of other entities. As a result, these systems can provide uniform protection to entire subnetworks.

Setting up security
associations   Security associations that are defined in the SPD are generally negotiated and set up based on version 1 or 2 of the IKE protocol (IKEv1 or IKEv2). Version 1 is based on a generic protocol for key negotiation referred to as *Internet Security Association Key Management Protocol (ISAKMP)*. Since IKEv2 has not yet been fully established and IKEv1 is also of interest for the development processes of IKEv2, we will first describe ISAKMP and IKEv1.

As already indicated, the ISAKMP [MSS⁺98] only defines a generic framework for entity authentication, key exchange and negotiation of parameters for SAs. It does not identify a specific authentication protocol, but stipulates the 'language' for defining such protocols by specifying fundamental items such as packet formats, retransmission timers, message construction requirements, etc. In principle, ISAKMP is defined as a generic protocol for the authentication and negotiation of security parameters, independently of IPsec. RFC 2407 [Pip98] explains the use of ISAKMP for negotiating pairwise IPSec associations in detail, and separately from the actual protocol definition. In addition, ISAKMP can also be used for setting up group associations [WRH11].

Internet Security Association Key Management Protocol

IKEv1 specified in RFC 2409 [HC98] defines a concrete authentication and key exchange protocol, which is compliant with ISAKMP and can deal with the negotiation of SAs for IPsec. This negotiation takes place in two phases: In the first phase a so-called *IKE SA* is set up, which specifies how other SAs for protecting concrete data streams are to be negotiated between the two peer entities in the second phase.

IKE version 1

IKEv2, the successor standard specified in RFC 5996 [KHN⁺10], can deal with the same tasks as IKEv1 and also involves two phases. However, ISAKMP is no longer used since the generic protocol made the IKEv1 standard unnecessarily complicated.

IKE version 2

Once the SAs have been established, one of the two security protocols deals with protection of the actual user data.

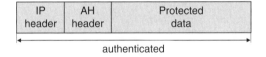

IP header	AH header	Protected data

authenticated

Figure 12.6

Structure of an IP packet with Authentication Header

The security protocol *Authentication Header (AH)* [Ken05a] implements the security service of data origin authentication with replay protection for IP packets. As the name indicates, the protection is provided through a protocol header inserted between the IP protocol header and the user data of the IP packet (see also Figure 12.6).

Header Authentication

In contrast, the security protocol *Encapsulating Security Payload (ESP)* [Ken05b] offers optional data origin authentication with packet replay protection as well as optional confidentiality for transmitted user data. Selection of at least one of the two optional security services is necessary for an SA. The protocol implementation involves an additional protocol header and a trailer, with the

Encapsulating Security Payload

user data of the IP packet encapsulated between them (see also Figure 12.7).

Figure 12.7

Structure of an IP packet with Encapsulating Security Payload

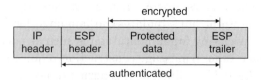

Replay protection Both security protocols AH and ESP carry a sequence number that is used to provide replay protection for IP packets. This sequence number is initialised with the value 1 when an SA is established and incremented by 1 with each packet sent. A new key is needed to replace the session key agreed for the SA before a wraparound of the 32-bit or 64-bit long sequence number occurs. Because this sequence number is always included in the computation of the MAC, any modification of it by an attacker will be detected.

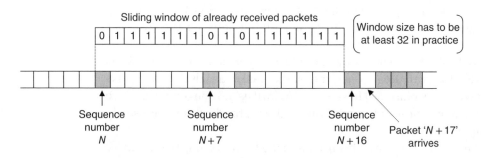

Figure 12.8

Example of a sliding window before updating

The receiver of an IPsec-protected packet always verifies that the sequence number contained in the packet is within a range of acceptable numbers. This range is called a 'sliding window'. The reason an entire window is used is that in the Internet the order of IP packets can change during transmission of IP packets via different routes, even during normal operation. Therefore, later packets may possibly arrive at the receiver sooner than packets that were sent earlier. If receivers were to insist upon a strict sequence of the numbers, they would have to discard IP packets that unintentionally end up in the wrong sequence, which would result in an unnecessary reduction of the data throughput in the Internet. Consequently, a receiver only accepts IP packets if they are not 'too old', that is, if newer IP packets with significantly higher sequence numbers have not already been accepted. This situation is illustrated in Figures 12.8 and 12.9.

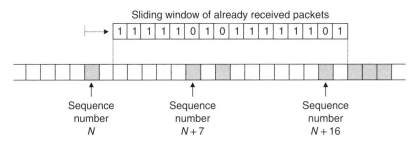

Figure 12.9
Example of a sliding window after a window is updated

Figure 12.8 shows an example of a size 16 receiving window. The packets that have not yet been received are indicated in the grey boxes and the vector of the packets that have already been received shows a 0 in these places and a 1 in the other places. Assuming that $N + 15$ is the sequence number of the most recently received packet, the packet with sequence number N is still acceptable. However, if the packet with sequence number $N + 17$ arrives before this packet, the window is advanced by two positions (see Figure 12.9) so that the packet with sequence number N is now placed to the left of the receiving window and therefore discarded as being too old by the time it is received.

RFC 4302 as well as RFC 4303 specifies a minimum window *Actions of the receiver* size of 32 with the value 64 recommended as the default. On receipt of an IP packet, the receiving system performs the following actions depending on the sequence number:

- If the sequence number is to the left of the receiving window, the receiver discards the packet.
- If the sequence number is inside the receiving window and not marked to be received already, the receiver verifies the MAC and accepts the packet if the verification is successful.
- If the sequence number is to the right of the receiving window, the receiver verifies the MAC and, if the verification is successful, accepts the packet and advances the window to the right.

There are a number of options for the implementation of IPsec. *Implementation* The host itself already offers the two alternatives shown in *options for IPsec* Figure 12.10: *integration of IPsec in the protocol processing func-* *within a device* *tions of the operating system* and *integration as intermediate layer between the IP layer and the access protocol layer*. The latter mode is mainly used when the operating system itself cannot be modified, for example when its source code is not available. However, for performance reasons direct integration into an operating system is clearly the method of choice since it avoids duplication of protocol functionality. Another reason for using an intermediate layer is a direct, tamper-proof realisation of the IPsec functionality in the network card. However, this approach has not proved popular with the mass market because of the high costs associated with it.

Figure 12.10
Integration
alternatives for IPsec
in end systems

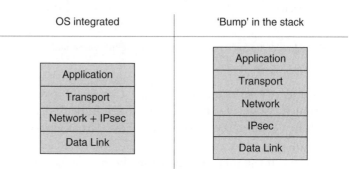

IPsec implement-
ation modes

As explained above, IPsec can be implemented in hosts as well as in gateway systems. The two separate implementation modes exist for both cases. The main advantage of IPsec implementation in a host is the provision of real end-to-end security. Furthermore, there is the availability of specific security services for each individual data stream, and the fact that either transport or tunnel mode can be used.

Implementa-
tion in a host

Implementation in
gateway systems

The advantage of IPsec implementation in gateway systems is that IP packet exchange between two subnetworks over the public Internet can be uniformly secured, thereby enabling the construction of *virtual private networks (VPNs)*. Furthermore, IPsec implementation and configuration is not necessary in each host in this case and the ability exists for IP traffic flowing between remote users and subnetworks to be uniformly secured and authorised. In particular, with proper configuration it is even impossible for compromised clients to simply send data to outside systems. This setup is therefore resistant against so-called covert channels.

The two alternatives shown in Figure 12.11 are used to implement IPsec in gateway systems: *integration directly into the switching system* and *insertion of external units*. With the first alternative IPsec functionality is directly integrated into the protocol functions of the switching system, whereas with the second alternative additional IPsec modules are inserted before each protected input or output of a gateway system. Direct integration is usually preferable for efficiency reasons, so the second alternative is only considered to be a temporary solution

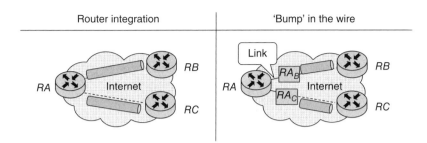

Figure 12.11

*Integration
alternatives for
IPsec in gateway
systems*

for non-IPsec-enabled switching systems. Exceptions are systems
with an extremely high security standard that perform an IPsec
protection by independent and potentially certified instances.
Furthermore, it may be necessary for load balancing reasons to
terminate SAs already in front of the actual router.

12.3   Use of Transport and Tunnel Modes

This section takes a detailed look at the differences between transport mode and tunnel mode, and explains specific usage scenarios.
First we need to distinguish between the two terms *communication
end point* and *cryptographic end point*.

Definition 12.1 *The* **communication end points** *of a data
stream denote the source and destination system of IP packet exchanges. In contrast, systems that generate and process the AH or
ESP protocol headers of IP packet exchanges within the framework
of an SA are called* **cryptographic end points***.*

*Communication
end points and
cryptographic end
points*

These two terms make it easy to distinguish between the usage
areas of transport and tunnel modes:

*Transport and tunnel
mode usage*

- ■ Transport mode can only be used when the cryptographic end
  points are the same as the communication end points (see also
  Figure 12.12).
- ■ Tunnel mode is normally deployed when at least one crypto-
  graphic end point is not a communication end point (see also
  Figures 12.13 and 12.14).

In most cases the communication end points are located in hosts
(PCs, servers, mobile devices), but not necessarily. For example, if
a gateway system is managed by a management station via the
Simple Network Management Protocol (SNMP), then the IP packet
exchanges are addressed to or sent by the gateway system.

Figure 12.12
End-to-end security
with transport mode

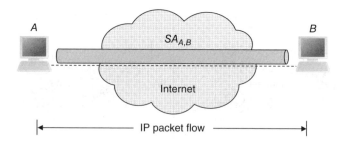

Figure 12.13
Use of tunnel mode
in gateway systems

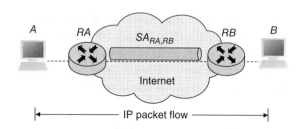

Packet structure

IP header	IPsec header	IP header	Protected Data
Src = RA Dst = RB		Src = A Dst = B	

Intranet scenario   Figure 12.13 illustrates the use of tunnel mode in gateway systems and the structure of packet exchanges between two hosts A and B in the Internet. When packets are transmitted from A to B, the gateway system RA refers to its local security policy to decide whether the packets should be secured based on an SA negotiated with RB. It then generates an appropriate IPsec protocol header (AH or ESP) that is placed in front of the *entire IP packet including the original protocol header*. It also generates a new IP protocol header that is addressed to RB and placed in front of the IPsec protocol header. The original IP packet is therefore transported in a tunnel between RA and RB through the Internet, which also accounts for the term 'tunnel mode'. In practice this sort of configuration is mainly found when two private subnetworks at different locations are networked over the public Internet *(Intranet scenario)*.

'Road warrior'   Figure 12.14 shows a different usage scenario for tunnel mode
scenario   in which the two hosts A and B communicate with one another but this time with the packets being secured between A and RB. Because the cryptographic end point RB is not the same as communication end point B, the packets between A and RB are

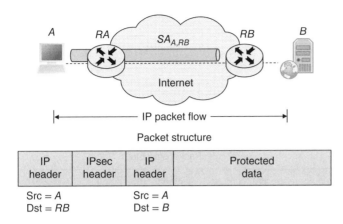

Figure 12.14
Use of tunnel mode
between a host and a
gateway

completely encapsulated. A typical example of this configuration is the *road warrior scenario* in which employees of a company have to access the services of the private subnetwork of the company when they are at remote locations, for example hotel rooms.

Security associations can also be nested, as shown in Figure 12.15. A sample application of nesting is when data exchanged between A and RB is basically authenticated and in addition all data exchanges between RA and RB are encrypted and, therefore, confidentiality is performed at the subnetwork level. As the illustration also shows, a separate IPsec protocol header and a separate IP protocol header are added to the packets for each SA.

Nesting of security associations

It is important when SAs are nested that no overlapping of tunnel segments occurs ('correct bracketing'). Figure 12.16 presents an example of two validly nested associations.

In contrast, the SAs shown in Figure 12.17 are not correctly nested. The packets are transported in a tunnel between RB and RD in such a way that RC is not able to process and strip the IPsec protocol header added by RA for it. Furthermore, after the outer protocol header has been stripped in gateway system RD, the IP packet finds itself at a topologically incorrect position in the network so that it has to be 'routed back' in the direction RC.

12.4 IPsec Protocol Processing

As clarified in the preceding sections, the IPsec architecture allows IP packets to be secured in hosts as well as in gateways. The additional processing procedures required to support IP protocols are listed below. What is evident is that hosts and gateways essentially

Figure 12.15
Nesting of security associations

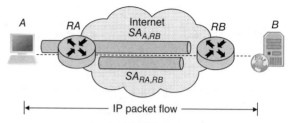

IP header	IPsec header	IP header	IPsec header	IP header	Protected data
Src = RA		Src = A		Src = A	
Dst = RB		Dst = RB		Dst = B	

Figure 12.16
Valid nesting of two security associations

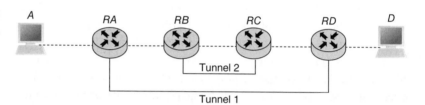

Packet structure

IP header	IPsec header	IP header	IPsec header	IP header	Protected data
Src = RB		Src = RA		Src = A	
Dst = RC		Dst = RD		Dst = D	

Figure 12.17
Example of two SAs with invalid nesting

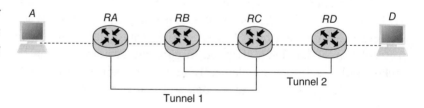

Packet structure

IP header	IPsec header	IP header	IPsec header	IP header	Protected data
Src = RB		Src = RA		Src = A	
Dst = RD		Dst = RC		Dst = D	

both provide the same functions for IPsec so that the only distinction required is between outgoing and incoming packets.

Consider a system that has to send a specific IP packet to another system. The following procedures are required for valid IPsec processing:

IPsec processing of outgoing packets

1. *Determine whether the IP packet has to be secured:* This decision is made on the basis of the local security policy that is stored in the security policy database (SPD). Depending on the action specified in the corresponding SPD entry, the packet is discarded, sent without any further protection or secured before it is sent.
2. *Determine the SA to be used for the IP packet:* If an SA does not yet exist with the corresponding peer entity, a request for authentication and parameter negotiation is sent to the key management entity.
3. *Read SA parameters:* The parameters of the newly generated SA are read from the SADB.
4. *Perform security measures specified in the SA:* This step results in the generation of an AH or ESP protocol header and a new IP protocol header when tunnel mode is used. Depending on which security services were negotiated for the SA, the related user data is encrypted and/or protected with a MAC. All necessary parameters and keys are stored in the corresponding entry in the SADB.
5. *Start IPsec processing for resulting packet:* Once the initial IP packet is ready, normal protocol processing continues as for all other IP packets (see step 1). The reason is that multiple IPsec protocol headers may have to be added in the same system when SAs are nested (look at the direction of B to A in gateway system RB in Figure 12.15).

The following procedures are performed in a system to process incoming IP packets:

IPsec processing of incoming packets

1. *Verify whether the packet contains an IPsec protocol header that the system needs to process:* This verification only considers the most outer IPsec header in each step as IPsec headers always have to be stripped from the outside to the inside.
2. *Process the outer IPsec header:* If the outer IPsec header is stipulated for this particular system, the next step will involve requesting the corresponding SA from the SADB. If the correct SA does not exist in the local system, the packet is

dropped. If the correct SA can be found, the packet is processed accordingly. The packet is also discarded if an error occurs, e.g. false MAC.

3. *Decide whether the packet is correctly secured:* The corresponding entry for the packet is searched in the SPD. Depending on the action specified in the security policy, the packet is either discarded or processed. Another check is required to determine whether an additional IPsec header needs to be processed. In addition, state information has to be stored until the packet has been completely processed (payload conveyed to appropriate transport entity, resulting IP packet forwarded to next router or packet discarded). This state information enables a decision on whether the packet was secured as specified in the security policy after all IPsec headers have been stripped.

Selection of appropriate security policy   As the discussion highlights so far, the security policy plays an important role in processing supported by the IPsec protocol. The following *selectors* are the basis for selecting the appropriate entries for IP packets in the SPD:

- *IP source address:* This can be the address of an individual system, a network prefix, an address range or a wildcard.
- *IP destination address:* This address is specified in the same way as the IP source address. With encapsulated IP packets (tunnel mode), it is always the outer IP packet headers that are evaluated for the source and destination addresses. The inner addresses are, however, also registered in the database.
- *Protocol:* This denotes the protocol identification of the transport protocol for the considered packet. ESP-encrypted user data first has to be decrypted before a decision is possible on whether or not the packet is properly secured.
- *Port of application protocol:* If accessible, the service access point identification of the application protocols can be included in the selection of a security policy.

Content of security policy entries   The entry for a packet is selected in the SPD on the basis of the characteristics mentioned. The entries contain the following information:

- *Identification of own and remote system:* This can be record of the domain name system (DNS) or another name type as defined in the IPsec-specific definitions for authentication protocols, e.g. RFC 2407 [Pip98] for ISAKMP. These names are only evaluated for the purpose of negotiating SAs.

■ A reference on how a so-called Phase-I-SA or IKE SA should be negotiated, for example with main mode or quick mode, or which cryptographic algorithms should be used (see Sections 12.7 and 12.8).

■ Details on which security services should be provided for IP packets, including:

● selectors that themselves identify individual data streams;

● the executable action for these data streams (discarding, direct routing or security);

● security attributes for secured data streams, such as the security protocol (AH or ESP), the protocol mode (transport or tunnel mode), information about the security algorithms and their parameters as well as other parameters such as the lifetime of SAs and the window size for replay protection.

If an SA is already established with a security policy, its identification is referenced in the SPD so that it can be requested efficiently from the SADB.

12.5   The ESP Protocol

The ESP protocol is a generic security protocol that may provide the following security services for IP packets:

ESP security services

■ *confidentiality* through encryption of payload (transport mode) or of complete IP packets (tunnel mode);

■ *data origin authentication* and *packet replay protection* achieved through the addition of a MAC and a sequence number.

Both security services are optional and can be combined with one another, but at least one of the two options must be selected for an SA. Sequence number checks can be activated or deactivated independently of authentication. This, however, only makes sense if an authentication exists, otherwise sequence numbers could be forged arbitrarily.

Although the standard does make provision for using ESP without authentication, it needs to be pointed out explicitly that ESP should not be used in this way. If the CBC mode is used for

Using ESP without authentication is insecure

encryption without authentication, the content of messages can be reconstructed through active attacks [PY06]. The combination of a separate ESP authentication and ESP encryption in two SAs is also insecure [DP10].

As already indicated, the ESP specification is subdivided into several parts: the definition of the actual protocol in RFC 4303 [Ken05b], the application of specific cryptographic algorithms with ESP, for example encryption with AES-CBC in RFC 3602 [FGK03], and message authentication with HMAC-SHA-2 in RFC 4868 [KF07].

Figure 12.18
Packet format of ESP

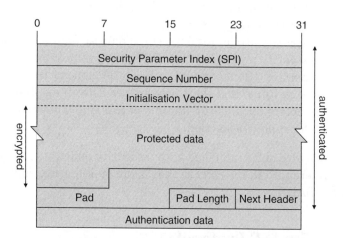

The base protocol definition for ESP in RFC 4303 contains a specification for the protocol header and trailer, fundamental steps for processing the protocol and procedures for transport and tunnel mode. Figure 12.18 shows the packet format for the encapsulating security payload.

ESP protocol fields   The ESP protocol header shown immediately follows an IP protocol header or a different IPsec protocol header, with the 'next header' field of the preceding protocol header using the value 50 to indicate that it is an ESP protocol header. The protocol fields of ESP have the following significance:

Security Parameter   ■ The *Security Parameter Index (SPI)* field identifies which SA
Index   should be used for a packet. The value entered in this field is always determined by the receiving side during SA negotiation because it is the receiver that must provide unique identification of the SA based on the SPI. Valid SPI values are always greater than or equal to 256. All lower values are reserved.

■ As explained before, the *sequence number* provides replay protection for IP packets.

Sequence number

■ If the cryptographic algorithm being used requires an *initialisation vector (IV)*, the IV is transported in plaintext in each IP packet so that each packet can be processed independently of other packets.

Initialisation vector

■ The *Pad* field ensures that the payload being encrypted is padded to a length that is equivalent to an integer multiple of the block size of the algorithm used and that the two following fields end up in the higher-order 16 bits of a 32-bit word. Furthermore, it is possible to use the pad to obfuscate the true length of the transported messages in order to make traffic flow analyses more difficult.

Pad

■ The *Pad Length* field indicates the number of octets added to obtain a multiple of the block length.

Pad Length

■ The *Next Header* field indicates the protocol type of the contained payload, e.g. TCP or UDP.

Next Header

■ The optional *Authentication Data* field contains a MAC, if available.

Authentication Data

Figures 12.19 and 12.20 show the processing procedures for preparing outgoing ESP packets.

Protocol processing of outgoing packets

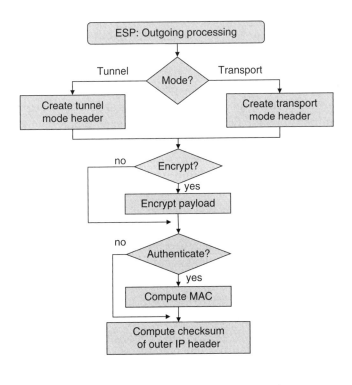

Figure 12.19
Preparation of outgoing ESP packets (1/2)

Figure 12.20

Preparation of outgoing ESP packets (2/2)

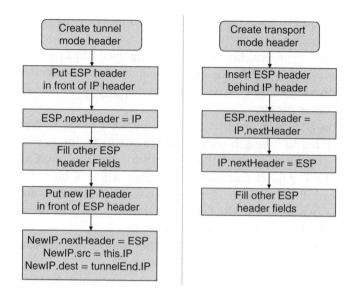

Based on the SA specified by the security policy, a determination is first made about whether to protect the packet in transport or in tunnel mode. Once the appropriate protocol headers have been generated, it has to be determined whether the packet is to be encrypted, and if so encryption is performed. Verification is also required to decide whether the packet should be authenticated, and if so a MAC is computed. As already discussed, at least one of the protection modes is obligatory. Lastly, the checksum of the outer IP protocol header is computed if necessary.

Preparation of protocol headers

Figure 12.20 illustrates how protocol headers are prepared for transport and tunnel mode. In tunnel mode an ESP protocol header with the next-header field set to 'IP' is placed before the existing IP protocol. Once the other ESP-specific fields are filled, a new IP protocol header is placed before the ESP header, which has its next-header field set to 'ESP' and its source and destination fields filled with the addresses of the two tunnel end points.

In transport mode an ESP header is inserted between the IP header and the payload. The next-header field of the ESP header is set to the value of the corresponding field in the IP header before the next header field of this header is set to the value 'ESP'. Afterwards the remaining ESP fields are filled.

Protocol processing of incoming packets

Both Figures 12.21 and 12.22 show the procedures for processing incoming ESP packets.

Verification is required with incoming packets to ensure that all fragments belonging to a specific packet are already available

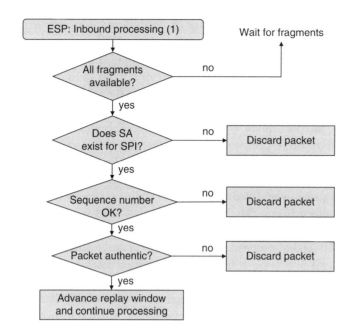

Figure 12.21
Processing incoming ESP packets (1/2)

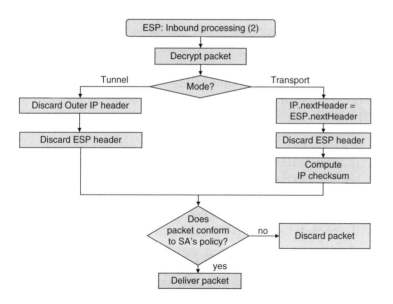

Figure 12.22
Processing of incoming ESP packets (2/2)

because processing cannot commence until all fragments have been received. The SA being used for the packet is then read or the packet is discarded if this association does not exist locally. A further check is applied to ensure that the sequence number is in the window or to the right of the window of acceptable sequence numbers. If not, the packet is discarded. Depending on the result of the MAC verification, the packet is either discarded or the replay window is advanced to the right and the processing of the packet continues.

Figure 12.22 shows how the processing of the packet continues. The payload of the packet is first decrypted and then checked to determine the mode in which the packet was secured. If it was in tunnel mode, then only the two outer protocol headers are stripped. If it was in transport mode, the original value of the next-header field is restored in the IP protocol header before the inserted ESP header is removed and the checksum of the IP protocol header is recomputed. With both modes the packet is checked to determine whether the security measures stipulated in the security policy were used to protect it before it is either discarded or conveyed to the appropriate protocol entity.

Handling of fragmented packets

An IP packet processed and reconstructed in this way can sometimes turn out to be a fragmented packet. This can occur, for instance, if a gateway system applies ESP in tunnel mode to already fragmented packets. A gateway system cannot fully decide how to treat a fragmented packet in accordance with the local security policy unless it has actually received all fragments of the packet or at least the fragments that contain the parts of the packet being evaluated, for example up to and including the port fields of the transport protocol header. It is possible that only those packets that are being sent to a specific port may be exchanged within an SA. The port information that needs to be evaluated for this purpose is only available in the first fragment of the IP packet.

Routing alternatives

The following alternatives are available for routing received packets in the context of ESP processing:

- If another IPsec protocol header is detected that requires attention by this system then IPsec processing is continued.
- If a packet was secured in tunnel mode and the system performing the processing is not the communication end point of the packet, then the packet is routed according to local routing information.
- If the received packet is destined for the system itself, it is forwarded to the appropriate transport entity (e.g. TCP or UDP).

Use of cryptographic algorithms

As explained earlier, the ESP specification is divided into a definition of the base protocol and a description of the use of specific cryptographic algorithms with ESP. The following RFCs were approved:

- *Confidentiality:* The use of DES in CBC mode specified in RFC 2405 [MD98] is no longer being recommended because of the short key length. However, this deficiency was already general knowledge when the RFC was approved in 1998. RFC 2451 [PA98] defines format and processing procedures for the use of various block ciphers in CBC mode with ESP. In principle, each block cipher can be used according to this RFC. The algorithms explicitly mentioned are Blowfish, CAST-128, 3DES, IDEA and RC5. Furthermore, there are explicit RFCs for AES [FGK03] and Camellia [KMK05], which describe the implementation of the CBC mode in ESP. The initialisation vector is transmitted in plaintext in each packet to avoid synchronisation problems (see also Section 2.5). The initialisation vectors must always be chosen randomly or at least pseudo-randomly. Constructing vectors deterministically, e.g. by forming them from the last computed ciphertext, may lead to risks regarding internal attackers. They might inject specially constructed packets to set a controlled initialisation vector for the following packets. A similar setting led to a security problem in TLS, which will be described in the next chapter.

■ *Data origin authentication:* The same algorithms are used to compute MACs for ESP as for AH (see also the section below).

■ *Authenticated Encryption (AEAD):* More recent IPsec implementations allow for the use of AES in GCM [VM05] or CCM mode [Hou05] and thereby efficiently provide confidentiality as well as authentication.

If within the framework of an SA ESP provides confidentiality as well as data origin authentication, each security service must use different keys if they are not realised by the same AEAD mode anyway.

12.6   The AH Protocol

The AH specified in RFC 4302 [Ken05a] is a generic security protocol that provides the following security services for IP packets:

AH security services

■ *Data origin authentication:* A MAC is computed and added to each protected packet.

■ *Replay protection for IP packets:* The acceptance of a sequence number in the AH protocol header and the inclusion of this number in the MAC computation enables a receiver to check the freshness of the received IP packets.

As with ESP, the AH specification is divided into two parts: a definition of the base protocol and use of cryptographic algorithms with AH. The protocol specification [Ken05a] defines the format of the protocol header, the fundamental processing procedures and operation in transport and in tunnel mode.

If both ESP and AH are to be applied to an IP packet by the same system, then ESP should always be applied first. This makes AH the outer of the two protocol headers and also enables it to protect the ESP header from modification. As an SA basically can only use one of the two protocols AH or ESP, two separate SAs are required per direction.

Figure 12.23

Packet format of AH

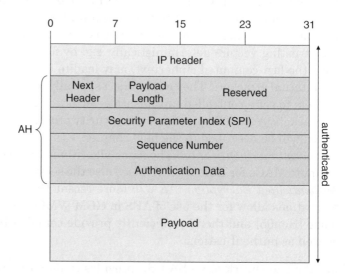

AH protocol fields   Figure 12.23 shows the structure of an IP packet secured with AH and the AH protocol fields:

Next Header   ■ The *Next Header* field contains the protocol identification of the payload transported in the packet, e.g. TCP, UDP.

Payload Length   ■ The length of the AH payload is contained in the *Payload Length* field. This easily confused labelling refers to the two integrity-securing fields *Sequence Number* and *Authentication Data* that, depending on the cryptographic algorithm used and the negotiated parameters, can in principle be of various lengths.

Reserved   ■ The protocol field labelled *Reserved* is reserved for future uses and set to 0.

Security Parameter Index   ■ The *Security Parameter Index (SPI)* together with the IP destination address and the protocol identifier AH uniquely identifies the SA used to receive this packet.

Sequence Number   ■ As explained above, the *Sequence Number* is used to detect intentional packet replay.

■ The *Authentication Data* field contains the MAC that is computed over the entire IP packet including parts of the IP protocol header. In contrast to ESP, AH is also able to protect the immutable parts of the outer IP protocol header from modification.

Authentication data

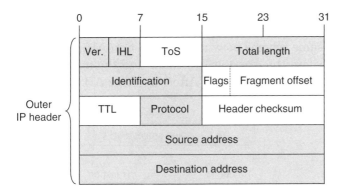

Figure 12.24
Variable and immutable fields of an IPv4 packet header

In Figures 12.24 and 12.25 the variable and the immutable fields of the IPv4 and IPv6 protocol headers are distinguished from one another through different background colours. The fields with a white background can change during the transport of an IP packet from source to destination (Type of Service, Flags, Fragment offset, Traffic Class, Flow Label) or in principle are subject to change in each gateway (Time to Live, Header checksum, Hop Limit). These fields naturally cannot be included in the MAC, as the IP packets would otherwise inevitably be discarded by the receiver. The value 0 is therefore assumed for variable fields in the MAC computation.

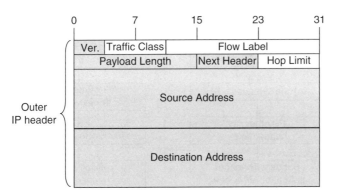

Figure 12.25
Variable and immutable fields of an IPv6 packet header

If IP option fields are used, it depends on their meaning if they may be modified. Details can be found in RFC 4302 and are not discussed further here.

Protocol processing
of outgoing packets

Figures 12.26 and 12.27 show the procedures for processing outgoing IP packets secured with AH.

As with ESP protocol processing, the packet is checked to determine whether it should be secured in transport or in tunnel mode. After the appropriate protocol headers are created, the message authentication code is prepared and then the checksum of the outer IP protocol header is recomputed, if IPv4 is used.

The protocol headers shown in Figure 12.27 are created using the same scheme as with ESP. First an AH protocol header is placed before the existing IP header and the next-header field of the AH header is set to 'IP'. After the other AH fields are filled, a

Figure 12.26
Preparation of
outgoing AH
packets (1/2)

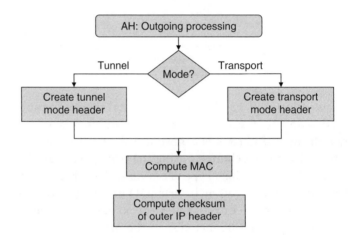

Figure 12.27
Preparation of
outgoing AH packets
(2/2)

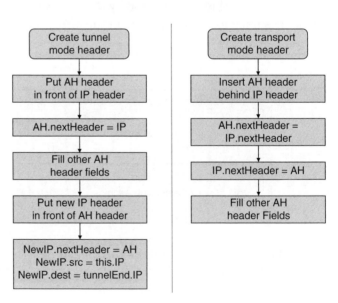

new IP header is created and placed in front of the AH header. The next-header field of the new IP header is set to the value 'AH' and its source and destination address fields are filled with the addresses of both cryptographic end points.

The processing of incoming packets secured with AH is illustrated in Figures 12.28 and 12.29.

Protocol processing of incoming AH packets

When processing incoming packets, the first thing to determine is whether all fragments for the AH protocol data unit being processed

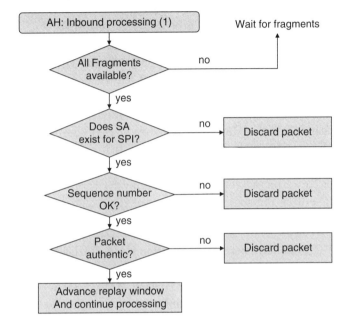

Figure 12.28
Processing of incoming AH packets (1/2)

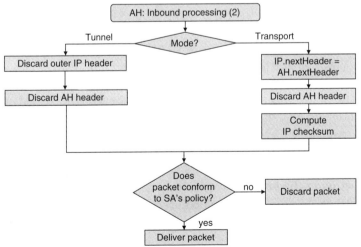

Figure 12.29
Processing of incoming AH packets (2/2)

are available since processing cannot continue until all fragments have been received. When all fragments are available, clarification is needed to establish whether the SA referenced in the packet is available locally, and if it is not, the packet is dropped.

Afterwards the freshness of the sequence number contained in the packet is checked and the packet dropped if this number is to the left of the current receiving window. The message authentication code is then computed and compared with the contained value. If the two values differ, the packet is dropped. The receiving window may then be updated and the processing is continued.

If the SA concerned is operating in tunnel mode, the outer IP header and the AH header are stripped. In the case of a transport mode SA, the next-header field of the IP header first has to be restored before the AH header can be removed. In the case of an IPv4 packet, the checksum of the IP header is then recomputed. Finally, the packet is checked to ensure that it complies with the requirements of the local security policy. If it does, it is routed to the appropriate protocol entity; otherwise it is discarded.

Cryptographic algorithms   Four RFCs have been approved so far for computing the message authentication codes on the basis of HMACs that are inserted into AH and ESP packets:

- RFC 2403 defines the construction HMAC-MD5-96 with a key length of 128 bits [MG98a];
- RFC 2404 defines the construction HMAC-SHA-1-96 with a key length of 160 bits [MG98b];
- RFC 2857 defines the construction HMAC-RIPEMD-160-96 with a key length of 160 bits [KP00];
- RFC 4868 defines the constructions HMAC-SHA-256-128, HMAC-SHA-384-192 and HMAC-SHA-512-256 with a respective key length of 256, 384 and 512 bits [KF07].

All the above message authentication codes use the HMAC construction defined in RFC 2104 [KBC97]. The suffix in the algorithm, for example '-96', means that the output of the hash construction is truncated to the higher-order 96, 128, 192 or 256 bits. This value fulfils the security requirements stated in RFC 2104 and allows a reduction in the protocol overhead.

Other mechanisms to calculate authentication codes on the basis of block ciphers include:

- RFC 3566 defines the usage of AES in XCBC mode [FH03] called AES-XCBC-MAC-96;

- RFC 4494 defines the usage of AES in CMAC mode [SPL06] called AES-CMAC-96;
- RFC 4543 defines the usage of AES in GMAC mode [MV06].

The two mentioned earlier are truncated to 96 bits, while the last one may only be used with a full tag length of 128 bits for security reasons.

12.7   The ISAKMP Protocol

Before data packet exchanges between two systems can be protected with IPsec, two opposite SAs are set up between the respective cryptographic end points. These IPsec SAs can basically use one of two options, either *manual* or *dynamic establishment*. Manual establishment involves the use of system management methods by hand, which are normally implemented differently from system to system. As this method is not only time-consuming but also error prone, it should only be used in very manageable configurations, for example between two dedicated gateways at different locations. However, in this case the replay protection is difficult to implement as distributed systems are usually restarted independently of each other and the replay protection state is not persistent. Furthermore, sequence number counters cannot be reset and overflow without changing the key material. A manual configuration also gives attackers better opportunities to place cryptographic attacks because deployed keys are usually changed irregularly. The use of manually configured SAs in combination with algorithms that require initialisation vectors not to be reused, like GCM, is extremely problematic. The manual configuration should therefore only be considered in cases where a dynamic method is not available in a specific system, although this situation should be occurring less and less.

Manual establishment of SAs is time consuming, error prone and less secure than dynamic methods

   IPsec hence defines standardised methods for the dynamic establishment of SAs. The most commonly used IKE version 1 is handled through the following two protocol specifications:

- The *Internet Security Association and Key Management Protocol (ISAKMP)* [MSS+98] defines generic protocol formats and procedures for the negotiation of security parameters and for entity authentication. The actual application of this protocol for the negotiation of pairwise parameters for IPsec SAs is presented in detail in the *IPsec Domain of Interpretation (IPsec DOI)* [Pip98]. A second protocol to establish group keys

ISAKMP

the *Group Domain of Interpretation (GDOI)* will not be discussed here, but details can be found in RFC 6407 [WRH11] and Section 23.2.2 also takes up this subject again.

IKE ■ *Internet Key Exchange (IKE)* defines the standard authentication and key exchange protocol for IPsec. The first version of the protocol [HC98] is based on ISAKMP.

ISAKMP is discussed in detail below. Version 1 of the IKE is covered in Section 12.8.

The ISAKMP specification defines two basic categories of exchanges: *Phase 1 exchanges*, which are used to negotiate *master SAs*, and *Phase 2 exchanges*, which use master SAs to establish other SAs.

Figure 12.30

Frame format of ISAKMP data units

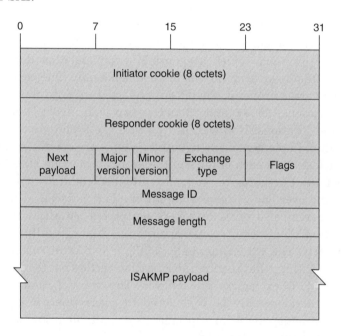

Figure 12.30 shows the basic structure of an ISAKMP message. It contains the following message elements:

Initiator and responder cookie ■ The *initiator and responder cookie* uniquely identifies an ISAKMP exchange or an ISAKMP-SA and also provides limited protection against denial-of-service attacks (explanation follows).

Next payload ■ *Next payload* specifies which ISAKMP payload type follows the protocol header.

Major and minor version ■ *Major and minor version* identifies the protocol version of the current message.

- *Exchange type* indicates the type of ISAKMP exchange that is conducted with the current message. There are five pre-defined generic exchange types; other types can be negotiated in DOI specifications.

- *Flags* contain bits to indicate specific characteristics. The *encrypt* bit indicates whether the payload following the message header is encrypted, the *commit* bit indicates a key change and the *authenticate only* bit indicates that the payload of the message is authenticated but not encrypted.

- *Message ID* identifies messages that belong to different protocol runs and therefore allows a simultaneous negotiation of multiple SAs.

- *Message length* indicates the total length of the current message, including the ISAKMP protocol header and all payloads.

- *ISAKMP payload* contains the message payload. An ISAKMP message can actually contain multiple 'chained' payloads. The payload type of the following message is always indicated in the next payload field of the preceding payload or in the ISAKMP protocol header.

In addition to identifying a protocol run or an ISAKMP-SA, the two message elements *initiator cookie* and *responder cookie* provide limited protection against *denial-of-service* attacks that are aimed at reducing system availability. The motivation for this protection mechanism is as follows. Depending on the authentication scheme used, authentication and key management can involve some very computationally intensive operations, e.g. exponentiation with large integers for the Diffie–Hellman protocol. By deliberately provoking such computations, attackers can cause such an increase in system load that the system is not available to deal with other tasks or with legitimate authentication requests from other systems. Attackers then try to keep their own system load as low as possible, for example by only participating in a protocol run until they have triggered a computationally intensive operation in the attacked system. These simulated authentication exchanges are consequently not successful. To a limited degree a system can protect itself from such attacks by not responding to a specific system's requests after a certain number of aborted attempts have been made and only sending a local error message.

However, this is not an effective measure if an attacker produces a request using a forged source address, which then triggers a computationally intensive operation. The two cookies contained in ISAKMP protocol headers can be used to reduce these particular risks. Each of the two systems participating in a protocol run sends the other system information that only the sender can generate and quickly verify, and only performs computationally intensive operations if the peer entity includes this information in its protocol messages:

■ The initiating ISAKMP entity creates an initiator cookie:

$$CKY\text{-}I = H(Secret_{Initiator}, Address_{Responder}, t_{Initiator})$$

■ The responder creates its own cookie:

$$CKY\text{-}R = H(Secret_{Responder}, Address_{Initiator}, t_{Responder})$$

Each of the two entities inserts both cookies into its protocol messages and verifies its own cookie before performing a computationally intensive operation. This protection mechanism is effective at fending off attacks with forged source addresses, as described above. An attacker who is unable to intercept the message while it is being transported between the attacked system and the forged source address will not have a valid cookie for this address to respond. The ISAKMP protocol specification defines no exact method for creating cookies. However, it is important that each entity has the information necessary to verify its own cookies (e.g. time stamp). More details to this approach will be given in Chapter 18.

Figure 12.31
Protocol header for
an ISAKMP payload

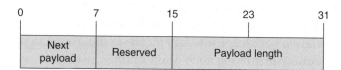

ISAKMP protocol
header

All ISAKMP payloads begin with the protocol header shown in Figure 12.31:

■ the *next payload* field indicates the type of the next payload;
■ the *reserved* field is reserved for future applications;
■ the *payload length* field contains the total length of the payload, including the protocol header.

ISAKMP payloads

The ISAKMP specification defines a range of different payloads (see [MSS+98] for a complete list):

■ *generic payloads* are of general usability, such as the payloads *hash, signature, nonce, vendor ID* and *key exchange*;

- *specific payloads* satisfy certain functions within an authentication exchange and include the payloads *SA, certificate, certificate request* and *identification*;
- *dependent and encapsulated payloads* are only used in conjunction with certain other payloads and provide further detail about the corresponding payload, e.g.:
  - *proposal payload*, which specifies a proposal for SA negotiation;
  - *transform payload*, which is part of a proposal payload and describes a specific security transformation;
- the *generic attribute payload* is not a self-contained ISAKMP payload and only occurs within other payloads.

All attribute payloads share the same structure as shown in Figure 12.32. Short attributes, where the length does not exceed 16 bits, are displayed with a '1' set in the highest-order bit. This is followed by a 15-bit long specification of the *attribute type* and then a 16-bit long *attribute value*. Longer attributes are indicated with a '0'. With long attributes, the type specification is followed by an *attribute length* field to indicate the length of the following *variable length attribute value*.

　　Figure 12.33 shows the structure of an SA payload, which initiates the specification of the desired SA parameters. The *Domain*

Structure of attribute payloads

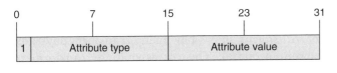
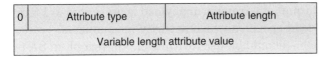

Figure 12.32
Short and long format for ISAKMP attributes

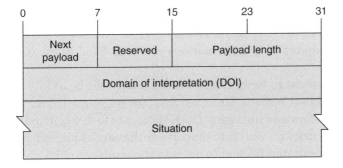

Figure 12.33
Structure of SA payload

of *Interpretation (DOI)* field, which follows the standard payload header, always carries the value 1 defined in RFC 2407 for the negotiation of IPsec-SAs. The *situation* field identifies the specific situation under which a current request is taking place, such as 'normal' or for 'emergency calls'. Such situations, however, do not play an important role in IPsec usage. A series of proposal payloads always follow an SA payload.

Figure 12.34
Structure of the
proposal payload

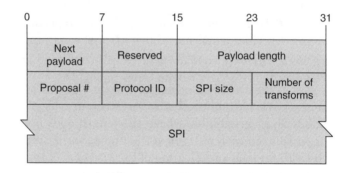

Linking multiple proposals   The structure of a proposal payload is illustrated in Figure 12.34. The *proposal #* field is used to communicate the security policy and negotiate separate proposals. If two or more proposal payloads carry the same number, it displays a logical 'AND'. If the proposal numbers have different values, a logical 'OR' is triggered with descending priority. The *protocol ID* specifies which security protocol should be used for the current negotiation (with IPsec: AH or ESP). The *SPI size* field indicates the length of the SPI and *number of transforms* shows how many transform payloads belong to the current proposal. The corresponding transform payloads directly follow the proposal payload.

Transform payloads specify which security mechanism should be used   The format of a transform payload is presented in Figure 12.35. This payload specifies which security mechanisms – called transformations – should be used within the context of an SA (or a proposal for it). Each transformation listed within a proposal carries a unique *transform #* and a *transform ID*, for example for 3DES, AES, SHA-1 or SHA-256, to identify its type. Transform IDs are defined in the DOI specifications for IPsec RFC 2407 [Pip98]. Specific attributes of transformations can be defined in the *SA attributes* field.

Negotiation of protection suites   The message formats introduced above will be used to explain how different options for IPsec-SAs are negotiated. The proposal payload allows an initiating ISAKMP entity to notify its peer entity of the security measures it supports or that are required for the currently negotiated SA and to do so in the sequence of its preference.

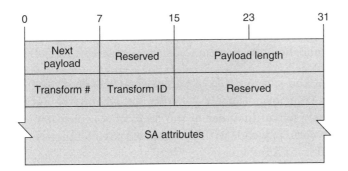

Figure 12.35
Structure of the
transform payload

The same proposal number can be used to combine multiple security mechanisms into a combined *protection suite*. However, these proposal payloads must also be considered as a unit within the ISAKMP message and cannot be separated by a proposal payload carrying a different payload number.

The following two examples help to illustrate the basic idea involved.

Examples

1. Assume that an initiator wants to negotiate a combined protection suite using ESP and AH, selecting either 3DES or AES for ESP encryption and using the SHA-1 algorithm for integrity protection. The initiator inserts the SA payload followed by the proposal and transform payloads into the ISAKMP message:

   ■ [Proposal 1, ESP, (Transform 1, 3DES, . . .), (Transform 2, AES)]
   ■ [Proposal 1, AH, (Transform 1, HMAC-SHA-1)]

   If this proposal is accepted by the responder, then two SAs result in each direction: one for ESP and one for AH. The IP packets exchanged within the framework of these associations are protected with 3DES and HMAC-SHA-1 or with AES and HMAC-SHA-1.

2. Two different protection suites should be proposed for the second example. The first suite requires the use of AH with HMAC-SHA-1 and ESP with 3DES, whereas the second suite only requires ESP with either 3DES or AES. The initiator sends the following proposal and transform payloads:

   ■ [Proposal 1, AH, (Transform 1, HMAC-SHA-1, . . .)]
   ■ [Proposal 1, ESP, (Transform 1, 3DES, . . .)]
   ■ [Proposal 2, ESP, (Transform1, 3DES, . . .), (Transform 2, AES, . . .)]

Again for the first protection suite two SAs are required per direction, whereas with the second one only one SA has to be established per direction.

Note that the specification of transformations does not allow two different transformations (e.g. 3DES and AES) to be defined simultaneously for an instance of the protocol specification, e.g. ESP. The transform payloads within a proposal payload therefore always carry different numbers.

The responder selects a proposal

The responder selects a proposal from those offered and responds with an ISAKMP message that (among other things) comprises an SA payload and the proposal and transform payloads of the selected proposal. The proposal payload can only contain a transform payload that originates from the list of transformations previously offered to this proposal. To simplify the protocol processing for the initiator, the responder should also select the same numbers for the proposal and transform payloads as appeared in the original message of the initiator. On receipt of this message, the initiator verifies that the returned proposal and transform payloads match the combination it used in its own message before it continues with the protocol processing.

Negotiated session keys

Four different session keys are negotiated with ISAKMP for a Phase 1 exchange (see Section 12.8):

- *SKEYID* is a string only known to the two entities actively involved in the authentication and is used as the *master key* to derive additional keying material. The computation of this key depends on the authentication method.
- *SKEYID_e* is the encryption key with which ISAKMP entities encrypt their payloads to protect the confidentiality of their messages (the 'e' denotes encrypt).
- *SKEYID_a* is used by ISAKMP entities to authenticate protocol message exchanges (the 'a' denotes authenticate).
- *SKEYID_d* is the keying material used to derive keys for non-ISAKMP SAs (the 'd' denotes derive).

12.8   Internet Key Exchange Version 1

Based on the message formats and procedures provided by ISAKMP, IKEv1 specifies a protocol for negotiating IPsec SAs. IKEv1 defines the following exchange types, which can be divided into three categories:

- *Phase 1 exchanges* used to negotiate IKE SAs:
  - *Main mode exchange* negotiates an SA through the exchange of six messages.
  - *Aggressive mode exchange* only requires three messages to do the same thing but cannot guarantee certain security properties of main mode exchange (details follow).
- *Phase 2 exchanges* used to negotiate IPsec SAs, which are also
  called Child SAs:
  - *Quick mode exchange* exchanges three messages to negotiate additional IPsec associations based on an existing IKE SA.
- Other exchanges for various purposes:
  - *Informational exchange* is used to communicate status and error messages between two IKE entities.
  - *New group exchange* is used to negotiate a new Diffie–Hellman group.

IKE provides detailed specifications for computing the four session
keys described in the ISAKMP specification and listed in the previous section. *SKEYID* computation, on the other hand, is dependent
on the actual authentication method and is therefore explained below. The following definitions are valid for the other three session
keys:

$$SKEYID\_d := H(SKEYID, g^{x \times y}, CKY\text{-}I, CKY\text{-}R, 0)$$

$$SKEYID\_a := H(SKEYID, SKEYID\_d, g^{x \times y},$$
$$CKY\text{-}I, CKY\text{-}R, 1)$$

$$SKEYID\_e := H(SKEYID, SKEYID\_a, g^{x \times y},$$
$$CKY\text{-}I, CKY\text{-}R, 2)$$

The $g^{x \times y}$ denotes the negotiated shared Diffie–Hellman secret and
$CKY\text{-}I$ and $CKY\text{-}R$ denote the initiator or responder cookie.

If the key length of a cryptographic algorithm requires more
bits than are computed by the hash function, the keys mentioned
above are 'expanded' according to the following rule:

$$K = (K_1, K_2, \dots) \text{ with } K_i = H(SKEYID, K_{i-1}) \text{ and } K_0 = 0$$

However, this 'expansion' is not able to increase security significantly since the input entropy is not changed. For example, if MD5
is used as a hash function H in combination with an AES-256 encryption, an attacker only needs to check only 2^{127} keys despite

the construction. The cryptographic weakness is that the relatively long Diffie–Hellman secret is not used as an input to the round function.

12.8.1   Negotiation of an ISAKMP-SA

Authentication based on hash values

IKE Phase 1 exchanges are authenticated using two hash values computed by the *initiator* and the *responder* once it has acquired the respective message elements:

$$Hash\text{-}I := H(SKEYID, g^x, g^y, CKY\text{-}I, CKY\text{-}R,$$

$$SA\text{-}offer, ID\text{-}I)$$

$$Hash\text{-}R := H(SKEYID, g^y, g^x, CKY\text{-}R, CKY\text{-}I,$$

$$SA\text{-}offer, ID\text{-}R)$$

In the computation above, g^x and g^y denote the two exchanged public Diffie–Hellman values, *ID-I* and *ID-R* the identity of the initiator and the responder, and *SA-offer* the SA, proposal and transform payloads exchanged during the SA parameter negotiation. IKEv1 supports four methods of authentication for peer entities and message exchanges:

- *Pre-shared key:* With this method the initiator and the responder know a shared secret $K_{Initiator, Responder}$ which, together with the random numbers $r_{Initiator}$ and $r_{Responder}$ selected by both entities, is included in *SKEYID* computation:

$$SKYEID = H(K_{Initiator, Responder}, r_{Initiator}, r_{Responder})$$

- *Public key encryption:* Public key encryption is supported in two methods where the *SKEYID* master key is always computed in the same way:

$$SKEYID = H(H(r_{Initiator}, r_{Responder}), CKY\text{-}I, CKY\text{-}R)$$

- *Digital signature:* With this method the two hash values Hash-I and Hash-R also have to be signed by the initiator or the responder because *SKEYID* itself provides no authentication. The value *SKEYID* is computed in this case as follows:

$$SKEYID = H(r_{Initiator}, r_{Responder}, g^{x \times y})$$

The different versions of Phase 1 exchanges are briefly presented below and distinguished according to the differences between them.

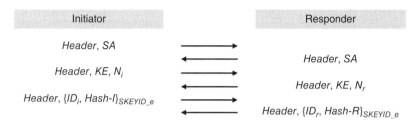

Initiator		Responder
Header, SA	→	
	←	Header, SA
Header, KE, N_i	→	
	←	Header, KE, N_r
Header, {ID_i, Hash-I}$_{SKEYID\_e}$	→	
	←	Header, {ID_r, Hash-R}$_{SKEYID\_e}$

Figure 12.36
Process for main mode exchange with pre-shared key

Figure 12.36 illustrates the process for the main mode exchange with authentication using a pre-shared key. For space reasons the IKE notation N_i and N_r is used for the random numbers ($r_{Initiator}$, $r_{Responder}$) selected by the initiator and the responder. In addition, *Header* denotes the ISAKMP protocol header, SA the exchanged SA, proposal and transform payloads, ID_i and ID_r the identity of the initiator and the responder, and KE (denoting key exchange) the transmitted public Diffie–Hellman values.

The messages exchanged are authenticated on the basis of the hash values in the last two messages. Because the value SKEYID is included in the computation of both Hash-I and Hash-R, after checking these hash values both peer entities can be assured that the respective other entity also knows the SKEYID value. However, because knowledge of the shared secret $K_{Initiator,Responder}$ is required for the computation of SKEYID, each entity is able to conclude that its peer entity also knows this secret and therefore is authentic. As all key message elements of the prior message exchange, including the two current random numbers N_i and N_r, are included in the computation of both hash values, both sides have the assurance that none of the messages exchanged was forged, modified or replayed by an attacker. A problem remains however: attackers may run man-in-the-middle attacks to obtain valid hashes and subsequently try to recover the used password locally. The pre-shared keys therefore need to have sufficiently high entropy to guarantee a secure operation.

Authentication with pre-shared key

The encryption of the ISAKMP payloads in the last two messages also protects the two identities ID_i and ID_r from possible eavesdropping. This measure is particularly useful if the identities cannot be derived from the source and destination addresses of the IP packets that are transporting the ISAKMP messages, e.g. with delegated SA negotiation through intermediate systems.

Identity confidentiality

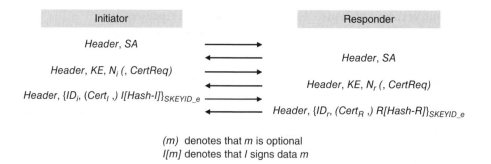

(m) denotes that *m* is optional
I[m] denotes that *I* signs data *m*

Figure 12.37 Figure 12.37 illustrates the message flow in main mode exchange
Process of main with authentication using digital signatures. The contained
mode exchange certificate requests (*CertReq*) and responses (*Cert_I*, *Cert_R*) are
with signatures in parentheses because they are optional. The notation $I[m]$ and
$R[m]$ identifies that message element m is signed by the initiator
or the responder. This type of exchange requires explicit digital
signatures for the actual authentication procedure because no
knowledge of specific keys is needed to compute the two hash
values. The two peer entities therefore cannot rely on the hash
values to conclude whether an attacker has computed them. The
encryption of the ISAKMP payloads in the last two messages
protects the confidentiality of the two identities.

Figure 12.38
Process of main
mode exchange with
public key encryption
(Method 1)

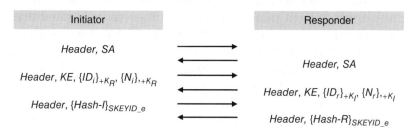

$\{m\}_{+K_I}$ denotes that *m* has been encrypted with public key $+K_I$

Authentication with The first authentication method using public key encryption with
public key encryption main mode exchange is illustrated in Figure 12.38. The notation
$\{m\}_{+K_I}$ denotes encryption of message element m with public key
$+K_I$ of entity I. This method proves authenticity by requiring
an entity to have knowledge of private key $-K_R$ or $-K_I$ that
is needed to decrypt random number N_i or N_r. Computation
of the master key SKEYID and consequently the hash values
Hash-R and Hash-I is not possible without knowledge of the two
random numbers. This means that an attacker has no possibility

of successfully participating in a complete protocol run using eavesdropped or modified messages.

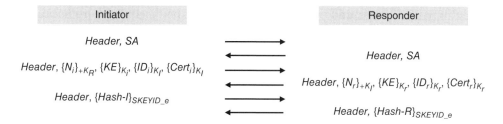

The second method of authentication using public key encryption as part of a main mode exchange is illustrated in Figure 12.39. The notation $\{m\}_{K_i}$ and $\{m\}_{K_r}$ denotes use of secret key K_i or K_r for the encryption of message element m.

Figure 12.39
Process of main mode exchange with public key encryption (Method 2)

These keys are computed as follows by initiator and responder:

$$K_i = H(N_i, CKY\text{-}I)$$
$$K_r = H(N_r, CKY\text{-}R)$$

The required random numbers N_i and N_r are not transmitted in plaintext but encrypted with the public key $+K_R$ or $+K_I$ and then sent. Consequently, an attacker cannot compute these keys without knowing the corresponding private key. Both initiator and responder therefore prove authenticity by including both values into the SKEYID computation that is then entered into HASH-I or HASH-R. Encryption with keys K_i and K_r protects the confidentiality of the identity of both entities. The reason for using a symmetrical encryption scheme for this task is the higher processing speed that can be achieved with symmetric encryption.

Figure 12.40
Process of aggressive mode exchange with pre-shared key

Figure 12.40 shows an aggressive mode exchange with authentication using a pre-shared key. Because the identities of both the initiator and the responder have to be sent before a session key can be established between the entities, aggressive mode exchange is not able to protect the confidentiality of the identities from eavesdropping attackers. However, as it only needs half as many messages as compared with main mode exchange, this mode is normally used in cases where identity confidentiality is not important or cannot be protected anyway.

Other modes Similar modes exist for authentication based on digital signatures and public keys but will not be discussed here because they do not involve any new aspects.

12.8.2 Negotiation of IPsec SAs

After an ISAKMP SA is established between two ISAKMP entities as the result of a Phase 1 exchange, it can be used to negotiate specific IPsec SAs to be used for data transport. These are also referred to as Child SAs. An ISAKMP SA allows multiple of these IPsec associations to be negotiated simultaneously. Therefore, in principle both peer entities must be able to allocate individual ISAKMP messages to the respective SA negotiations and to synchronise the cryptographic state needed, for example initialisation vectors for the encryption of ISAKMP payloads.

Figure 12.41

Process of quick mode exchange

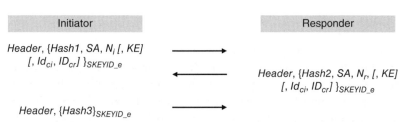

Compared with the diverse combinations available with the different authentication methods using main mode and aggressive mode in Phase 1 exchanges, the specification for negotiating an IPsec SA with IKE is relatively narrow. Figure 12.41 illustrates the process of such a negotiation that is always executed in *quick mode*. The hash values used in quick mode exchange are defined as follows:

$$Hash1 = H(SKEYID\_a, M\text{-}ID, SA, N_i\ [, KE]\ [, ID_{ci}, ID_{cr}])$$

$$Hash2 = H(SKEYID\_a, M\text{-}ID, N_i, SA, N_r\ [, KE]\ [, ID_{ci}, ID_{cr}])$$

$$Hash3 = H(SKEYID\_a, 0, M\text{-}ID, N_i, N_r)$$

$M\text{-}ID$ denotes the message identification contained in the ISAKMP message ID protocol field and used to allocate a message to a specific protocol run. This identification and the cookies in the ISAKMP protocol header identify the state belonging to the protocol run. Among other things, the state enables the calculation of the initialisation vector used to encrypt the payload.

The optional inclusion of identities ID_{ci} and ID_{cr} allows ISAKMP entities to negotiate SAs on behalf of other clients ('gateway scenario'). The optional key exchange payloads enable a new Diffie–Hellman exchange to be performed if the property of perfect forward secrecy is necessary for the IPsec SA being established (see also Definition 7.4).

Delegated SA negotiation

The keying material for deriving session keys is computed according to the following rule by both entities on successful completion of the exchange:

$$SessionKeyMaterial = H(SKEYID\_d, [g^{x \times y},] \, protocol, SPI, N_i, N_r)$$

12.9 Internet Key Exchange Version 2

A common criticism of IPsec is the comparatively high complexity (e.g. see [FS03]), which is also reflected in the key negotiation, where the basic case is split into three RFCs and the six IKE modes. The successor standard IKEv2 was therefore fundamentally simplified, and the documentation was reduced to a single document [KHN+10].

Nevertheless, although there is no direct reference to ISAKMP, the actual protocol sequence is still based on ISAKMP. In particular, the frame format already shown in Figure 12.30 is identical. This should simplify the migration from IKEv1 to IKEv2. Having said that, there are significant differences due to the following attributes:

- For each protocol step there is a fixed *request/reply scheme*. This means that one party initiates a query and the other party invariably responds. This also significantly simplifies the retransmission after errors. The requester is always responsible for retransmissions.

  Request/reply protocol

- In IKEv2 the attributes are generally coded independently of the length. The option to code attributes with a length of less than 16 bits in the length field was omitted in the interest of simplification, apart from one infrequent exception.

  Simpler coding

- Attributes can be marked as *critical*. Only then do they have to be interpreted by the counterpart. In this way it is possible to limit support for a particular implementation to a few important attribute types, without jeopardising security.

  Critical attributes

- Simultaneous negotiation of nested SAs, such as encapsulation of AH ESP, is no longer possible. However, if nested structures are required, it is still possible to negotiate two SAs consecutively.

  No simultaneous negotiation of nested SAs

Flexible configuration of algorithms

■ IKEv2 enables flexible coding of transform attributes, since combinations of encryption and authentication algorithms can be specified. If, for example, the following list 3DES-CBC, AES-CBC, SHA-1, SHA-256, AES-GCM is transmitted any combination of the encryption and authentication methods described above can be used. It goes without saying that only authenticated encryption methods (AES-GCM) are used without an explicit authentication method.

Encryption with explicit IV

■ The encryption and authentication within the IKE protocol itself is similar to the process in ESP packets. In particular, an explicit initialisation vector is transferred, which, unlike with IKEv1, is not dependent on previous packets. This makes the method more robust against packet losses.

Figure 12.42
Key exchange sequence in IKEv2

Analysing and processing of the IKEv2 protocol is therefore significantly simpler compared with version 1, resulting in a much-reduced risk of security-critical errors. The key exchange itself was also simplified. Instead of the six IKEv1 dialogues described above, only a single dialogue has to be implemented. As shown in Figure 12.42, it consists of two message pairs, which even have the same structure.

With IKEv2 the negotiation of an SA takes place in two phases. The first phase is unsecured and referred to as `IKE_SA_INIT`. The parties exchange their Diffie–Hellman values g^i and g^r, their supported cryptographic algorithms and two nonces Ni and N_R. The Diffie–Hellman values relate to certain predefined groups and are referred to as KE (for key exchange) in the standard. The second phase, `IKE_AUTH`, is then already secured. It is used to exchange the actual identities and an authenticated signature. The public certificates can also be sent, if they had been requested in the first phase. This is optional. IKEv2 also makes provision for 'piggyback' transfer of an IPsec SA negotiation, so that secure communication can commence directly after successful completion of the two phases.

Keys used in IKEv2

From the second phase, IKEv2 uses seven different keys, SK_d, SK_ai, SK_ar, SK_ei, SK_er, SK_pi and SK_pr, for further protection. Apart from SK_d, which is used to derive further key material for the actual IPsec SAs, these keys always exist in pairs for the initiator and responder. The keys SK_ei and SK_er are used for encrypting IKE traffic, and SK_ai and SK_ar are used for calculating message authentication values. The keys SK_pi and SK_pr are used to authenticate the packets exchanged in the IKE_AUTH phase. All keys are calculated together using a function for message authentication values, PRF:

Derivation of key material

$$\text{SKEYSEED} = \text{PRF}(N_i \,||\, N_r, g^{ir})$$

$$(SK\_d \,||\, SK\_ai \,||\, SK\_ar \,||\, SK\_ei \,||\, SK\_er \,||\, SK\_pi \,||\, SK\_pr) =$$

$$\text{PRF} + (\text{SKEYSEED}, N_i \,||\, N_r \,||\, SPI_i || SPI_r)$$

The function PRF+ describes an iterative application of the PRF function, similar to the way in which it was used in IKEv1, and is defined as follows:

$$\text{PRF} + (K, S) = T1 \,||\, T2 \,||\, T3 \,||\, T4 \,||\, \cdots$$

$$T1 = \text{PRF}(K, S \,||\, 1)$$

$$T2 = \text{PRF}(K, T1 \,||\, S \,||\, 2)$$

$$T3 = \text{PRF}(K, T2 \,||\, S \,||\, 3)$$

$$T4 = \text{PRF}(K, T3 \,||\, S \,||\, 4)$$

$$\vdots$$

A disadvantage of the construction – similar to the construction in IKEv1 – is that the comparatively high entropy of the Diffie–Hellman secret is reduced to the output length of PRF before the keys are generated. If, for example, PRF_HMAC_MD5 is negotiated as PRF, on average an attacker only has to try 2^{127} keys, even though AES-256 is used for the actual encryption. Since the PRF is only executed relatively infrequently, it is appropriate to use a method that is as strong as possible, such as PRF_HMAC_SHA2_512. In any case, the output of the PRF should at least be as long as the respective individual key lengths.

Unnecessary waiving of entropy when long keys are generated

Different mechanisms can be used for the actual authentication of instances within the dialogue, for example the IKE_AUTH messages can contain an RSA or ECDSA signature. Another option is password-based authentication. In this case the exchanged 'signature' is a message authentication value. A special feature is the option of EAP-based authentication [ETS10]. In this case a further phase is inserted between the two authentication dialogue phases, in which the EAP data are 'tunnelled' (using IKEv2) from the initiator to the authentication server via the responder. After

Instances authentication

a successful EAP dialogue the two parties know a shared key, which they can then use to authenticate themselves during the `IKE_AUTH` phase.

Integration of PAKE schemes

Alongside the EAP authentication already mentioned, there are efforts to integrate further password authentication methods in IKEv2. Recently three IKE variants for the PAKE schemes Dragonfly [Har12], AugPAKE [SK12] and PACE [KS12], were adopted. All three variants are based on the Secure Password Framework [Kiv11], whose application is negotiated during the `IKE_INIT` phase. The PAKE-specific part follows in the `IKE_AUTH` phase, in which the semantics of the IKE protocol, including the number of messages, can be changed. All three variants require four messages in the `IKE_AUTH` phase. They either work on elliptic curves or $\mathbb{Z}_p$ and are patent-free or at least free to use, so that the method can be chosen purely from a security perspective. In contrast to Dragonfly and PACE, AugPAKE is an augmented PAKE method. PACE has been very thoroughly examined by the German Federal Office for Information Security and is also used in identity cards. The DH-EKE and SRP methods discussed in Section 7.7 can only be used via EAP.

Protection against denial-of-service attacks

Another special feature, which can lead to additional exchange of messages, is optional protection against denial-of-service attacks. Similar to IKEv1, the problem requiring resolution is that the responder has to calculate the actual Diffie–Hellman secret after the initiator. However, in order to start the new key exchange, it has to apply an exponentiation for each `IKE_SA_INIT` query originating from a new source address. In a situation where an attacker floods the responder with forged `IKE_SA_INIT` queries for random IP addresses, the responder may have to execute a large number of calculations, which may impact on its responses to legitimate queries. If the responder detects such a situation, it responds to `IKE_SA_INIT` queries without the field for a Diffie–Hellman exchange and with a marker to indicate that an attack is suspected. The initiator responds with a new `IKE_SA_INIT` query, which contains a special value of the counterpart, that is, a cookie. Based on the cookies, the responder detects that it was already in contact with the initiator, and the possibility of a forged IP address can therefore be ruled out with high probability. Consequently it can carry out the complex calculation for the Diffie–Hellman exchange and implement a rate limit for each IP address, if necessary. Further details on the use of cookies are discussed in Section 18.3.1. The only disadvantage of the method is the additional round-trip time required for legitimate negotiations in the event of an attack.

12.10   Other Aspects of IPsec

We have learned that the IKE protocols provide flexibility for the negotiation of SAs and that the IPsec architecture offers numerous options (transport or tunnel mode, AH, ESP, diverse supported cryptographic algorithms, etc.). On this basis the previous sections have shown how this architecture can be used to secure specific IP data streams. This discussion is now supplemented with some other aspects.

12.10.1   Interaction with Compression

Note that if transmitted data packets are encrypted, the encrypted data usually cannot be compressed any further. This means that the desired reduction in data volume may not be achieved if compression is subsequently performed on the IP packets in the link layer, for example when connection is via a radio link. It may therefore be necessary for the data to be compressed before encryption via the ESP protocol.

Compression in the context of IPsec

To deal with situations where compression of the IP packet payload is required, IETF specified the *IP Payload Compression Protocol (IPComp)* [SMP⁺01]. This protocol can be used in conjunction with IPsec. Its use can be defined within the framework of IPsec policies and it can also be proposed and negotiated for proposal payloads with IKE-agreed SAs.

12.10.2   Interaction with Firewalls and Intrusion Detection Systems

Another aspect of IPsec is the interoperability with protocol functions in intermediate systems. Use of end-to-end security measures in particular can lead to a range of problems with the evaluation or partial modification of protocol headers in gateways.

Interoperability with protocol functions in intermediate systems

This leads to interoperability issues with Internet firewalls (see also Chapter 21) since, due to end-to-end encryption of IP packets, they prevent legitimate inspection of the protocol headers, which is a necessity for network operators in many cases. This makes it impossible to detect whether only legitimate services are used. Similarly, the ability of intrusion detection systems (see Chapter 22) to detect attacks or report the distribution of viruses is also severely limited.

Analysis in firewalls

As a consequence, many firewalls block the forwarding of IPsec-protected traffic. In some cases this results in problems for

IPsec users that are difficult to detect. If, for example, only ESP packets are discarded while UDP packets can pass through on port 500, which is designated for IKE, SAs can be established correctly. However, no data exchange is possible.

12.10.3   Handling of Network Address Translation

Application of NAT

A similar problem occurs in the so-called *Network Address Translation (NAT)* scenarios, in which router IP addresses are converted to IP packets, so that several devices can share a public IP address. In order to have sufficient information for the retransformation, the UDP and TCP port numbers are usually also modified when NAT is used in IPv4 scenarios.

AH and NAT are essentially incompatible

If encapsulation with the aid of AH is used, a NAT transformation must be avoided, since the IP addresses are authenticated at the same time and the cryptographic checksum is no longer correct after the conversion. By definition it is therefore not possible to use AH in NAT scenarios, since the methods have conflicting objectives.

UDP encapsulation for NAT devices: NAT-T

Even if ESP is used, the problem still exists that the NAT router cannot read or modify fields in the layer 4 protocol headers. The router is therefore not able to 'store' information in the packets pertaining to the end system to which they belong. To resolve this problem RFC 3948 [HSV+05] proposes adding a further UDP header between the IP and ESP headers, if required. For both modes this results in a protocol structure as shown in Figure 12.43. The sole purpose of the method referred to as *NAT-Traversal* is to appear transparent for NAT devices. With only 8 bytes of additional overhead, it is also adequately efficient.

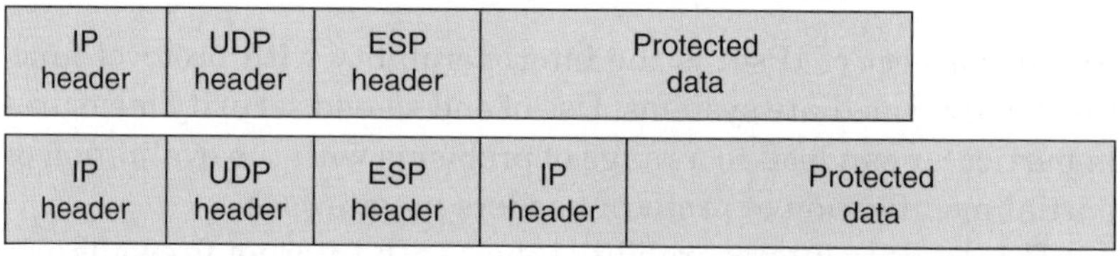

Figure 12.43
Protocol structure for application of NAT-T in transport mode (top) and tunnel mode (bottom)

IP header	UDP header	ESP header	Protected data	

IP header	UDP header	ESP header	IP header	Protected data

Detecting of NAT situations

The IKE implementations can use different techniques for detecting whether or not a NAT situation exists. One way is to activate NAT-T if one of the two sides detects that the source port number of the counterpart no longer has the designated IKE value of 500. Another option is explicit transmission of the source IP addresses during the IKE key exchange. If the real address differs from the expected value, NAT-T has to be activated. After the negotiation the

IKE software has to deal with another task when NAT-T is used: it has to maintain the state in the NAT router through periodic sending of pseudo-packets. Otherwise the port number assignment would be cancelled after a while if no traffic were sent via the SA.

Periodic sending of packets

For SAs in ESP tunnel mode NAT-T resolves the incompatibility with NAT routers in a satisfactory manner. However, in transport mode further issues have to be addressed. One of these is that the checksum of the inner TCP or UDP packet has to be repaired when the ESP header is removed, since it includes the original IP address, and the NAT router is therefore unable to modify it itself, due to the IPsec protection. A greater technical challenge is addressing several VPN devices behind one and the same NAT router. For security reasons the address issued by the NAT router to the devices cannot be used for addressing from outside. However, if the external address of the NAT router is used, unique identification of the devices is not possible in some cases. The only standardised option for resolving the problem is to issue virtual IP addresses for the devices. To ensure that these can be transferred with each packet, it is necessary to use the IPsec tunnel mode, even if the communication is only between two devices.

Limitations of NAT-T in transport mode

Use of tunnel mode is unavoidable in many cases

12.11 Summary

IPsec is the security architecture for the IP developed by the Internet Engineering Task Force (IETF). It provides the following security services for IP packets:

IPsec security services

- *data origin authentication* and *data integrity* in connection with *replay protection*;
- *confidentiality* of payload or entire IP packets with a limited protection against traffic flow analyses.

Securing IP packets exchanged between two systems requires that both systems define the methods and parameters to be used in the form of two *security associations (SA)* (one SA per direction). These associations also store the cryptographic context (session key, replay counter, etc.) for securing the packets.

Security associations

IPsec can be implemented in hosts and in gateways. Depending on whether the *cryptographic end points* of an SA coincide with the *communication end points* of the protected data stream, the IP packets concerned are secured in either *transport* or *tunnel mode*.

Transport and tunnel modes

The latter mode performs a complete encapsulation of the IP packets.

IPsec defines two fundamental security protocols:

Authentication header
- *authentication header (AH)*, which ensures the authenticity and freshness of IP packets, including the immutable parts of their outer protocol header;

Encapsulating security payload
- *encapsulating security payload (ESP)*, which optionally allows the encryption and authentication of the payload but cannot protect the authenticity of the immutable fields of the outer protocol header.

Use ESP only with authentication
For the very uncertain advantages of an authenticated IP header, in most scenarios solely ESP is deployed. It is important to always use an authentication as well as encryption, as the use of ESP for pure encryption without authentication may be insecure [PY06].

Entity authentication with ISAKMP, IKEv1 and IKEv2
The two mutually complementary protocols *Internet Security Association and Key Management Protocol (ISAKMP)* and *Internet Key Exchange version 1 (IKEv1)* were initially defined for the negotiation of SAs in connection with entity authentication. ISKAMP specifies fundamental data formats and protocol procedures whereas IKEv1 defines specific authentication protocols. The subsequent standard IKEv2 is also adopted. However, it is only inspired by ISAKMP and contains significant simplifications.

Remaining problem: How to deal with IPsec in complex infrastructures?
Despite the possibility of using the IKE protocols for a dynamic and automated key derivation an often criticised difficulty of IPsec remains: the high complexity if large infrastructures need to be configured. This issue will be covered in more detail in Section 23.2.

12.12   Supplemental Reading

[FGK03]   FRANKEL, S.; GLENN, R.; KELLY, S.: *The AES-CBC Cipher Algorithm and Its Use with IPsec*. September 2003. – RFC 3566, IETF, Status: Proposed Standard, https://tools.ietf.org/html/rfc3602

[HC98]   HARKINS, D.; CARREL, D.: *The Internet Key Exchange (IKE)*. November 1998. – RFC 2409, IETF, Status: Proposed Standard, https://tools.ietf.org/html/rfc2409

[Ken05a]   KENT, S.: *IP Authentication Header*. December 2005. – RFC 4302, IETF, Status: Proposed Standard, https://tools.ietf.org/html/rfc4302

[Ken05b]   KENT, S.: *IP Encapsulating Security Payload (ESP)*.
             December 2005. – RFC 4303, IETF, Status: Proposed
             Standard,
             https://tools.ietf.org/html/rfc4303
[KHN+10]   KAUFMAN, C.; HOFFMAN, P.; NIR, Y.; ERONEN, P.:
             Internet Key Exchange Protocol version 2 (IKEv2).
             September 2010. – RFC 5996, IETF, Status:
             Proposed Standard,
             https://tools.ietf.org/html/rfc5996
[KS05]   KENT, S.; SEO, K.: *Security Architecture for the
             Internet Protocol*. December 2005. – RFC 4301, IETF,
             Status: Proposed Standard,
             https://tools.ietf.org/html/rfc4301
[MSS+98]   MAUGHAN, D.; SCHERTLER, M.; SCHNEIDER, M.;
             TURNER, J.: *Internet Security Association and Key
             Management Protocol (ISAKMP)*. November 1998. –
             RFC 2408, IETF, Status: Proposed Standard,
             https://tools.ietf.org/html/rfc2408
[Pip98]   PIPER, D.: *The Internet IP Security Domain of
             Interpretation for ISAKMP*. November 1998. – RFC
             2407, IETF, Status: Proposed Standard,
             https://tools.ietf.org/html/rfc2407
[VM05]   VIEGA, J.; MCGREW, D.: *The Use of Galois/Counter
             Mode (GCM) in IPsec Encapsulating Security
             Payload (ESP)*. June 2005. – RFC 4106, IETF,
             Status: Proposed Standard,
             https://tools.ietf.org/html/rfc4106
[WRH11]   WEIS, B.; ROWLES, S.; HARDJONO, T.: *The Group
             Domain of Interpretation*. October 2011. – RFC 6407,
             IETF, Status: Proposed Standard,
             https://tools.ietf.org/html/rfc6407

12.13   Questions

1. Why are the principle of connectionless data transmission and
    the requirements for secure communication not compatible
    with one another, and which temporary measure is used in
    the IPsec security architecture to compensate for this short-
    coming?
2. Would it be possible to implement secure data transmission
    more efficiently in a connection-oriented communication ar-
    chitecture and, if yes, in which respect?

3. Why is the authentication header not able to protect all fields of the outer IP packet header?

4. Explain the tasks of the two conceptual databases, the security association database and the security policy database.

5. Why is the security parameter index for a security association in principle allocated by the receiving system?

6. Compare the task and function of the sliding window method for the correction of transmission errors with IPsec replay protection.

7. What are the uses of transport mode and tunnel mode, and how do they differ?

8. Can you give a reason why it can be useful to operate an ESP SA in tunnel mode although the cryptographic end points coincide with the communication end points?

9. What are the main disadvantages of nested IPsec security associations in terms of efficiency?

10. Can IPsec also be used to implement access control functions and, if yes, how?

11. In the case of IPv4, why does the checksum of the outer IP protocol header have to be recomputed when an ESP or an AH protocol header is created?

12. Why does it make sense when processing incoming IPsec packets to verify that the sequence numbers are acceptable before continuing with other cryptographic tests?

13. Is it possible that an IP packet has to run through IPsec protocol processing multiple times in one and the same system?

14. Why is the authenticity of an AH or an ESP packet always verified before the replay window is advanced?

15. Explain the protective effects of the ISAKMP cookie mechanism.

16. Explain how the logical functions 'AND' and 'OR' are realised when a protection suite is negotiated with ISAKMP.

17. Compare the four modes of ISAKMP main mode with respect to the complexity created through cryptographic operations.

18. Is compressed data transmission using the IP payload compression protocol combined with ESP disadvantageous compared to compression directly performed by a protocol of the data link layer?

19. Read about the so-called Bound-End-to-End-Tunnel (BEET) mode [NM08] and discuss how it can be used to avoid addressing issues with peers behind NAT gateways, while still not inducing the protocol overhead of an IPsec tunnel mode security association.

13 Transport Layer Security Protocols

Unlike the network layer, which enables communication between *Transport layer tasks* hosts, the transport layer implements communication between application processes. Its main tasks include:

- isolation of higher-order protocol layers from the technology, structure and deficiencies of the deployed communication technology;
- transparent transmission of user data;
- global addressing of application processes independently of the addressing formats of the lower communication layers.

The overall goal is to provide an efficient and reliable transmission service.

The security protocols of the transport layer enhance the service of the transport layer by assuring additional security properties. As security protocols usually require and are run on a reliable transport service, they actually represent *session layer protocols* in accordance with the OSI model for open communication systems.

However, because the OSI model has not been en vogue since around the mid-1990s, the session layer protocols are usually referred to as *transport layer security protocols*. This chapter deals with the most common protocols in this category: the *Secure Socket Layer (SSL)*, the protocols derived from *Transport Layer Security (TLS)* and *Datagram Transport Layer Security (DTLS)* as well as the independently developed protocol *Secure Shell (SSH)*.

13.1 Secure Socket Layer

The *Secure Socket Layer (SSL)* protocol was originally designed with the primary goal of protecting sessions of the *Hypertext*

Security in Fixed and Wireless Networks, Second Edition.
Guenter Schaefer and Michael Rossberg.

S-HTTP was a competitor to SSL

Transfer Protocol (HTTP). In the early 1990s a similar competing approach existed called the *Secure HTTP (S-HTTP)* protocol. However, as S-HTTP-capable web browsers were not free of charge, whereas SSL version 2.0 was included at no additional cost in the Netscape Communications browsers, SSL quickly became the dominant security protocol for HTTP.

PCT was another competitor

As version 2.0 of the protocol contained a number of deficiencies, Microsoft developed another competitive protocol called *Private Communication Technology (PCT)*. However, Microsoft's web browsers were not well established at the time and so the improved SSL version 3.0 [FKK96] from Netscape Communications managed to hold its ground as the standard protocol for securing HTTP traffic.

SSL was also standardised as TLS

Despite its origins as a security protocol for HTTP, SSL can be used to secure any application run over the transport protocol TCP. In 1996 the Internet Engineering Task Force therefore decided to develop a generic *Transport Layer Security (TLS)* protocol based on SSL.

13.1.1   Security Services and Protocol Architecture

SSL version 3.0 provides the following security services:

- *Entity authentication:* Prior to any communication between client and server, an authentication exchange is performed to verify the identity of the peer entity either only to the client or also to the server. After successful authentication, an *SSL session* is established between the two entities.
- *Confidentiality of user data:* If agreed during negotiation of the SSL session, the user data is encrypted. SSL offers a range of algorithms for this purpose, e.g. RC4, 3DES and IDEA, the use of which can be negotiated during session establishment.
- *Data origin authentication and data integrity:* Each message is secured with a MAC that is computed using a cryptographic hash function. SSL Version 3.0 originally used *prefix–suffix mode* for this purpose. There were some security concerns about this so a revised version that uses HMAC constructions was specified. Either MD5 or SHA-1 can be negotiated as the underlying cryptographic hash function.

Session and connection state

SSL uses the concept of *sessions* that was already anchored in the OSI model. Prior to actual communication, client and server establish a session in which the parameters for securing the communication are negotiated. As in the OSI model, a session can run over multiple transport layer connections if it is negotiated as a 'resumable' session. SSL makes a clear distinction between the following two state sets:

- ■ The *session state* stores the following data:

  Session state

  - ● *Session identifier:* a byte sequence chosen by the server to identify the session.
  - ● *Peer certificate:* an (optional) X.509v3 certificate from the peer entity.
  - ● *Compression method:* denotes the data compression algorithm used before encryption.
  - ● *Cipher spec:* specifies the cryptographic algorithms and their parameters.
  - ● *Master secret:* a 48-byte long secret negotiated between client and server.
  - ● *Is resumable:* indicates whether the session can be resumed or duplicated, i.e. multiple transport connections supported simultaneously.

- ■ In *connection state* the following information is provided over the current transport layer connection(s):

  Connection state

  - ● *Server and client random:* contains random byte sequences chosen by the server or the client.
  - ● *Server write MAC secret:* is included by the server in its MAC computations.
  - ● *Client write MAC secret:* the same as above but for client messages.
  - ● *Server write key:* the key for encrypting and decrypting messages from the server.
  - ● *Client write key:* the same as above but for messages from the client.

The SSL protocol itself is structured as a layered and modular protocol architecture as shown in Figure 13.1.

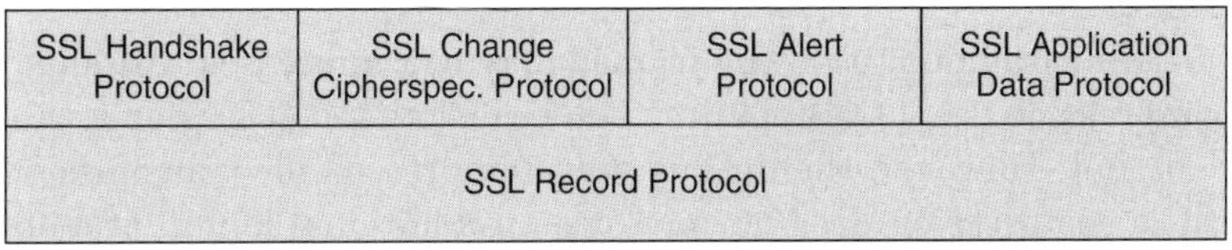

SSL Handshake Protocol	SSL Change Cipherspec. Protocol	SSL Alert Protocol	SSL Application Data Protocol
SSL Record Protocol			

Figure 13.1
Architecture of the secure socket layer protocol

The *Record protocol* is used as the basis for data exchange in SSL sessions. Its tasks include the fragmentation of user data into

Record protocol

plaintext blocks – called 'records' – with a maximum length of 2^{14} octets, the optional compression of plaintext blocks and the optional encryption and authentication of plaintext blocks.

SSL sub-protocols   The *handshake protocol* is used for entity authentication and session negotiation. The *change cipher spec protocol* signals changes in certain cryptographic parameters (session keys, algorithms, etc.) and the *Alert protocol* signals error conditions. The *Application data protocol* is a transparent interface to the record protocol and is used by applications for data unit exchanges with an SSL protocol entity.

Figure 13.2
Frame format of
the SSL record
layer protocol

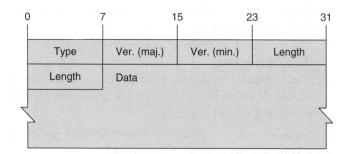

13.1.2   The Record Protocol

Figure 13.2 illustrates how an SSL record is structured. The *(content) type* field identifies the SSL protocol contained in the record: change cipher spec (20), alert (21), handshake (22) or application data (23). The *version* identifies the SSL protocol version (major = 3, minor = 0) and the *length* field contains the length of user data in octets. The maximum user data length is $2^{14} + 2^{10}$ bytes.

Record protocol   The protocol of the sending entity is processed according to the
processing procedures following procedure. First the user data (or the data of the handshake protocol, change cipher spec protocol or alert protocol) is fragmented into frames of a maximum length of 2^{14} octets. More than one message of the same protocol type can be assembled in one frame.

Compression   After fragmentation the frames may be compressed. Although compression is not the default, it can be negotiated at session establishment. However, the data is only compressed for transmission if the compression does not produce an additional length of more than 2^{10} bytes. A lengthening can occur, for example, if the data was already compressed, as with a JPEG file.

After compression a MAC is computed ('$||$' denotes concatenation): *MAC computation*

$$MAC := H(WriteMacSecret \ || \ pad_2 \ ||$$
$$H(WriteMacSecret \ || \ pad_1 \ || \ seqnum \ ||$$
$$length \ || \ data))$$

The sequence number included in the MAC computation is not transmitted because it is implicitly known to the receiving side. In contrast to the already discussed IPsec this is a valid assumption, as the reliable TCP protocol is used to implement the underlying transport layer connection so that any loss or reordering of data units is detected.

The compressed data with the MAC is then encrypted with *Encryption* the method negotiated at session establishment. Depending on the method used, the data first has to be expanded to a multiple of a specific block length. The data is then sent to the service interface of the transport protocol.

On the receiving side the data is successively decrypted, its au- *Processing at the* thenticity is verified and it is decompressed, reassembled and sub- *receiver* sequently delivered to the appropriate application or the higher layer parts of the SSL protocol.

13.1.3 The Handshake Protocol

The SSL handshake protocol is used to negotiate SSL sessions. *Negotiation of SSL* As mentioned earlier, a session can be negotiated so that it can *sessions* be duplicated or resumed at a later time, thus allowing an established cryptographic context to be reused. This feature was partic- *Resumption of* ularly important for the efficiency of protecting the formerly widely *sessions* spread HTTP 1.0 communication since each unit of a hypertext document, for example an HTML document with references to graphics, sound, etc., was transported in a separate TCP connection. If a separate complete authentication protocol with flexible negotiation of cryptographic parameters were required each time, this would have a negative effect on data throughput and latency. Session resumption, on the other hand, allows the use of shorter exchanges. Meanwhile HTTP 1.1 is the predominant web protocol, which also supports so-called persistent TCP connections that are not immediately closed after the transport of a single object. However, also with HTTP 1.1 TCP connections may be torn down and

Figure 13.3
Full exchange
for negotiating
an SSL session

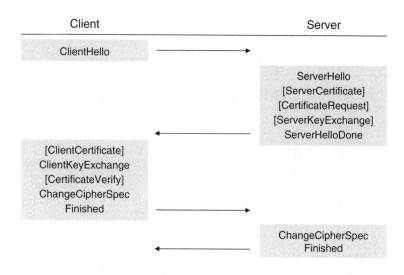

[...] denotes optional message elements

re-established, for example after waiting for a user action, therefore currently there may also be advantages in resuming SSL sessions.

Protocol run   Figure 13.3 presents an overview of a detailed exchange for
First message   negotiating an SSL session. The first message contains a
from client   *ClientHello*, which combines the protocol version used by the client, a random number, possibly a session ID, a list of *cipher suites* supported by the client and a list of allowable compression methods.

First message   The server responds to this message with a *ServerHello*, the op-
from server   tional message elements *ServerCertificate*, *CertificateRequest* and *ServerKeyExchange* as well as a *ServerHelloDone* that concludes the response. The *ServerHello* combines the protocol version supported by it, a random number, possibly a session ID along with the *cipher suite* selected by the server for the session and a designated compression method.

If the session ID contains the value 0, the server is signalling that it is not storing the connection and therefore the connection can neither be duplicated nor resumed at a later time. A value other than 0 means that the client can resume the session at a later time (see below). The certificate included by the server enables the cli-
The server is usually   ent to verify the identity of the server. The server is usually not
not interested in the   interested in the identity of the client, for example if it is merely
identity of the client providing information to a client or it delivers an explicit login page independently of an SSL authentication. However, certain applications also require an SSL-based authentication of the client. In such cases the server also requests a certificate from the client.

Depending on the method used to negotiate the session keys, the server also sends information for the key negotiation, for example its public Diffie–Hellman values or a public RSA key. The *ServerHelloDone* contains no further information and is only used to signal that the server is now waiting for a response from the client. This message is necessary because the client otherwise has no way of knowing whether the server is still going to send an optional message element or whether its response should be regarded as being complete.

The client responds to the message from the server with its certificate (if required), a *ClientKeyExchange*, an optional *CertificateVerify* and the message elements *ChangeCipherSpec* and *Finished*. The *CertificateVerify* enables the client to prove that it has a private key that matches the public key certified in its certificate – provided this certificate was transmitted and certifies a key with signing capability. The client uses *ChangeCipherSpec* to signal that all subsequent message elements it sends are protected with the negotiated cryptographic protection suite. The first message element protected in this way is therefore the element *Finished*, sent immediately after ChangeCipherSpec containing a hash value computed over the shared secret (see below) negotiated during the exchange and all message elements (including ClientHello) sent previously by the client.

Second message from client

The server responds to this message with a *ChangeCipherSpec* and a *Finished*. After the client and the server have both sent a Finished message and have verified the Finished message of their respective peer entity, they consider the session as established and can begin sending protected user data.

Second message from server

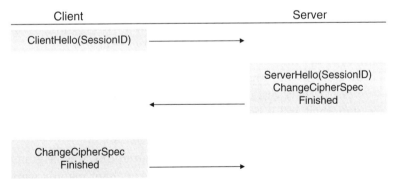

Figure 13.4
Abbreviated exchange for negotiating an SSL session

Figure 13.4 shows an abbreviated exchange for resuming or duplicating a session. In this case the client sends the session ID of the session being resumed in its ClientHello message. If the server has

Resuming a session

stored the session locally and is receptive to resuming the session, it includes the message elements ChangeCipherSpec and Finished immediately after its ServerHello response. The verification of authenticity in this case is solely based on the hash values in the Finished messages, which include the random numbers contained in the Hello messages and thus guarantee the freshness of the message exchanges. If the server is not receptive to resuming the session, it responds with the message elements shown in Figure 13.3, thereby initiating a full exchange between client and server.

Cipher suites   The exchanged *cipher suites* in the Hello messages always reference a combination of cryptographic schemes for establishing and protecting the subsequent session. To do this, the initial SSL specification defines a list of explicitly allowed combinations of encryption and authentication methods. Nevertheless, many current SSL implementations offer additional algorithms, such as AES, that were actually only defined for the succeeding TLS standard.

13.1.4   Authentication and Negotiation of Session Keys

Negotiation of
pre-master secret   A fully compliant SSL implementation would support three methods for negotiating a *pre-master secret* from which other session keys are derived:

RSA-protected
negotiation
- ■ *RSA-protected negotiation:* With this method a pre-master secret is randomly created by the client, encrypted using the public key of the server and sent to the server. The server does not send a separate KeyExchange message element of its own to the client as it is not actively involved in creating the shared secret.

Diffie–Hellman
- ■ *Diffie–Hellman:* This involves executing a conventional Diffie–Hellman key negotiation protocol with the pre-master secret derived from the shared secret $g^{x \times y} \bmod p$.

Fortezza
- ■ *Fortezza:* This is a non-published method that was developed by the NSA and supports key escrow for US government agencies. As there are justified security concerns about this type of method and it has never been widely deployed, we will not cover it in this book.

Securing
HTTP traffic   As mentioned at the beginning of this chapter, SSL was originally designed to secure HTTP traffic. Therefore, a client usually wants to access a web server and have assurance of its authenticity. Consequently, the web server sends a certificate of its public key right after its ServerHello message. This certificate can optionally contain the public Diffie–Hellman values of the server (cyclical group

and primitive root of group, also see Section 4.5). In this case the client must support the same group and primitive root, which can become a problem if the client has also had its public Diffie–Hellman values certified and they turn out to be based on a different cyclical group. Alternatively, the server can send its public Diffie–Hellman values in a KeyExchange message element to the client. In each of the cases mentioned, the client verifies the certificate of the server and uses it either for RSA, Diffie–Hellman or Fortezza-based key negotiation to establish the pre-master secret.

As the next step, the pre-master secret together with the two random numbers of the ClientHello and ServerHello messages are used to derive the 48-byte long *master secret* according to the following rule (the character '$||$' denotes again a concatenation):

Computation of pre-master secret

$$
\begin{aligned}
\textit{master-secret} := \ &\text{MD5}(\textit{pre-master-secret} \ || \\
&\text{SHA-1}(\,'A' \ || \ \textit{pre-master-secret} \ || \\
&\textit{ClientHello.random} \ || \ \textit{ServerHello.random})) \ || \\
&\text{MD5}(\textit{pre-master-secret} \ || \\
&\text{SHA-1}(\,'BB' \ || \ \textit{pre-master-secret} \ || \\
&\textit{ClientHello.random} \ || \ \textit{ServerHello.random})) \ || \\
&\text{MD5}(\textit{pre-master-secret} \ || \\
&\text{SHA-1}(\,'CCC' \ || \ \textit{pre-master-secret} \ || \\
&\textit{ClientHello.random} \ || \ \textit{ServerHello.random}))
\end{aligned}
$$

The use of the two hash functions MD5 and SHA-1 was defined with the intention that the scheme should still be secure even if cryptographic deficiencies are discovered with one of the two hash functions.

A sufficiently long *key block* is derived from the master secret and the random numbers of the two Hello messages. The necessary session keys and initialisation vectors are extracted from the master secret without overlapping.

Derivation of session keys

A key block is constructed using the following computation rule:

$$
\begin{aligned}
\textit{kb} := \ &\text{MD5}(\textit{master-secret} \ || \ \text{SHA-1}(\,'A' \ || \ \textit{master-secret} \ || \\
&\textit{ClientHello.random} \ || \ \textit{ServerHello.random})) \ || \\
&\text{MD5}(\textit{master-secret} \ || \ \text{SHA-1}(\,'BB' \ || \ \textit{master-secret} \ || \\
&\textit{ClientHello.random} \ || \ \textit{ServerHello.random})) \ || \\
&[\cdots]
\end{aligned}
$$

The following session keys and initialisation vectors are then extracted from this:

$$ClientWriteMacSecret := kb[\,1, CipherSpec.HashSize]$$

$$ServerWriteMacSecret := kb[\,i_1, i_1 + CipherSpec.HashSize - 1]$$

$$ClientWriteKey := kb[\,i_2, i_2 + CipherSpec.KeySize - 1]$$

$$ServerWriteKey := kb[\,i_3, i_3 + CipherSpec.KeySize - 1]$$

$$ClientWriteIV := kb[\,i_4, i_4 + CipherSpec.IvSize - 1]$$

$$ServerWriteIV := kb[\,i_5, i_5 + CipherSpec.IvSize - 1]$$

Aspects of authentication The pre-master secret from which the session keys are derived is used to authenticate the server and possibly also the client.

RSA-protected negotiation Using RSA-protected negotiation, the client encrypts the pre-master secret with the public key of the server. As the client can verify the authenticity of this key by evaluating the server certificate, it has the assurance that only the server is able to decrypt the pre-master key. When the client receives the server's Finished message, which contains a hash value over all exchanged message elements and the master secret derived from the pre-master secret, it can conclude that the server is authentic. However, this method does not allow the server to verify the authenticity of the client because any arbitrary client is able to send it a pre-master secret encrypted with the public key of the server. If verification of the authenticity of the client is also required, the client uses RSA-protected negotiation to send an additional client certificate and a CertificateVerify message, which contains a hash value (computed with MD5 or SHA-1) over the master secret and all previously sent message elements.

Diffie–Hellman key exchange If Diffie–Hellman key exchange with certified public Diffie–Hellman values is used, the authenticity of the server can be directly deduced from the negotiated master secret that is included in the hash value of the Finished message. In case the client also sends a certificate with public Diffie–Hellman values that match those of the server, its authenticity can be directly verified on the basis of its Finished message.

Anonymous key negotiation SSL also supports anonymous key negotiation without authentication although in principle this version cannot offer protection against potential man-in-the-middle attacks. It is therefore advisable for it to be deactivated in the local configuration.

13.1.5 A Shortcoming in the Handshake Protocol

In 1998 Bleichenbacher discovered a shortcoming in the encryption standard *PKCS #1* (Version 1.5), which is used in the SSL handshake protocol [BKS98]. Attackers who use RSA-protected negotiation to obtain a pre-master secret are able to exploit this shortcoming.

In this case the client formats the pre-master secret prior to encryption with the RSA algorithm using the standard PKCS #1, which formats and encrypts a message M as follows:

Formatting based on PKCS #1

$$EM := 0x02 \,||\, PS \,||\, 0x00 \,||\, M$$

$$C := RSA(+K_{Server}, EM)$$

PS above denotes a 'padding string' with a minimum of eight randomly generated octets that are always unequal to $0x00$ and should add a random component to the plaintext and pad it to the length of the RSA module being used.

After the server deciphers the ciphertext C, it verifies whether the first octet of the plaintext is equal to $0x02$ and whether the plaintext also contains an octet with a value equal to $0x00$. If the verification is unsuccessful, the server responds with an error message. It is precisely this error message that an attacker can use to execute an *Oracle attack*.

With this type of attack, the attacker Eve tries to discover the pre-master secret negotiated in a previously eavesdropped handshake exchange between Alice (client) and Bob (server) as well as all the session keys derived from it. So Eve has eavesdropped on ciphertext C and wants to recover the corresponding plaintext *EM*.

Operation of an Oracle attack

She therefore generates a series of ciphertexts C_i, which she sends to Bob as part of a bogus SSL session establishment. These have a specific relationship to one another (e and n are the two values of Bob's public key):

$$C_i = C \times R_i^e \;(\mathrm{mod}\; n)$$

The R_i values are constructed in a way that depends on previous 'good' R_i values that were processed by Bob without generating an error message. This indicates they were decrypted to valid plaintexts using PKCS #1. From the information that specific C_i have resulted in valid 'PKCS #1' plaintexts, Eve can now deduce certain bits of the corresponding message $M_i \equiv C_i^d \equiv M \times R_i \;(\mathrm{mod}\; n)$.

From the inferred bits of $M \times R_i \,\mathrm{mod}\, n$ for a sufficient number of R_i, Eve is able to reduce the size of the interval containing message M. Each 'good' ciphertext halves the interval in question so that with a sufficient number of 'good' values R_i Eve is able to determine message M and, consequently, the pre-master secret agreed between Alice and Bob.

With a 1024-bit module length an attacker only needs around 2^{20} requests to compute a plaintext!

With version 1.5 of PKCS #1 used in SSL version 3.0, approximately one of 2^{16} to 2^{18} values of R_i proves to be 'good'. On the basis of the formerly common RSA keys that had a 1024-bit module length, with this method Eve will require approximately 2^{20} ciphertexts and requests Bob to recover a plaintext. Therefore, after approximately one million bogus handshake exchanges, all of which are disrupted by Bob (because of the 'not good' R_i) or Eve (in case of 'good' R_i), Eve is able to discover the pre-master secret previously negotiated between Alice and Bob, and all the session keys derived from it.

In summary, this type of attack shows that *subtle protocol interactions (here between PKCS #1 and SSL) can result in the failure of a protocol even if the basic cryptographic algorithm (here RSA) is not broken itself.*

Possible countermeasures

Various countermeasures exist to combat this type of attack. A naïve but effective measure is to change the asymmetric keys regularly so that attackers are unable to try out sufficient C_i to determine the source text that belongs to C. However, a considerable effort is required as the public key of the server must be certified to enable the client to verify its authenticity.

Frequent key changes

Limit error feedback

Another approach is to reduce the probability of an attacker finding 'good' ciphertexts. This can be done by carefully checking the format of received plaintexts and showing identical behaviour (error notification, time behaviour, etc.) to prevent the client from misusing the server as an Oracle. A further recommendation is to require that the client can prove it knows the plaintext belonging to a ciphertext before it receives information as to whether the ciphertext could be decrypted into a valid plaintext. One possibility for implementing these two ideas is the addition of a strict structure to plaintexts, for example through the concatenation of a cryptographic hash value on each plaintext message. However, it is important that no weaknesses are introduced that can be exploited for another category of attacks [CFP+96].

The client should prove it knows the encrypted plaintext

Optimal Asymmetric Encryption Padding

The best countermeasure to protect against Oracle attacks on protocols using the RSA algorithm is to change the asymmetrical encryption protocol, in this case PKCS #1. Version 2.1 of the standard provides for the plaintext to be prepared using a method called *Optimal Asymmetric Encryption Padding (OAEP)* prior to actual encryption. The aim of this type of preparation is to prevent attackers from producing valid ciphertexts if they do not know the corresponding plaintexts. This property of the modified 'PKCS #1' protocol is called *plaintext aware*.

However, SSL's follow-up standard TLS, which will be presented in the following section, only advises servers to react to detected attacks by using a random pre-master secret. Thus attackers are not able to measure a change of reaction of the server.

13.2   Transport Layer Security

In 1996 the IETF founded a working group to specify a security protocol called *Transport Layer Security (TLS)*. Officially, the protocols SSL, SSH and PCT were to be used as the common input, but it was quickly decided that the protocol SSL version 3.0 with the following modifications should be adopted as TLS:

TLS is based on SSL version 3.0

- The prefix–suffix construction originally used in SSL version 3.0 to compute cryptographic hash values should be replaced by the HMAC construction.
- To calculate the keys MD5 and SHA-1 are not nested, but independently calculated with the results being XORed to each other. The weaknesses of MD5 should therefore have no impact.
- The cipher suites based on Fortezza should be removed from the protocol because they are based on a non-published and potentially insecure technology.
- The handshake protocol should be enhanced to include an authentication version based on the Digital Signature Standard (DSS).
- The protocol specification should be modularised and the record and handshake protocols in particular specified in separate documents.

The last requirement was not actually implemented so the first draft of the TLS specification largely resembles SSL version 3.0. This also applies to RFC 2246, which was adopted in 1999 [DA99].

13.2.1   Cryptographic Algorithms used in TLS

In order to attain a global export permit for TLS-compliant products, several cipher suites were defined in the original TLS standard that stipulate the use of keys with a maximum entropy of 40 bits. These cipher suites contain the word 'Export' in their

Adaptations for attaining a global export permit

symbolic labels. In actual fact these methods provide hardly any protection against attackers, since nowadays brute-force attacks on 40-bit long keys can be executed on standard computers with adequate processing speeds. As a result of the change in US export policy regarding cryptography, these cipher suites have lost their significance and they are no longer included in the current TLS 1.2 specification [DR08].

Supported crypto-graphic algorithms and protocols

In terms of protocol functions there is little difference between TLS and SSL, although version 1.2 of the protocol supports a number of other cipher suites with the following cryptographic algorithms and protocol elements:

- *Authentication and key exchange:* A Diffie–Hellman key exchange (DH and ECDH) can be implemented with or without digital signatures (DSA, ECDSA or RSA). Alternatively, the Diffie–Hellman key exchange, either via $\mathbb{Z}_p$ or via elliptic curves, can be authenticated with certified public values. A comparatively new option is the use of SRP for client and server authentication [TWM+07]. In principle it is also possible to re-use passwords on the client side, since certificate-based authentication can be offered as well. Assuming pairwise different passwords, SRP also offers a method to verify the server identity that is independent of CAs. The most common method remains RSA-protected transfer of the pre-master secret by the client.

- *Encryption algorithms:* 3DES and AES are supported in CBC mode. The 'alternative' encryption algorithms Camellia [KKK10] and ARIA [KLP+11] can also be used in CBC mode. ARIA is a Korean cipher which, like AES, can also be operated in GCM. Alternatively, the protection can be negotiated through RC4 (key length 128 bits) or no encryption. Although the use of IDEA and (Single-)DES in CBC mode is specified in the separate RFC 5469 [Ero09], it is not recommended.

- *Message authentication values:* In addition to HMAC structures based on MD5 and SHA-1, TLS 1.2 also makes provision for SHA-224, SHA-256, SHA-384 and SHA-512. The use of HMAC-MD5 is no longer recommended. The verification of message authentication values can only be dispensed with in two special cases: (a) no protection through TLS is required, and at the same time no encryption is used, or (b) an AEAD algorithm is used.

- *Derivation of key material:* From TLS 1.2 the MD5 SHA-1 structure is no longer used for calculating the keys. Instead, functions have to specified explicitly for the cipher suites. Currently SHA-256 tends to be used.

13.2.2 Attacks on Selectable Initialisation Vectors

If ciphers are used in CBC mode with TLS version 1.0 or SSL, the initialisation vector for a record is always determined by the last block of the ciphertext of the previous record. In contrast to IPsec, where packets can be lost, TLS/SSL provides a reliable TCP connection so there are no functional disadvantages. However, if attackers can send records themselves, there is a security problem [Bar06] since they may then be able to decrypt records that were sent independently. In practice this may occur in VPN based on TLS/SSL, for example, where attackers can introduce packets via a compromised computer in order to decipher the packets of other computers. Furthermore, in 2010 a method referred to as Browser Exploit Against SSL/TLS (BEAST) emerged [DR11], in which the attacker uses a JavaScript in the victim's browser to construct web queries with a view to restoring data from a TLS-protected HTTP transfer.

Selection of IVs in TLS/SSL and attack scenarios

During the initial attack phase, records are sent via the attacked TLS/SSL connection, resulting in fixed cipher values. If an attacker is able to insert complete records arbitrarily, this is comparatively simple. If, for example, the plain text of the record starts with the last ciphertext, the result is always a zero block that has to be encrypted, while the rest of the record is always mapped to the identical ciphertext. If fixed frame formats are required, the attack becomes more complex but is still feasible. One source for further details is [DR11].

Checking the IV

The next attack phase begins once the attacker has intercepted sensitive traffic that was encrypted with this initialisation vector. The attacker can now use a targeted trial and error approach using plaintexts at the block boundaries, based on repeated reconstruction of the initialisation vector.

Targeted trying of data

Figure 13.5 shows a simplified example of such an attack. The attacker uses a JavaScript in the victim's browser to send queries to a server, for example the server of a bank. The attacker can embed the JavaScript via a man-in-the-middle attack when the victim visits unprotected web pages, for example. With each JavaScript query a cookie is transferred, which the server uses to identify the victim as a legitimate user and whose content (1234secsec23423) the attacker wants to find out in our example.

Simple eavesdropping is inadequate for this purpose since the records are protected by a CBC cipher with blocks that are 128

Figure 13.5

Simplified sequence

of an attack on the

CBC mode in TLS 1.0

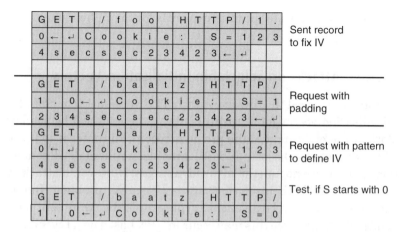

bits long. In Figure 13.5 each row corresponds to a block. The attacker initially sends a query, which ensures that the record ends with a certain ciphertext. In the next step the attacker sends another query, which is constructed in such a way that the first byte of the cookie is just before a block boundary. The ciphertext of the record is then registered. This is followed by a further query, which initially generates a ciphertext again, whose last block is used to set the defined IV. This is followed by the content of the second server query. The attacker does not know the value of the cookie but guesses that the cookie starts with '0' and detects that another ciphertext is generated. This enables the attacker to conclude that the cookie does not start with '0' and to continue the systematic guessing. The attacker can then generate a new query, in which the second character before the block boundary is encrypted, and try and guess that character.

Attack analysis   In summary, this attack clearly has to be regarded as very complex, so that, in practice, such attacks are unlikely to occur regularly. Nevertheless, it impressively demonstrates how different components of a cryptographic protocol can interact in an undesirable manner and lead to a weakness. New rules for the use of initialisation vectors were introduced in TLS 1.1. Each record must now be preceded by a randomly selected explicit initialisation vector. This prevents the type of attack described above.

13.2.3   Renegotiation Attack

In 2009 a further possible attack on TLS and SSL was published, in which the option of renegotiating sessions is misused. One source for further details is [Zol11]. In concrete terms, this loophole enables attackers to intervene between server and victim, and exchange messages with the server before the server/victim communication. The actual communication continues to take place confidentially and authentically.

Whether this behaviour leads to actual security problems strongly depends on the respective application protocol. However, despite being fairly complex, such attacks can be realised for web services with relative ease. A possible scenario is described below:

Effects depend on the application protocol

1. The victim establishes a TLS/SSL connection with the server and logs in on the web page.
2. The attacker sends a TCP reset packet on behalf of the server and the TLS/SSL connection is closed.
3. In the next operation the victim establishes a new TLS/SSL connection. This time the attacker intercepts the TCP connection and waits for a TLS/SSL handshake.
4. The attacker buffers the values and uses the parameters to establish a session with the server. This is easily possible, since with TLS/SSL usually only the server authenticates itself. The attacker can now send a specially configured query to the server, e.g.:
    ```
    GET /ebank/transfer?what=LotsOfMoney&to=eve
    HTTP/1.1 <crlf>
    X-Ignore: <no crlf>
    ```
    The attacker then initiates a renegotiation of the keys.
5. The weakness lies in the fact that the attacker can now trick the victim into continuing the session started by the attacker and to accept the renegotiated parameters as a new connection. The actual victim/server communication via the attacker will be secure, although any query sent by the victim will be appended to the values already sent. At the server, the query
    ```
    GET /ebank/start.html HTTP/1.1<crlf>
    Cookie: S=a40da433e30e79012617ac03<crlf>
    ```
    thus becomes
    ```
    GET /ebank/transfer?what=LotsOfMoney&to=eve
    HTTP/1.1 <crlf>
    X-Ignore: GET /ebank/start.html HTTP/1.1<crlf>
    Cookie: S=a40da433e30e79012617ac03<crlf>
    ```

In other words, the attacker uses the victim's cookie to carry out an action without having to use the weak spot to obtain knowledge of the cookie itself.

Effects and countermeasures

Once again it becomes apparent that TLS/SSL is a very complex protocol, where interaction between the components can result in problems with security. Although these may initially appear to be of little effect, they may have catastrophic consequences within the context of an application protocol. In addition to HTTPS, other affected protocols include SMTP and FTP-S, while protocols such as IMAP, POP or EAP-TLS are not affected. A number of other types of attack are known for HTTPS, which allow JavaScript to be executed on the victim's computer within the security context of the web server [Zol11].

A standardised countermeasure is described in RFC 5746 [RRD+10]. It involves an extension of the TLS protocol to link initial and renegotiated sessions through cryptographic measures.

13.2.4　Problems with Compression in TLS

A further problem relating to TLS/SSL and the interaction with the protection of HTTP was published in 2012 [DR12]. In this case the problem lies in the simple fact that TLS traffic can be compressed, which means that potentially all TLS/SSL versions are affected. In an attack scenario that is similar to the BEAST attack discussed above, a JavaScript is started in the victim's browser, for example by embedding the JavaScript in uninvolved, unprotected pages via a man-in-the-middle attack. The JavaScript then sends queries to a secure web page and the attacker checks how well the query was compressed. The name of the attack, *Compression Ratio Info-leak Made Easy (CRIME)*, is derived from this side channel.

Example of an attack

In the simplest case the attacker once again uses the CRIME attack to extract the value of a cookie. To this end the JavaScript can be used to issue the following query, for example:

```
GET /S=3 HTTP/1.1<crlf>
Cookie: S=31d6cfe0d16ae931b73c59d7<crlf>
```

Through observation of the network the attacker can detect that the query is smaller than other queries, for example after /S=2, since it is more compressible. In this way the attacker can use a targeted character-by-character trial and error approach to reconstruct the cookie. Further forms of attack that are more complex and better developed are described in [DR12].

The browser makers have responded to the attack by disabling the compression option. However, each application protocol has to be assessed to ascertain whether TLS-based compression represents a potential vulnerability.

TLS compression disabled in web browsers

13.2.5   Timing Attacks on the CBC Mode in TLS

In February 2013 a further attack on TLS was published [AP13], which enables reconstruction of plaintext blocks if ciphers are used in CBC mode. In this case, a combination of TLS/SSL procedures turned out to be problematic. In contrast to IPsec, TLS/SSL first authenticates the plaintext of a record, then appends a padding and finally encrypts the data. The padding is not authenticated, although it has to have a certain form, and each byte of the padding must correspond to the padding length minus one. For example, if the padding block comprises 3 bytes, the padding is expected to be 0x02 0x02 0x02. The implementation is where the actual problem arises. The processing times tend to differ, depending on whether or not a padding is correct. Since the processing duration does not depend on the cipher but on the plaintext, attackers can measure the duration and use it to their advantage. In particular, the attack is still possible, despite some countermeasures. These are even described explicitly in the TLS standard, for example initial authentication is invoked, even if the padding is incorrect. The authentication duration differs depending on whether or not the padding is correct because a different number of HMAC calls is required.

TLS authentication takes place after decryption

A highly simplified attack to reconstruct a ciphertext block C_n can take place as follows. The length field of the record is changed so that C_n is the last block. In addition, the block preceding C_n, that is, C_{n-1}, is linked with a value Δ via an XOR operation. For the attacker this results in unpredictable changes in the deciphered $\tilde{P}_{n-1}$ and predictable changes in $\tilde{P}_n$, which is now also linked with Δ via an XOR operation. If, for example, $\Delta = \texttt{0x0005}$ is selected and a valid padding is generated as in $\Delta = \texttt{0x1005}$, it is highly probable that the unmodified plain text P_n ends with 0x05. The test with $\Delta = \texttt{0x1005}$ serves to eliminate the possibility that the last bytes of $\tilde{P}_n$ were 0x01 0x01, for example. In this case the packet authentication is almost certainly likely to fail, despite the attacker's ability to measure differences in error message delays.

Modification of ciphertexts for generating valid paddings

The authors of the attacks carried out extensive tests and identified numerous TLS/SSL implementations that are vulnerable. In particular, the types of attack can be refined further with BEAST-like methods. The only quick solution to the problem is

Eliminating the problem

to avoid the CBC encryption mode in TLS/SSL, for example by using RC4 or AES-GCM. However, RC4 is problematic due to its cryptographic weaknesses. AES-GCM, on the other hand, is not yet supported by all TLS implementations. The medium-term solution involves eliminating the side channel, which arose due to the TLS/SSL specification, from the implementations by ensuring that the processing duration is only dependent on the packet length.

13.3   Datagram Transport Layer Security

The TLS protocol described above is popular due to the fact that it can be used in custom applications without having to modify the operating system or network components. However, it invariably requires a reliable connection, as provided through TCP. This limits the application options, particularly in cases where:

- voice or video data is to be transported in real time, and therefore time-consuming retransmissions are to be avoided or
- reliable protocols are to be tunnelled securely on the transport layer, e.g. via TCP connections in a TLS-based VPN.

For this reason the IETF decided to standardise a variant of TLS that also works via unreliable transport protocols such as UDP. The method referred to as *Datagram Transport Layer Security (DTLS)* is currently defined in RFC 6347 [RM12] as a complement to TLS version 1.2 and also offers many analogies to IPsec and IKE.

Modifications for   To account for the fact that messages may be lost, mechanisms
unreliable channels for the retransmission of handshake packets were developed. In addition, messages are explicitly tagged with sequence numbers, and a sliding window method is implemented for dealing with potential replays. Also, like IPsec, RC4 cannot be used with DTLS due to the lack of a resynchronisation mechanism. In order to prevent possible sabotage attacks on DTLS services based on a large number of forged queries, the method stipulates implementation of a protection mechanism against denial-of-service attacks like the one in IKEv2 (see Section 12.9). Thus, storage and calculation of values should only commence once the client address has been verified. Like IPsec, DTLS is also potentially affected by NAT situations. Such situations do not directly cause problems, as it is a transport layer protocol. However, here too, it may result in the state of the
Transmission NAT routers being lost if there are long gaps between packet ex-
of heartbeats changes. One of the procedures suggested in RFC 6520 [STW12] is

to use periodic *heartbeat messages* to check whether the parties can still reach each other correctly.

A noteworthy difference compared with IPsec is that DTLS attempts to avoid fragmentation at IP level by distributing plaintext data over several records. This may have positive effects on resistance against sabotage attacks, since the packets only have to be buffered or assembled after successful authentication.

Custom fragmentation mechanism

13.4 Secure Shell

The protocol *Secure Shell (SSH)* was specially designed to allow for a remote login to computers and developed by Ylönen at Helsinki University in Finland. As the author also provided a free implementation with source code for general use, the protocol was quickly widely used in the Internet. Although the author subsequently commercialised the development of SSH, free implementations of the current protocol version still exist, with *OpenSSH* being the one most widely used.

Version 2.0 of the SSH specification was submitted to the IETF in 1997 and since then has been refined on a regular basis in a series of updated Internet drafts. It took over nine years of redesign and in 2006 the RFCs were finally published [YL06a, YL06b, YL06c, YL06d].

Standardisation in IETF

SSH was designed with the goal of creating a secure replacement for the *R-Tools (rlogin, rsh, rcp, rdist)* in the *Unix* operating system. It thus represents an application layer or session layer protocol. However, as it also contains a generic security protocol for transport connections and supports the encapsulation of transport connections (tunnelling), it is referred to in this chapter as a transport layer security protocol.

Goal of SSH

Version 2 of the SSH specification is divided into four documents:

- The Secure Shell (SSH) Protocol Architecture [YL06c];
- The Secure Shell (SSH) Transport Layer Protocol [YL06d];
- The Secure Shell (SSH) Authentication Protocol [YL06a];
- The Secure Shell (SSH) Connection Protocol [YL06b].

The protocol architecture is based on a client/server approach. Each server has at least one public key that is used for the entire computer. SSH supports two fundamental trust models. With the simple model, each client has access to a local database that stores the public key for each computer known to it. SSH also supports the

Protocol architecture

Trust models

Negotiation of protocol mechanisms allocation of public keys to servers on the basis of certificates. In this case clients know the public key(s) of one or more certification entities that certify the public keys of the servers. In addition, the protocol enables a flexible negotiation of the protocol mechanisms used in a session, including encryption, data integrity, key negotiation and compression, along with the respective algorithms and parameters.

13.4.1 SSH Transport Protocol

SSH security services The SSH transport protocol runs on top of a reliable transport protocol (usually TCP) to provide the following security services for data exchanged in a session:

- server authentication (host-related);
- user data encryption (after optional prior compression);
- data origin authentication.

Cryptographic algorithms and protocols The servers may be authenticated using RSA, DSA or ECDSA signatures. A session key is usually agreed with authenticated Diffie–Hellman exchange at the same time. The latter one can also be performed by $\mathbb{Z}_p$ arithmetic or with the help of elliptic curves [SG09]. The algorithms 3DES, Blowfish, Twofish, AES, Serpent, IDEA and CAST in cipher block chaining mode and RC4 are supported for the encryption of the user data. For data integrity authentication the hash values are computed using the HMAC construction alternatively with MD5, SHA-1 or in newer implementations with SHA-2 [BB12]. Furthermore, there is also the possibility in SSH to implicitly authenticate data using AES in GCM [IS09].

Protocol fields Figure 13.6 shows the frame format of the SSH transport protocol. The meaning of the protocol fields contained in the frame is as follows:

Packet length
- *Packet length* denotes the number of octets in the frame minus this field.

Pad length
- *Pad length* indicates how many octets were used to lengthen the packet before encryption and must contain a value between 4 and 255.

Payload
- *Payload* contains the actual payload of the frame. If encryption of the user data was negotiated at the time of session establishment, the payload is encrypted after optional compression and computation of the MAC.

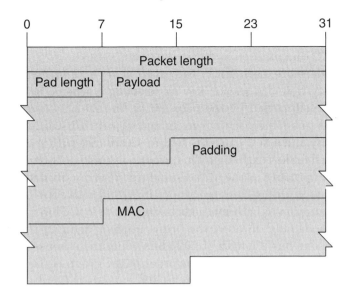

Figure 13.6
Frame format of SSH transport protocol

■ *Padding* denotes randomly selected octets that are used to pad the payload to an integer multiple of 8 or the block length of the encryption scheme (depending on which value is higher). *Padding*

■ *MAC* contains the optional authentication value of the message that is computed according to the following rule: *MAC*

$$MAC := HMAC(SharedSecret, SeqNum \parallel PlainPacket)$$

SeqNum denotes a 32-bit sequence number incremented for each frame and *PlainPacket* denotes the entire unencrypted frame without the MAC field.

Like the SSL record protocol, the frames with the SSH transport protocol are not aligned to 32-bit boundaries. Such an alignment is particularly important for protocols up to the network layer because it usually enables protocols to be processed efficiently in gateway systems. As protocol data units above the transport layer are no longer processed in gateway systems, this is something that can be eliminated without significantly impacting performance. *No alignment to 32-bit boundaries*

13.4.2 Parameter Negotiation and Server Authentication

When an SSH transport protocol connection is established, client and server agree on the cryptographic scheme that should be used.

Each peer entity sends a packet referred to as *Kexinit* with a specification of supported schemes in the order of local preference. Both entities then iterate over the list of the client and *Negotiation of supported scheme and preferences* select the first scheme that is also supported by the server. This enables schemes to be negotiated for server authentication, encryption, MAC computation and user data compression.

Key negotiation   Furthermore, each entity can attach a *key exchange packet* for the negotiation of a session key by selecting a scheme it assumes also to be supported by the peer entity. In case this assumption turns out to be false, the key exchange packet is discarded by the peer entity and a new packet is sent in accordance with the scheme negotiated for key exchange. This situation should not occur too frequently in practice as the initial standard [YL06d] only defined two methods with Diffie–Hellman groups in $\mathbb{Z}_p$ and with SHA-1 and the implementation of both methods being mandatory. More precisely the methods only differ in the prime number defining the group in which one has a length of 1024 bits while the other is 2048 bit long. The generator is 2 and the order of the group is $(p-1)/2$ in both cases. However, RFC 5656 [SG09] extends the initial standard by Diffie–Hellman exchanges over elliptic curves. It mandates the implementation of three NIST curves with $\mathbb{Z}_p$ arithmetic and recommends the support of all additional nine curves.

If the peer entity supports the scheme used in the key exchange packet, it processes the packet as the first packet for the key exchange. This saves one full round-trip time between client and server.

Protocol run   The scheme for key negotiation and server authentication specified in [YL06d] with the group given above comprises the following protocol procedures:

1. The client selects a random number x, computes $e := g^x \bmod p$ and sends e to the server.
2. The server selects a random number y, computes $f := g^y \bmod p$ and sends f to the client. The server does not have to wait for the first packet from the client with the value e and instead can execute this operation in parallel with the first protocol step of the client.
3. Upon receipt of e the server also computes:

$$K := e^y \bmod p \text{ as well as the hash value}$$

$$h := H(ver_C, ver_S, kexinit_C, kexinit_S, +K_S, e, f, K)$$

The message elements *ver* and *kexinit* denote the protocol version and the initial message for the algorithm negotiation of the client or the server. The server signs the hash value h with its private key $-K_S$, i.e. it computes $s := E(-K_S, h)$ and sends the message $(+K_S, f, s)$ to the client.

4. On receipt of this message the client verifies the authenticity of the public key $+K_S$ (either by querying its local database or by verifying the key certificate belonging to $+K_S$). It then computes $K := f^x \bmod p$ and the hash value h. It also verifies the signature over the hash value h. If the verification is successful, the client is assured that it has negotiated a shared secret K with the server in possession of key $-K_S$.

However, the server cannot use this exchange to deduce the authenticity of the client; the SSH authentication protocol described in the next section is used for this purpose.

The following session keys ($EK \stackrel{\wedge}{=}$ encryption key, $IK \stackrel{\wedge}{=}$ integrity key) are then derived by both sides from the negotiated secret K and hash value h, with hash value h of the initial key exchange also used as the session ID:

Derivation of session keys

$$IV_{Client2Server} := H(K, h, \; 'A', SessionId)$$

$$IV_{Server2Client} := H(K, h, \; 'B', SessionId)$$

$$EK_{Client2Server} := H(K, h, \; 'C', SessionId)$$

$$EK_{Server2Client} := H(K, h, \; 'D', SessionId)$$

$$IK_{Client2Server} := H(K, h, \; 'E', SessionId)$$

$$IK_{Server2Client} := H(K, h, \; 'F', SessionId)$$

The bits for the key are extracted from the beginning of the output of the cryptographic hash function. If additional bits are required to those produced by the cryptographic hash function, the keys are 'lengthened' using the following method:

Key 'lengthening'

$$K_1 := H(K, h, x, SessionId) \; \text{with} \; x = \; 'A', \; 'B', \; \ldots$$

$$K_2 := H(K, h, K_1)$$

$$K_3 := H(K, h, K_1, K_2)$$

$$XK := K_1 \| K_2 \| \; \ldots \; \text{with} \; XK = IV, EK, IK$$

13.4.3 Client Authentication

The SSH authentication protocol verifies the identity of the client and is run over the the SSH transport protocol. The default supports the following authentication methods:

Supported authentication methods

■ *Public key:* The client generates a signature that is created with the private key of the user $-K_{User}$ and sends the

Public key

following message to the server:

$$Client \rightarrow Server: \{SessionId, 50, ID_{User}, Service,$$
$$'public\text{-}key', True, PubKeyAlgName,$$
$$+ K_{User}\}_{-K_{User}}$$

Password

■ *Password:* With this method the password of the client is presented to the server. With this authentication method there has to be an assurance that the SSH connection was negotiated with encryption so that the password cannot be sniffed during transmission.

Host-based public key

■ *Host-based public key:* Similar to the public key method described above but with the key of the client computer being used.

None

■ *None:* This method is mainly used to query the schemes supported by the server. If the server does not demand client authentication, it can also respond with a 'success' message.

If verification of the authentication message is successful, the server responds with the message SSH_MSG_USERAUTH_SUCCESS.

13.4.4   Connection Control Within A Session

Connection control within an SSH session is run by the SSH connection protocol that provides the following services:

■ interactive login sessions;
■ remote command execution;
■ encapsulation and routing of TCP/IP connections;
■ encapsulation and routing of X11 connections.

For each of the services listed above one or more channels, which are all multiplexed into a single encrypted and integrity-protected SSH transport connection, are constructed between client and server. Each of the two peer entities can request that a new channel be opened. Numbers identify the separate channels at sender and receiver, and each channel is typed: session, x11, forwarded-tcpip, etc. Flow control using a sliding window mechanism is performed for each channel and data can only be sent if a window credit is granted by the receiving side.

Opening of a channel

The message SSH_MSG_CHANNEL_OPEN with the following parameters opens a new channel:

■ *Channel type* is a character string that specifies one of the channel types listed above.

■ *Sender channel* is a 32-bit long integer value for the local identification of a channel and is provided by the requesting entity.

■ *Initial window size* defines the initial sending credit granted by the initiator of the channel of the responding entity.

■ *Maximum packet size* defines the maximum PDU size that the initiator wants to receive over this channel.

■ Other parameters are possible and are specific to the requested channel type.

In the case that the receiver of this message does not want to accept the channel request, it needs to respond with the message SSH_MSG_CHANNEL_OPEN_FAILURE, which is parameterised as follows:

Rejection of a channel request

■ *Recipient channel* contains the identification number defined by the sender of the OpenRequest message.

■ *Reason code* carries one of the values defined in [YL06b] for signalling the reason.

■ *Additional textual information* enables the sending of an error message that is readable by the user.

■ *Language tag* is a character string indicating the language in which the textual information is composed.

If the receiver of an OpenRequest message also agrees to open a new channel, it answers with a message called SSH_MSG_CHANNEL_OPEN_CONFIRMATION, which contains the following parameters:

Acceptance of a channel request

■ *Recipient channel* contains the identification number allocated by the initiator to the channel.

■ *Sender channel* indicates an identification number defined by the responder.

■ *Initial window size* is the initial sending credit granted to the initiator of a channel.

■ *Maximum packet size* defines the maximum packet size the responder will accept in a channel.

■ Other parameters can be contained and are specific to the channel type requested.

After a channel has been opened successfully, data transfer is possible, channel-specific requests can be made and the channel can finally be closed. In addition, both peer entities regularly send an appropriate message to renew the sending credit.

Communicating how data should be handled

Before data is sent, channel-specific requests may have to be negotiated in order to agree how the data should be handled on the receiving side. This requires the message SSH_MSG_ CHANNEL_REQUEST. As parameters it contains the identification number of the channel being requested on the receiving side, a request type that is formatted as a character string, an indication of whether an explicit response is expected to the request (want reply) and possibly other parameters that are specific to the request type. The responding entity can use the two message types SSH_MSG_CHANNEL_SUCCESS and SSH_MSG_CHANNEL_FAILURE to report on the processing results of the request. The establishment and configuration of specific channel types is explained using examples below.

Establishing an interactive session and starting a command interpreter

The first example illustrates how an interactive session is established with the starting of a command interpreter. Figure 13.7 shows the message exchanges involved. First a session type channel is opened. In the example shown the initiator of the channel defines the local identification number '20' for the channel, grants an initial sending credit of 2048 bytes and specifies a maximum packet size of 512 bytes. The responder replies to this message referring to identification number 20 and defines the value 31 as its own local identification number. It grants an initial sending credit of 1024 bytes and defines 256 bytes as the maximum size for packets sent to it.

The initiator responds using a SSH_MSG_CHANNEL_REQUEST message typed pty-req to request the establishment of a *pseudo terminal*. As it does not yet expect an explicit response, it sets the value of the message field *want reply* to 'false'. It then immediately requests that environment variables be set within the session, for example the variable *HOME* should be set to the value like /home/username. The initiator asks that a command interpreter be started (the *shell*, with Unix systems this results in the start of 'Default Shell', for example /bin/sh, which is specified for each user in /etc/password) this time requesting an explicit acknowledgement that confirms whether the processing was successful. The responder acknowledges this request with an SSH_MSG_CHANNEL_SUCCESS message.

Tunnelling of X11 data streams

The second example involves tunnelling X11 data streams. The client system, which must have an X11 server running on it, opens a session type channel. It then sends an SSH_MSG_CHANNEL_REQUEST message typed x11-req to request

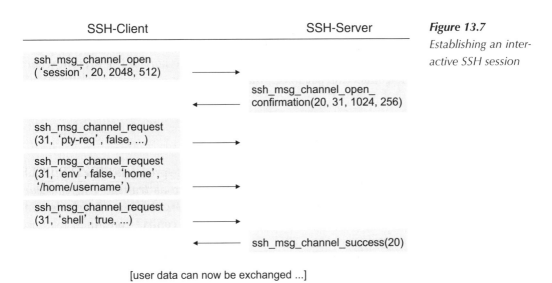

Figure 13.7
Establishing an inter-
active SSH session

the tunnelling and routing of X11 data streams. If an X11 application is started on the server later, then its input/output must be
encapsulated by the SSH process and sent to the client system.
The SSH process on the client system routes this input/output to
the local X11 server that has the 'impression' the X11 application
is running on the local computer. A separate x11 type channel is
opened for the data of each X11 application. The server system
takes the initiative for this because it is the first system to have
knowledge of the application.

The final example relates to the tunnelling and routing of *Tunnelling and routing*
TCP/IP traffic, where a distinction is made for the client between *of TCP/IP traffic*
incoming and outgoing connections.

For outgoing connections the client does not need to make an *Outgoing connections*
explicit request for tunnelling in advance and instead can directly
request that the server opens a new direct-tcp type channel. The
channel-type-specific parameters specified by the client are the IP
address and the port of the desired target system along with the IP
address and the port of the source system.

In contrast, with incoming connections the client must send *Incoming connections*
an explicit request for tunnelling to the server so that it has
knowledge of this requirement. The client consequently sends an
SSH_MSG_GLOBAL_REQUEST message typed tcpip-forward. In
the type-specific parameters the client specifies the source addresses from which connections should be accepted (the address
0.0.0.0 indicates that arbitrary systems can be set) and under which
port number the server should accept the connections. If a connection setup request for this port arrives at the server later, the server

opens a new `forwarded-tcpip` type channel. The parameters conveyed to the client are the port number where the connection arrived along with the IP address and the port of the system where the connection setup originated.

13.5   Summary

Within the meaning of the OSI model, the protocols SSL/TLS/DTLS and SSH, which are usually referred to as *transport layer security protocols*, are actually session layer protocols, as clearly demonstrated by the mechanisms for session control contained in these protocols.

TLS and SSH similarly suite to secure communication above transport layer

TLS and SSH are similarly suitable for securing Internet communication above the transport layer. Both protocols operate on a reliable transport service provided by the TCP protocol. DTLS is a security protocol specifically designed for protecting connectionless transport protocols such as UDP.

Computer-based authentication

Although SSH operates above the transport layer, server authentication is computer-based and is not executed with reference to a specific application process. In this respect SSL/TLS/DTLS support multiple certificates and consequently multiple identities within a server system. Regarding the security it needs to be noted that all of the presented protocols are much more complex than the previously discussed IPsec, which in turn has been widely criticised for its complexity. This results in the high quantity of reveal attacks. All in all, if SSL/TLS/DTLS or SSH is to be used, each individual scenario should be evaluated as to whether there may be unwanted side effects and which of the mechanisms may be deactivated.

Secure end-to-end communication between applications

If used correctly, the current security protocols of the transport layer implement secure end-to-end communication between application processes. SSH additionally allows application process-related tunnelling and routing of TCP data streams. Furthermore,

Limited firewall compatibility

to a limited degree both protocols can also interoperate with the packet filtering in Internet firewalls (see also Chapter 21) and in many cases present a very good option for securing Internet communications.

However, as these protocols in principle cannot secure the protocol headers of the lower communication layers, they offer no protection against attacks on actual network infrastructure and

therefore cannot replace but only complement the security protocols of the lower communication layers.

13.6   Supplemental Reading

[BKS98]   BLEICHENBACHER, D.; KALISKI, B.; STADDON, J.:
            *Recent Results on PKCS #1: RSA Encryption
            Standard.* 1998. – RSA Laboratories' Bulletin 7

[CFP⁺96]   COPPERSMITH, D.; FRANKLIN, M. K.; PATARIN, J.;
            REITER, M. K.: Low Exponent RSA with Related
            Messages. In: MAURER, U. (Hrsg.): *In Advances in
            Cryptology – Eurocrypt'96 Proceedings,*
            Springer-Verlag, 1996. – Vol. 1070 of Lectures Notes
            in Computer Science

[DR08]   DIERKS, T.; RESCORLA, E.: *The Transport Layer
            Security (TLS) Protocol version 1.2.* August 2008. –
            RFC 5246, IETF, Status: Proposed Standard,
            `https://tools.ietf.org/html/rfc5246`

[FKK96]   FREIER, A. O.; KARLTON, P.; KOCHER, P. C.: *The SSL
            Protocol version 3.0.* 1996. – Netscape
            Communications Corporation

[RM12]   RESCORLA, E.; MODADUGU, N.: *Datagram Transport
            Layer Security version 1.2.* January 2012. – RFC
            6347, IETF, Status: Proposed Standard,
            `https://tools.ietf.org/html/rfc6347`

[YL06a]   YLONEN, T.; LONVICK, C.: *The Secure Shell (SSH)
            Authentication Protocol.* 2006. – RFC 4252, IETF,
            Status: Proposed Standard,
            `https://tools.ietf.org/html/rfc4252`

[YL06b]   YLONEN, T.; LONVICK, C.: *The Secure Shell (SSH)
            Connection Protocol.* 2006. – RFC 4254, IETF, Status:
            Proposed Standard,
            `https://tools.ietf.org/html/rfc4254`

[YL06c]   YLONEN, T.; LONVICK, C.: *The Secure Shell (SSH)
            Protocol Architecture.* 2006. – RFC 4251, IETF,
            Status: Proposed Standard,
            `https://tools.ietf.org/html/rfc4251`

[YL06d]   YLONEN, T.; LONVICK, C.: *The Secure Shell (SSH)
            Transport Layer Protocol.* 2006. – RFC 4253, IETF,
            Status: Proposed Standard,
            `https://tools.ietf.org/html/rfc4253`

13.7   Questions

1.   Which security services are provided by the SSL/TLS protocols?

2.   Why is it that for SSL/TLS it is often only the server that authenticates itself to the client?

3.   Which concepts of the session layer based on the OSI model are implemented by SSL/TLS?

4.   The default in the SSL record protocol does not provide for data compression. Why is this an advantage?

5.   Which other security property is protected in the SSH transport protocol as a result of the MAC being computed over the plaintext before the plaintext is encrypted (instead of the equally conceivable sequence in which encryption is performed before the MAC is computed)?

6.   In an exchange based on the SSL/TLS handshake protocol, what convinces a client of the authenticity of the server when key negotiation uses Diffie–Hellman?

7.   Which cryptographic property is referred to as 'plaintext aware'?

8.   SSL VPN are usually much more inefficient compared to IPsec VPN. Why are they used despite this drawback?

9.   Why is it impossible to port the CRIME attack to the compression method used in IPsec (IPComp)?

10.   What are the advantages and disadvantages of DTLS in comparison to IPsec?

11.   Why is TLS used in EAP exchanges and not DTLS?

12.   To which layers of the OSI model can the SSH protocol be related? Give the appropriate protocol functions for each instance.

13.   What advantage is derived from the fact that specific Diffie–Hellman parameters are specified for SSH? Are there also potential disadvantages?

14.   Why does SSH provide a password-based authentication of the client?

15.   What is the purpose of the sending credits granted in SSH? Could this function not be handled by the underlying transport protocol?

16.   Compare SSH with SSL/TLS (listing similarities as well as differences).

17.   Compare the methods for 'extending' the length of session keys of SSH and IKEv1 in IPsec (Chapter 12) with respect to the entropy of derived session keys.

Part III

Secure Wireless and Mobile Communications

14 Security Aspects of Mobile Communication

Part III of this book is devoted to aspects of security specific to mobile communication. This chapter first examines some general aspects and the subsequent chapters discuss specific system examples. Chapter 15 describes security mechanisms in wireless local area networks (WLANs) based on the IEEE 802.11 standard, focusing particularly on the security shortcomings of the standard and potential alternatives. Chapter 16 deals with the security of wireless wide-area networks, with specific emphasis on the security mechanisms of GSM, UMTS and LTE networks, which all use similar principles.

14.1 Threats in Mobile Communication Networks

Any comprehensive study of the engineering discipline of network security will raise the issue of the extent to which the circumstances and technical characteristics of mobile communication introduce new security aspects and solutions for mobile communication networks. The first thing to note is that mobile communication is naturally a target for all the threats that occur in fixed network communication, that is, masqueraded identities, authorisation violations, eavesdropping, data loss, modified and falsified data units, repudiation of communication processes and sabotage. Consequently, similar measures to those in fixed networks should be taken in mobile communication networks.

Do mobile communication networks introduce new security aspects?

Security in Fixed and Wireless Networks, Second Edition.
Guenter Schaefer and Michael Rossberg.
Copyright © 2014 by dpunkt.verlag GmbH, Heidelberg, Germany.
Title of the German original: Netzsicherheit   ISBN 978-3-86490-115-7
Translation Copyright © 2016 by John Wiley & Sons, Ltd., All rights reserved

Specific aspects   However, some aspects do not occur in the same form in fixed networks and are caused by the mobility of users and their devices, as well as by the existence of wireless communication links.

Increase in risk potential
- Some of the threats that already exist in fixed networks form a greater risk potential for mobile networks, e.g. wireless transmission links are easier to eavesdrop than are wired transmission media due to the ease of gaining direct physical access. Likewise, the lack of a physical connection makes it easy for unauthorised entities to use the services of a wireless network if adequate security mechanisms are not in place.

New difficulties arise in providing security services
- Some new difficulties arise in providing security services, e.g. the authenticity of a mobile device has to be verified again by the respective network access point each time it changes the network access point, i.e. performs a *handover*. Key management is also more complicated because the respective peer entities generally cannot be determined in advance as they depend on the movements of the user.

Global infrastructures
- In mobile networks with a global backbone, like the GSM networks, users need to be authenticated securely, even though users and providers of foreign networks are not fully trustworthy.

Movement profiles
- Ultimately a completely new threat arises: the current location of a device and, consequently, also of its user provides much more interesting information than in fixed networks and therefore should be protected against eavesdropping.

The first three aspects are handled in detail in the discussion covering specific system examples in the following chapters. In terms of the last aspect, protecting the identity of a user's current location, existing architectures show the shortcomings and rudiments of solutions that at best in addressing this requirement. This subject is still mostly being dealt with in research and adequate solutions are being sought for use in mobile communication architectures. The following section therefore treats this aspect in general terms independently of any concrete system examples.

14.2 Protecting Location Confidentiality

As the following chapters show, the mobile communication networks that operate today do not incorporate effective measures for adequately protecting information about the current location of mobile devices *(location privacy)*. This aspect is examined in detail in the following chapters, but the major shortcomings are as follows:

- In WLANs there is no protection of the identity of mobile *WLANs* devices against local eavesdropping on the radio interface since the globally unique MAC address of a network adapter is basically included in plaintext in each transmission frame. If it is not used for an authentication (which is insecure in any case), the MAC address could theoretically be changed at each login into a WLAN, although in practice such a measure is not used widely. If a device has several radio interfaces, for example Bluetooth (which is not described in detail in this book), or a if user has several devices with radio interfaces, the addresses of all interfaces would have to be changed simultaneously, otherwise the address information could easily be linked.

- In GSM, UMTS and LTE networks active attackers can query *GSM, UMTS and* the globally unique IDs (so-called IMSI) of mobile devices if *LTE* they are able to send forged signalling messages to the devices via the radio interface and receive such messages from them. Furthermore, the operator of a 'visited' access network can monitor the movements of devices currently registered with it and relate this information to their unique ID. In fact, the contractual network operator — thus the home network operator — of a mobile device can monitor all movements of the device since it receives signalling requests and accounting data records from 'visited' networks for all devices that are contractually bound to it. In contrast, the current location of a mobile device remains hidden from its communication partners because in practice this information is only accessible to network operators and, usually upon court order, to prosecution services.

- In the context of mobile usage of Internet services a further *Mobile Internet usage* aspect relating to confidentiality of the user location has to be considered: can movement profiles for the user be created each time the mobile computer communicates? In this respect access via WLAN generally offers good opportunities for the corresponding computer to draw inferences about the present location since in many cases the externally visible IP addresses in such networks can be mapped to a few geographic areas, such as large cities. For mobile networks, on the other hand, the IP addresses assigned to a mobile device generally only allow relatively patchy inferences about its current location, e.g. the network operator and therefore the country where it is being used.

Conflict in goals between reachability and untraceability   The basic problem with the design of mobile communication systems in terms of confidentiality of mobile device location is a conflict in goals. On one hand, each mobile device should be reachable for incoming communication requests; on the other hand, no (single) entity in the network should be able to track the current location of the device in the network.

In recent years various fundamental approaches have been proposed to address this problem [MR99]:

Broadcast   ■ *Broadcast messages:* All messages are sent to all potential receivers so that the location of the receivers does not have to be known. If the confidentiality of the messages being sent is also to be protected, then all messages are encrypted with a public key. In this case, all potential receivers have to decrypt all received messages to filter out the messages meant for them. It is obvious that this approach does not scale well for large networks or for high message loads.

Temporary pseudonyms   ■ *Temporary pseudonyms:* With this approach, all mobile devices do not use their actual identities but instead are contacted through pseudonyms that are regularly changed. An entity is necessary to map the current temporary pseudonym to the device to ensure that the mobile device can be reached. However, in principle this entity can track and record the history of the temporary pseudonyms of a specific device.

Mix networks   ■ *Mix networks:* Messages are routed over entities in the network, with each entity only able to discover one part of the message route. These are called *communication mixes*.

Details about these approaches will be examined in the following sections.

14.2.1   Broadcast Communication

Explicit vs implicit addresses   Broadcast communication also distinguishes between *explicit* and *implicit addresses* for mobile devices. With explicit addresses, for example IP addresses, each entity that 'sees' a particular message is able to determine the addressed entity. In contrast, what distinguishes implicit addresses is that they do not identify a specific device or a specific location and instead only name an entity without any further meaning attributed to the name. Implicit addresses are usually selected randomly from a large address space to minimise the probability of random collisions.

With implicit addresses a further distinction is made between *open (visible)* and *hidden (invisible)* implicit addresses. The difference between the two versions is that each entity that sees multiple occurrences of the same visible address can check the equality of the visible address, whereas only the addressed entity can check invisible implicit addresses for equality.

Open and hidden implicit addresses

Hidden implicit addresses are implemented by using public key operations. The addressed entity A selects random number r_A and makes it known, together with its public key $+K_A$, to potential communication partners. Whenever entity B wants to send a message to A later on, it selects a fresh random number r_B and prepares the following hidden implicit address for A: $ImplAddr_A = \{r_B, r_A\}_{+K_A}$. If this address is sent in a broadcast message, A is the only entity that can determine that it was addressed in it because it is the only entity that can correctly decrypt the address.

Implementation of hidden implicit addresses

14.2.2 Temporary Pseudonyms

The basic idea of using temporary pseudonyms to protect the confidentiality of the current location of a mobile device is that the current location of the device is no longer stored together with its identification ID_A but with a changing temporary pseudonym $P_A(t)$ instead. A trusted entity maps the identity ID_A to the current temporary pseudonym $P_A(t)$, but this entity does not have to know where the device is located at a particular time.

Basic idea of temporary pseudonyms

When an incoming message is forwarded to the current location of device A, two procedures are needed to execute this operation:

Message forwarding

1. First, the identity ID_A is mapped to the current temporary pseudonym $P_A(t)$ and the addressing information is adapted accordingly in the message.
2. During the second procedure, the message is forwarded to the current location of the device (e.g. by checking the database for the current locations of all temporary pseudonyms).

In the case that the two functionalities are performed by independent entities, there is an assurance that no individual entity can prepare movement profiles of mobile devices.

Provisioning by independent entities

What is important, of course, is that the entities that forward the message after mapping to the temporary pseudonym cannot discover the actual identity ID_A of the receiver from the message payload.

The communication mix explained below can be used to provide additional protection against attacks in which multiple attackers exchange information in order to discover information about the movement profile of a mobile device.

14.2.3 Communication Mixes

Basic idea of communication mixes

The concept of communication mixes was invented in 1981 by David Chaum for untraceable e-mail communication [Cha81]. A communication mix uses the following measures to hide the communication relationships between sender and receiver:

Function of communication mixes

- It buffers incoming messages that are encrypted with its public key.
- It changes the appearance of the messages by decrypting them with its private key.
- It changes the sequences of the messages and always forwards them in batches ('batch processing').

Provided that a sufficiently high traffic load is processed, it can be ensured that even an attacker who can read all the incoming and outgoing messages of a communication mix is still not able to relate incoming messages to outgoing ones, therefore no information can be deduced about the relationships between senders and receivers.

Cascading communication mixes

If, however, an attacker succeeds in compromising a communication mix, no further protection can be offered. This danger can be countered through an additional cascading of communication mixes. For example, in principle sender A can transmit message m to receiver B without being traced by including the two communication mixes $M1$ and $M2$:

$$A \rightarrow M_1: \ \{r_1, M2, \{r_2, B, \{r_3, m\}_{+K_B}\}_{+K_{M2}}\}_{+K_{M1}}$$

$$M_1 \rightarrow M_2: \ \{r_2, B, \{r_3, m\}_{+K_B}\}_{+K_{M2}}$$

$$M_2 \rightarrow \ B: \ \{r_3, m\}_{+K_B}$$

Required message volume

However, the security of this scheme depends on all communication mixes processing a sufficient volume of messages. The way to understand this concept is by imagining a network of communication mixes through which, in an extreme case, a single message is routed. Although the message is recoded in each mix, an attacker who can eavesdrop on all communication connections can follow the route of the message through all the cascaded mixes. Furthermore, all messages should be of the same length. The idea of cascaded networks has already been applied conceptually to mobile communication systems [MR99].

14.3 Summary

Mobile communication networks and wireless local area networks face the same threats as fixed networks. The existence of wireless transmission links contributes considerably towards increasing the threat potential. Device mobility also makes it difficult to implement the necessary security services, for example key management for authentication in the access network area.

Increase in existing risk potential

Furthermore, the mobility of devices and their users introduces a new threat, which is the generation of movement profiles for individual devices. A range of theoretical concepts were proposed in the past to counter this threat: message transfer per broadcast, the use of temporary pseudonyms and the use of cascaded communication mixes that hide the connection between incoming and outgoing messages. So far these ideas have only been applied to mobile communication networks at a conceptual level. The next chapters in Part III are devoted to specific system examples.

New threat posed by generation of movement profiles

14.4 Supplemental Reading

[MR99] MÜLLER, G.; RANNENBERG, K. (Eds): *Multilateral Security in Communications*. Addison-Wesley-Longman, 1999

[Sch03] SCHILLER, J.: *Mobile Communications*. Second edition, Pearson Education, 2003
This book is recommended to readers who are interested in a comprehensive introduction to the fundamental principles of the system examples discussed. The discussion in the following chapters only focuses on security aspects.

14.5 Questions

1. What are the new threats and difficulties in terms of communication and network security faced by mobile communication systems compared with fixed network communication?

2. Why should the authenticity of a terminal be verified again if a mobile terminal executes a handover from one base station to another?

3. How well does the method of hidden (invisible) implicit addresses scale as the number of transmitted messages increases?

4. Discuss the usage possibilities of cascaded communication mixes for interactive applications such as Internet telephony or video conferencing services.

15 Security in Wireless Local Area Networks

Over the last 15 years the IEEE 802.11 standard [IEE12] has established itself as the key standard in the area of WLANs. As the standard proposed by the *IEEE-802-LAN/MANS Standardisation Committee*, it defines medium access control (MAC) and the physical characteristics of WLANs. The term 'Wi-Fi', while actually referring to the Wi-Fi Alliance, an organisation to promote WLAN products, is usually synonymously used.

This chapter mainly examines the security properties of the standard. After the introduction of the standard at the end of the 1990s and up until a series of serious shortcomings in the standard were published, most vendors of standard-conformant wireless network components claimed that this original version of IEEE 802.11 'is as secure as a wired network'. These security flaws are explained in detail in the first part of the chapter because they represent an excellent textbook example of a failed attempt at 'securing' a communication protocol. The repair schemes that were developed by the 802 committee are particular interesting and presented in the second part of the chapter. The chapter concludes with a discussion of security threads in public WLANs, often called *hotspots*, and a short summary.

15.1 The IEEE 802.11 Standard for WLANs

The current 802.11 standard comprises a significant number of different options to transmit signals on the physical layer. Currently transmission speeds between 1 and 600 Mbit/s may be

Physical layer

achieved. To do this different modulation techniques, such as *Direct Sequence Spread Spectrum (DSSS)* and *Orthogonal Frequency Division Multiplexing (OFDM)*, may be used in frequency bands around 2.4 and 5 GHz.

Medium access control sublayer

The MAC sublayer supports operation in infrastructure mode under the control of a base station as well as *ad hoc* communication between independent systems. Furthermore, it is possible to configure point-to-point connections between base stations, so-called *wireless distribution systems (WDS)*. The latter will be of less importance in this chapter, however.

Figure 15.1

Components of an infrastructure network based on IEEE 802.11

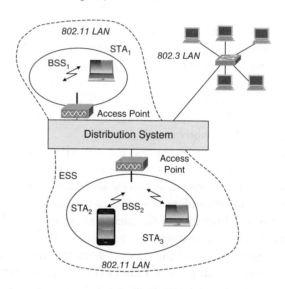

Figure 15.1 shows the components of an 802.11 WLAN when communication is in infrastructure mode:

Station
- A *station (STA)* is a system with access mechanisms to a wireless medium and radio contact to a base station.

Access point
- An *access point (AP)* is a base station containing special protocol functions for MAC that is usually incorporated into the wireless network as well as into a wired network, i.e. Ethernet.

Basic service set
- A *basic service set (BSS)* is a group of stations that can reach each other using the same radio frequency.

Distribution system
- A *distribution system* is an interconnection network that combines multiple basic service sets into one logical network, also called an *extended service set (ESS)*.

Figure 15.2 shows how communication is handled in *ad hoc* networks. In such networks, systems are only able to communicate

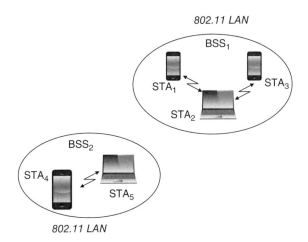

Figure 15.2

Ad hoc *communication based on IEEE 802.11*

with one another within a restricted radius, as no infrastructure for connecting separate basic service sets exists.

The IEEE 802.11 standard uses the following security functions. *Entity authentication* serves to verify the legitimate association with base stations. The *Wired Equivalent Privacy (WEP) Protocol*, *Temporal Key Integrity Protocol (TKIP)* and *CTR with CBC-MAC Protocol (CCMP)* provide the security services *confidentiality*, *data origin authentication* and *data integrity* as well as *access control* (in conjunction with layer management).

Security functions of IEEE 802.11

For these security functions the original 802.11 standard only defined the WEP protocol using the algorithms *RC4* (also see Section 3.4) and *cyclic redundancy check (CRC)*, which is actually an error-checking method and therefore does not meet the requirements outlined here. TKIP, which has been developed due to these insufficiencies, was designed to be backward compatible to a certain degree, that is, it was supposed to work with hardware that originally was only designed for WEP. Nevertheless, it should reach an 'adequate' level of security. In contrast CCMP has been developed to be a long-term substitute for WEP. It uses authenticated encryption based on the AES cipher.

The following three sections explain the standard's security functions in detail.

15.2 Entity Authentication

The IEEE 802.11 standard contains a rudimentary authentication function. Authentication is performed between stations (terminals) and base stations (access points), and optionally can also be performed between arbitrary terminals.

IEEE 802.11 provides four authentication schemes:

- *Open system authentication:* The standard itself [IEE12, Section 11.2.3.2.1] states: *'Open system authentication is a null authentication algorithm'*. This algorithm therefore cannot offer any security regarding the identity of a communication partner. Nevertheless, many networks use Open System Authentication, but allow only access to a virtual 'uncontrolled' 802.1X port. Only after a successful 802.1X authentication can arbitrary data be exchanged.

- *Shared key authentication:* With the help of WEP this scheme uses a shared key to 'prove' that a user belongs to the group that possesses this key. The standard does not regulate how the key is negotiated and distributed, but it is explicitly assumed that the shared key was delivered to the stations over a secure channel independently of IEEE 802.11. The scheme may only be used in conjunction with an encryption of user data with WEP.

- *Fast transition (FT) authentication:* To allow stations to quickly switch between base stations within the same BSS, IEEE 802.11r introduced a mechanism to perform fast authentications. With the help of a key hierarchy stations are enabled to prove that they have been associated to a different base station, and may use services without reconfirmation by another 802.1X procedure. As this mechanism is not yet widely deployed, we refrain from a description of further details in this book.

- *Simultaneous authentication of equals (SAE):* IEEE 802.11s specified the so-called *mesh networks*, which are groups of base stations that may forward packets over multiple intermediate systems. SAE was specified to allow for the password-based authentication between members of such a mesh.

15.2.1   Shared Key Authentication

When shared key authentication is performed, one of the two stations acts as *requestor* and the other one as *responder*. The requestor starts the authentication process by asking the responder to conduct the following challenge-response exchanges:

$$A \rightarrow B\colon \ (\textbf{\textit{Authentication}}, 1, ID_A)$$

$$B \rightarrow A\colon \ (\textbf{\textit{Authentication}}, 2, r_B)$$

$$A \rightarrow B\colon \ \{\textbf{\textit{Authentication}}, 3, r_B\}_{K_{A,B}}$$

$$B \rightarrow A\colon \ (\textbf{\textit{Authentication}}, 4, \textbf{\textit{Successful}})$$

This exchange authenticates the requestor to the responder. Two separate protocol runs — one per direction — would be needed for mutual authentication. This is, however, not provided by IEEE 802.11. The encryption in the third protocol step is performed according to the WEP protocol (details follow).

Unfortunately, the authentication exchange described offers no security for the identity of the communication partner because it contains a serious cryptographic error. This error is particularly serious because it is so easy to discover and should therefore have been noticed by the authors of the standard. *Insecure authentication protocol*

The protocol failure originates from a combination of two properties of the deployed mechanisms: a deficiency in the WEP protocol on how initialisation vectors needed to generate an RC4 keystream are selected and the general characteristic of all OFB ciphers of supplying the corresponding keystream of a ciphered message with its plaintext in XOR operations.

Looking at the second and third steps in the protocol specification above, one may easily notice that a potential attacker who is able to eavesdrop on a wireless medium knows the entire plaintext of the third authentication message ($\textbf{\textit{Authentication}}, 3, r_B$) and may therefore determine the keystream used to encrypt the message. *Determining keystreams*

As the WEP protocol also does not restrict the reuse of initialisation vectors and, consequently, the keystream (more details follow), an attacker is able to use this keystream for his or her own authentication procedure without knowing the key $K_{A,B}$. This makes the 802.11 authentication exchange totally useless. *Reuse of initialisation vectors*

15.2.2 Simultaneous Authentication of Equals

The SAE dialogue is significantly more complex. It secures the authentication dialogue through a method that is also known as *Dragonfly* and was published in [Har08]. Dragonfly is a PAKE method (see Section 7.7), which derives a session key with high entropy from a password with minimum entropy. It is based on asymmetric cryptography, optionally via $\mathbb{Z}_p$ or elliptic curves over $\mathbb{Z}_p$, and *Simultaneous Authentication of Equals* is said to offer properties that are similar to the Diffie–Hellman key exchange. In particular, the method ensures Perfect Forward Secrecy and – like other PAKE methods – is said to prevent efficient dictionary attacks, despite the fact that simple passwords are used. The dialogue itself does not differentiate between requester and responder. Instead, both parties mutually authenticate themselves in a simultaneous dialogue with identical message types. An SAE sequence normally has two phases, which follow the station identification based on probes:

$$A \rightarrow B: \quad Probe$$

$$B \rightarrow A: \quad Response$$

$$A \rightarrow B: \quad SAE\ Authentication - Commit$$

$$B \rightarrow A: \quad SAE\ Authentication - Commit$$

$$A \rightarrow B: \quad SAE\ Authentication - Confirm$$

$$B \rightarrow A: \quad SAE\ Authentication - Confirm$$

The order of commit and confirm messages is irrelevant. Commit messages consists of two values, which differ slightly depending on the group arithmetic used. The following section initially focuses on SAE with elliptic curves over $\mathbb{Z}_p$.

Construction of a point from a password
    Both A and B have to convert their password into a point on the curve. This is based on the following iterative calculation (similar to the method described in Section 4.8.4), which continues until an x coordinate of a valid point is found for the counter variable c:

$$seed = \mathrm{HMAC}(max(\mathrm{Addr}_A, \mathrm{Addr}_B) \parallel min(\mathrm{Addr}_A, \mathrm{Addr}_B),$$

$$password \parallel c)$$

$$x = \mathrm{KDF}(seed, \text{'SAE Hunting and Pecking'})$$

The variables Addr_A and Addr_B indicate the WLAN addresses of stations A and B. KDF stands for *key derivation function*, which generates a pseudo-random number of a certain length required for a particular situation by linking HMAC function calls. Once a valid x coordinate has been found, a point P can be determined. Since there are two possible y coordinates, the last bit of the *seed* variable is used to decide whether the larger or smaller y value is used. The calculation is deterministic, which means all parties using the same password calculate the same point P.

Generating commit messages
    To generate a commit message, each station first generates two random numbers between 0 and the number of points on curve n.

A then calculates the scalar cs_A and the point ce_A, which are both transferred in the commit message:

$$cs_A = (r_{1,A} + r_{2,A}) \bmod n$$

$$ce_A = -(r_{2,A}P)$$

Station B does likewise, so that the two parties can then calculate a shared secret K. Specifically, B calculates K using a function F, which extracts the x coordinate of a point:

Calculation of a shared secret

$$K = F(r_{1,B}(cs_A P + ce_A))$$
$$= F(r_{1,B}(((r_{1,A} + r_{2,A}) \bmod n)P - r_{2,A}P))$$
$$= F(r_{1,B}(r_{1,A}P + r_{2,A}P - r_{2,A}P))$$
$$= F(r_{1,B}r_{1,A}P)$$

A is assigned the same key due to commutativity of the point addition, provided the passwords were identical and no attack has occurred.

Using the secret K, both sides prepare confirm messages to verify that they possess the correct password. To this end they create two keys based on a KDF: the *key confirmation key (KCK)* and the *pairwise master key (PMK)*, which makes the subsequent communication secure. The KCK is used to authenticate the content of the exchanged commit messages, based on an HMAC construction. Data authentication at A and B takes place in a different sequence to ensure that different values are transferred in the two confirm messages, in order to prevent attackers replaying the confirm message of the counterpart.

Generating confirm messages

The process for the SAE variant based on number field Z_p is similar. First, a natural number $P < p$ is determined from the password, based on a deterministic process. The subsequent process is similar to the ECC-based dialogue, whereby scalar point multiplications are replaced by exponentiations, and point additions by multiplications. A therefore calculates the two values cs_A and ce_A as follows:

SAE with number field Z_p

$$cs_A = (r_{1,A} + r_{2,A}) \bmod n$$

$$ce_A = P^{-r_{2,A}}$$

B calculates the secret K, which is shared between A and B, using the following formula:

$$K = (P^{cs_A} \times ce_A)^{r_{1,B}} \pmod{p}$$
$$= (P^{(r_{1,A}+r_{2,A}) \bmod n} \times P^{-r_{2,A}})^{r_{1,B}} \pmod{p}$$

$$= (P^{r_{1,A}+r_{2,A}-r_{2,A}})^{r_{1,B}} \pmod{p}$$

$$= P^{r_{1,A}r_{1,B}} \pmod{p}$$

Thanks to the commutativity characteristic, A can calculate K in the same way.

Security of SAE   An interesting aspect of the SAE protocol is that keys with relatively high entropy can be derived securely from comparatively short passwords. Usually, the use of passwords with adequately high entropy is very complex for applications with demanding cryptographic requirements, that is, more than 256 bits, since the passwords have to be very long. SAE is supposed to enable the use of shorter passwords as it is only feasible to actively try out passwords, whereas offline calculation, which would be more efficient, is said to be impossible. It is very important to check messages received in the commit step, for example to verify that the transferred point does in fact lie on the curve. Attacks are possible if these checks are not carried out correctly [CH13]. Some of these checks are also stipulated in the 802.11 standard, although the current SAE standard has a weak spot that enables offline attacks.

Offline attack on   In order to try out possible passwords offline, an attacker E
$\mathbb{Z}_p$-based SAE   first has to initiate a $\mathbb{Z}_p$-based SAE handshake, during which the specified protocol is not fully complied with. Passwords can then be tried out relatively efficiently based on the values received from the counterpart. The complexity of the required calculations essentially depends only on the entropy of the password. The attacker E selects a value $ce_E = 1$. The value for cs_E can also be 1. For other values the attack has to be modified accordingly. Counterpart A complies with the protocol and sends $cs_A = (r_{1,A} + r_{2,A}) \bmod p - 1$ and $ce_A = P^{-r_{2,A}}$. A now calculates K as follows:

$$K = (P^{cs_E} \times ce_E)^{r_{1,A}} \equiv (P^1 \times 1)^{r_{1,A}} \equiv P^{r_{1,A}} \pmod{p}.$$

Flawed group   Based on the KCK derived from K, A now calculates an authentic-
size verification   ation value via the exchanged messages and sends it to E, along with cs_A and ce_A. The problem of SAE is that it does not need to be verified that the value ce_E is not 1 and that a sufficiently large subgroup is generated in in $\mathbb{Z}_p$. This enables the attacker to efficiently check whether an element in a set of passwords was used by calculating the corresponding number $\hat{P}$ for each password. The attacker can then calculate $\hat{P}^{cs_A} ce_A \equiv \hat{P}^{r_{1,A}} \pmod{p}$ for all $\hat{P}$ and
Preventing the attack   check for a valid KCK. The attack could quite easily have been prevented in the standard by making $ce_E > 1$ a condition. Also, like

the standard correctly requires, it needs to be verified that the generated subgroup of ce_A has the expected size n through calculation of $ce_A^n \bmod p \equiv 1$.

15.3 Wired Equivalent Privacy

The WEP protocol defines a way to encrypt and integrity-protect protocol data units in the MAC sublayer. Within the original 802.11 standard WEP has been the only security mechanism to ensure data confidentiality and authentication. The following sections explain the operations of WEP and its shortcomings.

15.3.1 Operation and Linearity of CRC

The WEP protocol provides integrity protection based on a CRC. This method uses an error check code that was actually developed as a statistical means of discovering random errors.

Mathematical basis of CRC

The mathematical basis of CRC is the division by a defined, irreducible polynomial $G(X)$ using $GF(2^n)$ arithmetic. Therefore, a message M is interpreted as polynomial $M(x)$ and polynomial arithmetic modulo 2 is used so that the addition and subtraction correspond to a bitwise XOR operation. The details of this mathematical structure, called Galois field, were presented in Section 4.8.3.

Operation of CRC

Now consider the division of $M(x) \times 2^n$ by the generator polynomial $G(x)$:

$$\text{As} \quad \frac{M(x) \times 2^n}{G(x)} = Q(x) + \frac{R(x)}{G(x)} \quad \text{is also} \quad \frac{M(x) \times 2^n + R(x)}{G(x)} = Q(x)$$

with $R(x)$ being the remainder of $M(x) \times 2^n$ when divided by $G(x)$.

The remainder $R(x)$ after division by $G(x)$ is simply attached as a error checksum to message $M(x)$. The result $Q(x)$ of the division is not of further interest as the only thing considered in the verification of a received message $M(x) \times 2^n + R(x)$ is whether the remainder 0 results from division by $G(x)$.

Let us now consider the two messages M_1 and M_2 with the CRC values R_1 and R_2:

$$\text{As} \quad \frac{M_1(x) \times 2^n + R_1(x)}{G(x)} \quad \text{as well as} \quad \frac{M_2(x) \times 2^n + R_2(x)}{G(x)} \quad \text{are both divi-}$$

sible with remainder 0, $\dfrac{M_1(x) \times 2^n + R_1(x) + M_2(x) \times 2^n + R_2(x)}{G(x)}$

also divides with remainder 0.

CRC is a linear function

What this proves is that CRC is a linear function, that is, $CRC(M_1) + CRC(M_2) = CRC(M_1 + M_2)$. This property allows controlled modifications to messages and the corresponding CRC values and, therefore, makes CRC inappropriate for cryptographic purposes.

15.3.2 Operation of the WEP Protocol

Encryption using the RC4 algorithm

The WEP protocol uses the RC4 algorithm as a pseudo-random bit generator to derive a keystream that is solely dependent on the key and an initialisation vector. A new 24-bit long initialisation vector IV is selected for each protected message M and concatenated with a shared key K_{BSS} that is normally known to all the stations of a basic service set. The resulting value serves as the input for the RC4 algorithm, which uses it to generate an arbitrarily long keystream (also see Section 3.4).

The CRC method is also used to compute an *integrity check value* (ICV) that is appended to message M. The resulting message ($M \parallel ICV$) is XORed ('$\oplus$') with the keystream $RC4(IV \parallel K_{BSS})$ and the initialisation vector in plaintext is placed in front of the resulting ciphertext. Figure 15.3 shows this process as a block diagram.

Figure 15.3

Block diagram of WEP encryption

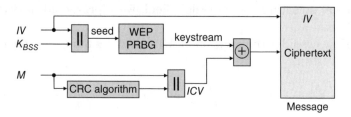

Self-synchronisation

As the initialisation vector is sent in plaintext with each message, each receiver that knows the key K_{BSS} can reproduce the appropriate plaintext. This process assures the property of *self-synchronisation* that is particularly important in wireless networks.

The decryption and integrity-verification process at the receiver essentially consists of the reverse processing sequence and is illustrated in Figure 15.4.

Security goals of WEP protocol

The WEP protocol was designed with the intention of assuring the following security goals:

- *Confidentiality:* Only those stations in possession of key K_{BSS} can read WEP-protected messages.

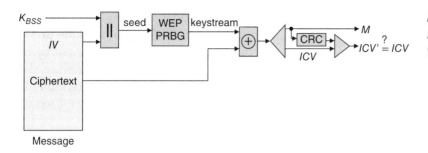

Figure 15.4
Block diagram of WEP decryption

- *Data origin authentication and integrity:* The receiver can detect malicious modifications to WEP-protected messages.
- *Access control in conjunction with layer management:* If preset as such in layer management, receivers only accept WEP-protected messages, which means that only those stations that know key K_{BSS} can send to these receivers.

The following section explains how WEP unfortunately does not achieve any of these goals.

15.3.3 Flaws in the WEP Protocol

The WEP protocol has security flaws in the following five areas:

1. Lack of key management.
2. Inadequate protection against messages being read by unauthorised parties.
3. Insecure data origin authentication and integrity protection.
4. Insufficient access control.
5. Key computation based on eavesdropped messages.

IEEE 802.11 originally did not define any specifications for *key management* and merely recommended the shared use of group keys. As already discussed in Chapter 8, shared group keys are considered to be inadequate from a security perspective because their distribution is difficult, if not impossible, to control, and any member of a group can pretend to be another member of the group. Furthermore, due to the lack of key management, in practice group keys are seldom, if ever, changed and in many cases the 802.11 security functions were even switched off.

Key management

Another point is that many WLAN products of the first generation only support 40-bit long keys, and today this provides little protection against attackers who try out all possible keys to find the right one. Although some products do support 104-bit long keys,

Brute-force attacks on 40-bit long keys

they are not interoperable with the 40-bit versions. Consequently, when a WLAN was introduced a decision had to be made at the outset about which devices are to be procured if they are not be replaced in the future. The products with the longer keys were also often marketed with the misleading claim '128-bit encryption'. In reality, the key length is only 104 bits because 24 bits are used for the initialisation vector.

Messages read by unauthorised parties

Even if keys are properly distributed and sufficiently long in length, the WEP protocol does not *adequately protect messages from being read by unauthorised parties*. One reason for this is the reuse of the keystream [BGW01], which is a direct outcome of the short initialisation vectors and lack of key management. With WEP encryption each message triggers a resynchronisation of the state of the pseudo-random bit generator by generating and adding a new 24-bit long initialisation vector IV in front of the group key K_{BSS}, and executing the initialisation procedures of the RC4 algorithm.

Reuse of initial-isation vectors

Consider two messages M_1 and M_2 that were randomly encrypted using the same initialisation vector IV_1:

$$C_1 = M_1 \oplus RC4(IV_1, K_{BSS})$$
$$C_2 = M_2 \oplus RC4(IV_1, K_{BSS})$$

Therefore the following also holds:

$$C_1 \oplus C_2 = M_1 \oplus RC4(IV_1, K_{BSS}) \oplus M_2 \oplus RC4(IV_1, K_{BSS})$$
$$= M_1 \oplus M_2$$

Known-plaintext attack

If, for example, an attacker knows the values M_1 and C_1, he or she can compute plaintext M_2 from ciphertext C_2. The WEP protocol is therefore susceptible to known-plaintext attacks if initialisation vectors happen to be reused with the same key K_{BSS}.

This situation occurs relatively frequently in practice because many implementations choose the initialisation values poorly, for example hardware is often initialised starting again with '0'. However, even if the initialisation values are selected in an ideal manner, the short 24-bit length remains a major problem. A busy WLAN base station, for example, exhausts its available IV space within half a day if transmission is only at 11 Mbit/s.

Vulnerable data origin authentication

Because of to the linearity of the CRC and the encryption function, an attacker can easily undermine WEP integrity-protection and data origin authentication. Let us consider a message sent from sender A to receiver B that is intercepted by attacker E:

$$A \rightarrow B: \quad (IV, C) \text{ with } C = RC4(IV, K_{BSS}) \oplus (M, CRC(M))$$

Even without knowing key K_{BSS}, attacker E can construct a cipher-text C' that is decrypted to a plaintext $(M', CRC(M'))$ with a valid CRC value. The attacker chooses an arbitrary message Δ and uses it to compute C' as follows:

$$
\begin{aligned}
C' &= C \oplus (\Delta, CRC(\Delta)) \\
&= RC4(IV, K_{BSS}) \oplus (M, CRC(M)) \oplus (\Delta, CRC(\Delta)) \\
&= RC4(IV, K_{BSS}) \oplus (M \oplus \Delta, CRC(M) \oplus CRC(\Delta)) \\
&= RC4(IV, K_{BSS}) \oplus (M \oplus \Delta, CRC(M \oplus \Delta)) \\
&= RC4(IV, K_{BSS}) \oplus (M', CRC(M'))
\end{aligned}
$$

Because the attacker does not know the original message M, he or she also does not know the resulting message M'. However, what is known is that a '1' in a specific position in message Δ produces a 'flipped' bit in the corresponding position in M'. The attacker can therefore make controlled changes that will not be detected by the receiver.

Controlled modifications

The access control function using WEP can also easily be bypassed by attackers. All they need is a sufficiently long plaintext–ciphertext pair (M, C) (the IV value can be deduced from the eavesdropped message since it appears in front of the ciphertext). There are two main reasons why the access control function fails: the integrity verification function CRC is not parameterised with a key and there is a lack of requirements for the reuse of initialisation values for RC4.

Inadequate access control

Because attacker E knows message M and ciphertext $C = RC4(IV, K_{BSS}) \oplus (M, CRC(M))$, she can compute the keystream $RC4(IV, K_{BSS})$ that matches the IV from it. If she wants to send her own message M' in the future, she uses the same initialisation value IV for transmission and computes the ciphertext of her message with the previously calculated and possibly shortened keystream:

$$
E \to B: (IV, C') \text{ with } C' = RC4(IV, K_{BSS}) \oplus (M', CRC(M'))
$$

As the reuse of arbitrary initialisation values is possible without triggering any alarms at the receiver, the attacker succeeds in creating valid messages that are accepted by any receiver in the WLAN.

This attack technique can be applied to make unauthorised use of network resources, for example an attacker can send IP packets that are routed to the public Internet from the underlying network infrastructure of the WLAN. Even if the attacker cannot read the

Unauthorised use of network resources

response packet, as he does not know K_{BSS}, he or she will have already gained free access to the Internet and some 'useful applications'. These include the execution of *denial-of-service attacks*, where attackers are often not interested in the responses from receivers of their packets.

Recovery of
K_{BSS} using a
related key attack

As already sketched in Section 3.4, an attack on WEP was published in August 2001 [FMS01] that is based on related keys. It enables the key K_{BSS} to be retrieved after a sufficient volume of packets has been eavesdropped. This attack and several further developed techniques can retrieve a shared key seconds after the eavesdropping of around 0.25 to 2 million packets [TWP07]. The attack is based on the following properties of RC4 and the usage of RC4 in the WEP protocol:

1. RC4 is vulnerable to the deduction of individual key bits if a large number of messages are encrypted using a keystream computed from a variable initialisation value and a fixed key, and if the respective initialisation vector as well as the first two plaintext octets of each message are known.
2. With WEP, the initialisation value is transmitted in plaintext with each message.
3. The first two octets of each message can easily be guessed in WLANs because the first octets of the transmitted LLC frames are easily to predict.

R. Rivest published the following comment on this attack technique [Riv01]: *'Those who are using the RC4-based WEP or WEP2 protocols to provide confidentiality of their 802.11 communications should consider these protocols to be broken [...]'*

Conclusion: WEP
is totally insecure!

The overall conclusion is that the WEP protocol is totally insecure and users are urgently advised to use alternative security measures.

15.4   Robust Secure Networks

After the publication of the security problems relating to WEP it quickly became clear that the standard had to be revised. In response, the IEEE *802.11 Task Group I* originally developed the 802.11i amendment to the WLAN standard, which in the meantime is included in the main document. Devices that are compatible with 802.11i are generally marketed as *Wi-Fi Protected Access (WPA)* or WPA2.

Secure WLANs that comply with this successor standard are referred to in the standard as *Robust Secure Networks (RSN)*. Instead of using static group keys, the traffic is generally secured based on pairwise keys between user and base station, which are managed through automatic key management and changed regularly. Another option is to install group keys for broad- and multicast packets and to use *Station-To-Station-Link keys* (STSL) for radio contact between base stations. All these keys are either derived from a *Pairwise Master Key (PMK)* or centrally generated and securely transmitted to the devices. Two different modes can be used for negotiating the key:

RSN feature key management

- In *personal mode* all base stations and terminal devices continue to have a shared secret. A 256-bit long PMK is explicitly specified by entering 64 hexadecimal characters. Since this is too complex in most cases, alternatively a password with a minimum of 8 characters can be used. In this case the PMK is calculated as follows:

$$PMK = PBKDF2(\text{password, SSID, } 4096, 256),$$

  where PBKDF2 is the *Password-Based Key Derivation Function 2* from RFC 2898 [Kal00]. For calculating the PMK this involves 4096 times calculation of two HMAC SHA1 calls, and in addition the PMK is linked to the name of the WLAN, the so-called *SSID*. Both measures are intended to make dictionary attacks against the used password very complex. In contrast to the SAE handshake described above, passive attacks are still possible.
- *Enterprise Mode* can be used in environments with many users. In this case users have to register with an authentication server through 802.1X via the base stations and negotiate a shared *Master Session Key (MSK)* via EAP. The upper 256 bits of the MSK are then interpreted as PMK by the base station and the STA.

In any case, open system authentication takes place before the cryptographic authentication, which means users initially associate themselves with a base station without a password. However, the 'port', which only exists virtually, still operates in restricted mode ('uncontrolled') and only allows processing of EAP or EAPOL packets for mutual authentication and key installation.

RSNs are based on open system authentication and use EAP for enabling a controlled 'port'

The basic procedure for installing key material via EAPOL based on a four-way handshake is as follows:

1. $BS \rightarrow STA : (r_{BS})$

2. $STA \rightarrow BS \;\; : (r_{STA}, MAC_{KCK})$

3. $BS \rightarrow STA : (r_{BS}, MAC_{KCK}, \{GTK\}_{KEK})$

4. $STA \rightarrow BS \;\; : (r_{STA}, MAC_{KCK})$

Temporary keys are derived from the PMK   The base station initiates the key negotiation (as well as periodic renegotiations) and transmits a nonce r_{BS}. The user station responds by creating its own nonce r_{STA} and calculates a *Pairwise Transient Key (PTK)* via the PMK, the two nonces and the WLAN addresses of the parties:

$$PTK = \text{PRF}(PMK, \text{'Pairwise key expansion'},$$
$$min(Addr_{BS}, Addr_{STA}) \;||$$
$$max(Addr_{BS}, Addr_{STA}) \;||$$
$$min(r_{BS}, r_{STA}) \;||\; max(r_{BS}, r_{STA}))$$

The pseudo-random function (PRF) used for this purpose essentially links HMAC calls via the input data and a counter until the required key length is reached. The calculated PTK is then regarded as concatenation of three different pairwise keys:

- a 128-bit *Key Confirmation Key (KCK)*,
- a 128-bit *Key Encryption Key (KEK)* and
- a *Temporal Key (TK)* of variable length (minimum 128 bits).

Authentication of EAPOL messages   From the second EAPOL message, the KCK is used to calculate a message authentication value and convinces the respective counterpart that the same PMK is known and no attack is taking place. In addition to the HMAC method, the AES-CMAC mode can also be *Secure key transfer*   used for calculating the message authentication value. In the third message the base station transfers the so-called *Group Temporal Keys (GTK)* for making broad- and multicast packets secure. These are protected through the KEK, whereby either RC4 is used or AES in so-called *Key Wrap Mode* [SH02].

Which encryption and authentication algorithms are used in EAPOL depends on which method is used for making the actual data traffic secure. In any case, the key material used, that is, the TK and the GTK, is available after a successful EAPOL exchange.

15.4.1 Temporal Key Integrity Protocol

The aim of the development of the Temporal Key Integrity Protocol (TKIP) was to provide a quick solution to the security problems that emerged with WEP. The TKIP was designed for straightforward retrofitting on base stations and terminal devices through a software update. It is marketed as *Wi-Fi Protected Access (WPA)*. The main challenge was the fact that, for reasons of speed, the actual RC4 encryption of WEP was usually realised in hardware and therefore not easily exchangeable. Also, it was not possible to simply realise an alternative cipher in software, since the processors used in access points were often running at only 25 or 33 MHz and were therefore inadequate for the additional processing power required for software-based calculation of AES.

TKIP is a compromise between security and compatibility

The idea was to continue to use the existing hardware-based RC4 encryption, if possible, and to implement the following extensions, alongside the key management described above:

WEP extension

- The transmitted messages are no longer just protected through the ICV, but also through a *Message Integrity Code (MIC)*, which is the term chosen by the IEEE for the message authentication code, in order to avoid confusion with Medium Access Control (MAC). The *Michael* calculation method developed specially for this purpose is intended to be adequately fast while offering a degree of protection against forged messages.
- Since Michael cannot provide the same level of security as a full message authentication method, packets with faulty values are not only discarded, but rate limitation is implemented as an additional measure.
- The initialisation vectors are not determined randomly, but serve as sequence numbers. In this way repetition is avoided, while at the same time protection against replays is afforded.
- In addition to regular key changes, so-called *key mixing* is used, which means the RC4 keys are modified with each packet.

The procedure for encryption with TKIP is illustrated in Figure 15.5. Together with the sequence number and the destination address of the packet, the current *traffic key* (TK) is transformed to an initialisation vector and a packet key using two key mixing functions. The background to the splitting of the key mixing functions is that only the higher-order bytes of the sequence number are used in the phase 1 function, and the

TKIP transmission sequence

Figure 15.5

TKIP protection

sequence

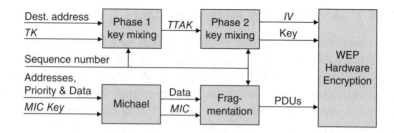

resulting TTAK value (*TKIP-mixed Transmit Address and Key*) can be held in the buffer. The MIC can be prepared in parallel with the preparation of the WEP key. In addition to the SDU, Michael also authenticates the source and destination addresses as well as the packet priority. Since the resulting packets may be too large, the actual securing through WEP may take place after a fragmentation, if required.

Figure 15.6

Schematic diagram

of the Michael

rounds function

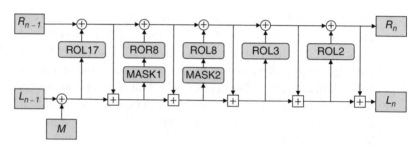

Of particular interest from a cryptographic perspective is the Michael function, which was specifically developed for TKIP. The aim was to make it very fast while still offering adequate security. Figure 15.6 shows a schematic diagram of the algorithm, which operates on two 32-bit wide registers, L and R. These registers are initialised with the *MIC key* and output as MIC at the end. The mapped rounds function is always called with 32-bit input data M, which are initially linked with L via an XOR operation. The contents of L and R are then alternately linked with each other. R is always linked via an XOR operation with a value that results from the content of L. Cyclic shift operations by 17, 8, 3 or 2 positions are used as derivation functions. The result in R is then added to L (with respect to $\mathbb{Z}_{2^{32}}$). The resulting MIC values have a length of 64 bits, although the security of the method is much lower. During the design phase the effective length was estimated at around 20 bits [Fer02].

In view of the fact that the security margin of the MIC is therefore very low, WLAN devices have to implement additional security measures. To this end 802.11 specifies that packets with invalid MIC should not only be discarded, but the standard also stipulates that such an error should only occur once per minute at most, otherwise the attacked device switches off for one minute and discards all temporary keys. The complete receiving process is shown schematically in Figure 15.7.

Countermeasures for forged MICs

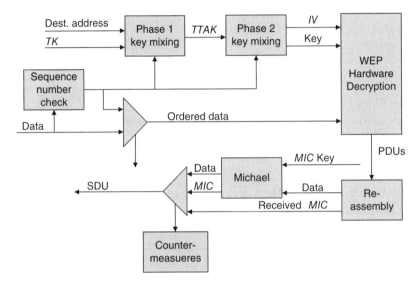

Figure 15.7
TKIP receiving routine

The security of the resulting TKIP protocol has been the subject of considerable speculation, although, notwithstanding the 'adverse' circumstances, it has met its security goals well over the last 10 years. Although certain attacks have been documented [TB09, OM09], they are far more complex than the attacks on WEP described above. In particular, they preclude restoration of the key, so that they have simply become less attractive for attackers. Nevertheless, the IEEE advises against the use of TKIP and instead recommends the CCMP method described in the following section.

15.4.2   CTR with CBC-MAC Protocol

The *CTR with CBC-MAC Protocol (CCMP)* was developed as a long-term substitute for the WEP method. It uses AES as encryption algorithm and is marketed under the name *Wi-Fi Protected*

CCM is marketed as WPA2.

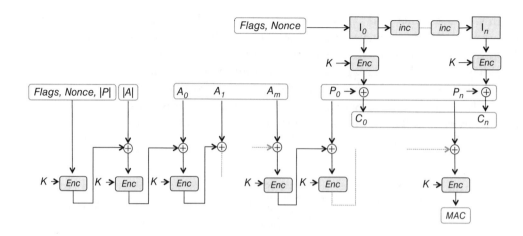

Figure 15.8
Simplified CCM encryption procedure

Access 2 (WPA2). Originally the standard envisaged an alternative block cipher mode referred to as *Offset Codebook Mode (OCB)*, although this has now been completely removed from the standard due to patent issues.

Principle of CCM mode

In CCMP the AES cipher is operated in CCM mode, which was developed specifically for this protocol. As it serves for authenticated encryption no other cryptographic algorithms are required. Figure 15.8 shows a simplified version of such a process at the sender, as proposed in RFC 3610 [WHF03]. The basic idea of CCM is the use of CBC-MAC for message authentication and counter mode for encryption. In order to prevent CBC-MAC attacks of the type described in Section 5.3.2, the lengths of the data to be authenticated and the data additionally to be encrypted are included in the first two authenticated blocks. In addition, a nonce and flags are used for encoding the MAC code length, for example. During encryption these latter values are also used in the upper bits of the counter for the counter mode. Similar to the original counter mode, the security of this methods depends on avoiding the repeated use of nonces. In addition, the CCM calculations are very complex, compared with other modes for authenticated encryption (approximately twice as many block cipher calls as for GCM). Another factor is that the authentication part is difficult to parallelise.

The CCMP frame format

In 802.11, AES-CCM is used to generate the frame shown in Figure 15.9. A CCMP header with 8 bytes is added directly after the header of the media access protocol. It mainly contains the 6 bytes of the sequence number, referred to as the *packet number (PN)*. It also contains the index of the current key. The 'ExtIV' bit must be set. It indicates that the header used for the encryption consists of 8 bytes (i.e. not 4 bytes, as for WEP). The actual data is followed by

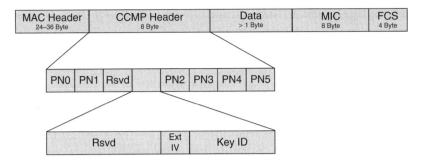

Figure 15.9

Structure of a 802.11 frame for CCMP

the MIC. The packet also contains a CRC checksum referred to as *Frame Check Sequence (FCS)*.

In addition to the user data, much of the header, including the addresses used, is also authenticated. Only the user data is encrypted. In both cases a concatenation of flags, sender address and sequence number is used as nonce, so that its uniqueness can be guaranteed. However, this fixed calculation rule has led to some criticism since it enables the first value of the counter for the first packet to be determined in advance. In principle, this could be used to prepare a dictionary attack [JMI06]. However, such an attack can be regarded as unrealistic since the key should have a high entropy, thanks to the automatic key management, and in view of the fact that the precalculations have to be performed separately for each source address.

15.5   Security in Public WLANs

Because the 802.11 technology is in widespread use and offers high speed compared with mobile networks, public WLANs are operated at many public locations. Some of these *hotspots* are free to use and some are charged for, with payments made by credit card, for example. The main problem with hotspots is that, for reasons of user-friendliness, operators are unable to use the security measures provided in 802.11. These include obligatory use of passwords and corresponding connection setups. In contrast, hotspot operators want to be able to reach users who are unable to configure WLAN connections or do not want to keep personal access information.

Public hotspots cannot use the security systems of 802.11

A common approach taken by hotspot operators is to emulate the main functionality of 802.1X: the hotspot WLAN is operated without a security mechanism and all users can connect via Open System Authentication without further configuration. Packets

Hotspots emulate 802.1X and use web pages for authentication

originating from an unknown STA are not forwarded. This is similar to the approach used for the uncontrolled port of IEEE 802.1X. In contrast to 802.1X, no access to an authentication server via EAPOL is required. Instead, packet transfer to a DNS server is permitted and all HTTP queries are diverted to an internal page. Since users invariably visit this web page, they are notified that they are using a hotspot and can activate the access by entering payment data. The activation takes place for the MAC address of the client and typically remains active for several hours, or until client inactivity leads to automatic deactivation.

Access control and protection of login data via TLS

In terms of the security aspects of this approach, only the requirements of the hotspot operators are considered. The access control ensures that the Internet usage is paid for. In many cases the page asking for user or payment data redirects to a TLS-protected web page in order to avoid eavesdropping via the mobile network. The subsequent Internet traffic of the client is not affected by this protection at the application level. The problem is that the encryption at the data link layer cannot be activated retrospectively.

Threats to user data

Users of such hotspots are therefore subject to a number of threats. The sent packets can be monitored, modified, suppressed or freely generated by an attacker. In contrast to a wired Internet connection, this is particularly easy via the air interface. In a public WLAN it is therefore advisable to only use services that provide cryptographic protection at the application level. In particular, the background services of the client should also be configured accordingly, so that no e-mail passwords are transferred in plain text, for example. A better approach is to use an IPsec VPN, in which all IP packets are first encrypted and sent to a trusted point in the network before being forward in unencrypted form to the actual destination.

Attackers can impersonate users in order to hide illegal activities

However, one particular problem remains: since there is no cryptographic link between user and hotspot, an attacker can impersonate the user. In the simplest case, an attacker merely has to wait until the user leaves the hotspot area and then use the user's MAC address as their own. The hotspot continues to regard the user as authenticated. This results in two potential problems:

- with time-based payment methods the user has to pay for the Internet time used by the attacker;
- if the attacker uses the access for illegal activities, there may be consequences for the user.

A manual logout option is no guarantee that such an attack is not possible, since the attacker may try to suppress the corresponding packets. Alternatively, the attacker may use a man-in-the-middle attack to use the access at the same time as the user. The lack of security architecture at public hotspots means that even security-conscious users are unable to adequately protect themselves. It is therefore advisable to use public WLANs that require an authentication with caution.

15.6 Summary

Because of the increased threat potential to radio transmission links, special security measures are required for WLANs. In the past, the IEEE 802.11 standard, which is the standard most frequently used with such networks, did not provide adequate protection due to the following security flaws:

Security flaws in WEP

- The lack of key management makes it difficult to use the provided security functions. The result in practice is that keys are seldom changed, if ever, and security functions are often never activated.
- Entity authentication based on Shared Key Authentication and encryption are based on the use of shared group keys, the distribution of which is difficult to control. They also do not allow the protection of individual data streams on a device-specific basis. The authentication exchange is also totally useless as an attacker only needs to eavesdrop on a single authentication procedure to obtain the required keystream to replay such an exchange.
- Many products only provided for 40-bit long keys, thus essentially offering no protection against brute-force attacks.
- The reuse of initialisation values for RC4 encryption makes it easy for known-plaintext attacks.
- The linearity of the integrity checking function CRC allows controlled and undetected changes to be made to messages.
- The access control function can be bypassed an arbitrary number of times using a sufficiently long known plaintext–ciphertext pair.
- A weakness in the key schedulling for the RC4 algorithm enables the key to be computed using eavesdropped messages.

As a rule, IEEE-802.11 WLANs should be protected with methods that are referred to as *Robust Secure Networks (RSN)* in the standard. Protection based on the *Temporal Key Integrity Protocol (TKIP)* as an interim solution should generally be avoided, since

Security measures in Robust Secure Networks

nowadays virtually all WLAN components support the application of *CTR with CBC-MAC Protocol (CCMP)*. In addition to the currently more trusted AES cipher, the latter also has the advantage that safe message authentication values can be calculated. Plus, denial-of-service attacks based on replaying of packets with invalid Michael checksums are no longer possible. A key characteristic of RSN is dynamic key management, which makes it much more difficult for an attacker to compromise a network.

Protection of static passwords
    In terms of static passwords, 802.11 includes special security measures. On the one hand, dictionary attacks are slowed down significantly through the *Password-Based Key Derivation Function 2 (PBKDF2)* in RSN. On the other hand, the SAE handshake currently does not allow offline dictionary attacks, that is, only trial and error 'on the device' is possible, at least if ECC is used. Particularly for the latter, a careful implementation is required, that is, all special cases should be considered in the protocol handling.

User protection offered by hotspots is inadequate
    Public WLAN access points, so-called *hotspots*, pose an increased risk of attacks, mainly because it is not possible to use the security mechanisms offered by 802.11 since authentication with user name and password is too inflexible. There is no provision for a direct login, for example via payment data. As a result, no protection based on the data link layer is implemented.

15.7 Supplemental Reading

[BGW01]   BORISOV, N.; GOLDBERG, I.; WAGNER, D.: Intercepting Mobile Communications: The Insecurity of 802.11. In: *Proceedings of ACM MobiCom*, 2001. – http://www.cs.berkeley.edu/~daw/papers/wep-mob01.ps

[FMS01]   FLUHRER, S.; MANTIN, I.; SHAMIR, A.: Weaknesses in the Key Scheduling Algorithm of RC4. In: *Selected Areas in Cryptography, Lecture Notes in Computer Science* Bd. 2259, Springer-Verlag, 2001, pp. 1–24

[IEE12]   IEEE INSTITUTE OF ELECTRICAL AND ELECTRONICS ENGINEERS: *Wireless LAN Medium Access Control (MAC) and Physical Layer (PHY) Specifications*. The Institute of Electrical and Electronics Engineers (IEEE), IEEE Std 802.11-2012, 2012

[Riv01]   RIVEST, R.: *RSA Security Response to Weaknesses in Key Scheduling Algorithm of RC4*. 2001. –

http://www.rsa.com/rsalabs/technotes
/wep.html

[TWP07]   TEWS, E.; WEINMANN, R. P.; PYSHKIN, A.: Breaking
          104 bit WEP in less than 60 seconds. In: *Information
          Security Applications* (2007), pp. 188–202

15.8   Questions

1. Can you track down the errors in the shared key authentica-
    tion protocol by conducting a formal analysis using GNY logic?
2. Why, with WEP, is the initialisation vector (IV) sent with each
    MAC-PDU instead of being implicitly extracted from the last
    MAC-PDU of the same sender to the same receiver?
3. Why is the combination of the integrity protection function
    (CRC), which is not parameterised with a key, and the cipher-
    ing algorithm (RC4), which is operated in OFB mode, not ad-
    equate for executing effective access control?
4. Explain, why an implementation of SAE needs to check if ce_A
    is a valid curve point, e.g. not $\mathcal{O}$.
5. Give alternative options for implementing access control in
    wireless LANs.
6. Can the use of IEEE 802.1X compensate for the security flaws
    in WEP?
7. How can an attacker obtain possession of a plaintext–
    ciphertext pair if he or she knows that certain public visible
    IP addresses are used in the WLAN being attacked?
8. Which property leads to non-linearity of the Michael al-
    gorithm?
9. How high is the probability that Michael recognises an error,
    when only bit errors are assumed and they are not caused by
    attackers?
10. Is it possible that nonces are reused in CCMP? Does this lead
    to a security issue?
11. How would you evaluate WLANs based on IEEE 802.11 in
    terms of location privacy?

16 Security in Mobile Wide-Area Networks

The main difference between wireless local area networks and mobile wide-area networks are the functions for true mobility support that produce a range of qualitatively new aspects. This chapter explains the most important architectures currently being used in this area, *GSM*, *UMTS* and *LTE*, with special emphasis on their security functions.

16.1 Global System for Mobile Communication

The acronym GSM stands for the current leading standard for mobile telecommunications in the world. Standardised since the early 1980s by the *European Telecommunications Standards Institute (ETSI)*, it was originally specified as the acronym for the *Groupe Spéciale Mobile* in 1982 (at a time when the French language still played an important role in European telecommunications). GSM was renamed *Global System for Mobile Communication* due to its success on the international stage in the 1990s.

GSM is a pan-European standard that was introduced in three phases in 1991, 1994 and 1996 by the European telecommunication administrations simultaneously. It enables the use across Europe of the services offered, referred to as *roaming*. Now GSM-based networks are being operated in more than 200 countries in Africa, America, Asia, Australia and Europe. GSM allows 'true' mobile communication with no regional restrictions and supports the service types speech and data communication. GSM services can be

Pan-European standard

Now being used in more than 200 countries

used worldwide through a uniform address — the international telephone number.

The description of GSM in this chapter mainly focuses on its security functions *confidentiality on the radio interface* and *access control and user authentication* (actually in the sense of device authentication). The GSM standards comprise the following security services [TG93, TS94]:

Security services of GSM

- *Subscriber identity confidentiality:* Potential attackers should not be able to determine which user happens to be using given radio resources (data and signalling channels) simply by listening to the radio interface. Consequently, devices normally use a temporary pseudonym when they register. This provides certain protection against tracing a user's location through listening to the radio interface.

- *Subscriber identity authentication:* Prior to using the services of a network, each device must prove its identity in a simple authentication exchange.

- *Signalling information element confidentiality:* The confidentiality of signalling information exchanged between mobile devices and the access network is protected through the encryption of the signalling messages on the radio interface.

- *User data confidentiality:* Like signalling information, user data is encrypted on the radio interface.

The definitions of the security services listed above indicate that GSM measures mainly take into account passive attacks on the radio interface.

Architecture of a GSM network

Before the operation of the security services can be explained, a brief overview is needed of the GSM network architecture. A detailed explanation of all components and their functions would take too much space in this chapter and readers are therefore referred to the relevant literature, for example [Sch03], for in-depth coverage.

Figure 16.1 presents an overview of the components of a GSM network. The acronyms of GSM terminology used in the illustration and other acronyms relevant to this chapter can be found in Table 16.1.

The signalling information and user data exchanged between mobile devices are encrypted in the area called *radio subsystem (RSS)*. To be more precise, encryption and decryption is performed by the mobile devices *(mobile station, MS)* and the base stations *(base transceiver station, BTS)*. The main tasks of the latter components include coding and decoding information

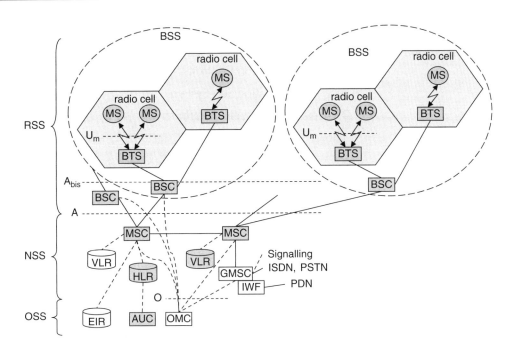

Figure 16.1
Architecture of a GSM network

transmitted on the radio interface as well as the appropriate modulation/demodulation and transmission.

A *base station controller (BSC)* normally controls multiple BTS. The BSC is also responsible for routing and forwarding calls between the *mobile switching center (MSC)* and the base stations, as well as allocating the resources used on the radio interface.

The two databases *home location register (HLR)* and *visited location register (VLR)* play a central role in the forwarding of incoming calls. The HLR contains information about the users administered by the network operator. This includes a user's identification *international mobile subscriber identification (IMSI)*, his/her mobile telephone number *mobile subscriber international ISDN number (MSISDN)* and other data on subscribed services. The HLR also stores the VLR number where a user is currently registered so that incoming calls can be routed to the appropriate network as well as the authentication vectors required for user authentication. These will be explained in more detail later.

The VLR is connected to one or multiple MSCs and registers the users that are currently located within a specific geographical zone, called the *location area (LA)*. The VLR stores information about registered users similar to the HLR, but with the addition of a *temporary mobile subscriber identity (TMSI)*, which is a temporary pseudonym to protect the identity of a user on the radio interface.

Acronym	Meaning
AuC	Authentication Center
BSC	Base Station Controller
BSS	Base Station Sub-System
BTS	Base Transceiver Station
EIR	Equipment Identity Register
GMSC	Gateway Mobile Switching Center
HLR	Home Location Register
IMSI	International Mobile Subscriber Identity
ISDN	Integrated Services Digital Network
IWF	Interworking Function
LAI	Location Area Identifier
MS	Mobile Station (e.g. mobile telephone)
MSC	Mobile Switching Center
MSISDN	Mobile Subscriber International ISDN Number
NSS	Network Subsystem
OMC	Operation and Management Center
OSS	Operation Subsystem
PDN	Packet Data Network
PSTN	Public Switched Telecommunication Network
RSS	Radio Subsystem
TMSI	Temporary Mobile Subscriber Identity
VLR	Visitor Location Register

Figure 16.2 presents an overview of the principle involved in the authentication of mobile devices in GSM networks. After a mobile device inputs its IMSI to signal to an access network that it wants to use the services of the network, the MSC obtains the information required for the authentication from the HLR responsible for the device. The HLR does not generate this information itself; the *authentication center (AuC)* that periodically or upon request sends the HLR a supply of authentication vectors for the device is responsible for this task.

Authentication vector　　In GSM networks such an authentication vector consists of a triple $(r_i, SRES_{*i}, K_{BSC,MS:i})$. The r_i denotes a random number

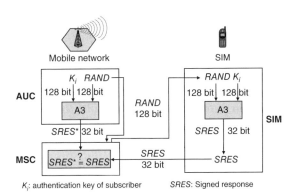

Figure 16.2
Authentication in
GSM networks

selected from the AuC and $SRES*_i$ is a *signed response*, that is, $SRES*_i := A3(r_i, K_{MS})$, that the AuC computes by applying an algorithm called $A3$ to the random number r_i and the user-specific authentication key K_{MS}. After a mobile device has been successfully authenticated, the session key $K_{BSC,MS:i}$ is used to encrypt the signalling messages and the user data on the radio interface. This key is computed by the AuC from the random number r_i and the authentication key K_{MS} through use of the algorithm $A8$, that is, $K_{BSC,MS:i} = A8(r_i, K_{MS})$.

Cryptographic
algorithms

The two algorithms A3 and A8 implement non-invertible functions, that is, cryptographic hash functions. They are, however, not further specified, but they may be arbitrarily chosen by system vendors and network operators. In fact A3 and A8 are only algorithm identifiers, and a range of different algorithms exist that are designed to meet all the properties specified in the GSM standards. The situation of the encryption algorithm A5 is similar: it has been specified from the beginning, but it was not publicly accessible. It could only be obtained from system vendors, network operators or similar organisations by signing a confidentiality declaration from the GSM standardisation committee.

Storage of authentica-
tion key in subscriber
identity module (SIM)

The authentication key K_{MS} is stored additionally in the manipulation-safe *subscriber identity module (SIM)* of the mobile device. For authentication verification the access network (represented by the MSC and the BSC or the BTS) sends the mobile device the random number r_i of an authentication vector. The mobile device asks its SIM to use the random number and the stored key to compute the signed response that belongs to the random number and also to compute the session key: $SRES_i := A3(r_i, K_{MS})$; $K_{BSC,MS:i} := A8(r_i, K_{MS})$.

The mobile device then responds to the access network with $SRES_i$. This $SRES_i$ denotes the response computed by the mobile device and only matches $SRES*_i$ if the correct key exists in the SIM. On receipt of this message the access network verifies whether or not the response from the mobile device matches the expected response $SRES*_i$ (e.g. by the MSC as the GSM standard does not define which of the entities BTS, BSC, MSC or VLR performs this comparison). If the two values $SRES*_i$ and $SRES_i$ match, the authentication verification was successful.

After this verification the encryption is activated on the radio interface and the access network notifies the mobile device of the *location area identifier* (LAI_{VLR1}) for the current region and the new temporary pseudonym $TMSI_{MS:n}$. Thus, the authentication exchange can be summarised as follows:

1. $MS \rightarrow MSC : (IMSI_{MS})$
2. $MSC \rightarrow HLR : (IMSI_{MS})$
3. $HLR \rightarrow MSC : (IMSI_{MS}, r_{[i,j]}, SRES*_{[i,j]}, K_{BSC,MS:[i,j]})$
4. $MSC \rightarrow MS : (r_i)$
5. $MS \rightarrow MSC : (SRES_i)$
6. $MSC \rightarrow MS : (\{LAI_{VLR1}, TMSI_{MS:n}\}_{K_{BSC,MS:i}})$

The HLR normally does not transfer one but a series of authentication vectors (5 is considered a normal number and is shown as the notation '$[i, j]$' above) to the MSC to avoid the need for contact between the access network and the HLR for every authentication procedure. After successful authentication of the mobile device, all other protocol data units transmitted over the radio interface are encrypted and thus protected from potential eavesdropping attacks.

Handover within
a location area
The procedure described so far is used when a mobile device 'initially' registers in a specific access network, for example after the device is switched on. If the device has already registered once in the access network, the IMSI is not required for a new authentication. The authentication is performed according to the following scheme:

1. $MS \rightarrow MSC : (LAI_{VLR1}, TMSI_{MS:n})$
2. $MSC \rightarrow MS : (r_i)$
3. $MS \rightarrow MSC : (SRES_i)$
4. $MSC \rightarrow MS : (\{LAI_{VLR1}, TMSI_{MS:n+1}\}_{K_{BSC,MS:i}})$

After each successful authentication procedure a new temporary pseudonym is allocated to the mobile device. Therefore, an attacker who merely listens to the radio interface cannot find out which devices are active in the respective radio cell nor even allocate consecutive authentication requests (and thus service uses) to individual devices.

The location area identifier sent with each re-authentication request allows devices coming from other access network areas to be identified. If the old and the new region happen to fall under the control of the same network operator, a handover can be executed with a change of the VLR. This takes place according to the following scheme:

Handover between two location areas

1. $MS \rightarrow VLR2 : (LAI_{VLR1}, TMSI_{MS:n})$
2. $VLR2 \rightarrow VLR1 : (LAI_{VLR1}, TMSI_{MS:n})$
3. $VLR1 \rightarrow VLR2 : (TMSI_{MS:n}, IMSI_{MS}, K_{BSC,MS:n}, r_{[i,j]},$
$SRES*_{[i,j]}, K_{BSC,MS:[i,j]})$
4. $VLR2 \rightarrow MS : (r_i)$
5. $MS \rightarrow VLR2 : (SRES_i)$
6. $VLR2 \rightarrow MS : (\{LAI_{VLR2}, TMSI_{MS:n+1}\}_{K_{BSC,MS:i}})$

On receipt of the first message, the *VLR2* (or the BSC or MSC processing the message) determines that the LAI contained in the message falls under the responsibility of a different VLR. It then requests information about the device identified by $TMSI_{MS:n}$ from the appropriate VLR. The queried *VLR1* responds with the IMSI of the mobile device and the remaining authentication vectors. Afterwards the authentication exchange between *VLR2* and the mobile device can continue as explained above.

If the *VLR1* has no more unused authentication vectors for the mobile device, in other words, an allocation of a TMSI to the IMSI of the device is no longer possible, for example if a device has been switched off for a long time, *VLR2* explicitly asks the mobile device for its IMSI in order to execute the already described initial authentication procedure. The mobile device cannot encrypt the IMSI, which means that a potential attacker has the possibility of listening to the device's IMSI. An attacker can also exploit this weakness for an explicit retrieval of the IMSIs of mobile devices. Because mobile devices do not have the possibility of verifying the entities of an access network, they are unable to detect or prevent this kind of attack. This weakness may be used by government agencies, for example, to obtain positioning information for mobile devices within a network cell. Specialised devices, so-called IMSI catchers, are, however, already affordable for private enthusiasts.

Recourse to an initial authentication exchange

Active attack to reveal an IMSI

To summarise GSM security mechanisms, GSM authentication is based on a challenge-response procedure that only establishes

Achieved security properties

the identity of mobile devices to the access network. Mobile devices themselves have no possibility of verifying the identity of the entities of an access network. The periodic allocation of temporary identities at least enables the identity of these mobile devices to be protected from passive attackers on the radio interface. However, active attackers form a serious threat as they may bypass this protection by explicitly sending requests to mobile devices.

A5/4 can protect the confidentiality of conversations, but has to be deactivated

The current A5/4 encryption algorithm is a KASUMI cipher with 128-bit keys. After successful authentication of a mobile device, encryption of the data units based on this algorithm offers protection against attackers eavesdropping on the radio interface. As already explained in Section 3.5, the predecessor algorithms A5/1 and A5/2, which had been kept secret, no longer offer adequate protection. Waiving the authentication of GSM networks leads to another significant problem with confidentiality: with relatively little effort, attackers can operate BSCs themselves and simply deactivate user encryption to eavesdrop on conversations. Very few mobile phones alert users when a conversation is not encrypted. It is therefore quite likely that such an attack will remain undetected.

However, within the GSM network and also at the gateway into other network areas (e.g. ISDN) data units are always exchanged unencrypted and no further security measures are taken (e.g. no authentication of signalling entities). The underlying model for the security mechanisms of GSM basically implies that all network operators can trust one another and that the signalling network is secure from attackers. In conclusion, GSM networks are designed to be only as secure as conventional (non-secured) telecommunication networks.

16.2   Universal Mobile Telecommunications System

The acronym *UMTS* stands for *Universal Mobile Telecommunications System* and denotes a third-generation mobile communication system that was mostly developed in Europe. As such, it is part of the worldwide standardisation under the umbrella *International Mobile Telecommunications (IMT)*, which is coordinated by the *International Telecommunication Union (ITU)*. UMTS is thus a technology for IMT-2000 that is standardised within the framework of the ITU.

The telecommunications industry as well as European politicians had good reason for great hopes in UMTS, which continues the success of European GSM technology into the age of the mobile information society.

For reasons of space this chapter only looks at the security concepts of UMTS and readers are referred to [Les03], for example, for a more detailed introduction to the technology. This section predominantly discusses the most current version of the UMTS specification, the so-called *Release '11*. However, the differences to other releases are often only marginal. As in the presentation of GSM, a particular emphasis is put on the important aspects of device authentication and UMTS key negotiation in the following.

UMTS provides the following security services [3GP12b]: *Security services*

■ *User identity confidentiality* to pursue the following specific security goals:
  ● User identity confidentiality: The permanent identity of a user (his or her IMSI) cannot be eavesdropped on the radio interface.
  ● User location confidentiality: The current presence of a user in a particular geographic region cannot be discovered through eavesdropping on the radio interface.
  ● User untraceability: Potential attackers cannot eavesdrop on the radio interface to determine whether multiple services are being provided simultaneously to a particular user.

User identity confidentiality

■ *Entity authentication* will be available in two versions:
  ● User authentication should prove the identity of a user (or his or her device) to the access network currently being used.
  ● Network authentication should enable a user to verify that he or she is connected to the access network authorised by the respective home network to offer services (this incorporates the freshness of this authorisation).

Entity authentication

■ *Confidentiality* with the following specific security goals or properties:
  ● Algorithm negotiation (cipher algorithm agreement) on a manipulation-safe basis between a mobile device and the access network it aims to connect to.
  ● Key negotiation (cipher key agreement) for the session keys used by a mobile device and the access network.
  ● Confidentiality of user data to ensure that user data cannot be eavesdropped on the radio interface.

Confidentiality of user data

- Confidentiality of signalling information to ensure that it cannot be eavesdropped on the radio interface.

Data integrity   ■ *Data integrity*, which pursues the following goals:

- algorithm negotiation (integrity algorithm agreement);
- key negotiation (integrity key agreement);
- data origin authentication and data integrity of signalling information so that each entity receiving signalling information (mobile device or access network entity) can verify prior to a message being processed whether it actually originates from the entity indicated as the sender and was not manipulated on the radio interface during transmission.

Like GSM, UMTS *also mainly considers* *the security needs of* *the network operator* What is clear from the enumeration above is that the security mechanisms of UMTS mainly focus on eavesdropping attacks. Aside from protecting authentication exchanges (details follow) from active attackers on the air interface, it only offers integrity protection for signalling data. This means that the system mainly considers those security aspects that are fundamentally important to network operators. However, unlike GSM, mobile devices can at least gain assurance of the 'trustworthiness' of the current access network during an authentication exchange.

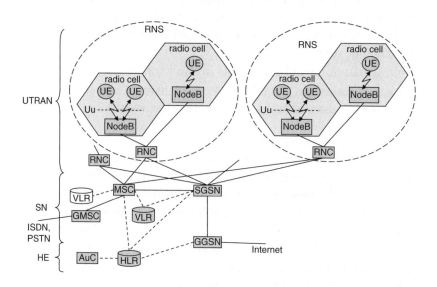

Figure 16.3 *Overview of the* *architecture of a* *UMTS network* In comparison to GSM, some of the architectural notations change to take the additional functionalities of the components into account. As depicted in Figure 16.3, however, many of the devices have different names, but still provide similar services.

For example, Base Transceiver Stations are called NodeB in the context of UMTS. The biggest difference of UMTS, in comparison to the original GSM, is the adoption of packet distributing network components from GPRS, that is, packets may be transported from the users via SGSN and GGSN directly to the Internet. The newly introduced acronyms that are commonly used in conjunction with the authentication and key negotiation functions of UMTS are listed in Table 16.2.

Acronym	Meaning
AK	Anonymity Key
AMF	Authentication Management Field
AUTN	Authentication Token
AV	Authentication Vector
CK	Confidentiality Key
GGSN	Gateway GPRS Support Node
GPRS	General Packet Radio Service
HE	Home Environment
IK	Integrity Key
RAND	Random Challenge
RNC	Radio Network Controller
SGSN	Serving GPRS Support Node
SN	Serving Network
SQN	Sequence Number
UE	User Equipment (analogous to MS in GSM)
USIM	Universal Subscriber Identity Module
UTRAN	UMTS Terrestrial Radio Access Network
XRES	Expected Response

Table 16.2
Common abbreviations used with UMTS authentication

Figure 16.4 shows a UMTS authentication exchange. As with GSM, three principal actors can be identified: (1) the mobile device, called User Equipment (UE) in UMTS, (2) the network (serving network, SN) currently being used by the mobile device and represented by one of the two entities VLR or SGSN (= serving GPRS support node, which provides mobility functions for data services in some parts similar to those provided by a VLR for voice service) and (3) the

UMTS authentication

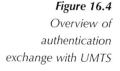

Figure 16.4
Overview of authentication exchange with UMTS

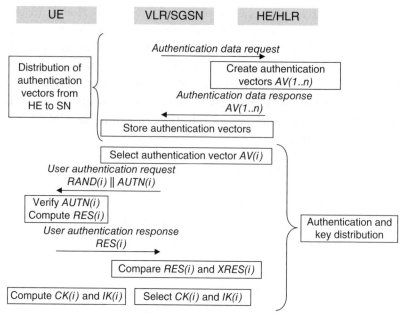

home network of the mobile device, represented either by the HLR or the Home Environment (HE).

Phases of UMTS authentication

UMTS authentication is divided into the two phases *transport of authentication vectors* and the actual *authentication and key negotiation*. As is the case with GSM, the first phase is triggered when a mobile device wants to use the services in a particular network and the access network establishes that it has to request authentication vectors (AV) for the device. Once these vectors are received and stored, actual authentication and key negotiation can be performed for a specific connection. This procedure, called *authentication and key agreement (AKA)* in UMTS terminology, follows a pattern similar to GSM but with some specific differences.

UMTS authentication exchange

The responsible entity of the access network sends a random number $RAND(i)$ (according to UMTS terminology) and an authentication token $AUTN(i)$ to the mobile device. The mobile device computes a response $RES(i)$ from the random number and the key K stored in its Universal Subscriber Identity Module (USIM) and using $AUTN(i)$ verifies whether the access network entity was authorised by its home network (see below). If this verification is successful, the mobile device sends the response $RES(i)$ to the access network. The mobile device then has its USIM compute the two session keys $CK(i)$ (confidentiality key) and $IK(i)$ (integrity key) from the random number and key K, which is stored in the USIM.

The access network compares the response received with the expected response $XRES(i)$. If the two values do not agree, the access network discontinues the communication. On the other hand, if the values are equal the access network extracts the two session keys $CK(i)$ and $IK(i)$ from the authentication vector $AV(i)$ and activates integrity protection and encryption on the radio interface.

One important innovation offered by UMTS, but not available with GSM, is the possibility given to a mobile device to verify whether its communication partner in an authentication exchange actually has the information generated by its home network, and whether this information is current. Section 7.2 explained that there are basically two possibilities for verifying the freshness of messages during an exchange: random numbers and time stamps. Note that time stamps do not necessarily have to contain absolute times and instead can also be sequence numbers. With UMTS the mobile device checks the freshness of the network's answer message during an authentication exchange using sequence numbers, whereas the freshness check by the network is performed on the basis of random numbers.

Authenticating access network to the mobile device

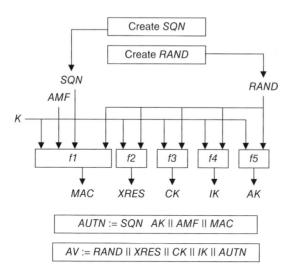

Figure 16.5
Generating authentication vectors with UMTS

Figure 16.5 presents an overview of how authentication vectors are generated. The HE/HLR or AuC (authentication center) first generates a new random number $RAND$ and increments the sequence number SQN that is synchronised between the mobile device and the HE/AuC. These two numbers are used with five standardised functions $f1_K, \ldots, f5_K$ that are always parameterised with the key K of the mobile device to compute the following values:

Generating authentication vectors

- message authentication code
  $MAC := f1_K(SQN\|RAND\|AMF)$
- expected response $XRES := f2_K(RAND)$
- confidentiality key $CK := f3_K(RAND)$
- integrity key $IK := f4_K(RAND)$
- anonymity key $AK := f5_K(RAND)$

The authentication token is constructed from these values according to the following rule:

$$AUTN := SQN \oplus AK\|AMF\|MAC$$

Encryption of sequence numbers   The task of the anonymity key is to protect sequence numbers from potential eavesdropping attacks on the radio interface during transmission. Otherwise the sequence numbers could be used to conclude that consecutive authentication procedures are being executed by one and the same mobile device. AMF denotes the *authentication and key management field*. The UMTS standards do not include any compulsory specifications regarding its tasks and its use is on an operator-specific basis.

The authentication vector comprises the following components:

$$AV := RAND\|XRES\|CK\|IK\|AUTN$$

Figure 16.6
*Client-side processing
with authentication*

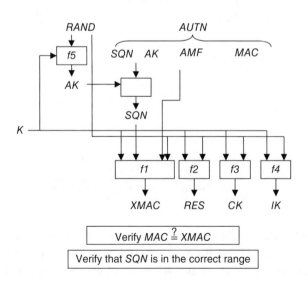

Figure 16.6 shows the processing performed in an authentication exchange in a mobile device. On receipt of the random number *RAND* and the authentication token *AUTN*, the device computes

the anonymity key $AK := f5_K(RAND)$. It then uses this key to extract the sequence number from the authentication token.

At this point the sequence number can already be used to perform a freshness test of the received message, whereas the authenticity check first requires a verification of the MAC. The device computes the expected MAC $XMAC := f1_K(SQN||RAND||AMF)$ and compares it to the received value MAC. If both values agree and the sequence number is sufficiently recent (the UMTS standard recommends that the sequence number should originate from a range of 32 numbers), the device assumes that the current access network has received the tuple $(RAND, AUTN)$ from its home network and therefore has authorisation from it to provide services. If the sequence number does not fall within the correct range but the MAC is correct, the mobile device sends the message *synchronisation failure* with an appropriate parameter for resynchronising the sequence numbers.

Protection against replay attacks

After this verification the mobile device computes its response $RES := f2_K(RAND)$, the confidentiality key $CK := f3_K(RAND)$ and the integrity key $IK := f4_K(RAND)$, and sends the value RES to the access network.

As mentioned earlier, the peer entity in the access network then verifies whether the received value RES agrees with the expected value $XRES$. If this verification is successful, integrity protection and encryption are activated on the radio interface and a new temporary identity $(TMSI_n, LAI_n)$ is forwarded to the mobile device.

16.3 Long-Term Evolution

The 3rd Generation Partnership Project (3GPP) adopted *Long-Term Evolution (LTE)* as successor standard for UMTS. This standard is based on GSM/UMTS standards, so that the structure of LTE networks is similar to those already described. In addition to higher data rates, there is a further significant change: for the first time network operators only use packet-switched components. To do so the Internet protocol is used, mainly for cost reasons.

Figure 16.7 illustrates the configuration of LTE networks, indicating highly simplified structures, for example NodeBs and RNCs were consolidated to eNodeBs. Avoiding circuit-switched components also simplifies the core network, now referred to as *Evolved Packet Core (EPC)*. A transition to the conventional telephone network is realised via the *IP Multimedia Subsystem (IMS)*. HLR and AuC were also consolidated into a single component,

Structure of LTE networks

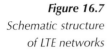

Figure 16.7

Schematic structure
of LTE networks

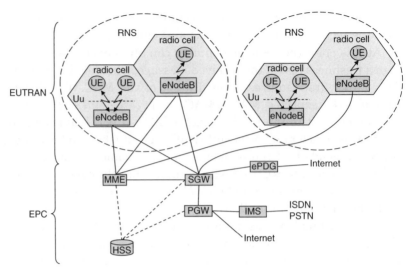

referred to as *Home Subscriber Server (HSS)*. The VLR tasks are largely handled by the *Mobility Management Entity (MME)*. The *Evolved Packet Data Gateway (ePDG)*, which offers a transition to the public Internet, presents a security challenge. In contrast to the *Packet Data Network Gateway (PGW)* or GGSN, users should be able to access LTE network functions from the public network via ePDGs in order to enable a handover between LTE and WLAN, for example.

LTE and UMTS
have the same
security goals

In terms of the security goals there are no significant changes with LTE. The relevant document [3GP12c] largely refers to the corresponding sections in the UMTS standard. In particular, data transferred by the user is not authenticated. This kind of protection is only obligatory for signalling messages.

Although the LTE key exchange differs from the UMTS variant, the conceptual differences in the actual AKA are relatively minor, as shown in Figure 16.8. When a UE links to the network it sends an attach request, which usually contains its *Globally Unique Temporary ID (GUTI)*. Essentially this is the equivalent of the TMSI. The IMSI is only used on first contact. For emergency calls without a SIM card the *International Mobile Station Equipment Identity (IMEI)* can be transmitted, which unambiguously identifies the UE. The eNodeB then establishes a connection with the relevant MME, which identifies the user based on the GUTI. If the resolution fails, the user IMSI can be requested explicitly via an identity request. On initial contact the MME has to obtain authentication vectors, just like for GSM and LTE. This task is handled by the HSS,

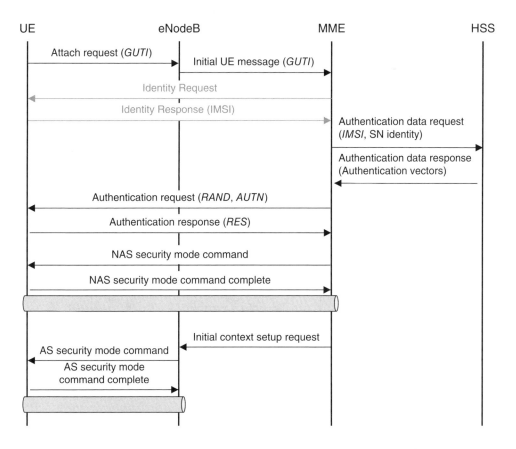

Figure 16.8
Security-related messages on UE login into an LTE network

based on the user ID and the identification number of the serving network (SN), to which the MME belongs. If the HSS trusts the MME making the request, it transfers the authentication vector, which the MME can use to identify itself with the UE and to derive shared keys. As in UMTS, this is followed by the actual authentication dialogue between the MME and the UE, based on a challenge-response technique. If this dialogue is successful, the MME uses a *NAS Security Mode Command* to activate the encryption and data authentication between the UE and the MME. In order to secure the actual air interface between the UE and the eNodeB, the MME shares key material for the UE with the eNodeB. The eNodeB can then activate this material via an *AS Security Mode Command*. User data can now be encrypted between the UE and the eNodeB. Signalling messages are encrypted and their integrity is protected with two separate keys.

Additional keys are required, compared with UMTS, due to the fact that the protection goes beyond solely encrypting the radio channel. In contrast to UMTS, these keys are derived via a key

The LTE key hierarchy

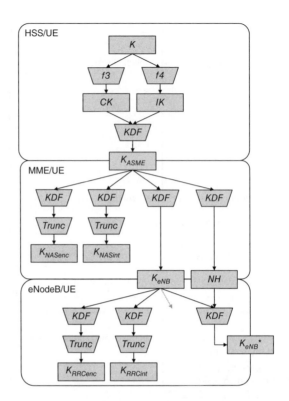

hierarchy from the key shared by AuC and UE K. AuC and UE calculate the keys of the second hierarchy level, that is, the 128-bit CK and IK, based on the functions f3 and f4 known from UMTS, as shown in Figure 16.9. HSS and UE then calculate the 256-bit master key K_{ASME} for the LTE functions from a concatenation of CK and IK. A Key Derivation Function (KDF) [3GP12f], which takes into account the identity of the serving network, is used for this purpose. Currently the HMAC construction of SHA-256 is the only standardised KDF. In a further hierarchy level MME and UE then use the KDF to derive four further keys from the K_{ASME}. These are the 128-bit long K_{NASenc} and K_{NASint}, which are used for encryption and authentication of messages between MME and UE, the 256-bit K_{eNB}, which the MME transfers to the current eNodeB in order to determine keys for securing the air interface K_{RRCenc} and K_{RRCint}, and a value referred to as NH, which the MME calculates from K_{ASME} via the KDF and which is also transferred to the eNodeB. It is used for calculating a new key $K_{\mathrm{eNB}}*$ for handover processes between eNodeBs. One source for further details regarding the calculation of the key hierarchy is [3GP12c].

For the actual encryption and authentication LTE makes provision for the use of the AES for the first time, in addition to the SNOW-3G stream cipher, which was originally developed for UMTS. Counter mode (EEA2) is used for encryption, while the CMAC method (EIA2) is used for authentication. An additional stream cipher described in the LTE standard is ZUC, which is used in China where foreign ciphers are not permitted as they are against regulations there.

Ciphers in LTE

Little has changed since GSM with regard to protecting provider networks. Although the use of IPsec is now stipulated for coupling between networks of different providers [3GP12a, 3GP12g], providers still have to trust one another with issues such as billing, data protection and user security.

Protecting provider networks

In addition to the native air interface, LTE also makes provision for communication between the core network and the UE via other network technologies [3GP12e]. These include WIMAX networks operated by the same provider, but also untrusted connections, for example to the public Internet. EAP-based authentication between the core network and the UE is always required in such cases [3GP12d]. Two subtypes were specified as RFCs in order to meet the requirements for LTE networks: EAP-AKA [AH06] and EAP-AKA' [ALE09]. For trusted access networks they take on the role of authenticator. The authentication server is part of the LTE core network, since it has to communicate directly with the HSS to check the identity of the UE. For access via a network area classified as untrusted by the provider, LTE stipulates data protection between UE and core network with IPsec tunnels. These terminate at the ePDG, which also takes on the role of EAP authenticator.

Linking non-3GPP networks

16.4 Summary

The international standards GSM, UMTS and LTE are of central importance in the area of radio-based wide-area networks. Their security properties share a range of basic similarities.

All architectures are based on the assumption that network operators within wired network areas can trust each other and no attacks will be made on transmitted data. The architectures therefore deploy security measures that mainly apply to user and device authentication and transmission security over the radio interface. Only LTE and later versions of UMTS provide a specification to secure the interfaces between providers with the help of IPsec.

With GSM, UMTS and LTE the different network operators have to trust one another

Device authentication   Device authentication for the three architectures is also based on similar principles. A trustworthy entity, the AuC or HSS, generates authentication vectors that contain challenge-response pairs as well as session keys. These vectors are provided to a visited access network upon request, although the transmission of these vectors is usually not secured in the signalling network. The signalling network selects one of these vectors and sends the contained random number to the mobile device being authenticated. The device reacts with a response, which it computes from the random number and the key stored in its security module. The session key(s) are generated in the same way. In LTE it is required to compute the deployed key hierarchy to derive these keys.

Use of temporary   The architectures deploy temporary pseudonyms to conceal the
pseudonyms   identity of mobile devices on the radio interface during authentication. However, this measure does not protect against active attackers as all protocols explicitly allow access networks to request the permanent identity of a mobile device at any time. Furthermore, with GSM, UMTS and LTE the confidentiality of transmitted data is only protected on the radio interface.

Innovations of   UMTS additionally offers integrity protection for signalling
UMTS vis-à-vis GSM   information on the radio interface and gives mobile devices the possibility to verify the authenticity, as well as the freshness, of the data sent by an access network during an authentication exchange.

Innovations of LTE   LTE furthermore allows the establishment of secure tunnels to
vis-à-vis UMTS   the core network of the provider. Thus, it is no longer required to fully trust eNodeBs with regard to accounting relevant information, for example.

In summary, all three systems were designed with the aim of providing a level of security comparable to a fixed network without explicit security measures.

16.5   Supplemental Reading

[3GP12a]   3GPP: *3G Security; Network Domain Security (NDS); IP network layer security (Release 12)*. 3rd Generation Partnership Project, Technical Specification Group Services and System Aspects, 3GPP TS 33.210, V12.2.0, December 2012

[3GP12b]   3GPP: *3G Security: Security Architecture (Release 11)*. 3rd Generation Partnership Project, Technical Specification Group Services and System Aspects, 3GPP TS 33.102, V11.5.0, December 2012

[3GP12c]   3GPP: 3GPP *System Architecture Evolution (SAE); Security Architecture (Release 12)*. 3rd Generation Partnership Project, Technical Specification Group Services and System Aspects, 3GPP TS 33.401, V12.6.0, December 2012

[Les03]   LESCUYER, P.: *UMTS: Origins, Architecture and the Standard*. Springer, 2003

[Sch03]   SCHILLER, J.: *Mobile Communications*. Pearson Education, 2003

[TG93]   TC-GSM, ETSI: *GSM Security Aspects (GSM 02.09)*. European Telecommunications Standards Institute (ETSI), Recommendation GSM 02.09, Version 3.1.0, June 1993

[TS94]   TC-SMG, ETSI: *European Digital Cellular Telecommunications System (Phase 2): Security Related Network Functions (GSM 03.20)*. European Telecommunications Standards Institute (ETSI), ETS 300 534, September 1994

16.6   Questions

1. Which new security services does UMTS offer compared to GSM?
2. Which new security services does LTE offer compared to UMTS?
3. What is the purpose of the location area identifier of GSM?
4. For what purpose do GSM and UMTS use a TMSI? Why must a mobile device send an IMSI upon request?
5. How does a mobile terminal retrieve the current session key for communication with the base station?
6. Why is communication with GSM not encrypted end-to-end and only on the radio interface?
7. What would be the disadvantage if random numbers were also used as part of the freshness test performed by a mobile device during an authentication exchange under UMTS or LTE?
8. What is the purpose of the anonymity key with UMTS authentication?
9. What is the effect of the loss of synchronisation of the sequence numbers used by the home network to prove the freshness of its messages to a mobile device?
10. Assume that the temporary identity of UMTS and LTE is also used for the home network so that a visited network cannot

discover the IMSI. What potential difficulties could this cause in actual network operations? Which category of cryptographic schemes would have to be used in such a case to provide secure identity of the mobile device?

11. Formulate the authentication protocol of UMTS according to the notation mainly used in this book (see also Chapter 7 and particularly Table 7.1).

12. Why does LTE not use EAP-TLS or EAP-TTLS to authenticate UEs in foreign networks?

Part IV

Protecting Communications Infrastructures

17 Protecting Communications and Infrastructure in Open Networks

The continuously evolving information society constantly poses key challenges to IT security. In the last 20 years the global Internet and the ubiquitously available mobile communication networks have completely changed not only the ways in which we communicate, but our entire society. Whether it is a matter of executing business processes in companies and government agencies, regulating the European electricity market or political opinion-forming, most of these processes involve the use of complex and frequently even open IT networks. The continuing trend towards increasingly mobile lifestyles and ways of working intensify these effects still further. Judging from current research projects ranging from simple sensor networks up to intelligently acting cities, we can only imagine what role IT network infrastructures will play in the future.

However, these developments do not only offer new opportunities, but also new threats and risks as our society becomes more and more dependent on the *availability* of the networks and support services. In particular, this requires resistance not only to random and correlated failures, but against intelligently acting attackers. This security objective and its implementation in networks is one of the core issues of this fourth part of the book.

The availability of IT networks is a key challenge.

For this purpose, we will initially address the systematic analysis of large IT infrastructures, as they form the basis for assessing the security of complex systems. The second part of the chapter discusses the software security of end systems and routers, as this is an important prerequisite for the security of communications infrastructures.

Security in Fixed and Wireless Networks, Second Edition.
Guenter Schaefer and Michael Rossberg.
Copyright © 2014 by dpunkt.verlag GmbH, Heidelberg, Germany.
Title of the German original: Netzsicherheit   ISBN 978-3-86490-115-7
Translation Copyright © 2016 by John Wiley & Sons, Ltd., All rights reserved

This is followed in Chapter 18 by an introduction to attacks on the availability of data transport and general countermeasures against such attacks. Chapter 19 discusses the security of protocols for routing in the Internet, and Chapter 20 explains methods for safeguarding name resolution in the Internet. In Chapter 21 Internet firewalls for access control in packet-switched networks are introduced. Chapter 22 describes basic methods for automated intrusion detection and the response to attacks. Using two examples, Chapter 23 finally focuses on the management of security mechanisms in complex communications infrastructures.

17.1   Systematic Threat Analysis

A common, although not very systematic, method for evaluating the security of a system is to compile an unstructured list of threats by, for instance, brainstorming. For a hospital information system, it might look like this:

- Alteration of patient information
- Alteration of invoice information
- Disclosure of confidential patient information
- Compromising of internal service plans
- Non-availability of confidential patient information

Completeness and consistency are difficult to ensure

This naïve approach has some very obvious problems. First, it is questionable whether all relevant threats were actually registered. In particular, there is no method for deriving threats that are not known in advance or are self-evident. On the other hand, it is difficult to identify potential inconsistencies in threats. In the hospital information system, for example, there needs to be a balance between the disclosure and the non-availability of confidential patient information, otherwise a doctor who is not actually responsible for a patient might, in an emergency, have to help without having sufficient information.

One systematic method for conducting a threat analysis is to compile a threat tree [Amo94].

Definition 17.1 *A **threat tree** is a tree structure with nodes that describe threats at different levels of abstraction, and sub-trees, each of which represents a complete refinement, or decomposition, of its predecessor node.*

The construction of threat trees is initially based on a very rough and approximate threat, for example 'System X is being compromised'. This threat forms the root node of the threat tree. The threat is subsequently refined, for instance by division into 'The system is being compromised by internal attackers' and 'The system is being compromised by external attackers'. This refinement by child nodes is continued iteratively until elementary events are reached. Some examples of these threats modelled as leaves are 'An e-mail infected with an unknown virus is opened in the office' or 'An attacker gains access to a router password'. In the refinement of the threats, it is important that in each refinement step it is clearly evident that all relevant threats have been registered. One basic idea of this method is to defer as far as possible the creation of a list of the specific individual threats. Figure 17.1 shows an example of a threat tree for some threats that may occur in packet-oriented networks. A more complex example can be found in [ERG$^+$07].

Construction of threat trees

In order to quantify the often very complex threat-scenarios and in this way to identify particularly vulnerable areas, extensions of the threat trees can be used. As shown in Figure 17.2, partial threats can be linked either by conjunction or disjunction. In the first case, both partial threats must exist before the threat becomes real. In the second case just one of the two partial threats is sufficient. These different types of links have implications if we are to estimate the cost to an attacker of actually creating a threat. In the case of conjunction, the effort for attackers will always be at least as large as it is to create the more complex of the two partial threats. In the disjunction case, the task facing attackers is easier. They can search for the objective that is easier for them to compromise and then implement just that single one of the two partial threats.

Logical linking of partial threats

For the actual quantification of threats, the individual threats are assigned two values once the threat tree has been created. One value is the estimated effort that an attacker must apply in order to realise the threat, for example, *low = 1, medium = 2* and *high = 3*. For the second one, we estimate the damage that would occur with the onset of the threat and assign it a value between 1 and 6, for instance. The risk posed by any individual threat can now be expressed by the ratios of damage and effort:

Quantification of threat trees

$$\text{risk} = \frac{\text{damage}}{\text{effort}}$$

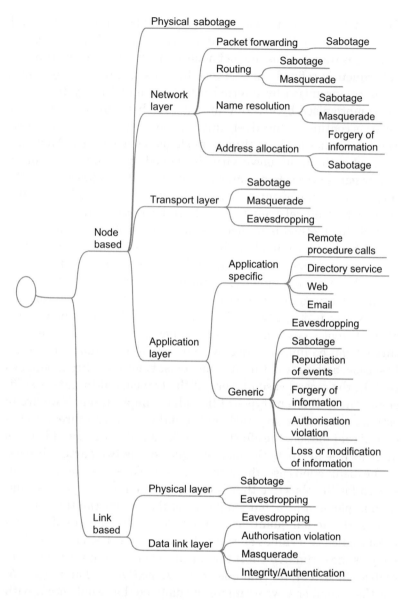

Figure 17.1

Example of a simplified threat tree for packet-oriented networks

Starting with the risk from the individual threats, the threat to the overall system can then be derived.

Other methods
of analysis   In addition to threat trees, there are a number of other similar methods. Thus, for example, in the Threat Vulnerability Risk Analysis (TVRA) [ETS06] the objects to be protected, termed the *assets*, are first catalogued and then the threats to the individual components and the security goals are systematised. In contrast to the simple threat-tree model that has been described, in the TVRA assumptions are also made about the attacker. Consequently the

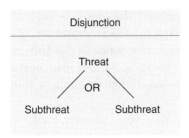
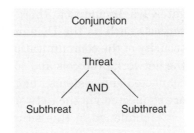

Figure 17.2
Types of threat
refinements: logical
AND- and OR linking

risk is also approximately weighted with the expertise required by the attacker.

If the overall risk that has been determined does not fall within acceptable limits, there is a need for action such as measures that will minimise the potential damage caused by an attacker. In general, however, the effort required by an attacker will be increased by introducing new security measures. In principle, there are two options for doing this:

Minimising the overall risk

- *Prevention:* The attacker could be proactively kept from carrying out certain attacks, for example by cryptographic mechanisms or packet filtering. By definition, these measures must always be performed, even when no attack is taking place.
- *Attacker detection and response:* Alternatively, it is also possible to identify attacks either as they start or very soon afterwards. This is done by regularly evaluating network traffic and analysing log files. If an attack is detected, countermeasures must be initiated that disable the attack and, if possible, also have a deterrent effect on the attacker. Only in this way will the cost for attackers become higher, because they now have to avoid detection. The response must bear in mind that precisely these types of fully automatic responses may also be intentionally provoked by an attacker.

With the practical implementation of any measures it usually makes sense to prioritise them by the reduction in risk they offer and their resource requirement. When measures are implemented, the security analysis must always be rerun because new threats may arise as a result of the measures themselves.

Perform further analyses until an acceptable risk is achieved

17.2 Security of End Systems

Communications infrastructures consist mainly of network connections and connecting components, such as switches, routers or gateways. In addition, there are components that provide support services such as the Domain Name System (DNS). However, the security of the communications infrastructure depends not only on the network protocols and components themselves, but also on the connected end systems, that is, the servers and client devices that are connected via the networks.

The number of known security vulnerabilities greatly complicates the safeguarding of end systems

A challenge in this situation is that, given the complexity of hardware and software, even the security of just individual end systems is itself difficult to analyse and so to ensure. A core problem here, particularly during software development, is that short release cycles and high cost pressure result in scant attention being paid to the security of the implementation. This is reinforced by the widespread use of programming languages that foster certain security problems, for example the lack of memory checking in C and C++ programs frequently results in problems. Because of these factors, end users and system administrators are faced with a large number of security vulnerabilities and associated updates. Figure 17.3 shows the number of security vulnerabilities that have been reported in recent years and have been assigned a globally unique number, called the Common Vulnerabilities and Exposures (CVE) Number. Around 5000 security vulnerabilities per year have been reported over the past few years. This results in an enormous amount of work for administrators and end users if they want to protect themselves against all currently known threats.

In addition to the published vulnerabilities, there may be other weak points that are known to only a small group of people and of whose existence the manufacturer is completely unaware. Protection against these so-called *zero-day exploits* is almost impossible for the average end user or administrator.

*Figure 17.3
Number of published security vulnerabilities with CVE numbers over the last few years*

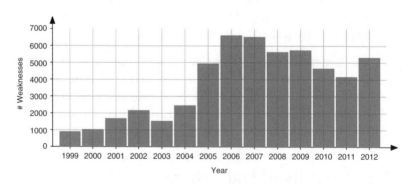

As well as the absolute number of weak points, the number of affected systems is crucial for threat assessment. Because of the dominance of the Microsoft Windows platform in client computers, Unix operating systems in the server field and Cisco IOS in routers, individual weak points can be particularly well exploited when they affect one of these operating systems.

Monoculture of software systems fosters the exploitation of vulnerabilities

The following sections give an brief introduction to some common classes of security vulnerabilities that can lead to an attacker taking control of IT systems. As a general rule these relate to end systems, but compromised end systems today represent a significant hazard for communications systems. In addition, routers and switches can in principle also be affected by these vulnerabilities.

17.2.1 Buffer Overflows

Because network services and components are usually programmed in C or C++, the buffer overflows that are facilitated by these programming languages are among the most common and well-known types of attack on systems that can be reached through the network. The main reason is that in both programming languages array access is not automatically checked for length. If an attacker succeeds in passing to a program a string that is longer than the buffer allocated, and this case is not explicitly being handled by the programmer, then the parts of the memory in which other data is stored are overwritten. Depending on the memory area affected, it is distinguished between *heap overflows* and *stack overflows*.

Buffer overflows are among the most common vulnerabilities

The overwriting of the memory can have very different effects, depending on the program structure and the contents of the buffer:

Effects of buffer overflows

- In the best case, the overwritten memory is not used anymore and the program execution is not disrupted.
- Uncontrolled changes usually result in a program crash.
- If the attacker can control the changes in the memory, variables may possibly be changed, which alter the subsequent program execution, e.g. the attacker could try to alter variables that control his privileges in the system.
- Especially with stack overflows, it is often possible for the attacker to alter the contents of code pointers. If these code pointers are used for jumps in the subsequent program execution, then under certain circumstances attackers can execute their own code and so take control of the program. With stack overflows, the return address of the executing function is usually overwritten, so that when the function has completed the program will jump to the attacker's code.

Executing exploit code   The goal of most attacks that use buffer overflows is to deploy the attacker's own program code – a so-called *exploit* – and execute it. In the simplest case, the buffer itself is used to transfer the program and it is transmitted along with the new jump address. The attacker has to take into account some constraints. For example, the code cannot contain 'null' characters because in C and C++ they mark the end of a string and thus overwriting of the memory will be terminated. However, there are ready-made program segments in which commands with null characters have been replaced by others. For example, a register is initialised to 0 by being XORed with itself. Sometimes there are also other constraints, for instance that the string may not exceed a specified total length. If attackers cannot accurately determine the memory address of the resident code, techniques known as *NOP slides* are often used. Here, valid commands are written before the actual exploit; these have the sole function of making the program longer and increasing the chance of guessing a correct jump address.

Non-executable memory areas   The frequency with which buffer overflows have been utilised has led to the development of a series of countermeasures. For example, in x86 processors the so-called *non-executable flag* (NX flag) was introduced for marking memory areas that must not be executed. Since programs do not, as a rule, reload or generate code dynamically, stacks and heaps can be marked in this way so that the direct execution of infiltrated exploits is therefore prevented.

No comprehensive protection by NX flags   But the NX flag cannot prevent attacks completely. On the one hand, not all programs can be protected in this way because just-in-time compilers, to take one example, generate and execute program code dynamically. On the other hand, *Return Oriented Programming (ROP)* is an attack technique that does not require any code of its own to be introduced. Instead, complex functions are assembled from code fragments that are already loaded in the victim's memory. For this purpose, the attacker will typically write a number of return addresses on the stack, which are then processed.

Return-oriented programming

Address Space Layout Randomisation   ROP attacks, in turn, have also resulted in the development of generic defence strategies against them. Best known in this context is the technique known as *Address Space Layout Randomisation (ASLR)*. Here, we randomly select the memory addresses that system libraries, heaps and stacks in the memory of programs are loaded to. In this case, the attacker would need extraordinarily good luck to choose the correct jump addresses. One problem with ASLR is that the actual program code is often not randomised, as this requires compiler support to implement absolute jumps in the program code with random offsets. In this case attackers have significantly less code available to them, from which they can construct their exploit. In addition, ASLR should only be used in combination with the NX flag because otherwise attackers can once again greatly increase their chances by using large NOP slides and a conventional injection of code. In addition, ASLR is substantially more secure on 64-bit systems because only here can the large number of possible memory addresses provide sufficient entropy for real protection.

In addition to generic methods for preventing buffer-overflow attacks, programs can also be hardened by the compiler. This is usually done by generating code for building and verifying *canary values*, as they are known. In an allusion to the canaries used by miners to warn of mine gas, these are values that are written to the stack at runtime with each function call. Before each return, the program itself checks if the canary value is still correct. Should this not be the case, the stack must have been modified by an attacker and the program exits before an exploit can be activated. A disadvantage of the method is the loss of efficiency when many function calls are made because all checks are done at runtime and the canary values must also be sufficiently long. In addition, the canaries, like ASLR and the NX bit, do not give general protection against the overwriting of other function pointers and variables on stacks and heaps.

Compiler-based protection for buffer overflows

Forgetting all the generic facilities, the development process should in any case take care to ensure that no buffer overflows are produced. For example, all calls from C functions without length-checking – such as gets() or strcpy() – should be replaced by versions with such a check. For the examples given these are fgets() and strncpy(). In addition, it is often sensible to limit any user inputs to a maximum length. Another way of finding security-critical buffer overflows is the static code analysis. Here, other programs carry out fully automatic searches for obvious problems in the source code. Because of the undecidability of the problem, not all buffer overflows can be found in this way, but the overhead associated with the method is also relatively low. Somewhat more complicated, but still capable of being automated, is the *Fuzzing* [Oeh05] procedure, as it is known. Randomised inputs are fed into a program until it crashes or causes memory corruption. This type of dynamic code analysis can theoretically find more vulnerabilities than static analysis, but it usually requires more resources. Additional information on buffer overflows can be found in [Kle03], for example.

Securing implementations

17.2.2   Format String Attacks

Incorrectly used format string calls are a risk

Along with buffer overflows, format string attacks are another well-known type of attack aimed primarily at C and C++ programs. The causal problem is the calling of a function with a variable number of arguments with an unchecked format specification. For example, if a programmer, instead of using `printf("%s", Input);` calls `printf(input);` to output user input on the command line, this will work for many inputs. However, if a command such as `%d` is given, the `printf` method assumes that an integer is to be printed, and that this value was passed as another argument. Because this is not the case, however, a stack location containing other values is read and output. Depending on the program structure this may be other variables or stack pointers. By using more complex format statements, any location in the stack can be read and output. Furthermore, many format string libraries also accept `%n` and allow the number of previously formatted bytes to be written to a variable. With clever design of the format statement, an attacker can use several pieced write operations to write any values on the stack. Likewise, through the targeted overwriting of return addresses or other function pointers, format string attacks can enable the attacker's code to be executed.

Thanks to the possibilities of being able to not only sequentially overwrite memory, but also read and manipulate stack data at any location, format string attacks are very powerful. Generic methods such as ASLR or canaries, which ward off buffer overflows, therefore provide limited protection. Vulnerable points in program code can be found relatively easily using static analysis, however. Many compilers offer the option of checking the relevant function calls, but for attackers it is also relatively easy to find exploitable function calls in binary code.

17.2.3   Exploiting Race Conditions and Confidence in the Operating System Environment

Using SUID programs to elevate privileges

As well as attacks aimed at altering the memory and executing program code, there are other types of attacks that can be used to execute code with elevated privileges in a system.

Ideal for such attacks are the widespread UNIX systems, where programs can be provided with the *Set User ID (SUID) Flag*. Programs that have this flag will run not with the privileges of the user, but with the privileges of the user who owns the file. This is normally the user 'root', who generally has no privilege restrictions.

A prominent example of such a program is `passwd`, which allows users to change their password and notes the changes in the system password file with administrator privileges.

Popular attacks on programs of this type exploit weaknesses that are combined under the term *time-of-check, time-of-use (TOC-TOU)*. Here, an attacker uses a typical race condition to trick the SUID program. In the vulnerable category are some programs that, before writing to a file, check that the file actually exists in order to then open it with another command and begin the write operation. During the interval, that is, immediately after the check and before the opening, attackers can create a link to a file to which they have no access privileges. Since the SUID program has these privileges, however, the file is then overwritten. Depending on what data has been written to the file, the impact can range from a simple denial-of-service attack to an authorisation violation. To find and rectify race conditions in general is very complex. However, many situations can be avoided by first opening files and then executing security-relevant function calls only with file descriptors. An example is avoiding the `stat()` function by instead calling `fstat()`. In this case, an attacker can no longer replace the file by another one [LC05].

Security problems from race conditions

Another common error that is found in SUID programs is unjustified confidence in the operating system environment. For example, if external programs are called and no absolute path information is used, attackers can alter the `PATH` environment variable so that their own program is called instead of the intended program. However, the task of reliably deducing the path of an external program in relation to one's own program in order to call a program in the same directory is not a trivial one. If attackers call such an SUID program via a file link, for example, they can control which external programs are called. The inheritance of environment parameters also applies to other characteristics such as `umask` – a bitmask that specifies the default privileges of newly created files. If this value is not set explicitly by the SUID program, an attacker can use this to alter established files retrospectively.

Unjustified confidence in program environment

17.2.4 SQL Injections and Cross-site Scripting

Meanwhile, in many security-relevant incidents attackers have scarcely any 'real' access to the computer systems being attacked. Taking the example of web requests, attackers embed SQL commands or JavaScripts in the HTTP request sent to the server. If the server uses the variables thus passed without further examination

In many cases, attackers do not need full access

to then construct database queries or personalise web pages, the transferred code may possibly be executed. In the techniques known as *SQL injections* skilful design of the SQL queries can enable databases to be copied, manipulated or simply deleted. If the attacker embeds JavaScript in other websites, we talk of *cross-site scripting (XSS)*. For an attack to be successful, attack victims must open a specially crafted link and then find themselves on a web page whose content is controlled by the attacker, without this fact being visible from the displayed URL, for example.

In addition to injecting SQL and JavaScript commands, similar types of attack are also conceivable in other languages. Slightly less-well known, for example, are LDAP injections [ABB+08], where usernames or passwords are furnished with LDAP control characters. The goal in this case is to alter authorisation requests in such a way that an attacker without permission is granted access anyway.

Ultimately, even format string attacks are similar in type because here, too, control characters are not handled correctly. However, the impacts from the direct memory manipulation are even more significant.

17.2.5   Malware

A way of penetrating computer systems that is steadily increasing in importance is the targeted placement of malicious programs. Derived from the word 'malicious', these are usually referred to as *malware*. They can be distributed in different ways, for example:

- bogus e-mails containing malware are sent;
- infected USB sticks are left around in the hope that users will plug them into their workstations;
- web sites are modified so that they deploy manipulated programs;
- as in the case of the Flame malware, automatic Windows software updates are modified [Kus13].

Malwares are distinguished by their distribution and conceal functions

Depending on the distribution mechanism and the refinement of the concealment of the malicious code, the following major types of malware can be distinguished:

- **Backdoors:** In the simplest case, the malware has no distribution function of its own and, undocumented, resides inside a program that works as intended. Only after some time has passed or it is triggered by an external event such as network packets from the attacker is the malicious function activated.

- **Trojan horses:** Specialised software that has the main task of producing malicious functions is often referred to as a Trojan horse because it is usually installed under false pretences. In contrast to backdoors in 'useful software', Trojan horses usually install themselves as a background process in the operating system environment so that they do not to need to be specially activated by the user. Common malicious functions include the sending of files and spam, spying on the user – using a microphone and webcam, for example – and the tapping of credit card information.

Trojan horses run independently of useful software

- **Rootkits:** In some cases Trojan horses can be detected and removed very easily. Software that can conceal itself in a better way is usually referred to as a rootkit. Once again, there is a wide range of gradations here. In the simplest case, commands such as `ls` are exchanged in order to hide the files of the rootkit. More complex rootkits try to camouflage themselves by altering the system calls of the operating system. As a result, software that uses these calls can no longer detect the rootkit. As far back as 2006, *Blue Pill* was presented as a rootkit [Rut06] that migrates the host operating system, during its operation, into a virtual machine, while the rootkit itself works virtually undetectably as a hypervisor. More recent operations hide malicious code in microcontrollers on the motherboard [TW09] or in the debugging and management functions of processors [ESZ08].

Rootkits are hidden deeply in operating system or hardware controllers

- **Viruses:** If malicious code has the ability to replicate itself via USB data-storage devices and similar media, it is referred to as a virus.

Viruses and worms have independent distribution functions

- **Worms:** Some programs have the ability to infect other computers over networks. They are referred to as worms. When a collective of such computers is in turn remote controlled to attack other computers in a network we talk of *Bots*, which is derived from the word robot. Bots and the botnets formed from them will be cover in greater depth in the next chapter.

Malicious code can be countered only by various preventive and monitoring measures. The major approaches are as follows:

Countermeasures

- By using *virus scanners* and *network monitoring*, known malware and suspicious code fragments and activities can potentially be detected. Further details about network monitoring are given in Chapter 22.

Signed programs

- The sourcing of *software from trusted sources* and executing only *signed code* helps to further lower the threat from backdoors and Trojan horses. In particular, software updates should be performed regularly to close known vulnerabilities. Again, the signature of the code is an important prerequisite, so that attackers do not simply replace legitimate software with malicious code. Nevertheless, it must be assumed that advanced attackers will gain access, at least from time to time, to valid code signing keys, so revocation mechanisms, for example, should be provided.

Attackers can gain access to code signing keys

- Ultimately, backdoors can only be found by regular *software audits* and by *monitoring the operating system functions invoked*.

- To counter the 'accidental' execution of programs in e-mails or from dubious websites and media, an important measure is appropriate *user training* in order to raise awareness and lower the risk of unconscious execution of malicious code.

- With the enforcement of the *Least Privilege Principle*, that is, that users and processes only get the privileges they actually need, the impacts of malicious code can at least be reduced.

The problem of malicious code is a very deep one, however, and it cannot be resolved even by the comprehensive analysis of the source code of all programs executed. To illustrate this, in the following we use a number of considerations from a seminal article by Ken Thompson [Tho84].

Observation 1: It is possible to write software that can reproduce its own source code.

On this topic, Thompson himself gave an example of a C program, which is shown in Figure 17.4. The program outputs a source code that generates a program that can output itself. These *Quine* programs, as they are known, can also be designed in a much more compact form, and in particular they can be generated automatically.

Observation 2: Compilers can be written so that they are able to translate themselves.

Particularly in the case of C compilers, it is normal that they are written in C and can translate themselves. Of course, there is a certain 'chicken and egg' problem here, but in principle it is possible

to translate a compiler with its own source code, as long as you use
a different C compiler for the first pass.

```
char s[] = {
    '\t',
    '0',
    '\n',
    '}',
    ';',
    '\n',
    '\n',
    '/',
    '*',
    (about 200 lines deleted)
    0
};

/*  The string is a representation of
    the body of this program from '0'
    to the end. */

main() {
    int i;
    printf("char s[] = {\n");
    for (i=0: s[i]; i++)
        printf("\t%d, \n", s[i]);
    printf("%s",s);
}
```

Figure 17.4

A self-replicating C program

```
    . . .
    c = next();
    if(c != '\\')
        return(c);
    c = next();
    if(c == '\\')
        return('\\');
    if(c != 'n')
        return('\n');
    if(c != 'v')
        return(11);
    . . .
```

⇨

```
    . . .
    c = next();
    if(c != '\\')
        return(c);
    c = next();
    if(c == '\\')
        return('\\');
    if(c != 'n')
        return('\n');
    if(c != 'v')
        return('\v');
    . . .
```

Figure 17.5

New backslash escape sequence. The first C compiler requires the code on the left. All subsequent ones can use the code on the right and adopt the interpretation of the first code.

Observation 3: Compilers adopt interpretation rules from the compiler that translated them.

Thompson demonstrates this observation in a small example in which a new backslash escape sequence \v for strings is introduced in the compilers. In the original compiler this sequence is not yet defined and must – as shown in the left part of Figure 17.5 – be included in the source code of the new compiler as a number. However, the new C compiler can also translate the source code on the right and even use the escape sequence to replace the string during the translation process. In this process, the interpretation used by the first compiler is inherently adopted.

Observation 4: Malicious compilers can detect that they are translating a targeted program and insert additional code.

If an attacker succeeds in planting a malicious compiler with a user, it could insert additional or slightly altered code into the binary file subsequently generated, for example password requests could be modified to always accept certain default passwords. This can even be done independently of the translated program because password requests in C are often carried out by calling the `getpass()` function.

Observation 5: Compilers can detect that they are translating a compiler.

Malicious compilers can replicate themselves during the translation of uncompromised compilers

Based on characteristic lines of code, such as those shown in Figure 17.5, a compiler can detect that it is translating either itself or a similar compiler. Even at this instant, a malicious compiler could change its behaviour. As noted in Observation 1, a malicious compiler can replicate the source code of malicious functions and insert it in the original source code. After it has been compiled, the new compiler also contains the malicious functions. This is regardless of whether the binary file was generated for a different processor architecture. Attackers can also adapt their malicious functions to different compilers so that the malicious functions do not disappear if different compilers are repeatedly translated with each other. It is even conceivable that malicious compilers could also modify the compilers for other programming languages.

Software backdoors can only be ruled only through the immense complexity of a binary code analysis

These considerations should make it especially clear that even by checking the source code it is not possible to conclude that there are no backdoors. By incorporating a self-replicating backdoor in a compiler, even the repeated translation of a backdoor-free compiler source code does not enable the re-creation of a compiler without a backdoor. The only guaranteed effective measure would be to completely verify a questionable program at the level of the machine code. There are some tentative methods for doing this [SBY$^+$08, BJA$^+$11], but they are not yet a self-evident protective measure. However, the question of whether backdoors cannot be so well hidden that finding them in sufficiently complex programs becomes simply too expensive, is still to be answered. Because of these relationships, the often-made statement that open source software is fundamentally 'safer' than proprietary software appears in a different light.

17.3   Summary

In making complete communications infrastructure secure, the cryptographic protection between endpoints that was covered previously is not sufficient. In this context, the availability of services gains more importance. Naturally, this includes securing transmission paths and also end systems.

Cryptographic protocols alone are not sufficient for secure operation

In order to achieve an adequate level of protection at acceptable costs, a systematic threat analysis is essential. The threat trees that were introduced are such a possibility – another one is the TVRA method, for example. The core of all threat analyses is the estimation of the overall risk, which consists of the probability of occurrence and the expected damage, among other factors.

The starting point of any security measure should be the estimation of the overall risk

A necessary condition for the operation of secure and, in particular, available communications infrastructures is the security of end systems against being compromised. This chapter summarised in overview some basic software errors and threats in this context. In essence, these are buffer overflows, format string attacks, race conditions and the untested use of passed strings, such as in SQL injections. But even without exploitable vulnerabilities in sufficiently complex systems one cannot simply infer the absence of malicious code. There are a number of distribution channels for these, such as e-mails, USB sticks or infected web sites. Countermeasures, such as virus scanners, code analysis and user training, provide a way of reducing the risk of malicious code, but cannot rule it out completely.

The security of individual systems is an important prerequisite for the safe operation of communications infrastructures

17.4   Supplemental Reading

[Amo94]   AMOROSO, E. G.: *Fundamentals of Computer Security Technology*. Prentice Hall, 1994
Chapter 2 includes an introduction to threat trees.

[ETS06]   ETSI TISPAN: *Methods and protocols; Part 1: Method and proforma for Threat, Risk, Vulnerability Analysis*. European Telecommunications Standards Institute (ETSI), Technical Specification 102 165-1 Version 4.2.1, Dec 2006

[Kle03]   KLEIN, T.: *Buffer Overflows und Format-String-Schwachstellen: Funktionsweisen, Exploits und Gegenmaßnahmen [Buffer overflows and format string vulnerabilities: Modes of operation, exploits and countermeasures]*. dpunkt.verlag, 2003

Not quite up to date, but offers a comprehensive introduction to buffer overflows and format string attacks.

[Tho84]   THOMPSON, K.: Reflections on Trusting Trust. In: *Communications of the ACM* 27 (1984), No. 8, pp. 761–763

17.5   Questions

1. Develop a threat tree for possible attacks on a WLAN hotspot.
2. What problems do you anticipate in the systematic analysis of threats?
3. For what reason is the security of the end systems a prerequisite for the safe operation of communications infrastructures?
4. What distinguishes buffer overflows from SQL injections in relation to their risk for further attacks?
5. Explain why, while Java and Flash programs themselves should not include buffer overflows, the frameworks are a popular target for these attacks.
6. Using *Trusted Platform Modules* (TPM), programs can detect whether they were started in a 'secure' environment, that is, whether the only code segments that were loaded were signed by trusted instances. Can we therefore conclude that there is no attack code, even if no code signing keys were compromised?
7. Why is it sensible to generate code signatures even when we assume that valid signature keys will, from time to time, end up in the hands of the attackers?
8. What makes rootkits that are hiding in management functions of motherboards so dangerous?
9. Suppose that the build server of a development team for an operating system was temporarily compromised. What dangers must be assumed if you take into account Ken Thompson's observations? What measures are required in such a case?

18 Availability of Data Transport

In addition to the classic security objectives of confidentiality, integrity and authenticity, in recent years public awareness has focused increasingly on the availability of communication means. The reason for this is the attackers' ability to disrupt communication systems very easily by so-called denial-of-service attacks without being identified and still cause significant harm (possibly also of a financial nature). The following sections will look first at classic denial-of-service attacks from one source, and then introduce the special features of multi-source attacks. Countermeasures to denial-of-service attacks will then be explained. The chapter concludes with a further section on tracing the sources of denial-of-service attacks.

18.1 Denial-of-Service Attacks

Definition 18.1   Denial-of-service attacks *(DoS attacks) refer to sabotage attacks in the ICT field and aim to make access to network resources and services more difficult or prevent such access altogether.*

Even if these attacks frequently do not enable the attacker to enrich themselves directly or access sensitive data, there are still a number of frequently mentioned motivations for denial-of-service attacks:

Motivation for denial-of-service attacks

- **'Fun':** As denial-of-service attacks are sometimes extremely easy to execute, they are often carried out by self-proclaimed hackers without a serious background reason, and usually also without these perpetrators being aware of the full damage caused. So-called **script kiddies** usually simply execute software originating from pertinent Internet sources, which generates the appropriate network packets.

- **Commercial advantages:** Denial-of-service attacks can lead to monetary benefits, such as by preventing competitors from obtaining information. As early as 1998, for example, servers of the US Bureau of Labor Statistics were overloaded [Cha98] just as they announced the current producer price index. Since this has a significant impact on the stock market, it is likely that this was intended to support specific manipulations.

- **Discrediting:** Unavailable mail or web servers may harm the reputation of the operators. Attackers can exploit this by means of sabotage.

- **Revenge:** Denial-of-service attacks are often used for retaliation purposes because they are easy to carry out. For example, there were reports of massive denial-of-service attacks on MasterCard after the freezing of transactions for WikiLeaks [PD11]. An attacker can also create a direct financial loss if higher charges for servers and network infrastructure become due as a result of increased use of the victim's resources.

- **Political reasons:** A number of cases are known in which increased denial-of-service attacks were carried out where political tensions existed. Examples include the conflict between Russia and Estonia in 2007 [Les07] and the Russo-Georgian War a year later [KK08].

Reasons for the significance of denial-of-service attacks

The many different motivations for denial-of-service attacks are only one aspect of the problem. The form of attack is also becoming more significant with the increasing level of networking and the degree to which our society relies on effective communication networks. To some extent the attack tools are also very easy to obtain and display a high level of automation. In addition, protection against denial-of-service attacks is often very difficult to implement and therefore expensive. In a study, 98% of the 400 corporate security experts surveyed said that they are worried about such attacks, and at least two thirds had experienced one or more failures due to denial-of-service in the previous year [For09].

18.1.1 Denial-of-Service Attacks with Permanent Effects

The following sections discuss the various forms of denial-of-service attacks on networks and refer in each case to better known attacks as examples. First, attacks where the effects continue to exist after the end of the attack or where maintaining the attack costs the attacker barely any resources are examined.

Permanent Destruction and Reservation of Resources

In the best case for the attacker, he is able to render servers, routers and other important network components permanently unusable for other users. This is made possible by two types of attacks: destruction of the components or reservation of resources by the attacker.

In relation to the destruction alone, there are again a number of basic possibilities. In addition to physical destruction, for example, destruction by means of software commands is possible in many cases. In the simplest case, the hard disk will be wiped after a successful intrusion into a computer system. However, implementation bugs in the operating system or in server applications can also often be exploited to cause them to crash and so make them inaccessible. The better known attacks of this kind that have occurred in the past include:

Examples of attacks that cause systems to crash

- **Ping of Death:** According to [Inf81], IP packets have a maximum size of 65.535. However, under certain circumstances when IP fragments are assembled they may produce larger packets which, in the late 1990s, were incorrectly handled by many IP implementations. By overwriting the buffer areas, the affected operating systems crashed and attackers were able to persistently disrupt services by means of a few specially designed IP packets. As ICMP echo requests were often used, the term 'Ping of Death' has become widely accepted.
- **Teardrop attack:** A teardrop attack also targets a vulnerability that was common in the IP processing of operating systems in the late 1990s. In this case, the attacker generated two IP fragments that did not contain consecutive packet areas, as is normally the case. Instead, one fragment was contained completely in the other fragment and a negative number was obtained when calculating an offset in the course of assembling the packet. However, as the implementations assumed unsigned numbers, overflows occurred and the result was interpreted as an extremely large number. The succeeding memory operation led to the operating system to crash.
- **LAND attack:** The problem that is exploited with the so-called LAND attack on old systems is similar to a teardrop

attack. In this case, the attacker initiates the establishment of a TCP connection to the victim. However, the corresponding SYN packet is provided with a forged source address, in this case the address of the victim itself. Because of implementation errors in the IP stack of the affected systems, the machine continuously replies to itself, thus creating an endless loop. This results in a crash.

Attacks on applic-
ation processes
In addition to the attacks described, which affect the victim's operating system, specific applications in particular, such as web servers, are attacked over and over again. However, these are often less seriously affected because under certain circumstances applications can be restarted and not as many systems are affected.

Illegitimate Resource Reservation

Blocking by means of
resource reservation
In addition to blocking attacks aimed at the destruction of resources, resources can be fully used up by frequent reservation, so they are not available to legitimate users [HR06]. Web servers which limit the number of parallel sessions to a fixed value are a classic example [AN97]. If an attacker establishes this maximum number of connections to the server, legitimate users can no longer use the service. Interestingly, such limitations of simultaneous connections are often configured specifically because the system should be protected against overload situations.

Even if the attacked system drops the inactive connections after a short time, it is usually easy for the attacker to delay the victim long enough by means of slow responses. An interesting way to keep TCP connections open at the victim's end was described in 2008 [CER09]. In this case, the attacker first establishes a TCP connection normally and announces a flow control window of size 0. The victim's system then waits until the attacker is again able to accept data and keeps the connection resources available.

18.1.2   Resource Exhaustion

In addition to attacks which lead to a permanent disruption of network services, there are a number of other ways to implement denial-of-service if the attacker also invests resources continuously. As soon at these attacks are prevented, the attacked systems usually recover by themselves. Depending on how the attacker proceeds, the victim's memory, computing capacity or communication bandwidth may be exhausted.

Memory Exhaustion Attacks

In memory exhaustion attacks, a process of the victim is forced to use a lot of working memory or disk space. Depending on the implementation, the processing of requests slows down so much that the service is in fact no longer available to other users. In attacks aimed at exhausting memory, these effects are sometimes more drastic as the load increases. The attacked systems react even more slowly as data is swapped to the hard disk due to the lack of memory. Sometimes the transitions to resource destruction are also fluid because, when the lack of memory is very acute, the Linux operating system, for example, reacts by terminating user processes. Since the processes are not relaunched after the end of the attack, the effects may be permanent.

Aim: extreme slowdown of services

Smooth transition to resource destruction

Frequent memory exhaustion attacks at network and transport level include, for example, the following:

Memory exhaustion attacks at network and transport level

- **TCP-SYN flooding:** The memory reserved for network connections can be relatively easily exhausted in many systems by sending TCP-SYN packets to the victim. In conventional TCP implementations, in response to such packets a connection context, which is maintained for a few minutes at least, is kept in the memory. The destination system will be overloaded if the attacker uses random, forged sender addresses or a very large number of computers send many connection requests.

- **IP fragment attacks:** A similar principle can be followed by sending a high number of random IP fragments. In this case, the victim's system must reserve resources to reconstruct the full datagrams from the fragments. However, if the attacker does not send any full datagrams, the attacked system has to wait for a timeout.

Often, memory exhaustion attacks can also be carried out on the application layer. Examples of this are compressed archives that contain extremely large but very compressible files. Anti-virus scanners, for example, can be loaded in this way if they decompress content without further examination. Similar attacks are also possible on software or online tools that process images, if they only check the transmitted file size and are instructed to process extremely compressible images with a huge number of pixels, such as unicolour PNG files.

Attacks on the application layer

Exhaustion of Computing Resources

Exhaustion of computing resources occurs on higher layers

In addition to the exhaustion of memory, denial-of-service attacks can also exhaust the computing capacity of a system. However, relatively little processing power is required for processing packets at network and transport level, the more so as the calculation of checksums often takes place in the actual network cards. Attacks therefore tend to focus on the higher layers and particularly on cryptographic operations.

Attacks on SSL/TLS

Unlike IPsec (see Chapter 12), the widely used SSL/TLS protocol, for example, which was presented in Section 13.1, possesses no inherent protection against denial-of-service attacks. It is relatively easy for attackers to put the server under load as a result of cryptographic operations by establishing many connections. However, improved versions of the attack are also conceivable: a method is described in [The11] in which an attacker forces frequent cryptographic renegotiations of the same connection and thus blocks the server.

Bandwidth Exhaustion

Attacks on the victim's memory or processor resources are no longer possible if the attacker's packets are dropped. In this case, however, communication may also be disrupted by simply overloading the network. In the simplest case, significantly more data is sent to the victim than its connection to the Internet can pass on. In addition to pure communication bandwidth, however, there is a further limitation: the packet rate. By creating as many small packets as possible, attackers can usually use the packet processing capacity well below the maximum bandwidth. Since most applications also use the reliable TCP and TCP performs congestion control, legitimate users withdraw automatically when packets are lost because their congestion control windows are reduced by the losses occurring, therefore the attack traffic prevails.

TCP congestion control exacerbates effects

It is often possible for attackers who proceed intelligently to increase the bandwidth they use. In these so-called *amplification attacks*, the attacker sends packets with a forged source address to uninvolved third parties. They respond to the specified source address and so ensure an increase in the effect when larger or greater numbers of response packets are generated.

Amplification due to many parallel responses

■ **Smurf attack:** In IP networks, a so-called broadcast address, which addresses all the devices, exists for each subnet. In a Smurf attack [TFr97] it is precisely this behaviour that is exploited, in that the attacker sends a packet to the broadcast address of a subnet that is as large as possible. If computers respond to these requests without rate limiting or similar tests, a high number of responses will be directed to the victim through the use of forged source addresses in the requests. In the original attack, this method was implemented using ICMP echo requests. However, the principle can also be applied to all connectionless services that can be globally accessed via broadcast and multicast addresses.

■ **TCP Bang attack:** In addition to the ability to generate many responses in parallel, overload situations can also arise when a request triggers several responses over a longer period. An attack circulating under the name *Bang* [HR06] exploits precisely this behaviour. In this case, the attacker sends TCP-SYN packets with the source address of the victim to uninvolved third parties – so-called *reflectors*. They respond to the victim with confirmation by means of SYN-ACK packets. Unlike TCP-SYN floods, the victim is therefore overloaded with packets of the second phase of the TCP connection establishment. The TCP standard requires that systems without proper TCP connection may terminate the connection state in the reflector by sending a TCP reset packet. However, stateful firewalls often suppress such packets. In addition, the victims cannot respond to all SYN-ACK packets in large-scale attacks. If resets are not carried out, the reflectors respond by retransmitting the SYN-ACKs and thus reinforce the attack.

Amplification by many sequential responses

■ **DNS amplification:** To generate more bandwidth, it is not necessarily imperative to generate more packets. Instead, it is enough to make even small requests to uninvolved servers on behalf of the victim if they respond with very large packets. A popular means for such attacks is the Domain Name System (DNS), in which extremely small requests, each provoking responses of several kilobytes, can be formulated via a connectionless service [DKB+11].

Amplification due to large response packets

■ **Bounce attacks:** In addition to the possibility of using uninvolved parties to generate traffic, it is also possible with an incorrect configuration to get the victims themselves to make a significant contribution to the volume of traffic. A classic example is use of the `chargen` [HR06] or `echo` service [Pos83]. Both services react to receiving UDP datagrams by sending a response and are actually supposed to be used for diagnosing errors in networks. If, by forging the source address and source port, an attacker succeeds in convincing

Amplification by involving the victim

such a service to respond to an uninvolved echo or chargen server, the two services send each other messages until a packet is lost at some point. A similar technique is also used at the application level where, with an incorrect configuration, mail servers are persuaded to deliver mails to each other. Examples of this include out-of-office messages that are sent without further examination. In this case, the attacker only needs to send one e-mail with a forged sender address from an address with the out-of-office message to an address to which an out-of-office address has also been applied. The situation is similar with mailing lists whose e-mail addresses have been mutually registered as members or in case error e-mails are sent in response to other error e-mails.

Using TCP conges-
tion control to
increase effectiveness

Added to the problem that, under certain circumstances, attackers can generate a multiple of their own bandwidth, there is a further issue: user processes frequently use TCP to transport data reliably. As already mentioned, TCP reacts to lost packets by throttling the speed so that legitimate users limit themselves in the transmission rate. With a completely reduced rate, TCP sends only one packet and then waits for a timeout or confirmation. Although the minimum timeout values are implementation-dependent, they are usually fixed, which means that packet transmissions always take place at fixed intervals. An attacker may take advantage of this situation: in so-called *low-rate DoS attacks* [KK03], bandwidth utilisations are not carried out continuously, but only periodically. The time in which TCP carries out retransmissions is chosen as the period so that it always causes an overload situation at exactly this point in time. It is interesting in this case that the retransmissions of TCP messages automatically synchronise to the attack times. Two things are achieved by using the pulsed method: firstly, other targets can be attacked in the meantime and, secondly, these attacks are more difficult to detect because the network load, on average, does not have to rise sharply to cause damage and flow-based monitoring mechanisms only detect aggregated measures.

18.2   Distributed Denial-of-Service Attacks

Resource exhaustion
by single sources
often not sufficient

In order to carry out the bandwidth exhaustion envisioned, attackers must also incur significant expenses, since the targets of the attacks are usually well-connected server systems. However, even if they have very good internet connections, the large volume of data at a point is relatively conspicuous and can often be filtered well by the Internet Service Provider (ISP). At the end of the 1990s, therefore, an advanced form of denial-of-service attacks became prevalent: the so-called *distributed denial-of-service* (DDoS). In principle the same methods are used here as in the attacks from one source referred to above. However, the traffic is not generated by one system but by many thousands simultaneously, which attackers have previously brought under their control. Derived from the word robot these are known as *botnets* and consist of magnitudes of compromised systems. They are mostly made up of poorly secured end systems, which in turn have a limited communication bandwidth. Nevertheless, the amount of traffic generated is significant due to the sheer number of sources and is difficult to filter due to the diversity.

Use of botnets

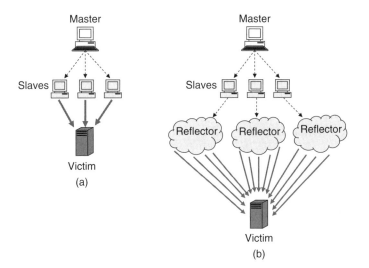

Figure 18.1

Classic scenarios for distributed denial-of-service attacks: (a) master–slave victim; (b) master–slave reflector victim

Figure 18.1 shows classic command and traffic flows which play a role in distributed denial-of-service attacks. In the simplest case, an attacker uses one or more master systems – often also referred to as *command-and-control servers* (C&C servers) – to send commands to compromised hosts, which then start a resource exhaustion attack. The second case is somewhat more subtle: if reflectors are additionally used, it is even more difficult for the victim to isolate the attack. This form of attack coordination has been used since the late 1990s. Examples of early representatives are *Trinoo* or *TFN2K* [LRS+00, BT00]. Despite their simple construction, these tools were able to interfere significantly with

First tools for distributed denial-of-service attacks

well-known websites like Ebay or Yahoo. Additionally, already with these first developments emphasis was placed on obscuring the control communication and protecting against hostile takeover of the botnets.

Peer-to-peer-based botnets

Today botnets have made significant progress in terms of concealment and protection against takeovers [RAW+13]. The reason for this development is the ongoing professionalisation of the botnet operators, who rent them for targeted denial-of-service attacks, for example. In particular, various peer-to-peer communication forms have prevailed instead of direct communication between master and slave. Generally speaking, to do this the botnet members each connect via cryptographically secure connections to a few other members. Commands are then sent by the attacker to only one or a few members and they cooperate among each other for dissemination using gossip protocols. This procedure has several advantages. Firstly, the method is scalable, so today's botnets can grow to hundreds of thousands of members. Secondly, the structure of the botnet and the identity of the attacker is even better disguised, making it de facto no longer possible to identify botnet operators based on traffic observations. Since in general the commands now have asymmetric signatures, it is only rarely possible for even law enforcement authorities and researchers to completely disable botnets and so stop distributed denial-of-service attacks.

18.3 Countermeasures

Hardening of implementations and overprovisioning

As a result of the many different ways of carrying out denial-of-service attacks, it is usually necessary to take a number of countermeasures to prevent them or at least to reduce their damage. These include obvious ways, such as systematically identifying and resolving software problems, as happened, for example, in the Ping of Death referred to previously. It is sometimes possible to guard against resource exhaustion attacks by so-called overprovisioning, that is, keeping many additional resources available. In addition to extra communication bandwidth, memory and processing power, for example, special hardware for fast computation of cryptographic operations could be used or services could be outsourced to cloud providers, who keep sufficient resources available for extremely severe attacks. However, it is also possible by intelligently designing software and network protocols to minimise the effects of denial-of-service attacks.

18.3.1   Cookies and Stateless Protocol Design

An elegant way of preventing memory exhaustion attacks like the aforementioned TCP-SYN flooding is to store as little state as possible about the opposite party. In the best case, it is thus possible to identify the communication partner before data on them is stored. In this way, quotas can be set up for each partner and capacity exhaustion by one communication partner has little effect on the others.

Preventing the storage of data

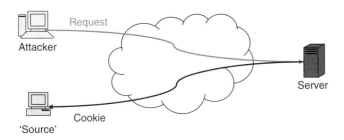

Figure 18.2
Scenario for using TCP-SYN cookies

The so-called *TCP-SYN cookies* [BS96] have probably become the most widely accepted approach in this context. As illustrated in Figure 18.2, in this case the server responds to the request to establish a TCP connection with a SYN-ACK packet. It is already possible in the standard TCP to rule out that the illustrated forging of source addresses will be successful for the third packet (ACK) following on from the SYN-ACK packet. To do so the server checks for incoming ACK packets that the correct sequence numbers match those of the SYN-ACKs. If these 32-bit long sequence numbers are chosen at random, the attacker can only try and guess them, and cannot therefore specify any source address for which he is *off-path*, that is to say not on the network path between the victim and the address he has stated. However, in TCP the calculated sequence numbers at least are usually kept as a state for each SYN packet.

TCP standard: sequence numbers prevent the successful forging of IP addresses

This behaviour is modified in the case of TCP-SYN cookies. Instead of random sequence numbers, a pseudo-random value is generated using a cryptographic hash value via the important TCP parameters, such as the sender's address, and a secret of the server. The pseudo-random value, however, does not need to be saved, but is recomputed for the incoming ACK and compared with the specified sequence number. If they match, the sender must have received the SYN-ACK packet, since he would not have been able to calculate the correct sequence number without the server's secret.

Stateful operation	Stateless operation
1. $C \rightarrow S$: Msg_1	1. $C \rightarrow S$: Msg_1
2. $S \rightarrow C$: Msg_2　　　S stores $State_{S1}$	2. $S \rightarrow C$: Msg_2, $State_{S1}$
3. $C \rightarrow S$: Msg_3	3. $C \rightarrow S$: Msg_3, $State_{S2}$
4. $S \rightarrow C$: Msg_4　　　S stores $State_{S2}$	4. $S \rightarrow C$: Msg_4, $State_{S3}$
...	...

Figure 18.3
Stateful and
stateless protocols

Cookies are also used
in IKEv2

After verifying the address of a communication partner — at least for IPv4 — it is possible to keep state without risk, as memory can then be associated to each communication partner. In IPv6 networks this assignment must be made to subnetworks because attackers can easily change their address within a subnet. Very similar methods are used, for example, as part of the IKEv2 protocol to identify communication partners in overload situations (see Section 12.9). In this case, however, a further round-trip time is required for the exchange of cookies.

The cookie mechanism prevents the investment of memory or processing power before being able to exclude, with a high degree of probability, that the address is forged. However, this principle can also be generalised: as shown in Figure 18.3, it is possible to transform stateful protocols into stateless protocols. The queried server transmits its state in each of the response packets to the client. The client in turn sends the current state with each request.

Protecting the
state with MAC

If the application must prevent an attacker from changing the state on the client side, it should be protected using a MAC. Again, the server uses a secret that is known only to it and in which the client address has been included. The latter ensures that clients cannot pass on states among themselves. One problem that remains is possible resetting of the state by the client: if the secret for the MAC has not changed in the meantime, it can simply import a previous state. For countermeasures, such as the checking of sequence numbers, some memory at least would be required. A continuing disadvantage is that a lot of communication bandwidth and time for message processing has to be used due to transmitting the state completely in each case. It should also be borne in mind that the first server-generated packet is not significantly larger than the client's request, otherwise the server may be used for amplification attacks. Because of the disadvantages, approaches that only rely in the first step on a stateless cookie mechanism and then limit the reserved memory have become more widespread.

18.3.2 Client Puzzles

The cookie mechanism presented here ensures that the addresses of clients can be verified before state information is created or complex calculations are started. However, if the attacker controls large address ranges or is located in the victim's immediate vicinity, overload situations may still be generated without creating any significant effort for the attacker. To increase the effort for the attacker as well, when using *client puzzles* [JB99] requests are only processed if the client can prove that it has also experienced significant effort when formulating the request. This effort is generated artificially and serves only to eliminate the asymmetry in respect of memory or CPU load.

Cookies are inadequate if attackers control large address ranges

A number of functional requirements are made on client puzzles: they must be easy for a server to generate and check. Solving a puzzle must require considerable effort from the clients and it should be possible to adjust this effort to the server's load. So if there is no overload condition in the server, there should also be no effort for the clients. Only in the event of overload should effort arise adaptively; in this case, however, it is essential to load even legitimate users with the solving of client puzzles.

Requirements for client puzzles

A very well thought-out scheme for client puzzles was proposed in [ANL01]. In this case, the server specifies a nonce N_S and a level of difficulty k at regular intervals, with the latter depending on the load situation on the server. With this information, each client C can derive and calculate a unique puzzle for itself. For this purpose, he also first chooses a nonce N_C and calculates a value X for a given cryptographic hash function H so that the following is valid:

Client puzzles with cryptographic hash functions

$$H(C, N_S, N_C, X) = 0^k Y$$

The hash value over the input must therefore begin with k zero bits. The rest of the value Y plays no further role. As inverting H is very difficult by construction, trying a large number of candidates is the easiest way to determine a valid value X. On average, 2^{k-1} calculations of H are required so that the server, by increasing k, can make the task exponentially more difficult. In contrast, only a single calculation of H is required for checking the calculation on the server side.

The method presented offers even more advantages. The communication effort of the protocol increases only minimally in practice as, for a feasible $k < 64$, the X values do not grow significantly over eight bytes. The server does not need to cache any

Advantages and disadvantages of client puzzles

client-specific values, so it is possible to dispense with simultaneous use of cookies. The inclusion of C in the hash function ensures that although all clients use the same value N_S, no solutions can be transferred among themselves. Because of the periodically changing values of N_S, at the same time the server also prevents the precalculation of solutions. For their part, by reselecting N_C, clients can create new puzzles within the lifetime of N_S and thus make roughly parallel requests. This, however, requires that the server caches and checks the nonces N_C for the successful solutions.

The general disadvantage of calculation-based client puzzles continues, however, to exist: even legitimate users have to perform the calculations. Particularly in mobile devices, this can mean higher energy consumption and longer waiting times. If this disadvantage is acceptable, client puzzles provide good protection against exhaustion of memory and computing resources.

18.3.3   Filtering, Partitioning and Redundancy

Exhaustion of communication bandwidth is very difficult to prevent

The measures previously presented relate mainly to resource destruction and resource exhaustion of computing power and memory. Protection against the exhaustion of communication resources is considerably more difficult to implement. The fundamental problem in the latter case is that the exhaustion generally occurs outside the victim's control. The communication link from ISP to server is therefore often overloaded and the filtering of attack packets would have to take place on the ISP's part. Even the connections between the ISPs may be affected in very large attacks.

Filtering of traffic by ISP and specialised providers

Very exposed operators of Internet services often have contracts with specialised ISPs which install filters in the event of attacks [Pri13]. In addition, there are also specific providers who pull the victim's traffic to themselves in the case of denial-of-service attacks by means of changes in the Internet routing, filter it and then forward the traffic that is now freed from attack traffic to the former victim. The success of these measures largely depends in each case on the quality of the filters. In simple attack tools, however, filtering is often easy because one can search for unusual recurring patterns in the packets, for example when the options set in TCP-SYN packets are not the options set by the popular operating systems. However, if it is possible for the attacker to simply simulate a legitimate user, this approach will reach its limits. One example is VPN traffic generated by the attacker that cannot be distinguished from real traffic by filters at external partners because the cryptographic keys are not known.

If the filtering of traffic proves inadequate, services can be designed redundantly so that a failure in one part of the network has no effect on the rest. In contrast to conventional redundant systems, it is extremely important in this case that in the event of failure due to denial-of-service the workload of the attacked system is not transferred to the rest. Otherwise, the attack on the remaining systems will be continued and they will also be affected by the attack. The majority of DNS root servers use such an approach, for example. They were frequently beset by denial-of-service attacks in the past and are now usually implemented via anycast [SPT06]. This means that there are a number of globally distributed servers with the same IP address. Packets to this destination are each forwarded to the next server. If a server fails due to denial-of-service attacks, the other servers carry on working for their respective region. At the same time, during distributed denial-of-service attacks, the load of the individual bots is spread, since in general they are also distributed globally. This method will also be addressed again in Section 20.3.

Redundant isolated services

18.3.4   IP Traceback*

All the outlined measures that can reduce the impact of bandwidth utilisation are very complex, however, and as a result only very few hosts in the Internet can provide them. Hence it is sensible to make the sources of bandwidth exhaustion attacks easier to identify and to contain the problem using reactive measures. In many cases it would be sufficient to prevent the forging of IP addresses, which would make it considerably easier to filter traffic and identify bots as well as attackers. Using forged IP addresses, however, can only be prevented by the attacker's provider. In the core of the Internet this is not possible for performance reasons. The filtering of incorrect IP addresses at the provider, so-called *ingress filtering*, has been recommended as best practice even in an RFC [FS00] for quite some time. However, it was shown in [BBH+09] that about 33% client computers are still able to specify any address as the sender and 77% of the remaining client machines are still able to use addresses from their subnet. The fundamental problem with ingress filtering is that the Internet service providers of the bots and attackers may have no real incentive to implement it consistently.

Filtering of forged IP addresses is inadequately implemented by providers

An alternative, which has at least been discussed in the scientific world, is to make packets traceable despite possible incorrect source addresses. The so-called *IP traceback mechanisms* can rely on the fact that core network routers are not compromised

in general and the routes through the network during the trace-
backs are usually rather stable, but it is essential that they take
into account a number of constraints:

- It must be assumed that attackers know the traceback mechanism.
- Attackers can generate arbitrary packets to disrupt the process, particularly packets such as the ones generated by the
  traceback system.
- In this case, the attacker-controlled systems can be located in
  various places on the Internet and operate in a coordinated
  fashion.
- The generated attack packets that lead to the denial-of-
  service attack may be rearranged on the way to the victim
  or may sometimes be lost.
- The number of packets that are generated may be extremely
  high.
- Resources that can be introduced by routers to support a
  traceback are very limited.
- In particular, the process must not give rise to any new vulnerabilities.

At the same time, traceback mechanisms should have the following
properties:

- As far as possible it should not be necessary to involve Internet service providers, as they may have no great interest in
  cooperation.
- The process should require as few packets as possible from
  attackers to be able to trace them, for example in the case of
  resource destruction attacks.
- A traceback should be possible even if it is only partially supported by the core network. Even if only a few ISPs or router
  manufacturers implement a traceback method, it should still
  be possible for these 'islands' to work together.
- As few resources as possible should be used – this relates particularly to processing power and memory requirements in the
  routers and the necessary network bandwidth.
- It should only be possible to bypass traceback measures with
  difficulty or not at all.
- The approach to traceability should be scalable, that is, it
  should also work in scenarios where very large numbers of

attackers or communication flows are present. Furthermore, the configuration effort must not increase significantly in large networks.

To be able to trace packets, there are two possible approaches in principle. First, packets can be logged on the way through the Internet. In the event of an attack, requests to databases can then be used to determine which route the packet was passed along. With a continuous attack flow, it is also possible to search for similar packets without any individual packets being stored. Second, the path taken by packets can be made measurable for the destination node. Both options are explained below in more detail with some examples.

Logging of Packets in Gateway Systems

It would be a very naïve approach to cache traffic in routers over a period of time within which the routers can be asked whether they have forwarded a certain packet. However, at many hundreds of gigabits per second, the network throughput of routers is so high that traffic cannot be cached even for a few seconds. Even if a continuous attack flow is present, path reconstruction may be time-consuming as the path must be traced from router to router.

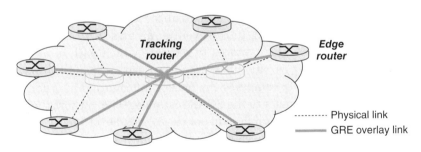

Figure 18.4

Centertrack: concentration of DoS traffic on a router for better traceability

Beyond this, there is another technical problem: many inexpensive routers simply do not have the ability to examine data flows in the CPU. In the *centertrack* method [Sto00] shown in Figure 18.4, it is therefore proposed to redirect the traffic to a victim through GRE tunnels to a powerful core network router, the so-called *tracking router*. It is easier then to analyse centrally where the suspicious traffic originates from. In addition, the route to the attacker has fewer intermediate stations due to the GRE tunnel, so the path is more easily reconstructed. For scalability reasons, there should be recourse to a whole network of tracker systems. Despite

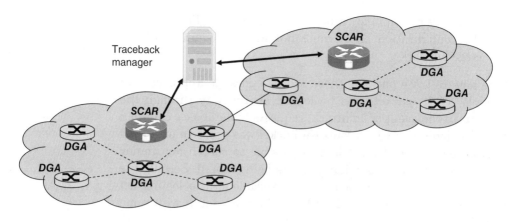

these optimisations, the method only works within a single provider network and for a limited amount of attack traffic as forwarding through tunnels may even worsen the overload situation. For large providers, the configuration effort cannot be disregarded either. The method is also not suitable for tracing sporadic attack packets because traffic cannot be recorded proactively for reasons of speed.

To address this problem, a complex method called the Source Path Identification Engine (SPIE) is proposed in [SPS$^+$02] for proactively logging packets. As shown in Figure 18.5, packets from routers are logged, and in this context they are referred to as Data Generation Agents (DGA). The information obtained is compressed and forwarded to decentralised SPIE Collection and Reduction Agents (SCAR). In the event of an attack, it is possible by querying the SCAR instances to recreate which path a packet has taken. To what extent this method can work depends on how much it is possible to compress the packet information in order to justify proactive transfer to the SCAR instances. The authors therefore use only the immutable fields of the IP header (16 bytes) and the first 8 bytes of the packet. For the signature of each packet, it is noted in a hash table with multiple hash functions, a so-called Bloom filter, that this packet has passed the DGA. This can drastically reduce the effort for storage and transmission of the packet

Collection of information. For large core network routers, however, it remains
traceback data doubtful whether traffic can be logged for more than a few mil-
in Bloom filters liseconds. Caching is only useful if attacks which do not take place periodically can be traced. Thus, it would have to be possible to bridge at least the time for manual detection of an attack, identification of the attack packet and triggering of the traceback.

Reconstruction of Network Paths by the Receiver

As an alternative to the approaches presented, mechanisms could be developed for end systems to trace packets without querying service providers.

A method documented in [BC00] manages this task even without additional protocol interfaces. To do this, in the case of overloading due to attack traffic, the victim should also generate a high traffic load which, forwarded via reflectors, systematically produces additional overload situations at various places on the Internet. If the intensity of the attack traffic decreases, it is the authors' belief that the site of the new overload is on the path to the attacker. However, creating new overload situations is problematic, especially if the method were to be used widely and the administrators of the artificially overloaded systems were then also to try to locate the cause for the further overload. Furthermore, disrupting routers in the backbone is much more difficult than overloading end systems due to the bandwidth required.

Controlled flooding of the Internet

A better way to make paths reconstructable is represented by messages regularly sent by routers to the destination. It was proposed in [BLT03], for example, that routers should randomly announce their identity to the packet destination approximately every 20,000 packets in an ICMP message. These so-called *ITRACE* messages contain not only the header of the trigger packet and the address of the router but also time stamps and, if available, information about the router's affected network interfaces. The TTL field of each ITRACE is set to 255 to estimate the receiver's distance from the trigger router. Since this is the maximum value of the field and the value in each subsequent gateway system is necessarily reduced, an attacker can only forge ITRACE messages to a limited extent. In particular, no ITRACE messages can be forged for routers that are closer to the destination than the attacker is. If the attacker controls systems in the vicinity of the victim, traceability could be disrupted by generated ITRACE messages. Therefore, an authentication mechanism is provided for ITRACE messages which, similarly to the TESLA method that was presented in Section 8.3.3, is based on a signed later disclosure of symmetrical keys. A disadvantage of the method is that additional traffic is generated and, due to the low probability of packet generation, tracing is only successful in long-lived communication flows.

In ITRACE, router information is probabilistically sent to the destinations of IP packets in the network

In addition to the ability to send separate messages for the traceback, it is also possible to integrate them directly into the IP

Figure 18.6

Embedding of the traceback in- formation in IPv4 packets

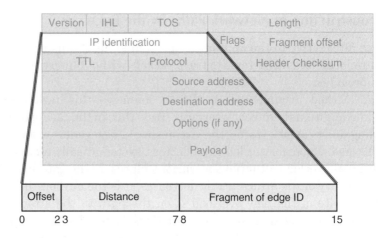

packets [SWK⁺01]. In the simplest case this is done by recording the IP addresses of each router passed in an IP option field. However, the packet size rises slightly in each hop, and gradually packets would possibly have to be fragmented several times. Alternatively, it is suggested that only one router is noted and with a certain amount of probability the following routers will overwrite the IP address entered with their own IP address. Since in this case the packet size is also increased in the first router at least, it may still be necessary to carry out fragmentation as appropriate. It is therefore proposed in the article to encode the traceback information in the identification field of IPv4 packets. As outlined in Figure 18.6, edge numbers — essentially with XOR-linked IP addresses of neighbouring routers — and hop information are embedded. Because of the short length of the identification field of only 16 bits, the edge numbers are fragmented and distributed across several packets. The coding has no effect on the majority of IP packets on the Internet because it is only used for the reassembly of fragments and modern Internet applications try to avoid fragmentation anyway. If IP fragments are nevertheless transferred, an ITRACE-like behaviour must be accessed in the process and additional ICMP packets will be generated. Overall, the process must be regarded as very complex, especially if it is necessary to detect the forged packets of attackers or take different transport pathways into consideration in the receiver. Furthermore, it is questionable whether the encoding of edge numbers can be reversed if routers have several different IP addresses, which is the normal case.

Conclusion Regarding IP Traceback

Unfortunately, the various methods for making IP packets traceable all have significant weaknesses. Despite relatively complex measures, they scale relatively poorly if service providers are involved, such as the barely adequate reduction by Bloom filters in SPIE. Methods which probabilistically mark or insert packets seem to be a better alternative. However, these are not implemented and they only work well if attack flows are very long-lasting. In addition, open questions remain during authentication of the router addresses sent. Thus, even for the simplest case — denial-of-service attacks which exhaust the bandwidth — there is often no automated way of tracing the attack traffic.

18.4 Summary

In our modern knowledge-based society, the constant availability of data networks is becoming increasingly important and is also taken more and more for granted. As described in this chapter, at the same time we are putting ourselves in a fragile dependency, as effective denial-of-service attacks can be carried out relatively easily. The basic problem here is the very open design of IP networks that permits denial-of-service attacks to be carried out that are hard to combat using generally applicable solutions and prove to be very difficult to trace.

Denial-of-service attacks are a significant threat to today's IP networks

Nevertheless, standard methods can be used to at least limit the potential for successful attacks and to protect against many kinds of denial-of-service attacks. This includes, for example, the hardening of software against vulnerabilities, the use of firewalls and network monitoring on the part of administrators. During the development of network protocols, it is important from the outset to be aware of possible utilisation of the protocol behaviour for denial-of-service attacks. Stateless protocols, cookie mechanisms, client puzzles and cryptographic measures for authentication can completely eliminate the risk of overloading the memory or computing resources if used carefully.

In the future, the demand for securely-designed protocols will continue to increase, since IP is also being used increasingly in traditional telephone and mobile networks. Similar developments can also be observed in the field of industrial and home automation. Freely programmable terminal devices, such as smartphones and tablet computers, will also be involved in botnets in the future and may therefore also be able to disrupt the ordinary telephone network. If new software defined radios catch on, completely new developments could also become possible due to targeted interference with radio communications. In addition, attackers will continue to refine their approach to conventional denial-of-service attacks and, for example, will imitate legitimate user behaviour more accurately, so that the filtering of requests becomes more complicated.

18.5   Supplemental Reading

[ANL01]   AURA, T.; NIKANDER, P.; LEIWO, Jussipekka: DOS-Resistant Authentication With Client Puzzles. In: *Security Protocols,* Springer-Verlag, 2001, p. 170–177

[BC00]   BURCH, H.; CHESWICK, B.: Tracing Anonymous Packets to Their Approximate Source. In: *Proceedings of the 14th Conference on Large Installation System Administration Conference (LISA),* 2000, p. 319–327

[BLT03]   BELLOVIN, S.; LEECH, M.; TAYLOR, T.: *ICMP Traceback Messages.* 2003. – IETF, Status: Expired Internet-Draft, https://tools.ietf.org/html/draft-ietf-itrace-04

[HR06]   HANDLEY, M.; RESCORLA, E.: *Internet Denial-of-Service Considerations.* 2006. – RFC 4732, IETF, Status: Informational, https://tools.ietf.org/html/rfc4732

[RAW+13]   ROSSOW, C.; ANDRIESSE, D.; WERNER, T.; STONE-GROSS, B.; PLOHMANN, D.; DIETRICH, C. J.; BOS, H.: SoK: P2PWNED – Modeling and Evaluating the Resilience of Peer-to-Peer Botnets. In: *IEEE Symposium on Security and Privacy (SP),* 2013, p. 97–111

[SPS+02]   SNOEREN, A. C.; PARTRIDGE, C.; SANCHEZ, L. A.; JONES, C. E.; TCHAKOUNTIO, F.; SCHWARTZ, B.; KENT, S. T.; STRAYER, W. T.: Single-Packet IP Traceback. In: *IEEE/ACM Transactions on Networking* 10 (2002), no. 6, p. 721–734

[Sto00]   STONE, R.: Centertrack: An IP Overlay Network for Tracking DoS Floods. In: *Proceedings of the 9th Conference on USENIX Security Symposium,* 2000

[SWK⁺01] SAVAGE, S.; WETHERALL, D.; KARLIN, A.; ANDERSON, T.: Network Support for IP Traceback. In: *IEEE/ACM Transactions on Networking* 9 (2001), no. 3, p. 226–237

18.6 Questions

1. What qualitatively distinguishes bandwidth exhaustion denial-of-service attacks from CPU or memory exhaustion attacks?
2. Explain how an amplification attack can be carried out by downloading large files from a server. Take into account that TCP acknowledgement packets can also be sent 'blind', i.e. without having received the actual packet.
3. Why do filters fail during bandwidth exhaustion attacks on VPN?
4. How high is the probability of establishing a TCP connection with forged sender addresses if TCP-SYN cookies are used?
5. Why must a protocol be suitable for a stateless design? Which state information has to be kept in almost every case in the server?
6. What problems arise during IP traceback due to controlled flooding?
7. Would IP traceback help in containing resource-destroying attacks, such as a Ping of Death?

19 Routing Security

Automatic determination of paths for data packets is a basic service in computer networks. This so-called *routing* generally takes place in IP networks by means of distributed algorithms. In this context, a distinction is essentially made between *distance-vector* and *link-state* protocols. The former are characterised in that routers notify each other about destinations that they can reach and the costs associated with this. The routers, if necessary, also notify their other neighbours about route changes, and subsequently send their packets to the destination via the neighbour with the lowest path costs. Examples of distance-vector protocols are the Routing Information Protocol (RIP) and the proprietary Interior Gateway Routing Protocol (IGRP). With link-state protocols on the other hand, routers distribute the link cost descriptions in the entire network by means of flooding. Consequently, every router knows the entire network and can calculate the shortest paths through the network with the help of Dijkstra's algorithm. The most prominent representative of the link-state family is the Open Shortest Path First Protocol (OSPF).

Overview of routing with Interior Gateway Protocols

All the routing protocols mentioned so far have one thing in common: they are *Interior Gateway Protocols*, which means that they are only used inside an autonomous system of the service provider (see Figure 19.1). Between IP networks that are subject to different administrative authorities, the Border Gateway Protocol (BGP) is the de facto standard routing protocol. BGP is a path-vector protocol, which means that it essentially behaves like a distance-vector protocol, but complete paths to the individual destinations are exchanged with neighbours and not just the path costs. This allows for a prevention of routing loops.

BGP is the predominant routing protocol between providers

Security in Fixed and Wireless Networks, Second Edition.
Guenter Schaefer and Michael Rossberg.
Copyright © 2014 by dpunkt.verlag GmbH, Heidelberg, Germany.
Title of the German original: Netzsicherheit   ISBN 978-3-86490-115-7
Translation Copyright © 2016 by John Wiley & Sons, Ltd., All rights reserved

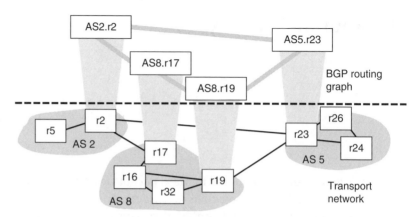

*Protection of
BGP routers*

For security reasons, routers are usually situated in physically protected locations and are only operated by trained staff. The threat situation in respect of attacks on routing protocols inside organisations is estimated to be low. The situation throughout the Internet is more difficult as here several thousand different organisations exchange routing information among each other with the help of BGP. Essentially threats can be differentiated as follows [BMY06]:

*General distribution
of BGP attacks*

- **Source of an attack:** An attack on a routing protocol may take place on the link between two routers, for instance by modifying exchanged packets. Alternatively, an attacker may compromise one or several routers or add routers to the system without authorisation.
- **Extent of an attack:** Depending on the structure of the network and the attacker's position and procedure, it may be only individual routers, specific network areas or the entire Internet that is affected.
- **Consequence of an attack:** The information regarding how computer networks are constructed in detail is usually confidential and therefore even discovering routing information can be a problem. Furthermore, routers may be deceived by messages that are not authentic, with the result that the normal routing operations are either disrupted or the attacker is enabled to control traffic, for instance by gaining access to traffic that would not normally be directed through it.
- **Duration of the consequences of an attack:** The consequences may only exist at the time of the attack or they may last until the network stabilises. With BGP — because of the complex policies with which routes are forwarded or held

back — it is even theoretically possible that a manual intervention will be necessary for convergence.

From a network point of view, the following basic threats exist in detail with regard to availability:

Breakdown of denial-of-service attacks on BGP routing

- **Congestion:** Because of re-routing of traffic, congested situations may occur in parts of the network with the result that packets sometimes get lost.
- **Black hole attacks:** If an attacker causes packets to be forwarded to a router that has no valid route to the destination, the packets will be dropped.
- **Routing loops:** If an attacker can arrange that two or more routers forward traffic to one destination circularly over each other then, on one hand, a congestion situation occurs for other packets that have identical path segments and, on the other hand, packets to the destination are dropped after reaching the maximum number of hops.
- **Logical network partitioning:** An attacker may, under certain circumstances, manipulate parts of the network in such a way that it appears that there is no valid path to the rest of the network. In this case, packets cannot reach the relevant subnetwork.
- **Frequent routing changes:** Paths through the network can be constantly changed by means of frequent routing changes and thus cause fluctuations in the delay and reorder packets for the end user.
- **Instabilities during convergence of the routing:** Because of the attacker's manipulations, the routing protocol may, under certain circumstances, be barred from a convergence and an adaptation of the paths concerned may be prevented.
- **Overload due to the routing protocol:** Because of changes in the routing, on one hand a significant bandwidth may be required for the routing protocol itself and, on the other hand, the routers may be loaded to such an extent that they can only respond very slowly to legitimate changes. In this context, the term *BGP update storm* is used.

Alongside this, attackers can also manipulate routing to redirect traffic to themselves. In this way, the traffic that would otherwise be inaccessible can be monitored or manipulated by them. The following two threats are often referred to in this context:

BGP attacks aimed at re-routing traffic

- **Sinkhole attack:** If attackers, by giving bogus addresses or metrics, for example, draw more traffic to themselves than would normally be the case, this is generally referred to as a sinkhole attack.
- **Wormhole attack:** It may be possible under certain circumstances for attackers to simulate a connection between distant routers that does not actually exist, for instance by forwarding traffic through tunnels. Thus, more traffic is forwarded via the routers as the connection is perceived as a shortcut between the various network areas.

Effect on end systems From the point of view of the end systems concerned, the effects of these global threats appear somewhat different:

- **Delay and jitter:** Delay and jitter of the transmitted packets increase if the traffic takes longer or overloaded paths to certain destinations. The attacker can also forward packets via compromised systems and delay them there artificially. This type of attack, sometimes referred to by the name *Jellyfish*, is very difficult to detect and reduces the throughput rate significantly in some cases.
- **Unavailability:** Packets may get lost under certain circumstances because parts of the network believe that they cannot reach the destination or because a routing loop exists.
- **Monitoring of traffic:** The traffic between two parties may possibly be monitored although the attacker is not on a shortest path between two communication partners. Even if encryption methods are used, it is usually possible for the attacker to carry out a traffic flow analysis and determine which parties are communicating, when and with what intensity. It may even be possible to reconstruct the application based on packet size and communication patterns.
- **Controlled delivery:** Attackers may be able to specifically discard individual packets. In addition, even if cryptographic protection takes place, it is often also possible for identification and targeted suppression to take place, based for instance on the application and depending on the communication pattern. This form of attack is described in the literature as a *grey hole attack*.

The large number of threats and their complexity illustrate the challenges faced when protecting a routing infrastructure. Compared to securing the transmission, with the help of IPsec for example, the basic problem here is that it is not only necessary to deal with attackers between end systems, but the aim is also to achieve a consensus between routers, with some routers possibly being compromised. The development of security measures is focused particularly on BGP as the protocol has a global influence and, due to the large number of organisations involved, it is reasonable to expect the majority of attacks for it.

Attacks on BGP are rarely documented as such and are more often passed off as 'misconfigurations'. In 2013, however, it was possible to reconstruct an apparent man-in-the-middle attack in a detailed manner [Cow13]. In this case, over a period of several months, the White Russian provider GlobalOneBel repeatedly used BGP to announce 1500 address blocks at various intervals for which it actually had no authorisation. As a result, the corresponding traffic was attracted by the GlobalOneBels provider in Moscow and routed to it. After 'inspection', the traffic of GlobalOneBel was forwarded to a different provider in Frankfurt/Main that had not taken over the bogus routes and had delivered the traffic to the original destination. As the changes are usually only temporary and hard to reconstruct even using traceroutes, such attacks are very difficult to detect and also difficult to prevent as the following sections will illustrate.

BGP attack by GlobalOneBel 2013

19.1   Cryptographic Protection of BGP

BGP routers communicate with each other via TCP connections on port 179. As BGP dispenses with mutual authentication, it is conceivable that attackers will simply connect to a router and purport to be a router that announces its own routes to possible destinations. In the simplest case, it is possible to use the so-called *BGP TTL Security Hack* [GHM03] to prevent this. As most BGP routers are connected without further intermediate routers, it is possible to establish that BGP connections are only established to routers that are adjacent. To do this, all routers are configured so that they send packets with the TTL of 255 and do not accept packets that possess a TTL of 254 or less. Depending on the operating system architecture, a value of 254 must also be allowed if the operating system decrements the TTL before the packet is passed onto the application process. As attackers cannot generate any packets with a higher TTL and the value is necessarily reduced in every gateway system, they must therefore control a system in the immediate vicinity of the router to be able to connect themselves at all.

Many attacks are prevented by filtering packets that obviously do not originate from neighbours

With the *Generalized TTL Security Mechanism* [GHM$^+$07] there exists a further development of the approach in which lower TTL values are also essentially accepted for some sources if the administrator explicitly configures this and considers it to be secure. Moreover, the same process is standardised for the hop limit field for analogous use of the process under IPv6.

19.1.1   Authentication of Data Transmission

BGP sessions are frequently protected by cryptographic check values in the TCP

Naturally, checking of the TTL can only offer limited protection as attackers who have access to the router's local network or who can even carry out man-in-the-middle attacks continue to be able to announce any routes. For this reason, cryptographic safeguarding of the TCP connections has been implemented at BGP for some time by providing TCP packets with a cryptographic checksum. The so-called *TCP-MD5 Signature Option* [Hef98] uses statically defined passwords between the parties to calculate a hash value including the actual payload and the protocol fields of the TCP segments, and therefore protect packets against unidentified modification. The checksum is transmitted with every packet as a TCP option field in its full length of 16 bytes. Among other things, the aim of directly protecting the TCP protocol is to prevent attackers from using TCP reset packets to disrupt existing BGP connections and thus to trigger routing instabilities. However, there are some weak spots in this. On the one hand, the protocol is no longer reasonable due to being fixed to the usage of MD5 and, on the other hand, replay protection is only guaranteed on the basis of the TCP sequence numbers. Thus, with the *TCP Authentication Option*, a successor [TMB10] was developed that eliminates these drawbacks. Compared to protection at network level by IPsec (see Chapter 12), however, this option also offers less security and flexibility, especially as the key material used is relatively static and it is not possible to carry out any regular updates automatically. IPsec has dynamically negotiated security associations, but for large routers with a high number of neighbours the drawback is that a considerable volume of asymmetrical cryptographic operations have to be carried out after a possible reboot, and this therefore increases the convergence time significantly. For this reason one has to weigh up whether full protection by IPsec for safeguarding the BGP connections is preferable to the weaker protection of the TCP Authentication Option.

IPsec may lead to performance bottlenecks on central BGP routers

In spite of the options outlined for making BGP routers inaccessible for uninvolved third parties, it has been shown that some of them can nevertheless be contacted from outside [CKV11]. Not least for this reason it must be assumed that attackers are able to participate in BGP routing and also to influence it using bogus information. Proceeding against such internal attacks is very complicated and the following two services have to be considered in detail:

Some BGP routers are accessible in spite of the recommended security measures

- Secure authentication of the party that has initially sent the BGP UPDATE is generally referred to as *Secure Origin Authentication (SOA)* and for its part comprises three subitems:
  - **Verification of the ownership of IP addresses:** It must be possible to check whether a subnetwork of the Internet – a so-called *Autonomous System* (AS) – is responsible for an IP address range. Only in this case may routers of the AS represent these IP address ranges towards other routers.
  - **Verification of the ownership of AS numbers:** As BGP IP address ranges link to the number which identifies the original AS, routers must be able to check whether and to whom the specified AS numbers were assigned.
  - **Authentication of routers:** When communicating with other routers, it must additionally be possible to check whether they may represent a specific AS in BGP. This implies that it must be possible to verify which AS numbers and IP addresses they are responsible for.
- Secure authorisation of the paths used in BGP messages consists of two essential tasks:
  - **Authorising the announcement of routes:** As not only is knowledge of adjacent routers recorded in a routing protocol, but it is also possible to transitively deduce which paths exist through the network, for secure routing it must be possible to check whether an announced route exists and may also be used. In particular, it should not be possible for attackers to artificially reduce the cost of individual routes in order to pull additional traffic to them in this way.
  - **Authorisation of the withdrawal of routes:** The withdrawal of routes must also be protected in a similar way to the announcement of routes, as attackers could

otherwise withdraw routes in order to make their own routes more attractive.

19.1.2 The Secure Border Gateway Protocol

The S-BGP extension can protect BGP by the systematic use of cryptography

The crucial problems that arise due to the verification of routing messages can be solved by the systematic use of asymmetrical cryptography. This is shown by the BGP expansion S-BGP [LMS03]. Mandatory protection of all BGP connections by IPsec is an important prerequisite to ensure a basic level of security, such that communication is performed exclusively to the determined neighbours. Subsequently, all BGP UPDATE messages exchanged are checked with regard to their legitimacy. So-called *Attestations* are used for this, which provide evidence of the entitlement to represent certain addresses and AS numbers, but also to announce specific routes with the help of certificates. In addition, as is always necessary for the secure use of certificates, Certificate Revocation Lists (CRLs) must be used to check whether a certificate that is used might have been revoked.

Construction of certification hierarchies for verification of the ownership of IP addresses and AS number

To demonstrate the ownership of AS numbers and IP addresses, S-BGP provides for the construction of two certification hierarchies, each of which comes from a root certificate of the Internet Assigned Numbers Authority (IANA). In the following levels, subsets of the relevant address ranges are assigned to issuing bodies, such as RIPE NCC, through to the 'owners' of the IP address range or the AS number. The address ranges in this case are each directly embedded in the certificates in X.509 extensions [LKS04] and are checked for consistency during verification of the certificate chain. In particular, the IP addresses or AS numbers listed must each be a subset of the IP addresses or AS numbers of the higher level certificate. The certificates relating to the ownership of AS numbers and IP address ranges may then be used to confirm to an AS, by means of a digital signature, that it may represent these addresses in the BGP routing. This confirmation is referred to in the S-BGP *address attestation*. If the AS operator provides every router with a certificate which identifies it as a legitimate router of the AS, it is possible with the help of a signature of the router and all relevant certificates to reconstruct that this router is responsible for certain IP addresses and routes may terminate there. The security service provided is thus the *secure origin authentication*.

Checking of routes by route attestations

For verifying the propagated routes, *route attestations* are additionally introduced by S-BGP. As illustrated in Figure 19.2, the last router of an AS inserts a signature for this purpose and proves with this that it has received the UPDATE message from

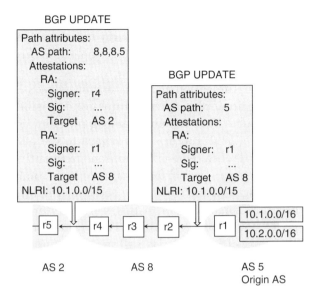

BGP UPDATE

| Path attributes: |
| AS path: 8,8,8,5 |
| Attestations: |
| RA: |
| Signer: r4 |
| Sig: ... |
| Target   AS 2 |
| RA: |
| Signer: r1 |
| Sig: ... |
| Target   AS 8 |
| NLRI: 10.1.0.0/15 |

BGP UPDATE

| Path attributes: |
| AS path: 5 |
| Attestations: |
| RA: |
| Signer: r1 |
| Sig: ... |
| Target   AS 8 |
| NLRI: 10.1.0.0/15 |

r5 ← r4 ← r3 ← r2 ← r1   10.1.0.0/16   10.2.0.0/16

AS 2   AS 8   AS 5
                                Origin AS

Figure 19.2
Extension of BGP
UPDATE messages by
route attestations

the previous AS and is ready to forward traffic on this route. The first router of an AS must check in each case whether all route attestations are valid and that the original AS possesses the entitlement, based on the address attestations, to represent the address block listed in the Network Layer Reachability Information (NLRI). To do this, the router requires and checks in detail:

- an address attestation from every organisation that owns IP addresses in the address block named in the NLRI;
- a confirmation certificate from each of these organisations that the original AS may currently use the address attestation;
- a routing attestation for every AS on the path;
- a certificate with which the relevant AS confirms the identity of the issuing router on the path;
- the relevant CRLs of all certificates involved in order to rule out that a certificate in the hierarchy has been revoked.

However, as a result of the extensive security measures, not only does the size of the UPDATE messages increase rapidly due to the routing attestations, but so does the computing and communication effort involved in verifying the certificates and attestations. S-BGP therefore provides for a large number of optimisation measures. On one hand, many decisions can be stored temporarily, for example because many routes repeatedly use identical path segments. On the other hand, address attestations, certificate databases and CRLs are supposed to be held in replicated servers in the relevant AS so that the routers do not necessarily have to store them

S-BGP provides for
extensive measures
to reduce the effort
involved in the routers

themselves. These servers can also verify the information held so that the routers merely have to carry out a check on the route attestations. In this case, the mentioned replicated servers have to be trusted as well.

The effort for the verifications in S-BGP has led to doubts about practicability

Despite the optimisation measures envisaged by S-BGP and the development of numerous demonstrators and feasibility studies, considerable doubts have remained among the administrators and manufacturers of BGP routers with regard to the effort involved in the S-BGP approach. One of the reasons frequently cited is the reduced convergence speed if, for instance, a high number of routes have to be changed at the same time because of failures. Furthermore, there are some routers in the present Internet that have thousands of neighbouring routers. They would be very heavily loaded by the use of S-BGP despite all the optimisations. Construction of the necessary certification hierarchies is another problem. Although here S-BGP suggests that IANA takes this over, whether this organisation, which is mainly under US control, should carry out such tasks was and is the subject of controversial discussions.

S-BGP can be further optimised by generating signatures via several messages

Despite S-BGP not being widely accepted and its complexity, it offers the most comprehensive protection against routing attacks on BGP. Beyond this there are other possibilities for increasing the efficiency of S-BGP [NSZ03]. In the approach known as *Signature Amortisation Across Peers*, every router arranges its neighbours in a permutation that it announces to them. If a BGP UPDATE message then has to be forwarded, it is no longer signed and forwarded individually for each child. Instead, a bit vector is inserted into the message in which each bit represents a neighbour according to the permutation. The bits that represent neighbours to receive the message are set and a single signature is created. Because of the bit vector, it is possible to send the same route attestation to all relevant neighbours and yet to check cryptographically which destinations the message was determined for. It is additionally suggested that the RSA algorithm be used instead of the DSA as a signature algorithm for route attestations. When using suitable exponents in the public key that are characterised by very few set bits, for example 65,537, signatures can be verified at a higher speed. As signatures are checked more frequently than generated by the Signature Amortisation Across Peers approach, this reduces the convergence time of S-BGP.

An approach known as Signature Amortisation Across Buffers was introduced at the same time as and complementary to Signature Amortisation Across Peers. In this case a different property of the BGP routing was exploited. UPDATE messages are usually

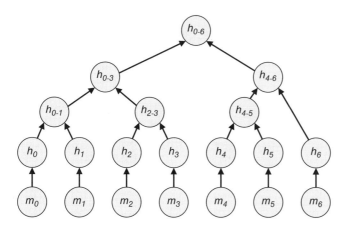

Figure 19.3
Example of a Merkle Hash Tree over seven messages $m_0, \ldots, m_6$. Every parent node is the hash value of its child nodes. The signature takes place via the root node.

sent in bulk because changes in the network generally apply to many paths simultaneously and, for convergence reasons, are only propagated after a *Minimum Route Advertisement Interval* (MRAI) has expired. As a result, UPDATE messages could also be signed and verified in bulk. To be able to forward messages only to specific neighbours, there is no creation of a single hash over all the messages but rather a so-called *Merkle Hash Tree* is constructed. Figure 19.3 shows an example for the aggregated signature of seven messages. If, for example, a neighbour should only receive message m_3, then in addition to the message and the signature it is also sent the hash values h_{0-1}, h_2, h_{4-6}. With these it can reconstruct h_{0-6} and check the signature. By using the tree structure, with n messages, it is always only necessary to include $\mathcal{O}(\log n)$ hash values for verification.

With Merkle Hash Trees, several messages can be signed in a block and efficiently verified independently of each other.

19.1.3   The Secure Origin Border Gateway Protocol

A number of alternative methods have been developed due to the reservations regarding S-BGP. The *Secure Origin BGP Protocol* (soBGP) [Whi06a, Whi06b, Ng04] has probably attracted the most attention. Compared to S-BGP, the main aim here was to dispense with a centralised certificate hierarchy. Although certificates are used in soBGP, for example the so-called *AuthCerts* and *EntityCerts*, which provide the approximate function of S-BGP address attestations and AS certificates, they are not issued by a PKI but are signed by 'adjacent' providers. As a result of transitive trust in the signed relationships, a structure is generated that is comparable to the *Web of Trust* in e-mail coding (see also

Central PKI is replaced by Web of Trust

Figure 19.4

Trust relationships between providers in soBGP. Unbroken lines symbolise direct trust and dashed lines indirect trust.

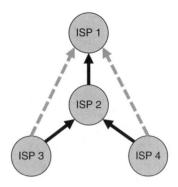

Figure 19.4). The soBGP approach envisages limiting certificate chains to a maximum depth freely configurable by each provider.

soBGP uses a new SECURITY message type

Certificates, signatures and revocation information are exchanged in soBGP by means of the newly introduced SECURITY message type. On the one hand, UPDATE messages are not changed as a result and — unlike S-BGP — soBGP can be introduced incrementally. On the other hand, no functioning routing is required in order to access a PKI and this increases the robustness of the approach. The *ASPolicycerts*, which are intended to verify paths instead of the route attestations, are another way in which soBGP differs from S-BGP. In these certificates an AS can securely publish direct connections to other ASes and mark whether these ASes are permitted to forward the traffic of the publishing AS. If a provider wants to keep its peering information secret in some cases at least, then in soBGP distinct ASPolicycerts are propagated to different neighbour nodes. These certificates are intended to check whether two adjacent ASes in a route are actually adjacent at all in the BGP topology. As a result, however, policies specified by providers for path-specific withholding of routing information are not recorded, which means that the ASPolicycerts do not offer the same security as route attestations in S-BGP. It is advantageous, however, that the peering information rarely changes, leading to less verification effort.

19.1.4   Interdomain Route Validation

IRV uses servers to verify BGP routes

At approximately the same time as soBGP, the proposal was developed to delegate the verification tasks to specific servers inside each AS. As a result, this [GAG⁺03] method, referred to as *Interdomain Route Validation (IRV)*, does not add to the load of BGP routers; they simply reconcile information gained from the BGP with a local server. As illustrated in Figure 19.5, the IRV servers for

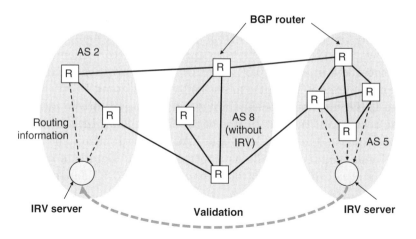

Figure 19.5
Interdomain Route
Validation with
external servers

their part contact the IRV servers of other ASes via cryptographically secured connections in order to verify the routes. While the
advantage of IRV is that it can be introduced incrementally, the
server-based approach suffers from some inherent problems. If, for
instance, routes to an AS are dropped because the IRV server dis-
covers discrepancies, then it may no longer be possible to reach
the remote IRV server in order to resolve these discrepancies again
later. In addition, the IRV server represents a central point of failure with respect to the relevant AS.

19.1.5   BGPSEC and the Resource Public Key Infrastructure

At present the IETF Working Group for Secure Inter-Domain Routing (SIDR), including the developers of S-BGP, is striving towards
comprehensive standardisation of a cryptographic approach to safeguarding BGP. The *Resource Public Key Infrastructure (RPKI)*
[LK12] and the *BGPSEC* protocol [LT13] were recently adopted
as RFCs or are still in the standardisation process. Both components when combined will offer approximately the same services as
S-BGP although a few design weaknesses have been avoided and
attention has been paid to separating the verification of the original
AS and path. The RPKI is essentially used for secure origin authentication and thus provides the same security properties as the
address attestations in S-BGP or to a lesser extent the EntityCerts
in soBGP. The RPKI is technically a database that is mirrored and
synchronised between servers. BGP routers or local servers which
take over the verification for the BGP routers can cache information from the database via the Resource Public Key Infrastructure

*The RPKI is an
infrastructure with
which the IP address
prefixes and AS
numbers can be
verified*

to Router Protocol (RPKI-RTR) [BA13]. Forced verification is not yet possible despite support from the major router manufacturers, as fewer than 5% of the IP address prefixes have corresponding certificates and in around 0.5% of all IP address prefixes certified information and BGP routes are actually inconsistent. Furthermore, the IANA has not published any valid root certificate so far, with the result that the certificates of the five regional Internet registries, such as the RIPE NCC and LACNIC, each have to be added and managed individually as a root certificate. Details of the current status can be found, for example, in the RPKI dashboard at `http://rpki.surfnet.nl`.

BGPSEC allows path validation based on RPKI information

For validating paths, the BGPSEC protocol [LT13, Lep13] is proposed. Its use can be negotiated when opening a BGP session. The signatures are distributed via BGP UPDATE messages in a non-transitive attribute so that BGP routers which do not support any BGPSEC are not given these attributes. The content of the attribute essentially equates to the data of a route attestation in S-BGP. Thus, the effort to be anticipated for generating and verifying BGPSEC-secured messages corresponds approximately to that of S-BGP and only the future will show whether BGPSEC will find widespread adoption.

19.2   Identification of Routing Anomalies*

Consistency checking of routes as complementary protection

In addition to elaborate cryptographic protection of BGP, it is often possible to increase the security of the routing process significantly by using simple consistency checks and filtering mechanisms. To some extent such approaches should also be considered as complementary to cryptographic approaches since they cannot offer any protection against a number of identified threats, such as frequent route changes, delaying the convergence of routing or overload due to routing messages. On the contrary, as a result of the elaborate checking and forwarding of secured BGP messages the global routing infrastructure will become even more susceptible to overload-based denial-of-service attacks.

BGP messages from stubs can easily be filtered

In the simplest case, filtering already takes place in *stub ASes*. These are ASes that do not forward any traffic and merely send their own traffic via one or more upstream providers. The providers can filter for both AS properties and the IP address prefixes announced, and can thus severely limit the attackers' opportunities as only routers in transit networks have unchecked access to the BGP infrastructure.

It is extremely time-consuming to enforce filters in the transit areas and this is barely achievable manually. Therefore, various proposals have been developed for automating this task. One option is to query the *whois* databases, which are provided by the Internet registries for IP addresses and AS numbers, to examine the details of the original AS. They can be queried automatically, for example via the Routing Policy Specification Language (RPSL) [AVG+99] or the Routing Policy Specification Language next generation (RPSLng) [BDP+05], and contain information regarding to whom AS numbers and IP address prefixes belong. Unlike the RPKI, however, this database is not cryptographically secured and is also not intended for safeguarding BGP. As a result, the entries are frequently not up to date and accurate enough to implement filters directly.

Filtering of routes in transit networks cannot be carried out manually with justifiable effort

19.2.1 Geographic Filtering

The whois databases can be used for filtering illegitimate routes. It is suggested in [KMR+03] that these databases can be used to extract the addresses of contacts for the AS in order to make a statement about the relevant geographical position of the AS. In addition, information from so-called *Looking Glass Servers*, which make their respective view of the BGP infrastructure freely accessible on the Internet, are used to create an AS graph. This can be used in turn to distinguish between a core network area and peripheral areas. As illustrated in Figure 19.6, routes can then be filtered if they cross the core network area more than once. A different configuration that favours an attack is routes which leave a geographical area — a so-called *cluster* — and lead to a different geographical cluster. The authors propose selecting a diameter of 300 km for clusters, that is to say a distance that is typically only bridged by transit networks. Using this approach, it is possible to find routes for which a compromised AS specifies short paths to a destination, for example.

Extraction of addresses from whois databases

The suggested approach is comparatively easy to implement and to some extent can considerably increase the routing's security as routes are also checked when no direct proximity to the attacker exists. However, the manner in which the geographical data are determined requires relatively extensive processing. It is probable that manual corrections will be necessary in this case to eliminate obvious errors in the whois databases and to define exceptions to the 300 km rule. In addition, a static distinction is drawn between the core and peripheral areas of the network. Although dynamic

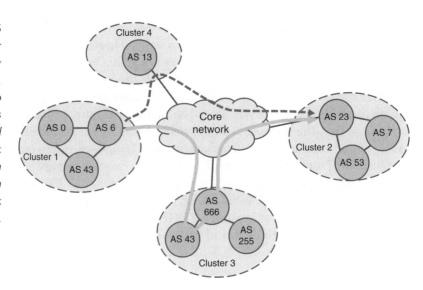

Figure 19.6
Example for geographically improbable paths. A path via two geographical clusters that is not directed via the core network (top) and a path that passes through the core network twice (bottom).

generation of AS graphs is conceivable, it must nevertheless be possible to guarantee that no attack is in progress at the time of adaptation. Otherwise an attacker might, for example, emulate belonging to the core area of the BGP infrastructure. No attacks can be filtered within geographical clusters with this approach. This presents a problem because the information about the contacts – and therefore the geographic information – deduced from the whois database may be forged. Therefore, in the case of long-term attacks, it is initially possible to claim a geographical position close to the destination in order to remain undetected.

19.2.2   Temporary Withholding of Unknown Routes

Consistency testing of routes based on historical AS graphs

A mechanism complementary to geographic anomaly identification was suggested in [QGR+07]: instead of using geographical correlations, it is proposed here, among other things, only to use and forward 'suspicious' routes after a configurable grace period. This approach is based on the observation that misconfigurations and attacks in the BGP infrastructure are usually identified and eliminated very quickly. First of all an AS graph structure is reconstructed from historical databases to determine whether a route might be illegitimate. Unlike the previous approach, however, it uses a directed graph to better represent BGP policies. Incoming UPDATE messages can be verified against this model of the BGP network. In this case, the path is checked iteratively by the verifying AS. It is marked as suspicious as soon as a link is found that was not previously part of the AS graph. Additionally, a check is carried out to discover whether the original AS has already announced a given IP address prefix in the past. At the same time, the approach takes into account the aggregation and disaggregation of address ranges. However, if no valid mapping can be determined, the UPDATE is also withheld.

Routes that have been erroneously identified as legitimate or were only legitimate for a time are regularly removed from the AS graph and the prefix database to improve the identification of attacks. For this, both the assignment of IP prefixes to ASes and also the existence of links between ASes are kept available as soft state, thus it is assumed for valid topology information that this will be announced regularly in the BGP.

Transient routes are removed from the database

Since 'suspicious' routes may actually be legitimate changes to the AS graph or prefix assignment, a variety of heuristics are used so that not too many routes are withheld. So, for instance, it is assumed that changes that merely lengthen paths are always legitimate because an attacker cannot draw traffic to itself in this way. Changing an IP address prefix to an AS that was already on the path to the former destination is also considered as valid for a similar reason. In this case, an attacker would already have had access to the traffic anyway. Among other things, the problem here is the assumption that the attacker only wants to attract traffic. Thus, it is not possible in this way to identify attackers who want to cause overload situations or black holes. A different heuristic relates to the IP address allocation policies of the address issuing registries, which assign address blocks that are as contiguous as possible to every AS to keep routing and forwarding tables as small as possible. For this reason the IP address range that is announced by an AS may grow to a certain degree without the UPDATE message being marked as suspicious. At the same time, it was observed that Internet providers in the same region often share the same customers and therefore announce the same prefixes, which is why such routes are also not withheld. Both heuristics introduce the risk that certain attacks will not be identified if they originate from neighbouring systems or from routers of an AS with similar addresses.

Another complementary heuristic of the approach is based on the observation that BGP UPDATE messages are often received in bulk that are attributable to a common event. If some of these events are identified as suspicious, then there is an increased probability that the other messages are also illegitimate and will be withheld. It should be possible as a result of this heuristic to configure other heuristics so that it is not necessary to identify

Bulk-based identification of suspicious routes

all illegitimate UPDATE messages. The main disadvantage is the attacker's opportunity to suppress legitimate routing messages in other parts of the network by injecting obviously bogus messages at the same time. As a result, the legitimate messages would also be withheld.

19.2.3   Automated Revocation of Illegitimate Routes

Listen and Whisper works reactively and attempts to correlate illegitimate routes to missing traffic

The *Listen and Whisper* approach [SRS+04] proposes a heuristic orthogonal to cryptographic security which, unlike the methods presented previously, works reactively. This means that route updates are always committed initially. However, the effects on the existing data traffic, particularly on TCP data, are observed. If it is discovered that connections are interrupted, the mechanism assumes reachability problems and switches to an alternative route.

One challenge when detecting data streams is the fact that BGP routes are only valid in one direction. Consequently, a data stream flowing back and forth usually takes two different paths through the core network. Thus, a core network router can often only observe one direction of the data streams. The Listen and Whisper approach therefore concentrates on TCP streams as they should only run correctly if bi-directional communication takes place. It ascertains whether at least one successful TCP handshake takes place within a time period t; in this case, the destination is assumed to be reachable. A TCP handshake is successful specifically if a TCP data packet follows within two minutes of a TCP-SYN packet. The time t is at least as long as a preconfigured minimum time T. In addition, incomplete TCP handshakes to at least N different destination addresses have to be observed in order to prevent false alerts caused, for example, by failed end systems.

Countermeasures against possible bypass methods

Attackers who know that the Listen and Whisper system is used to control data streams might try to simulate valid TCP handshakes. It is merely necessary to inject TCP-SYN messages and subsequent ACK packets in the direction of the attacked system. The authors therefore suggest randomly dropping SYN packets in the router and checking whether they and only they are repeatedly transmitted as this is the way a completely functional TCP connection would respond. This approach, however, considerably complicates statistically significant identification. If too few SYN packets are dropped, assessment of the situation may take too long. If, on the other hand, too many packets are dropped, establishing TCP connections will be slowed down in the case of legitimate changes. Moreover, there are possibly cascading effects if many routers use the system and drop packets or if attackers intentionally simulate a 'bogus connection' and simply continuously reinject SYN packets. The approach would then detect bypassing of the identification and would drop a possibly legitimate route change. In addition, during a sinkhole attack an attacker might simply respond to connection queries from end systems by generating valid SYN-ACK packets and thus devalue the approach significantly.

19.3 Summary

Guaranteeing the security in a routing protocol is a very complicated and resource-intensive task because, unlike protocols where only secure data transmission has to be guaranteed, here the aim is network-wide consensus between routers. This is the main reason that so far protection against internal attackers has barely found its way into routing protocols used in practice.

Guaranteeing an acceptable security level in routing protocols is extremely time-consuming

Despite the large number of threats, such as the injection of bogus routes, illegitimate announcement of IP address prefixes or possible denial-of-service attacks, Internet routing is still comparatively reliable at present. This is mainly attributable to the fact that BGP routers are relatively well separated from the rest of the Internet, for instance by the Generalised TTL Security Mechanism or by BGP connections secured by TCP-MD5. Physical measures also lower the probability of occurrence for many threats, some of which are mentioned in more detail in [BFM+10].

BGP routers are generally well protected

Thanks to the global spread of the Internet, however, the number and global distribution of the systems in the BGP infrastructure is growing. As a result, it is to be expected that the probability of internal attacks or 'misconfigurations', as the disruptions in the BGP are almost always presented as, will continue to increase in future. Also in the future, political conflicts may well be anticipated as triggers.

The threat to the BGP infrastructure is growing

One possible way out is to cryptographically safeguard the BGP by certifying the IP address prefixes announced and attesting the paths used. The first comprehensive protocol with this aim is *S-BGP*, which was unable, however, to establish itself, mainly due to reservations with respect to resource consumption. Other protocols, such as *soBGP*, have therefore tried to reduce the effort and as a result provide fewer security guarantees. At present, *BGPSEC*, a successor of S-BGP, is in the process of standardisation by the Internet Engineering Task Force. Here, the *Resource Public Key Infrastructure (RPKI)* should be highlighted. The Internet registries

In future BGP could be protected by cryptographic measures

can already use it to cryptographically sign the binding between IP address prefixes and the origin ASes. However, as the distributed database constructed for this is poorly maintained, it is not possible so far to filter IP address ranges meaningfully on this basis. It remains to be seen whether or not router manufacturers and operators will invest in the cryptographic effort of BGPSEC.

Heuristic methods can be used complementary to cryptographic security approaches   Alternatively to cryptographic safeguarding, routes in BGP exchanges can be filtered on the basis of heuristics in order to prevent attacks. The approaches presented here are based on very different ideas, such as geographical or chronological plausibility checks. Compared to cryptographic mechanisms, they are each relatively resource-saving, can be implemented locally by individual Internet providers and can even to some extent protect against attacks that are not eliminated by cryptographic mechanisms. The majority of heuristic approaches, however, have the problem that an attacker that operates cautiously may actually exploit them to carry out novel attacks, for example because legitimate routes are no longer taken into account.

19.4   Supplemental Reading

[BFM⁺10]   BUTLER, K.; FARLEY, T. R.; MCDANIEL, P.; REXFORD, J.: A Survey of BGP Security Issues and Solutions. In: *Proceedings of the IEEE* 98 (2010), No. 1, p. 100–122

[BMY06]   BARBIR, A.; MURPHY, S.; YANG, Y.: *Generic Threats to Routing Protocols*. 2006. – RFC 4593, IETF, Status: Standard, https://tools.ietf.org/html/rfc4593

[GHM⁺07]   GILL, V.; HEASLEY, J.; MEYER, D.; SAVOLA, P.; PIGNATARO, C.: *The Generalized TTL Security Mechanism (GTSM)*. 2007. – RFC 5082, IETF, Status: Standard, https://tools.ietf.org/html/rfc5082

[KMR⁺03]   KRUEGEL, C.; MUTZ, D.; ROBERTSON, W.; VALEUR, F.: Topology-based detection of anomalous BGP messages. In: *Recent Advances in Intrusion Detection (RAID)*, 2003, S. 17–35

[LK12]   LEPINSKI, M.; KENT, S.: *An Infrastructure to Support Secure Internet Routing*. 2012. – RFC 6480, IETF, Status: Proposed Standard, https://tools.ietf.org/html/rfc6480

[LMS03] LYNN, C.; MIKKELSON, J.; SEO, K.: *Secure BGP (S-BGP)*. 2003. – IETF, Status: Expired Internet-Draft, https://tools.ietf.org/html/draft-clynn-s-bgp-protocol-01

[LT13] LEPINSKI, M.; TURNER, S.: *An Overview of BGPSEC*. 2013. – IETF, Status: Internet-Draft, https://tools.ietf.org/html/draft-ietf-sidr-bgpsec-overview-04

[QGR⁺07] QIU, J.; GAO, L.; RANJAN, S.; NUCCI, A.: Detecting bogus BGP route information: Going beyond prefix hijacking. In: *SecureComm 2007*, 2007, S. 381–390

[SRS⁺04] SUBRAMANIAN, L.; ROTH, V.; STOICA, I.; SHENKER, S.; KATZ, R.: Listen and Whisper: Security Mechanisms for BGP. In: *Symposium on Networked Systems Design and Implementation (NSDI)*, 2004

[Whi06a] WHITE, R.: *Architecture and Deployment Considerations for Secure Origin BGP (soBGP)*. 2006. – IETF, Status: Expired Internet-Draft, https://tools.ietf.org/html/draft-white-sobgp-architecture-02

19.5 Questions

1. For what reason is the protection of a routing protocol more complex than is the case with other cryptographic protocols, such as IPsec or TLS?

2. In the BGP TTL security hack, why are the packets not provided with TTL 1 and automatically dropped by gateway systems?

3. Discuss why, in the case of S-BGP, certificates with very short lifespans are not used to bypass the necessity of checking Certificate Revocation Lists.

4. Why is there no significant increase in efficiency as a result of the simultaneous use of Signature Amortisation Across Peers and Signature Amortisation Across Buffers?

5. Can the Merkle hash tree mechanism be optimised by sending only the root element in addition to the signature?

6. Why does the use of dedicated servers in the IRV approach reduce the routing's availability, even if they are replicated locally?

7. Why can geographical filtering of BGP routers protect against worm hole attacks? Why are such attacks possible even when S-BGP is deployed?

8. Assess the threat tree specified in [CCF04] for the BGP infrastructure in respect of completeness.

20 Secure Name Resolution

The Domain Name Service (DNS) is probably one of the most important services on the Internet since it converts domain names, which are comparatively easy for humans to remember, into IP addresses. Among other purposes, the DNS is used to identify the mail server(s) responsible for a domain. Without a functioning DNS, the Internet would be unusable for most people and applications. Availability of the DNS system has therefore been a primary security objective since day one. Additionally, authenticity, integrity and confidentiality are desirable characteristics in connection with the DNS.

A functioning Domain Name Service is a commonly assumed prerequisite for the operation of an IP-based infrastructure

The following sections provide a brief summary of the operation of the DNS and discuss potential threats. This is followed by a description of measures for the secure use of conventional DNS and the DNSSEC security mechanism. Finally, a number of alternative methods for secure name resolution are discussed, such as the DNSCurve and the Peer Name Resolution Protocols.

20.1 The DNS Operating Principle

The DNS system is essentially a decentralised database whose data is stored and queried redundantly over a number of servers. Each of these servers is referred to as the *Authoritative Server* for the respective part of the namespace for which it is responsible. The structure of the namespace and the server structure follow the hierarchy outlined in Figure 20.1, with the aim of making the DNS system scalable and resistant to failures. The names in the DNS are formed starting from the *root zone*, which is referred to by a single dot. Subsidiary names are concatenated and separated

Security in Fixed and Wireless Networks, Second Edition.
Guenter Schaefer and Michael Rossberg.
Copyright © 2014 by dpunkt.verlag GmbH, Heidelberg, Germany.
Title of the German original: Netzsicherheit   ISBN 978-3-86490-115-7
Translation Copyright © 2016 by John Wiley & Sons, Ltd., All rights reserved

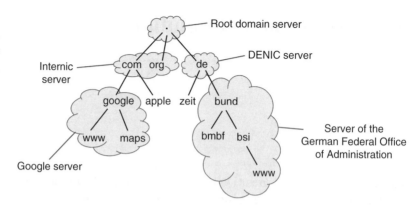

by further dots. An example is `www.bsi.bund.de`. In the interest of simplicity the last dot is usually omitted, since all names refer to the root zone.

*Authoritative servers
form a tree structure
that follows the DNS
namespace scheme*

The hierarchical server structure basically follows the name structure. Only a few servers are responsible for the root zone. The IP addresses of these servers are rather static and they are fixed in DNS server configurations. Queries are referred to servers that are provided by the operator of the queried top-level domain (TLD). Names ending with `.de.`, for example, are servers operated by DENIC eG. They refer in turn to servers operated by the operator of the respective subdomain, and so on. In principle, other servers may be responsible for each additional partial domain, although queries can also be answered directly if a server is responsible for several consecutive stages in a subtree. For redundancy reasons, the contents of the authoritative servers are usually mirrored on backup servers whose addresses are also stored in the higher zone, so that in case of a server failure another server can respond to the query. The actual mirroring of the data is also solved by DNS and is achieved via so-called *zone transfers*, which enable complete parts of the database to be queried by the backup servers.

*Caching servers
respond to client
queries by querying
the DNS hierarchy*

In addition to servers that actively maintain parts of the DNS database, there are so-called *recursive* or *caching servers*. These are not part of the DNS hierarchy, but serve as proxies for local systems. They buffer the responses to queries so that they can be made available quickly to other clients. If the data is not available, caching servers can query the DNS hierarchy iteratively to answer the client's query directly with a single response packet. In this case the query processing is referred to as *recursive*, since it is delegated from the client to the caching server.

The software that generates the actual DNS queries is referred to as a *resolver*. It is usually integrated directly into the operating

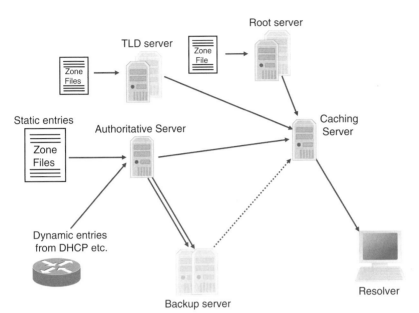

Figure 20.2
Flow of information within a DNS zone. A caching server queries the root, TLD and authoritative servers of a domain for a client.

system of the client. As already indicated, it is not necessary that DNS is implemented in its full complexity: in the case of recursive queries only, these can be sent via a so-called *stub resolver* to a local caching server. The resulting flow of information is illustrated in Figure 20.2.

20.2   Security Objectives and Threats

With regard to security, the security objectives introduced in Chapter 1 also apply to name services. In some cases, however, the weighting may differ substantially from the protocols presented so far.

- **Data integrity and accountability:** Since the IP addresses resolved in the DNS are largely used for communications, which are themselves not secured cryptographically, securing the data integrity and accountability is the primary objective. If attackers are able to manipulate name mappings unnoticed or send illegitimate records to the client, these can then be redirected to systems controlled by the attacker. In contrast to the protocols considered so far, when it comes to accountability it is not the identity of the server that is crucial, but the entity that created the record.

- **Availability:** Since the DNS infrastructure is needed for almost every communication process on the Internet, it is itself a frequent target of attacks on availability. As already described in Section 18.1.2.3, the DNS protocol itself is often also used to amplify denial-of-service attacks, resulting in adverse side effects on the DNS system.

- **Confidentiality:** For most DNS operators and developers confidentiality plays a subordinate role. Since the service is to be made available to everyone in any case, the individual mappings do not have to be protected. However, consideration should be given to the fact that the operators of caching servers are able to closely monitor client behaviour based on their queries. In addition, zone transfers have frequently been used in the past to enumerate the network systems of organisations in order to prepare attacks.

- **Controlled access:** Similarly to confidentiality, in the operation of DNS systems little thought is often given to the objective of controlled access. However, zone transfers, for example, and dynamic updates of the DNS mappings should be restricted. Furthermore, caching servers should only be made available to trusted clients for the reasons explained in the next section. In practice, access control in these contexts is done almost exclusively via IP address filtering.

Primary security objectives are integrity and authenticity The most severe consequences for users of the DNS are therefore attacks on the integrity and authenticity of name mappings. Because of the complex arrangement of the DNS infrastructure, attackers have the opportunity in principle to exert influence on these mappings at a whole series of points, as shown in Figure 20.3. Essentially, these are:

- **Attacks on the infrastructure of the provider:** If an attacker succeeds in compromising the provider's DNS server or one of the backup servers, the current name mappings can be changed and clients can be redirected accordingly. Until a few years ago such attacks were of greater significance because the implementation security of the DNS servers being used was very poor. However, in recent years such attacks have become rather rare. Furthermore, securing communications with backup servers and distribution of dynamic name updates can be implemented with standard tools such as IPsec, for example. Alternatively, a DNS-specific security method can be used that involves the Transaction SIGnatures

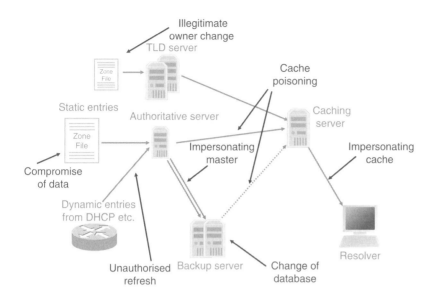

Figure 20.3

*Possible threats
to data integrity
and authenticity at
various points of the
DNS infrastructure*

(TSIG) of the *Secret Key Transaction Authentication for DNS*
[VGE⁺00].

- **Attacks on the TLD operator:** In principle, the infrastructures of TLD operators can be attacked by the same means.
  However, due to the great leverage these have, they are well
  secured and monitored. In the past, most cases that were
  reported involved attackers managing to convince the TLD
  operator of a change of domain ownership and thereby taking
  it over. Nowadays, such changes tend to be verified cryptographically, so security problems on the part of the TLD operators are less likely.

- **Attacks on the client network:** If an attacker manages to
  access the local network of a client, for example via its DSL
  router, caching servers can be taken over or DNS queries can
  be redirected to the attacker's caching servers via fake DHCP
  responses. The probability of such threats can be greatly reduced with conventional security measures, such as the introduction of 801.1X.

- **Attack on Internet data:** Recent attacks on the integrity
  and authenticity of DNS therefore frequently focus on the
  communication between caching servers and authoritative
  servers at different levels of the DNS infrastructure. Because
  of the low latency requirements in this context – dialogues in
  the DNS consist merely of a simple query and the according
  response – it is not possible to simply use security protocols

such as IPsec, which means that man-in-the-middle attacks, for example, pose a serious threat. Even more problematic are *cache poisoning* attacks, which are presented in the following section.

Cache poisoning attacks aka DNS spoofing

In so-called *cache poisoning* attacks, an attacker uses packets with forged IP addresses to forestall the response of a DNS server to a query sent by himself in order to control the cache when the victim performs a query. During this process the attacker is *off-path*, which means that no access to the routers or lines between the DNS servers or clients is required; instead he exploits the connectionless communication of the DNS protocol. A classic DNS cache poisoning attack involves the steps shown in Figure 20.4:

1. First, the attacker sends a query to the caching server responsible for the victim, a query which can be answered only by a DNS server controlled by the attacker.
2. The caching server recursively queries the attacker's DNS server using a specific UDP source port and a query ID in order to be able to map any response to the triggering query.
3. The attacker's DNS server reports the query ID and the source port to the attacker. Whether or not the query is answered is irrelevant for the remainder of the attack.
4. The attacker sends a further query to the victim's caching server. This time, the query relates to the domain that the attacker wants to take over.
5. The caching server forwards the query to the authoritative server that is responsible for the domain. It uses the same UDP port number as in the query to the attacker's server.

Figure 20.4

Classic DNS cache poisoning sequence

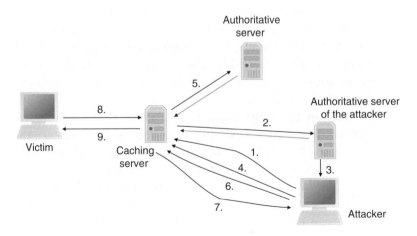

In some DNS servers the query ID is simply selected in ascending order so that in a fast query sequence the new query ID is one greater than the previous query.

6. Directly after the query the attacker sends a forged response in the name of the authoritative server. Since the attacker has a high probability of predicting the source port and query ID correctly, the caching server will be unable to distinguish the forged response from the correct one and will accept the mappings it contains into its cache. The subsequently arriving 'second' response from the genuine authoritative server is usually ignored as a presumed duplicate.

7. After the response by the assumed authoritative server, the caching server will communicate the name mapping to the attacker. The attacker is thus even able to verify that the attack was successful.

8. If victims now want to access the respective domain, they send their query.

9. The response will contain the mapping manipulated by the attacker because this has been stored in the cache in the meantime. The 'poisoning' of the cache may go back some time. The exact upper limits depend on the software configuration, but the time period may well be up to a week.

Since cache poisoning attacks require no access to lines or intermediate systems and essentially exploit a protocol weakness, they are very dangerous if no countermeasures are taken. One simple measure is the use of random query IDs. Because cache poisoning attacks are only possible if the cache has no valid mapping already, and this period is often up to 24 hours, in the 'naïve' case attempts to change a specific name can only succeed once during the period. Many DNS operators therefore assume that the search space for the attacker is too large to be able to perform efficient cache poisoning, despite the fact that the query ID field stipulated in the DNS protocol comprises only 16 bits.

Current DNS servers use random query IDs to increase the space that the attacker needs to search

However, the attacker could, for example, deliberately overload the server actually responsible in order to suppress the legitimate response and thus have a higher number of attempts to send the 65,536 possible values. A further method was published in 2008 [Kam08]. In this case the attacker sends queries about random, non-existent subdomains of the attacked domain to the caching server, for example `kslkskdf.bank.com`. The caching server always has to forward these queries to the authoritative server, with the result that in each case the attacker has a slight chance to

The query ID field in the DNS does not have sufficient entropy to fend off complex poisoning attacks

take over the corresponding domain. At this point a trick can be used so that the actual target, for example www.bank.com, can be redirected. To this end, the attacker sends a forwarding response and indicates that the caching server should contact the actual target via DNS in order to resolve the random name. In addition, the IP address of the supposed DNS server, as specified by the attacker, is already included in the response. In simple terms, the response in the example could be as follows: 'I do not know kslkskdf.bank.com. Please contact www.bank.com, which you will find under 1.2.3.4', where 1.2.3.4 is actually an IP address under the attacker's control. As a result of this more complex approach the attacker has the opportunity to undertake a whole series of poisoning attempts, so the 65,536 possible values of the query ID field do not provide adequate protection.

Random source ports significantly increase security

Newer DNS servers therefore also use a random source port for the queries in addition to a random query ID. This greatly increases the attacker's search space to almost 2^{32} possibilities. Another method [DAV$^+$08] proposes to make caching servers exploit the fact that DNS does not distinguish between uppercase and lowercase letters. They can randomly change the case of individual letters in the queried domain and compare it with the case in the response. Since the attacker then also has to guess these correctly, the complexity increases to 2^{32+n} possibilities, with n being the number of letters in the domain name.

Because of fragmentation at the network level, countermeasures can be bypassed

For these measures, only the caching server has to be changed in each situation, and the search space for the attacker is significantly increased, so in most cases a simple bruteforce attack will not be successful. In some cases, however, the attacker can use even more skillful procedures to greatly reduce the search space again. In [HS13b] a method is described in which the caching server's queries require very long responses, which are larger than the Maximum Transmission Unit (MTU) for the network. Depending on the scenario, the attacker may even be able to control this parameter by means of fake ICMP messages. In the case of UDP messages that are too large, as well as the DNS responses that they provoke, the Internet protocol breaks these down into several fragments. The recipient – in this case, the caching server – reassembles them and identifies related fragments using a 16-bit ID in the IP protocol header. The attacker's objective is now to generate a query in such a way that the name mappings to be used as fakes are in the second fragment, while the random components, that is, query ID, source port number and domain name, the latter with optionally modified upper/lower case properties, are transmitted in the first fragment.

He can now – before the triggering query is sent – send multiple packets with different fragment IDs to the caching server. When the first packet arrives with the response from the Authoritative Server, the supposedly full packet is assembled complete with the fake mappings, and the real second fragment is ignored. The procedure that the attacker has to follow has now become much more complex as a result of the countermeasures that have been introduced, but the fragmentation problem shows very clearly how unforeseen interactions between protocols can be exploited again and again.

20.3 Secure Use of Traditional DNS

It is virtually impossible to make the conventional DNS protocol completely secure, especially when sophisticated attacks are being used. Nevertheless, with the help of a hardened environment, the risk of successful attacks can still be considerably reduced. The following measures help in this respect:

- **Using up-to-date software:** Just as with other services, it is equally important with DNS to be using the latest software. This is the only means to reduce the risk of the exploitation of classic security vulnerabilities such as buffer overflows. This is particularly important because the DNS system, while highly redundant with respect to the hardware, is homogeneous in terms of the server software used, and any security problem in this software may cause extremely high levels of damage due to the number of affected systems. In addition to the classic security vulnerabilities, more recent DNS servers and clients usually also avoid newly discovered DNS-specific problems, e.g. by the use of random source ports and query IDs, as has been described. A comprehensive overview for implementers can be found in RFC 5452 [HM09].

- **Disabling the Path MTU Discovery:** To impede attacks on the DNS system, actions should also be taken on the part of the operating system environment. One possibility, for instance, is disabling the Path MTU Discovery on the DNS server to hamper the fragmentation attack described earlier. With the `IP_PMTUDISC_INTERFACE` option, newer Linux systems even offer the possibility of doing so only for certain network sockets.

Figure 20.5

Split-horizon DNS

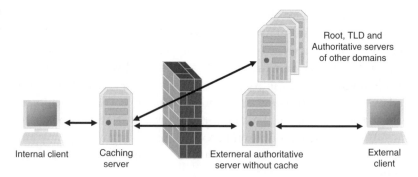

*Separation of external
and internal services*

- **Split-horizon DNS:** Probably the the most comprehensive protection is offered by separating the cache server from external clients. As shown in Figure 20.5, by using a firewall, for example, it becomes impossible for external attackers to send queries to the cache server themselves. To launch a successful attack, they would have to accurately anticipate a query from the client, which means that using random query IDs and source-port numbers gives no significant probability that a cache-poisoning attack would be successful. In order to make statically configured name mappings available to external parties, another DNS server is used, which is separated either physically or possibly just logically from the caching server, where a second DNS server process with another IP address is implemented on the same host. Attacks launched by internal clients are still possible in this scenario, so the network areas for which a caching server is responsible should, from a security perspective, be as small as possible.

- **Redundant DNS infrastructure:** As mentioned earlier, denial-of-service attacks are a significant threat to DNS. The DNS servers responsible for a domain should therefore be configured with the greatest possible spatial and network-topological redundancy to ensure the availability of at least one server. In the case of the root servers, this is ensured by a global anycast service, for instance. Several servers are configured with the same IP addresses and the corresponding IP address range is announced by various autonomous systems via BGP. In this way, a different server responds depending on its position in the network, and any attack always affects just one part of the network. An overview of the currently active servers can be found at http://www.root-servers.org. Particularly in the case of medium-sized domains, it may prove difficult to operate DNS servers with availability guarantees that are comparable to the availability of all terminals for which names are being served. In such cases, (partial) outsourcing to an external service provider may be worthwhile.

■ **Filtering illegitimate queries:** DNS servers that respond to recursive queries without authentication represent a significant risk to the availability of other Internet participants. For this reason, recursive queries should be performed only by caching servers and only for their own clients. Otherwise, attackers can use the server as a proxy server to disguise, or spoof, their identity and increase the effectiveness of their attack. The filtering will become more complex if the presumption of compromised clients has to be made, such as when bot software generates a very large number of queries that cannot be answered directly from the cache. Such attacks can only be contained by monitoring and a targeted deactivation of the originating clients.

With particular regard to authenticity and integrity, however, there still remains a risk of successful attacks through the use of the traditional DNS system. This is especially the case when on-path attackers must be considered, as it is impossible to mitigate man-in-the-middle attacks.

20.4   Cryptographic Protection of DNS

Only cryptographic methods offer meaningful relief against attacks on the authenticity and integrity of DNS data. A selection of these techniques is presented in the following sections.

20.4.1   TSIG

The first method that has been standardised in this context is *Secret Key Transaction Authentication for DNS (TSIG)* [VGE⁺00], which makes it possible to embed a cryptographic checksum for previous records in a *TSIG resource record*. The generation of the checksum was initially restricted to HMAC-MD5, but HMACs based on SHA-1 and SHA-2 have also been standardised [Eas06]. TSIG uses manually distributed keys or automatically negotiates these through the use of Kerberos, for example [Eas00]. However, as it does not contribute any way to build chains of trust, TSIG can only be used in locally restricted scenarios, for example to update backup servers. TSIG is not suitable for comprehensively securing queries

TSIG is a first simple approach in cryptographic DNS protection.

to authoritative servers because with n DNS parties up to $n(n-1)/2$ keys would have to be configured.

20.4.2 DNSSEC

DNSSEC builds a DNSSEC has been designed from the outset for worldwide use and
trust hierarchy in the is fundamentally different from TSIG since it does not rely on ex-
DNS system itself ternal key management [AAL+05a, WB13]. Instead, starting from
the root zone and corresponding to the DNS hierarchy, a key hierarchy is established to authenticate the responses of DNS servers
and enable their integrity to be verified. This applies from end to
end, starting from the operators of this root zone. Although there
is strict enforcement of the use of asymmetric cryptography, the
name mappings are only signed, that is, they are not encrypted, so
no online calculations are required.

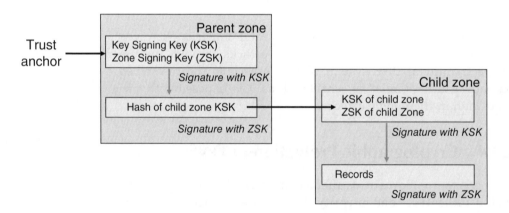

Figure 20.6   The security stems from asymmetric signatures covering groups of
Chain of trust in   name assignments, so-called *Resource Records*, where in each DNS
the use of DNSSEC   hierarchy level the checksums of the keys of the next lower level
are published. Since these are also signed, a chain of trust is built
up, as shown in Figure 20.6. The root of the chain of trust is formed
by the *Key Signing Key (KSK)* of the root zone, which signs the *Zone
Signing Key (ZSK)* of the root zone. In return, this ZSK is used to
protect the actual groups of resource records in the root zone, where
among other things the checksums of the KSK of the lower zones
are located.

The separation into   The subdivision into KSK and ZSK is done because, for speed
KSK and ZSK allows   reasons, DNSSEC dispenses with the time-consuming examination
for different security   of CRLs or changes in the name mappings. To reduce the potential
levels within a zone   for misuse of compromised keys or replayed name mappings, the

signatures used are given a very short validity period, for example one day. This procedure, however, requires that, for administrative reasons, the private key is stored on a system connected to the network in order to be able to perform changes in an automated manner. The separation of KSK and ZSK allows for differentiation of the security levels. Thus, the private part of the KSK can be generated and stored in a safe place, and the signature for the ZSK is regenerated only every few months. The ZSK, on the other hand, is used to sign more frequently changing resource records in an automated process with short lifetimes.

The aforementioned KSK for the root zone forms the trust anchor for DNSSEC. The private part of the key is retained in two *Hardware Security Modules (HSM)*, which can be activated in each case by a group of seven recognised international experts. From these seven so-called *Crypto Officers*, any three together can, with the help of a secret sharing protocol, issue new signatures for the respective ZSKs of the root zone. To do this, they need to meet every three months at one of two secure sites in the USA. In the case of a catastrophic event, the KSK can be recovered by a third group of seven experts. To do this, five of these *Recovery Key Share Holders* must bring their part of a symmetric key and meet at a secret location where there is an encrypted copy of the KSK. Details of this procedure can be found in [ICA10], for instance. The actual signature of the mappings of the root zone is made with the private part of the corresponding ZSK, which is produced and used by the American company Verisign.

In order to increase the trust and confidence in the root-zone KSK, it is controlled by international experts.

Resource Records of DNSSEC

Technically, DNSSEC is implemented by new resource-record types that are published alongside the resource records that are used for the name mapping [AAL+05b]. The necessary key material is published in DNSKEY records with the type number 48. In addition to the public keys, they contain a bit field and a protocol field that marks the key as a DNSSEC key. Also published is the type of signature algorithm for which the key is intended. Currently, there are a number of standardised methods: DSA/SHA1, RSA/SHA-1, DSA-NSEC3-SHA1, RSASHA1-NSEC3-SHA1, RSA/SHA-256, RSA/SHA-512, GOST R 34.10-2001, ECDSA P-256 with SHA-256 and ECDSA P-384 with SHA-384. Although only the implementation of RSA/SHA-1 is mandatory [Ros13], RSA/SHA-256 is already required for the verification of the root zone, so all RSA- and ECDSA-based methods should be implemented. DSA-based

Public keys are published as DNSKEY records.

signatures are not widespread due to the lower efficiency of verification in comparison with RSA. GOST R 34.10-2001 is the Russian equivalent of the US ECDSA standard and is similarly optional. Signatures based on RSA/MD5 were originally standardised, but their use is no longer permitted.

References to the keys of lower zones are implemented by publication of the cryptographic hash values

References to the public keys in lower zones are implemented by *Delegation Signer (DS) records* with the type number 43. In addition to the name of the zone, they contain the algorithm of the key and a short, not cryptographically secure, hash value, which will enable the verifying entity to find the DNSKEY records quickly. The actual mapping is done via a cryptographic hash value by means of the DNSKEY record of the lower zone. The hash function used for this purpose is likewise published in the record. This may concern SHA-1 and SHA-256 as well as SHA-384 or the optional Russian standard GOST R 34.11-94.

Cryptographic signatures are coded by the type number 46 and are referred to in standards and applications as `RRSIG` records. In addition to the actual signature, the records have the following content:

- the type of the signed record (`A`, `AAAA`, `CNAME`, . . .);
- the signature algorithm used;
- the number of parts of the DNS name;
- the TTL of the record in the Authoritative Server;
- the period over which the signature is valid;
- an identification number for the signature key;
- the name of the signing entity.

The number of parts of the DNS name indicates which parts of the DNS name are to be included in the signature verification, and provides support for wildcard domains. In the example of `www.icann.org` this field is three, whereas with `*.icann.org` it is two. In the latter case, arbitrary subdomains may be authenticated by the signature, too. The TTL of the record is also transmitted just to enable the signature-verifying entity to calculate the original data because the TTL may be reduced in intermediate caching servers.

NSEC records authenticate responses that indicate the non-existence of a name

The records described here and the related verification mechanisms are sufficient to determine whether a name mapping that has been received is authentic and complete. However, an attacker could also try to pretend that a domain is non-existent and thus trigger undesirable behaviour. DNSSEC therefore provides for authenticating even responses such as these. This property is referred to as *Authenticated Denial of Existence*. The implementation of this requires more records, where in the original standard *NSEC records* were initially provided with the type number 47. For each DNS name they include a mapping to the next DNS name in the same zone in lexicographic order. The last name contains a reference to the first name. Since they are also signed, a recipient can exclude the possibility that a name exists if it is lexicographically between the names of a mapping. A disadvantage of this method is that all the name mappings of a DNS server can be systematically queried. In the procedure known as *Zone walking*, attackers iteratively request the next NSEC record to obtain all the DNS names of an institution, and they use these in the preparation of further attacks. One possible relief is described in RFC 4470 [WI06], in which the DNS server generates NSEC records online and, as regards the predecessor and successor names, responds to the query with the lexicographically next values in each case. For a query about www.example.org, an NSEC record of wwv.example.org with a mapping to wwx.example.org is returned, for instance. However, this allows relatively simple denial-of-service attacks on the computing power of the server and can also overload caching servers, where applicable.

Using NSEC attackers can draw conclusions about all the DNS names in a domain

A supposedly better solution is denoted by the *NSEC3 records* introduced in RFC 5155 [LSA$^+$08]. In this case, the uncovering of the DNS name should be prevented by the repeated application of a cryptographic hash function. In addition, a random so-called *salt value* can be appended to the host name, which should handicap any systematic trial-and-error probing. The basic idea corresponds to the PBKDF2 function mentioned in Section 15.4, where the host name is the 'password'. The resulting hashes are now ordered as with the conventional NSEC and then circularly linked, so that a verifying entity only has to check if the hash of the queried DNS name lies between the two returned values. For host names and passwords, however, completely different conditions apply: passwords should be long and complex, but host names should be easy to memorise and as short as possible. Despite the possibility of iterating the hash function several times and using salt values, the resulting hash values may still be very easily found by systematic trial-and-error probing. In addition, long salt values and high numbers of iterations have little practical relevance. For example, the servers that are responsible for .com currently use only one iteration and dispense altogether with salt values. Tools have therefore been developed in recent years that run zone walking automatically even where NSEC3 records are being used.

Cryptographic safeguarding of names with NSEC3

In practice, NSEC3 offers no significant security benefit

Security Discussion

Despite the initially simple-seeming approach, the use of DNSSEC conceals an extremely high complexity because a large number of parameters have to be set and the management of keys by the separation of KSK and ZSK, for example, or by a key change is not a trivial matter. Common errors include short signature lifetimes with a long TTL. As a result, the signatures of caching servers continue to be cached even though they are no longer current. The verification fails and due to the misconfiguration the system is no longer accessible. The use of DNSSEC requires very precise planning. Useful parameters and methods can be found in RFC 6781 [KMG12], for example, or in a report from the European Data Protection Agency ENISA [Sar10].

In particular, the division into ZSK and KSK seems to bring only a questionable security benefit. While signatures with the ZSK have only a short validity, KSK signatures have a longer validity period. If the ZSK becomes compromised, secure replacement is not simple due to the long validity of the signature. A more sensible procedure would seem to be a combined replacement of KSK and ZSK because the signature issued by the parent ZSK for the DS record is likely to expire sooner.

In addition, DNSSEC, as well as other conventional PKIs, forms a strictly hierarchical structure. A compromised key in one level causes a complete loss of security in this and all lower levels. Cross-certifications are not provided. This characteristic becomes blatant with the ZSK of the root zone: while the use of the root-zone KSK is handled rather transparently, the private part of the ZSK is in the possession of a single US company. This may be considered a severe issue as – completely analogous to the KSK – the security of the entire DNSSEC construct depends on the ZSK being used righteously.

With reference to the authenticity and integrity of DNSSEC, it must be noted that an incremental rollout of DNSSEC brings only a minor increase in security because the attacker can always attack unsigned mappings. While this problem is obvious, it seems nevertheless that well-known domains such as paypal.com are also affected by this issue [HS13a]. A similar problem is that many clients still accept unsigned responses even though a DS record is available in the parent zone. In this case, too, the security guarantees of DNSSEC are completely lost.

The fact remains, however, that the activation of DNSSEC greatly improves the integrity and authenticity of DNS. Just the simple act of verifying signatures in the caching server may achieve a significant increase in security in relation to cache poisoning attacks. In this case, however, communication between the cache and a (non-verifying) client must be secured by physical or cryptographic measures such as the use of split-horizon techniques or TSIG.

Even a gradual roll-out to caching servers strengthens authenticity and integrity

The introduction of DNSSEC does not address some security objectives, however, and in some cases it even worsens the characteristics significantly. The confidentiality of queries is not addressed, so that the traffic to and from DNS servers is still suitable for user tracking. Because of the weaknesses introduced in terms of zone walking, DNS hierarchies can be browsed relatively efficiently, particularly since the increase in security from the Authenticated Denial of Existence is not entirely clear. Current software systems use DNS to resolve names and check if there is an error; in most cases, however, it does not matter whether a name was authentically signalled as non-existent or the responses were simply suppressed.

DNSSEC does not address other security objectives and can even make matters worse

In relation to availability, the introduction of DNSSEC has lead to massive concerns that have proven to be largely justified. Because of the usually very long signatures in DNS responses, amplification attacks (see Section 18.1.2.3) can be performed much better. Ultimately, this can be avoided effectively only by monitoring and reactive, selective filtering. Another option for at least reducing the impacts is the use of ECDSA-based signatures, which – for the same security – are much shorter and thus amplify less.

DNSSEC simplifies amplification attacks

At present DNSSEC looks as if it will slowly establish itself as a standard resource. Thus, according to ICANN[1] in the spring of 2014, 298 out of 494 TLDs were equipped with a valid DNSSEC signature. At the same time, however, StatDNS[2], for example, reported only 322,055 out of 112,606,960 .com domains as being DNSSEC-secured. That is only around 0.29%, so currently there is no possibility of enforcing DNSSEC security.

Insignificant spread of DNSSEC

20.4.3 DNSCurve*

Developed by the well-known cryptographer Daniel J. Bernstein as an alternative to DNSSEC, DNSCurve [Ber09b, Dem10] has led to some controversial debates.

Unlike DNSSEC, DNSCurve secures the connection between DNS participants

---

[1]http://stats.research.icann.org/dns/tld_report
[2]http://www.statdns.com

The DNSCurve Operating Principle

In contrast to DNSSEC, here the records are not signed offline, but – in a similar fashion to TLS – the communication between DNS servers is secured. However, because TLS and similar protocols are too slow for DNSSEC, DNSCurve uses a custom development. A query *Request* is sent encrypted from the client C to the server S, which then sends the *Reply*:

$$C \rightarrow S\colon (+K_C, r_C, B[r_C, -K_C, +K_S, Request])$$
$$S \rightarrow C\colon (r_C, r_S, B[r_C \| r_S, -K_S, +K_C, Reply])$$

The function $B[n, -K_1, +K_2, m]$ relates to what Bernstein referred to as *box*, a cryptographic operation [Ber09a] that first secures a message m with a symmetrical method. The used key K_s is derived from the public/private-key pairs and is processed together with a nonce n as well as the encrypted message to generate an authenticated hash value. The following applies:

$$K_s := H(\{+K_2\}_{-K_1}, 0) = H(\{+K_1\}_{-K_2}, 0)$$
$$B[n, -K_1, +K_2, m] := H_2(\{m\}_{g(K_s, n)}) \| \{m\}_{f(K_s, n)}$$

The cryptographic operations for DNSCurve are rigidly defined

For DNSCurve, the parameters of the box function are rigidly defined. For asymmetric encryption and decryption or signature operations a cryptosystem designated as *Curve25519* is used. This is the elliptic curve $y^2 = x^3 + 486662x^2 + x$ over $\mathbb{Z}_{2^{255}-19}$ with other related parameters. According to present knowledge, this provides the same security as other 256-bit ECC systems, but is comparatively fast to compute and can be implemented in a manner that is resistant to side-channel attacks. The symmetric encryption and decryption are performed in DNSCurve with *Salsa*, a fast stream cipher, and the required hash function is based on *Poly1305*, which is likewise marked out by its high speed. The nonce values r_C and r_S sent in the DNSCurve protocol also go through the box function in the key test. By means of two Salsa20 calls, each of which determines the first 20 bytes of the keystream of a Salsa cipher, they are used with K_r to generate the real key for the Salsa cipher (designated as $f(k, n)$ in the formulas).

DNSCurve can be tunnelled through conventional DNS queries

Because DNSCurve is a fundamentally different security protocol, a direct introduction would imply a significant change to the DNS infrastructure, especially when load balancers, firewalls and similar intermediate systems that intervene in the DNS system must continue to function. Bernstein therefore proposes that the DNSCurve protocol should be tunnelled through DNS. To do this, queries and responses are coded in dynamic TXT records that were originally specified to be able to provide additional data about the DNS infrastructure.

The key hierarchy can be implemented in DNSCurve similar to DNSSEC. However, instead of the reference by means of DS records, a simpler route is chosen. Thanks to its relatively short length, the public key of a DNSCurve server can be anchored directly in the host name. Thus, instead of referencing the DNS server ns.example.org in a subzone, the server could simply be called uz5xgm1kx1zj8xsh51zp315k0rw23csgyabh2sl7g8tjg25ltcv hyw.example.org. The first three characters uz5 indicate that it is a DNSCurve name. The remaining characters encode the public key. This host name is used only for references within the DNS and the user does not need to know or learn anything about this 'trick'. In contrast to DNSSEC, thanks to this procedure the user does not have to completely rely on the secure operation of the root zone and TLD zones. If links are published on websites, for instance, and the link host names include DNSCurve keys, it can be verified, quite independently of the root zone, that the responsible DNS server is always the same.

DNSCurve publishes public keys via the host name

Security and Functionality Implications

In terms of security, DNSCurve does not suffer from some of the limitations of DNSSEC, that is, the transmission overhead for queries and responses in the proposed protocol is approximately equal, which means that DNS reflection attacks do not result in a higher attack efficiency. Furthermore, queries and responses are transmitted confidentially. Even negative responses, when a host does not exist, are authenticated without making zone walking possible. By being able to use secure host names, parent zones need not be completely trusted.

DNSCurve addresses additional security objectives

With respect to the cryptographic operations used, it should be noted that these are tightly integrated into the DNSCurve protocol. Although this excludes the misconfigurations that frequently occur with DNSSEC, the method cannot be easily replaced in the event that security issues are identified. In addition, all three operations are Bernstein's proprietary designs. Although these are either relatively well studied (Curve25519 and Salsa20) or there is a security proof for equivalence to the security of AES (Poly1305), the events of the past have nevertheless shown that ciphers are broken time and again. For such an important infrastructure as the DNS system,

The cryptographic primitives used are an integral part of DNSCurve

using a fixed specification of cryptographic primitives is therefore not a sound procedure.

Compromised devices represent a significant security risk

In contrast to DNSSEC, DNSCurve does not provide end-to-end security, which means that compromised caching servers can pass on any records to clients. Furthermore, DNSCurve signs and decrypts online, so the private keys must be in the server. This is a significant drawback, particularly in root and TLD zones, because the anycast approach means that there are many DNS servers, and the compromising of just one of these servers is sufficient to defeat all security services implemented via DNSCurve. This also has implications for the confidentiality of past queries, since DNSCurve cannot provide Perfect Forward Secrecy.

With regard to functionality, further disadvantages are often listed: queries are said to be difficult to cache and to increase the delay greatly. These objections are only partially applicable or justified because caching servers can still cache internal mappings, for example. Moreover, similar delay times should be expected when using DNSSEC because of the signature checks.

On the whole, DNSCurve has to be regarded as an interesting concept and good to use for protecting communications between client and caching server, for example. It is not a complete substitute for DNSSEC. For completeness, it should be noted that DNSSEC can be operated in a mode similar to DNSCurve. Thus, a reverse proxy server with access to the ZSK can be used for the ad hoc and transparent signing of the zones of conventional DNS servers and to issue NSEC3 records as required. If, in addition, ECDSA is deployed and the same key is used for ZSK and KSK, the size of the response packets can be reduced. The authentication of DNS servers via the host name can likewise be added [Kam10].

20.4.4   Distributed Name Resolution*

Distributed approaches to name resolution could provide better resistance to DoS attacks

The protocols on name mapping introduced earlier are based on DNS and are thus directly dependent on the availability of core components, for example the root servers. Although these are redundantly configured, they constitute – at least logically and organisationally – an exposed point of failure. Fully distributed systems in principle offer better availability and often more limited possibilities for the controlled exertion of influence, but they are also frequently more difficult to manage. On the following pages we introduce the Peer Name Resolution Protocol (PNRP) and the GNU Name System (GNS), two alternatives to DNS that have the objective of creating services with a high availability level.

Peer Name Resolution Protocol

The Peer Name Resolution Protocol (PNRP) [Mic13] is a Microsoft development that has even found its way into the company's operating systems in recent years. Because it is disabled by default and requires IP version 6, it has so far played only a very minor role and is just used for some special applications. Technically, PNRP is based on the structured peer-to-peer network *Pastry*, in which all participants build a logarithmic number of connections to others, which in turn ensure that any value-key pairs can be found in logarithmic time [RD01]. Thus, exactly the same algorithm runs in all participating systems, and each participant stores a portion of the total namespace. Which name mappings participants are responsible for depends on their identity, the 256-bit *PRNP ID*. This includes, among others, a hash value of their name and parts of their IPv6 address. An extensive caching concept is designed to prevent the overloading of individual participants and counteract node failures.

Because there is no hierarchical allocation of names in PRNP, the names within the system are also 'flat'. Transparently from the operating system, all registered names are virtually linked into the DNS structure under `name.pnrp.net`. Because of the flat namespace, however, the global uniqueness of the names is also not automatically guaranteed. In particular, attackers, too, can easily register names that may possibly be resolved. For this reason, PRNP also offers the possibility of registering *secure names*. These can no longer be easily reproduced by people, however. The structure of these names is `pnamep-authority.pnrp.net`. The term `authority` here refers to the hexadecimal representation of an SHA-1 hash value covering the name and the public key of the registering entity. Much as with the DNSCurve protocol, the name itself can therefore be used as a trust anchor.

PRNP supports the use of insecure, memorable as well as secure names with high entropy

As well as a global namespace, PNRP can also handle local namespaces. Microsoft calls these *clouds*. Standard practice is to differentiate between global, site and local clouds. The differentiation relates to the IPv6 prefixes used, and all clouds can be independently searched. In addition, there is also the possibility to design one's own private clouds, for example for all the computers in a company. With regard to security, this differentiation only offers advantages when the integrity of all participating computers can be ensured.

The namespace can be structured in 'clouds'

On the whole, the assessment of PNRP security is relatively complex. The use of insecure names outside of local networks

Insecure names should not be used

should be completely avoided. With respect to the confidentiality of queries and responses, PNRP provides no protection mechanisms whatsoever, so attackers may be able to acquire comprehensive information simply by passive eavesdropping. Because the identities of the participants are not certified cryptographically, attackers can also try to register PRNP IDs in the vicinity of a victim in order to gain a greater impact. With regard to availability, PNRP is not dependent on individual subsystems. In particular, local and site clouds can continue to operate without a global cloud. However, the peer-to-peer protocol itself may possibly be attacked in order to mark particular participants as unavailable. The standard provides some countermeasures on its own, such as a check of the source-node address on acquiring the information in the local cache. A comprehensive, perhaps even formal, analysis of the system is not available, however, particularly since Microsoft has only partially published the caching strategies.

GNU Name System

The GNU Name System (GNS) is part of the GNUnet initiative, which aims to provide a comprehensive framework for serverless, secure use of the Internet based on peer-to-peer technologies. As with PNRP, GNS uses a structured peer-to-peer network to provide data on a distributed basis. In comparison with PRNP, however, more measures were implemented for availability [EG11]. The protocol is also protected by cryptographic measures against attacks by external parties.

The proposition of Zooko's triangle implies that name services cannot be distributed and secure if they allow easy-to-remember names

Perhaps the most interesting thing about GNS is how it handles *Zooko's triangle*, a proposition that is attributed to the security researcher Zooko Wilcox-O'Hearn. According to the proposition, name resolution should:

1. be secure;
2. be implemented in a distributed manner;
3. allow names that people can remember easily.

However, of these three characteristics only two can be achieved simultaneously. With DNSSEC, characteristics (1) and (3) are achieved. DNSCurve can fulfil (1) and (3) or (1) and (2), depending on the naming scheme. The insecure names in PNRP satisfy the characteristics (2) and (3), the secure names (1) and (2).

GNS circumvents this problem by using cryptographic names, but providing a system for secure aliases. The cryptographic names themselves are hash values of public keys and thus globally virtually unique. Much as with PRNP, they are represented in the form of `hash.zkey` in the 'normal' DNS namespace. To enable users to memorise these names, local aliases can be assigned. In English, they are also called *Pet Names* and are similarly incorporated in the DNS namespace in the form `alias.gnu`. The advantage of GNS is a recursive use of these aliases, so `bob.alice.gnu` would be mapped on the system, which designates `alice` locally as `bob`. In this way, a graph structure is developed, which reflects the trust in the naming. The disadvantage is that the names no longer have to be globally unique. In globally accessible URLs, it would therefore be necessary to continue to use names that are not human-readable.

20.5   Summary

Much like with a phone book, in the Internet human-understandable names must be converted into network-specific addresses. Particularly when using unsecured communication protocols, this service, generally implemented by the DNS infrastructure, is of great importance for secure network operation because users and systems use the names to make assumptions about who their respective communication partner is.

Secure name mapping is particularly important when using unsecured protocols

DNS, developed in the early 1980s, provides no adequate protective measures and contains a large number of vulnerabilities [AA04]. To counter cache-poisoning attacks in particular, it has been necessary to develop multiple, complex countermeasures.

DNSSEC builds on the existing DNS infrastructure and provides a hierarchical certification of public keys to overcome these shortcomings. DNSSEC is relatively complex with respect to implementation and operation, but provides end-to-end security of the name mappings in terms of authenticity and integrity. The confidentiality and availability of the data is degraded by DNSSEC, however.

DNSSEC addresses the two key security objectives: authenticity and integrity of the mapped names

The DNSCurve protocol is a protocol that complements DNSSEC and protects packets by means of session keys and does not sign offline. Thanks to this procedure, confidentiality can in principle be improved, but there remain open questions regarding maintainability, such as when cryptographic methods need to be replaced by new, more secure methods.

DNSCurve is a security protocol that complements DNSSEC

The distributed mapping of names offers the theoretical advantage that the systems can be more robust with regard to failures and malicious surveillance of participants can be severely restricted. To what extent these methods, such as the PRNP or GNS that have been described, establish themselves remains to be seen, particularly because they bring a higher response delay with them and DNS, despite its hierarchical structure, has previously shown itself to be comparatively resistant to failures.

20.6 Supplemental Reading

[AAL⁺05a]   ARENDS, R.; AUSTEIN, R.; LARSON, M.; MASSEY, D.; ROSE, S.: *DNS Security Introduction and Requirements*. 2005. – RFC 4033, IETF, Status: Proposed Standard, https://tools.ietf.org/html/rfc4033

[AAL⁺05b]   ARENDS, R.; AUSTEIN, R.; LARSON, M.; MASSEY, D.; ROSE, S.: *Resource Records for the DNS Security Extensions*. 2005. – RFC 4034, IETF, Status: Proposed Standard, https://tools.ietf.org/html/rfc4034

[DAV⁺08]   DAGON, D.; ANTONAKAKIS, M.; VIXIE, P.; JINMEI, T.; LEE, W.: Increased DNS forgery resistance through 0x20-bit encoding: security via leet queries. In: *Proceedings of the 15th ACM conference on Computer and Communications Security*, 2008, S. 211–222

[HM09]   HUBERT, A.; MOOK, R. van: *Measures for Making DNS More Resilient against Forged Answers*. 2009. – RFC 5452, IETF, Status: Proposed Standard, https://tools.ietf.org/html/rfc5452

[HS13a]   HERZBERG, A.; SHULMAN, H.: DNSSEC: Security and availability challenges. In: *IEEE Conference on Communications and Network Security (CNS)*, 2013, S. 365–366

[HS13b]   HERZBERG, A.; SHULMAN, H.: Fragmentation Considered Poisonous, or: One-domain-to-rule-them-all.org. In: *IEEE Conference on Communications and Network Security (CNS)*, 2013, S. 224–232

[KMG12]   KOLKMAN, O.; MEKKING, W.; GIEBEN, R.: *DNSSEC Operational Practices, Version 2*. 2012. – RFC 6781, IETF, Status: Proposed Standard, https://tools.ietf.org/html/rfc6781

[WB13]   WEILER, S.; BLACKA, D.: *Clarifications and Implementation Notes for DNS Security (DNSSEC)*. 2013. – RFC 6840, IETF, Status: Proposed Standard, `https://tools.ietf.org/html/rfc6840`

20.7 Questions

1. Why are cache-poisoning attacks the most significant threat in traditional DNS infrastructures?
2. Do long or short time-to-live fields in DNS records benefit cache poisoning?
3. NAT is often used in many private households. Is it more advantageous in such scenarios to trust the DNS caching server on the NAT router or to operate a caching server on the clients themselves? In your argument discuss the fact that NAT modifies source ports.
4. Why, in certain circumstances, are DNSSEC records advantageous to cache poisoning as described due to fragmented responses?
5. Why is a three-way handshake not used to prevent amplification attacks in the DNS protocol?
6. Justify the need for synchronous clocks in the use of DNSSEC. What does this mean for the use of the Network Time Protocol (NTP)?
7. Why, with NSEC3, is an extremely high number of iterations (e.g. 10,000) not used to make it harder for the attacker to perform trial-and-error probing?
8. Find out what the salt value is that is currently used in the protection of NSEC3 records in the .de zone.
9. Using a system for distributed name resolution, in which order of magnitude can the latencies be expected?
10. With transactions, majority voting between participants in a distributed system can be implemented. In this case, a transaction is regarded as completed when the majority of the participants have confirmed the content. Explain how the registration of easily remembered names could be realised securely and in a distributed manner with transactions, despite the proposition of Zooko's triangle. Why is such a system not used for name resolution?

21   Internet Firewalls

The preceding chapters in this part of the book mainly deal with directly protecting systems and packets from attacks. This chapter expands on that discussion and is devoted to the task of protecting certain parts of a network from the intrusion of 'undesirable' data units.

In building construction, the word *firewall* has become the established term for describing the task of protecting certain parts of a building from the spread of fire. Based on this term, the components used for protecting specific subnetworks from potential attack from other network parts are referred to as *Internet firewalls*. This term may not be totally accurate from a technical standpoint since Internet firewalls, unlike normal firewalls, should not be completely impenetrable (disconnecting the physical network connection would suffice in this case). However, it does convey an intuitive understanding of the necessary task.

Analogy to firewalls in building construction

21.1   Tasks and Basic Principles of Firewalls

Because an Internet firewall should not be completely impenetrable, it can easily be compared to the drawbridge of a medieval castle [ZCC00]. A drawbridge typically had the following functions:

Tasks

- It forced people to enter a castle at one specific location that could be carefully controlled.
- It prevented attackers from getting close to other defence components of the castle.
- It forced people to exit the castle at one specific location.

Internet firewalls provide access control at the subnetwork level

For obvious reasons, an Internet firewall is normally installed at the network gateway between a protected trusted subnetwork and an untrustworthy network, which allows it to monitor incoming and outgoing data traffic. An example of this is the point where a corporate local area network is connected to the global Internet, see Figure 21.1. All systems of a protected subnetwork are normally protected by the same means, that is, from the same undesirable data packets. Thus, an Internet firewall implements access control at the subnetwork level.

Figure 21.1
Firewall placement between a protected network and the Internet

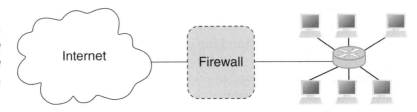

Functions of Internet firewalls

An Internet firewall therefore provides a central point where access control decisions are made and implemented [Sem96]. It is also an effective means of monitoring the Internet activities of subnetworks and preventing certain security problems from proliferating from one network area to another.

Limit to protection provided by Internet firewalls

Firewalls can – if at all – only provide limited protection against malicious insiders who are determined to bypass the security strategy of a subnetwork. In particular, a firewall cannot influence any data traffic that is not passing through it. This self-evident fact is often overlooked. An example of this is an open WLAN access point that is set up with a system placed behind the corporate firewall, enabling attackers to gain unrestricted access. A firewall furthermore cannot protect against totally new attack patterns and also only offers limited protection against the intrusion of software viruses.

A differentiation is made between two diametrically opposed approaches to the basic security strategy that can be implemented by an Internet firewall [WC95, SH09]:

Default-Deny Strategy

- The *Default-Deny Strategy* is based on the principle that 'Anything that is not explicitly permitted is denied'. First an analysis is undertaken to determine which network services users of the protected subnetwork require and how these services can be made available in a secure way. Only those services for which a legitimate need exists and that can be supplied in a secure manner are provided. All other services are blocked by technical means. An example of this approach is permitting the transmission of HTTP traffic to any arbitrary systems and SMTP traffic to an e-mail gateway. All other data traffic would be blocked by the firewall. The advantage of this strategy from the perspective of security is that it also provides limited protection from unknown threats.

■ The *Default-Permit Strategy* follows an opposite approach, which is 'Anything that is not explicitly forbidden is permitted'. With this approach services categorised as high risk or contravening local security strategies are explicitly blocked by appropriate measures in the firewall. All other services are considered permissible and not blocked by the firewall. For example, such a strategy could mean that traffic from the *Server Message Block (SMB) protocol* and *Simple Mail Transfer Protocol (SMTP)* protocols are generally blocked to prevent the connections to Windows shares and restrict the sending of unwanted mails. Additionally, SSH connections could only be permitted to specific hosts that are known to be solely accessible for administrators with complex passwords. This approach is preferred by most users because it usually gives them more flexibility. However, this strategy can, in principle, only offer protection from known threats.

Default-Permit Strategy

As the description of these two approaches indicates, each Internet service blocked or permitted by a firewall always has to be examined specifically. The following section provides a brief overview of popular Internet services and their transport within the framework of the TCP/IP protocol family.

21.2 Firewall-Relevant Internet Services and Protocols

In practice, the following Internet services are of particular importance in the context of Internet firewalls:

Internet services

■ *File Exchange* often takes place on the basis of the *Server Message Block (SMB) Protocol*, the *File Transfer Protocol (FTP)* and *Web-based Distributed Authoring and Versioning (WebDAV)*. In closed UNIX environments, the *Network File System (NFS)* is also used in some cases.

■ The *accessing of websites* takes place on the basis of the *Hypertext Transfer Protocol (HTTP)* or the secure version *HTTPS*.

■ *E-mails* are usually sent with the *Simple Mail Transfer Protocol (SMTP)* and received using the *Post Office Protocol (POP)* or the *Internet Message Access Protocol (IMAP)*.

In addition, there are a number of other popular applications and protocols:

■ *chat applications* such as *ICQ* or *Jabber-based methods* such as *Google Talk*;

■ *real-time-enabled conferencing systems* such as *Skype* or *Adobe Connect*;

■ *name services*, which are provided in the Internet through the *Domain Name System (DNS)*;

■ *network management* based on the *Simple Network Management Protocol (SNMP)*;

■ *clock synchronisation* using the *Network Time Protocol (NTP)*;

■ *remote terminal access* and *remote command execution* using the *Secure Shell (SSH)*;

■ *terminal services*, most commonly represented by the *Independent Computing Architecture (ICA)* and the *Remote Desktop Protocol (RDP)*;

■ *printing services*, based, for example, on the *Internet Printing Protocol (IPP)*;

■ *voice-over-IP (VoIP)* systems, which normally make use of the *Session Initiation Protocol (SIP)* and the *Real Time Transport Protocol (RTP)*.

These services are often implemented by client-server programs. In other cases, peer-to-peer concepts are used. Examples are represented by Skype or by directly communicating VoIP participants. In both concepts, programs communicate using application protocols and exchange either *segments* via a TCP connection or *datagrams* using the UDP protocol. TCP segments and UDP datagrams are transported in IP packets that in turn are sent in protocol data units of the Link Layer Protocols used on the different communication links between source and destination computer, for example, the Ethernet.

Addressing of application processes   The two tuples *(source-IP address, source port)* and *(destination-IP address, destination port)* are used to address individual application processes. A *port* represents a number, comprising two octets, which explicitly identifies the Service Access Point (SAP) of an application process within an end system.

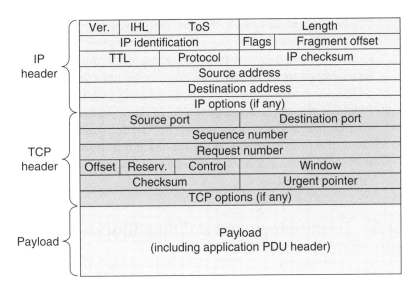

Figure 21.2
Frame format of an
IP packet with a TCP
segment

Figure 21.2 shows the frame format of an IPv4 packet that is transporting a TCP segment. The following protocol fields are of particular importance for Internet firewalls:

Firewall-relevant
protocol fields

- Fields of the access protocol ('Link layer protocol', not shown):
  The fields of particular interest are those that identify the contained network layer protocol (usually IPv4 or IPv6) and the
  source addresses of the access protocol, e.g. MAC addresses in
  Ethernet.
- Fields of the IP protocol (here in version 4): Of special
  interest here are the source and destination addresses, the
  flags, which also contains one bit to indicate IP fragments,
  the protocol identification of the user data contained (e.g.
  TCP, UDP) and possible options such as the stipulation of the
  transmission path by the source. However, at least in IPv4
  options are rarely used for anything other than attacks.
- Fields of the TCP protocol: The fields of particular interest are
  the source and destination ports that have a limited influence
  on determining the sending and receiving application, since
  many popular Internet services use well-defined port numbers. In addition, individual bits of the control field have an
  effect on connection control. An ACK bit is set in all PDUs except in the first connection establishment PDU, which means
  that an ACK bit that has not been set identifies a connect
  PDU. A SYN bit is set in all PDUs except in the first two PDUs
  of a connection. A packet with a set ACK bit and a set SYN bit

therefore identifies the PDU accepting the connection. Lastly, an RST bit permits a connection to be terminated immediately without displaying a further error message, and can therefore be used to terminate a connection without providing additional information.

■ Fields of the application protocol: In some instances it may also be necessary or meaningful for the Internet firewall to check the protocol fields of an application protocol. However, these vary from application to application and therefore will not be discussed here.

21.3   Terminology and Building Blocks

Internet firewalls are usually made up of certain building blocks that fulfil specific tasks and possess certain characteristics. This section briefly introduces the relevant terminology.

Internet firewall   An *Internet firewall* (hereafter simply referred to as a firewall for short) is a component, or a group of components, that restricts access between a protected network and the Internet or another untrustworthy network. In this context access refers to the exchange of data packets. Even if the term may appear to be an unusual choice at first glance, it should convey that, from the point of view of security, access control decisions are made and implemented on the basis of a firewall.

Packet filtering   *Packet filtering* specifies the actions taken by a specific system when selectively controlling the flow of data packets from and to a specific network. Packet filtering is an important basic technique for implementing access control at the subnetwork level in packet-oriented networks such as the Internet. The packet filtering process is also referred to as *screening*.

Bastion host   A *bastion host* is a computer that has special security requirements due to the network configuration that makes it more vulnerable to certain attacks than the other computers in a subnetwork. A bastion host that is directly attached to a firewall often represents the main point of contact between application processes within a protected network and the processes of external hosts.

Dual-homed host   A computer is identified as a *dual-homed host* if it has at least two network interfaces and is therefore part of two subnetworks.

Proxy   A *proxy* is a program that deputises for the clients of a protected subnetwork and communicates with external servers. Proxies relay approved requests from internal clients to the actual servers and in return also forward server responses to the internal clients.

The term *perimeter network* identifies a subnetwork that is inserted between an external and an internal network to create an additional security zone. Perimeter networks are often referred to as *demilitarized zones (DMZs)*.

As already touched on many times in previous chapters, *Network Address Translation (NAT)* is a technique in which an intermediate system deliberately modifies address fields in a data packet in order to implement an address conversion between internal and external addresses. For example, with this technique a large number of systems can be connected to the Internet on the basis of a small number of externally valid addresses, that is, globally valid in the Internet. Although NAT is not actually a security technique, it offers the advantage from a security perspective that the internal addresses will not be known to external attackers. This makes it more difficult for deliberate attacks to be executed to individual internal systems from the outside. With NAT the 'initiative' for specific data streams must in most cases originate from internal systems, otherwise the application processes of internal systems do not become visible to the outside.

21.4   Firewall Architectures

As mentioned above, Internet firewalls can be built from one component or a group of components. As a result, a number of firewall architectures have established themselves over the years. The structures of some popular ones will be explained in this section.

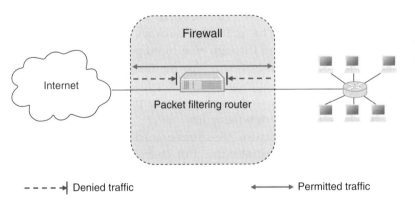

Figure 21.3
Architecture of a packet filter firewall

The simplest of these architectures consists solely of one packet filter and is illustrated in Figure 21.3. This architecture can be built either with a commercially available server computer using two network interfaces or with a dedicated router that also incorporates basic packet filter functions. The protection function of this architecture is based solely on filtering undesirable data packets between a protected network and the Internet (or other untrustworthy subnetwork). In Figure 21.3 (and in other figures in the rest of this section) a straight arrow shows the 'permitted' data traffic and a dotted line the 'blocked traffic'.

Figure 21.4
Dual-homed-host
architecture

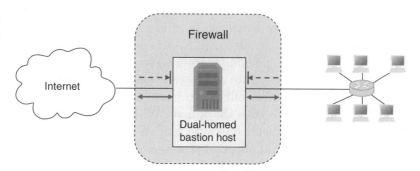

Figure 21.4 illustrates the minimally more complex *dual-homed host architecture*. Although there may be no difference between the hardware configuration of this architecture and a packet filter (if the packet filter is implemented on a workstation computer), the software on the dual-homed host provides additional security functions because its main task is not limited to pure packet filtering.

A dual-homed
host provides
proxy services

A dual-homed host provides proxy services to internal and external clients, so IP packets do not need to be routed directly into and out of the protected subnetwork, which may give a certain security advantage. The protected network in this case is only attached to the Internet through monitored proxy services. In some cases, the dual-homed host can also handle routing functions for IP packets. However, appropriate packet filter functionality must then also be implemented on the host to prevent the protective effects of the firewall from being lost.

A dual-homed host
should be secured
as a bastion host

With this architecture the dual-homed host is the central attack point for potential attackers therefore it should be regarded as a bastion host and protected accordingly (compare also Section 21.6).

The drawback of this architecture is that, depending on the size of the protected subnetwork and the bandwidth of the Internet connection, a dual-homed host can develop into a performance bottleneck.

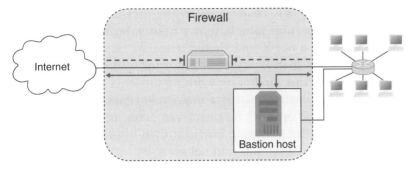

Figure 21.5
Screened-host archi-tecture

Figure 21.5 shows a *screened-host architecture*, which spreads the functionality of the packet filter and the proxy server over two components. The packet filter allows permitted traffic to pass between the Internet and the internal bastion host, and blocks all direct traffic between other internal computers and the Internet. In some cases certain traffic streams can also be permitted directly between the internal computers and the Internet, but this can introduce potential vulnerabilities. The bastion host in turn provides proxy services for communication between internal computers and the Internet.

Screened-host architecture

Two main advantages can be gained from separating packet filter functionality and proxy services into two consecutively switched devices:

Advantages of separating packet filtering and proxy services

- In terms of security, a bastion host will be better protected from attacks on potentially available services that should not be accessible from outside. Furthermore, compared with proxy services, relatively simple software can be used to implement packet filter functionality, which means that a relatively compact software installation is all that is required on the respective system. This is particularly an advantage because complexity is the main obstacle in the construction of secure systems.
- Another benefit of this architecture is that it can also provide a performance advantage. When certain data streams, e.g. Internet telephony, are routed directly into an internal network, they do not have to 'cross through' the same computer that also provides the proxy services.

In terms of the physical structure of the networking, it should be noted that a bastion host could sometimes also be connected to the same internal subnetwork for which it provides security services. In this case, its relationship to the firewall tends to be of a logical

Physical networking structure

nature since it is only conditional on the packet filter rules. It is particularly important to note that a bastion host essentially has special protection needs and should therefore be more difficult to access physically than the systems protected by it (also see Section 21.6). However, this kind of networking presents a security problem even if the bastion host is a physically separate installation: depending on the networking technique used, attackers who are able to compromise a bastion host can then directly sniff or even modify the traffic in the internal network.

Sniffing threat when bastion host compromised!

Figure 21.6
Screened-subnetwork architecture

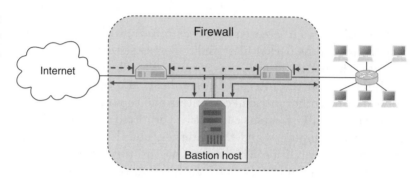

The *screened-subnetwork architecture* illustrated in Figure 21.6 counters the particular threat of a potentially compromised bastion host by setting up a *demilitarised zone*, also referred to as a *perimeter network*. This zone is created using two packet filters between which one or more bastion hosts is embedded for the purpose of providing proxy services. This zone is also available for the connection of the servers that provide services to external computers, such as web or mail services. The main task of the second packet filter is to protect the internal network from the threat of a possibly compromised bastion host.

Perimeter network

Figure 21.7
Split-screened subnetwork architecture

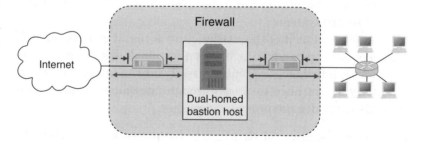

The *split-screened subnetwork architecture* shown in Figure 21.7 is an even more sophisticated architecture in terms of security. In this

Split-screened subnetwork architecture

architecture, a dual-homed bastion host divides the demilitarised zone into two separate subnetworks. Using proxy services, the bastion host is better able than a simple packet filter to exercise finely granulated control over the data streams.

Furthermore, an outer packet filter protects the bastion host from external attackers and an inner packet filter protects the internal subnetwork from the bastion host if it is compromised. The architecture thus provides an 'in-depth defence' comparable to that of a knight's castle, where attackers normally have to surmount several protective walls before they can penetrate the interior.

'In-depth defence'

21.5 Packet Filtering

As our discussion on the different firewall architectures has shown, the packet filtering function plays a central role in securing individual subnetworks. This section takes a detailed look at the role of packet filtering.

The first question in this context is which protective functions can IP packet filtering provide for access control?

Theoretically, protective measures of any complexity are feasible because all data exchanged between two or more entities in the Internet is ultimately transported in IP packets. In practice, however, the two basic considerations listed below have proven useful in the decision criteria for designing protective measures:

Proxy service or packet filtering?

1. Selection operations, which require detailed knowledge about the functioning of higher level protocols or a comprehensive evaluation of the protocol data units transmitted in previous IP packets, are often easier and more secure to implement as specific proxy services.
2. Simple selection operations that have to be executed quickly and always evaluate individual IP packets can be implemented more efficiently through the use of packet filters.

This kind of *basic packet filtering* uses the following information to make its selection decision:

Basic packet filtering

- ■ source IP address;
- ■ destination IP address;
- ■ transport protocol;
- ■ source port;
- ■ destination port;

- in some cases, specific protocol fields (e.g. TCPs ACK-bit and SYN-bit);
- network interface where packet was received.

Stateful packet filtering   In addition to these basic functions, *stateful packet filtering* is also often used in selection decisions. This variant, also referred to as *dynamic packet filtering*, ensures that incoming packets are only allowed to pass if they are a response to previously observed outgoing packets. This even works for connectionless protocols, for example UDP or ICMP. Another example of stateful packet filtering is the rate limitation of certain packet types.

Basic protocol check   Lastly, packet filters can also handle basic *protocol checks*. An example is the checking of IP packets that are sent to a DNS port for correct formatting in accordance with the DNS protocol. Another related point is that packets containing an HTTP-PDU in their data part should definitely not be forwarded to certain IP addresses.

Increasing complexity means additional resources!   The design of packet filter functions should take into account that the more complex they become, the more resources they require for execution. Therefore, it is always important to consider whether a two-step approach using a simple packet filter and application-specific proxy services would produce a more efficient mechanism for the checking process.

Packet filter actions   Based on the filtering rules configured in it, a packet filter decides how to proceed with each packet it looks at. This involves the following actions:

- forwarding the packet;
- dropping the packet;
- modifying the packet (e.g. removing certain IP options);
- in some cases, logging either an entire packet or parts of it;
- possibly sending an error message to the sender, taking into account that error messages could be helpful to any attackers who are preparing further attacks.

Specification of basic filter rules   Because packet filters normally attempt to separate a protected subnetwork from a less trustworthy network, an implicit understanding of the traffic direction is required for the specification of filter rules. Therefore, IP packets that are received from a network interface located outside the protected network are referred to as *inbound traffic*. Accordingly, packets that are received from the network interface of a protected subnetwork are considered to be *outbound traffic*. When packet filter rules are specified, the information identifying which network interface received the IP packet is usually based on one of the three alternatives 'inbound', 'outbound' or 'either'.

Subnet masks can be used to specify multiple source and destination IP addresses at once. For example, '125.26.0.0/16' refers to all IP addresses that begin with the prefix '125.26.'.

Use of subnet masks

The IP addresses in the following examples are often simply indicated as *'internal'* or *'external'* to keep the discussion neutral in terms of any particular network topology. Often, when the source and destination ports are given, entire ranges are specified, for example '>1023' for all port numbers higher than 1023.

One basic assumption is that packet filter rules are evaluated in the sequence in which they are specified and that the first rule applicable to a packet determines the action to be taken. Over the years it has been proved that this method is the easiest one for system administrators to understand and the best one for keeping errors in rule specification to a minimum.

Sequence of evaluating packet filter rules

The set of packet filter rules developed below illustrates the concepts described so far and is aimed at ensuring that only e-mail traffic is allowed between a protected subnetwork and the Internet (example according to [ZCC00]).

Example of a packet filter specification

Internet e-mail is exchanged between two SMTP servers in TCP connections. The initiative for the exchange originates from the server that is delivering the e-mails. This server establishes a TCP connection to destination port 25 of the receiving SMTP server for this purpose, selecting a number higher than 1023 as the source port. Since incoming as well as outgoing e-mails are allowed, packet filter rules have to be designed for both directions.

Table 21.1
Example of a packet filter specification

Rule	Direction	Src. addr.	Dest. addr.	Protocol	Src. port	Dest. port	ACK	Action
A	Inbound	External	Internal	TCP		25		Permit
B	Outbound	Internal	External	TCP		>1023		Permit
C	Outbound	Internal	External	TCP		25		Permit
D	Inbound	External	Internal	TCP		>1023		Permit
E	Either	Any	Any	Any		Any		Deny

Table 21.1 shows the first approach that can be taken. The two rules A and B are used to transmit incoming e-mails and rules C and D fulfil the same task for outgoing e-mails. Rule E is aimed at denying all other data traffic (Default-Deny Strategy).

First approach

Rule A allows inbound IP packets that are being sent to destination port 25 and are transporting TCP segments as payload. For the TCP connection to be established and maintained between the two SMTP servers the corresponding response packets of the server receiving the e-mails must be allowed to pass outside. Rule B therefore allows outbound IP packets to port numbers higher than 1023.

Protection function of the first approach

The following examples help to explain the protection function of these rules:

- Assume that an IP packet with a forged internal source address is being sent to the protected subnetwork from the outside. Since inbound packets are only forwarded if they have external source addresses and internal destination addresses (Rules A and D), this sort of attack will be successfully defeated. The same applies to outgoing packets from an internal attacker making use of external source addresses (Rules B and C).
- This filter specification is also effective at blocking incoming SSH traffic because SSH servers normally wait at port 22 for incoming connections and incoming traffic is only allowed by the packet filter if it is being sent either to port 25 or to a port higher than 1023 (Rules A and D). On the basis of Rules B and C, the same applies to outgoing SSH traffic.

Drawback of first approach

However, this rule set is not fully effective. For example, it does not block either incoming or outgoing traffic of RDP sessions. A terminal server supporting RDP usually waits at port 3389 for incoming connections and the corresponding client programs use destination ports from the set of numbers above 1023. Because of Rule B, inbound RDP PDUs can therefore pass the packet filter and, because of Rule D, outbound RDP PDUs are not blocked either. This possibly provides potential attackers with an attractive opportunity because the RDP protocol allows an attacker, after guessing a password, to remotely access screen information and perform keyboard as well as mouse input, therefore he will gain full control over the machine.

Table 21.2
Inclusion of source port in a packet filter rule set

Rule	Direction	Src. addr.	Dest. addr.	Protocol	Src. port	Dest. port	ACK	Action
A	Inbound	External	Internal	TCP	>1023	25		Permit
B	Outbound	Internal	External	TCP	25	>1023		Permit
C	Outbound	Internal	External	TCP	>1023	25		Permit
D	Inbound	External	Internal	TCP	25	>1023		Permit
E	Either	Any	Any	Any	Any	Any		Deny

Second approach: including a source port

This problem can be dealt with through the inclusion of the source port in the filter specification. Table 21.2 shows the resulting filter rules. With this rule set outbound packets are only permitted to ports higher than 1023 if they originate from source port 25 (Rule B). Therefore, PDUs from internal RDP client or RDP server programs are blocked. Similarly, Rule D blocks incoming traffic to RDP client or RDP server programs.

Drawback of second approach

In practice, however, one cannot assume that an attacker will not use port 25 as the source port for his RDP client. In this instance the packet filter would allow the traffic to pass.

Table 21.3

Inclusion of an ACK bit in the packet filter rule set

Rule	Direction	Src. addr.	Dest. addr.	Protocol	Src. port	Dest. port	ACK	Action
A	Inbound	External	Internal	TCP	>1023	25	Any	Permit
B	Outbound	Internal	External	TCP	25	>1023	Yes	Permit
C	Outbound	Internal	External	TCP	>1023	25	Any	Permit
D	Inbound	External	Internal	TCP	25	>1023	Yes	Permit
E	Either	Any	Any	Any	Any	Any	Any	Deny

Table 21.3 shows an improved version of the filtering specification that also incorporates the ACK bit of the TCP protocol header and includes Rules B and D. Since the ACK bit is assumed to be set in Rule B, this rule can no longer be used to open an outgoing connection (the TCP connection request is identified by an ACK bit not set). Similarly, the stipulation of a set ACK bit in Rule D prevents the opening of incoming TCP connections sent to ports with a number higher than 1023.

Third approach: including a TCP-ACK bit

As a basic guideline it should be noted that each packet incoming filter rule designed to allow TCP-PDUs for outgoing connections (or the reverse) should request a set ACK bit.

If the firewall contains a bastion host, then the SMTP server should preferably be run on this system or the SMTP host be regarded as a bastion host. Incorporating the IP address of the bastion host into the packet filter rule set can increase the security of the protected subnetwork because in this instance attacks on the SMTP server program will only affect the bastion host. Table 21.4 shows the resulting packet filter rule set.

Fourth approach: including address of SMTP server

Table 21.4

Inclusion of bastion host in packet filter rule set

Rule	Direction	Src. addr.	Dest. addr.	Protocol	Src. port	Dest. port	ACK	Action
A	Inbound	External	Bastion	TCP	>1023	25	Any	Permit
B	Outbound	Bastion	External	TCP	25	>1023	Yes	Permit
C	Outbound	Bastion	External	TCP	>1023	25	Any	Permit
D	Inbound	External	Bastion	TCP	25	>1023	Yes	Permit
E	Either	Any	Any	Any	Any	Any	Any	Deny

With a screened subnetwork firewall, two packet filters have to be equipped with the appropriate rule sets: one for the traffic between the Internet and the bastion host and one for the traffic between the bastion host and internal subnetwork.

21.6   Bastion Hosts and Proxy Servers

Point of contact between internal and external systems

As explained in Section 21.3, the bastion host is the main point of contact between application processes within a protected network and the processes of external systems. Depending on the firewall architecture, it is responsible for the task of packet filtering and/or provides dedicated proxy services for specific applications. As the principal point of contact for the protected network to external systems, a bastion host has a higher exposure to threats than the systems to which it provides security functions.

Even though a dedicated packet filter can be used to reduce these risks, special measures should also be taken to secure the proxy server itself. This section begins by presenting some general observations on securing bastion hosts and concludes by briefly reviewing how proxy services are implemented.

Configuration of a bastion host

The principles applied to building a 'secure' bastion host are ultimately merely extensions to the strategies used for securing any key system in a network. The basic rule is that the system configuration of a bastion host should be kept *as simple as possible*. If there are any services that do not have to be offered on the bastion host, they should not even be installed on it.

Potential compromising of bastion host

One should also basically anticipate the fact that a bastion host might be compromised. Internal systems should therefore not place more trust in the bastion host than is absolutely necessary. For example, no file systems should be exported to the bastion host, no login should be enabled from the bastion host to internal systems, etc. If possible, the bastion host should be integrated into the network infrastructure in such a way that it is unable to eavesdrop on data traffic in the internal subnetwork. This can be done through the use of another packet filter to separate the network or by a MAC address filter in the inner switch.

Event logging for attack detection

In addition, extensive event logging should take place on the bastion host to ensure early detection of any attacks or successful compromising of the host. Note that a successful attacker should not be able to tamper with event logging at a later time. One possibility is to transfer the event entries over a dedicated interface to a separate log-computer that does not have a network interface itself.

Unattractive attack target

As long as no important reasons exist to the contrary, the bastion host should preferably be an 'unattractive' target for potential attackers. Therefore, the only software tools that should be installed on it are those that are essential to its operation. Above all, no user accounts should be available on a bastion host that are also used in the internal network. This will reduce the risk of a successful reconnaissance or executing password attacks.

Lastly, a bastion host should definitely be installed in a secure location where general physical access is not allowed to ensure that the risk of manipulation is kept to a minimum. Its system configuration should be backed up at regular intervals. A routine reinstallation of the system from a security copy can also be considered for the purpose of correcting any possible manipulation that has occurred. However, it is important to be aware that any existing weakness in a system configuration that has already been exploited by an attacker can be used again for gaining access to the system. A reinstallation of the system therefore does not significantly reduce the risk of it being compromised.

Installation in a secure location

A bastion host equipped with proxy services can give users of a protected subnetwork the illusion that all systems in this network are able to access Internet services although in reality it is only the bastion host that has access. In this case also the outside server has the illusion of exchanging data with the bastion host only.

Proxy services

There are two main different types of proxy services:

- If a proxy server analyses the commands of the application protocol and interprets its semantics, it is referred to as an *application level proxy*.

  Application level proxy

- If, on the other hand, the proxy server is restricted to forwarding application PDUs between client and server, it is called a *circuit level proxy*.

  Circuit level proxy

A web proxy that automatically removes advertisements and viruses is a typical example of an application level proxy. Other possible protocols include DNS and SMTP. An example for a circuit level proxy is a SOCKS proxy, which allows games or other specialised, often interactive, applications to communicate. Circuit level proxies are mostly installed when no application level proxy exists for the particular protocol. As there is no significant security gain compared to NAT deployments, their relevance has decreased in recent years. The only advantage is the possibility of authenticating and authorising internal users.

If a proxy service is used, applications-specific data streams have to be rerouted to the proxy server. Furthermore, the proxy server must be informed of which application server it is to use

Different variants of proxy services

for the connection. The following four implementation possibilities exist:

User procedures

■ *Proxy-aware user procedures:* An example of this variant is the use of SSH proxies. Here the user first registers on the bastion host and from there establishes a SSH session to the actual desired server.

Client software

■ *Proxy-aware client software:* In this case the client software is responsible for transferring the corresponding data to the proxy server. This approach is used, for example, with proxy-enabled web browsers where client software only has to be configured once with the name or address of the web proxy.

Operating system

■ *Proxy-aware operating system:* With this variant the operating system (using the appropriate configuration data) is responsible for the redirection of transfers to the proxy server. In this deployment scenario the configuration data could be automatically distributed via DHCP in combination with the Web Proxy Autodiscovery Protocol (WPAD), therefore no user interaction is required.

Routers

■ *Proxy-aware router:* This variant transfers the task of activating the proxy to an intermediate system, which transparently reroutes connections initiated by internal client computers to a proxy computer and also sends the necessary address data to the computer. As this approach does not require support by users or devices it is usually called *r proxy*.

21.7   Other Aspects of Modern Firewall Systems

The mechanisms and properties of Internet firewalls that have been introduced so far are of a very basic nature. Modern firewalls offer a number of other technical tricks with the aim of increasing security. Some examples of such mechanisms and concepts are:

Data diodes

■ So-called *data diodes* or *one-way gateways* are used to separate high-security areas from the Internet. These are firewall systems that implement physical measures to demonstrably transport data in only one direction, e.g by using a fibre optic cable with just one fibre. On the one hand, systems of this kind can be used to transmit highly confidential data in a secure zone. On the other hand, monitoring data can be retrieved from areas that require a high level of integrity, such as the monitoring of power stations.

■ The concept of the *Remote-Controlled Browser System (Re-CoBS)* is intended for similarly high-security environments: In this scenario, a specially hardened terminal server runs on the Bastion Host of a screened subnet, and within this server the clients on the local network can use a web browser. The firewall for the local network also inspects the exact protocol sequence of the terminal service protocol. For ReCoBS there is a Common Criteria Protection Profile from the German Federal Office for Security in Information Technology [BSI08].

Remote-Controlled Browser System

■ At the same time, firewalls are featuring more and more technologies for *Deep Packet Inspection*, which is the detailed examination of protocol sequences and the transmitted user data. One difficulty for these approaches is the increasing use of encrypted connections. For this reason, many commercial firewalls offer the possibility of breaking up SSL/TLS or SSH connections. Known as *SSL inspection* or *SSH inspection*, in essence this technology implements an automated man-in-the-middle attack. In the systems of the local network, the firewall's main certificate is therefore configured as a valid certificate authority in order to indicate the legitimacy of the procedure to them.

Deep Packet Inspection

Interrupting cryptographic connections

■ Another persistent trend is the integration of firewalls in comprehensive network security solutions, including connection to the user management, virus scanners and VPN access management, to increase the maintainability while simultaneously enabling correlations to be established. Thus, for example, network access can be blocked when no user is logged in to a system or when the current status of a system's operating system is inadequate. These efforts are currently being discussed under a whole range of keywords. The most common are *Network Access Control (NAC)* [Ser10] or *Unified Threat Management (UTM)* when the security systems are combined on one physical system.

Integrated solutions

21.8   Summary

Internet firewalls provide access control at the subnetwork level. For this purpose Internet firewalls are normally installed between a protected subnetwork and a less trustworthy network, such as the public Internet.

Access control at the subnetwork level

At the same time it should be noted that an Internet firewall is only capable of monitoring those data streams that pass through it and it cannot provide any protection from internal attackers.

Firewall architectures

Depending on the level of security being sought and the resources available, an Internet firewall can be constructed using either a single or a group of components. Over time a number of architectures have evolved as a result, each offering specific security features. In practice, the *packet filter*, the *dual-homed-host*, the *screened-host*, the *screened-subnetwork* and the *split-screened-subnetwork* architectures are the most popular.

Central elements are packet filters and proxy servers

The central elements used by all these architectures are *packet filters*, which make access decisions for each IP packet routed through them, and *proxy servers*, which enable an applications-specific monitoring of data streams. The computing systems with specific functions installed in a firewall are called

Bastion hosts

bastion hosts. Because they have a high level of exposure to attackers, bastion hosts must be installed with particular care and constantly monitored.

21.9   Supplemental Reading

[BSI08]   BSI (BUNDESAMT FÜR SICHERHEIT IN DER INFORMATIONSTECHNIK, FEDERAL OFFICE FOR SECURITY IN INFORMATION TECHNOLOGY): *Common Criteria Protection Profile for Remote-Controlled Browsers Systems (ReCoBS)*. BSI PP BSI-PP-0040. Version: 2008

[Sem96]   SEMERIA, C.: *Internet Firewalls and Security*. 1996. – 3Com Technical Paper

[SH09]   SCARFONE, K.; HOFFMAN, P.: *Guidelines on Firewalls and Firewall Policy*. NIST Special Publication 800-41. Version: 2009

[ZCC00]   ZWICKY, E.; COOPER, S.; CHAPMAN, B.: *Building Internet Firewalls*. Second Edition, O'Reilly, 2000
A recognised standard work in this field that not only offers in-depth explanations of the principle functions of firewall components but also provides detailed practical information on packet filtering and securing the most popular Internet services. It is a little bit old-fashioned unfortunately.

21.10   Questions

1.   What basic information is normally necessary for access control decisions that identify whether or not an IP packet should be routed?
2.   What further tests can be carried out and which type of components should be used for this purpose?
3.   Does a bastion host always have to be a dual-homed host? Is the opposite conclusion correct?
4.   Why should information identifying which network interface card received a packet be included in the generation of packet filter rules?
5.   Use of packet filtering for access control.

   ■ What is the main underlying assumption in the use of packet filtering for access control?
   ■ Can this lead to potential security risks?
   ■ If yes, how can one deal with these risks?
   ■ Can you give some reasons why the use of packet filters still makes sense?

6.   Why should packet filter rules always be applied in the sequence of their specification?
7.   Research, e.g. using the appropriate Internet RFC, the information required for packet filtering of the SNMPv3 protocol and list the packet filter rules for blocking SNMPv3 data streams.
8.   Which restriction can you implement in packet filtering through an appropriate evaluation of the ACK bit of TCP?
9.   Why do you always have to allow two traffic directions with TCP-based services?
10.   Is there a functional difference between firewalls that track the TCP connections state and firewalls that monitor the direction of TCP connections with the help of the SYN flags?
11.   How can you protect your network so that a possibly compromised bastion host is not misused for eavesdropping on your internal traffic?
12.   Microsoft's Secure Socket Tunneling Protocol (SSTP) [Mic14] establishes PPP-based VPN connections over HTTPS. Why does the approach use HTTP over TLS and not pure TLS? What does this mean for the achievable security properties?

22 Automated Attack Detection and Response

The security measures described in the previous chapters are aimed primarily at preventing security incidents and reducing the associated risk of such incidents. The idea is to use cryptographic techniques to completely prevent an attacker from executing an attack. As already mentioned in Section 17.1, however, this approach is not always sufficient or appropriate for several reasons:

Preventive measures are often too expensive, inflexible, wrongly planned or not feasible for regulatory reasons

- **Cost:** Proactively safeguarding a system against all possible attacks can generate extremely high costs and a huge amount of technical effort, although many of the threats never become relevant.
- **Low flexibility:** Restrictive access rules in firewalls and proxies, forcing complex passwords and similar measures, only theoretically increase the security of networks. If the efforts for users are too high, they will circumvent the security guidelines. Complex passwords written down on the monitor or stuck under the keyboard are a common example of this.
- **Error of judgement:** Even if a systematic threat analysis was conscientiously carried out and an acceptable risk was identified, some threats may simply have been underestimated. The risk assessment can change significantly, especially if new attack techniques are employed or if certain types of attackers – e.g. politically motivated – were previously not taken into account.
- **Compliance:** Sometimes distinct individuals or enterprises have no direct way of eliminating security problems because

Security in Fixed and Wireless Networks, Second Edition.
Guenter Schaefer and Michael Rossberg.
Copyright © 2014 by dpunkt.verlag GmbH, Heidelberg, Germany.
Title of the German original: Netzsicherheit   ISBN 978-3-86490-115-7

Figure 22.1
PDRR process. The
success of preventive
measures is veri-
fied by attack de-
tection. Short- and
long-term measures
are implemented to
adapt it as necessary

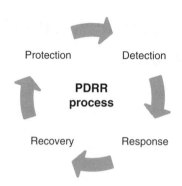

no patches are available, only certified devices are allowed to be used or certain standards have to be observed.

It is therefore useful in vulnerable infrastructures to carry out attack detection and response in addition to pure attack prevention. The security risk is assessed and adapted in this case by means of an ongoing process. An example of such an approach is shown in the PDRR process illustrated in Figure 22.1. Preventive measures (protection) are monitored by means of attack detection (detection). If a successful attack is detected, initially short-term measures are introduced to counter the attack (response), such as blocking relevant IP addresses in the firewall or involving police and prosecutors. The security of the infrastructure is subsequently restored (recovery). In the longer term, the preventive measures are adapted to rule out further attacks.

22.1   Operating Principle and Objectives of Intrusion Detection Systems

The detection
of attackers is
only meaningful
if this reduces the
IT security risk

The aim of an *intrusion detection system* (IDS) is to monitor electronic equipment and the communication infrastructure in order to detect relevant attacks. Attacks are usually only relevant if they are not already prevented by standard prevention mechanisms (applies particularly to untargeted, automated attacks) and:

- they lead to identification of the identity of an attacker and thereby discourage further attackers;
- they allow conclusions to be drawn regarding previously unknown threats and attack techniques;
- they contribute to the prevention of major damage.

To enable attack identification lead to any positive effects, damage must be averted as a result of response and recovery mechanisms subsequent to the detection of an attack. Attack detection is of little value without an appropriate cycle. In any case, it should be irrelevant whether attacks have an internal or external origin.

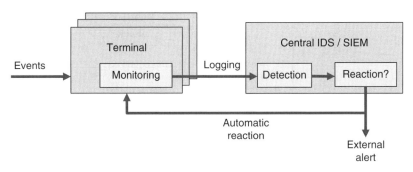

Figure 22.2
Function blocks in an IDS

Figure 22.2 shows the basic sequence of any IDS: first, a variety of events in the systems involved are recorded and evaluated locally. If a suspicious action is suspected on checking, the information is transmitted to a central component. In some configurations, this is also referred to as *security information and event management (SIEM)*. An external alarm is raised after checking again and, where appropriate, correlating with other events. In *intrusion prevention systems* (IPS), automatic prevention of communication relationships can also be initiated.

Any IDS used should have the following characteristics:

Goals and requirements

- **High accuracy:** An IDS should raise an alarm if and only if a relevant attack exists. This requirement may initially sound simple, but it actually conceals a complex task: as illustrated in Figure 22.3, an IDS is used to categorise events as suspicious and unsuspicious. Any error will result either in a false alarm *(false positive)* or an unidentified attack, a so-called *false negative*. Even false alarms pose a problem that can have significant consequences, such as when countermeasures are taken automatically. To make matters worse, the administrator is usually only interested in 'serious' attacks, i.e. those that are not prevented by proactive measures anyway, and processing of irrelevant and false alarms takes up valuable time.
- **Easy integration:** It must be easy to integrate IDSs into an existing networking environment to prevent any further

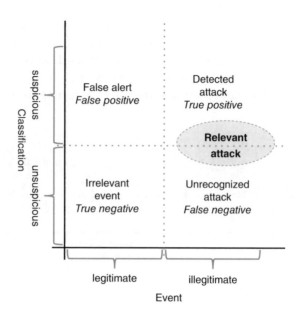

increase in complexity and so that the reorganisation when IDSs are retrofitted does not alert attackers already in the network.

■ **Simple configuration and management:** Easy operation of such systems is a requirement for preventing configuration errors and for acceptance of an IDS.

Attacks must also be recognised in cases of failure

■ **Autonomous and fault-tolerant operating:** On one hand, attackers may cause targeted failures in networks and, on the other hand, attackers may wait until a random failure exists so as to infiltrate a system. It is therefore important that IDSs work autonomously even without connection to central components and that any potential attacks are revealed after elimination of the fault.

■ **Low resource consumption:** If IDSs are not working on dedicated systems, low resource consumption is a premise so as not to interfere with other applications. Even on dedicated systems, which mostly operate centrally, it is important to be able to handle an extremely large number of events quickly otherwise an attack may be disguised in a flood of legitimate events.

IDSes are consistently used as an attack vector

■ **Self protection:** Attackers must not easily be able to target an IDS itself and thus evade recording of the events triggered. In the past, IDSs repeatedly showed security vulnerabilities themselves that actually made intrusion possible. Such problems are obviously unacceptable.

IDSs can be divided into two principal categories: in *host-based IDSs (HIDSs)*, software is installed on the end-systems and either continuously or at least periodically checks to see whether suspicious actions are being carried out. In contrast to this, *network-based IDSs (NIDSs)* work on dedicated systems at exposed areas on the network and observe the traffic. Both variants are complementary and can also be combined. In this case, the term *hybrid IDS* is used.

A distinction is drawn between host-based and network-based IDSs

HIDSs process a wide variety of information that they find in the systems, for example by:

- analysing log data from the operating system and application processes;
- checking the system files for unauthorised modification;
- logging access errors;
- recording times of login attempts and inputs of invalid userames or passwords, etc.;
- statistically evaluating resource use;
- searching for viruses, Trojans and rootkits;
- checking the confidentiality requirements of files that are written to external data carriers.

NIDSs, on the other hand, can only observe network traffic and therefore focus on:

- detecting the characteristic packets of certain attack patterns;
- analysing the construction and degradation behaviour of connections;
- the occurrence of error messages, such as ICMP destination unreachable messages;
- detecting deviations in protocol procedures;
- determining transmitted volumes, services used and hosts involved.

The specific advantages and disadvantages of HIDSs and NIDSs also emerge directly from the usage scenarios and events to be detected. Naturally, only HIDSs can capture attacks not carried out by the network, for example by illegally copying data to a USB stick. However, to do this an HIDS must be installed at every endpoint of a network to reliably detect all relevant events. NIDSs, on the other hand, only have to run on a few systems. The installation and maintenance effort is accordingly lower. In addition, a NIDS is therefore also able to monitor non-cooperative systems, for example systems that are under the attacker's control or because they – like routers

Advantages and disadvantages of NIDSs and HIDSs

or printers – simply cannot run arbitrary application software. At the same time, NIDSe are also easier to protect as with HIDSs there is a risk that they will be disabled or manipulated after a successful attack or will be deactivated by physical access.

By observing network flows, NIDSs can additionally detect network-specific attacks which cannot be measured on the individual hosts, for example the systematic probing of port numbers (so-called *port-scanning*), DoS-triggering packets or the use of incorrect IP addresses. It is often easier in NIDSs to correlate certain events they are already collected in one place. For HIDSs, an additional SIEM system, which provides a central repository for IDS data, is inevitably required for such correlations.

The following section deals exclusively with NIDSs As a NIDS component must necessarily be used to monitor the communications infrastructure, the following section deals exclusively with NIDSs. For detailed information on HIDSs, reference is made to [BC08], a description of the popular HIDS *OSSEC*.

22.2   Design and operation of network-based IDSs

NIDSs usually work – as already mentioned – on dedicated systems and initially carry out passive monitoring of the network traffic. As shown in Figure 22.4, these systems can be set up at various positions in the network:

1. upstream of an organisation's firewall on the open Internet;
2. in the demilitarised zone;
3. in the networks of workstations.

Depending on the location, various things can be measured, thus NIDSs in the DMZ are by nature particularly suited to monitoring servers. NIDSs upstream of the firewall, by comparison, will also observe many untargeted attacks that are often not relevant to the administrator. However, they offer better ways of watching previously unknown attacks. Network traffic on the other hand, particularly between the workstations, should be less diverse. Here, for example, a NIDS can monitor that no devices apart from those authorised by the administrator are operated. This is not the same level of security as achieved in a 802.1X authentication (see Section 11.2) but it does enable basic protection.

In large networks, systems are often placed at various points, so-called *probes*, each monitoring a subnetwork and reporting

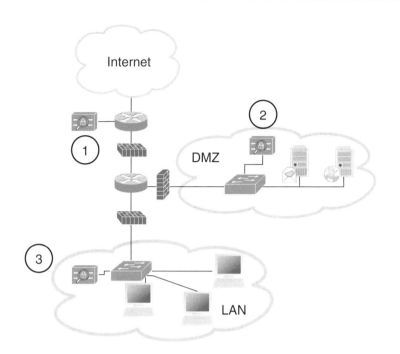

Figure 22.4
Possible positioning of a NIDS: on the open Internet, in the DMZ or internal networks

events to a central point for correlation. It is of course important to ensure that an IDS cannot be circumvented, for example because not all Internet-uplinks are monitored.

As NIDSs even have security vulnerabilities themselves from time to time, it is advisable to connect the probes to a monitor port on the upstream switch and to allow traffic to flow in one direction only. Communication to the central management should be done through a virtual or, better still, physically separate network. Many IDSs control the import and export of messages in the XML-based Intrusion Detection Message Exchange Format (IDMEF) [DCF07] so the aggregation of data in centralised systems no longer presents a significant functional problem.

Operation of physically separated networked probes is useful in real networks

How the individual probes identify attackers can be very varied. There are essentially three categories: signature- and behaviour-based methods, and methods that identify abnormal traffic flows based on self-learning processes. These are presented in more detail in the following sections.

22.2.1   Signature-based Identification

The idea behind the signature-based identification of attackers is comparatively easy. Packet patterns that are known to be involved

Example of a simple attack signature

Signature-based NIDSs require robust reconstruction of IP packets and TCP flows

in attacks are stored in the NIDS. An event is generated if a packet of the examined traffic flows matches a pattern.

An example of such a pattern for the widespread signature-based NIDS *Snort* is the following rule:

```
alert icmp $EXTERNAL_NET any -> $HOME_NET any
  (msg: "Ping-of-Death detected";
   dsize: > 10000;
   sid: 3737844653)
```

It states that all ICMP datagrams that are directed from an external IP address to an internal IP address should be examined for their size. If they exceed 10,000 bytes, an alarm is generated because a ping of death packet may be present (details can be found in Section 18.1.1.1). The keyword sid gives the event a unique identification number so that a correlation and aggregation of events can be carried out.

Even in this small example, a basic problem of the approach becomes clear: datagrams more than 10,000 bytes in size are not usually transmitted directly via the Internet. Since the maximum transmission unit (MTU) is typically 1500 bytes, the datagram is split into at least seven packets which then have to be put together not only in the end system but also in the NIDS in order to identify the attack.

In addition to defragmenting IP packets, TCP data streams must also be reassembled and, where necessary, normalisations are carried out at application level. If all of this is successful, however, it is possible to record even relatively complex situations with such rules. The following example is taken from the official Snort rule set and attempts to detect buffer-overflow attacks on SMTP virtual servers:

```
alert tcp $EXTERNAL_NET any -> $SMTP_SERVERS 25
  (msg:"SERVER-MAIL RCPT TO overflow";
   flow:to_server,established;
   content:"rcpt to|3A|";
   nocase;
   isdataat:256,relative;
   pcre:"/^RCPT TO\x3a\s*\x3c?[^\n\x3e]{256}/im";
   classtype:attempted-admin;
   sid:654;
   rev:23;)
```

Here, TCP flows from external to internal systems are viewed on port 25. In addition, the flows are further restricted by additional rules so that only the direction of flow to an internal server is more closely examined and only the flows which contain the keyword 'rcpt to:'. Based on the specification of SMTP, it is irrelevant whether the keyword is written in upper or lower case. Only when these rules are satisfied and there are at least another 256 bytes in the data stream does the actual verification begin on the buffer-overflow by means of the regular expression `/^RCPT TO\x3a\s*\x3c?[^\n\x3e]{256}/im`. This triggers an event if a user specifies a recipient that is longer than 255 characters. In this case, staggering of the rules is supposed to increase efficiency as evaluating regular expressions is relatively time-consuming.

The two examples already reveal the advantages and disadvantages of signature-based NIDSs. Because of the specific rules, the meaning of triggered alarms can easily be interpreted by an administrator. In addition, it is also possible in principle to suppress false alarms easily during normal operation by adapting the rules to the relevant network. The following points, however, are a disadvantage:

Alarms of signature-based NIDSes are often easily understood

- **False alarms:** Even the simple example rule for the potential buffer overflow attack can lead to false alarms, in that a corresponding line is simply written in an e-mail because the NIDS does not differentiate between SMTP commands and transported messages. In this way, the actual attack can be disguised in a variety of false alarms. Even carefully creating rules does not mean that false alarms can be excluded entirely.
- **Extensive quantities of rules:** Since for each potential security issue one or more specific NIDS rules must be created, the approach requires a rather large number of rules that should not be underestimated in their complexity. This creates a significant amount of maintenance and administration effort.
- **Large number of special plug-ins:** Many attacks and threats can be extremely difficult to detect with simple rules. For this reason NIDSs have plug-ins which detect special attacks and threats, e.g. for detecting port scans.
- **Resource requirements:** The assembly of IP packets and TCP streams leads to a considerable amount of overhead in terms of storage and processing load. This is significant in that attackers could initially generate a great deal of legitimate traffic in order to increase the chances of evading

the detection of their ultimate attack due to a resource bottleneck.

■ **Evading detection:** The complex rules and regulations often provide attackers with ways to code their attack traffic in such a way that this kind of NIDS no longer covers them with signatures. This problem is similar to that of anti-virus software, which is repeatedly confronted by slightly modified viruses. Details of such techniques are presented in Section 22.4. In signature-based NIDSs there is the additional problem that the complex rule sets often come from central databases. Attackers can therefore test their actions in advance to see whether they will be detected. In addition, a signature-based NIDS can only inspect data streams if they are unencrypted. Encryption can frequently be used at the application level to conceal attacks.

■ **No identification of unknown attacks:** Novel attacks cannot be detected by signature-based methods. In practice, it often helps to subscribe to rule sets from commercial providers who specialise in maintaining and updating NIDS rulesets and quickly incorporate attack descriptions when they become known. This approach, however, does not help against targeted attacks on unknown vulnerabilities, known as *zero-day exploits*.

22.2.2   Detection of Deviations from Defined Behaviour Models

Based on the NetSTAT project [VK98], another method for identifying attacks has become established, even if it is not directly used in its original form. In this case, all permitted flows are modelled at individual points of a network. Deviations from this behaviour are detected by probes and regarded as an attack. A distinction is made between a static set of rules, which are specified by an administrator, and dynamic state information, for which the administrator can, however, define state transitions.

Behaviour of network flows   A system currently distributed commercially that acts according to this idea is Lancope StealthWatch [Cha12, FN09]. Unlike other NIDSs, it not only has probes that are used for detecting attackers, but flow information is additionally imported from network switches. In this way flows can be completely reconstructed in the network and compared with security policies. StealthWatch additionally features integration with user databases so that the expected behaviour can change when different users are logged onto the computers. In particular, the system can thus identify traffic originating from any local user.

Another complementary example for the modelling of network functionality is the *Bro security monitor* [Pax99] project that has now been actively developed for more than 15 years. It focuses on providing tools for the most detailed traffic analysis possible at one or a few points of the network. The behaviour of each individual message stream can be modelled exactly using a scripting language. In particular, all states of the protocol state machines may be reproduced.

Behaviour of protocols

Despite their very different approaches, the NIDSs that have normal behaviour modelled by administrators have similar properties. They can be adapted very well to the network conditions and therefore produce very few false alarms. As they detect behaviours that are outside the modelling, it is not possible to evade them by slightly varying the attack patterns. Depending on the level of detail of the modelling, however, the processing effort is either extremely high or the accuracy of attack detection drops significantly; when observing flows, buffer overflows, for example, cannot be detected at all. In any case, the creation and continuous maintenance of models requires a significant administrative effort, which is not often invested in practice.

Behaviour models generate a significant administrative effort

If no effort is spared, there is still the question of whether the model will immediately be bindingly enforced. Here, in research at least, a convergence can be observed between firewall systems and NIDS components. Probably best known in this context is Ethane [CFP+07], a system that enforces security policies based on network flows in the data link layer.

In some special cases, attack detection on the basis of behavioural models offers serious advantages, for example *honeypot systems* or whole *honey nets* are communication systems that legitimate users simply do not access at all. It can be assumed that traffic which arrives there is caused directly by attackers or by responses to attacks with forged source addresses, so-called *backscatter*. Various concepts are conceivable at this point. For example, specialised software systems can be used, which for their part emulate standard software, or conventional virtual machines can be equipped with standard software and monitored by an external monitoring system. Depending on the effort which the operator puts in, honeypots can model the behaviour of real components very realistically. In any case, it is important to ensure that attackers cannot use the honeypots in order to compromise them and abuse them for further attacks.

Normal users do not access honeypot systems at all

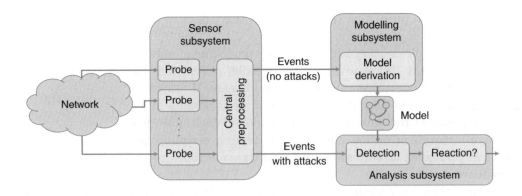

Figure 22.5
Model of NIDSs with
automatic anomaly
detection [EGD04]

22.2.3   Self-learning Systems for Anomaly Detection

It is an obvious idea to avoid the hassle of manual modelling by having this modelling carried out by an automatic process. Assuming that no attacker is currently active on the network, the 'normal behaviour' is 'learned' by means of some very complex methods and subsequently deviations from the behaviour pattern created are assessed as an attack. A NIDS structure such as that illustrated in Figure 22.5 emerges.

The advantage of this approach is that it is even possible to capture very complex correlations which cannot realistically be analysed by manual procedures due to their high level of complexity. *Very complex situations can be detected by means of automatic learning* An obvious disadvantage is the premise that there are no attackers in the system during the learning phase. This may be verified by manual audits during initial commissioning. However, because in practice most networks change significantly over time, models have to be adapted regularly or even continuously. As permanent manual auditing is not realistic, there is always the inherent risk with automatically learning NIDSs that attack traffic will also be considered normal as time passes. In addition, any possibly normal behaviour has to be detected in the learning phase so as not be classified as an attack later on. If a full backup of all devices is made once a month, the NIDS must be able to detect this situation, by means of multiple observations if necessary. This may lead to rather long learning periods.

Three basic categories of anomaly For the automatic detection of anomalies, three cases can be distinguished depending on the structure of the data [CBK09]:

■ **Point anomalies:** If the measured values associated with an entity are embedded in a multidimensional space, it is usually possible to generate various clusters that group the entities with identical characteristics. If some individual points cannot be allocated to a group without a major error or if individual clusters are very small, it can be assumed that these are anomalies. The number of causal relations examined in this case should not be too high as otherwise the data points become difficult to compare. We refer here to the *curse of dimensionality*.

■ **Contextual anomalies:** The behaviour of communication flows depends heavily on the scenario considered so it is perfectly normal for servers to send large amounts of data, but such behaviour is not usually to be expected of workstations. The context in this case can also be temporal in nature: a sudden collapse of the data rate in the peak period suggests an anomaly, while a low data rate is normal at night.

■ **Collective anomalies:** Some anomalies relate to elements of a set or series which materialise suddenly or in an unknown sequence. Examples in the context of NIDSs are an event indicating the download of files without a prior event of a successful login or the appearance of new IP addresses in a network segment.

With regard to possible algorithms for detecting the three categories of anomalies, a variety of completely different methodologies have been proposed:

There are many different algorithms for anomaly detection

■ **Statistical profiling:** Deviations from the normal behaviour can be detected by various statistical tests such parameterising distributions of normal behaviour using maximum likelihood estimates and interpreting significantly different parameters as outliers. Another possibility is the determination of regression functions. In this case, values deviating significantly from the function represent abnormal behaviour. In the simplest case, the frequency of events is counted and significant changes trigger an alarm.

■ **Neural networks:** All three established categories of anomalies can be detected using methods found in neuroinformatics. Depending on the specific task, different network types, such as self-organising maps (SOM), can be used to detect point abnormalities.

■ **Bayesian networks:** Using this method from the field of artificial intelligence, it is possible to determine probabilities for causal chains in order to subsequently draw conclusions from the frequency with which events occur.

- **Support vector machines:** Data points whose entities are assigned to different categories can often be separated by functions. In the simplest case, a linear equation may be specified so that the data points of two categories are each in one of the two half-spaces. For example, if one knows for some systems that they have been compromised, for example in the past, then it may be possible later to find equally compromised systems by determining that their measuring points are in the same half-space, given a good separation.
- **Rule-based learning:** By analysing events, it may be possible to learn rules that distinguish normal behaviour from anomalies. Decision trees are an example of such an approach.
- **Clustering:** As already mentioned under point anomalies, one method of accounting for them is to create data clusters. The basic assumption in this case is that attacks are much less common than legitimate behaviour and therefore form smaller clusters. A typical algorithm used here is *k-means clustering*.
- **Calculation of neighbours:** A simple, fast method of detecting point anomalies is to determine the distances from each point to its k-nearest neighbours. If these distances are much greater than for other points, an anomaly may be assumed as the point is set apart.
- **Spectral analysis:** In anomaly detection the term 'spectral analysis' is understood to be two completely different procedures depending on context. On one hand it is – typically with time-related data – the transformation of data series in the frequency range in order to evaluate recurring patterns such that, for example, the transfer of large amounts of data at unusual times attracts attention. On the other hand, spectral analysis describes reducing the dimensionality of large matrices, such as by means of eigenvalue analyses.
- **Information-theory consideration:** In some cases it is assumed in anomaly studies that the 'complexity' of the communication patterns and events increases due to the attack. The term 'complexity' covers different parameters such as the Kolmogorov complexity or entropy.

Lack of acceptance   The different methods each have different advantages and disadvantages regarding the data to be analysed with them, their computational complexity and their robustness to outliers. Details can be found in [CBK09]. In principle, they can be used to detect even completely unknown attacks and insider threats. However, all previous

NIDS-based approaches that rely on an unsupervised learning process are characterised by such a high false alarm rate that they have not found their way into commercial products. The problem is mainly that too many special cases occur in 'normal' communication networks, which cannot be represented adequately by a learning phase. In addition, it is often not clear in learning processes exactly why certain communication flows have led to the triggering of an alarm, for example when using neural networks. This lowers acceptance even further.

An anomaly detection system currently used in research projects is the Internet Analysis System (IAS) of the German Federal Office for Information Security [Wai09]. Building on the ideas of PHAD [MC01], here the headers of packets are analysed at various points in German government networks. Since the project focuses on the early warning of completely new attacks and the underlying infrastructure is extremely complex, only self-learning algorithms can be used at this point. The detection of anomalies is documented when the data points exceed a normal range defined with the help of Chebyshev's inequality. A simple threshold value is used, which results from the sum of the measured mean value over the past four weeks and the empirical standard deviation determined in the same manner multiplied by a constant adjustment factor. The procedure is applied to a large number of possible header values, such as destination port numbers of TCP flows. As a result, widespread port scans by worms can be detected, for example. The procedure cannot warn, however, against targeted or chronologically very precisely coordinated attacks. In addition, well-trained operators are generally required to select and interpret the data.

Self-learning anomaly detection systems can be used for situational recognition

22.3   Response to Attacks and Automatic prevention

Regardless of how attacks are detected, an automatic response is also triggered by current IDSs. In the simplest case, events are gathered centrally, evaluated and, where appropriate, an administrator is notified about the incident, for example by SMS. This poses the question as to whether the alarm and the manual intervention of an administrator makes sense in any case. There are primarily two reasons against manual intervention:

Automated attacks also necessitate an automatic response

■ **Volume of events:** Nowadays many attacks are triggered automatically and randomly, e.g. by worms or by systematically trying passwords. As a result, a large number of attack events occur and manual intervention creates too much administrative effort.

- **Speed:** Because of the high degree of attack automation, damage can quite simply already have occurred before the administrator has had a chance to respond.

Virtually all current NIDSs have automated defence options

For these reasons, automated response systems, usually known as *intrusion prevention systems (IPSs)*, have been developed. Nowadays, the distinction between IDSs and IPSs is mainly a marketing tool because all the better known IDSs also have a defence component.

The suppression of illegitimate intrusion attempts can be achieved by means of various technical measures:

- **Suppression in the IDS:** If the traffic is routed through the IDS itself — so-called 'inline operation' — the relevant flow can easily be suppressed there. Some systems even only concentrate on filtering malicious content in HTTP streams or in e-mails. One advantage of this method is the ease of its implementation by IDS manufacturers and a high level of security because it is ensured for each forwarded packet that the IDS has not detected an attack. Robustness is a problem to some extent since the availability of the overall network depends on the IDS working correctly and no hardware defect being present. In some scenarios, introduction of the IDS components into existing networks is not desirable because the downtime during setup and maintenance is unacceptable.

- **Firewall reconfiguration:** IDSs that are easier to maintain reconfigure otherwise operationally independent central firewalls so that the attack flow is not forwarded. However, selective filtering of content, like removing viruses, cannot be guaranteed in this way. Additionally, in most cases the first packets of the attack will already have passed through the firewall and the attack will have had at least partial success. This becomes a real problem if a single packet is sufficient for the attack, as in the case of the *SQL Slammer worm* [CR04].

- **Sending of TCP reset packets:** If the IDS is intended to work without any interaction with existing network infrastructure components, it is possible to interrupt TCP flows by targeted sending of TCP reset packets. Other transport protocols cannot automatically be protected in this case.

■ **Isolation of the attacking end system (quarantine):** If the origin of an attack is located in the internal network, there is the additional possibility of isolating the host in the network on the data link layer and thus of completely preventing any further attacks. This is useful, for example, if the IDS has discovered botnet activities on a computer.

In addition to preventing a further packet flow from the attacker, other countermeasures may be initiated which may prevent further attacks or at least make them more difficult. So it is conceivable, for example, to redirect the attacker's traffic to a non-productive system. This method, known as *deflection*, is used on one hand to keep the attacker busy without disrupting the productive system and on the other to learn something about his approach or his goals.

Attackers can be redirected to a honeypot system

A similar technique, which generates less administrative effort but only slows down automated attacks, goes by the name *tarpit*. In this case the TCP connections to the attacker are slowed down significantly, for example by the TCP flow control not allowing any further packets or all further packets after the SYN-ACK being suppressed. This method is generally used to slow down the spread of worms or the sending of spam.

Active Defense or *hack-back* are two names for a very extreme countermeasure: manual or automated 'hitting back' against the attacker in which the defender attacks the end system that the original attack appears to come from. Fortunately, this may be not an option for most administrators for ethical and legal reasons, but such ideas are discussed frequently and are also implemented. As early as in the mid 1990s, for example, the US Air Force applied such methods to trace attackers via several 'stepping stones' [SH95]. The term 'stepping stones' refers to systems that are under the attacker's control and are used as proxy servers for concealing its identity.

Some operators discuss 'hacking back' as a possible response

It should be obvious that active measures can lead to problems, and even if false alarms do not immediately lead to an attack, they can cause damage by preventing communication processes. As a result, the question of whether automatic countermeasures should be used becomes a pure risk assessment: will the amount of damage prevented by filtering of attacks be higher than is caused by misconducts due to false alarms? In any case, it must be considered in such assessments that attackers might deliberately trigger countermeasures, for example by sending attack packets from forged IP addresses to suppress communication to a legitimate system.

The use of IPS requires a comprehensive risk assessment

22.4   Techniques for Evading NIDSs

In addition to specially adapted techniques, generic techniques to evade IDSs exist

As already indicated in several sections, attackers can try to evade NIDSs by using various techniques. This is referred to as *IDS evasion*. In anomaly-based methods, this is achieved mainly by proceeding slowly during times where there is already a high load in the network. With signature-based IDSs, evasion can frequently be effected by means of customised exploits.

However, there are also a number of generic methods for evading NIDSs by cleverly exploiting protocols on the network or transport layer [SP03]. These are especially dangerous because they enable an at least partially automated approach by the attacker.

IP reassembly algorithms which work in different ways lead to different states in the IDS and the destination system

A well-known example for the evasion of IDSs on the network layer is the use of IP fragments. As already established in Section 22.2.1, these must be assembled by the IDS in order to detect attacks reliably. However, there is no clear ruling on how to deal with fragments when they overlap. As a consequence the various operating systems behave differently if there is inconsistent data in the overlapping parts. Ideally, the IDS should exactly replicate the behaviour of each end system in order to prevent the attack from taking full effect in the end system only. Even if it is possible to partially automate operating system detection, the administration effort and the potential for errors rises sharply as a result. One basic way to avoid this error is to discard any overlapping fragments as they should not occur in normal data communication.

Estimating TTL timeouts in the destination network

With other techniques, however, such a simple prevention strategy does not work. For example, the attacker can provide his packets with different TTL values; if other routers are located between the NIDS and the destination, then without further information the NIDS cannot easily determine which packets actually reach the destination and which are discarded by gateway systems. Ergo, in this case the NIDS is unable to reconstruct the data stream correctly. Enforcing a certain minimum TTL would be an obvious solution to the problem, but then traceroutes, for example, would no longer work.

Homogeneous MTU sizes must be present in the network infrastructure

The behaviour is similar if different MTUs are used in the attacked network. If the attacker prohibits fragmentation of its packets by using the DF field, then some large packets may not reach the destination without this being easy for the IDS to detect.

Proper estimation of potential timeouts in the destination systems by the IDS is even more complex. As illustrated in Figure 22.6 based on the example of IP fragmentation, other semantics can arise due to incorrect estimates and attacks go undetected.

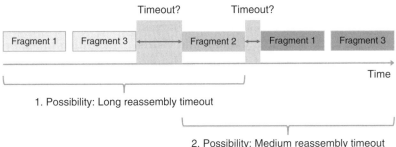

Similar options which can be used to conceal attacks are added on the transport layer. For example, various operating systems interpret TCP-RST packets differently so that IDSs cannot simply distinguish whether or not a TCP stream has been interrupted. Similarly to the assembly of IP fragments, TCP segments can also overlap and provoke inconsistent behaviour depending on the IDS and the destination system's operating system.

Similar evasion strategies exist on the transport layer as on the network layer

Even if it were possible to completely reconstruct TCP streams, application-level attacks may still be concealed. Popular examples of bypassing signature-based NIDSs are recoding of exploits and URLs in the HTTP [CLL+12].

In the recoding of exploits, many signature-based IDSs recognise exploits by characteristic byte patterns. For example, a sequence of 0x90 values may be a sign of a NOP slide (details can be found in Section 17.2.1). The idea of attack evasion now consists of using other commands, which also have no significance for the sequence of the exploit, instead of the NOP command. An example would be a sequence of 0x0c0c commands, which on x86 systems perform a bitwise OR operation of the value 12 and the register AH. Detection of such attacks is made much more difficult due to the large number of possibilities.

Recoding of exploit code

The procedure of recoding hostile URLs is similar. It is used to conceal malicious code which is transported in them. The standard allows the insertion of common ASCII characters directly into a URL, but they can be coded in hex notation too, so the letter a can also be transmitted as %61. Some applications additionally allow transmission as UTF-16 characters in the form %u0061. By constantly changing the coding method, attacks can be almost arbitrarily varied in their shape and the signatures in IDSs can thus be bypassed if they do not provide any explicit normalisation.

Recoding of URLs

At application level there is sometimes another way of escaping detection by a NIDS. As they often have fewer resources available than the actual application servers, the relevant protocols are sometimes not fully implemented in IDS systems or cannot be completely analysed due to a lack of resources. One such possibility is the compression of highly redundant content in addition to the actual attack code, so that data cannot be decompressed by the NIDS for further inspection.

22.5   Summary

IDSs are intended to reduce costs and provide knowledge about attack techniques

Intrusion detection systems should be used as a supplement to proactive protection measures and enable a reactive response to attacks. This should ultimately reduce the costs for IT security measures and obtain knowledge about attackers. In principle, a distinction is made between host- and network-based IDSs. This chapter has concentrated on the latter because they can also monitor components of the network itself.

NIDSs identify attack signatures or 'behavioural' abnormalities

NIDSs can be differentiated into *signature-* and *anomaly-based* methods, where in the latter case there is a conceptual difference between systems that build on a manually configured knowledge base and those that are supposed to learn normal behaviour autonomously. The major problem with existing NIDSs is that they can either only detect already known attacks or have a high rate of false alarms.

Intrusion Prevention Systems

Because of the increase in automated attacks, it is common practice to link IDSs to components for automatic intervention. As emphasised in Section 22.3, however, when using IPSs consideration must always be given to appropriateness, since the risk of wrong decisions is sometimes significant. In any case, IPSs do not represent a protective measure to adequately secure IT communication infrastructures that is sufficient on its own. This especially holds since there are a variety of ways to evade such systems. The reliable estimation of timeouts in particular represents a significant problem for IDSs but is required for correct attack detection.

Problems when used in practice

During practical use of IDSs, other problems may also arise that do not affect security directly and which we therefore did not cover within the scope of this book. For example, it is difficult to compare the IDSs of different manufacturers because there are no standardised benchmarks. While there are some network recordings which allow researchers to validate their systems, they are relatively old and are only partially suitable for the assessment of current systems. Another problem, particularly in a commercial environment, is data privacy. The question as to what extent user

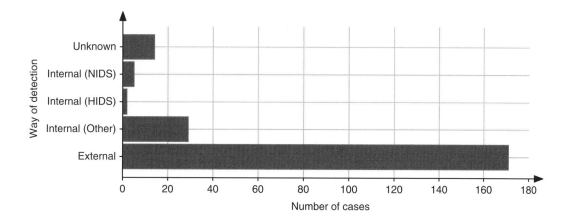

behaviour may be recorded and how this should be done in a privacy preserving manner is almost impossible to answer in general.

If one looks closely at the 'success' of IDSs after more than 20 years of research, the result is at best sobering. Figure 22.7 shows several sources for the discovery of attackers from a study by the Verizon security team. Of 221 attacks discovered, only seven were found by an intrusion detection system. Most of the attacks (171) were not reported by the operators of a service but rather by third parties.

According to this data, IDSs have had hardly any effect in reality. One can only speculate at this point about the reasons. The basic problem, however, is that targeted attacks are rarely detected and the administrators are desensitised by the high number of false alarms. However, it can be useful to use IDSs in very controlled environments with a significant proportion of communication processes between machines, such as in the industrial environment or in the fixed network area of mobile networks.

Figure 22.7
Ratio of the discovery of attackers by means of external or internal measures according to [Ver13]

22.6 Supplemental Reading

[BC08]   BRAY, R.; CID, D.: *OSSEC Host-Based Intrusion Detection Guide*. Syngress Media, 2008

[CBK09]   CHANDOLA, V.; BANERJEE, A.; KUMAR, V.: Anomaly Detection: A survey. In: *ACM Computing Surveys (CSUR)* 41 (2009), No. 3, p. 15
Worth reading these very extensive reviews on the detection of anomalies.

[CLL⁺12] CHENG, T.-H.; LIN, Y.-D.; LAI, Y.-C.; LIN, P.-C.: Evasion Techniques: Sneaking through Your Intrusion

Detection/Prevention Systems. In: *IEEE
Communications Surveys & Tutorials* 14 (2012), No. 4,
p. 1011–1020

[EGD04]   ESTEVEZ-TAPIADOR, J. M.; GARCIA-TEODORO, P.;
DIAZ-VERDEJO, J. E.: Anomaly detection methods in
wired networks: a survey and taxonomy. In: *Computer
Communications* 27 (2004), No. 16, p. 1569–1584

[FN09]   FRY, C.; NYSTORM, M.: *Security Monitoring: Proven
Methods for Incident Detection on Enterprise
Networks*. O'Reilly Media, 2009

[SP03]   SHANKAR, U.; PAXSON, V.: Active Mapping: Resisting
NIDS Evasion Without Altering Traffic. In:
Symposium on Security and Privacy, 2003, p. 44–61

[Ver13]   VERIZON: *2013 Data Breach Investigations Report*.
http://www.verizonenterprise.com/DBIR/2013.
Version: 2013

22.7   Questions

1. Why does a high rate of false alarms lead in practice to a lower
    detection rate for real attacks?
2. Why can unknown attack methods only be found with a great
    deal of administrative effort?
3. Develop a Snort rule with which Smurf attacks on a network
    are detected. Details about Smurf attacks can be found in Sec-
    tion 18.1.2.3 or on relevant web sites. Why is it impossible to
    specify a generic rule that works in every network?
4. Describe the permitted communication flows within your
    home network or the LAN of a small business.
5. What are the problems for NIDS caused by peer-to-peer applic-
    ations such as Skype? Look at and elaborate the reservation
    of port numbers and the IP addresses of the endpoints.
6. To which system should TCP reset packets be sent by an IPS,
    the external one or the internal one?

23 Management of Complex Communication Infrastructures*

The methods and security protocols described in the previous chapters are well suited to protect individual end systems or small networks. For large infrastructures, however, scaling issues are to be expected with manual configuration due to the sheer number of systems. This is because administrators not only have to set up, monitor and maintain systems, but in the worst case there are also a quadratic number of communication relationships that require to be taken care of. Furthermore, the increased manual effort also increases the risk of safety-critical configuration errors, and the larger number of parties involved leads to a higher risk for internal attackers being present.

The scalable and secure configuration of security services is a significant challenge in large networks

For these reasons it is often necessary to automate the management processes for network security services and to do so in a secure and scalable manner. As examples of the many tasks involved, this chapter describes in more detail methods for

- automatic management of certificates;
- configuration of large VPNs.

23.1 Automatic Certificate Management

In large communication infrastructures, the operation of the PKI is a significant challenge. Figure 23.1 shows an overview of various components and external interfaces of a typical PKI. PKIs essentially consist of the actual *Certificate Authority* (CA), a *Registration Authority* (RA) and a *Validation Authority* (VA). The different components facilitate functional separation and thus a high level of

Security in Fixed and Wireless Networks, Second Edition.
Guenter Schaefer and Michael Rossberg.
Copyright © 2014 by dpunkt.verlag GmbH, Heidelberg, Germany.
Title of the German original: Netzsicherheit   ISBN 978-3-86490-115-7
Translation Copyright © 2016 by John Wiley & Sons, Ltd., All rights reserved

security, at least in principle. The CA merely provides a signature service for the RA and VA, which in turn contain interfaces to the users.

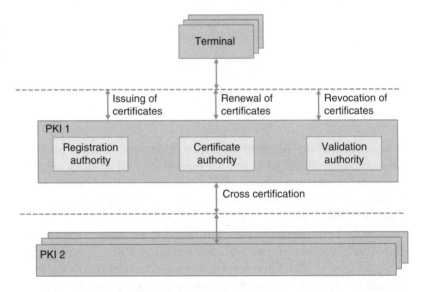

The VA provides services for validation of certificates The VA provides a public service that enables not necessarily authenticated entities to check whether certificates have been revoked. As already pointed out, for example in Chapter 19, this is an essential service in view of the fact that certificates are valid for long periods, but the corresponding private keys may be compromised before this expiration. In the simplest case, validity checking involves the distribution of signed CRLs so that the requirements with respect to confidentiality, integrity and authenticity are relatively easy to implement by the VA.

The CA can be made to issue certificates via the RA In addition, in large communication infrastructures – such as those providing VPN or VoIP services – all devices and users must be initially equipped with certificates based on a standardised and at least partially automated process, and these certificates must also be renewed at regular intervals. To do this, the RA handles *Certificate Signing Requests* (CSR) from authenticated users or devices, checks information such as names and addresses, and forwards the request to the CA. The revised CSRs are then signed by the CA and the certificate is passed back to the user.

Where appropriate, there is further external interface to other CAs in cases where regular cross-certification with other PKIs is required.

In the following a number of protocols are presented that implement these interfaces and protocols.

23.1.1   Mirroring of Certificate Revocation Lists

In the simplest case, in a small PKI, certificates are generated in a manual process and distributed offline to end users and devices. Even in these cases it should be possible to guarantee that certificates can be revoked automatically when there is the possibility of a compromise of a private key, in order to ensure secure operation.

If the number of certificates that are revoked is small, it makes sense to publish a complete list of invalid certificates, referred to as the CRL, as introduced in Section 7.5. A procedure that has become established quite widely involves noting one or more Uniform Resource Identifiers (URIs) of *CRL Distribution Points* as an X.509 extension in all certificates issued by a PKI [CSF+08]. To verify the revocation status of a certificate, the CRL can be loaded and checked automatically from the location specified within it. The scheme is defined independently of transport protocols; typically, however, open networks simply use HTTP for data transfer, although publication on an LDAP server is also conceivable.

Automatic loading and checking of revocation lists

The main disadvantage of this approach is the additional communication overhead resulting from the fact that the CRLs contain the serial numbers of all revoked certificates, the reason for the revocation and the date of the revocation. Despite the space-saving ASN.1 encoding, CRLs can quickly grow to several hundreds of kilobytes because all certificates have to be listed until they expire.

To reduce the communication overhead, the standard contains a mechanism to distribute so-called *Delta CRLs*. In this case only changes to the list are transferred, which are each individually signed. Entities that perform verifications can buffer the individual Delta CRLs, although they must ensure that the latest version of the entire list is available for each verification. A special case is the withdrawal of a certificate revocation, for instance when a user manages to find a smart card that had been reported as lost. In this case the reason for the revocation is changed to `removeFromCRL` in the Delta CRL and the serial number is removed from the individual copies.

Delta CRLs can reduce the communication overhead

Despite mechanisms for transferring Delta CRLs, terminal devices always have to provide and check the entire CRL for verification of certificates. Particularly when many PKIs are trusted – as is common for most of today's consumer devices – the transfer may cause significant communication overhead. This is especially undersirable as most of the revocation information is never needed.

CRL administration generates significant overhead

23.1.2   Online Certificate Status Protocol

OCSP off-loads checking for revocations to a server

The *Online Certificate Status Protocol* (OCSP) [SMA⁺13] takes a slightly different approach. Keeping track of the revocation status of a certificate is handled by a sever referred to as an *OCSP Responder*. OCSP is intended to replace the CRL mechanism, or at least complement it, in cases where CRLs are not continuously updated.

Like the mechanism used to distribute CRLs, OCSP uses ASN.1 to encode the exchanged messages and is defined independently of the transport protocol. Nevertheless, it is often used over HTTP, in order to be able to pass through firewalls and proxy servers. Here too, the corresponding reference URL is passed on to the verifying entity through a X.509 certificate extension.

OCSP dialogue sequence

The protocol itself uses a simple request/response scheme: the verifying entity queries whether a set of certificates is valid, which are identified based on hash values over the name and public key of the issuer and the serial number. Optionally, this request can be signed to authenticate to the server, although usually this is omitted. If OCSP is used over HTTP, requests can be sent based on GET or POST methods. If GET is used, the request is simply appended to the URL in hexadecimal encoding. If POST is used, the OCSP request is transmitted in binary form in the body of the HTTP request. The server responds with a status code, for example 'successful' or 'tryLater', and, if successful, with the signed status of the requested individual certificates. These may be classified as 'good', 'revoked' or 'unknown'. It is imported to interpret any unsuccessful responses (e.g. 'tryLater') as certificate verification errors otherwise they could be provoked in a man-in-the-middle attack in an attempt to make a revoked certificate appear valid [Mar09].

OCSP reduces availability and makes communication relationships observable

A disadvantage of OCSP is that constant access to the OCSP servers of the PKI is required. As a result, much of the benefit of asymmetric cryptography, compared with direct negotiation of symmetric authentication keys using a TTP, is lost. Not only are the robustness and availability of the communication reduced, the individual communication acts also become traceable, since the OCSP servers can keep track of which partners communicate with each other.

23.1.3   Server-based Certificate Validation Protocol

Centralised certificate management

The *Server-based Certificate Validation Protocol* (SCVP) [FHM⁺07] extents the concept of off-loading verification tasks to a server. Clients delegate the whole verification task to a trusted server through a request/reply protocol. The server holds CRLs and can make

OCSP requests. SCVP is also based on ASN.1-encoded messages, which are exchanged over a reliable transport or application protocol, typically HTTP. In contrast to OCSP, all messages are encapsulated using the *Cryptographic Message Syntax* (CMS) [Hou09] and thus are protected against undetected manipulation by means of asymmetric signatures.

SCVP exchanges CMS-secured request/reply messages

The protocol defines two message dialogues. One is used to query the local verification policies of the server, such as permitted signature algorithms. The other is used for complete verification of certificates on the server. To this end the relevant certificates are passed by address reference or directly embedded into the request and transferred to the server jointly with a client-side verification policy. The latter indicates whether revocation information is to be checked or how to deal with wildcards in domain names, for example. The response contains, among other fields, a status code to indicate whether the server has been able to handle the request and the according verification result, if applicable. If specified in the request, revocation information and the trust chain found by the server can also be returned to the client.

Delegation of the verification operation to the server

Because of this approach, SCVP servers are trusted to a much greater extent than OCSP servers. Here too, availability is particularly problematic. However, these drawbacks can be handled well when SCVP servers are solely used within a closed organisation, and in this case SCVP offers profound possibilities to control certificate checks centrally, for example a defined minimum key length can easily be enforced for all services.

23.1.4 Simple Certificate Enrollment Protocol

The *Simple Certificate Enrollment Protocol* (SCEP) [PNV11] primarily pursues a somewhat different task, that is, the initial issuing or renewal of certificates, although it can also be used to obtain revocation information. SCEP was developed by Cisco and VeriSign and is quite widely used in practice. However, the IETF standardisation comities did not approve the protocol for several reasons. They favour protocols that are described later in this chapter.

SCEP also uses a simple request/response mechanism and HTTP as the communication protocol. The requests are implemented in `GET` operations in the form `/pkiclient.exe?operation=` `OPERATION&message=MESSAGE`, with the binary strings encoded using base64. The response messages are transported in the body of the HTTP replies.

SCEP exchanges messages over HTTP, secured with PKCS #7

Operations

The defined operations are represented by the strings GetCACert, PKIOperation or GetNextCACert. The command GetCACert is used to query the current CA certificate. GetNextCACert is used to obtain a future CA certificate. The protocol does not assure that the distributed initial CA certificate is authentic, so this task must be carried out 'out-of-band'. The renewal of a new CA certificate may be authenticated with the old certificate. The case of a CA being compromised is therefore not covered.

The authenticity of the transmitted CA certificates must be verified externally

As already mentioned, the main purpose of SCEP is to issue an initial certificate. To secure the message the PKCS #7 [Kal98] standard is used in this case, which essentially represents a predecessor to the CMS used in SCVP, and enables the encryption and signature of data by using asymmetric cryptography. In contrast to the intrinsic objectives of the standard, clients are allowed to use self-signed certificates until they have received a globally valid certificate from the CA. To initiate the issuing of a certificate, the client first generates a key pair and starts a PKIOperation, in which a CSR, which has been generated from the public key, is sent to the SCEP server in PKCS #10 format. The server responds with the status SUCCESS and a certificate if the operation was successful, or with FAILURE in the event of a rejection. In addition, it is possible to instruct a client to resubmit a request later by sending the PENDING code. This is particularly useful if issuing of the certificate by policy requires an manual confirmation on the server side.

User authentication can only be performed based on passwords

The core problem of SCEP is that users of the service are not authenticated directly with reference to the values they specified in the CSR. PKCS #10 only offers an option to protect the CSRs through a challenge password, which the CA Server can use indirectly to check whether the identity stated by the user is correct. However, this procedure requires administrators to assign sufficiently long, individual passwords for each user. For security reasons, it should only be possible to use such a password once, in order to prevent an attacker from generating new certificates after compromising a client.

Overall, SCEP offers only moderate security benefits since it either has to be used in a secure environment or administrators have to install the CA certificate securely on the rolled-out devices and also issue sufficiently long one-time passwords to the individual users. In the light of the significant effort required for a secure operation, the question arises why the certificates are not issued manually in the first place.

23.1.5 Certificate Management over CMS

The aims of *Certificate Management over CMS* (CMC) [SM11, Sch11] are similar to SCEP, especially regarding the initial issuing of certificates. Like the other protocols described before, it uses a simple request/response mechanism and can be run directly over HTTP or bare TCP, for example [SM08]. It is predominantly used in Microsoft products.

CMC distinguishes between two modes of operation. When issuing a 'Simple PKI Request' a client sends a CSR containing its name and public key to the server in PKCS #10 format. The request is signed with the private key of the user, although this is of limited use in so far as the server may not trust the binding of the public key and therefore cannot use this signature for authentication. The server can respond with a 'Simple PKI Response', which is encapsulated in CMS and contains a *SignedData* object, in which the issued certificate and all required intermediate certificates are listed. Optionally, information on CRLs can be transported at the same time. The answer is not secured by a signature, so that the standard explicitly stipulates that, in this case, self-signed CA certificates must not be trusted implicitly. Thus, both CSR and response must be verified manually in client and server, and an automated, secure use of the method can only be expected in trusted environments, for example those that are physically secured.

CMC offers a simple, unauthenticated operating mode

More complex queries are referred to as 'Full PKI Request' and may also contain CSRs or CMS-encapsulated data. Using this scheme clients may also transmit CSRs in alternative formats, such as the CRMF (Certificate Request Message Format), which is also standardised by the IETF [Sch05]. Additional functionality includes retrieving of revocation information or automated invalidation of certificates. In contrast to the simple scheme, the server must respond to every 'Full PKI Requests' — at least with an error code — and the response must be signed by a CA or RA. Even if the more complex scheme is used, the initial issuing of certificates is not sufficiently authenticated so manual confirmation is required.

More complex methods are encapsulated in CRMF messages

23.1.6 Enrollment over Secure Transport

The latest IETF protocol for secure roll-out of certificates is *Enrollment over Secure Transport* (EST) [PYH13]. Essentially, this refers to the use of CMC with some extensions to support a server-side generation of keying material, whereas HTTPS is used as a secure transport protocol. The purpose of this approach is a significant

EST is based on CMC and requires an authenticated HTTPS communication

simplification of the CMC protocol and additional support for a secure initial roll-out of certificates. In EST, implementation of 'Full PKI Requests' and responses is optional, while a simplified dialogue without authentication by the CMC protocol is the standard procedure. The mutual authentication of client and server is simply based on the HTTPS certificates or passwords. The simplicity and the use of standard cryptographic mechanisms make the protocol unique. In view of the fact that the development is quite new, it remains to be seen to what extent the protocol will become established in the coming years. Nevertheless, it is expected to prevail as an alternative to SCEP. This especially holds when used with TLS-SRP because in this case client and server can authenticate mutually and without prior configuration of trusted certificates by means of the shared secret.

23.1.7   Certificate Management Protocol

CMP is a fully comprehensive protocol for the operation of PKI, although very complex to implement

The *Certificate Management Protocol* (CMP) [AFK⁺05] is probably the most comprehensive standardised PKI management protocol. It covers almost all aspects of PKI operation and, like all protocols adopted by the Public Key Infrastructure Working Group of the IETF, is defined completely independently of the underlying transport protocol. As with CMC, a bare TCP connection may be used directly, but the forwarding via HTTP is common practice [KP12]. Technically, it is also implemented as a request/response protocol using messages in ASN.1 encoding, and the CMS-based CRMF is used for encapsulation. CMP-enabled software is distributed primarily by manufacturers whose products do not rely on a Microsoft environment.

The functional and technical differences compared with CMC are relatively small. A distinction is, however, the trust model during the initial issuing of certificates, where explicit authentication of client and server is stipulated for CMP. An externally transferred shared key is used for this purpose. The protocol makes no provision for insecure transfers. In addition, CMP offers further mechanisms compared with CMC, such as cross-certifications. The main disadvantage of CMP is its high complexity, which explains why the protocol has not become widely established so far.

23.2   Automatic VPN Configuration

The approaches for (semi-)automated processing of PKI tasks presented in the previous section show that, although controllability of large IT security infrastructures can be achieved in principle, the associated complexity is not to be underestimated. Similar challenges arise in the operation of large VPNs. Here too, although the basic mechanisms for secure communication are specified in various standards (such as IPsec, see Chapter 12), the administrative effort associated with large VPNs is significant. This includes PKI operations, but additionally requires the configuration of IP addresses in remote stations as well as the specification of authorised communication relations between them. These tasks should be realised in an automated process.

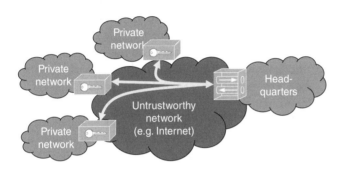

Figure 23.2

Hub-and-spoke architecture: the parties link up to a central coordinator

Essentially, two different VPN architectures have been established for interconnecting trusted networks, so-called *red networks*, and end points over untrusted networks, so-called *black networks* [RS11]. Most VPNs use *hub-and-spoke topologies*, as shown in Figure 23.2. Here, all devices participating in the VPN – be it gateways for whole trusted networks or individual endpoints – are linked to a central *VPN concentrator*, which forwards packets between the systems. The name of the topology originates from an analogy with wheels: the concentrator represents the *hub* of the imaginary wheel, while the connections of the other participants are compared to *spokes*. The other architecture is *fully meshed VPNs*. Here, each VPN participant is connected to all others, as shown in Figure 23.3. Furthermore, hybrid topologies are possible, which represent more interconnected topologies, but do not establish a connection between all devices.

VPNs are usually fully meshed or form a hub-and-spoke topology

Some advantages and disadvantages of these two main approaches are evident. In a hub-and-spoke VPN the concentrator represents not only a potential bottleneck, but also a single point of failure. In addition, the latency is higher than in a scenario where the VPN participants can communicate directly among each

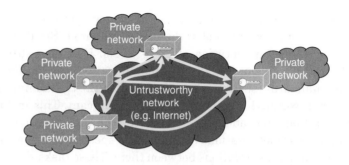

Figure 23.3
Fully-meshed
VPN: all parties
are connected
to each other

other. Regarding the security, it must be noted that commonly no end-to-end protection of the forwarded flows can be guaranteed, so that a compromised concentrator can read and manipulate all traffic. Fully-meshed VPN topologies do not have these disadvantages. They do, however, have other drawbacks. With n participating parties, $n(n-1)/2$ pairwise security associations have to be established, instead of n as in hub-and-spoke topologies. With manual approaches this results in an increased risk of misconfigurations (transposed digits, wrong subnet masks etc.), but also in an agility problem because it is not easily possible to adapt the IP addresses of the nodes in the black network.

Protocol layer of
implementation

In addition to the topology, VPNs can also be distinguished in terms of the protocol layer in which they are implemented:

- **VPNs on the data link layer** (see Section 11.6) by definition offer high flexibility, since they are transparent to the higher layers. However, the scalability properties in terms of the number of participating parties are generally low due to their security characteristics. The core problem is that the address space used is 'flat', i.e. a security policy is not able to capture which addresses may be used by a remote station. Thus, a single compromised device in one of the subnets represents a significant risk to the overall system.
- **VPNs on the network layer** are generally realised with IPsec (Chapter 12) and are characterised by a high degree of flexibility and security. The main disadvantage is high administrative complexity.
- **VPNs on the transport layer** are often implemented through protocols of the SSL and TLS family (details can be found in Section 13.1 and the following sections). Compared with IPsec VPNs, they should offer improved operability. In return, many SSL VPNs do not offer a gateway functionality, but can only integrate individual end points. However, a

certain convergence between the functionality of IPsec VPNs and transport layer VPNs can be observed in that IPsec VPNs can now also pass NAT devices, for example. The performance of SSL VPNs has also increased due to the deployment of DTLS, which avoids the disadvantages of having a TCP congestion control for services that should be connectionless in practice.

The following sections mainly focus on IPsec-based VPNs because they are in widespread use and at the same time offer high flexibility thanks to the IPsec standard, for example tunnel mode and nested tunnels. The often criticised complexity of a secure IPsec configuration should be hidden from administrators and end users by the use of automation techniques.

The IETF itself has recognised the need for autoconfigured VPNs and has compiled a list of requirements [MH13]. The main requirements from [RS11] are summarised below:

Requirements for VPN autoconfiguration

- **Easy operability:** VPNs should work without extensive manual configuration. In particular, it should not be necessary to set up all possible communication partners at each cryptographic end point.

- **Coverage of any scenario that may be configured manually:** Autoconfiguration mechanisms for VPNs should be able to configure gateways as well as individual end points, and they should support tunnel-in-tunnel scenarios, NAT-T and QoS. Within red networks it should be possible to provide private IP address ranges. At the same time, they must not depend on special transport network functionality such as native multicast support, routing of private addresses or the like.

- **Robustness:** The mechanisms for autoconfiguration should not entail a single point of failure and remain operational in the event of partial transport network failures, e.g. during network partitioning, within the physical possibilities.

- **Scalability:** Large VPNs can comprise several thousand end points and gateways. Even such extensive VPNs should be manageable with reasonable administrative and communication overhead.

- **Fast adaptation:** VPNs can change very quickly due to churn induced by mobility, node and link failures or denial-of-service attacks. An autoconfiguration approach should quickly adjust the topology and routing information to new situations, but without requiring the whole network to be flooded with messages for each change.

■ **Security:** Autoconfigured VPNs should not be less secure than manually configured VPNs. In particular, this means that compromising of a device should not lead to a loss of security at other points (graceful degradation). In addition, mechanisms should ensure:

- end-to-end security;
- Perfect Forward Secrecy;
- resistance to covert channels;
- authenticity of the red addresses;
- system availability.

Within the IETF recurring attempts were made to standardise an autoconfiguration system for network layer VPNs [SC02, SHM⁺13]. However, these efforts have not been successful so a variety of proprietary approaches have emerged. Some representative examples of these are presented in the following sections, together with their advantages and disadvantages.

23.2.1   Centralised Distribution of VPN Policies

In the simplest case, IPsec policies can be created and managed centrally. When a new party joins the VPN, it first connects to a central server and loads its configuration. Such servers may be realised by an LDAP system, for example, or the system could be based on Windows group policies. The exact implementation is relatively unimportant for the characteristics of such approaches.

Central approaches are easy to implement, but have functional deficits

The approach is mainly characterised by its simplicity. It offers centralised control and monitoring, which probably explains its dominance in the military sector. However, it has a number of obvious drawbacks. Tunnel-in-tunnel configurations are not possible, since in such cases it is not possible to access the central server initially. Furthermore, its robustness, scalability and availability are questionable. A fast adaptation of the VPN topology requires a 'push' mechanism from the server to all participants. However, in situations with high mobility, this would lead to high load.

23.2.2   Group Encrypted Transport VPN

Cisco is marketing a system under the name *Group Encrypted Transport VPN* (GET-VPN) [Cis07, Bha08], which is based on the IKEv1 variant *Group Domain of Interpretation (GDOI)* [WRH11]. Here, all VPN participants initially establish a security association

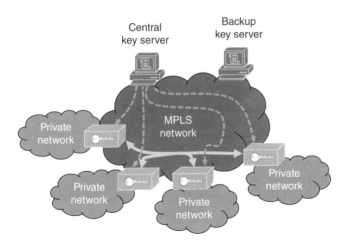

Central
key server

Backup
key server

MPLS
network

Private
network

Private
network

Private
network

Private
network

Figure 23.4
Topology of a Group
Encrypted Transport
VPN

with a central key server or one of up to seven permanently configured backup servers.

Using this security association, two symmetric keys are distributed to the participants: a Traffic Encryption Key (TEK) and a Key
Encryption Key (KEK). The TEK is used to encrypt all traffic within
the VPN and to provide packets with a MAC, respectively. The KEK
in turn is used by the key servers to protect periodic messages for
renewal of the TEK and the KEK. Since all VPN parties share the
same keys, they can exchange data with each other transparently.
This results in the scenarios exemplified in Figure 23.4.

*GET negotiates two
symmetric keys with
GDOI*

In addition to the key configuration, GET also greatly simplifies
the connection configuration. To do this, the GET servers send the
configuration data for a security policy jointly with the TEK and
the KEK. This includes instructions on which traffic should be
protected with which algorithm. The actual protection of user data
is based on the ESP tunnel mode, whereby Cisco deviates from
the standardised processing rule. In GET jargon this approach
is referred to as 'tunnel-less encryption'. This is somewhat
misleading, since the outer tunnel header is still present. However,
parts of the inner header are reused to form the outer IP header,
as illustrated in Figure 23.5. Specifically, these are the TOS field,
the IP identification field, the source and destination addresses,
as well as the DF and reserved bit from the fragmentation fields.
This copying procedure avoids the need for a separate tunnel
configuration. The decision on which packet is forwarded to which
gateway falls to the routing process of the transport network.

*'Tunnel-less' encryp-
tion*

A further difference to the standardised IPsec approach relates
to protection against replay attacks. The use of a single security
association per group induces that the window-based process no

*Time-based
protection against
replay of packets*

Figure 23.5

Tunnel-less Encryp-
tion: GET copies
parts of the inner
IP header to the
outer header

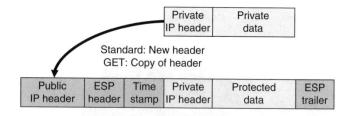

longer works because the senders cannot synchronise the used sequence numbers. Therefore, a different mechanism is used in GET: a further proprietary protocol is encapsulated in the IPsec header, which produces 12 bytes of additional data per packet and contains a time stamp. This time stamp is used to implement a time-based protection mechanism that involves discarding packets with old time stamps. The tolerated divergence is at least 1 second because the systems are not fully synchronised and the maximum latency between a sender and a receiver has to be taken into account. Attackers may arbitrarily replay packets within this window, however.

GET simplifies
VPN management

Because it diverges from the IPsec standard, the method has several significant administrative advantages, for example it offers excellent scaling in terms of number of participants, it is relatively easy to configure and it can even protect transported multicast traffic.

GET significantly
weakens the
security of IPsec

A key drawback is the fact that the security properties are changed completely [RS09]. It should be obvious that all network traffic is only protected by a single key. If just a single device is compromised, even a passive attacker can decrypt all the traffic in the VPN, including unicast traffic between actually uncompromised devices. Since the keys are renewed using symmetric cryptography, the attacker can read and decrypt the corresponding messages too. This means the attacker is not locked out of the system when the initially compromised device is removed from the VPN. Active attackers can even use the group key approach to impersonate any participating parties for an indefinite period. The aim of graceful degradation is thus totally subverted.

Lack of resistance to
covert channels

Even if an attacker only manages to compromise clients, resistance to covert channels is not given. Clients may send packets to any external addresses and transmit data directly in the copied IP header fields. This creates a covert channel with a rather large capacity. Communication into GET-protected networks is also possible, for example attackers can send packets with forged addresses that trigger an ICMP error message in another VPN gateway.

Forging the address results in the ICMP message, which contains the original message, to be encrypted and sent to the client. Thus, the aim of a mandatory encryption is not fully complied with and hence there is no sufficient resistance to covert channels.

In addition, there are other potential issues. The time-based protection against replays induces that any packets can be replayed within that window. For most applications this may have no significant consequences, but, for example, lessons learned from a similar weakness in WEP lead to a more differential picture. The property allows for the generation of additional traffic, which can speed up attempts to breach the cryptography. The impact of weaker protection may therefore not be immediately obvious. It is not possible to use NAT-T, Path MTU Discovery or private addresses if they cannot be forwarded in the non-trusted part of the network. In addition, the key servers represent a good target for denial-of-service attacks. The method should therefore only be used in very controlled environments.

Consequences of weaker protection against replays?

23.2.3 DNSSEC-based VPN

An option to configure VPNs in a more decentralised way, without the need to change the standardised IPsec procedures, was proposed in [RR05, MGM+06], for example. The basic idea is to take advantage of an existing DNSSEC infrastructure. Before establishing security associations, participants first perform a DNS lookup with the host name of their counterpart or a reverse DNS lookup with the respective IP address. As a premise for this approach, a DNSKEY record is published alongside the name, whose content is a public key to be used by other devices for negotiating IPsec associations. Because of the signatures introduced by DNSSEC, attackers cannot change the keys without this fact being noticed, and the keys may therefore be used for authentication.

Publication of IPsec keys in the DNS hierarchy

However, the method has several significant functional disadvantages. It does not work if NAT is involved, and it cannot establish tunnels, so that it can only be used in 'flat' scenarios, where all participants are directly connected to the untrusted network. In terms of security, it is only possible to establish VPNs that offer the same level of security as the DNSSEC infrastructure. Among others, this means that the company Verisign (details can be found in Section 20.4.2) and one's own ISP must be trusted, since it publishes the reverse DNS records. It is not possible to establish VPNs with an independently operated protection mechanism. In addition, the availability of at least one server in each DNS zone, from the

Simple method with mainly functional disadvantages

root zone to the zones of the authenticating devices, must be ensured. Nevertheless, compared with centralised approaches such as GET-VPN, it is comparatively easy to replicate the directory data securely and flexibly.

23.2.4   Dynamic Multipoint VPN and FlexVPN

Using a conventional routing protocol on IPsec tunnels

Cisco markets another autoconfiguration system for IKEv1-based IPsec VPNs under the name *Dynamic Multipoint VPN (DMVPN)* [Cis08, Flu07]. Many of the ideas and protocols of DMVPN can also be found in slightly modified form in the *FlexVPN* [Cis13] approach, which is Cisco's 'IKEv2 Framework' and designated successor of DMVPN. Figure 23.6 shows a DMVPN example topology. It is characterised by a comparatively static hub structure, which is essentially represented by the routers of an institution's main sites. They are interconnected by manually configured IPsec associations to forward traffic among each other. The decisions on which paths are to be used is made by conventional routing protocols, such as BGP or OSPF. The dynamic nodes connect to one or more hubs and initially only transfer traffic to the VPN via the hub(s). In addition there is the possibility to use the *Next Hop Resolution Protocol (NHRP)* [LKP+98] to dynamically establish so-called *spoke-to-spoke* tunnels between devices with dynamic addresses in the untrusted network.

NHRP for establishing dynamic links

DMVPN is a very complex, but also powerful, framework for setting up IPsec VPNs. In contrast to the previously described systems, it is able to redirect traffic inside the network. By doing so, it allows for the usage of addresses that are not forwarded in the

Figure 23.6
DMVPN: configuration of a static hub structure and flexible spoke associations

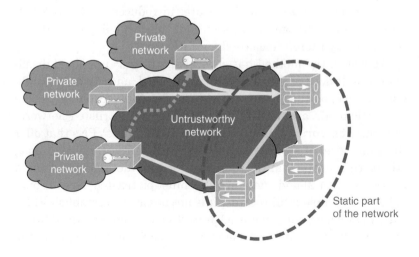

untrusted area of the network, that is, private IP address ranges. Also, it can cope better with failures by re-routing traffic. Depending on the configured topology, DMVPN scales well and can react quickly to changing situations. The performed security-related compromises are less significant than in GET. The DMVPN or FlexVPN devices use pairwise, standard-compliant IPsec associations. However, here too the graceful degradation property is problematic: if a participating device is compromised, it might influence the internal routing, for example via the NHRP, OSPF protocol or BGP. Essentially, all generic routing threats described in Chapter 19 are relevant in this case. As a result, attackers can also impersonate addresses allocated for other users, since they are not authenticated. There is no end-to-end protection of the traffic so the transmitted user data can potentially be eavesdropped or modified by compromised intermediate hubs in the VPN.

Lack of address authentication and end-to-end protection

23.2.5 Tunnel Endpoint Discovery

The method marketed by the name *Tunnel Endpoint Discovery (TED)* [Flu00] was also developed by Cisco. In contrast to the previously presented approaches, it operates in a fully distributed manner that uses neither dedicated servers nor hubs. TED works in four phases, as shown in Figure 23.7:

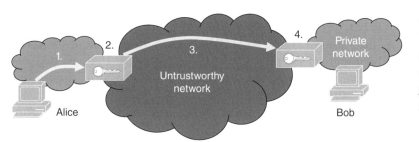

Figure 23.7

TED: establishment of IPsec associations between IPsec gateways, initiated by client traffic

1. A client (Alice) sends traffic to another client (Bob) via its VPN gateway.
2. The VPN gateway checks if a valid security association exists. If this is not the case, the gateway discards the packet.
3. In contrast to the standardised behaviour of IPsec, the gateway transmits a packet to establish an IKE association to the packet destination (Bob).

4. The VPN gateway of the destination intercepts the IKE packet and responds to the initiation request to set up the association. Further packets, and in particular retransmissions of the original packet, can then reach the destination through the created tunnel.

The underlying mechanism of TED is therefore very simple. However, some constraints are placed on the scenario, for example nested scenarios, and those involving NAT or addresses that are not forwarded in the untrusted area, are inherently impossible. There are some minor limitations with regard to the achievable level of security compared with manually configured VPNs. Because the allocation of client addresses and gateways is based on the transport network routing, compromised gateways may claim any address ranges within the VPN. Also, clients can establish covert channels to attackers that are not on a path used by the VPN. To this end they send packets to the IP address of the attacker, thus triggering the sending of IKE packets to the attacker. In this way data can slowly be 'morsed' to the outside.

23.2.6   Proactive Multicast-Based IPSEC Discovery Protocol

PMIDP is a simple method to announce VPN gateways in military networks

The *Proactive Multicast-Based IPSEC Discovery Protocol* (PMIDP) [Tra06, AGM⁺08] is a proposal from the military sector. In many military networks it is possible to use native IP multicast in untrusted areas, for example to transmit video and audio conference data. As illustrated in Figure 23.8, PMIDP uses this technique to periodically announce the presence of IPsec gateways. If a new gateway is detected, the other gateways set up a static security association utilising a fixed password in order to query the address ranges of the trusted networks the gateway is responsible for. Dynamic security associations can then be established based on a key negotiation protocol, as required. If some of the periodic multicast messages are no longer received, the gateway is automatically detected as failed, and all security associations with it are removed.

The scalability and security characteristics of PMIDP are questionable

PMIDP thus represents a very pragmatic solution for the special requirements of the military. However, there are a number of disadvantages. The method is inherently dependent on a functioning multicast service in the underlying transport network and does not work if NAT is involved, for example. For the sender side,

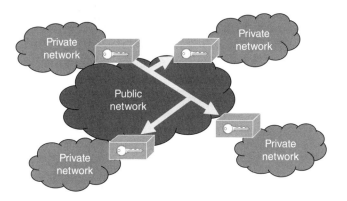

Figure 23.8
With PMIDP,
gateways announce
their presence
using regular
multicast messages

scalability is ensured by multicast, although messages still have to be received by all other participants during each period. The same is true if the red network areas are queried via unicast. The objective of a high availability is not considered by the approach. The lack of protection against replaying due to the use of static security associations means that not only old announcements, but also old network mappings may be sent. As a result, the configuration mechanism might no longer work correctly. In addition, multicast is inherently relatively vulnerable to denial-of-service attacks, since the sending of packets to the multicast address can potentially result in a network-wide bandwidth exhaustion. In terms of the graceful degradation characteristic, it is not clear how the specified address ranges of the trusted networks are authenticated. The protection realised by the fixed symmetric group key is not sufficient for this purpose.

23.2.7   Secure Overlay for IPsec Discovery

In contrast to the previously presented approaches, *Secure Overlay for IPsec Discovery (SOLID)* [RSS10] uses a fully distributed configuration mechanism with explicit mechanisms for gateway discovery, routing and in particular topology control. It is planned to be commercially available in autumn 2015 as part of the SINA product line of the German company secunet Security Networks AG. For scalability reasons, and in order to ensure fast adaptation, the system only establishes a few security associations proactively. To be able to search for other participants efficiently within the VPN despite this limitation, SOLID uses the established concept

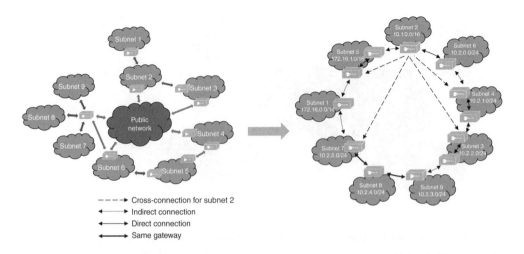

---→ Cross-connection for subnet 2
◄·········► Indirect connection
◄──────► Direct connection
◄──────► Same gateway

Figure 23.9

SOLID maps complex transport networks in a ring structure

of peer-to-peer overlays [SMK+01, For03] within IPsec infrastructures (see also Section 20.4.4).

SOLID's topology control initially sets up only two IPsec associations per VPN device proactively, so that an ordered ring structure is formed (see Figure 23.9). Since the participating devices within this structure are ordered according to the IP address ranges of their private subnets, the destination device responsible for a data packet can always be found by sending a search message along the ring. The VPN devices responsible for multiple networks arrange themselves several times in the ring, as needed. This search always terminates, but with n subnets it requires $\mathcal{O}(n)$ overlay steps. Therefore, once the ring has been established, it forms a logarithmic number of cross-connections for each participant to reduce the search to a logarithmic number of steps. Initially this basic structure differs only to a limited extent from Chord or I3, except in terms of security characteristics [SAZ+04]. However, in SOLID-VPNs, the participants are not arranged based on random IDs or IDs determined by hashing, since this would not allow subnet masks of variable length for the VPN subnets, therefore samples over the address space of the subnets are collected to enable optimum choice of cross-connections. In particular, the cross-connections are set up in such a way that the search space is halved at each hop through the VPN.

Basic principle: proactive establishment of ordered ring structures

Setting up complex topologies

However, the principle of Chord is not fully applicable for complex topologies with VPN participants located behind others, or when local failures in the transport network must be expected, due to the fact that not all participants can communicate directly with all others. For this reason, the SOLID mechanism establishes indirect connections between participants without a direct

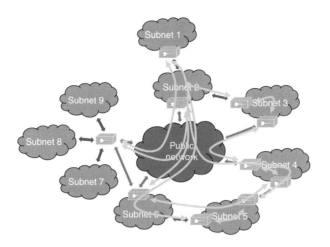

Figure 23.10
*Example of connected
paths for SOLID
ring topology*

communication option. These connections are established via virtual paths through the VPN itself. In contrast to normal routing mechanisms, no broadcast information is used to do this. Instead, the paths are constructed iteratively based on greedy optimisation of the overlay metric. To establish a new connection in the VPN, a search is initially started within the VPN. If a target is found, but no direct communication is possible, the found, indirect overlay path is used initially. However, since this may involve $\mathcal{O}(\log n)$ steps and may therefore take too long, optimisation measures are carried out that lead to provable efficient results in common VPN topologies. The optimised paths are minimised in terms of the number of overlay steps, since both delay and bandwidth are usually dominated by cryptographic operations that need to be performed in every intermediate. In this way SOLID is able to map, and thus configure, even complex topologies in a logical ring topology (see Figure 23.10).

*Setting up indirect
paths and successive
optimisation*

In terms of the functionality of the autoconfiguration process it should be emphasised that it places no special demands on the transport network and also works in scenarios with NAT, for example. Of all the methods presented here it is the only method that is able to establish tunnel-in-tunnel configurations. The non-functional properties referred to above can be realised through the distributed construction and the dispensation with global knowledge. The system is able to scale for several thousand systems and can even handle failures of large parts of the VPN without significant effects on the remaining VPN. Frequently changing security associations, for example as a result of repeated activation and deactivation caused by a 'loose link', do not cause route changes that have to be propagated through the entire VPN. Partial

*SOLID meets
extensive functional
and non-functional
requirements*

transport network failures can be circumvented through indirect paths, and if network partitions are present, the VPN parts configured by SOLID can continue to operate autonomously.

Dealing with the complexity of the approach

Because of the complexity of the tasks and requirements, distributed approaches carry an inherent risk that the achievable level of security is significantly reduced due to the sophisticated software required for the configuration. SOLID counteracts this risk at different levels:

- **Control of unmodified IPsec components:** Neither IPsec processing nor the IKE daemon require significant modifications. The IKE daemon is merely instructed as to which associations are to be established.
- **End-to-end security:** All user data is always protected from end to end, which means that even compromised VPN devices cannot eavesdrop on forwarded traffic or modify it without evidence.
- **Address attestation:** Within the VPN, participants can only act for addresses listed in their certificate. Together with end-to-end security this achieves the graceful degradation property, since even compromised parties can only read and generate traffic for which they are either target or source.
- **IPsec protection for configuration messages:** Even the configuration messages exchanged by SOLID are secured through IPsec, so that external attackers cannot modify them without this being detected. This means that even threats to routing are limited to internal attackers, which are limited by the fact that they are restricted to using authentic addresses.

Resistance to denial-of-service attacks

The fully distributed configuration and routing within VPN also enhances the resistance against denial-of-service attacks because partial failure of the VPN can be tolerated or responded to. Furthermore, administrators can influence the established VPN topologies such that important VPN areas can be separated from less important areas if denial-of-service attacks originate from them [BRS09].

23.3 Summary

In large IT infrastructures it is impossible to configure security protocols manually

The aim of this chapter is to highlight problems that can arise with the operation of security protocols in large IT infrastructures, and to discuss certain solutions for cases in which manual configuration methods are no longer feasible. The initial 'roll-out' and updating of certificates, which forms the basis of most cryptographic methods, is described as a first example. The second part of the chapter refers to large IPsec VPNs.

The main components of a PKI are explained with regard to certificate management. In addition to the *Certificate Authority (CA)*, these are the *Registration Authority (RA)* and the *Validation Authority (VA)*. The VA offers revocation of certificates as a basic service that has become widely established. In addition to the *Certificate Revocation Lists (CRL)*, the *Online Certificate Status Protocol (OCSP)* has become established as a method for explicit validation of a particular certificate. The disadvantages are that the VA must be available and the use of certificates can be centrally monitored. The *Server-based Certificate Validation Protocol (SCVP)* can be used by devices with limited resources to delegate the verification of certificates, including checking against CRLs, to a trusted server. This can also be used to enforce institution-wide requirements for certificates.

Validation of freshness of certificates

A number of PKI protocols exist to issue and renew initial certificates and perform cross-certification, if required. The most widely used is the *Simple Certificate Enrollment Protocol (SCEP)*, although this can only be used in trusted environments. In principle, *Certificate Management over CMS (CMC)* is more suitable, although it is relatively complex. A simplified, standardised version of CMC is *Enrollment over Secure Transport (EST)*, which is encapsulated within HTTPS and is intended to facilitate the initial issuing of certificates for closed systems such as routers. Finally, the *Certificate Management Protocol (CMP)* is presented, which provides a framework for all essential tasks within a PKI. CMP is very complex to implement and there is partial overlap with CMC. Here too, the question of how to build initial trust between client and PKI is shifted to external processes so that for large IT infrastructures significant personnel resources must be provided for issuing and renewing certificates.

A number of protocols can support PKI operation

Significant personnel resources are required for PKI operations

The second example scenario examines the automatic configuration of IPsec VPNs, which is required in cases where traditional hub-and-spoke architectures are no longer suitable due to scalability and robustness issues. The lack of recognised standards in this area has led to a number of different approaches in recent years. This book describes a selection of centralised, decentralised and fully distributed approaches. At the time of writing, most of these methods are characterised by limited functionality, poor security properties and/or high complexity. For example, the simple *Group Encrypted Transport VPN (GET VPN)* offers transparent multicast support and scales very well. However, due to the group key

Most VPN configuration systems have shortcomings in terms of functionality, security and/or complexity

approach the level of security is reduced significantly compared with traditional IPsec VPNs. The graceful degradation property is of fundamental importance in large infrastructures because it has to be assumed that compromised individual devices are present. However, an attestation of addresses in combination with a mandatory end-to-end protection enables complex configuration methods to be used, and yet the goal of graceful degradation can be achieved.

The fully distributed SOLID method is such a complex approach, where each VPN participant performs the same configuration algorithm. It was designed with a view to avoid impairment of the security properties that may be achieved with a properly configured standard IPsec VPN by the autoconfiguration process itself. Thereby, it fulfils the set security objectives as well as other non-functional goals such as scalability and robustness.

23.4   Supplemental Reading

[CSF+08]   COOPER, D.; SANTESSON, S.; FARRELL, S.; BOEYEN, S.; HOUSLEY, R.; POLK, W.: *Internet X.509 Public Key Infrastructure Certificate and Certificate Revocation List (CRL) Profile*. May 2008. – RFC 5280, IETF, Status: Proposed Standard, https://tools.ietf.org/html/rfc5280

[FHM+07]   FREEMAN, T.; HOUSLEY, R.; MALPANI, A.; COOPER, D.; POLK, W.: *Server-Based Certificate Validation Protocol (SCVP)*. December 2007. – RFC 5055, IETF, Status: Proposed Standard, https://tools.ietf.org/html/rfc5055

[MGM+06]   MUÑOZ MERINO, P. J.; GARCÍA-MARTÍNEZ, A.; MUÑOZ ORGANERO, M.; DELGADO KLOOS, C.: *Enabling Practical IPsec Authentication for the Internet*. In: *On the Move to Meaningful Internet Systems 2006: OTM 2006 Workshops*, 2006, pp. 392–403

[MH13]   MANRAL, V.; HANNA, S.: *Auto-Discovery VPN Problem Statement and Requirements*. September 2013. – RFC 7018, IETF, Status: Informational, https://tools.ietf.org/html/rfc7018

[PNV11]   PRITIKIN, M.; NOURSE, A.; VILHUBER, J.: *Simple Certificate Enrollment Protocol.*, 2011, September. – Expired Draft, IETF, Intended Status: Historic,

        https://tools.ietf.org/html/draft-nourse-
        scep-23

[PYH13]   PRITIKIN, M.; YEE, P.; HARKINS, D.: *Enrollment over Secure Transport*. October 2013. – RFC 7030, IETF, Status: Proposed Standard,
        https://tools.ietf.org/html/rfc7030

[RR05]   RICHARDSON, M.; REDELMEIER, D. H.: *Opportunistic Encryption using the Internet Key Exchange (IKE)*. RFC 4322, IETF, Status: Informational,
        https://tools.ietf.org/html/rfc4322, 2005

[RS11]   ROSSBERG, M.; SCHAEFER, G.: *A Survey on Automatic Configuration of Virtual Private Networks*. In: *Computer Networks Journal* 55, 2011, pp. 1684–1699

[RSS10]   ROSSBERG, M.; SCHAEFER, G.; STRUFE, Th.: *Distributed Automatic Configuration of Complex IPsec-Infrastructures*. In: *Journal of Network and Systems Management* 18, 2010, No. 3, pp. 300–326

[Sch05]   SCHAAD, J.: *Internet X.509 Public Key Infrastructure Certificate Request Message Format (CRMF)*. September 2005. – RFC 4211, IETF, Status: Proposed Standard,
        https://tools.ietf.org/html/rfc4211

[SHM⁺13] SATHYANARAYAN, P.; HANNA, S.; MELAM, S.; NIR, Y.; MIGAULT, D.; PENTIKOUSIS, K.: *Auto Discovery VPN Protocol*. October 2013. – Expired Internet Draft,
        https://tools.ietf.org/html/draft-sathyanarayan-ipsecme-advpn-03

[SM11]   SCHAAD, J.; MYERS, M.: *Certificate Management over CMS (CMC)*. June 2011. – RFC 5272, IETF, Status: Proposed Standard,
        https://tools.ietf.org/html/rfc5272

[SMA⁺13] SANTESSON, S.; MYERS, M.; ANKNEY, R.; MALPANI, A.; GALPERIN, S.; ADAMS, C.: *X.509 Internet Public Key Infrastructure Online Certificate Status Protocol - OCSP*. June 2013. – RFC 6960, IETF, Status: Proposed Standard,
        https://tools.ietf.org/html/rfc6960

[Tra06]   TRAN, T.: *Proactive Multicast-Based IPSEC Discovery Protocol and Multicast Extension*. In: *Proceedings of the IEEE Military Communications Conference (MILCOM)*, 2006

23.5 Questions

1. What is the reason why PKIs are split into components?
2. What is the advantage of request/reply mechanisms in cryptographic protocols?
3. Why is ASN.1 encoding used in most PKI protocols?
4. Should the reissuing of certificates be secured through existing certificates?
5. When is it necessary to ensure confidentiality of the transmission for secure initial configuration of keys and certificates? In which device are the keys generated in this case? Is Perfect Forward Secrecy suitable in this case?
6. What advantage does hub-and-spoke architecture offer for the integration of mobile users?
7. What is the reason why the replay window mechanism standardised for IPsec does not work for group associations, as in GET?
8. Use an IKE daemon (e.g. strongSwan) to establish an IPsec tunnel between two nodes. Use certificates from a certification authority that is hosted by yourself for this purpose. Based on this experience, explain the difficulty of maintaining a VPN with 100 nodes. Which configuration components must be adapted regularly?
9. What security problems may occur if the routing of VPN data relies on transport network mechanisms, such as in TED and GET?
10. Can the Internet-wide use of PMIDP be accomplished in a meaningful manner?
11. Compare the security properties of PMIDP with an approach in which the IKE daemons announce their presence via Zeroconf or mDNS. Look up these protocols using a search engine if you do not know them.
12. What does the use of structured peer-to-peer methods imply for the routing in respect to sinkhole attacks?
13. Are routing attacks more likely in the transport network or in a VPN? What are the respective effects, e.g. if DMVPN is used?

Bibliography

[3GP12a]   3GPP: *3G Security; Network Domain Security (NDS); IP network layer security (Release 12)*. 3rd Generation Partnership Project, Technical Specification Group Services and System Aspects, 3GPP TS 33.210, V12.2.0, December 2012

[3GP12b]   3GPP: *3G Security: Security Architecture (Release 11)*. 3rd Generation Partnership Project, Technical Specification Group Services and System Aspects, 3GPP TS 33.102, V11.5.0, December 2012

[3GP12c]   3GPP: *3GPP System Architecture Evolution (SAE); Security Architecture (Release 12)*. 3rd Generation Partnership Project, Technical Specification Group Services and System Aspects, 3GPP TS 33.401, V12.6.0, December 2012

[3GP12d]   3GPP: *3GPP System Architecture Evolution (SAE); Security aspects of non-3GPP accesses (Release 11)*. 3rd Generation Partnership Project, Technical Specification Group Services and System Aspects, 3GPP TS 33.402, V11.4.0, June 2012

[3GP12e]   3GPP: *Access to the 3GPP Evolved Packet Core (EPC) via non-3GPP access networks; Stage 3 (Release 11)*. 3rd Generation Partnership Project, Technical Specification Group Services and System Aspects, 3GPP TS 24.302, V11.5.0, December 2012

[3GP12f]   3GPP: *Generic Authentication Architecture (GAA); Generic Bootstrapping Architecture (GBA) (Release 11)*. 3rd Generation Partnership Project, Technical Specification Group Services and System Aspects, 3GPP TS 33.220, V11.4.0, September 2012

[3GP12g]   3GPP: *Network Domain Security (NDS); Authentication Framework (AF) (Release 11)*. 3rd Generation Partnership Project, Technical Specification Group Services and System Aspects, 3GPP TS 33.310, V11.2.0, December 2012

[AA04]   ATKINS, D.; AUSTEIN, R.: *Threat Analysis of the Domain Name System (DNS)*. August 2004. – RFC 3833, IETF, Status: Informational, `https://tools.ietf.org/html/rfc3833`

[AAL+05a]   ARENDS, R.; AUSTEIN, R.; LARSON, M.; MASSEY, D.; ROSE, S.: *DNS Security Introduction and Requirements*. March 2005. – RFC 4033, IETF, Status: Proposed Standard, `https://tools.ietf.org/html/rfc4033`

[AAL+05b]   ARENDS, R.; AUSTEIN, R.; LARSON, M.; MASSEY, D.; ROSE, S.: *Resource Records for the DNS Security Extensions*. March 2005. – RFC 4034, IETF, Status: Proposed Standard, `https://tools.ietf.org/html/rfc4034`

[ABB+08]   ALONSO, J. M.; BORDON, R.; BELTRAN, M.; GUZMAN, A.: LDAP Injection Techniques. In: *11th IEEE Singapore International Conference on Communication Systems*, 2008, pp. 980–986

[ABV+04]   ABOBA, B.; BLUNK, L.; VOLLBRECHT, J.; CARLSON, J.; LEVKOWETZ, H.: *Extensible Authentication Protocol (EAP)*. June 2004. – RFC 3748, IETF, Status: Proposed Standard, `https://tools.ietf.org/html/rfc3748`

[AFK+05]   ADAMS, C.; FARRELL, S.; KAUSE, T.; MONONEN, T.: *Internet X.509 Public Key Infrastructure Certificate Management Protocol (CMP)*. September 2005. – RFC 4210, IETF, Status: Proposed Standard, `https://tools.ietf.org/html/rfc4210`

[AGM+08]   AURISCH, T.; GINZLER, T.; MARTINI, P.; OGDEN, R.; TRAN, T.; SEIFERT, H.: Automatic multicast IPsec by using a proactive IPsec discovery protocol and a group key management. In: *Journal of Telecommunications & Information Technology* (2008), No. 2

[AGM+09]   AOKI, K.; GUO, J.; MATUSIEWICZ, K.; SASAKI, V.; WANG, L.: Preimages for Step-Reduced SHA-2. In: *Advances in Cryptology – ASIACRYPT'09*, 2009, pp. 578–597

[Agn88]   AGNEW, G. B.: Random Sources for Cryptographic Systems. In: *Advances in Cryptology – Eurocrypt '87 Proceedings*, Springer-Verlag, 1988, pp. 77–81

[AH06]   ARKKO, J.; HAVERINEN, H.: *Extensible Authentication Protocol Method for 3rd Generation Authentication and Key Agreement (EAP-AKA)*. January 2006. – RFC 4187, IETF, Status: Informational, `https://tools.ietf.org/html/rfc4187`

[ALE09]   ARKKO, J.; LEHTOVIRTA, V.; ERONEN, P.: *Improved Extensible Authentication Protocol Method for 3rd Generation Authentication and Key Agreement (EAP-AKA')*. May 2009. – RFC 5448, IETF, Status: Informational, `https://tools.ietf.org/html/rfc5448`

[Amo94]   AMOROSO, E. G.: *Fundamentals of Computer Security Technology*. Prentice Hall, 1994

[AN97]   AURA, T.; NIKANDER, P.: Stateless connections. In: *Information and Communications Security* (1997), pp. 87–97

[ANL01]   AURA, T.; NIKANDER, P.; LEIWO, J.: DOS-resistant Authentication with Client Puzzles. In: *Security Protocols*, Springer-Verlag, 2001, pp. 170–177

[AP13]   ALFARDAN, N. J.; PATERSON, K. G.: *Lucky Thirteen: Breaking the TLS and DTLS Record Protocols*. 2013

[AT&86]   AT&T: *T7001 Random Number Generator*. Data Sheet, August 1986

[ATM97a]   ATM Forum Technical Committee: *BTD-SIG-SEC-01.00: UNI 4.0 Security Addendum*. February 1997. – ATM Forum/97-0019

[ATM97b]   ATM Forum: *Phase I ATM Security Specification*. April 1997. – (Draft Version 1.02)

[ATM99]   ATM FORUM: *ATM Security Specification Version 1.0*. February 1999. – AF-SEC- 0100.000

[AVG+99]   ALAETTINOGLU, C.; VILLAMIZAR, C.; GERICH, E.; KESSENS, D.; MEYER, D.; BATES, T.; KARRENBERG, D.; TERPSTRA, M.: *Routing Policy Specification Language (RPSL)*. 1999. – RFC 2622, IETF, Status: Proposed Standard, `https://tools.ietf.org/html/rfc2622`

[BA13]   BUSH, R.; AUSTEIN, R.: *The Resource Public Key Infrastructure (RPKI) to Router Protocol*. 2013. – RFC 6810, IETF, Status: Proposed Standard, `https://tools.ietf.org/html/rfc6810`

[BAN90]   BURROWS, M.; ABADI, M.; NEEDHAM, R.: A Logic of Authentication. In: *ACM Transactions on Computer Systems* 8 (1990), February, No. 1, pp. 18–36

[Bar06]   BARD, G. V.: A challenging but feasible blockwise-adaptive chosen-plaintext attack on SSL. In: *SECRYPT* (2006), pp. 7–10

[BB12]   BIDER, D.; BAUSHKE, M.: *SHA-2 Data Integrity Verification for the Secure Shell (SSH) Transport Layer Protocol*. July 2012. – RFC 6668, IETF, Status: Proposed Standard, `https://tools.ietf.org/html/rfc6668`

[BBH+09]   BEVERLY, R.; BERGER, A.; HYUN, Y.; CLAFFY, kc: Understanding the efficacy of deployed internet source address validation filtering. In: *Proceedings of the 9th ACM SIGCOMM conference on Internet measurement conference*, 2009 (IMC '09), pp. 356–369

[BBK08]   BARKAN, E.; BIHAM, E.; KELLER, N.: Instant Ciphertext-Only Cryptanalysis of GSM Encrypted Communication. In: *Journal of Cryptology* 21 (2008), March, No. 3, pp. 392–429

[BBM09]   BRECHER, T.; BRESSON, E.; MANULIS, M.: Fully Robust Tree-Diffie-Hellman Group Key Exchange. In: *Cryptology and Network Security* Bd. 5888. 2009, pp. 478–497

[BBP+12]   BRUMLEY, B. B.; BARBOSA, M.; PAGE, D.; VERCAUTEREN, F.: Practical realisation and elimination of an ECC-related software bug attack. In: *Proceedings of CT-RSA*, 2012, pp. 171–186

[BC00]   BURCH, H.; CHESWICK, B.: Tracing Anonymous Packets to Their Approximate Source. In: *Proceedings of the 14th Conference on Large Installation System Administration Conference (LISA)*, 2000, pp. 319–327

[BC08]   BRAY, R.; CID, D.: *OSSEC Host-Based Intrusion Detection Guide*. Syngress Media, 2008

[BDK05]   BIHAM, E.; DUNKELMAN, O.; KELLER, N.: A Related-Key Rectangle Attack on the Full KASUMI. In: *Advances in Cryptology – ASIACRYPT'05*, Springer-Verlag, 2005, pp. 443–461

[BDP+05]   BLUNK, L.; DAMAS, J.; PARENT, F.; ROBACHEVSKY, A.: *Routing Policy Specification Language next generation (RPSLng)*. 2005. – RFC 4012, IETF, Status: Proposed Standard, `https://tools.ietf.org/html/rfc4012`

[BDP+11a]   BERTONI, G.; DAEMEN, J.; PEETERS, M.; ASSCHE, G. V.: *Cryptographic sponge functions*. Research report. Version 0.1, 2011

[BDP+11b]   BERTONI, G.; DAEMEN, J.; PEETERS, M.; ASSCHE, G. V.: *The Keccak reference*. Research report. Version 3.0, 2011

[Ber09a]   BERNSTEIN, D. J.: Cryptography in NaCl. In: *Networking and Cryptography library* (2009)

[Ber09b]   BERNSTEIN, D. J.: *DNSCurve: Usable security for DNS*. `http://dnscurve.org`. Version: 2009

[BF03]   BONEH, D.; FRANKLIN, M.: Identity-Based Encryption from the Weil Pairing. In: *SIAM Journal of Computing* 32 (2003), pp. 586–615

[BFM+10]   BUTLER, K.; FARLEY, T. R.; MCDANIEL, P.; REXFORD, J.: A Survey of BGP Security Issues and Solutions. In: *Proceedings of the IEEE* 98 (2010), No. 1, pp. 100–122

[BGW01]   BORISOV, N.; GOLDBERG, I.; WAGNER, D.: Intercepting Mobile Communications: The Insecurity of 802.11. In: *Proceedings of ACM MobiCom*, 2001. – `http://www.cs.berkeley.edu/~daw/papers/wep-mob01.ps`

[Bha08]   BHAIJI, Y.: *Network Security Technologies and Solutions*. 1st. Cisco Press, 2008. – ISBN 978–1–58705–246–0

[Bie90]   BIEBER, P.: A Logic of Communication in a Hostile Environment. In: *Proceedings of the Computer Security Foundations Workshop III*, IEEE Computer Society Press, June 1990, pp. 14–22

[BJA+11]   BRUMLEY, D.; JAGER, I.; AVGERINOS, T.; SCHWARTZ, E. J.: BAP: A Binary Analysis Platform. In: *Computer Aided Verification* Bd. 6806. 2011, pp. 463–469

[BK12]   BARKER, E.; KELSEY, J.: *Recommendation for Random Number Generation Using Deterministic Random Bit Generators*. NIST Special Publication 800-90A, 2012

[BK14]   BARKER, E.; KELSEY, J.: *Recommendation for Random Number Generation Using Deterministic Random Bit Generators*. DRAFT NIST Special Publication 800-90A, Rev. 1, 2014

[BKR11]   BOGDANOV, A.; KHOVRATOVICH, D.; RECHBERGER, C.: Biclique cryptanalysis of the full AES. In: *Proceedings of the 17th international conference on The Theory and Application of Cryptology and Information Security*, Springer-Verlag, 2011, pp. 344–371

[BKS98]   BLEICHENBACHER, D.; KALISKI, B.; STADDON, J.: *Recent Results on PKCS #1: RSA Encryption Standard*. 1998. – RSA Laboratories' Bulletin 7

[BKY93]   BETH, T.; KLEIN, B.; YAHALOM, R.: Trust Relationships in Secure Systems: A Distributed Authentication Perspective. In: *Proceedings of the 1993 Symposium on Security and Privacy*, IEEE Computer Society Press, May 1993, pp. 150–164

[BLR08]   BERNSTEIN, D.; LANGE, T.; REZAEIAN FARASHAHI, R.: Binary Edwards Curves. In: *Cryptographic Hardware and Embedded Systems (CHES)* Bd. 5154. Springer-Verlag, 2008, pp. 244–265

[BLT03]   BELLOVIN, S.; LEECH, M.; TAYLOR, T.: *ICMP Traceback Messages*. 2003. – IETF, Status: Expired Internet-Draft, `https://tools.ietf.org/html/draft-ietf-itrace-04`

[BM92]   BELLOVIN, S.; MERRITT, M.: Encrypted Key Exchange: Password-Based Protocols Secure Against Dictionary Attacks. In: *IEEE Computer Society Symposium on Research in Security and Privacy*, 1992, pp. 72–84

[BM93]   BELLOVIN, S.; MERRITT, M.: *Cryptographic protocol for secure communications*. 1993. – US Patent 5,241,599

[BMY06]   BARBIR, A.; MURPHY, S.; YANG, Y.: *Generic Threats to Routing Protocols*. 2006. – RFC 4593, IETF, Status: Standard, `https://tools.ietf.org/html/rfc4593`

[Bre89]   BRESSOUD, D. M.: *Factorization and Primality Testing*. Springer-Verlag, 1989

[BRS09]   BRINKMEIER, M.; ROSSBERG, M.; SCHAEFER, G.: Towards a Denial-of-Service Resilient Design of Complex IPsec Overlays. In: *Proceedings of International Conference on Communications (ICC)*, 2009

[Bry88]   BRYANT, R.: *Designing an Authentication System: A Dialogue in Four Scenes*. 1988. – Project Athena, Massachusetts Institute of Technology, Cambridge, USA

[BS90]   BIHAM, E.; SHAMIR, A.: Differential Cryptanalysis of DES-like Cryptosystems. In: *Journal of Cryptology* 4 (1990), No. 1, pp. 3–72

[BS93]   BIHAM, E.; SHAMIR, A.: *Differential Cryptanalysis of the Data Encryption Standard*. Springer-Verlag, 1993

[BS96]   BERNSTEIN, D. J.; SCHENK, E.: *TCP SYN cookies*. `http://cr.yp.to/syncookies.html`. Version: 1996

[BSI08]   BSI (BUNDESAMT FÜR SICHERHEIT IN DER INFORMATIONSTECHNIK): *Common Criteria Protection Profile for Remote-Controlled Browsers Systems (ReCoBS)*. BSI PP BSI-PP-0040. `https://www.bsi.bund.de/SharedDocs/Downloads/DE/BSI/Zertifizierung/ReportePP/pp0040b_pdf.pdf?__blob=publicationFile`. Version: 2008

[BSI12]   BSI (BUNDESAMT FÜR SICHERHEIT IN DER INFORMATIONSTECHNIK): *Elliptic Curve Cryptography*. 2012. – Technical Guideline TR-03111

[BSW10]   BEUTELSPACHER, A.; SCHWENK, J.; WOLFENSTETTER, K.-D.: *Moderne Verfahren der Kryptographie: Von RSA zu Zero-Knowledge.* Vie″-weg+Teubner Verlag, 2010

[BT00]   BARLOW, J.; THROWER, W.: *TFN2K – an analysis (Revision: 1.3).* 2000

[BT11]   BRUMLEY, B. B.; TUVERI, N.: Remote timing attacks are still practical. In: *Proceedings of the 16th European conference on Research in computer security (ESORICS'11)*, 2011, pp. 355–371

[CBK09]   CHANDOLA, V.; BANERJEE, A.; KUMAR, V.: Anomaly Detection: A survey. In: *ACM Computing Surveys (CSUR)* 41 (2009), No. 3, pp. 15

[CC89]   CHIOU, G.; CHEN, W.: Secure Broadcasting Using the Secure Lock. In: *IEEE Transactions on Software Engineering* 15 (1989), pp. 929–934

[CCF04]   CONVERY, S.; COOK, D.; FRANZ, M.: *An Attack Tree for the Border Gateway Protocol.* 2004. – IETF, Status: Expired Internet-Draft, `https://tools.ietf.org/html/draft-ietf-rpsec-bgpattack-00`

[CER09]   CERT-FI VULNERABILITY COORDINATION: *CERT-FI Advisory on the Outpost24 TCP Issues.* September 2009. – Information on CVE-2008-4609, `https://www.cert.fi/haavoittuvuudet/2008/tcp-vulnerabilities.html`

[CFP+96]   COPPERSMITH, D.; FRANKLIN, M. K.; PATARIN, J.; REITER, M. K.: Low Exponent RSA with Related Messages. In: MAURER, U. (Hrsg.): *In Advances in Cryptology – Eurocrypt'96 Proceedings*, Springer-Verlag, 1996. – Vol. 1070 of Lectures Notes in Computer Science

[CFP+07]   CASADO, M.; FREEDMAN, M. J.; PETTIT, J.; LUO, J.; MCKEOWN, N.; SHENKER, S.: Ethane: Taking control of the enterprise. In: *ACM SIGCOMM Computer Communication Review* 37 (2007), No. 4

[CGI+99]   CANETTI, R.; GARAYT, J.; ITKID, G.; MICCIANCIOSAND, D.; NAORE, M.; PINKASLL, B.: Multicast Security: A Taxonomy and Some Efficient Constructions. In: *IEEE Infocom*, 1999

[CH13]   CLARKE, D.; HAO, F.: *Cryptanalysis of the Dragonfly Key Exchange Protocol.* 2013. – Forschungsbericht

[Cha81]   CHAUM, D.: Untraceable electronic mail, return addresses, and digital pseudonyms. In: *Communications of the ACM* 24 (1981), February, No. 2

[Cha98]   CHANDRASEKARAN, R.: False Requests Flood, Shut BLS Web Site. In: *Washington Post* (1998), January. `http://www.washingtonpost.com/wp-srv/national/longterm/fedguide/stories/fig010998.htm`

[Cha12]   CHAPPLE, M.: *NetFlow Security Monitoring For Dummies, Lancope Special Edition.* John Wiley & Sons, 2012

[Cis07]   CISCO SYSTEMS, INC.: *Cisco Group Encrypted Transport VPN.* Cisco Feature Guide. `http://www.cisco.com/en/US/docs/ios/12_4t/12_4t11/htgetvpn.pdf`. Version: 2007

[Cis08]   CISCO SYSTEMS, INC.: *Cisco IOS DMVPN Overview.*

	`http://www.cisco.com/c/dam/en/us/products/collateral/` `security/dynamic-multipoint-vpn-dmvpn/DMVPN_Overview.` `pdf`. Version: 2008
[Cis13]	CISCO SYSTEMS, INC.: *FlexVPN and Internet Key Exchange Version 2 Configuration Guide, Cisco IOS XE Release 3S*. `http://www.cisco.` `com/c/en/us/td/docs/ios-xml/ios/sec_conn_ike2vpn/` `configuration/xe-3s/sec-flex-vpn-xe-3s-book.pdf`. Version: 2013
[CJR+10]	CHAUM, D.; JAKOBSSON, M.; RIVEST, R. L.; RYAN, P. Y. A.; BENALOH, J.; KUTYLOWSKI, M.; ADIDA, B.: *Towards Trustworthy Elections*. Springer-Verlag, 2010
[CKV11]	CAVEDON, L.; KRUEGEL, C.; VIGNA, G.: Are BGP Routers Open to Attack? An Experiment. In: *Open Research Problems in Network Security* Bd. 6555. Springer-Verlag, 2011, pp. 88–103
[CLL+12]	CHENG, T.-H.; LIN, Y.-D.; LAI, Y.-C.; LIN, P.-C.: Evasion Techniques: Sneaking through Your Intrusion Detection/Prevention Systems. In: *IEEE Communications Surveys & Tutorials* 14 (2012), No. 4, pp. 1011–1020
[CLR01]	CORMEN, T. H.; LEISERSON, C. E.; RIVEST, R. L.: *Introduction to Algorithms*. B&T, 2001
[Cow13]	COWIE, J.: *The New Threat: Targeted Internet Traffic Misdirection*. `http://www.renesys.com/2013/11/mitm-internet-hijacking`. Version: 2013
[CP05]	CRANDALL, R.; POMERANCE, C.: *Prime numbers: A computational perspective*. Springer-Verlag, 2005
[CPS03]	CHAN, H.; PERRIG, A.; SONG, D.: Random Key Predistribution Schemes for Sensor Networks. In: *Proceedings of Symposium on Security and Privacy*, 2003, pp. 197–213
[CR04]	CHEN, T. M.; ROBERT, J.-M.: Worm Epidemics in High-Speed Networks. In: *Computer* 37 (2004), June, No. 6, pp. 48–53
[CSF+08]	COOPER, D.; SANTESSON, S.; FARRELL, S.; BOEYEN, S.; HOUSLEY, R.; POLK, W.: *Internet X.509 Public Key Infrastructure Certificate and Certificate Revocation List (CRL) Profile*. May 2008. – RFC 5280, IETF, Status: Proposed Standard, `https://tools.ietf.org/html/rfc5280`
[CU98]	CRELL, B.; UHLMANN, A.: *Einführung in Grundlagen und Protokolle der Quanteninformatik*. 1998. – NTZ Preprint 33/1998, Universität Leipzig, `http://www.uni-leipzig.de/~ntz/abs/abs3398.htm`
[DA99]	DIERKS, T.; ALLEN, C.: *The TLS Protocol Version 1.0*. January 1999. – RFC 2246, IETF, `https://tools.ietf.org/html/rfc2246`
[DAV+08]	DAGON, D.; ANTONAKAKIS, M.; VIXIE, P.; JINMEI, T.; LEE, W.: Increased DNS forgery resistance through 0x20-bit encoding: security via leet queries. In: *Proceedings of the 15th ACM conference on Computer and Communications Security*, 2008, pp. 211–222

[DCF07]   DEBAR, H.; CURRY, D. A.; FEINSTEIN, B. S.: *The Intrusion Detection Message Exchange Format (IDMEF)*. March 2007. – RFC 4765, IETF, Status: Experimental, https://tools.ietf.org/html/rfc4765

[Dem93]   DEMYTKO, N.: A New Elliptic Curve Based Analogue of RSA. In: *Advances in Cryptology – EUROCRYPT '93* Bd. 765. 1993, pp. 40–49

[Dem10]   DEMPSKY, M.: *DNSCurve: Link-Level Security for the Domain Name System*. February 2010. – Expired RFC-Draft, Intended Status: Proposed Standard,
https://tools.ietf.org/html/draft-dempsky-dnscurve-01

[Den76]   DENNING, D. E.: A Lattice Model of Secure Information Flow. In: *Communications of the ACM* 19 (1976), No. 5, pp. 236–243

[DH76]   DIFFIE, W.; HELLMAN, M. E.: New Directions in Cryptography. In: *Trans. IEEE Inform. Theory, IT-22* (1976), pp. 644–654

[DKB+11]   DESHPANDE, T.; KATSAROS, P.; BASAGIANNIS, S.; SMOLKA, S. A.: Formal Analysis of the DNS Bandwidth Amplification Attack and Its Countermeasures Using Probabilistic Model Checking. In: *International Symposium on High-Assurance Systems Engineering (HASE)*, 2011, pp. 360–367

[DKS10]   DUNKELMAN, O.; KELLER, N.; SHAMIR, A.: A Practical-Time Related-Key Attack on the KASUMI Cryptosystem Used in GSM and 3G Telephony. In: *Advances in Cryptology - CRYPTO 2010* Bd. 6223, Springer-Verlag, 2010, pp. 393–410

[DP89]   DAVIES, D. W.; PRICE, W. L.: *Security for Computer Networks*. John Wiley & Sons, 1989

[DP10]   DEGABRIELE, J. P.; PATERSON, K. G.: On the (in)security of IPsec in MAC-then-encrypt configurations. In: *Proceedings of the 17th ACM conference on Computer and communications security*, 2010 (CCS '10), pp. 493–504

[DR08]   DIERKS, T.; RESCORLA, E.: *The Transport Layer Security (TLS) Protocol Version 1.2*. August 2008. – RFC 5246, IETF, Status: Proposed Standard,
https://tools.ietf.org/html/rfc5246

[DR11]   DUONG, T.; RIZZO, J.: *Here Come The ⊕ Ninjas*. Unpublished Manuscript, 2011

[DR12]   DUONG, T.; RIZZO, J.: *The CRIME attack*. Presentation at Ekoparty, 2012

[DS81]   DENNING, D. E.; SACCO, G. M.: Timestamps in Key Distribution Protocols. In: *Communications of the ACM* 24 (1981), No. 8, pp. 198–208

[Dwo05]   DWORKIN, M.: *Recommendation for Block Cipher Modes of Operation: The CMAC Mode for Authentication*. NIST Special Publication 800-38B, 2005

[Dwo07]   DWORKIN, M.: *Recommendation for Block Cipher Modes of Operation: Galois/Counter Mode (GCM) and GMAC*. NIST Special Publication 800-38D, 2007

[Eas00]   EASTLAKE 3RD, D.: *Secret Key Establishment for DNS (TKEY RR)*.
           September 2000. – RFC 2930, IETF, Status: Proposed Standard,
           `https://tools.ietf.org/html/rfc2930`

[Eas06]   EASTLAKE 3RD, D.: *HMAC SHA TSIG Algorithm Identifiers*. August 2006.
           – RFC 4635, IETF, Status: Proposed Standard,
           `https://tools.ietf.org/html/rfc4635`

[EG11]   EVANS, N. S.; GROTHOFF, C.: R5N : Randomized Recursive Routing for
           Restricted-Route Networks. In: *Network and System Security (NSS)*, 2011,
           pp. 316–321

[EGD04]   ESTEVEZ-TAPIADOR, J. M.; GARCIA-TEODORO, P.; DIAZ-VERDEJO, J. E.:
           Anomaly detection methods in wired networks: a survey and taxonomy. In:
           Computer Communications 27 (2004), No. 16, pp. 1569–1584

[ElG85]   ELGAMAL, T.: A Public Key Cryptosystem and a Signature Scheme based
           on Discrete Logarithms. In: *IEEE Transactions on Information Theory* 31
           (1985), July, No. 4, pp. 469–472

[ERG+07]   EDGE, K.; RAINES, R.; GRIMAILA, M.; BALDWIN, R.; BENNINGTON, R.;
           REUTER, C.: The Use of Attack and Protection Trees to Analyze Security
           for an Online Banking System. In: *40th Annual Hawaii International
           Conference on System Sciences (HICSS)*, 2007

[Ero09]   ERONEN, P.: *DES and IDEA Cipher Suites for Transport Layer Security
           (TLS)*. February 2009. – RFC 5469, IETF, Status: Proposed Standard,
           `https://tools.ietf.org/html/rfc5469`

[ESC05]   EASTLAKE 3RD, D.; SCHILLER, J.; CROCKER, S.: *Randomness Requirements
           for Security*. 2005. – RFC 4086, IETF, Status: Best Current Practice,
           `https://tools.ietf.org/html/rfc4086`

[ESS+98]   ELSTNER, J.; SCHÄFER, G.; SCHILLER, J.; SEITZ, J.: A Comparison of
           Current Approaches to Securing ATM Networks. In: *Proceedings of the 6th
           International Conference on Telecommunication Systems*, 1998,
           pp. 407–415. – Nashville, TN, USA

[ESZ08]   EMBLETON, S.; SPARKS, S.; ZOU, C.: SMM Rootkits: A New Breed of OS
           Independent Malware. In: *SecureComm*, 2008

[ETS06]   ETSI TISPAN: *Methods and protocols; Part 1: Method and proforma for
           Threat, Risk, Vulnerability Analysis*. European Telecommunications
           Standards Institute (ETSI), Technical Specification 102 165-1 Version
           4.2.1, Dec 2006

[ETS10]   ERONEN, P.; TSCHOFENIG, H.; SHEFFER, Y.: *An Extension for EAP-Only
           Authentication in IKEv2*. September 2010. – RFC 5998, IETF, Status:
           Proposed Standard, `https://tools.ietf.org/html/rfc5998`

[ETS12a]   ETSI/SAGE: *Specification of the 3GPP Confidentiality and Integrity
           Algorithms; Document 2: Kasumi specification*. 3GPP Release 11., 2012

[ETS12b]   ETSI/SAGE: *Specification of the 3GPP Confidentiality and Integrity
           Algorithms UEA2 & UIA2*. 3GPP Release 11., 2012

[FB08]   FUNK, P.; BLAKE-WILSON, S.: *Extensible Authentication Protocol Tunneled Transport Layer Security Authenticated Protocol Version 0 (EAP-TTLSv0).* August 2008. – RFC 5281, IETF, Status: Informational, `https://tools.ietf.org/html/rfc5281`

[Fer02]   FERGUSON, N.: *Michael: an improved MIC for 802.11 WEP.* February 2002. – IEEE 802.11 doc 02-020r0

[Fer05]   FERGUSON, N.: *Authentication weaknesses in GCM.* Comments submitted to NIST Modes of Operation Process, 2005

[FGK03]   FRANKEL, S.; GLENN, R.; KELLY, S.: *The AES-CBC Cipher Algorithm and Its Use with IPsec.* September 2003. – RFC 3566, IETF, Status: Proposed Standard, `https://tools.ietf.org/html/rfc3602`

[FH98]   FERGUSON, P.; HUSTON, G.: *What is a VPN?* 1998. – The Internet Protocol Journal, volume 1, no. 1&2, Cisco Systems

[FH03]   FRANKEL, S.; HERBERT, H.: *The AES-XCBC-MAC-96 Algorithm and Its Use With IPsec.* September 2003. – RFC 3566, IETF, Status: Proposed Standard, `https://tools.ietf.org/html/rfc3566`

[FHM+07]   FREEMAN, T.; HOUSLEY, R.; MALPANI, A.; COOPER, D.; POLK, W.: *Server-Based Certificate Validation Protocol (SCVP).* December 2007. – RFC 5055, IETF, Status: Proposed Standard, `https://tools.ietf.org/html/rfc5055`

[FKK96]   FREIER, A. O.; KARLTON, P.; KOCHER, P. C.: *The SSL Protocol Version 3.0.* 1996. – Netscape Communications Corporation

[Flu00]   FLUHRER, S.: *Tunnel Endpoint Discovery.* Expired Internet Draft, 2000. – Expired Internet Draft, `https://tools.ietf.org/html/draft-fluhrer-ted-00`

[Flu07]   FLUHRER, S.: *System and method for protected spoke to spoke communication using an unprotected computer network.* United States Patent US 2007/0271451 A1, 2007

[FMS01]   FLUHRER, S.; MANTIN, I.; SHAMIR, A.: Weaknesses in the Key Scheduling Algorithm of RC4. In: *Selected Areas in Cryptography, Lecture Notes in Computer Science* Bd. 2259, Springer-Verlag, 2001, pp. 1–24

[FN09]   FRY, C.; NYSTORM, M.: *Security Monitoring: Proven Methods for Incident Detection on Enterprise Networks.* O'Reilly Media, 2009

[For94]   FORD, Warwick: *Computer Communications Security – Principles, Standard Protocols and Techniques.* Prentice Hall, 1994

[For03]   FORD, B.: Unmanaged Internet Protocol: Taming the Edge Network Management Crisis. In: *Second Workshop on Hot Topics in Networks*, 2003

[For09]   FORRESTER CONSULTING: *The Trends And Changing Landscape Of DDoS Threats And Protection.* `https://www.verisign.com/ddos-protection/resources/whitepaper-ddos-threats-protection-forrester.pdf.` Version: July 2009

[FS00]   FERGUSON, P.; SENIE, D.: *Network Ingress Filtering: Defeating Denial of Service Attacks which employ IP Source Address Spoofing.* May 2000. – RFC 2827, IETF, Status: Best Practice, `https://tools.ietf.org/html/rfc2827`

[FS03]   FERGUSON, N.; SCHNEIER, B.: *A Cryptographic Evaluation of IPsec.* December 2003

[GAG⁺03]   GOODELL, G.; AIELLO, W.; GRIFFIN, T.; IOANNIDIS, J.; MCDANIEL, P. D.; RUBIN, A. D.: Working around BGP: An Incremental Approach to Improving Security and Accuracy in Interdomain Routing. In: *NDSS*, 2003

[GH04]   GILBERT, H.; HANDSCHUH, H.: Security Analysis of SHA-256 and Sisters. In: *Lecture Notes in Computer Science* Bd. 3006/2004. 2004, pp. 175–193

[GHM03]   GILL, V.; HEASLEY, J.; MEYER, D.: *The BGP TTL Security Hack (BTSH).* 2003. – IETF, Status: Expired Internet-Draft, `https://tools.ietf.org/html/draft-gill-btsh-02`

[GHM⁺07]   GILL, V.; HEASLEY, J.; MEYER, D.; SAVOLA, P.; PIGNATARO, C.: *The Generalized TTL Security Mechanism (GTSM).* 2007. – RFC 5082, IETF, Status: Standard, `https://tools.ietf.org/html/rfc5082`

[GNY90]   GONG, L.; NEEDHAM, R. M.; YAHALOM, R.: Reasoning about Belief in Cryptographic Protocols. In: *Symposium on Research in Security and Privacy*, IEEE Computer Society, IEEE Computer Society Press, May 1990, pp. 234–248

[GS91]   GAARDNER, K.; SNEKKENES, E.: Applying a Formal Analysis Technique to the CCITT X.509 Strong Two-Way Authentication Protocol. In: *Journal of Cryptology* 3 (1991), No. 2, pp. 81–98

[Gud85]   GUDE, M.: Concept for a High Performance Random Number Generator Based on Physical Random Phenomena. In: *Frequenz* 39 (1985), pp. 187–190

[Gud87]   GUDE, M.: *Ein quasi-idealer Gleichverteilungsgenerator basierend auf physikalischen Zufallsphänomenen.* Dissertation, Universität Aachen, 1987

[Har08]   HARKINS, D.: Simultaneous Authentication of Equals: A Secure, Password-Based Key Exchange for Mesh Networks. In: *Second International Conference on Sensor Technologies and Applications (SENSORCOMM)*, 2008, pp. 839–844

[Har12]   HARKINS, D.: *Secure Pre-Shared Key (PSK) Authentication for the Internet Key Exchange Protocol (IKE).* June 2012. – RFC 6617, IETF, Status: Experimental, `https://tools.ietf.org/html/rfc6617`

[HC98]   HARKINS, D.; CARREL, D.: *The Internet Key Exchange (IKE).* November 1998. – RFC 2409, IETF, Status: Proposed Standard, `https://tools.ietf.org/html/rfc2409`

[HD03]   HARDJONO, T.; DONDETI, L. R.: *Multicast and Group Security.* Artech House, 2003

[HDW+12] HENINGER, N.; DURUMERIC, Z.; WUSTROW, E.; HALDERMAN, J. A.: Mining Your Ps and Qs: Detection of Widespread Weak Keys in Network Devices. In: *Proceedings of 21st USENIX Security Symposium*, 2012

[Hef98]   HEFFERNAN, A.: *Protection of BGP Sessions via the TCP MD5 Signature Option*. 1998. – RFC 2385, IETF, Status: Standard, `https://tools.ietf.org/html/rfc2385`

[HH99]   HARNEY, H.; HARDER, E.: *Logical Key Hierarchy Protocol*. 1999. – IETF, Status: Expired Internet-Draft, `https://tools.ietf.org/html/draft-harney-sparta-lkhp-sec-00`

[HM97a]   HARNE, H.; MUCKENHIRN, C.: *Group Key Management Protocol (GKMP) Architecture*. 1997. – RFC 2094, IETF, Status: Standard, `https://tools.ietf.org/html/rfc2094`

[HM97b]   HARNE, H.; MUCKENHIRN, C.: *Group Key Management Protocol (GKMP) Specification*. 1997. – RFC 2093, IETF, Status: Standard, `https://tools.ietf.org/html/rfc2093`

[HM09]   HUBERT, A.; MOOK, R. van: *Measures for Making DNS More Resilient against Forged Answers*. January 2009. – RFC 5452, IETF, Status: Proposed Standard, `https://tools.ietf.org/html/rfc5452`

[HMN+98] HALLER, N.; METZ, C.; NESSER, P.; STRAW, M.: *A One-Time Password System*. February 1998. – RFC 2289, IETF, Status: Draft Standard, `https://tools.ietf.org/html/rfc2289`

[Hou05]   HOUSLEY, R.: *Using Advanced Encryption Standard (AES) CCM Mode with IPsec Encapsulating Security Payload (ESP)*. December 2005. – RFC 4309, IETF, Status: Proposed Standard, `https://tools.ietf.org/html/rfc4309`

[Hou09]   HOUSLEY, R.: *Cryptographic Message Syntax (CMS)*. September 2009. – RFC 5652, IETF, Status: Proposed Standard, `https://tools.ietf.org/html/rfc5652`

[HPV+99] HAMZEH, K.; PALL, G.; VERTHEIN, W.; TAARUD, J.; LITTLE, W.; ZORN, G.: *Point-to-Point Tunneling Protocol*. July 1999. – RFC 2637, IETF, Status: Informational, `https://tools.ietf.org/html/rfc2637`

[HR06]   HANDLEY, M.; RESCORLA, E.: *Internet Denial-of-Service Considerations*. November 2006. – RFC 4732, IETF, Status: Informational, `https://tools.ietf.org/html/rfc4732`

[HS13a]   HERZBERG, A.; SHULMAN, H.: DNSSEC: Security and availability challenges. In: *IEEE Conference on Communications and Network Security (CNS)*, 2013, pp. 365–366

[HS13b]   HERZBERG, A.; SHULMAN, H.: Fragmentation Considered Poisonous, or: One-domain-to-rule-them-all.org. In: *IEEE Conference on Communications and Network Security (CNS)*, 2013, pp. 224–232

[HSV+05] HUTTUNEN, A.; SWANDER, B.; VOLPE, V.; DIBURRO, L.; STENBERG, M.: *UDP Encapsulation of IPsec ESP Packets*. January 2005. – RFC 3948, IETF,

Status: Proposed Standard, `https://tools.ietf.org/html/rfc3948`

[ICA10] ICANN: *Trusted Community Representatives – Proposed Approach to Root Key Management.* 2010. – Provisional TCR Proposal, `http://www.root-dnssec.org/wp-content/uploads/2010/04/ICANN-TCR-Proposal-20100408.pdf`

[IEE00] IEEE P1363 WORKING GROUP: *IEEE Standard Specifications for Public-Key Cryptography.* IEEE Std 1363-2000, 2000

[IEE06] IEEE (INSTITUTE OF ELECTRICAL AND ELECTRONICS ENGINEERS): *Standards for Local and Metropolitan Area Networks – Security.* The Institute of Electrical and Electronics Engineers (IEEE), IEEE Std 802.1AE-2006, 2006

[IEE10] IEEE (INSTITUTE OF ELECTRICAL AND ELECTRONICS ENGINEERS): *Standards for Local and Metropolitan Area Networks – Port Based Network Access Control.* The Institute of Electrical and Electronics Engineers (IEEE), IEEE Std 802.1X-2010, 2010

[IEE11a] IEEE (INSTITUTE OF ELECTRICAL AND ELECTRONICS ENGINEERS): *IEEE Standard for Local and metropolitan area networks – Media Access Control (MAC) Bridges and Virtual Bridged Local Area Networks.* The Institute of Electrical and Electronics Engineers (IEEE), IEEE Std 802.1Q-2011, 2011

[IEE11b] IEEE (INSTITUTE OF ELECTRICAL AND ELECTRONICS ENGINEERS): *Standards for Local and Metropolitan Area Networks – Security Amendment 1: Galois Counter Mode – Advanced Encryption Standard-256 (GCM-AES-256) Cipher Suite.* The Institute of Electrical and Electronics Engineers (IEEE), IEEE Std 802.1AEbn-2011, 2011

[IEE12] IEEE (INSTITUTE OF ELECTRICAL AND ELECTRONICS ENGINEERS): *Wireless LAN Medium Access Control (MAC) and Physical Layer (PHY) Specifications.* The Institute of Electrical and Electronics Engineers (IEEE), IEEE Std 802.11-2012, 2012

[Inf81] INFORMATION SCIENCES INSTITUTE, UNIVERSITY OF SOUTHERN CALIFORNIA: *Internet Protocol.* September 1981. – RFC 791, IETF, Status: Proposed Standard, `https://tools.ietf.org/html/rfc791`

[IS09] IGOE, K.; SOLINAS, J.: *AES Galois Counter Mode for the Secure Shell Transport Layer Protocol.* August 2009. – RFC 5647, IETF, Status: Informational, `https://tools.ietf.org/html/rfc5647`

[ISO13] ISO (INTERNATIONAL ORGANIZATION FOR STANDARDIZATION): *ISO/IEC 27001:2013 Information technology – Security techniques – Information security management systems – Requirements.* 2013

[IT87] ITU-T: *Draft Recommendation X.509: The Directory Authentication Framework, Version 7.* November 1987

[IT93] ITU-T: *X.509: Information Technology – Open Systems Interconnection – The Directory: Authentication Framework (4).* 1993

[JB99]   JUELS, A.; BRAINARD, J. G.: Client Puzzles: A Cryptographic Countermeasure Against Connection Depletion Attacks. In: *NDSS* Bd. 99, 1999, pp. 151–165

[JMI06]   JUNAID, M.; MUFTI, M.; ILYAS, M. U.: Vulnerabilities of IEEE 802.11i wireless LAN CCMP protocol. In: *Transactions on Engineering, Computing and Technology* 11 (2006)

[Jou06]   JOUX, A.: Multicollisions in Iterated Hash Functions. Application to Cascaded Constructions. In: *Advances in Cryptology – CRYPTO 2004* Bd. 3152. 2006, pp. 306–316

[KAF$^+$10] KLEINJUNG, T.; AOKI, K.; FRANKE, J.; LENSTRA, A.; THOMÉ, E.; BOS, J.; GAUDRY, P.; KRUPPA, A.; MONTGOMERY, P.; OSVIK, D.; TE RIELE, H.; TIMOFEEV, A.; ZIMMERMANN, P.: Factorization of a 768-bit RSA modulus. In: *Proceedings of the 30th annual conference on Advances in cryptology*, Springer-Verlag, 2010 (CRYPTO'10), pp. 333–350

[Kal98]   KALISKI, B.: *PKCS #7: Cryptographic Message Syntax*. March 1998. – RFC 2315, IETF, Status: Proposed Standard, `https://tools.ietf.org/html/rfc2315`

[Kal00]   KALISKI, B.: *PKCS #5: Password-Based Cryptography Specification Version 2.0*. September 2000. – RFC 2898, IETF, Status: Informational, `https://tools.ietf.org/html/rfc2898`

[Kam08]   KAMINSKY, D.: Black ops 2008: It's the end of the cache as we know it. In: *Black Hat USA* (2008)

[Kam10]   KAMINSKY, D.: *Phreebird Suite 1.0: Introducing the Domain Key Infrastructure*. `http://www.slideshare.net/dakami/phreebird-suite-10-introducing-the-domain-key-infrastructure`. Version: 2010

[KBC97]   KRAWCZYK, H.; BELLARE, M.; CANETTI, R.: *HMAC: Keyed-Hashing for Message Authentication*. February 1997. – RFC 2104, IETF, Status: Informational, `https://tools.ietf.org/html/rfc2104`

[Kem89]   KEMMERER, R. A.: Analyzing Encryption Protocols using Formal Description Techniques. In: *IEEE Journal on Selected Areas in Communications* 7 (1989), May, No. 4, pp. 488–457

[Ken05a] KENT, S.: *IP Authentication Header*. December 2005. – RFC 4302, IETF, Status: Proposed Standard, `https://tools.ietf.org/html/rfc4302`

[Ken05b] KENT, S.: *IP Encapsulating Security Payload (ESP)*. December 2005. – RFC 4303, IETF, Status: Proposed Standard, `https://tools.ietf.org/html/rfc4303`

[Ker83]   KERCKHOFF, A.: La Cryptographie Militaire. In: *Journal des Sciences Militaires* (1883), January

[KF07]   KELLY, S.; FRANKEL, S.: *Using HMAC-SHA-256, HMAC-SHA-384, and HMAC-SHA-512 with IPsec*. May 2007. – RFC 4868, IETF, Status: Proposed Standard, `https://tools.ietf.org/html/rfc4868`

[KHN⁺10]   KAUFMAN, C.; HOFFMAN, P.; NIR, Y.; ERONEN, P.: *Internet Key Exchange Protocol Version 2 (IKEv2)*. September 2010. – RFC 5996, IETF, Status: Proposed Standard, `https://tools.ietf.org/html/rfc5996`

[Kiv11]   KIVINEN, T.: *Secure Password Framework for Internet Key Exchange Version 2 (IKEv2)*. December 2011. – RFC 6467, IETF, Status: Informational, `https://tools.ietf.org/html/rfc6467`

[KK03]   KUZMANOVIC, A.; KNIGHTLY, E. W.: Low-rate TCP-targeted Denial of Service Attacks: The Shrew vs. The Mice and Elephants. In: *Proceedings of the Conference on Applications, Technologies, Architectures, and Protocols for Computer Communications (SIGCOMM)*, 2003, pp. 75–86

[KK06]   KELSEY, J.; KOHNO, T.: Herding Hash Functions and the Nostradamus Attack. In: *Advances in Cryptology – EUROCRYPT'06*, 2006

[KK08]   KASTENBERG, J. E.; KORNS, S. W.: Georgia's Cyber Left Hook. In: *Parameters* 38 (2008), No. 4, pp. 60–76

[KKK10]   KATO, A.; KANDA, M.; KANNO, S.: *Camellia Cipher Suites for TLS*. June 2010. – RFC 5932, IETF, Status: Proposed Standard, `https://tools.ietf.org/html/rfc5932`

[Kle03]   KLEIN, T.: *Buffer Overflows und Format-String-Schwachstellen: Funktionsweisen, Exploits und Gegenmaßnahmen*. dpunkt.verlag, 2003

[Kle08]   KLEIN, A.: Attacks on the RC4 stream cipher. In: *Designs, Codes and Cryptography* 48 (2008), September, No. 3, pp. 269–286

[Kli06]   KLIMA, V.: Tunnels in Hash Functions: MD5 Collisions Within a Minute (extended abstract). In: *Cryptology ePrint Archive: Report 2006/105*, 2006

[KLP⁺11]   KIM, W.; LEE, J.; PARK, J.; KWON, D.: *Addition of the ARIA Cipher Suites to Transport Layer Security (TLS)*. April 2011. – RFC 6209, IETF, Status: Proposed Standard, `https://tools.ietf.org/html/rfc6209`

[KMG12]   KOLKMAN, O.; MEKKING, W.; GIEBEN, R.: *DNSSEC Operational Practices, Version 2*. December 2012. – RFC 6781, IETF, Status: Proposed Standard, `https://tools.ietf.org/html/rfc6781`

[KMK05]   KATO, A.; MORIAI, S.; KANDA, M.: *The Camellia Cipher Algorithm and Its Use With IPsec*. December 2005. – RFC 4312, IETF, Status: Proposed Standard, `https://tools.ietf.org/html/rfc4312`

[KMR⁺03]   KRUEGEL, C.; MUTZ, D.; ROBERTSON, W.; VALEUR, F.: Topology-based detection of anomalous BGP messages. In: *Recent Advances in Intrusion Detection (RAID)*, 2003, pp. 17–35

[KNT94]   KOHL, J.; NEUMAN, B.; TS'O, T.: The Evolution of the Kerberos Authentication Service. In: BRAZIER, F. (Hrsg.); JOHANSEN, D. (Hrsg.): *Distributed Open Systems*, IEEE Computer Society Press, 1994

[Kob87a]   KOBLITZ, N.: *A Course in Number Theory and Cryptography*. Springer-Verlag, 1987

[Kob87b]   KOBLITZ, N.: Elliptic Curve Cryptosystems. In: *Mathematics of Computation* 48 (1987), pp. 203–209

[Koh89]   KOHL, J.: The Use of Encryption in Kerberos for Network Authentication. In: *Proceedings of Crypto'89*, Springer-Verlag, 1989

[KP00]   KEROMYTIS, A.; PROVOS, N.: *The Use of HMAC-RIPEMD-160-96 within ESP and AH*. June 2000. – RFC 2857, IETF, Status: Proposed Standard, `https://tools.ietf.org/html/rfc2857`

[KP12]   KAUSE, T.; PEYLO, M.: *Internet X.509 Public Key Infrastructure – HTTP Transfer for the Certificate Management Protocol (CMP)*. September 2012. – RFC 6712, IETF, Status: Proposed Standard, `https://tools.ietf.org/html/rfc6712`

[KPT04]   KIM, Y.; PERRIG, A.; TSUDIK, G.: Tree-based Group Key Agreement. In: *ACM Transactions on Information and System Security (TISSEC)* 7 (2004), No. 1, pp. 60–96

[KS05]   KENT, S.; SEO, K.: *Security Architecture for the Internet Protocol*. December 2005. – RFC 4301, IETF, Status: Proposed Standard, `https://tools.ietf.org/html/rfc4301`

[KS12]   KUEGLER, D.; SHEFFER, Y.: *Password Authenticated Connection Establishment with the Internet Key Exchange Protocol version 2 (IKEv2)*. June 2012. – RFC 6631, IETF, Status: Experimental, `https://tools.ietf.org/html/rfc6631`

[Kum98]   KUMMERT, H.: *The PPP Triple-DES Encryption Protocol (3DESE)*. September 1998. – RFC 2420, IETF, Status: Proposed Standard, `https://tools.ietf.org/html/rfc2420`

[Kus13]   KUSHNER, D.: The real story of stuxnet. In: *Spectrum, IEEE* 50 (2013), March, No. 3, pp. 48–53

[KW94]   KESSLER, V.; WEDEL, G: AUTOLOG – An Advanced Logic of Authentication. In: *Proceedings of the Computer Security Foundations Workshop VII*, IEEE Computer Society Press, 1994, pp. 90–99

[KY11]   KIRCANSKI, A.; YOUSSEF, A. M.: On the sliding property of SNOW 3G and SNOW 2.0. In: *IET Information Security* 5 (2011), No. 4, pp. 199–206

[Küh01]   KÜHN, U.: Cryptanalysis of Reduced-Round MISTY. In: *Advances in Cryptology - CRYPTO 2001*, Springer-Verlag, 2001 (Lecture Notes in Computer Science), pp. 325–339

[LC05]   LHEE, K.; CHAPIN, S.: Detection of File-Based Race Conditions. In: *International Journal of Information Security* 4 (2005), No. 1–2, pp. 105–119

[LD05]   LUCKS, S.; DAUM, M.: The Story of Alice and her Boss. In: *Rump session of EUROCRYPT'05*, 2005

[Lep13]   LEPINSKI, M.: *BGPSEC Protocol Specification*. 2013. – IETF, Status: Internet-Draft, `https://tools.ietf.org/html/draft-ietf-sidr-bgpsec-protocol-08`

[Les03]   LESCUYER, P.: *UMTS: Origins, Architecture and the Standard*. Springer, 2003

[Les07]   LESK, M.: The New Front Line: Estonia under Cyberassault. In: *IEEE Security & Privacy* 5 (2007), No. 4, pp. 76–79

[LK12]   LEPINSKI, M.; KENT, S.: *An Infrastructure to Support Secure Internet Routing*. 2012. – RFC 6480, IETF, Status: Proposed Standard, `https://tools.ietf.org/html/rfc6480`

[LKP⁺98]   LUCIANI, J.; KATZ, D.; PISCITELLO, D.; COLE, B.; DORASWAMY, N.: *NBMA Next Hop Resolution Protocol (NHRP)*. RFC 2332, IETF, Status: Proposed Standard, `https://tools.ietf.org/html/rfc2332`, 1998

[LKS04]   LYNN, C.; KENT, S.; SEO, K.: *X.509 Extensions for IP Addresses and AS Identifiers*. 2004. – RFC 3779, IETF, Status: Proposed Standard, `https://tools.ietf.org/html/rfc3779`

[LM10]   LOCHTER, M.; MERKLE, J.: *Elliptic Curve Cryptography (ECC) Brainpool Standard Curves and Curve Generation*. 2010. – RFC 5639, IETF, Status: Standard, `https://tools.ietf.org/html/rfc5639`

[LMS03]   LYNN, C.; MIKKELSON, J.; SEO, K.: *Secure BGP (S-BGP)*. 2003. – IETF, Status: Expired Internet-Draft, `https://tools.ietf.org/html/draft-clynn-s-bgp-protocol-01`

[LR92]   LONGLEY, D.; RIGBY, S.: An Automatic Search for Security Flaws in Key Management Schemes. In: *Computers & Security* 11 (1992), No. 1, pp. 75–89

[LRS⁺00]   LAU, F.; RUBIN, S. H.; SMITH, M. H.; TRAJKOVIC, L.: Distributed denial of service attacks. In: *IEEE International Conference on Systems, Man, and Cybernetics* Bd. 3, 2000, pp. 2275–2280

[LS92]   LLOYD, B.; SIMPSON, W.: *PPP Authentication Protocols*. October 1992. – RFC 1334, IETF, Status: Obsoleted by RFC1994, `https://tools.ietf.org/html/rfc1334`

[LSA⁺08]   LAURIE, B.; SISSON, G.; ARENDS, R.; BLACKA, D.: *DNS Security (DNSSEC) Hashed Authenticated Denial of Existence*. March 2008. – RFC 5155, IETF, Status: Proposed Standard, `https://tools.ietf.org/html/rfc5155`

[LT13]   LEPINSKI, M.; TURNER, S.: *An Overview of BGPSEC*. 2013. – IETF, Status: Internet-Draft, `https://tools.ietf.org/html/draft-ietf-sidr-bgpsec-overview-04`

[LTG05]   LAU, J.; TOWNSLEY, M.; GOYRET, I.: *Layer Two Tunneling Protocol – Version 3 (L2TPv3)*. March 2005. – RFC 3931, IETF, Status: Proposed Standard, `https://tools.ietf.org/html/rfc3931`

[LWW05]   LENSTRA, A.; WANG, X.; WEGER, B. de: Colliding X.509 Certificates. In: *Cryptology ePrint Archive: Report 2005/067*, 2005

[Man11]   MANUEL, M.: Classification and Generation of Disturbance Vectors for Collision Attacks against SHA-1. In: *Designs, Codes and Cryptography* 59 (2011), pp. 247–263

[Mar09]   MARLINSPIKE, M.: *Defeating OCSP With The Character '3'*. `http://www.thoughtcrime.org/papers/ocsp-attack.pdf`. Version: 2009

[Mat94]   MATSUI, M.: Linear Cryptanalysis Method for DES Cipher. In: *Advances in Cryptology – EUROCRYPT'93*, Springer-Verlag, 1994, pp. 386–397

[MB93]   MAO, W.; BOYD, C.: Towards Formal Analysis of Security Protocols. In: *Proceedings of the Computer Security Foundations Workshop VI*, IEEE Computer Society Press, 1993, pp. 147–158

[MC01]   MAHONEY, M. V.; CHAN, P. K.: *PHAD: Packet Header Anomaly Detection for Identifying Hostile Network Traffic*. 2001 (Technical Report CS-2001-04). – Forschungsbericht

[MCF87]   MILLEN, J. K.; CLARK, S. C.; FREEDMAN, S. B.: The Interrogator: Protocol Security Analysis. In: *IEEE Transactions on Software Engineering* 13 (1987), February, No. 2, pp. 274–288

[MD98]   MADSON, C.; DORASWAMY, N.: *The ESP DES-CBC Cipher Algorithm With Explicit IV*. November 1998. – RFC 2405, IETF, Status: Proposed Standard, https://tools.ietf.org/html/rfc2405

[Mea92]   MEADOWS, C.: Applying Formal Methods to the Analysis of a Key Management Protocol. In: *Journal of Computer Security* 1 (1992), No. 1, pp. 5–35

[Mea95]   MEADOWS, C.: Formal Verification of Cryptographic Protocols: A Survey. In: *Advances in Cryptology – ACRYPT'94*, Springer-Verlag, 1995 (Lecture Notes in Computer Science 917), pp. 133–150

[Men93]   MENEZES, A. J.: *Elliptic Curve Public Key Cryptosystems*. Kluwer Academic Publishers, 1993

[Mer83]   MERRIT, M.: *Cryptographic Protocols*. Ph.D Thesis, Georgia Institute of Technology, GIT-ICS-83, 1983

[Mer89]   MERKLE, R.: One Way Hash Functions and DES. In: *Proceedings of Crypto '89*, Springer-Verlag, 1989

[Mey96]   MEYER, G.: *The PPP Encryption Control Protocol (ECP)*. June 1996. – RFC 1968, IETF, Status: Proposed Standard, https://tools.ietf.org/html/rfc1968

[MG98a]   MADSON, C.; GLENN, R.: *The Use of HMAC-MD5-96 within ESP and AH*. November 1998. – RFC 2403, IETF, Status: Proposed Standard, https://tools.ietf.org/html/rfc2403

[MG98b]   MADSON, C.; GLENN, R.: *The Use of HMAC-SHA-1-96 within ESP and AH*. November 1998. – RFC 2404, IETF, Status: Proposed Standard, https://tools.ietf.org/html/rfc2404

[MGM⁺06]   MUÑOZ MERINO, P. J.; GARCÍA-MARTÍNEZ, A.; MUÑOZ ORGANERO, M.; DELGADO KLOOS, C.: Enabling Practical IPsec Authentication for the Internet. In: *On the Move to Meaningful Internet Systems 2006: OTM 2006 Workshops*, 2006, pp. 392–403

[MH13]   MANRAL, V.; HANNA, S.: *Auto-Discovery VPN Problem Statement and Requirements*. September 2013. – RFC 7018, IETF, Status: Informational, https://tools.ietf.org/html/rfc7018

[MHR12]   MARLINSPIKE, M.; HULTON, D.; RAY, M.: *Defeating PPTP VPNs and WPA2 Enterprise with MS-CHAPv2*. Talk at Defcon 20, 2012

[Mic13]   MICROSOFT: *Peer Name Resolution Protocol (PNRP) Version 4.0.* `http://download.microsoft.com/download/9/5/E/95EF66AF-9026-4BB0-A41D-A4F81802D92C/[MS-PNRP].pdf`. Version: 2013. – Technical Document, Version 14

[Mic14]   MICROSOFT: *[MS-SSTP]: Secure Socket Tunneling Protocol (SSTP)*. Open Specifications Documentation. Version 14.0. `http://download.microsoft.com/download/9/5/E/95EF66AF-9026-4BB0-A41D-A4F81802D92C/[MS-SSTP].pdf`. Version: 2014

[Mir02]   MIRONOV, I.: (Not So) Random Shuffles of RC4. In: *Proceedings of the 22nd Annual International Cryptology Conference on Advances in Cryptology*, Springer-Verlag, 2002, pp. 304–319

[Mit97]   MITTRA, S.: Iolus: a framework for scalable secure multicasting. In: *ACM SIGCOMM Computer Communication Review* 27 (1997), October, No. 4, pp. 277–288

[MLE+99] MAMAKOS, L.; LIDL, K.; EVARTS, J.; CARREL, D.; SIMONE, D.; WHEELER, R.: *A Method for Transmitting PPP Over Ethernet (PPPoE)*. February 1999. – RFC 2516, IETF, Status: Informational, `https://tools.ietf.org/html/rfc2516`

[MM78]   MATYAS, S. M.; MEYER, C. H.: Generation, Distribution and Installation of Cryptographic Keys. In: *IBM Systems Journal* 17 (1978), May, No. 2, pp. 126–137

[Mos89]   MOSER, L.: A Logic of Knowledge and Belief for Reasoning about Computer Security. In: *Proceedings of the Computer Security Foundations Workshop II*, IEEE Computer Society Press, June 1989, pp. 57–63

[MOV97]   MENEZES, A.; OORSCHOT, P. van; VANSTONE, S.: *Handbook of Applied Cryptography*. CRC Press LLC, 1997

[MR99]   MÜLLER, G. (Hrsg.); RANNENBERG, K. (Hrsg.): *Multilateral Security in Communications*. Addison-Wesley-Longman, 1999

[MSS+98] MAUGHAN, D.; SCHERTLER, M.; SCHNEIDER, M.; TURNER, J.: *Internet Security Association and Key Management Protocol (ISAKMP)*. November 1998. – RFC 2408, IETF, Status: Proposed Standard, `https://tools.ietf.org/html/rfc2408`

[MV06]   McGREW, D.; VIEGA, J.: *The Use of Galois Message Authentication Code (GMAC) in IPsec ESP and AH*. May 2006. – RFC 4543, IETF, Status: Proposed Standard, `https://tools.ietf.org/html/rfc4543`

[Ng04]   NG, J.: *Extensions to BGP to Support Secure Origin BGP (soBGP)*. 2004. – IETF, Status: Expired Internet-Draft, `https://tools.ietf.org/html/draft-ng-sobgp-bgp-extensions-02`

[NIS77]   NIST (NATIONAL INSTITUTE OF STANDARDS AND TECHNOLOGY): *FIPS (Federal Information Processing Standard) Publication 46: Data Encryption Standard*. 1977

[NIS88]   NIST (NATIONAL INSTITUTE OF STANDARDS AND TECHNOLOGY): *FIPS (Federal Information Processing Standard) Publication 46-1: Data Encryption Standard*. 1988. – Aktualisiert FIPS Publication 46

[NIS01]   NIST (NATIONAL INSTITUTE OF STANDARDS AND TECHNOLOGY): *FIPS (Federal Information Processing Standard) Publication 197: Specification for the Advanced Encryption Standard (AES)*. 2001

[NIS02]   NIST (NATIONAL INSTITUTE OF STANDARDS AND TECHNOLOGY): *Secure Hash Standard*. FIPS (Federal Information Processing Standard) Publication 180-2, 2002

[NIS12]   NIST (NATIONAL INSTITUTE OF STANDARDS AND TECHNOLOGY): *Recommendation for Key Management: Part 1: General (Revision 3)*. 2012. – NIST Special Publication 800-57

[NIS13]   NIST (NATIONAL INSTITUTE OF STANDARDS AND TECHNOLOGY): *Digital Signature Standard (DSS)*. 2013. – FIPS PUB 186-4 - Federal Information Processing Standards Publication

[NM08]   NIKANDER, P.; MELEN, J.: *A Bound End-to-End Tunnel (BEET) mode for ESP*. August 2008. – IETF, Status: Expired Internet-Draft, `https://tools.ietf.org/search/draft-nikander-esp-beet-mode-09`

[NS78]   NEEDHAM, R. M.; SCHROEDER, M. D.: Using Encryption for Authentication in Large Networks of Computers. In: *Communications of the ACM* 21 (1978), December, No. 12, pp. 993–999

[NS87]   NEEDHAM, R.; SCHROEDER, M.: Authentication Revisited. In: *Operating Systems Review* 21 (1987), No. 1

[NSZ03]   NICOL, D. M.; SMITH, S. W.; ZHAO, M.: *Efficient Security for BGP Route Announcements* / Dartmouth College, Computer Science. 2003 (TR2003-440). – Forschungsbericht

[NYH⁺05]   NEUMAN, C.; YU, T.; HARTMAN, S.; RAEBURN, K.: *The Kerberos Network Authentication Service (V5)*. 2005. – RFC 4120, IETF, Status: Standard, `https://tools.ietf.org/html/rfc4120`

[NZ80]   NIVEN, I.; ZUCKERMAN, H.: *An Introduction to the Theory of Numbers*. John Wiley & Sons, 1980. – 4th edition

[Oeh05]   OEHLERT, P.: Violating Assumptions with Fuzzing. In: *IEEE Security Privacy* 3 (2005), No. 2, pp. 58–62

[OM09]   OHIGASHI, T.; MORII, M.: A Practical Message Falsification Attack on WPA. In: *Procedings of Joint Workshop on Information Security, Cryptography and Information Security Conference System*, 2009

[Oor93]   OORSCHOT, P. van: Extending Cryptographic Logics of Belief to Key Agreement Protocols. In: ASHBY, V. (Hrsg.): *1st ACM Conference on Computer and Communications Security*, 1993, pp. 232–243

[OR87]   OTWAY, D.; REES, O.: Efficient and Timely Mutual Authentication. In: *Operating Systems Review* 21 (1987), No. 1

[PA98]   PEREIRA, R.; ADAMS, R.: *The ESP CBC-Mode Cipher Algorithms.*
            November 1998. – RFC 2451, IETF, Status: Proposed Standard,
            `https://tools.ietf.org/html/rfc2451`

[Pat97]   PATEL, S.: Number Theoretic Attacks On Secure Password Schemes. In:
            IEEE Symposium on Security and Privacy, 1997, pp. 236–247

[Pax99]   PAXSON, V.: Bro: a System for Detecting Network Intruders in Real-Time.
            In: *Computer Networks* 31 (1999), No. 23-24, pp. 2435–2463

[PD00]   PETERSON, L.; DAVIE, B.: *Computernetze – Ein modernes Lehrbuch.*
            dpunkt.verlag, 2000

[PD11]   PARKS, R. C.; DUGGAN, D. P.: Principles of Cyberwarfare. In: *IEEE
            Security Privacy* 9 (2011), No. 5, pp. 30–35

[Pip98]   PIPER, D.: *The Internet IP Security Domain of Interpretation for ISAKMP.*
            November 1998. – RFC 2407, IETF, Status: Proposed Standard,
            `https://tools.ietf.org/html/rfc2407`

[PM03]   PANNETRAT, A.; MOLVA, R.: Efficient Multicast Packet Authentication. In:
            Network and Distributed System Security Symposium (NDSS), 2003

[PNV11]   PRITIKIN, M.; NOURSE, A.; VILHUBER, J.: *Simple Certificate Enrollment
            Protocol.* (2011), September. – Expired Draft, IETF, Intended Status:
            Historic, `https://tools.ietf.org/html/draft-nourse-scep-23`

[PO95]   PRENEEL, B.; OORSCHOT, P. van: MDx-MAC and building fast MACs from
            hash functions. In: *Advances in Cryptology – CRYPTO'95*, 1995

[Pos83]   POSTEL, J.: *Echo Protocol.* May 1983. – RFC 862, IETF,
            `https://tools.ietf.org/html/rfc862`

[PPP09]   PRENEEL, B.; PAAR, C.; PELZL, J.: *Understanding cryptography: a textbook
            for students and practitioners.* Springer, 2009

[Pri13]   PRINCE, M.: *The DDoS That Almost Broke the Internet.* `http://blog.`
            `cloudflare.com/the-ddos-that-almost-broke-the-internet.`
            Version: 2013

[PSC⁺05]   PERRIG, A.; SONG, D.; CANETTI, R.; TYGAR, J. D.; BRISCOE, B.: *Timed
            Efficient Stream Loss-Tolerant Authentication (TESLA): Multicast Source
            Authentication Transform Introduction.* 2005. – RFC 4082, IETF, Status:
            Standard, `https://tools.ietf.org/html/rfc4082`

[PSS82]   PURDY, G. B.; SIMMONS, G. J.; STUDIER, J. A.: A Software Protection
            Scheme. In: *Proceedings of the 1982 Symposium on Security and Privacy*,
            IEEE Computer Society Press, April 1982, pp. 99–103

[PST⁺02]   PERRIG, A.; SZEWCZYK, R.; TYGAR, J. D.; WEN, V.; CULLER, D. E.: SPINS:
            Security Protocols for Sensor Networks. In: *Wireless Networks* 8 (2002),
            No. 5, pp. 521–534

[PY06]   PATERSON, K. G.; YAU, A. K.: Cryptography in Theory and Practice: The
            Case of Encryption in IPsec. In: *Advances in Cryptology - EUROCRYPT
            2006* Bd. 4004. Springer-Verlag, 2006, pp. 12–29

[PYH13]   PRITIKIN, M.; YEE, P.; HARKINS, D.: *Enrollment over Secure Transport*. October 2013. – RFC 7030, IETF, Status: Proposed Standard, `https://tools.ietf.org/html/rfc7030`

[PZ01]   PALL, G.; ZORN, G.: *Microsoft Point-To-Point Encryption (MPPE) Protocol*. March 2001. – RFC 3078, IETF, Status: Informational, `https://tools.ietf.org/html/rfc3078`

[QGR⁺07] QIU, J.; GAO, L.; RANJAN, S.; NUCCI, A.: Detecting bogus BGP route information: Going beyond prefix hijacking. In: *SecureComm 2007*, 2007, pp. 381–390

[Rae05]   RAEBURN, K.: *Advanced Encryption Standard (AES) Encryption for Kerberos 5*. 2005. – RFC 3962, IETF, Status: Standard, `https://tools.ietf.org/html/rfc3962`

[Ran88]   RANGAN, P. V.: An axiomatic Basis of Trust in Distributed Systems. In: *Proceedings of the 1988 Symposium on Security and Privacy*, IEEE Computer Society Press, April 1988, pp. 204–211

[RAW⁺13] ROSSOW, C.; ANDRIESSE, D.; WERNER, T.; STONE-GROSS, B.; PLOHMANN, D.; DIETRICH, C. J.; BOS, H.: SoK: P2PWNED – Modeling and Evaluating the Resilience of Peer-to-Peer Botnets. In: *IEEE Symposium on Security and Privacy (SP)*, 2013, pp. 97–111

[RD01]   ROWSTRON, A.; DRUSCHEL, P.: Pastry: Scalable, decentralized object location, and routing for large-scale peer-to-peer systems. In: *Middleware 2001*, 2001, pp. 329–350

[RE08]   RANKL, W.; EFFING, W.: *Handbuch der Chipkarten*. Hanser, 2008

[RH03]   RAFAELI, S.; HUTCHISON, D.: A Survey of Key Management for Secure Group Communication. In: *ACM Computing Surveys* 35 (2003), No. 3, pp. 309–329

[Ric92]   RICHTER, M.: *Ein Rauschgenerator zur Gewinnung von quasi-idealen Zufallszahlen für die stochastische Simulation*. Dissertation, Universität Aachen, 1992

[Riv90]   RIVEST, R.: Cryptography. In: VAN LEEUWEN, J. (Hrsg.): *Handbook of Theoretical Computer Science* Bd. 1, Elsevier, 1990, pp. 717–755

[Riv91]   RIVEST, R. L.: The MD4 Message Digest Algorithm. In: *Advances in Cryptology — Crypto '90 Proceedings*, Springer-Verlag, 1991, pp. 303–311

[Riv92]   RIVEST, R. L.: *The MD5 Message Digest Algorithm*, April 1992. – RFC 1321

[Riv01]   RIVEST, R.: *RSA Security Response to Weaknesses in Key Scheduling Algorithm of RC4*. 2001. – `http://www.rsa.com/rsalabs/technotes/wep.html`

[RM12]   RESCORLA, E.; MODADUGU, N.: *Datagram Transport Layer Security Version 1.2*. January 2012. – RFC 6347, IETF, Status: Proposed Standard, `https://tools.ietf.org/html/rfc6347`

[Ros13]   ROSE, S.: *Applicability Statement: DNS Security (DNSSEC) DNSKEY Algorithm Implementation Status*. April 2013. – RFC 6944, IETF, Status: Proposed Standard, `https://tools.ietf.org/html/rfc6944`

[RR05]   RICHARDSON, M.; REDELMEIER, D. H.: *Opportunistic Encryption using the Internet Key Exchange (IKE)*. RFC 4322, IETF, Status: Informational, `https://tools.ietf.org/html/rfc4322`, 2005

[RRD+10]   RESCORLA, E.; RAY, M.; DISPENSA, S.; OSKOV, N.: *Transport Layer Security (TLS) Renegotiation Indication Extension*. February 2010. – RFC 5746, IETF, Status: Proposed Standard, `https://tools.ietf.org/html/rfc5746`

[RS09]   ROSSBERG, M.; SCHAEFER, G.: Ciscos Group Encrypted Transport VPN – Eine kritische Analyse. In: *Proceedings of D-A-CH security, German*, 2009, pp. 351–360

[RS11]   ROSSBERG, M.; SCHAEFER, G.: A Survey on Automatic Configuration of Virtual Private Networks. In: *Computer Networks Journal* 55 (2011), pp. 1684–1699

[RSA78]   RIVEST, R.; SHAMIR, A.; ADLEMAN, L.: A Method for Obtaining Digital Signatures and Public Key Cryptosystems. In: *Communications of the ACM* (1978), February

[RSS10]   ROSSBERG, M.; SCHAEFER, G.; STRUFE, T.: Distributed Automatic Configuration of Complex IPsec-Infrastructures. In: *Journal of Network and Systems Management* 18 (2010), No. 3, pp. 300–326

[Rut06]   RUTKOWSKA, J.: Subverting Vista^{TM} Kernel For Fun And Profit. In: *Black Hat Briefings* (2006)

[RWR+00]   RIGNEY, C.; WILLENS, S.; RUBENS, A.; SIMPSON, W.: *Remote Authentication Dial In User Service (RADIUS)*. June 2000. – RFC 2865, IETF, Status: Draft Standard, `https://tools.ietf.org/html/rfc2865`

[SA09]   SASAKI, Y.; AOKI, K.: Finding Preimages in Full MD5 Faster Than Exhaustive Search. In: *Advances in Cryptology – EUROCRYPT'09*, 2009

[Saa11]   SAARINEN, M.: GCM, GHASH and Weak Keys. In: *Proceedings of ECRYPT II Hash Workshop*, 2011

[SAH08]   SIMON, D.; ABOBA, B.; HURST, R.: *PPP EAP TLS Authentication Protocol*. March 2008. – RFC 5216, IETF, Status: Proposed Standard, `https://tools.ietf.org/html/rfc5216`

[Sar10]   SARAGIOTIS, P.: *Good Practices Guide for Deploying DNSSEC*. 2010. – ENISA Good practices guide, `http://www.enisa.europa.eu/activities/Resilience-and-CIIP/networks-and-services-resilience/dnssec/gpgdnssec/at_download/fullReport`

[SAZ+04]   STOICA, I.; ADKINS, D.; ZHUANG, S.; SHENKER, S.; SURANA, S.: Internet indirection infrastructure. In: *IEEE/ACM Transactions on Networking (TON)* 12 (2004), No. 2, pp. 205–218

[SBY+08]   SONG, D.; BRUMLEY, D.; YIN, H.; CABALLERO, J.; JAGER, I.; KANG, M.; LIANG, Z.; NEWSOME, J.; POOSANKAM, P.; SAXENA, P.: BitBlaze: A New Approach to Computer Security via Binary Analysis. In: *Information Systems Security* Bd. 5352. 2008

[SC01]   SAMARATI, P; CAPITANI DI VIMERCATI, S. de: Access Control: Policies,
           Models, and Mechanisms. In: FOCARDI, R. (Hrsg.); GORRIERI, R. (Hrsg.):
           *Foundations of Security Analysis and Design; Lecture Notes in Computer
           Science* Bd. 2171, Springer-Verlag, 2001, pp. 137–196

[SC02]   SANCHEZ, L. A.; CONDELL, M. N.: *Security Policy Protocol*. January 2002. –
           Expired Internet Draft, `https://tools.ietf.org/html/draft
           -ietf-ipsp-spp-01`

[SCF+96]   SANDHU, R.; COYNE, E.; FEINSTEIN, H.; YOUMAN, C.: Role-Based Access
           Control Models. In: *IEEE Computer* 29 (1996), February, No. 2, pp. 38–47

[Sch85]   SCHOOF, R.: Elliptic Curves Over Finite Fields and the Computation of
           Square Roots mod p. In: *Mathematics of Computation* 44 (1985),
           pp. 483–494

[Sch96]   SCHNEIER, B.: *Applied Cryptography Second Edition: Protocols,
           Algorithms and Source Code in C*. John Wiley & Sons, 1996

[Sch98]   SCHÄFER, G.: *Effiziente Authentisierung und Schlüsselverwaltung in
           Hochleistungsnetzen*. October 1998. – Dissertation an der Fakultät für
           Informatik, Universität Karlsruhe (TH)

[Sch03]   SCHILLER, J.: *Mobile Communications*. Pearson Education, 2003

[Sch05]   SCHAAD, J.: *Internet X.509 Public Key Infrastructure Certificate Request
           Message Format (CRMF)*. September 2005. – RFC 4211, IETF, Status:
           Proposed Standard, `https://tools.ietf.org/html/rfc4211`

[Sch11]   SCHAAD, J.: *Certificate Management over CMS (CMC) Updates*. November
           2011. – RFC 6402, IETF, Status: Proposed Standard, `https://tools.
           ietf.org/html/rfc6402`

[Sem96]   SEMERIA, C.: *Internet Firewalls and Security*. 1996. – 3Com Technical
           Paper

[Ser10]   SERRAO, G.: Network access control (NAC): An open source analysis of
           architectures and requirements. In: *IEEE International Carnahan
           Conference on Security Technology (ICCST)*, 2010, pp. 94–102

[SF07]   SHUMOW, D.; FERGUSON, N.: *On the Possibility of a Back Door in the NIST
           SP800-90 Dual Ec Prng*. CRYPTO 2007 rump session, 2007

[SG09]   STEBILA, D.; GREEN, J.: *Elliptic Curve Algorithm Integration in the Secure
           Shell Transport Layer*. December 2009. – RFC 5656, IETF, Status:
           Proposed Standard, `https://tools.ietf.org/html/rfc5656`

[SH95]   STANIFORD-CHEN, S.; HEBERLEIN, L. T.: Holding intruders accountable on
           the Internet. In: *Proceedings of the IEEE Symposium on Security and
           Privacy*, 1995, pp. 39–49

[SH02]   SCHAAD, J.; HOUSLEY, R.: *Advanced Encryption Standard (AES) Key Wrap
           Algorithm*. September 2002. – RFC 3394, IETF, Status: Informational,
           `https://tools.ietf.org/html/rfc3394`

[SH09]   SCARFONE, K.; HOFFMAN, P.: *Guidelines on Firewalls and Firewall Policy*.
           NIST Special Publication 800-41. `http://csrc.nist.gov/`

publications/nistpubs/800-41-Rev1/sp800-41-rev1. pdf. version: 2009

[SHB95] STEVENSON, D.; HILLERY, N.; BYRD, G.: Secure Communications in ATM Networks. In: *Communications of the ACM* 38 (1995), February, pp. 45–52

[SHM⁺13] SATHYANARAYAN, P.; HANNA, S.; MELAM, S.; NIR, Y.; MIGAULT, D.; PENTIKOUSIS, K.: *Auto Discovery VPN Protocol*. October 2013. – Expired Internet Draft, https://tools.ietf.org/html/draft-sathyanarayan-ipsecme-advpn-03

[Sid86] SIDHU, D. P.: Authentication Protocols for Computer Networks: I. In: *Computer Networks and ISDN Systems* 11 (1986), No. 4, pp. 297–310

[Sim85] SIMMONS, G. J.: How to (Selectively) Broadcast a Secret. In: *Proceedings of the 1985 Symposium on Security and Privacy*, IEEE Computer Society Press, April 1985, pp. 108–113

[Sim94a] SIMMONS, G. J.: Cryptology. In: *Encyclopaedia Britannica*, Britannica, 1994

[Sim94b] SIMPSON, W.: *The Point-to-Point Protocol (PPP)*. July 1994. – RFC 1661, IETF, Status: Standard, https://tools.ietf.org/html/rfc1661

[Sim94c] SIMPSON, W.: *PPP in HDLC-like Framing*. July 1994. – RFC 1662, IETF, Status: Standard, https://tools.ietf.org/html/rfc1662

[Sim96] SIMPSON, W.: *PPP Challenge Handshake Authentication Protocol (CHAP)*. August 1996. – RFC 1994, IETF, Status: Draft Standard, https://tools.ietf.org/html/rfc1994

[SK12] SHIN, S.; KOBARA, K.: *Efficient Augmented Password-Only Authentication and Key Exchange for IKEv2*. June 2012. – RFC 6628, IETF, Status: Experimental, https://tools.ietf.org/html/rfc6628

[SM98a] SCHNEIER, B.; MUDGE: Cryptanalysis of Microsoft's Point-to-Point Tunneling Protocol (PPTP). In: *ACM Conference on Computer and Communications Security*, 1998, 132–141

[SM98b] SKLOWER, K.; MEYER, G.: *The PPP DES Encryption Protocol, Version 2 (DESE-bis)*. September 1998. – RFC 2419, IETF, Status: Proposed Standard, https://tools.ietf.org/html/rfc2419

[SM08] SCHAAD, J.; MYERS, M.: *Certificate Management over CMS (CMC): Transport Protocols*. June 2008. – RFC 5273, IETF, Status: Proposed Standard, https://tools.ietf.org/html/rfc5273

[SM09] SORNIOTTI, A.; MOLVA, R.: A provably secure secret handshake with dynamic controlled matching. In: *Computers & Security* (2009)

[SM11] SCHAAD, J.; MYERS, M.: *Certificate Management over CMS (CMC)*. June 2011. – RFC 5272, IETF, Status: Proposed Standard, https://tools.ietf.org/html/rfc5272

[SMA⁺13] SANTESSON, S.; MYERS, M.; ANKNEY, R.; MALPANI, A.; GALPERIN, S.; ADAMS, C.: *X.509 Internet Public Key Infrastructure Online Certificate Status Protocol - OCSP*. June 2013. – RFC 6960, IETF, Status: Proposed Standard, https://tools.ietf.org/html/rfc6960

[SMK⁺01]   STOICA, I.; MORRIS, R.; KARGER, D.; KAASHOEK, F.; BALAKRISHNAN, H.: Chord: A scalable peer-to-peer lookup service for internet applications. In: *ACM SIGCOMM Computer Communication Review* 31 (2001), No. 4, pp. 149–160

[SMP⁺01]   SHACHAM, A.; MONSOUR, B.; PEREIRA, R.; THOMAS, M.: *IP Payload Compression Protocol (IPComp)*. September 2001. – RFC 3173, IETF, Status: Proposed Standard, https://tools.ietf.org/html/rfc3173

[SMW99]   SCHNEIER, B.; MUDGE; WAGNER, D.: Cryptanalysis of Microsoft's PPTP Authentication Extensions (MS-CHAPv2). In: *International Exhibition and Congress on Secure Networking – CQRE [Secure]*, 1999

[Sne91]   SNEKKENES, E.: Exploring the BAN Approach to Protocol Analysis. In: *1991 IEEE Computer Society Symposium on Research in Security and Privacy*, 1991, pp. 171–181

[SO94]   SYVERSON, P.; OORSCHOT, P. C.: On Unifying Some Cryptographic Protocol Logics. In: *1994 IEEE Computer Society Symposium on Research in Security and Privacy*, 1994, pp. 14–28

[SP03]   SHANKAR, U.; PAXSON, V.: Active Mapping: Resisting NIDS Evasion Without Altering Traffic. In: *Symposium on Security and Privacy*, 2003, pp. 44–61

[SPL06]   SONG, J. H.; POOVENDRAN, R.; LEE, J.: *The AES-CMAC-96 Algorithm and Its Use with IPsec*. June 2006. – RFC 4494, IETF, Status: Proposed Standard, https://tools.ietf.org/html/rfc4494

[SPS⁺02]   SNOEREN, A. C.; PARTRIDGE, C.; SANCHEZ, L. A.; JONES, C. E.; TCHAKOUNTIO, F.; SCHWARTZ, B.; KENT, S. T.; STRAYER, W. T.: Single-Packet IP Traceback. In: *IEEE/ACM Transactions on Networking* 10 (2002), No. 6, pp. 721–734

[SPT06]   SARAT, S.; PAPPAS, V.; TERZIS, A.: On the Use of Anycast in DNS. In: *15th International Conference on Computer Communications and Networks (ICCCN)*, 2006, pp. 71–78

[SR97]   SEXTON, M.; REID, A.: *Broadband Networking – ATM, SDH and SONET*. Artech House Publishers, 1997

[SRS⁺04]   SUBRAMANIAN, L.; ROTH, V.; STOICA, I.; SHENKER, S.; KATZ, R.: Listen and Whisper: Security Mechanisms for BGP. In: *Symposium on Networked Systems Design and Implementation (NSDI)*, 2004

[Sta95]   STALLINGS, W.: *ISDN and Broadband ISDN with Frame Relay and ATM*. Prentice Hall, 1995. – Third Edition

[Sta98]   STALLINGS, W.: *High-Speed Networks – TCP/IP and ATM Design Principles*. Prentice Hall, 1998

[Sti06]   STINSON, D. R.: *Cryptography: Theory and Practice (Discrete Mathematics and Its Applications)*. CRC Press, 2006

[Sto00]   STONE, R.: Centertrack: An IP Overlay Network for Tracking DoS Floods. In: *Proceedings of the 9th USENIX Security Symposium*, 2000

[STW00]   STEINER, M.; TSUDIK, G.; WAIDNER, M.: Key Agreement in Dynamic Peer Groups. In: *IEEE Transactions on Parallel and Distributed Systems* 11 (2000), pp. 769–780

[STW12]   SEGGELMANN, R.; TUEXEN, M.; WILLIAMS, M.: *Transport Layer Security (TLS) and Datagram Transport Layer Security (DTLS) Heartbeat Extension.* February 2012. – RFC 6520, IETF, Status: Proposed Standard, `https://tools.ietf.org/html/rfc6520`

[SWK+01]   SAVAGE, S.; WETHERALL, D.; KARLIN, A.; ANDERSON, T.: Network Support for IP Traceback. In: *IEEE/ACM Transactions on Networking* 9 (2001), No. 3, pp. 226–237

[Syv90]   SYVERSON, P.: Formal Semantics for Logics of Cryptographic Protocols. In: *Proceedings of the Computer Security Foundations Workshop III*, IEEE Computer Society Press, June 1990, pp. 32–41

[Syv91]   SYVERSON, P.: The Use of Logic in the Analysis of Cryptographic Protocols. In: *1991 IEEE Computer Society Symposium on Research in Security and Privacy*, 1991, pp. 156–170

[Syv93a]   SYVERSON, P.: Adding Time to a Logic of Authentication. In: *1st ACM Conference on Computer and Communications Security*, 1993, pp. 97–101

[Syv93b]   SYVERSON, P.: On Key Distribution Protocols for Repeated Authentication. In: *ACM Operating System Review* 4 (1993), October, pp. 24–30

[SZT+11]   SHEFFER, Y.; ZORN, G.; TSCHOFENIG, H.; FLUHRER, S.: *An EAP Authentication Method Based on the Encrypted Key Exchange (EKE) Protocol.* February 2011. – RFC 6124, IETF, Status: Informational, `https://tools.ietf.org/html/rfc6124`

[TB09]   TEWS, E.; BECK, M.: Practical attacks against WEP and WPA. In: *Proceedings of the second ACM conference on Wireless network security*, 2009, pp. 79–86

[TFr97]   TFREAK: *smurf.c.* `http://www.phreak.org/archives/exploits/denial/smurf.c`. Version: 1997

[TG93]   TC-GSM, ETSI: *GSM Security Aspects (GSM 02.09).* European Telecommunications Standards Institute (ETSI), Recommendation GSM 02.09, Version 3.1.0, June 1993

[The11]   THE HACKER'S CHOICE: *THC SSL DOS.* `http://thehackerschoice.wordpress.com/2011/10/24/thc-ssl-dos/`. Version: 2011

[Tho84]   THOMPSON, K.: Reflections on Trusting Trust. In: *Communications of the ACM* 27 (1984), No. 8, pp. 761–763

[TMB10]   TOUCH, J.; MANKIN, A.; BONICA, R.: *The TCP Authentication Option.* 2010. – RFC 5925, IETF, Status: Standard, `https://tools.ietf.org/html/rfc5925`

[Tou91]   TOUSSAINT, M.-J.: *Verification of Cryptographic Protocols.* Ph.D Thesis, Université der Liège (Belgium), 1991

[Tou92a]   TOUSSAINT, M.-J.: Deriving the Complete Knowledge of Participants in Cryptographic Protocols. In: *Advances in Cryptology — CRYPTO '91 Proceedings*, Springer-Verlag, 1992, pp. 24–43

[Tou92b]   TOUSSAINT, M.-J.: Seperating the Specification and Implementation Phases in Cryptology. In: *ESORICS 92 – Proceedings of the Second European Symposium on Research in Computer Security*, Springer-Verlag, 1992, pp. 77–101

[Tra06]   TRAN, T.: Proactive Multicast-Based IPSEC Discovery Protocol and Multicast Extension. In: *Proceedings of the IEEE Military Communications Conference (MILCOM)*, 2006

[TS94]   TC-SMG, ETSI: *European Digital Cellular Telecommunications System (Phase 2): Security Related Network Functions (GSM 03.20)*. European Telecommunications Standards Institute (ETSI), ETS 300 534, September 1994

[TVR⁺99]   TOWNSLEY, W.; VALENCIA, A.; RUBENS, A.; PALL, G.; ZORN, G.; PALTER, B.: *Layer Two Tunneling Protocol (L2TP)*. August 1999. – RFC 2661, IETF, Status: Draft Standard, https://tools.ietf.org/html/rfc2661

[TW09]   TERESHKIN, A.; WOJTCZUK, R.: Introducing Ring -3 Rootkits. In: *Black Hat USA (2009)*

[TWM⁺07]   TAYLOR, D.; WU, T.; MAVROGIANNOPOULOS, N.; PERRIN, T.: *Using the Secure Remote Password (SRP) Protocol for TLS Authentication*. November 2007. – RFC 5054, IETF, Status: Informational, https://tools.ietf.org/html/rfc5054

[TWP07]   TEWS, E.; WEINMANN, R. P.; PYSHKIN, A.: Breaking 104 bit WEP in less than 60 seconds. In: *Information Security Applications* (2007), pp. 188–202

[Var89]   VARADHARAJAN, V.: Verification of Network Security Protocols. In: *Computers & Security* 8 (1989), August, No. 8, pp. 693–708

[Var90]   VARADHARAJAN, V.: Use of Formal Description Technique in the Specification of Authentication Protocols. In: *Computer Standards & Interfaces* 9 (1990), pp. 203–215

[Ver13]   VERIZON: *2013 Data Breach Investigations Report*. http://www.verizonenterprise.com/DBIR/2013/. Version: 2013

[VGE⁺00]   VIXIE, P.; GUDMUNDSSON, O.; EASTLAKE 3RD, D.; WELLINGTON, B.: *Secret Key Transaction Authentication for DNS (TSIG)*. May 2000. – RFC 2845, IETF, Status: Proposed Standard, https://tools.ietf.org/html/rfc2845

[VK98]   VIGNA, G.; KEMMERER, R. A.: NetSTAT: A Network-based Intrusion Detection Approach. In: *Proceedings of the 14th Annual Computer Security Applications Conference*, 1998, pp. 25–34

[VLK98]   VALENCIA, A.; LITTLEWOOD, M.; KOLAR, T.: *Cisco Layer Two Forwarding (L2F) Protocol*. May 1998. – RFC 2341, IETF, Status: Historic, https://tools.ietf.org/html/rfc2341

[VM05]   VIEGA, J.; MCGREW, D.: *The Use of Galois/Counter Mode (GCM) in IPsec Encapsulating Security Payload (ESP)*. June 2005. – RFC 4106, IETF, Status: Proposed Standard, https://tools.ietf.org/html/rfc4106

[VV96]   VOLPE, F. P.; VOLPE, S.: *Chipkarten — Grundlagen, Technik, Anwendungen*. Heise, 1996

[Wai09]   WAIBEL, F.: Das Internet-Analyse-System (IAS) als Komponente einer IT-Sicherheitsarchitektur. In: *11. Deutscher Sicherheitskongress*, 2009, pp. 281–296

[WB13]   WEILER, S.; BLACKA, D.: *Clarifications and Implementation Notes for DNS Security (DNSSEC)*. February 2013. – RFC 6840, IETF, Status: Proposed Standard, https://tools.ietf.org/html/rfc6840

[WC95]   WACK, J. P.; CARNAHAN, L. J.: *Keeping Your Site Comfortably Secure: An Introduction to Internet Firewalls*. 1995. – NIST Special Publication 800-10

[WFL+04] WANG, X.; FENG, D.; LAI, X.; YU, H.: Collisions for Hash Functions MD4, MD5, HAVAL-128 and RIPEMD. In: *IACR Eprint archive*, 2004

[WHA99]   WALLNER, D.; HARDER, E.; AGEE, R.: *Key Management for Multicast: Issues and Architectures*. 1999. – RFC 2627, IETF, Status: Standard, https://tools.ietf.org/html/rfc2627

[WHF03]   WHITING, D.; HOUSLEY, R.; FERGUSON, N.: *Counter with CBC-MAC (CCM)*. September 2003. – RFC 3610, IETF, Status: Informational, https://tools.ietf.org/html/rfc3610

[Whi06a] WHITE, R.: *Architecture and Deployment Considerations for Secure Origin BGP (soBGP)*. 2006. – IETF, Status: Expired Internet-Draft, https://tools.ietf.org/html/draft-white-sobgp-architecture-02

[Whi06b] WHITE, R.: *Secure Origin BGP (soBGP) Certificates*. 2006. – IETF, Status: Expired Internet-Draft, https://tools.ietf.org/html/draft-weis-sobgp-certificates-04

[WI06]   WEILER, S.; IHREN, J.: *Minimally Covering NSEC Records and DNSSEC On-line Signing*. April 2006. – RFC 4470, IETF, Status: Proposed Standard, https://tools.ietf.org/html/rfc4470

[WL93]   WOO, T. Y. C.; LAM, S. S.: A Semantic Model for Authentication Protocols. In: *1993 IEEE Computer Society Symposium on Research in Security and Privacy*, 1993, pp. 178–194

[WRH11]   WEIS, B.; ROWLES, S.; HARDJONO, T.: *The Group Domain of Interpretation*. October 2011. – RFC 6407, IETF, Status: Proposed Standard, https://tools.ietf.org/html/rfc6407

[Wu00]   WU, T.: *The SRP Authentication and Key Exchange System*. 2000. – RFC 2945, IETF, Status: Standard, https://tools.ietf.org/html/rfc2945

[Wu02]   WU, T. J.: *SRP-6: Improvements and Refinements to the Secure Remote Password Protocol*. http://srp.stanford.edu/srp6.ps. Version: 2002

[WYY05]   WANG, X.; YIN, Y. L.; YU, H.: Finding collisions in the full SHA-1. In: *Advances in Cryptology – CRYPTO'05*, 2005, pp. 18–36

[YL06a]   YLONEN, T.; LONVICK, C.: *The Secure Shell (SSH) Authentication Protocol*. 2006. – RFC 4252, IETF, Status: Proposed Standard, `https://tools.ietf.org/html/rfc4252`

[YL06b]   YLONEN, T.; LONVICK, C.: *The Secure Shell (SSH) Connection Protocol*. 2006. – RFC 4254, IETF, Status: Proposed Standard, `https://tools.ietf.org/html/rfc4254`

[YL06c]   YLONEN, T.; LONVICK, C.: *The Secure Shell (SSH) Protocol Architecture*. 2006. – RFC 4251, IETF, Status: Proposed Standard, `https://tools.ietf.org/html/rfc4251`

[YL06d]   YLONEN, T.; LONVICK, C.: *The Secure Shell (SSH) Transport Layer Protocol*. 2006. – RFC 4253, IETF, Status: Proposed Standard, `https://tools.ietf.org/html/rfc4253`

[Yuv79]   YUVAL, G.: How to Swindle Rabin. In: *Cryptologia* (1979), July

[ZC98]   ZORN, G.; COBB, S.: *Microsoft PPP CHAP Extensions*. October 1998. – RFC 2433, IETF, Status: Informational, `https://tools.ietf.org/html/rfc2433`

[ZCC00]   ZWICKY, E.; COOPER, S.; CHAPMAN, B.: *Building Internet Firewalls*. O'Reilly, 2000. – Second Edition

[Zol11]   ZOLLER, T.: *TLS & SSLv3 renegotiation vulnerability*. 2011

[ZRM05]   ZOU, X.; RAMAMURTHY, B.; MAGLIVERAS, S.: *Secure Group Communications Over Data Networks*. Springer-Verlag, 2005

Abbreviations

3GPP	3rd Generation Partnership Project
AAA	Authentication, Authorisation and Accounting
ACL	Access Control List
AEAD	Authenticated Encryption with Associated Data
AES	Advanced Encryption Standard
AH	Authentication Header
AK	Anonymity Key
AKA	Authentication and Key Agreement
AMF	Authentication Management Field
ANSI	American National Standards Institute
AP	Access Point
ARP	Address Resolution Protocol
ARPA	Advanced Research Project Agency
AS	Autonomous System
ASLR	Address Space Layout Randomisation
ASN.1	Abstract Syntax Notation 1
AuC	Authentication Center
AUTN	Authentication Token
AV	Authentication Vector
BEAST	Browser Exploit Against SSL/TLS
BGP	Border Gateway Protocol
BSC	Base Station Controller
BSS	Base Station Sub-System (in context of GSM)

Security in Fixed and Wireless Networks, Second Edition.
Guenter Schaefer and Michael Rossberg.
Copyright © 2014 by dpunkt.verlag GmbH, Heidelberg, Germany.
Title of the German original: Netzsicherheit   ISBN 978-3-86490-115-7
Translation Copyright © 2016 by John Wiley & Sons, Ltd., All rights reserved

BSS	Basic Service Set (in context of WLANs)
BTS	Base Tranceiver Station
BU	Binding Update
CA	Certification Authority
CBC	Cipher Block Chaining
CCM	Counter with CBC-MAC
CCMP	CTR with CBC-MAC Protocol
CFB	Ciphertext Feedback
CHAP	Challenge Handshake Authentication Protocol
CK	Confidentiality Key
CMAC	Cipher-based MAC
CMC	Certificate Management over CMS
CMP	Certificate Management Protocol
CMS	Cryptographic Message Syntax
CN	Corresponding Node
CRC	Cyclic Redundancy Check
CRIME	Compression Ratio Info-leak Made Easy
CRL	Certificate Revocation List
CRMF	Certificate Request Message Format
CSPRBG	Cryptographically Secure Pseudo Random Bit Generator
CSPRNG	Cryptographically Secure Pseudo Random Number Generator
CSR	Certificate Signing Requests
CTR	Counter (usually referring to Counter mode of block ciphers)
CV	Chaining Value
DDoS	Distributed Denial-of-Service
DES	Data Encryption Standard
DGA	Data Generation Agents
DHCP	Dynamic Host Configuration Protocol
DMZ	Demilitarised Zone
DOI	Domain of Interpretation
DNS	Domain Name System
DNSSEC	Domain Name System Security Extensions

DOD	Department of Defense
DSA	Digital Signature Algorithm
DSS	Digital Signature Standard
DSSS	Direct Sequence Spread Spectrum
DTLS	Datagram Transport Layer Security
EAP	Extensible Authentication Protocol
EAPOL	EAP over LANs
ECB	Electronic Code Book
ECC	Elliptic Curve Cryptography
ECDSA	Elliptic Curve Digital Signature Algorithm
ECDH	Elliptic Curve Diffie Hellman
ECGDSA	Elliptic Curve-based German Digital Signature Algorithm
ECN	Explicit Congestion Notification
ECP	Encryption Control Protocol
EIR	Equipment Identity Register
EKE	Encrypted Key Exchange
EPC	Evolved Packet Core
ePDG	Evolved Packet Data Gateway
ESP	Encapsulating Security Payload
ESS	Extended Service Set
EST	Enrollment over Secure Transport
FCS	Frame Check Sequence
FHSS	Frequency Hop Spread Spectrum
FTP	File Transfer Protocol
FTP-S	File Transfer Protocol over SSL/TLS
GC	Group Controller
GCD	Greatest Common Divisor
GCM	Galois/Counter Mode
GDH	Group Diffie–Hellman
GDOI	Group Domain of Interpretation
GGSN	Gateway GPRS Support Node
GMSC	Gateway Mobile Switching Center
GKM	Group Key Management
GKMP	Group Key Management Protocol

GMAC	Galois Message Authentication Code
GPRS	General Packet Radio Service
GRE	Generic Routing Encapsulation
GSA	Group Security Agent
GSC	Group Security Controller
GSI	Group Security Intermediaries
GSM	Global System for Mobile Communication
GTK	Group Temporal Key
HDLC	High-Level Data Link Control
HE	Home Environment
HIDS	Host-based IDS
HLR	Home Location Register
HSS	Home Subscriber Server
HMAC	Hashed Message Authentication Code
HTTP	Hypertext Transfer Protocol
HTTPS	Hypertext Transfer Protocol Secure
IANA	Internet Assigned Numbers Authority
ICMP	Internet Control Message Protocol
ICV	Integrity Check Value
IDEA	International Data Encryption Algorithm
IDS	Intrusion Detection System
IEEE	Institute of Electrical and Electronics Engineers
IETF	Internet Engineering Task Force
IGRP	Interior Gateway Routing Protocol
IHL	IP Header Length
IK	Integrity Key
IKE	Internet Key Exchange
IMS	IP Multimedia Sub-System
IMSI	International Mobile Subscriber Identity
IMT	International Mobile Telecommunications
IP	Internet Protocol
IPComp	IP Payload Compression Protocol
IPS	Intrusion Prevention System
IPsec	IP security Architecture
IPv4	Internet Protocol Version 4

IRV	Internet Route Validation
ISAKMP	Internet Security Association and Key Management Protocol
ISDN	Integrated Services Digital Network
ISO	International Organization for Standardization
ISP	Internet Service Provider
ITU	International Telecommunications Union
IV	Initialisation Vector
IWF	Interworking Function
KCK	Key Confirmation Key
KDF	Key Derivation Function
KEK	Key Encryption Key
KSK	Key Signing Key
L2F	Layer 2 Forwarding Protocol
L2TP	Layer 2 Tunneling Protocol
LACNIC	Latin America and Caribbean Network Information Centre
LAI	Location Area Identifier
LAN	Local Area Network
LCP	Link Control Protocol
LEAP	Lightweight Extensible Authentication Protocol
LKH	Logical Key Hierarchy
LTE	Long Term Evolution
MAC	Medium Access Control (in the context of LANs and WLANs)
MAC	Message Authentication Code (in cryptographic protocols)
MAN	Metropolitan Area Network
MD	Message Digest
MDC	Modification Detection Code
MIB	Management Information Base
MIC	Message Integrity Code
MIPS	Million Instructions Per Second
MME	Mobility Management Entity
MPLS	Multi-Protocol Label Switching
MPOA	Multi-Protocol over ATM

MPPE	Microsoft Point-to-Point Encryption Protocol
MRAI	Minimum Route Advertisement Interval
MS	Mobile Station
MSC	Mobile Switching Center
MSISDN	Mobile Subscriber International ISDN Number
MSK	Master Session Key
MTU	Maximum Transmission Unit
NAI	Network Access Identifier
NAT	Network Address Translation
NAT-T	NAT-Traversal
NCP	Network Control Protocol
NFS	Network File System
NHRP	Next-Hop Resolution Protocol
NIDS	Network-based IDS
NIST	National Institute of Standards and Technology
NLRI	Network Layer Reachability Information
NSA	National Security Agency
NSS	Network Sub-System
NTP	Network Time Protocol
OAEP	Optimal Asymmetric Encryption Padding
OSI	Open Systems Interconnection
OCB	Offset Codebook Mode
OCSP	Online Certificate Status Protocol
OFB	Output Feedback
OFDM	Orthogonal Frequency Division Multiplexing
OMC	Operation and Management Center
OSI	Open Systems Interconnection
OSPF	Open Shortest Path First
OSS	Operation Sub-System
OTP	One Time Password
OUI	Organisational Unit Identifier
PAE	Port Access Entities
PAKE	Password-authenticated Key Exchange
PBKDF2	Password-Based Key Derivation Function 2
PAP	Password Authentication Protocol

PCBC	Propagating Cipher Block Chaining
PCT	Private Communication Technology
PDN	Packet Data Network
PDU	Protocol Data Unit
PGW	Packet Data Network Gateway
PHAD	Packet Header Anomaly Detection
PKCS	Public Key Cryptography Standards
PKI	Public Key Infrastructure
PMK	Pairwise Master Key
PMIDP	Proactive Multicast-Based IPSEC Discovery Protocol
PNRP	Peer Name Resolution Protocol
POP	Point of Presence
PPP	Point-to-Point Protocol
PPTP	Point-to-Point Tunneling Protocol
PRBG	Pseudo Random Bit Generator
PRF	Pseudo Random Function
PRNG	Pseudo Random Number Generator
PSTN	Public Switched Telecommunication Network
PTK	Pairwise Transient Key
RA	Registration Authority
RADIUS	Remote Authentication Dial In User Service
RAND	Random Challenge
RAS	Remote Access Server
RBG	Random Bit Generator
RC4	Rivest Cipher 4
RDP	Remote Desktop Protocol
RFC	Request for Comments
RIP	Routing Information Protocol
RIPE NCC	Réseaux IP Européens Network Coordination Centre
RNC	Radio Network Controller
ROP	Return Oriented Programming
RPKI	Resource Public Key Infrastructure
RPSL	Routing Policy Specification Language
RSA	Rivest, Shamir and Adleman
RSN	Robust Secure Network (WLAN)

RSS	Radio Sub-System
SA	Security Association
SADB	Security Association Database
SAE	Simultaneous Authentication of Equals
SAP	Service Access Point
S-BGP	Secure BGP
SCAR	SPIE Collection and Reduction Agents
SCEP	Simple Certificate Enrollment Protocol
SCVP	Server-based Certificate Validation Protocol
SDU	Service Data Unit
SGT	Service Granting Ticket
SGSN	Serving GPRS Support Node
SHA	Secure Hash Algorithm
SIM	Subscriber Identity Module
SLIP	Serial Line IP
SMB	Server Message Block (Protocol)
SMTP	Simple Mail Transfer Protocol
SMTPS	Simple Mail Transfer Protocol over SSL/TLS
SN	Serving Network
SNMP	Simple Network Management Protocol
SOA	Secure Origin Authentication
soBGP	Secure Origin Border Gateway Protocol
SOLID	Secure Overlay for IPsec Discovery
SPD	Security Policy Database
SPI	Security Parameter Index
SPIE	Secure Path Identification Engine
SQN	Sequence Number
SRP	Secure Remote Password
SSH	Secure Shell
SSID	Service Set Identifier
SSL	Secure Socket Layer
STSL	Station-To-Station Link
TCP	Transport Control Protocol
TED	Tunnel Endpoint Discovery
TEK	Traffic Encryption Key

TESLA	Timed Efficient Stream Loss-tolerant Authentication
TGDH	Tree-Based Group Diffie–Hellman
TGS	Ticket Granting Server
TGT	Ticket Granting Ticket
TLD	Top Level Domain
TK	Temporal Key
TKIP	Temporal Key Integrity Protocol
TLS	Transport Layer Security
TMSI	Temporary Mobile Subscriber Identity
ToS	Type of Service
TSIG	Secret Key Transaction Authentication for DNS, Transaction Signature
TTAK	TTAK TKIP Mixed Address and Key
TTL	Time To Live
TTP	Trusted Third Party
TVRA	Threat Vulnerability Risk Analysis
UDP	User Datagram Protocol
UE	User Equipment
UMTS	Universal Mobile Telecommunications System
URI	Uniform Resource Identifier
USIM	Universal Subscriber Identity Module
UTRAN	UMTS Terrestrial Radio Access Network
VA	Validation Authority
VLAN	Virtual Local Area Network
VLR	Visitor Location Register
VPN	Virtual Private Network
WDS	Wireless Distribution System
WEP	Wired Equivalent Privacy
WIMAX	Worldwide Interoperability for Microwave Access
WLAN	Wireless Local Area Network
WPA	Wi-Fi Protected Access
WPAD	Web Proxy Autodiscovery Protocol
XCBC	eXtended Cipher Block Chaining
XOR	Exklusive-Or
XRES	Expected Response
ZSK	Zone Signing Key

Index